3D GAME
PROGRAMMING
WITH C++

John De Goes

CORIOLIS

President, CEO
Keith Weiskamp

Publisher
Steve Sayre

Acquisitions Editor
Stephanie Wall

Marketing Specialist
Tracy Schofield

Project Editor
Greg Balas

Technical Reviewer
Harry Henderson

Production Coordinator
Laura Wellander

Cover Design
Jesse Dunn

Layout Design
April Nielsen

CD-ROM Developer
Robert Clarfield

The Coriolis Group, LLC
14455 North Hayden Road
Suite 220
Scottsdale, Arizona 85260

480/483-0192
FAX 480/483-0193
http://www.coriolis.com

Library of Congress Cataloging-in-Publication Data
De Goes, John.
    3D game programming with C++ / by John De Goes.
       p.   cm.
    ISBN 1-57610-400-1
       1. Computer games--Programming.   2. C++ (Computer program language).   I. Title.

QA76.76.C672 D44   2000
794.8'16693--dc21   99-043502

CIP

Printed in the United States of America
10 9 8 7 6 5 4 3 2 1

CORIOLIS

14455 North Hayden Road • Suite 220 • Scottsdale, Arizona 85260

Dear Reader:

Coriolis Technology Press was founded to create a very elite group of books: the ones you keep closest to your machine. Sure, everyone would like to have the Library of Congress at arm's reach, but in the real world, you have to choose the books you rely on every day *very* carefully.

To win a place for our books on that coveted shelf beside your PC, we guarantee several important qualities in every book we publish. These qualities are:

- *Technical accuracy*—It's no good if it doesn't work. Every Coriolis Technology Press book is reviewed by technical experts in the topic field, and is sent through several editing and proofreading passes in order to create the piece of work you now hold in your hands.

- *Innovative editorial design*—We've put years of research and refinement into the ways we present information in our books. Our books' editorial approach is uniquely designed to reflect the way people learn new technologies and search for solutions to technology problems.

- *Practical focus*—We put only pertinent information into our books and avoid any fluff. Every fact included between these two covers must serve the mission of the book as a whole.

- *Accessibility*—The information in a book is worthless unless you can find it quickly when you need it. We put a lot of effort into our indexes, and heavily cross-reference our chapters, to make it easy for you to move right to the information you need.

Here at The Coriolis Group we have been publishing and packaging books, technical journals, and training materials since 1989. We're programmers and authors ourselves, and we take an ongoing active role in defining what we publish and how we publish it. We have put a lot of thought into our books; please write to us at **ctp@coriolis.com** and let us know what you think. We hope that you're happy with the book in your hands, and that in the future, when you reach for software development and networking information, you'll turn to one of our books first.

Keith Weiskamp
President and CEO

Jeff Duntemann
VP and Editorial Director

Look For This Other Book From The Coriolis Group:

Game Architecture and Design
Andrew Rollings and Dave Morris

To the visionary men and women whose dedication and passion have made everything from printed books, to computers, to 3D computer games a reality.

—John

❧

About The Author

John De Goes is a freelance computer programmer and technical writer. In addition to writing several commercially available games and software utilities, he authored the book *Cutting Edge 3D Game Programming with* C++ and numerous articles on game and software development. In his spare time, he enjoys such intellectual pursuits as mathematics, physics, and philosophy, as well as physical activities including biking, hiking, stargazing, and martial arts.

Acknowledgments

Fortunately for writers like myself, a book of this size and scope doesn't just suddenly come into existence. It is the end result of vision, hard work, a team of dedicated people, and excellent resources. Here I would like to credit all those who have been closely involved in the creation of this book.

First on that list would be Stephanie Wall, who on behalf of The Coriolis Group urged me to write a sequel to my first book on 3D game programming, *Cutting Edge 3D Game Programming with* C++. Without her initiative, it is safe to say this book would still be nothing more than a dream in the eyes of all aspiring Direct3D game programmers.

Once the book was off the ground, no one could have done a better job organizing the project and keeping the chapters flowing than Greg Balas. My all-time favorite editor, Greg deserves a hats off for being keenly aware of the time restrictions of a part-time writer, and adapting the schedule and distributing the workload to meet those constraints.

Also instrumental to the completion of the book was editor Susan Holly, who made my oftentimes abstruse, convoluted, wording much more palatable, and technical reviewer Harry Henderson who caught more than one sleep-deprivation-induced slip.

A big thanks goes to André LaMothe, who wrote the thought-provoking foreword to this book. Given his well-deserved worldwide fame, people will probably end up buying the book just for the foreword. Thanks, André. Readers: If you get the chance, buy his books on 3D game programming—you won't regret it.

I owe a round of applause to the authors of the books *Calculus* (Thomas and Finney); *Computer Graphics: Principles and Practice* (Foley, van Dam, Feiner, and Hughes); *Elementary Linear Algebra* (Hill); and *Precalculus* (Larson and Hostetler). Applied programming books like mine are built largely on the theoretical foundations of books like these.

Lastly, I'm indebted to the readers of my last book, who bought enough copies to make this sequel worthwhile. Thank you all!

Contents At A Glance

Table Of Contents

Foreword

Today, we are crossing the threshold not only into a new millennium, but also into the most exciting chapter of computer gaming history that we will ever see. We are now close to creating computer games that are absolutely photo-realistic. Not only are games becoming photo-realistic, but also the physics and artificial intelligence in games have finally caught up with the 3D graphics. The only conclusion that we can make as game developers and programmers is that one day we will have the technology to create alternate realities, worlds like the one depicted in The Matrix, and more. 3D games and simulations are the building blocks of these dreams.

The ultimate goal of any game programmer is nothing less then creating another world, or universe in which a player can be completely submerged. Today, we are almost there. It might be 10 to 20 years before we can create a fully interactive neural connection with a human and a computer—but I assure you, it will happen.

By reading this book you are becoming part of these exciting times for game development, 3D graphics, and simulation. I remember when Direct3D first came out; it was nothing less of horrific. You couldn't do anything with Direct3D except maybe walk around a room with a spinning cube in it. Direct3D has come a long way since then, and the original engines, both software and hardware, that make up Direct3D have been completely rewritten over and over. At this point, I have to admit the argument over Direct3D and OpenGL is moot. They are both very good systems to write 3D games with on the PC platform. It's really a matter of taste now.

I can tell you from experience that the only problem with Direct3D is that there are simply no good books on the material. The Microsoft Direct3D SDK is no help, and every book I have read on the subject is a regurgitation of the SDK materials—right down to the code. Moreover, very few authors can write about game programming and or 3D graphics targeted toward the game programmer. It's not an easy thing to do. So there's simply no good way to learn Direct3D except through trial and error.

When John first asked me to write the foreword to his new 3D book, I thought to myself that John and I are competitors in a way, and what would the readers think? Well, I have known John for many years. I can remember him emailing me about vectors on CompuServe around the time of DOOM I. He is one of those special people who is not only very talented, but also wants to help others learn about game programming and 3D graphics. Alas, I am very supportive of his work, even if he writes books that compete in a way with mine. Moreover, when I read John's first book *Cutting Edge 3D Game Programming with C++*, I liked it very much. His book is the only 3D game programming book I ever refer people to in addition to my own, so his work is right on target.

John's latest book, *3D Game Programming with C++*, is what every Direct3D programmer has been looking for. The Direct3D coverage is simply the best I have ever read, and it is complete. I am so happy John wrote this book because it takes a giant load off of me. I have no interest in writing a book on Direct3D. Thanks John!

With *3D Game Programming with C++* in your hands, along with a good C++ compiler and 3D accelerator, you will become an expert in Direct3D in no time. John has made the complex and contrived subject matter of Direct3D simple to understand and fun to learn—and that's what it's all about. Of course, Direct3D Game Programming isn't just about Direct3D, there is coverage on artificial intelligence, basic physics, and DirectX foundations, along with a number of really helpful appendixes. Hence, the book is a great all around read and a must have for any game programmer's library.

So turn the page, and prepare to be 3D accelerated—Direct3D style!

—André LaMothe

PART I

THE FOUNDATIONS OF 3D PROGRAMMING

Chapter 1
What Are 3D Games?

The computer game world is now officially 3D. Action games have long existed outside the confines of two dimensions, but until recently, a vast number of games were two-dimensional, most notably adventure and strategy games. With the advent of the low-cost 3D accelerator, however, this has changed.

The Beast Within marked Sierra's last 2D Gabriel Knight adventure game; the third in the series, Blood Of The Sacred, Blood of the Damned (see Figure 1.1), is fully three dimensional, as will be any sequels. LucasArts' The Curse Of Monkey Island, a highly acclaimed adventure game and the third in the Monkey Island

Figure 1.1
A screen shot from Blood Of The Sacred, Blood Of The Damned, a 3D adventure game.

3

series, was the last of the strictly Disney-style games from the entertainment company. Grim Fandango, as well as Indiana Jones And The Infernal Machine, were designed from the start as realtime 3D games, with much applause from gamers.

Even strategy games, once entirely two-dimensional (as with Starcraft and Dominion, for example), have increasingly become three-dimensional. Force Commander, another LucasArts game, is just one example of this.

In this chapter, I introduce three-dimensional games by covering their most distinguishing features. If you are a gaming expert, than most of these will already be familiar to you.

DirectX

Microsoft developed a software development kit (SDK) specifically to promote hardware-assisted, high-performance games for Windows. This SDK, known as DirectX, consists of many components, each of which deals with a particular aspect of game development. Because DirectX is well supported and widely known, virtually all 3D games rely on it for the features they need. In this book, I assume that if you want to write a 3D game, you will want to use DirectX (and you definitely will when you see the number of features it supports).

The components of DirectX are divided into two groups: DirectX Foundation contains low-level components that supply basic functionality; DirectX Media contains high-level components that perform many complex operations. The next sections provide a quick overview of each component's features.

DirectX Foundation

DirectX Foundation consists of the following components: DirectDraw, DirectSound, DirectMusic, Direct3D Immediate Mode (IM), DirectInput, DirectSetup, and AutoPlay.

DirectDraw

DirectDraw provides a way for software developers to access the display's attributes—including the size of the desktop and how many colors can be displayed at once—and the display's features, such as playing back video, displaying images and bitmaps, and so on. DirectDraw is not a graphics library, in that it cannot draw lines, polygons, or text, but it is still nonetheless invaluable for all of today's 3D games.

DirectSound

DirectSound can play, mix, and apply effects to sounds on a variety of hardware devices. Many programmers rely on DirectSound for all of their sound output.

DirectMusic

DirectMusic, a recent addition to DirectX, supports the playback of MIDI files and other kinds of music.

Direct3D IM

Direct3D IM gives programmers direct access to a graphics card's 3D features. It is written with a minimal amount of code, thus requiring the programmer to do most of the work in displaying 3D environments.

DirectInput

DirectInput allows programmers to use existing and future input devices. It directly supports force-feedback joysticks, normal joysticks, mice, flight yokes, and any other input device developed with DirectInput support.

AutoPlay

AutoPlay allows a CD to start itself after being inserted into a CD-ROM drive, thus enabling software developers to create self-installing games and those that run themselves after being inserted.

DirectX Media

DirectX Media consists of only four components—Direct3D Retained Mode (RM), DirectPlay, DirectShow, and DirectAnimation—but each one contains a large amount of functionality.

Direct3D RM

Direct3D RM is a high-level component of DirectX. Rather than handling only the basics, as IM does, RM performs most of the tasks involved in displaying 3D scenes. Because it is high level, the changes from one version of RM to the next tend to be slight, allowing programmers to become more familiar with it.

DirectPlay

DirectPlay allows programmers to write multiplayer software that runs over LANs, modems, the Internet, and other networks.

DirectShow

DirectShow plays video files of all types—QuickTime, AVI, MPEG—according to the filters (video decoders) installed on the computer it is running on. This provides game developers with an easy way to introduce cinematic scenes into their games.

DirectAnimation

DirectAnimation is a component designed for Web and desktop animation.

The Features Of DirectX

Today's games use DirectX and so support many if not all of the graphical features provided by this SDK. The next sections describe some of these features, all of which are fully covered in this book.

Lights

Lights play an important role in games, casting shadows and illuminating important parts of scenes. Many games use a combination of *realtime lighting* and *prerendered lighting*. Realtime lighting is calculated while the game is playing—all the mathematics for generating shadows and other lighting effects is done by the game every time the 3D world is displayed. *Prerendered lighting* is calculated in advance by a 3D modeling program and applied to objects in the game world (this lighting type is faster, but cannot be used for moving lights).

Polygons

The main *primitive*—a simple geometric shape from which more complex shapes are formed—in 3D games is a convex polygon. A *polygon* is a bounded portion of a plane, which is, in turn, a shape infinitely wide in two dimensions and infinitely flat in the third.

A *convex polygon* has no two points through which a line can be drawn that passes outside the polygon (Figure 1.2a). This is contrasted with a *concave polygon*, which has at least two points through which a line *can* be drawn that passes outside the polygon (Figure 1.2b).

Nearly all objects in Direct3D games are composed of convex polygons. Objects with sharp edges, therefore, can be replicated exactly, while those with smooth edges can be simulated. Most games do not display plain, single-color polygons. Rather, they display polygons with a number of special effects to improve their realism.

Shading

Direct3D is capable of *shading* polygons realistically to enhance their appearance. It can shade polygons based on their positions and their orientations relative to one or more light sources.

Gouraud Shading

Gouraud shading is a fast method of simulating curved surfaces. The vertices of the polygon are shaded as if the polygon were curved, and these resulting shades are spread across the face of the polygon. This approach does not produce accurate results if a highlight from a

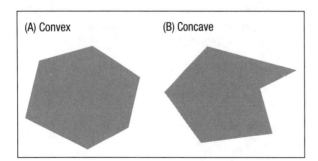

Figure 1.2
A convex polygon (a) and a concave polygon (b).

light falls in the center of the polygon (because only the shades at the vertices are calculated); but otherwise, it is fairly realistic.

Phong Shading

Although *Phong shading* is not currently implemented in Direct3D, it will be in future versions. Phong shading is more realistic than Gouraud and never misses highlights. It shades each pixel of the polygon as if it were curved; for this reason, it is slower than Gouraud shading.

Texture Mapping

Virtually all polygons have a *texture*—an image or bitmap—applied to them. This image is *mapped*, or painted, on the polygon. Usually, each vertex of the polygon is assigned a *texture coordinate*—a two-dimensional point indicating the pixel in the texture corresponding to the given polygon vertex.

Transparency

Transparency results from giving the texture map associated with the polygon a *stencil* (also called a *mask*) or an *alpha channel*. A stencil allows cutouts; portions of the polygon can be either fully transparent or fully opaque. An alpha channel is another component (added to the red, green, and blue components of each pixel) that specifies to what extent each pixel is transparent. Alpha channel transparency takes longer to compute than stenciling, but is hardware-accelerated in all of today's graphics cards, and so it is the preferred method of transparency.

Bump Mapping

Bump mapping refers to the process of modifying the appearance of a polygon so it seems bumpy. The bumps are specified by an image (sometimes called a *height* or *displacement map*), and the technique is usually used in combination with texture mapping.

Reflection Mapping

Reflection mapping is a method of simulating reflections. When a reflection map is applied to a polygon, the texture coordinates chosen depend on the viewer's location, and the texture map itself is an image that resembles the environment. This produces the illusion of a reflective surface.

Environmental Effects

In addition to the many effects applied to polygons, Direct3D supports *environmental effects*—those that are global and affect all objects in the game world.

Fog

Fog is a generic name for any type of color that distant objects converge to. It can be white to simulate real fog, black to simulate nighttime, or another color.

Shadows

Today's games increasingly make use of *shadows*, which Direct3D supports. Game designers usually decide that not all objects should have shadows—only select objects (like characters and moving vehicles, for example), because using shadows for *all* objects within a 3D world is computationally expensive.

Many objects, because they do not move, can be given textures with predrawn shadows, eliminating the computational cost at the expense of memory. Another technique involves modifying the intensities of the polygon's vertices (similar to Gouraud shading), making those that lie within shadow regions darker and those that do not, lighter. This technique crudely approximates real shadows, but is fast and universally supported by hardware.

Hardware

Another feature of Direct3D games is support for *hardware* acceleration. Every hardware device that includes solid DirectX drivers—and most such devices do—is instantly compatible with all existing DirectX games. This reduces user headaches and allows you, as a developer, to concentrate on game issues rather than hardware issues.

DirectX allows hardware acceleration for 3D graphics, 2D graphics, sound output, and input devices (some of which have miniature computers built inside to reduce strain on the CPU). As far as this book is concerned, the most important of these accelerated areas is 3D graphics.

3D Hardware Acceleration

Years ago, not even the fastest computer could produce a quality three-dimensional environment running at playable speeds by using an elegant C++ solution. Programmers who wanted to write 3D games were thus forced to use low-level and painstakingly optimized assembly language. Even the fastest assembly code was not fast enough; however, programmers had to go beyond this by using clever tricks that often restricted features. The computer game Doom, for example, didn't allow arbitrary polygonal shapes or even slanted walls to inhabit its worlds. It also restricted players to strictly two-dimensional maps—no two floors could exist at any one location. Players weren't even free to look in arbitrary directions (the looking up and down that did exist was noticeably faked).

Descent, the popular 3D space action game, went beyond Doom by allowing a truly three-dimensional world, but even it had its limitations: It ran in low resolution, with some constraints on the manner in which worlds were formed, and the texture mapping quality was crude.

Manufacturers of graphics cards were aware of the PC's lack of built-in 3D hardware and seized the opportunity to incorporate 3D hardware on their products. Though 3D graphics cards were standard equipment in the high-end workstations used by computer artists, such cards were new to the PC world. As the first few cards were released, gamers were disappointed when they discovered a Pentium could easily outperform the best of the pricey accelerators (with some degradation in image quality). Their outlook changed, however, around the time 3DFX released the Voodoo, an amazing chip capable of outperforming in both speed and quality the fastest Pentium. Other companies, such as nVidia, also released high-performance chips. Computer companies and gamers rushed to buy these second-generation accelerators, inducing other companies to make 3D cards. Thus was born a competitive, performance-driven market that continues today.

The Features Of Hardware

Today's average 3D card includes the following features, all of which can be relied on in Direct3D games:

- 16MB or more of video memory
- Texture mapping
- Transparency, shading, and bump mapping
- Geometry acceleration

Video Memory

Graphics cards use video memory to store geometric and graphical information. Direct3D, in particular, uses video memory for the following purposes:

- *For the video mode they run in*—Games usually run in full-screen mode, meaning the game chooses and sets its resolution and color depth, rather than using the one that Windows is using. Higher resolutions and color depths require more memory.

- *For storing the geometry of their objects*—Before cards can perform mathematical operations on geometry (such as polygons), the geometric information must be moved to video memory.

- *For the depth buffer*—The depth buffer is a piece of memory that stores one depth value for each pixel. It is used to allow close objects to obscure objects behind them, and it is implemented in most hardware. Depth buffers typically consume as much or more memory than that used by the video mode.

- *For graphical information*—Textures, bump maps, light maps, and other kinds of graphical information can be stored in video memory.

- *For alpha information*—Transparency data, such as stencils and alpha channels, can be stored in video memory.

Texture Mapping

Graphics cards can texture polygons in many different ways. The most common methods are referred to as *nearest point*, *bilinear filtering*, and *trilinear filtering* (bilinear and trilinear will be discussed later in this book). Each of these methods first calculates which pixel in the texture map should be mapped onto a given pixel on the polygon. Because this point is not whole (that is, it is a point containing fractions), the hardware must choose which pixel should be used. The nearest-point method rounds the fractional point to the nearest point. The other methods use parts of several surrounding pixels. Thus, the nearest-point method produces the lowest quality output, whereas the others produce much higher-quality polygons. The nearest-point method is no longer considered an acceptable texture-mapping method, because all new graphics cards support at bilinear and trilinear filtering. Many graphics cards also support hardware texture compression and decompression, allowing many more textures to fit into video memory.

Geometry Acceleration

Direct3D allows graphics cards to handle more than just graphical output. They can also accelerate the processing of geometry, which must occur before such data can be displayed. Few graphics cards fully accelerate geometry processing (but CPU extensions, such as AMD's 3DNow!, help with this); most, however, do at least *triangle set up*, which is the mathematical set up that must be performed immediately before a triangle can be displayed. (All polygons are broken down into triangles before being displayed.)

Transparency, Shading, And Bump Mapping

All of today's 3D graphics cards support alpha-channel transparency. Many also support stenciling, the faster method of transparency mentioned earlier. As a programmer, these methods allow you to use pixel-precise transparency in your games.

Another universal feature of graphics cards is their support for shading. They can display polygons shaded by lights, as well as perform Gouraud shading and fog effects.

Lastly, most graphics cards support hardware bump mapping, allowing an unprecedented level of realism for polygons.

Summary

The first step in becoming a three-dimensional game programmer is to understand what elements contribute to the graphics of three-dimensional games. For Windows programmers, those elements are usually the features supplied by Microsoft's DirectX, a high-performance COM SDK aimed specifically at the game-developer community. DirectX gives developers direct control over graphics accelerators, input devices, sound cards, and more.

Credit goes to the manufacturers of graphics accelerators for the radical new advances in the quality and performance of three-dimensional games. These graphics accelerators natively support a growing list of 3D features, enabling developers to produce games that are richly detailed and run at high speeds.

The next chapter takes you through the architecture of 3D games, covering some of the mathematics you will use when writing for Direct3D.

Chapter 2
Overview Of 3D Games

Key Topics:

- *Virtual worlds*
- *Characters*
- *Environmental effects*
- *Cameras*
- *Matrices*

The prospect of writing a 3D computer game is daunting. Few types of software require the programmer to be so well versed in as many different fields as does 3D game programming. The game programmer bold enough to venture into the third dimension must know trigonometry, matrix math, physics, artificial intelligence techniques, the nature of sound, input devices, the Windows operating system, DirectX, and a host of esoteric algorithms and procedures used only in 3D computer simulations.

Acquiring this wealth of knowledge does not come all at once: It comes in small, sure steps of incremental learning. In the last chapter you learned the terminology of 3D games and were introduced to Microsoft's DirectX, a library that simplifies the development of 3D games. In this chapter, I present an overview of the 3D game, a behind-the-scenes look at what it takes to create the stunning simulations of the third dimension found in today's hottest games. After you finish, you will have a solid understanding of the framework of every 3D game and know enough to start using DirectX with confidence.

Virtual Worlds

The world we live in is filled with sights, sounds, smells, and textures. Our senses perceive this information and create in our mind images of what the world is like. Three-dimensional computer games, to one degree or another, strive to emulate this experience. To do so, they display detailed scenes of their *virtual worlds* that have a sense of depth and look and act like their real-world counterparts. They enhance the illusion with audible sound effects that sound like they're coming from where they're supposed to be coming from (even when that's behind us). This realism is the magic that pulls us into these virtual worlds and allows us to believe, even if only for a short time, that we are *there*, in that place and at that time, doing whatever the game encourages us to do.

From your perspective as a programmer, three important elements go into all realistic virtual worlds: *objects*, *characters*, and *environmental effects*. The next few sections that follow take a closer look at each one of these.

Objects

An *object* in a virtual world is anything that has substance and is unified. This broad definition means that a chair, a fire hydrant, a rock, and a deforested mountain are all objects. All of these examples represent tangible and singular things.

On the other hand, a series of unconnected railroad cars, a ray of light shining through a small window, and a mountain filled with rocks, plants, and evergreens are all examples of elements in a virtual world that are *not* objects. Railroad cars are unconnected, and thus do not act as a whole (each railroad car is an object, but the whole is not). The ray of light lacks substance. And the objects on the mountain are not unified with the mountain: They are separate objects, resting on the mountain object.

Virtual world objects have more than just a shape. They also usually have the following properties:

♦ *Objects are often richly detailed*—In many cases, they use texture and bump maps taken from their real-world equivalents. It is typical, for example, to find actual satellite photos of terrain painted on the virtual terrain of computer flight simulators.

♦ *Objects sometimes have sound associated with them*—When you push a box in a computer game, for example, you almost certainly hear the sound of the box rubbing against the floor.

♦ *Objects may have real-world physical properties*—Especially in newer games, objects are often free to fall from heights, to collide with other objects, and even to deform when subject to force.

♦ *The sizes, shapes, positions, orientations, and surface details of many objects change*—When you press on a door in a game, for example, it swings open. A spider moves its legs as it scurries about on the floor.

These are the general properties that apply to most objects. Certain objects that have these properties but go beyond them are called *characters*.

Characters

A *character* is an object that represents an intelligent being, usually capable of animation and motion. The *main character* in a game is the one that represents the player. Other characters, often referred to as *Nonplayer Characters (NPCs)*, are usually controlled by artificial intelligence, but can also be controlled by other players using different computers across the Internet or other such network.

Environmental Effects

Environmental effects are nonobject elements that are closely bound to the game's virtual environment. In our world, we experience many environmental elements: sound, light, heat, cold, fog, haze, wind, and so forth. In the virtual world of 3D computer games, not all of these can be simulated. The following list describes some of the common environmental effects supported by games:

♦ *Sound*—Most games use high quality sound effects and play them to sound three-dimensional (the user hears the sound at the proper distance and coming from the right direction). Some games can even calculate audio sounds after they have traveled through the virtual world, bouncing off of and being absorbed by objects.

♦ *Light and shadow*—A wide variety of light sources are found in games, including spotlights and point lights. Some lights cast shadows, others do not.

♦ *Fog, haze, and other atmospheric perturbations*—For some time now games have been using these effects because they enhance realism and increase performance (objects deep in the fog or haze do not need to be drawn).

♦ *Other effects*—Some games simulate earthquakes, underwater turbulence, rain, and other environmental effects as called for by the game's story line.

Representing Virtual Worlds

Geometry, surface detail, and a number of other virtual world aspects are represented differently in the computer. In the next few sections, you will learn about how these aspects are dealt with digitally.

Representing Geometry

As noted in Chapter 1, games almost invariably represent objects with polygons. Polygons are compact (they don't use a lot of memory), general-purpose (they can represent almost any shape, with sharp or soft edges), and are extensively developed. Over the years graphics experts have devised many methods of drastically improving the realism of polygonal objects without substantially decreasing performance (texture mapping and bump mapping, mentioned in the last chapter, are two examples).

Note

For more information on how points are described and manipulated, see Appendix E.

Games represent polygons by storing their points. These points are defined in a Cartesian coordinate system known as the *model coordinate system* (also called an *object coordinate system*), or, synonymously, *model space*. Each object has its own model coordinate system, and the origin of this system corresponds to where the center of the object is located (see Figure 2.1). This is not necessarily the geometric center of the object, but rather, the point around which the object should be rotated and scaled.

Because the position of an object in model space is not the position of the object in the virtual world, it must be moved to its final location each time the virtual world is displayed. At first, this may seem an odd way to store objects. Why not just store all objects in one coordinate system, that of the virtual world, rather than giving each object its own separate coordinate system? There are two main reasons for this:

♦ *Animation*—With each object located in its own coordinate system, animation is much easier. Scale and rotation operations occur around the origin of a coordinate system, so if objects were defined in the virtual world, they would have to be moved to the origin every time they were rotated or scaled. But if each object has its own coordinate system, then they can be rotated and scaled around this before being moved to their final location in the virtual world.

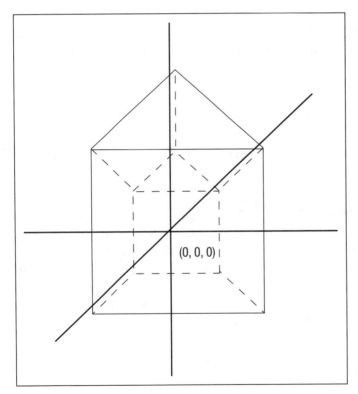

Figure 2.1
A house object defined in its model coordinate system.

♦ *Space*—If the virtual world has objects that are identical except for their position and orientation, then only one copy is needed: the one in model space. This copy can be used to generate all others, thus saving memory.

Note
Technically speaking, polygons usually aren't stored as a series of points, but rather, as a series of indices into a list of vertices. Why this strange convention? Consider a cube, which has six sides and so would be represented by six polygons. If the polygons were stored as a series of points, then the number of points stored would be 6 (the number of sides) times 4 (the number of points per side), or 24. But this is a waste of both memory and time, because the cube has only eight unique points. These eight points can be put in a list and associated with the object. The polygons can then be stored as a series of indices into this list. Thus the requirements are cut by a factor of three.

Representing Surface Detail

With a few exceptions, today's games don't display single-colored polygons. Instead, all polygons are given texture maps. These are usually high-color or true-color images. They can include transparency (*alpha*) information.

Texture Coordinates

Each vertex of every polygon is assigned (usually by a 3D modeling program) a *texture coordinate*. This coordinate identifies the pixel in the texture map (referred to as a *texel*) that should appear at that vertex. Texture coordinates are usually called (u, v) coordinates rather than (x, y) coordinates to identify them as texture coordinates. Typically, the coordinates are measured in a 0.0 to 1.0 range, where 0.0 corresponds to the left side (for the u coordinate) or the bottom side (for the v coordinate) and 1.0 corresponds to the right side (for u) or top side (for v). Values outside this range are often permitted; they can be dealt with in many ways, such as wrapping (adjusting the values to fit within the 0.0 to 1.0 range), or clamping (for example, using the texel at the side closest to the texture coordinate).

Other Surface Details

Multitexturing is a technique used by games that allows them to combine several different texture maps in a variety of ways. They add bump maps, light maps, reflection maps, or other textures to a polygon, increasing its realism. For every texture applied to a polygon, the polygon must have a set of texture coordinates, one for each vertex.

Representing Motion

From doors that swing in the wind, to trains that move on tracks, to characters, animation is absolutely essential for all computer games. There are three ways that games internally represent motion:

♦ *Key frames*—This approach, which is widely supported by 3D modelers, involves storing a series of 3D models to represent the object's animation. Each model, called a key frame, is a snapshot of the object at a given point in time. Some games can transform one model smoothly into another, cutting down on the required number of key frames and also enhancing playback of the animation.

♦ *Transformation lists*—This approach involves storing a list of transformations (involving rotations, scales, and so forth). One or more transformations are applied to the object in model space each frame. This technique, used by Direct3D Retained Mode, requires less space than key frame animation.

♦ *Physics modeling*—This approach, potentially the most realistic and immersive of the three, involves storing certain constants, like how heavy the object is, where its center of rotation is, what force it can exert in which directions, and so on. The game must then use this information to create the object's animation on a frame-by-frame basis.

Representing Environmental Effects

Environmental effects are represented in a variety of ways. Sounds are typically stored in an uncompressed WAV format, and music is often stored in MIDI format. Fog or haze requires only a single color (and perhaps a distance factor) to represent it.

A light source requires at the very least an intensity, although most lights emit a certain color. Some lights may point in a direction and spread light over a definite number of angles; these lights are stored with an additional vector (to identify the light's direction) and an angle.

Experiencing Virtual Worlds

Representing a virtual world is not the same as displaying it. To allow the user to experience a virtual world, you must go through a number of steps, such as loading the world, creating at least one camera, and then performing the many steps involved in graphically illustrating that 3D scene on the 2D window of a computer monitor. In the sections that follow, I will describe each of these steps in some detail.

Loading The Virtual World

Before you can begin viewing a virtual world, you must load it from disk or from a network into computer memory. Loading a virtual world means loading everything required to represent it at a given time, including geometry, animation, textures, and little details such as fog colors and so on. Once loading has completed, games will create at least one camera.

Defining A Camera

All virtual worlds have at least one *camera*. A camera, synonymously called a *viewport* or *viewer*, captures a view of the virtual world and stores it in memory, either for displaying on the screen (if the camera represents the user) or for texture mapping polygons.

Cameras are defined by two parameters: a 3D position, usually given in Cartesian coordinates; and something called a *viewing frustum*. A viewing frustum is a section of a pyramid that defines the space in the virtual world that the camera sees. An example of a viewing frustum is shown in Figure 2.2.

As you can see in Figure 2.2, six planes bound the viewing frustum. The front and back planes define the closest and farthest space the camera can see, respectively. The left, right, top, and bottom planes set limits on those respective sides of the camera. The angle between the left and right planes is called the *horizontal field of view*. The angle between the top and bottom planes is called the *vertical field of view*. Your choice of the horizontal and vertical fields of view depends both on the viewer you intend to represent and the scale of your world.

The choice of a camera's fields of view is very important when the camera represents the eyes of the game's user. Large angles tend to make the virtual world appear huge, while small ones usually make it appear tiny. Though monitors usually take up no more than 35 degrees horizontally and 25 degrees vertically of the user's view space (see Figure 2.3), these small angles tend to feel confining, and so angles of approximately 70 degrees and 50 degrees are usually chosen instead.

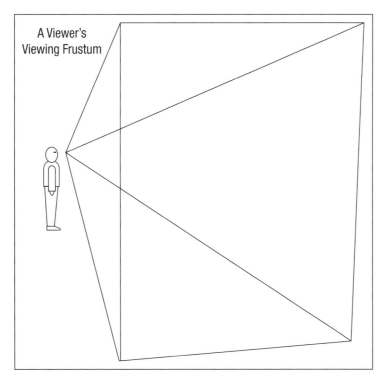

Figure 2.2
A viewing frustum.

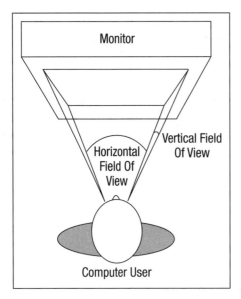

Figure 2.3
The space taken up by the monitor, measured in two angles.

The camera's settings are largely responsible for what units of measurement the user perceives when traveling through the virtual world. The near plane, the fields of view, and the speed with which the user moves all affect how large or small objects will appear in the virtual world.

Transforming Geometry

The transformation phase of displaying a virtual world has two key purposes: to animate geometry and to prepare the geometry for display. The first step, animating geometry, involves only rotating, scaling, and translating the points of the animated objects (the details of these steps, as performed under Direct3D, are discussed in chapters 6 and 7). These operations occur in model space.

The second step, preparing the geometry for display, is more complicated and consists of four distinct phases:

1. First, the objects are transformed from model space into *world space*. This involves rotating, scaling, and finally translating objects to their final orientation, position, and size in the virtual world.

2. Second, the objects are transformed from world space into *camera space*. Three-dimensional geometry cannot be directly displayed on a screen. First it must be transformed into suitable 2D shapes. This transformation is easy to do if the camera is centered on the origin and looking down the positive z-axis, but otherwise it is

computationally expensive. So this second step rotates and translates the world in such a way that a camera at the origin and looking down the positive z-axis would see exactly the same thing as the real camera would see. This is done by negating the position and rotation of the camera and then rotating and translating objects by these negated values.

3. Third, the geometry within the new camera's frustum (the camera located at the origin and looking down the positive z-axis) is warped into a cube shape. This first makes it easy to clip geometry that lies both inside and outside of the viewing frustum (clipping to a cube is much easier than clipping to a pyramid). Second, this transformation also applies perspective to scene, because objects close to the front of the frustum are expanded and objects close to the end are shrunk. After this step has been applied, the results are still 3D. One more step is needed to convert them to 2D shapes.

4. Fourth, the geometry is clipped to the cube shape and the resulting clipped geometry is then transformed into 2D (this involves merely dropping the z-coordinate and scaling the points so they correspond to screen coordinates).

Once all of these steps have been performed, the virtual world is ready to be displayed by the hardware. As you can see, this process involves a lot of rotations, translations, and scales. Performing each rotation separately, and then scaling and finally translating, would take a lot of time. Fortunately, a faster way enables one to concatenate many operations into a single one, by use of vectors.

Vector-Based Transformation

The faster method of transformation defines the location of points by a new coordinate system composed of three vectors: **i**, **j**, and **k**, each defined in terms of the x-, y-, and z-coordinate system. These vectors all intersect at the origin and are perpendicular to one another (see Figure 2.4). Points defined by this system are measured along these three vectors rather than along the x-, y-, and z-axes.

A point normally has an x-, y-, and z-value, but under this coordinate system, it has an **i**, **j**, and **k** value. These values indicate how far the point is from the origin along the **i**, **j**, and **k** vectors, respectively. In this system, the point (2, 1, 3) is interpreted as 2 **i** units from the origin in the direction of the **i** vector, 1 **j** unit from the origin in the direction of the **j** vector, and 3 **k** units from the origin in the direction of the **k** vector. The length of these units depends on the magnitude of the vectors **i**, **j**, and **k** (such as one **i** unit is a length equal to the magnitude of the **i** vector).

You can convert from points in the **i-j-k** system to points in the x-y-z system easily, because the vectors **i**, **j**, and **k** are defined in terms of x-, y-, and z-coordinates. The equation, which follows directly from the previous definition of the **i-j-k** coordinate system, is as simple as this

```
P = i * I + j * J + k * K
```

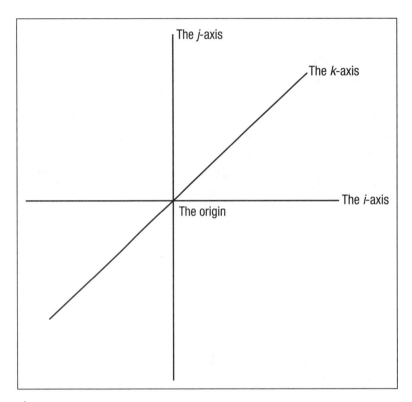

The *j*-axis

The *k*-axis

The *i*-axis

The origin

Figure 2.4
The **i**, **j**, and **k** coordinate system.

where **i**, **j**, and **k** are the vectors defining the **i-j-k** coordinate system, and I, J, and K are the coordinates of the points in the **i-j-k** coordinate system. P is the converted point that resides in the *x-y-z* coordinate system. Notice this equation involves multiplication of scalars (I, J, and K) by vectors (**i**, **j**, and **k**), and then their vector addition.

The neutral settings for the vectors **i**, **j**, and **k** are unit vectors directed along the positive *x*-, *y*-, and *z*-axes, respectively. In this case, the above equation is merely:

```
P = <1, 0, 0> * I + <0, 1, 0> * J + <0, 0, 1> * K
```

This simplifies to the point (I, J, K), which is exactly what you would expect. The real power of defining points in the **i-j-k** coordinate system, however, lies not when the vectors are unit and aligned to the *x*-, *y*-, and *z*-axes, but when they are rotated, scaled, or skewed. If you rotate the **i**, **j**, and **k** vectors, all points based on them, when converted to the *x*-, *y*-, and *z*-coordinate system, will also be rotated. This is true because the points are based on the **i**, **j**, and **k** coordinate system. Thus, if the coordinate system changes orientation, so do the points defined in it. Likewise, scaling (or skewing) the **i**, **j**, and **k** vectors results in all points in that coordinate system being scaled when converted to the *x-y-z* system. This means you can rotate, scale, and skew the **i-j-k** coordinate system as much as you want, and then use the resulting vectors in the above equation to produce any number of identically transformed points.

This savings becomes significant when you remember that each axis rotation involves four trigonometric functions, four multiplications, and two additions. Each axis scale involves another multiplication. If you are rotating and scaling on all three axes, that equals 12 uses of trigonometric functions, 15 multiplications, and six additions, *per point*. The above equation uses a scant nine multiplications and three additions per point, and after the vectors are set up, there is no need to employ trigonometric functions at all. The great power of vector transformation makes it easy to see why the above equation is used in virtually all 3D games made today.

Another great advantage of using vectors for point transformation is that you can concatenate (merge into one) multiple levels of transformations. For example, consider the steps required to spin a robot's head in a simple animation. The robot as a whole has an orientation, so you can first rotate an **i-j-k** coordinate system around the vertical axis to account for this orientation. You can then use this coordinate system to transform all points (except for the head) from model space to view space. For the head, which needs to spin, you can then take the same coordinate system, but rotate its **i** and **k** vectors *further*, around the **j** vector, by the amount the head should spin. You can then use the coordinate system to transform the head. Thus instead of rotating the head to the orientation of the body, and then further rotating it for animation, you only have to transform it once. The optimization is not limited to two transformations, either—any number of rotations, scales, and skews can be so joined into a single **i-j-k** coordinate system, thereby saving large amounts of time and system resources.

Homogenous Coordinates

You will notice that the vector transformation developed above does not support translation. This is because the **i**, **j**, and **k** vectors cannot be translated without changing their orientation. That is, if you add some vector (representing translation) to the **i**, **j**, and **k** vectors, their orientation will also change. The way around this involves defining points in *homogenous coordinates*.

In the homogenous coordinates, each point has a fourth component that measures distance along an imaginary fourth-dimensional axis called w. In this 4D space, all 3D points are represented by the section of 3D space located at $w = 1$. Thus the 4D point $(2, 1, 4, 1)$ represents the 3D point $(2, 1, 4)$. All multiples (fractional or whole) of a point whose w component is equal to 1 represent that same 3D point. Thus $(4, 2, 8, 2)$ represents the same 3D point as $(2, 1, 4, 1)$. So to convert a 4D point into a 3D point, you merely divide each component (x, y, z, and w) by w.

If we add this additional axis, **i**, **j**, and **k** have to be fourth dimensional vectors (in the neutral position, the w component of these vectors will be 0). Further, just three vectors will not suffice to describe a 4D point—we need another vector to describe distance on the *w*-axis. So instead of having just an I, J, and K component, measured along the **i**, **j**, and **k** vectors, each point will have an additional component L, measured along the **l** vector. The neutral orientation of the **l** vector points in the positive direction of the *w*-axis, and its neutral magnitude, like the other vectors, is 1.

For clarity, the neutral settings for all vectors are shown below:

```
i = <1, 0, 0, 0>
j = <0, 1, 0, 0>
k = <0, 0, 1, 0>
l = <0, 0, 0, 1>
```

The equation for translating a point defined in this **i**-**j**-**k**-**l** coordinate system to one in homogenous *x*-*y*-*z*-*w* coordinates is quite simple, and is listed below:

```
P = i * I + j * J + k * K + l * L
```

Points sent through this transformation will consist of *x*-, *y*-, *z*-, and *w*-components. To convert these to 3D points, divide all components by *w*.

How does this addition of an extra dimension help translation? To understand this, notice what happens if we define the vector **l** not as **<0, 0, 0, 1>**, but as **<t_x, t_y, t_z, 1>**, where **t_x, t_y,** and **t_z** are translation factors. Then using the neutral orientations and simplifying, we get the following equation for a homogenous point P:

```
P = (I + t_x, J + t_y, K + t_z, 1)
```

or the three-dimensional point

```
P = (I + t_x, J + t_y, K + t_z)
```

This is a translation, because **t_x, t_y,** and **t_z** are all added to I, J, and K, respectively. This works even when the vectors are not neutral, but are rotated, scaled, or skewed. For now, do not worry about cases where *w* is not equal to 1. I will return to this topic in Chapter 6.

As it turns out, the vector transformations seen above can be represented by matrices more conveniently. For this reason, the next section will introduce matrices and show how they can handle vector transformations.

Matrices

Matrices are rectangular arrays of numbers. An example of matrix notation for a 2×2 matrix is shown here:

```
|M₁₁   M₁₂|
|M₂₁   M₂₂|
```

Each of these symbols stands for a number. The upper-left element is known as m_{11}, because it is in the first row and the first column. The lower-left element is called m_{21}, because it is in the second row, first column.

Matrices are defined for addition, subtraction, multiplication (both with a scalar and with another matrix), and other operations. The main operation that concerns 3D programmers is multiplication, which for matrices **A**, **B**, and **C** (where **A** and **B** are the matrices being multiplied, and **C** is the result) is defined as:

$$C_{ij} = A_{i1}B_{1j} + A_{i2}B_{2j} + A_{i3}B_{3j} + \ldots + A_{in}B_{nj}$$

This definition of matrix multiplication is convenient because if you represent the quadruplet of vectors **i**, **j**, **k**, and **l** with one matrix, and a point by another, multiplying the two matrices together is equivalent to using the equation introduced earlier.

The benefit of using matrices is that you can also multiply one matrix (which represents an **i-j-k-l** coordinate system) with another matrix (which represents another **i-j-k-l** coordinate system). The resulting matrix, when multiplied by a point, will have the effect of transforming the point first by the *second* matrix, and then by the *first*. This powerful merging operation, called *concatenation*, is valid for any number of matrices.

Note
*The order of multiplication is important: Multiplying a point by the matrix (**B** x **A**) is not the same as multiplying it by the matrix (**A** × **B**). In the first case, the transformation **A** visually looks like it has been applied to the point first, followed by the transformation **B**. In the second case, the order is reversed: **B** looks like it has been applied first, followed by **A**.*

For this reason, developers almost invariably represent three-dimensional vector transformations by using matrices. You will often see the four vectors **i**, **j**, **k**, and **l** designated as the rows (or, in some texts, as the columns) of a 4×4 matrix, and a point designated as the elements of a four element, row matrix. Internally, programmers represent matrices by a series of floating-point numbers.

Common Matrices
A number of standard matrices enable you to transform points. These matrices are analogous to the equations used to rotate, scale, and translate points without using matrices. The following is the matrix, introduced earlier with four vectors, that allows you to translate a point:

$$\begin{vmatrix} 1 & 0 & 0 & 0 \\ 0 & 1 & 0 & 0 \\ 0 & 0 & 1 & 0 \\ t_x & t_y & t_z & 1 \end{vmatrix}$$

The scaling matrix is shown here:

```
|sx    0     0     0|
|0     sy    0     0|
|0     0     sz    0|
|0     0     0     1|
```

Rotation has three matrices—one for each axis. The one for the *x*-axis is as follows:

```
|1     0          0       0|
|0     cos θ      sin θ    0|
|0     -sin θ     cos θ    0|
|0     0          0        1|
```

This is the matrix for rotating points around the *y*-axis:

```
|cos θ        0           -sin θ    0|
|0            1           0         0|
|sin θ        0           cos θ     0|
|0            0           0         1|
```

Finally, the matrix for performing rotations around the *z*-axis is as follows:

```
|cos θ      sin θ      0    0|
|-sin θ     cos θ      0    0|
|0          0          1    0|
|0          0          0    1|
```

As mentioned earlier, you can multiply these matrices together to produce one transformation matrix that performs all of these operations simultaneously when multiplied by a point matrix.

Updating Surface Detail

Another important aspect of displaying virtual worlds is updating surface detail. Surface detail includes texture maps, bump maps, alpha maps, light maps, and all other details applied to 3D surfaces. For many surfaces, you have to do nothing at all. But sometimes your virtual world will include a movie playing on a virtual TV, slightly rippling water, or a shadow that changes shape. These effects require you to update the textures applied to the 3D shapes.

Updating Environmental Effects

While updating environmental effects, sounds may be modified, played, or stopped. Lights may change size, position, or strength. Fog may become less or more dense, or other effects, such as rain, snow, or wind, may change. Some of these effects are changed randomly (like rain), others algorithmically, and still others according to a predefined list of changes loaded with the virtual world.

Tactilely Representing The World

Games that use Force-feedback joystick have an additional aspect to update: the states of the Force-feedback devices. Force-feedback devices can apply different kinds of forces in different directions, and games employing such devices must take care to make what the user *sees* match what the user *feels*. On occasion this may happen automatically, because some joysticks support Force-feedback effects that are automatically triggered when one of the joystick's buttons are pressed (this is useful when the joystick represents a weapon). But for the most part, the application must constantly monitor the environment and report this information to the Force-feedback joystick in a way that is intuitive to the user.

Creating Virtual Worlds

An important part in writing 3D games is creating virtual worlds. Most software developers have a selection of custom 3D tools written in-house, which their sound and graphics artists use to create data or transform it into a format suitable for the game. But even so, there are a number of standard program types that nearly all developers use for creating their 3D content. These tools fall into three categories: 3D modeling tools, 2D paint tools, and sound tools.

3D Modeling Tools

Many artists use Caligari's trueSpace to create the 3D geometry for their virtual worlds, or, if geometry is scanned from a 3D source, to clean it up for use in the game. This program, a demo of which is included on the enclosed CD-ROM, supports the X file format (commonly used in DirectX programs), and polygon reduction (the operation of reducing the number of polygons a model uses, to enhance speed), two important features for programmers. Other popular choices include 3D Studio MAX and Microsoft's SoftImage.

All of these programs export files either in their native file formats or in standards such as DXF or X, so programmers usually must write plug-ins or utilities to convert from these file formats into a proprietary format that the game uses.

2D Paint Tools

A game's interface (including its menus, status bar, and so on) and all of its texture maps are two-dimensional. Artists often use 2D paint programs to create (or assemble and touch up from scanned photographs) this artwork. Some standards in the field include Jasc's Paint Shop Pro, Adobe's PhotoShop, and Metacreation's Fractal Design Painter. Though many games directly use BMP, TGA, and even JPEG images, others use a custom file format to prevent users from tampering with the game's look and feel.

Sound Tools

Most sounds that games use are recorded directly from real-world sounds. But for those that are not, and for retouching and modifying those that are, sound artists use tools like SoundForge. As with 2D artwork, many programmers devise utilities for converting standard WAV (or other file formats) into a proprietary file format used strictly by the game, but others simply use WAV files for convenience. For MIDI composition, which is used increasingly in games because of DirectMusic (which enables custom samples for MIDI instruments, thereby ensuring the music sounds the same for all computers), composers often use ACID Pro or another similar product.

Summary

Virtual worlds are composed of objects, characters, and environmental effects. Objects are unified and tangible things in the virtual world. Characters are a special kind of object, either driven by a player or by artificial intelligence.

Polygons are typically represented as a series of indices into a list of 3D points. This method conserves space and processing time. Motion can be stored as a series of models, which are either cycled or morphed through, as a series of transformations that are applied to parts of a model, or as physical formulas, which describe how the model would behave in the real world. Texture maps, bump maps, and other such details applied to 3D surfaces are stored in 2D bitmaps. Environmental effects are stored in a way that depends on the effect.

To display a virtual world, a number of steps are involved: loading the world, defining a camera with a viewing frustum and position, transforming points by using matrices so it can be displayed, updating the changing aspects of the virtual world, and (if necessary) applying Force-feedback effects to an input device.

The creation of a virtual world involves using 3D modeling tools, 2D paint programs (both possibly in combination with scanning), and sound tools. Added to this are often a collection of programs written by programmers to aid the transition from data generated by these tools to data the game will use when it ships.

In the next chapter, we will take a break from the third dimension and look at Microsoft's DirectDraw, a component essential to using Direct3D.

PART II

PROGRAMMING WITH DIRECTX

Chapter 3
Introduction To DirectDraw

Direct3D, both Immediate Mode and Retained Mode, relies heavily on one component of DirectX: DirectDraw. As discussed in Chapter 1, DirectDraw deals with two-dimensional graphics and allows developers to access many of a graphics card's 2D features, such as image copying (*blitting*), resolution changing, and texture creation.

Direct3D uses DirectDraw in several important ways:

♦ To manage the screen resolution and color depth

♦ To create texture maps and mipmaps (covered in the section titled "Bump Maps" later in this chapter)

♦ To create bump maps, luminescence maps, and environment maps

♦ To display texture-mapped video

♦ To manage palettes and, when the application runs in a window, to interface properly with other windows

Before you are introduced to DirectDraw, you must have a solid understanding of Microsoft's Component Object Model (COM), on which each component of DirectX rests.

Introduction To COM Principles

The Component Object Model, invented by Microsoft many years ago, champions the idea of object-oriented software—software composed of many small components, each of which serves a particular function. The advantages to this kind of software design are many:

◆ Parts (components) of an application can be individually updated without updating the entire application, as typically happens when the application consists of one large library rather than many smaller components. This enables software developers to fix bugs rapidly and introduce new functionality in one area of a program without hindering its other parts.

◆ Many different applications can share one component. For example, a spellchecking component can be shared across a word processor, spreadsheet, and database, without duplicating functionality.

◆ This modular method of writing software lends itself to such ideas as inheritance (where one version of a component inherits previous functionality) and complexity encapsulation (just as in C++, where an object can be trivial to use even if it provides much functionality).

◆ COM integrates well with the Web, because it supports self-installing components and those that work directly in Web browsers.

Not all of these benefits apply to DirectX, but because most do, and to keep in line with many other recent Windows developments that use COM, Microsoft decided to produce DirectX as a series of components.

Components And Interfaces

Components in COM are executables that support a list of features. The components of Direct3D, for example, are stored as executable code in a series of DLLs. The precise features supported by a component are described in that component's *interface*. An interface is a technical and exact description of all the features a component uses and how those features are accessed. In this way, *interfaces connect applications to components*. See Figure 3.1 for an illustration of this relationship.

Interfaces are very similar to C++ *classes*. In fact, when you work with interfaces in the C++ language, they *are* classes—pure, abstract base classes. These classes, provided by the designers of the components, are stored in C++ header files and provide your application with all the information it needs to know to use the components.

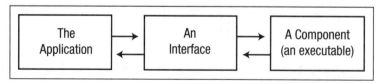

Figure 3.1
The relationship among interfaces, applications, and components.

Like a class, an interface does nothing in itself—that task is performed elsewhere. In C++, the class implementation does the work—the header (the class definition) never has any code. In COM, the components do the work, never the interfaces. The interface defines how objects are accessed: The components implement those definitions.

Also like many classes, interfaces do not allow direct access to data; rather, they expose the functionality of components, and the components in turn modify data. Further, the data created by a component is, as in C++, called an *object*. Interfaces, through components, create and manipulate this data just as C++ classes (through their implementations) create and manipulate data.

Despite these strong similarities, classes and interfaces differ in several major ways:

♦ Interfaces have no constructors or destructors. The objects created through interfaces by components are allocated and deallocated explicitly, by using certain functions.

♦ Interfaces cannot change. In C++, a class is free to undergo revision as necessary. Because this introduces compatibility problems with older programs, however, and thus generates bugs and unexpected program operation, Microsoft forbids interfaces from changing. Once an interface is defined, it must remain as defined forever; new functionality in COM is obtained by defining new interfaces (of course, bugs can be fixed without adding more interfaces). This allows old programs to use old interfaces and new programs to use new interfaces without any hassle.

Note

DirectX does not conform to COM perfectly. Often, the same interface changes slightly with new releases, and some of COM's advanced features are not found in DirectX.

♦ Interfaces can be *queried* to obtain earlier versions of themselves or other interfaces. All interfaces must support the IUnknown interface (covered in the section titled "The IUnknown Interface" later in this chapter).

♦ All interfaces must support at least three functions: **AddRef ()**, **Release ()**, and **QueryInterface ()**. These are management functions and are described in the next section.

♦ Each interface must have an identifier, called a Globally-Unique Identifier, or GUID, associated with it. This is a number that no other interface can have.

Note

One file in your program must include the header InitGuid.H. This causes the compiler to create the GUIDs for use later.

♦ Interfaces must make certain changes to the registry, so Windows is aware of them and can create them, given their GUID.

♦ Interfaces begin with the letter *I*, which stands for interface. The C++ class called **Time** would be named ITime in COM. Subsequent versions of an interface are numbered. The second version of the ITime interface would be ITime2.

These are the major features of interfaces that have no direct or intuitive correspondence in C++. These features are by no means comprehensive, but they should give you a deep enough understanding of COM to use DirectX.

Note

For more information on interfaces (and the many other aspects of COM), see the book Inside COM *from Microsoft Press.*

The IUnknown Interface

As mentioned, all interfaces must support the IUnknown interface. They are derived from this interface and so support its three functions (**QueryInterface ()**, **AddRef ()**, and **Release ()**). Interfaces must also return the IUnknown interface when queried for it.

The following sections detail the functionality of the IUnknown's three functions.

QueryInterface ()

QueryInterface() is the function through which other interfaces are queried. Its C++ declaration is as follows:

```
HRESULT QueryInterface ( REFIID riid, LPVOID* obp );
```

The parameter **riid** is a GUID that identifies the interface being queried.

The parameter **obp** is the address of a pointer, which, upon successful return of the function, will point to the object belonging to the interface (for example, DirectDraw interfaces create DirectDraw objects).

AddRef ()

Objects maintain a *reference count*, which is an integer that specifies how many times the objects are being referenced. Initially, after an object is created, this reference count is set to 1. When it falls to 0, the memory associated with the object is released. Applications *must*, according to COM regulations, call the **AddRef ()** function every time they create a new pointer to the object, and call **Release ()** when they dispose of such pointers.

The **AddRef ()** function increments an object's reference count. It is defined as follows:

```
ULONG AddRef ();
```

The function returns the new reference count.

Release ()

The other memory management function in all interfaces is **Release ()**, which decrements an object's reference count and returns the new count. It is declared as follows:

```
ULONG Release ();
```

As mentioned in the previous section, your application *must* call the **Release ()** function every time a pointer is discarded; otherwise, the object's memory will not be freed when it should be.

DirectDraw Basics

With the foundation of COM laid, you are ready to learn the basics of DirectDraw, starting with terminology and fundamental graphics principles.

Note

For detailed documentation on DirectX, including an exhaustive reference of those functions mentioned in this chapter, see Appendix A, the DirectX help file included with the DirectX Software Developer's Kit, or Microsoft's DirectX Web site at ***www.microsoft.com/directx****.*

Hardware Acceleration

DirectDraw supports hardware acceleration through the *Hardware Abstraction Layer (HAL)*. This is a piece of software, provided by the manufacturer of the graphics card, allowing access to all of the hardware's features. The HAL is a layer between DirectDraw and the graphics card. DirectDraw can, in some cases, emulate features not supported by the HAL by using DirectDraw's own *Hardware Emulation Layer (HEL)*, a software layer that supports many DirectDraw functions. A graphical representation of these layers and their functions is shown in Figure 3.2.

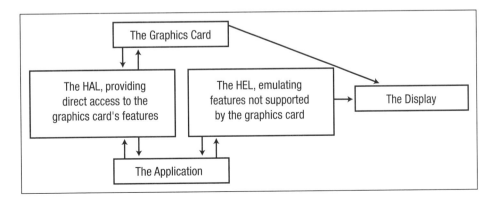

Figure 3.2
The HAL and HEL, pictured graphically.

In systems with one graphics card, applications do not need to concern themselves with HALs. For systems with multiple graphics cards (and this does happen, because some old cards provide 3D acceleration in concert with a 2D accelerator), an application must select which HAL, and thus which graphics card, it wishes to use for acceleration. Alternatively, an application can ignore the HAL and inform DirectDraw to use the HEL exclusively. This makes few features possible and substantially slows performance, but perhaps is necessary in systems that have flawed or no DirectDraw support.

Cooperative Level

The term *cooperative level* refers to the way an application behaves under DirectDraw. DirectDraw applications can run in full-screen mode, allowing the application to change the video mode (no other windows are visible and the application occupies the entire screen), or in windowed mode, where the application behaves as any other Windows application, sharing the display's resources. Cooperative mode also determines other factors, such as whether or not the application will respond to Ctrl+Alt+Delete.

Surfaces

A *surface* in DirectDraw is a rectangular piece of memory, located either on the video card itself or in system memory. This memory is used to store texture maps, bump maps, alpha maps, luminescence maps, mipmaps, the memory visible on the display, z-buffers, and other graphically related data.

DirectDraw surfaces have, in addition to width and height, a factor called *pitch*, which indicates the number of bytes from one scan line to the next. This is not the same as width. Surfaces located in video memory are allocated not in one contiguous block, but in a series of horizontal strips, evenly spaced apart (as seen in Figure 3.3); the pitch informs applications what this spacing distance is. Surfaces located in system memory are aligned to 8-byte boundaries, so the pitch indicates the number of bytes between each horizontal line even in these types of surfaces.

Surfaces all have a *pixel format*, which describes what format their data is in. For example, a 16-bits-per-pixel surface might have a pixel format where 5 bits are dedicated to each red, green, and blue component, and the remaining bit is not used.

DirectDraw surfaces, though all sharing these basic features, come in many different types— that is, the surface memory is used to store different kinds of information.

Basic Surface Types

A surface consisting of the memory visible on the display is called the *primary surface*. This surface always has the same pixel format as current video mode. Modifying the pixels on this surface immediately modifies what the display shows. Primary surfaces are always located in video memory.

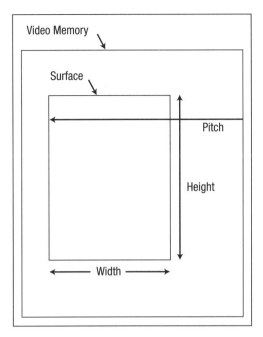

Figure 3.3
The surface's width is different than its pitch, which describes the distance between the rows.

Surfaces can be linked to form *explicit chains*, where one surface is attached to another that is attached to another, and so on. Such surfaces are explicitly attached to one another by DirectDraw functions. These explicit chains are useful for grouping related surfaces.

Another kind of chain is called a *complex surface*, which has a number of implicit surfaces attached to it. Mipmaps are examples of this: DirectDraw can create a texture map that has multiple versions of itself (each version is one-half smaller than the previous version) to improve performance and the quality of rendered images. This texture map is called a mipmap, and is created as a complex surface—one surface with a number of implicit surfaces attached to it. Complex surfaces are easier to use than explicitly attached surfaces, because DirectDraw manages all memory for a complex surface as if it were one surface (memory for explicitly attached chains must be managed individually).

One special kind of chain is a *flipping chain*, where the surface visible on the display alternates, or *flips*, between all surfaces within the chain. In a flipping chain, surfaces not presently visible are called *back buffers*, while the visible surface is called the *front buffer*. Flipping chains are used quite often; data is drawn to a back buffer, and then, when all drawing for the scene is complete, the chain is flipped, turning one of the back buffers into the front buffer (if the polygons were drawn to the primary surface directly, the user would see it and the animation would not appear smooth).

When a flipping chain is flipped, one of the back buffers actually becomes the new front buffer, and the old front buffer becomes a back buffer. This means you will always write to the back buffer and then flip it; you will not write to the back buffer, flip it, then write to the front buffer, flipping it, and so on.

Memory Management

Because all DirectX games run in Windows, they are subject to video mode changes. Users can, for example, press Alt-Tab to switch from a well-behaved DirectX game to the Windows desktop. These and other events cause the memory for all surfaces created in video memory to be *lost*—that is, irreparably freed for other uses. When the application is reactivated, the memory must be restored explicitly by calling DirectDraw functions. This, however, restores only the memory in those surfaces, not the contents of the surfaces, which must be restored by your application.

Restoring a complex surface restores all of its implicit surfaces, whereas restoring a surface in an explicit chain affects only that particular surface (though DirectDraw does provide a way to restore all surfaces at once).

Writing To And Reading From Surfaces

It would be disastrous for the operating system if, while your program was writing to the primary surface, the video mode was changed. To prevent this memory-access error, DirectDraw requires the primary surface to be *locked* before it can be used and *unlocked* when it is done being used.

Usually, when a surface is locked, no other software is allowed to run—only your program, effectively preventing any errors from occurring. Because no other software is running, however, the system will not be able to respond to the user or run critical software. This is always true for the primary surface when it is locked; other surfaces can request that DirectDraw not prevent other software from running.

For maximum performance, do not lock the primary surface for more than a small fraction of a second. To avoid errors, never forget to unlock your surfaces.

Many debuggers will not function if DirectDraw locks a surface. For this reason, many developers write their games to support windowed output, and then later add full-screen DirectDraw support.

Overlay Surfaces

Overlay surfaces are attached to the primary surface. When displayed, overlays float over the primary surface and do not disrupt its contents. Each overlay has a *z*-position, allowing some overlays to obscure others.

Overlay surfaces are implemented entirely in hardware (DirectDraw cannot emulate them) and always reside in video memory. Some hardware allows overlays to be placed anywhere on the primary surface (without being aligned to certain boundaries), to use color keys (covered later), and to use a different pixel format than the primary surface. Other, older hardware devices do not even support overlays.

Texture Map Surfaces

Texture map surfaces are merely those used for texture mapping. These surfaces are often stored in system memory and moved into video memory as required by Direct3D.

Texture maps consist of either red, green, and blue components for each pixel, or, in the case of textures with less than 15 bits per pixel, each pixel consists of an index into a palette associated with the texture map (see "Palettes" later in this chapter).

Environment Map Surfaces

Environment maps are textures specially mapped on a polygon to create the illusion of reflection. Typically, an environmental map will look like the environment of the object to which it is applied. When this likeness of the environment is mapped on an object in a certain way, it appears as if the object is reflecting the environment.

Sometimes, one or more bright highlights are painted on an environment map instead of the environment. If the environment map is then blended with a texture map and applied to an object, it looks like the object is reflecting light sources, adding realism to the scene. These kinds of environment maps play an important role in bump mapping, as you will learn in Chapter 6.

Luminescence Map Surfaces

Luminescence maps, also called *light maps*, are textures that contain lighting information. They are usually blended with texture maps and applied to polygons to create realistic lighting effects.

Luminescence maps come in two flavors: monochrome and color. No pixel in a monochrome luminescence map has red, green, or blue components. Rather, each pixel has an alpha component, and that alpha value determines the pixel's intensity. For color luminescence maps, each pixel has red, green, and blue components; they indicate both the pixel's intensity and its color.

Bump Maps

Bump maps are textures that displace the apparent height of pixels in a texture map. This produces texture mapped surfaces that are apparently bumpy or irregular. Each pixel in a bump map consists of a *u* delta, a *v* delta, and a luminescence value. These components will be explained in Chapter 6 when the mathematics behind bump mapping is covered.

Surface Blitting

Blitting is the process of transferring one surface, called the *source*, to another, called the *destination*. The *source rectangle* in such operations describes the part of the source surface that should be copied. The *destination rectangle* describes where on the destination surface the source is copied.

Copying rectangles is too limiting to create advanced effects, so DirectDraw supports color keys to copy portions of a rectangle from the source surface to the destination.

Color Keys

Color keys consist of a certain color or range of colors that indicate which parts of a surface should be visible. Because DirectDraw cannot yet blit surfaces with alpha components, color keys are the only method of implementing transparency in DirectDraw (Direct3D is an entirely different matter).

The two kinds of color keys in DirectDraw are source color keys and destination color keys. Source color keys specify one or more colors in the source surface that are transparent—they will not be visible on the destination surface after the blit. Destination color keys specify one or more colors in the destination surface that can be covered (pixels of other colors in the destination surface will not be covered).

Palettes

A *palette* in DirectDraw is an array of colors. Each color has an associated index (0 through the number of colors in the palette). Rather than defining pixels in terms of red, green, and blue color components, palettized images are defined in terms of references to a palette.

Palettes are still used for texture maps, which for reasons of speed and special effects are often created as 8-bit palettized textures, even though the video mode is set to 15 bits per pixel or greater. Palettes are not used for the primary surface, because no hardware supports palettized 3D graphics and palettized display modes do not provide enough colors for realistic 3D graphics.

Monitor Frequency And Vertical Blanks

The frequency of a monitor is also called its *refresh rate*—the rate at which the monitor refreshes (redraws) its pixels. The period between a monitor's refreshes is called the *vertical blank*. During this period, you can update the memory on the video card without image problems. If, however, you update the video card's memory while the monitor is refreshing its pixels, the video card will send the new data to the monitor, and the monitor will finish refreshing its pixels with the new data, producing a mix of old and new data. This problem is called *tearing* or *flickering*; both terms describe what the problem looks like.

Avoiding tearing by waiting to update the display until the monitor enters its vertical blank period produces the highest-quality image, but degrades performance somewhat because of the time lost by waiting. DirectDraw can update the display with or without waiting for the vertical blank interval.

FourCCs

Occasionally, the topic of FourCCs arises in discussions of DirectDraw. A *FourCC*— short for four-character code—consists of four characters that describe the software technology used to create graphical or sound information. An example is DXT1, a compressed texture format used by Microsoft in DirectX.

Clippers

Clippers play an important role in windowed DirectDraw applications. In Windows, each window has a *clip list* associated with it. A clip list describes all regions obscuring the window. Through a clipper, DirectDraw is informed of which regions should not be obscured by its blitting operations.

> **Note**
> *DirectDraw provides two functions for blitting:* **BltFast** *(), which ignores clip lists; and* **Blt** *(), which fully supports them.*

Although less common, you can also use clippers to define your own clip lists, unrelated to the ones Windows uses.

Interface Overviews

DirectDraw consists of eight objects managed by eight interfaces. Five of these objects are listed here:

♦ *DirectDraw*—The fundamental object in DirectDraw. All applications must create a DirectDraw object to use any of DirectDraw's features.

♦ *DirectDrawSurface*—Encapsulates a surface, which can be a texture map, bump map, alpha map, luminescence map, mipmap, the primary display device, or other memory-storing graphically-related data.

♦ *DirectDrawPalette*—Represents a palette of colors. It's used for video modes and surfaces with less than 15 bits per pixel.

♦ *DirectDrawClipper*—Allows DirectDraw applications to run in windowed mode. Usually, applications run in full-screen mode, where no other windows are visible.

♦ *DirectDrawVideoPort*—Allows applications to display, capture, and manipulate video (from, for example, a FireWire video camera or a file on disk).

The other three objects, DDVideoPortContainer, DirectDrawColorControl, and DirectDrawGammaControl, are minor and related to the DirectDrawVideoPort object.

The following sections explore the interfaces behind these objects (except for the DirectDrawVideoPort object, which is not covered here because it is not directly relevant to 3D graphics).

The IDirectDraw7 Interface

The IDirectDraw7 interface is a manager for DirectDraw. It interfaces with the graphics card, represented by the DirectDraw object, and it creates surface, clipper, and palette objects.

Table 3.1 lists the major functions of this interface and provides a brief description of what each one does.

Table 3.1   The major member functions of IDirectDraw7 and their descriptions.

Method Name	Description
SetCooperativeLevel ()	Sets the application's cooperative level
TestCooperativeLevel ()	Determines which cooperative level is set
CreateClipper ()	Creates a DirectDrawClipper object
CreatePalette ()	Creates a DirectDrawPalette object
CreateSurface ()	Creates a DirectDrawSurface object
GetCaps ()	Retrieves the capabilities of the chosen graphics card
EnumDisplayModes ()	Lists possible display modes for the graphics card
GetDisplayMode ()	Retrieves the display mode currently set
GetMonitorFrequency ()	Determines which frequency the monitor is set to
RestoreDisplayMode ()	Restores the DirectDraw application to its default setting after the application changes the display mode
SetDisplayMode ()	Sets the display mode for a full-screen application
WaitForVerticalBlank ()	Returns immediately after the monitor enters its next vertical blank
GetScanLine ()	Returns the row, measured from the top of the monitor, being redrawn
GetVerticalBlankStatus ()	Retrieves the status of the vertical blank
GetAvailableVidMem ()	Calculates the remaining free video memory for a certain type of surface
GetDeviceIdentifier ()	Retrieves information that identifies the graphics device
GetFourCCCodes ()	Retrieves the FourCCs supported by the graphics card
DuplicateSurface ()	Creates a duplicate of a DirectDrawSurface object
EnumSurfaces ()	Lists surfaces, whether existing or potential, for the DirectDraw object
FlipToGDISurface ()	Sets the surface used by the GDI (the Graphics Device Interface) to the primary surface, making it visible
GetGDISurface ()	Retrieves a surface whose memory the GDI is using as the primary surface
GetSurfaceFromDC ()	Retrieves the DirectDraw surface used to create a specific device context
RestoreAllSurfaces ()	Restores the lost memory for all surfaces

The IDirectDrawSurface7 Interface

The IDirectDrawSurface7 interface manages **DirectDrawSurface** objects. It provides functions for changing their attributes, modifying their contents, attaching them to each other, checking their status, restoring them, and numerous other functions. Table 3.2 lists the frequently used functions for this interface.

Table 3.2   The frequently used functions of IDirectDrawSurface7 and their descriptions.

Method Name	Description
IsLost ()	Determines whether the surface is lost
Restore ()	Restores the memory associated with the surface
AddAttachedSurface ()	Attaches another surface to the surface
DeleteAttachedSurface ()	Removes an attached surface from the surface
EnumAttachedSurfaces ()	Lists surfaces attached to the surface
GetAttachedSurface ()	Retrieves a particular attached surface
BltFast ()	Performs a rough blit, which is faster than **Blt** () when using software emulation
GetBltStatus ()	Determines the status of a blitting operation
GetColorKey ()	Retrieves the surface's color keys, both source and destination
SetColorKey ()	Sets the surface's color keys, both source and destination
GetDC ()	Retrieves a device context that the GDI can use
ReleaseDC ()	Releases a device context previously allocated with **GetDC** ()
GetFlipStatus ()	Retrieves the status of a flipping operation
Lock ()	Locks the surface
PageLock ()	Locks a system memory surface
PageUnlock ()	Unlocks a system memory surface
Unlock ()	Unlocks the surface
GetDDInterface ()	Obtains the DirectDraw object that created the surface
EnumOverlayZOrders ()	Lists overlays on the surface by their z-positions
GetOverlayPosition ()	Retrieves the position of an overlay surface
SetOverlayPosition ()	Sets the position of an overlay surface
UpdateOverlay ()	Updates the position or attributes of an overlay surface
UpdateOverlayZOrder ()	Changes the z-position of an overlay surface
GetCaps ()	Retrieves the capabilities of the surface
GetClipper ()	Retrieves the DirectDrawClipper object associated with the surface
SetClipper ()	Sets the DirectDrawClipper object for the surface
ChangeUniquenessValue ()	Forces a manual calculation of a unique number that identifies the surface based on the surface's contents
GetPixelFormat ()	Obtains the surface's pixel format
GetSurfaceDesc ()	Retrieves the surface description for the surface
GetUniquenessValue ()	Retrieves a number that uniquely describes the surface based on the surface's contents
SetSurfaceDesc ()	Sets the surface description for the surface
GetPalette ()	Obtains a DirectDrawPalette object previously associated with the surface
SetPalette ()	Associates a DirectDrawPalette object with the surface

The IDirectDrawPalette Interface

The IDirectDrawPalette interface communicates with DirectDrawPalette objects, changing their entries and retrieving their capabilities. Table 3.3 shows all but one of the functions of this interface.

The IDirectDrawClipper Interface

You can use the IDirectDrawClipper interface to check and change a **DirectDrawClipper's** clip list, in addition to associating a window with the clipper object and retrieving the window associated with it. Table 3.4 contains a list of this interface's most popular functions.

Getting Started With DirectDraw

Before you can use DirectDraw's interfaces or functions, you must include the DirectDraw header, "Ddraw.H:", in your application's source files and link the DirectDraw library (Ddraw.lib) to your project (if you use Microsoft Visual C++, add the file's location to the Project | Project Settings | Object/Library Modules text box). Then, according to COM standards, at least one file in your application must include "InitGuid.H", which initializes the GUIDs for use in the application.

Most applications you write will usually complete a number of steps. These steps, listed below in the order they occur, include basic initialization, surface creation, memory management, and, ultimately, object destruction:

1. The application optionally calls the function **DirectDrawEnumeratEx ()**, which lists all graphics devices (this allows an application to select the best device available, if the user has more than one).

Table 3.3   Most of IDirectDrawPalette's member functions and their descriptions.

Method Name	Description
GetCaps ()	Retrieves the capabilities of the palette
GetEntries ()	Sets the colors in the palette
SetEntries ()	Retrieves the colors in the palette

Table 3.4   The most popular member functions of IDirectDrawClipper and their descriptions.

Method Name	Description
GetClipList ()	Retrieves the clipper's clip list
IsClipListChanged ()	Determines whether or not the clip list has changed
SetClipList ()	Sets the clipper's clip list
SetHWnd ()	Associates a window with the clipper
GetHWnd ()	Retrieves the window associated with the clipper

2. The application calls **DirectDrawCreateEx ()**, given either the GUID produced in Step 1 or a default value, which selects the default graphics device. The result, if successful, is an interface to a DirectDraw object.

3. The cooperative level of the DirectDraw object is set, usually to full-screen exclusive mode.

4. If the application supports full-screen mode, the display mode is set.

5. The application creates the primary surface through **IDirectDraw4::CreateSurface ()**, using a flipping chain with one back buffer.

6. The application creates all of its textures, overlays, and other surfaces, and then loads this data from the disk.

7. The application runs until the user quits, restoring surfaces whenever they are lost, and, for each frame, writing to the back buffer and then flipping the primary surface, making the back buffer visible.

8. The application releases all objects.

You'll learn the details in this list in the next chapter.

Summary

The Component Object Model (COM) provides applications with a way to create reusable, upgradable software components. Used in DirectX for all of its components (DirectSound, Direct3D, DirectDraw, and so on), a basic understanding of COM is essential for 3D game development.

COM defines interfaces (roughly analogous to C++ classes), which interface to components (similar to C++ executables) and create objects (as in C++). Interfaces cannot change after they are created. They have a Globally-Unique Identifier (GUID, initialized by "InitGuid.H" in one of the application's source files) and are governed by many other regulations.

The main interfaces in DirectDraw include IDirectDraw4, IDirectDrawSurface4, IDirectDrawVideoPort, IDirectDrawPalette, and IDirectDrawClipper. These interface with DirectDraw, DirectDrawSurface, DirectDrawVideoPort, DirectDrawPalette, and DirectDrawClipper objects, respectively. The DirectDraw object represents a graphics card; its cooperative level must be set, and then the object can be used to set the display mode and create other objects, such as surfaces and clippers. DirectDraw surfaces can be of many types (overlays, for example) and can be connected to one another to form chains and flipping chains. Flipping chains are useful for animation, because a nonvisible surface in the chain, called a back buffer, can be written to and then made into the visible surface. Flipping is best done during a monitor's vertical blank (when no pixels are being refreshed) to avoid tearing.

Surfaces can be blitted, or copied, from a source rectangle to a destination rectangle, with transparency (through the use of source and destination color keys). They can also be read from and written to directly if they are locked. Applications must be careful to unlock surfaces and not keep them locked for long periods of time. Though palettized video modes are not used these days, some palettes are used for textures and other surface types, and for performance and rendered quality reasons.

DirectDraw clippers allow applications to run in windows without overwriting windows placed on top of them. They are not generally used in full-screen DirectDraw applications.

In the next chapter, I go into more detail about actually using DirectDraw.

Chapter 4
Working With DirectDraw

B ecoming familiar with DirectDraw is essential to your mastery of Direct3D—and, thus, to your mastery of 3D game programming. In this chapter, I present a tutorial of DirectDraw, showing you sufficient source code to begin writing your own DirectDraw applications. I also explain a high-level DirectDraw encapsulation in C++, one that takes much of the tedium from writing DirectDraw and Direct3D applications.

Note
Appendix A is a comprehensive reference for DirectDraw. Refer to this Appendix frequently when functions and structures are introduced throughout this chapter.

A Full-Screen DirectDraw Tutorial

Most 3D games run in full-screen mode, rather than in a window, because of its enhanced realism (it is easier to concentrate on gameplay when no distracting windows are in the background) and greater speed (some accelerators do not function or function slowly in windowed mode). For these reasons, this tutorial covers full-screen mode.

Making a full-screen DirectDraw application begins even before you call any DirectDraw functions. It begins with the creation of the application's main window, which you accomplish by using special flags.

Creating The Main Window

Creating a DirectDraw application requires special modifications to the main window's class and the main window itself (as created through **CreateWindowEx ()**). The following code is similar to what you will find in most DirectDraw applications:

```
WindowClass.style          = CS_HREDRAW | CS_VREDRAW;
WindowClass.lpfnWndProc    = WindowProc;
WindowClass.cbClsExtra     = 0;
WindowClass.cbWndExtra     = 0;
WindowClass.hInstance      = Instance;
WindowClass.hIcon          = LoadIcon ( Instance,
   MAKEINTRESOURCE ( IDI_MAIN_ICON ) );
WindowClass.hCursor        = LoadCursor ( NULL, IDC_ARROW );
WindowClass.hbrBackground  =
   ( HBRUSH ) GetStockObject ( BLACK_BRUSH );
WindowClass.lpszMenuName   = CLASS_NAME;
WindowClass.lpszClassName  = CLASS_NAME;

RegisterClass ( &WindowClass );

Window = CreateWindowEx (  WS_EX_TOPMOST,
                           CLASS_NAME,
                           WINDOW_TITLE,
                           WS_POPUP,
                           0,
                           0,
                           GetSystemMetrics ( SM_CXSCREEN ),
                           GetSystemMetrics ( SM_CYSCREEN ),
                           NULL,
                           NULL,
                           Instance,
                           NULL );
```

The source code modifies the **WINDOWCLASS** structure in two unusual ways:

♦ *It associates an icon with the application*—Although you cannot see this icon in the upper right corner of the application (because it is, after all, a full-screen mode application), Windows still uses the icon when you press the Alt+Tab combination to switch from one application to another. You can also see the icon on the task bar when the full-screen application is minimized.

♦ *It sets the background to black*—This ensures no background applications are visible and performs one other function. The window is created first, and then the display mode is set. If the screen were not painted black, it would distort and flicker when the application set the display mode. These problems are not visible when the application's window is entirely black.

The creation of a DirectDraw application's window differs from a non-DirectDraw application's main window in the following ways:

♦ *You use* **CreateWindowEx ()** *rather than* **CreateWindow ()**. This allows extended windows flags.

♦ *You create the window with the extended windows flag* **WS_EX_TOPMOST** *(allowed only in* **CreateWindowEx ())**. This makes the DirectDraw application's window the topmost window (no other window can display anything on top of it). Without this flag, other windows could interfere with the application's primary surface.

♦ *You use only one standard windows flag:* **WS_POPUP**. Though you can use menus, title bars, and other standard windows elements with full-screen DirectDraw applications, usually, for aesthetic reasons, a game allows user interaction through its own highly graphical menus, whose design matches the game's content.

♦ *You give your window a title, as with a regular (non-DirectX) application.* This title is used when you minimize the application and when you press Alt+Tab—though generally the window of a DirectDraw application has no title bar.

♦ *You make the size of the window the same as the size of the desktop.* This ensures that all of the desktop is painted black, thus eliminating the distortion and flicker caused when the display mode is changed while the display contains colors. It also ensures that when the display mode is changed, the window will be large enough so that no background windows will show.

Once an application has created a window, it is ready to initialize DirectDraw.

Initializing DirectDraw

The first step in preparing DirectDraw for graphical operations is to create a DirectDraw object with **DirectDrawCreate ()**, which obtains a pointer to the latest DirectDraw interface (**IDirectDraw7**).

A sample DirectDraw initialization follows:

```
HRESULT Result;
LPDIRECTDRAW7 DirectDraw7Ptr;
Result = DirectDrawCreate ( NULL, &DirectDraw7, IID IDirectDraw7, NULL );
if ( Result == DD_OK ) { // Creation was successful
}
else { /* Initialization failed */ }
```

Once the DirectDraw object is created, the application can set the cooperative level.

Setting The Cooperative Level

*Applications set the cooperative level by calling an **IDirectDraw7** function:*
***SetCooperativeLevel** ().*

The following code sets the cooperative level for a full-screen application:

```
Result = DirectDraw7Ptr->SetCooperativeLevel ( Window,
   DDSCL_EXCLUSIVE | DDSCL_FULLSCREEN |
   DDSCL_ALLOWREBOOT );
if ( Result == DD_OK ) {
   /* The cooperative level was set */
}
else { /* An error occurred */ }
```

Assuming a full-screen application, after the cooperative level is set, the application can determine which display modes the hardware supports.

Analyzing The Display Modes

Though not strictly necessary, determining if the hardware supports a video mode before trying to set that mode is good DirectDraw practice. The **IDirectDraw7**'s **EnumDisplay Modes** () function accomplishes this using a *callback function*. This is a function, defined by your application, which DirectX calls to exchange information.

The **EnumDisplayModes** () function can enumerate all video modes or just those matching a provided description. The following code searches for a 1024 × 768, 32-bits per pixel video mode:

```
DDSURFACEDESC2 SurfaceDesc;
bool FoundMode;
ZeroMemory ( ( void * ) &SurfaceDesc, sizeof SurfaceDesc );
SurfaceDesc.dwSize = sizeof ( DDSURFACEDESC2 );
SurfaceDesc.dwFlags = DDSD_HEIGHT | DDSD_WIDTH |
   DDSD_PIXELFORMAT;
SurfaceDesc.dwWidth = 1024;
SurfaceDesc.dwHeight = 768;
SurfaceDesc.ddpfPixelFormat.dwSize =
   sizeof ( DDPIXELFORMAT );
SurfaceDesc.ddpfPixelFormat.dwFlags = DDPF_RGB;
SurfaceDesc.ddpfPixelFormat.dwRGBBitCount = 32;
DirectDraw7Ptr->EnumDisplayModes ( 0, &SurfaceDesc,
   ( void * ) &FoundMode, CallbackFunction );
```

A sample callback function that simply stops the enumeration when the first video mode is found might look like this:

```
HRESULT WINAPI CallbackFunction (
    LPDDSURFACEDESC2 lpDDSurfaceDesc, LPVOID lpContext ) {
    *( ( bool * ) lpContext ) = true;
    return DDENUMRET_CANCEL; // Stop the enumeration
}
```

Once you find a suitable video mode, it's time to set that mode.

Setting The Display Mode

You can set the Display Mode by performing the following procedures:

```
Full-screen DirectDraw applications set the display mode
through the IDirectDraw7 interface's SetDisplayMode ()
function. Here is some code that sets the display mode
to 1,024 by 768 with 32 bits per pixel:

Result = DirectDraw7Ptr->SetDisplayMode ( 1024, 768, 24, 0,
    0 );
if ( Result == DD_OK ) { /* Display mode was set */ }
else { /* Display mode was not set */ }
```

The next step for DirectDraw applications is generally creating the primary surface (and, subsequently, any other surfaces they wish to use).

Creating The Primary Surface

The primary surface, as mentioned in Chapter 3, must match the display mode in pixel depth and configuration. A display mode of 800 by 600 with a color depth of 16 bits per pixel, for example, supports only a primary surface with these specifications (thus, you cannot specify width, height, and color depth when creating the primary surface).

An application creates the primary surface by calling the **IDirectDraw7::Create-Surface ()** function. Your application could create a primary, flippable surface with one back buffer using the following code:

```
HRESULT Val;
DDSURFACEDESC2 SurfaceDesc;
LPDIRECTDRAWSURFACE7 PrimarySurface;
ZeroMemory ( &SurfaceDesc, sizeof ( DDSURFACEDESC2 ) );
SurfaceDesc.dwSize  = sizeof ( DDSURFACEDESC2 );
```

```
SurfaceDesc.dwFlags = DDSD_CAPS | DDSD_BACKBUFFERCOUNT;
SurfaceDesc.dwBackBufferCount = 1;
SurfaceDesc.ddsCaps.dwCaps = DDSCAPS_COMPLEX | DDSCAPS_FLIP
|DDSCAPS_PRIMARYSURFACE | DDSCAPS_3DDEVICE |
DDSCAPS_VIDEOMEMORY;
Val = DirectDraw7->CreateSurface ( &SurfaceDesc,
&PrimarySurface, NULL );
if ( Val == DD_OK ) { /* Surface successfully created */ }
else { /* Surface not created */ }
```

The primary surface is usually not the only surface created. Your application will usually create other surfaces—texture maps, bump maps, light maps, and so on—after the primary surface, often using the same color depth and configuration as the primary surface. You create all other surfaces using the same function, merely modifying the **DDSURFACE-DESC2** structure passed to it.

After surfaces are created, you will sometimes want to modify their bits directly. DirectDraw refers to this process as *locking* a surface.

Locking Surfaces

You can lock a surface by calling its **IDirectDrawSurface7::Lock ()** member function, as shown in the following code:

```
bool LockSurface ( LPDIRECTDRAWSURFACE7 Surface7,
   RECT &Rect, DDSURFACEDESC2 &SurfaceDesc ) {
   HRESULT Val;
   ZeroMemory ( &SurfaceDesc, sizeof ( DDSURFACEDESC2 ) );
   SurfaceDesc.dwSize = sizeof ( DDSURFACEDESC2 );
   Val = Surface7->Lock ( &Rect, &SurfaceDesc,
      DDLOCK_NOSYSLOCK | DDLOCK_WAIT, NULL );
   if ( Val == DD_OK ) {
      // Pointer to bits is in SurfaceDesc.lpSurface
      return true;
   }
   else {
      /* Locking failed */
      return false;
   }
}
```

After you are done using a surface's bits, you must call **IDirectDrawSurface7::Unlock ()**, which unlocks the surface. The following code performs this rather straightforward action:

```
Surface7->Unlock ( &Rect );
```

Note

You can lock different portions of a surface at the same time. For example, an application could lock the upper half of a surface and subsequently lock the lower half of the surface without first unlocking the upper half.

A DirectDraw Encapsulation

To demonstrate many more things you can do with DirectDraw, and to simplify the operations your applications will typically perform, I have included a simple, easy-to-follow DirectDraw encapsulation.

The primary classes in this encapsulation are **DirectDrawManager** (which encapsulates a DirectDraw object) and **DirectDrawSurface** (which encapsulates a DirectDraw surface). The **DirectDrawManager** class initializes DirectDraw, sets the cooperative level and display mode, and creates surfaces. The **DirectDrawSurface** class provides a simplified means of locking surfaces and blitting them. Listings 4.1 (the header) and 4.2 (the implementation) show the source code for these classes, which are also available on the accompanying CD-ROM. Reference Tables 4.1 and 4.2 document these classes and should give you a good idea how to use them.

Listing 4.1   The DirectDraw.hpp file.

```
//
// File name: DirectDraw.hpp
//
// Description: The header file for a simple DirectDraw encapsulation.
//
// Author: John De Goes
//
// Project:
//
// Import libraries: Ddraw.lib
//
// Copyright (C) 1999 John De Goes -- All Rights Reserved
//

#ifndef __DIRECTDRAWHPP__
#define __DIRECTDRAWHPP__

#include <Stdio.H>
#include <Windows.H>
#include <DDraw.H>


bool PrintDirectDrawError ( HRESULT Error );
HRESULT WINAPI EnumModesCallback ( DDSURFACEDESC2 *SurfaceDesc, LPVOID AppData
);
```

```
class DirectDrawSurface;

class DirectDrawManager {
   protected:
            LPDIRECTDRAW7 DirectDraw7;

            LONG PropWidth, PropHeight, PropBPP;
        bool FullScreen;

        bool ConnectToDirectDraw ();
      public:
            DirectDrawManager ();
            ~DirectDrawManager ();

            bool CreateSurface ( DirectDrawSurface &Surface );

            bool SetDisplayMode ( LONG Width, LONG Height, LONG BPP );

            bool Initialize ( HWND Window );
            bool Uninitialize ();

        bool GetInterface ( LPDIRECTDRAW7 *Interface );
        bool GetBaseInterface ( LPDIRECTDRAW *Base );
};

class DirectDrawSurface {
   public:
        enum SurfaceType { Primary, Plain, Chain, Texture,
            ZBuffer, Alpha, Overlay, BumpMap, LightMap };

   protected:
        LPDIRECTDRAWSURFACE7 Surface7;

        bool TypeSet, Created, PropLum, PropAlpha,
            UseSourceColorKey, ShouldRepaint;

        LONG PropWidth,        PropHeight,        PropBPP,
            SurfWidth,        SurfHeight,        SurfPitch,
            PropChainCount;

        SurfaceType PropSurfaceType;

        friend class DirectDrawManager;

   public:
        DirectDrawSurface ();
        ~DirectDrawSurface ();
```

```
     bool StartAccess ( LPVOID *Pointer,
        RECT *Rect = NULL );
     bool EndAccess   ( RECT *Rect = NULL );

     bool SetSurfaceType ( SurfaceType Type );

     bool SetGeneralOptions ( LONG Width, LONG Height,
        LONG BPP );
     bool SetChainOptions ( LONG ChainCount );
     bool SetTextureOptions ( bool Alpha );
     bool SetBumpMapOptions ( bool Luminescence );

     LONG GetWidth  () { return SurfWidth;  }
     LONG GetHeight () { return SurfHeight; }
     LONG GetPitch  () { return SurfPitch;  }

     bool Show ();

     bool NeedsRepainting ();

     bool BlitTo ( DirectDrawSurface &Dest,
        RECT &DestRect );

     bool BlitPortionTo ( RECT &Portion,
        DirectDrawSurface &Dest, RECT &DestRect );

     bool BlitTo ( DirectDrawSurface &Dest,
        LONG DestX, LONG DestY );

     bool BlitPortionTo ( RECT &Portion,
        DirectDrawSurface &Dest, LONG DestX, LONG DestY );

     bool ClearToDepth ( DWORD Depth );
     bool ClearToColor ( DWORD Color );

     bool SetTransparentColorRange ( DWORD Color1,
        DWORD Color2 );

     bool GetInterface ( LPDIRECTDRAWSURFACE7 *Interface );

     bool GetBaseInterface ( LPDIRECTDRAWSURFACE *Base );
};

#endif
```

Listing 4.2 The DirectDraw.cpp file.

```
//
// File name: DirectDraw.cpp
//
// Description: The source for a simple DirectDraw
//              encapsulation.
//
// Author: John De Goes
//
// Project:
//
// Import libraries: Ddraw.lib
//
// Copyright (C) 1999 John De Goes -- All Rights Reserved
//

#include "DirectDraw.hpp"

DirectDrawManager::DirectDrawManager () {
    DirectDraw7 = NULL;
    FullScreen = false;

    // Establish connection to DirectDraw:
    ConnectToDirectDraw ();
}

DirectDrawManager::~DirectDrawManager () {
    DirectDraw7->Release ();
}

bool DirectDrawManager::ConnectToDirectDraw () {
    HRESULT Val;

    // Create a DirectDraw object:
    Val = DirectDrawCreateEx ( NULL,
        ( void ** ) &DirectDraw7,
        IID_IDirectDraw7, NULL );

    if ( FAILED ( Val ) ) {
            return PrintDirectDrawError ( Val );
    }

    // Successfully connected to DirectDraw

    return true;
}
```

```
bool DirectDrawManager::SetDisplayMode ( LONG Width,
      LONG Height, LONG BPP ) {
   bool CanSetMode = false;
   DDSURFACEDESC2 SurfaceDesc;

   // Set the display mode options to be used during
   // later initialization:

   FullScreen = false;

   PropWidth = Width; PropHeight = Height; PropBPP = BPP;

   SurfaceDesc.dwSize     = sizeof ( DDSURFACEDESC2 );
   SurfaceDesc.dwFlags    = DDSD_WIDTH | DDSD_HEIGHT;
   SurfaceDesc.dwWidth    = Width;
   SurfaceDesc.dwHeight   = Height;

   SurfaceDesc.ddpfPixelFormat.dwSize  =
      sizeof ( DDPIXELFORMAT );
   SurfaceDesc.ddpfPixelFormat.dwFlags = DDPF_RGB;

   SurfaceDesc.ddpfPixelFormat.dwRGBBitCount = BPP;

   // Make sure the specified display mode exists:
   DirectDraw7->EnumDisplayModes ( 0, &SurfaceDesc,
      &CanSetMode, ( LPDDENUMMODESCALLBACK2 )
      EnumModesCallback );

   if ( CanSetMode ) {
      FullScreen = true;
   }

   return FullScreen;
}

bool DirectDrawManager::Initialize ( HWND Window ) {
   HRESULT Val;

   // Set the cooperative level and display mode (if
   // so requested):
   if ( FullScreen ) {
      Val = DirectDraw7->SetCooperativeLevel ( Window,
         DDSCL_EXCLUSIVE | DDSCL_FULLSCREEN |
         DDSCL_ALLOWREBOOT );
```

```
            if ( FAILED ( Val ) )
                return PrintDirectDrawError ( Val );

            Val = DirectDraw7->SetDisplayMode ( PropWidth,
                PropHeight, PropBPP, 0, 0 );

            if ( FAILED ( Val ) )
                return PrintDirectDrawError ( Val );
        }
        else {
            Val = DirectDraw7->SetCooperativeLevel ( Window,
                DDSCL_NORMAL | DDSCL_ALLOWREBOOT );

            if ( FAILED ( Val ) )
                return PrintDirectDrawError ( Val );
        }

        return true;
    }

    bool DirectDrawManager::Uninitialize () {
        HRESULT Val;

        // If the display mode was set, restore it:
        if ( FullScreen ) {
            Val = DirectDraw7->RestoreDisplayMode ();

            if ( FAILED ( Val ) )
                return PrintDirectDrawError ( Val );
        }

        return true;
    }

    void SetColorBitDepth ( DDPIXELFORMAT &PF, LONG Depth,
            bool Alpha ) {

        // Set the bit depth for a color surface, optionally
        // with an alpha component.  Note that this function
        // uses common bit configurations, but there are others.

        ZeroMemory ( ( void * ) &PF, sizeof PF );
        PF.dwSize = sizeof ( DDPIXELFORMAT );
```

```
switch ( Depth ) {
   case 8:
      PF.dwFlags           = DDPF_PALETTEINDEXED8;

      PF.dwRGBBitCount  = 8;
   break;
   case 15:
      PF.dwFlags           = DDPF_RGB;

      PF.dwRBitMask     = 0x1F << 10;
      PF.dwGBitMask     = 0x1F <<  5;
      PF.dwBBitMask     = 0x1F <<  0;

      PF.dwRGBBitCount  = 16;
   break;
   case 16:
      PF.dwFlags           = DDPF_RGB;

      if ( Alpha ) {
         PF.dwFlags  |= DDPF_ALPHAPIXELS;

         PF.dwRBitMask        = 0x1F << 10;
         PF.dwGBitMask        = 0x1F << 5;
         PF.dwBBitMask        = 0x1F << 0;
         PF.dwRGBAlphaBitMask = 0x1  << 15;
      }
      else {
         PF.dwRBitMask     = 0x1F << 11;
         PF.dwGBitMask     = 0x3F << 5;
         PF.dwBBitMask     = 0x1F << 0;
      }

      PF.dwRGBBitCount  = 16;
   break;
   case 24:
      PF.dwFlags           = DDPF_RGB;

      PF.dwRBitMask     = 0xFF << 16;
      PF.dwGBitMask     = 0xFF << 8;
      PF.dwBBitMask     = 0xFF << 0;

      PF.dwRGBBitCount  = 24;
   break;
   case 32:
      PF.dwFlags           = DDPF_RGB;
```

```
         if ( Alpha ) {
            PF.dwFlags |= DDPF_ALPHAPIXELS;

            PF.dwRBitMask            = 0xFF << 16;
            PF.dwGBitMask            = 0xFF << 8;
            PF.dwBBitMask            = 0xFF << 0;
            PF.dwRGBAlphaBitMask = 0xFF << 24;
         }
         else {
            PF.dwRBitMask        = 0xFF << 16;
            PF.dwGBitMask        = 0xFF << 8;
            PF.dwBBitMask        = 0xFF << 0;
         }

         PF.dwRGBBitCount  = 32;
      break;
   }
}

void SetBumpMapBitDepth ( DDPIXELFORMAT &PF, LONG Depth,
      bool Light ) {

   // Set the pixel format for a bump map:

   ZeroMemory ( ( void * ) &PF, sizeof PF );
   PF.dwSize          = sizeof ( DDPIXELFORMAT );
   PF.dwFlags         = DDPF_BUMPDUDV;
   PF.dwBumpBitCount = Depth;

   switch ( Depth ) {
      // 15 and 8 bpp don't really make sense for bump maps,
      // so here they are ignored:
      case 16:
         if ( Light ) {
            PF.dwFlags |= DDPF_BUMPLUMINANCE;

            PF.dwBumpDuBitMask         = 0x1F << 0;
            PF.dwBumpDvBitMask         = 0x1F << 5;
            PF.dwBumpLuminanceBitMask  = 0x3F << 10;
         }
         else {
            PF.dwBumpDuBitMask         = 0xFF << 0;
            PF.dwBumpDvBitMask         = 0xFF << 8;
            PF.dwBumpLuminanceBitMask  = 0;
         }
```

```
         break;
         case 24:
         case 32:
            if ( Light ) {
               PF.dwFlags |= DDPF_BUMPLUMINANCE;

               PF.dwBumpDuBitMask        = 0xFF << 0;
               PF.dwBumpDvBitMask        = 0xFF << 8;
               PF.dwBumpLuminanceBitMask = 0xFF << 16;
            }
            else {
               PF.dwBumpDuBitMask        = 0xFF << 0;
               PF.dwBumpDvBitMask        = 0xFF << 8;
               PF.dwBumpLuminanceBitMask = 0;
            }
         break;
   }
}

void SetAlphaBitDepth ( DDPIXELFORMAT &PF, LONG Depth ) {
   // Set the pixel format for an alpha surface:

   ZeroMemory ( ( void * ) &PF, sizeof PF );
   PF.dwSize          = sizeof ( DDPIXELFORMAT );
   PF.dwFlags         = DDPF_ALPHA;
   PF.dwAlphaBitDepth = Depth;
}

void SetZBufferBitDepth ( DDPIXELFORMAT &PF, LONG Depth ) {
   // Set the pixel format for a z-buffer:
   ZeroMemory ( ( void * ) &PF, sizeof PF );
   PF.dwSize          = sizeof ( DDPIXELFORMAT );
   PF.dwFlags         = DDPF_ZBUFFER;
   PF.dwZBufferBitDepth  = Depth;

   switch ( Depth ) {
      case 8:
         PF.dwZBitMask = 0x000000FF;
      break;
      case 15:
         PF.dwZBitMask = 0x00007FFF;
      break;
      case 16:
         PF.dwZBitMask = 0x0000FFFF;
      break;
```

```
            case 24:
               PF.dwZBitMask = 0x00FFFFFF;
            break;
            case 32:
               PF.dwZBitMask = 0xFFFFFFFF;
            break;
        }
}


bool DirectDrawManager::CreateSurface (
         DirectDrawSurface &Surface ) {

    HRESULT Val;
    DDSURFACEDESC2 SurfaceDesc;
    DWORD EssentialCaps = 0, DesiredCaps = 0,
        EssentialCaps2 = 0, DesiredCaps2 = 0;

    if ( DirectDraw7 == NULL )
        return false;

    if ( !Surface.TypeSet )
        return false;

    if ( Surface.Created )
        return false;

    ZeroMemory ( &SurfaceDesc, sizeof ( DDSURFACEDESC2 ) );

    SurfaceDesc.dwSize  = sizeof ( DDSURFACEDESC2 );
    SurfaceDesc.dwFlags = DDSD_CAPS;

    switch ( Surface.PropSurfaceType ) {
       case DirectDrawSurface::Primary:
          // Create a primary surface with one backbuffer:

          SurfaceDesc.dwFlags |= DDSD_BACKBUFFERCOUNT;
          SurfaceDesc.dwBackBufferCount = 1;

          EssentialCaps  |= DDSCAPS_COMPLEX | DDSCAPS_FLIP |
             DDSCAPS_PRIMARYSURFACE | DDSCAPS_3DDEVICE |
             DDSCAPS_VIDEOMEMORY;

          EssentialCaps2 |= 0;

          DesiredCaps    |= DDSCAPS_LIVEVIDEO |
             DDSCAPS_TEXTURE;
```

```
      DesiredCaps2   |= 0;
break;

case DirectDrawSurface::Chain:
   // Create a surface chain:

   SurfaceDesc.dwFlags |= DDSD_WIDTH | DDSD_HEIGHT;
   SurfaceDesc.dwWidth  = Surface.PropWidth;
   SurfaceDesc.dwHeight = Surface.PropHeight;

   SurfaceDesc.dwFlags |= DDSD_PIXELFORMAT;

   SetColorBitDepth ( SurfaceDesc.ddpfPixelFormat,
      Surface.PropBPP, Surface.PropAlpha );

   SurfaceDesc.dwFlags |= DDSD_BACKBUFFERCOUNT;

   SurfaceDesc.dwBackBufferCount =
      Surface.PropChainCount;

   EssentialCaps  |= DDSCAPS_COMPLEX | DDSCAPS_FLIP |
      DDSCAPS_VIDEOMEMORY;

   EssentialCaps2 |= 0;

   DesiredCaps    |= DDSCAPS_LIVEVIDEO |
      DDSCAPS_TEXTURE | DDSCAPS_3DDEVICE;

   DesiredCaps2   |= 0;
break;

case DirectDrawSurface::Plain:
   // Create a plain surface:

   SurfaceDesc.dwFlags |= DDSD_WIDTH | DDSD_HEIGHT;
   SurfaceDesc.dwWidth  = Surface.PropWidth;
   SurfaceDesc.dwHeight = Surface.PropHeight;

   SurfaceDesc.dwFlags |= DDSD_PIXELFORMAT;

   SetColorBitDepth ( SurfaceDesc.ddpfPixelFormat,
      Surface.PropBPP, Surface.PropAlpha );

   EssentialCaps  |= DDSCAPS_LIVEVIDEO |
      DDSCAPS_OFFSCREENPLAIN;
```

```
        EssentialCaps2  |= 0;

        DesiredCaps     |= DDSCAPS_VIDEOMEMORY |
            DDSCAPS_TEXTURE;

        DesiredCaps2    |= 0;
    break;

    case DirectDrawSurface::Texture:
        // Create a texture:

        SurfaceDesc.dwFlags  |= DDSD_WIDTH | DDSD_HEIGHT;
        SurfaceDesc.dwWidth   = Surface.PropWidth;
        SurfaceDesc.dwHeight  = Surface.PropHeight;

        SurfaceDesc.dwFlags  |= DDSD_PIXELFORMAT;
        SetColorBitDepth ( SurfaceDesc.ddpfPixelFormat,
            Surface.PropBPP, Surface.PropAlpha );

        SurfaceDesc.dwFlags        |= DDSD_TEXTURESTAGE;
        SurfaceDesc.dwTextureStage = 0;

        EssentialCaps  |= DDSCAPS_TEXTURE |
            DDSCAPS_COMPLEX | DDSCAPS_MIPMAP;

        // With texture auto manage, we cannot specify
        // explicitly where the texture should be
        // located:
        EssentialCaps2 |= DDSCAPS2_TEXTUREMANAGE;

        DesiredCaps    |= DDSCAPS_LIVEVIDEO |
            DDSCAPS_3DDEVICE;

        DesiredCaps2   |= 0;
    break;

    case DirectDrawSurface::ZBuffer:
        // Create a z-buffer:

        SurfaceDesc.dwFlags  |= DDSD_WIDTH | DDSD_HEIGHT;
        SurfaceDesc.dwWidth   = Surface.PropWidth;
        SurfaceDesc.dwHeight  = Surface.PropHeight;

        SurfaceDesc.dwFlags  |= DDSD_PIXELFORMAT;
        SetZBufferBitDepth ( SurfaceDesc.ddpfPixelFormat,
            Surface.PropBPP );
```

```
      EssentialCaps  |= DDSCAPS_ZBUFFER;
      EssentialCaps2 |= 0;

      DesiredCaps    |= 0;
      DesiredCaps2   |= 0;
   break;

   case DirectDrawSurface::Alpha:
      // Create an alpha surface:

      SurfaceDesc.dwFlags |= DDSD_WIDTH | DDSD_HEIGHT;
      SurfaceDesc.dwWidth  = Surface.PropWidth;
      SurfaceDesc.dwHeight = Surface.PropHeight;

      SurfaceDesc.dwFlags            |= DDSD_PIXELFORMAT |
         DDSD_ALPHABITDEPTH;

      SurfaceDesc.dwAlphaBitDepth    = Surface.PropBPP;

      SetAlphaBitDepth ( SurfaceDesc.ddpfPixelFormat,
         Surface.PropBPP );

      EssentialCaps  |= DDSCAPS_ALPHA;
      EssentialCaps2 |= 0;

      DesiredCaps    |= DDSCAPS_VIDEOMEMORY;
      DesiredCaps2   |= 0;
   break;

   case DirectDrawSurface::Overlay:
      // Create an overlay:

      SurfaceDesc.dwFlags |= DDSD_WIDTH | DDSD_HEIGHT;
      SurfaceDesc.dwWidth  = Surface.PropWidth;
      SurfaceDesc.dwHeight = Surface.PropHeight;

      SurfaceDesc.dwFlags |= DDSD_PIXELFORMAT;
      SetColorBitDepth ( SurfaceDesc.ddpfPixelFormat,
         Surface.PropBPP, Surface.PropAlpha );

      EssentialCaps  |= DDSCAPS_OVERLAY;
      EssentialCaps2 |= 0;

      DesiredCaps    |= DDSCAPS_VIDEOMEMORY |
         DDSCAPS_LIVEVIDEO | DDSCAPS_3DDEVICE |
         DDSCAPS_TEXTURE;
```

```
        DesiredCaps2    |= 0;
    break;

    case DirectDrawSurface::BumpMap:
        // Create a bump map:

        SurfaceDesc.dwFlags |= DDSD_WIDTH | DDSD_HEIGHT;
        SurfaceDesc.dwWidth  = Surface.PropWidth;
        SurfaceDesc.dwHeight = Surface.PropHeight;

        SurfaceDesc.dwFlags |= DDSD_PIXELFORMAT;
        SetBumpMapBitDepth ( SurfaceDesc.ddpfPixelFormat,
            Surface.PropBPP, Surface.PropLum );

        SurfaceDesc.dwFlags          |= DDSD_TEXTURESTAGE;

        // WARNING: Code assumes bump map blending occurs
        // at the second stage. The environment map should
        // be located in the third stage.
        SurfaceDesc.dwTextureStage = 1;

        EssentialCaps  |= DDSCAPS_TEXTURE;
        EssentialCaps2 |= 0;

        DesiredCaps    |= DDSCAPS_LIVEVIDEO |
            DDSCAPS_3DDEVICE;

        DesiredCaps2    |= 0;
    break;

    case DirectDrawSurface::LightMap:
        // Create an RGB light map:

            SurfaceDesc.dwFlags |= DDSD_WIDTH | DDSD_HEIGHT;
        SurfaceDesc.dwWidth  = Surface.PropWidth;
        SurfaceDesc.dwHeight = Surface.PropHeight;

        SurfaceDesc.dwFlags |= DDSD_PIXELFORMAT;
        SetColorBitDepth ( SurfaceDesc.ddpfPixelFormat,
            Surface.PropBPP, false );

        SurfaceDesc.dwFlags          |= DDSD_TEXTURESTAGE;

        // WARNING: Code assumes light map blending occurs
        // at the second stage (this means bump mapping
```

```
        // and light mapping are incompatible operations,
        // since the above bump mapping code also uses
        // the second stage; change one stage number or
        // the other to fix this).
        SurfaceDesc.dwTextureStage = 1;

        EssentialCaps  |= DDSCAPS_TEXTURE;
        EssentialCaps2 |= DDSCAPS2_TEXTUREMANAGE;

        DesiredCaps    |= 0;
        DesiredCaps2   |= 0;
    break;
}

SurfaceDesc.ddsCaps.dwCaps  = EssentialCaps  |
    DesiredCaps;

SurfaceDesc.ddsCaps.dwCaps2 = EssentialCaps2 |
    DesiredCaps2;

// Try to get the most capabilities:
if ( DirectDraw7->CreateSurface ( &SurfaceDesc,
      &Surface.Surface7, NULL ) != DD_OK ) {

    SurfaceDesc.ddsCaps.dwCaps  = EssentialCaps;

    SurfaceDesc.ddsCaps.dwCaps2 = EssentialCaps2 |
        DesiredCaps2;

    Val = DirectDraw7->CreateSurface ( &SurfaceDesc,
        &Surface.Surface7, NULL );

    if ( FAILED ( Val ) ) {
        SurfaceDesc.ddsCaps.dwCaps  = EssentialCaps  |
            DesiredCaps;

        SurfaceDesc.ddsCaps.dwCaps2 = EssentialCaps2;

        Val = DirectDraw7->CreateSurface ( &SurfaceDesc,
            &Surface.Surface7, NULL );

        if ( FAILED ( Val ) ) {
            SurfaceDesc.ddsCaps.dwCaps  = EssentialCaps;
            SurfaceDesc.ddsCaps.dwCaps2 = EssentialCaps2;
```

```
                 Val = DirectDraw7->CreateSurface ( &SurfaceDesc,
                    &Surface.Surface7, NULL );

                 if ( FAILED ( Val ) ) {
                    return PrintDirectDrawError ( Val );
                 }
            }
        }
    }

    Surface.Created = true;

    // Grab the width, height, and pitch of the new surface:
    ZeroMemory ( ( void * ) &SurfaceDesc,
       sizeof ( DDSURFACEDESC2 ) );

    SurfaceDesc.dwSize = sizeof ( DDSURFACEDESC2 );

    Surface.Surface7->GetSurfaceDesc ( &SurfaceDesc );

    Surface.SurfWidth  = SurfaceDesc.dwWidth;
    Surface.SurfHeight = SurfaceDesc.dwHeight;
    Surface.SurfPitch  = SurfaceDesc.lPitch;

    return true;
}

bool DirectDrawManager::GetInterface (
        LPDIRECTDRAW7 *Interface ) {

    if ( DirectDraw7 == NULL )
       return false;

    ( *Interface ) = DirectDraw7;

    ( *Interface )->AddRef ();

    return true;
}

bool DirectDrawManager::GetBaseInterface (
        LPDIRECTDRAW *Base ) {

    // Retrieve the base interface:
    if ( DirectDraw7 == NULL )
       return false;
```

```
   return ( DirectDraw7->QueryInterface ( IID_IDirectDraw,
      ( void ** ) Base ) == S_OK );
}


DirectDrawSurface::DirectDrawSurface () {
   ShouldRepaint = UseSourceColorKey = TypeSet = Created = false;
   PropChainCount = 0;
   PropLum = PropAlpha = false;
   SurfWidth = SurfHeight = SurfPitch = 0;
}


DirectDrawSurface::~DirectDrawSurface () {
   if ( Created )
      Surface7->Release ();
}


bool DirectDrawSurface::StartAccess ( LPVOID *Pointer,
        RECT *Rect ) {

   LPDIRECTDRAWSURFACE7 Backbuffer;
   DDSURFACEDESC2       SurfaceDesc;
   DDSCAPS2             SurfaceCaps;
   HRESULT              Val;

   // Obtain a pointer to the surface's memory:

   ZeroMemory ( &SurfaceDesc, sizeof ( DDSURFACEDESC2 ) );

   SurfaceDesc.dwSize = sizeof ( DDSURFACEDESC2 );

   if ( !Created )
      return false;

   if ( Surface7->IsLost () != DD_OK ) {
      if ( FAILED ( Surface7->Restore () ) )
         return false;

      ShouldRepaint = true;
   }

   // If the surface is a primary surface, make sure we
   // obtain a pointer to the backbuffer, since that is the
   // surface the application probably wants to write to:
   if ( PropSurfaceType == Primary ) {

      SurfaceCaps.dwCaps = DDSCAPS_BACKBUFFER;
```

```
            Val = Surface7->GetAttachedSurface ( &SurfaceCaps,
               &Backbuffer );

            if ( FAILED ( Val ) )
               return PrintDirectDrawError ( Val );

            Val = Backbuffer->Lock ( Rect, &SurfaceDesc,
               DDLOCK_NOSYSLOCK | DDLOCK_WAIT, NULL );
      }
      else {
            Val = Surface7->Lock ( Rect, &SurfaceDesc,
               DDLOCK_NOSYSLOCK | DDLOCK_WAIT, NULL );
      }

      if ( FAILED ( Val ) )
         return PrintDirectDrawError ( Val );

      ( *Pointer ) = SurfaceDesc.lpSurface;

      return true;
}

bool DirectDrawSurface::EndAccess ( RECT *Rect ) {
   LPDIRECTDRAWSURFACE7 Backbuffer;
   DDSCAPS2             SurfaceCaps;
   HRESULT              Val;

   // End access to the surface:

   if ( !Created )
      return false;

   if ( PropSurfaceType == Primary ) {
      SurfaceCaps.dwCaps = DDSCAPS_BACKBUFFER;

      Val = Surface7->GetAttachedSurface ( &SurfaceCaps,
         &Backbuffer );

      if ( FAILED ( Val ) )
         return PrintDirectDrawError ( Val );

      Val = Backbuffer->Unlock ( Rect );
   }
   else {
      Val = Surface7->Unlock ( Rect );
   }
```

```
    if ( FAILED ( Val ) )
        return PrintDirectDrawError ( Val );

    return true;
}

bool DirectDrawSurface::SetSurfaceType (
        SurfaceType Type ) {

    if ( Created )
        return false;

    PropSurfaceType = Type;

    TypeSet = true;

    return true;
}

bool DirectDrawSurface::SetGeneralOptions ( LONG Width,
        LONG Height, LONG BPP ) {

    if ( Created )
        return false;

    PropWidth        = Width;
    PropHeight       = Height;
    PropBPP          = BPP;

    return true;
}

bool DirectDrawSurface::SetChainOptions (
        LONG ChainCount ) {

    if ( Created )
        return false;

    PropChainCount = ChainCount;

    return true;
}

bool DirectDrawSurface::SetTextureOptions ( bool Alpha ) {
    if ( Created )
        return false;
```

```
        PropAlpha = Alpha;

        return true;
    }

    bool DirectDrawSurface::SetBumpMapOptions (
            bool Luminescence ) {

        if ( Created )
           return false;

        PropLum = Luminescence;

        return true;
    }

    bool DirectDrawSurface::Show () {
        HRESULT Val;

        // Display the backbuffer of a primary surface:

        if ( !Created )
           return false;

        if ( PropSurfaceType != Primary )
           return false;

        if ( Surface7->IsLost () != DD_OK ) {
           if ( FAILED ( Surface7->Restore () ) )
              return false;

           ShouldRepaint = true;
        }

        Val = Surface7->Flip ( NULL, DDFLIP_WAIT );

        if ( FAILED ( Val ) )
           return PrintDirectDrawError ( Val );

        return true;
    }

    bool DirectDrawSurface::BlitTo ( DirectDrawSurface &Dest,
            RECT &DestRect ) {

        RECT Portion;
```

```
   if ( !Created )
      return false;

   Portion.left = 0; Portion.top = 0;
   Portion.right = PropWidth; Portion.bottom = PropHeight;

   return BlitPortionTo ( Portion, Dest, DestRect );
}

bool DirectDrawSurface::BlitPortionTo ( RECT &Portion,
        DirectDrawSurface &Dest, RECT &DestRect ) {

   DDBLTFX BlitFX;
   DWORD Flags = DDBLT_WAIT;
   HRESULT Val;

   if ( !Created )
      return false;

   if ( Surface7->IsLost () != DD_OK ) {
      if ( FAILED ( Surface7->Restore () ) )
         return false;

      ShouldRepaint = true;
   }

   ZeroMemory ( ( void * ) &BlitFX, sizeof ( DDBLTFX ) );
   BlitFX.dwSize = sizeof ( DDBLTFX );

   if ( UseSourceColorKey )
      Flags |= DDBLT_KEYSRC;

   Val = Dest.Surface7->Blt ( &DestRect, this->Surface7,
      &Portion, Flags, &BlitFX );

   if ( FAILED ( Val ) )
      return PrintDirectDrawError ( Val );

   return true;
}

bool DirectDrawSurface::BlitTo ( DirectDrawSurface &Dest,
        LONG DestX, LONG DestY ) {

   RECT DestRect;
```

```
            DestRect.left      = DestX;
            DestRect.right     = DestX + PropWidth;
            DestRect.top       = DestY;
            DestRect.bottom    = DestY + PropHeight;

            return BlitTo ( Dest, DestRect );
        }

        bool DirectDrawSurface::BlitPortionTo ( RECT &Portion,
                DirectDrawSurface &Dest, LONG DestX, LONG DestY ) {

            RECT DestRect;

            DestRect.left      = DestX;
            DestRect.right     = DestX + PropWidth;
            DestRect.top       = DestY;
            DestRect.bottom    = DestY + PropHeight;

            return BlitPortionTo ( Portion, Dest, DestRect );
        }

        bool DirectDrawSurface::ClearToDepth ( DWORD Depth ) {
            DDBLTFX BlitFX;
            RECT Portion;
            DWORD Flags = 0;
            HRESULT Val;

            if ( !Created )
                return false;

            if ( PropSurfaceType != ZBuffer )
                return false;

            if ( Surface7->IsLost () != DD_OK ) {
                if ( FAILED ( Surface7->Restore () ) )
                    return false;

                ShouldRepaint = true;
            }

            // Clear z-buffer to a specific depth:

            Portion.left = 0; Portion.top = 0;
            Portion.right = PropWidth; Portion.bottom = PropHeight;

            ZeroMemory ( ( void * ) &BlitFX, sizeof ( DDBLTFX ) );
            BlitFX.dwSize = sizeof ( DDBLTFX );
```

```
    Flags |= DDBLT_DEPTHFILL;

    BlitFX.dwFillDepth = Depth;

    Val = Surface7->Blt ( NULL, NULL, &Portion, Flags,
       &BlitFX );

    if ( FAILED ( Val ) )
       return PrintDirectDrawError ( Val );

    return true;
}

bool DirectDrawSurface::ClearToColor ( DWORD Color ) {
    DDBLTFX BlitFX;
    RECT Portion;
    DWORD Flags = 0;
    HRESULT Val;

    if ( !Created )
       return false;

    if ( Surface7->IsLost () != DD_OK ) {
       if ( FAILED ( Surface7->Restore () ) )
          return false;

       ShouldRepaint = true;
    }

    // Clear surface to a specific color:

    Portion.left = 0; Portion.top = 0;
    Portion.right = PropWidth; Portion.bottom = PropHeight;

    ZeroMemory ( ( void * ) &BlitFX, sizeof ( DDBLTFX ) );
    BlitFX.dwSize = sizeof ( DDBLTFX );

    Flags |= DDBLT_COLORFILL;

    if ( !PropAlpha ) {
       BlitFX.dwFillColor = Color;
    }
    else {
       BlitFX.dwFillPixel = Color;
    }
```

```
    Val = Surface7->Blt ( NULL, NULL, &Portion, Flags,
        &BlitFX );

    if ( FAILED ( Val ) )
        return PrintDirectDrawError ( Val );

    return true;
}

bool DirectDrawSurface::SetTransparentColorRange (
        DWORD Color1, DWORD Color2 ) {

    DWORD Flags = DDCKEY_COLORSPACE;
    DDCOLORKEY ColorKey;
    HRESULT Val;

    // Set the source color key range for the surface:

    if ( !Created )
        return false;

    if ( PropSurfaceType == Overlay ) {
        Flags |= DDCKEY_SRCOVERLAY;
    }
    else Flags |= DDCKEY_SRCBLT;

    ColorKey.dwColorSpaceLowValue  = Color1;
    ColorKey.dwColorSpaceHighValue = Color2;

    Val = Surface7->SetColorKey ( Flags, &ColorKey );

    if ( FAILED ( Val ) )
        PrintDirectDrawError ( Val );

    UseSourceColorKey = true;

    return true;
}

bool DirectDrawSurface::NeedsRepainting () {
    if ( ShouldRepaint ) {
        ShouldRepaint = false;
        return true;
    }
```

```
      return false;
}

bool DirectDrawSurface::GetInterface (
        LPDIRECTDRAWSURFACE7 *Interface ) {

   if ( Surface7 == NULL )
      return false;

   ( *Interface ) = Surface7;

   ( *Interface )->AddRef ();

   return true;
}

bool DirectDrawSurface::GetBaseInterface (
        LPDIRECTDRAWSURFACE *Base ) {

   return ( Surface7->QueryInterface (
              IID_IDirectDrawSurface,
              ( void ** ) Base ) == S_OK );
}

HRESULT WINAPI EnumModesCallback (
      DDSURFACEDESC2 *SurfaceDesc, LPVOID AppData ) {

   bool *CanSetMode = ( bool * ) ( AppData );

   // Possibly check surface description here for best
   // pixel configuration...

   ( *CanSetMode ) = true;

   return DDENUMRET_CANCEL;
}

bool FatalError ( TCHAR *Message ) {
   TCHAR ErrorMessage [ 200 ];

   sprintf ( ErrorMessage, "DirectDraw Error: %s",
      Message );

   MessageBox ( GetActiveWindow (), ErrorMessage,
      "DirectDraw Fatal Error", MB_OK | MB_ICONERROR );
```

```
        return false;
    }


    bool PrintDirectDrawError ( HRESULT Error ) {
        switch ( Error ) {
            case DD_OK:
                FatalError ( "DD_OK" );
            break;
            case DDERR_ALREADYINITIALIZED:
                FatalError ( "DDERR_ALREADYINITIALIZED" );
            break;
            case DDERR_BLTFASTCANTCLIP:
                FatalError ( "DDERR_BLTFASTCANTCLIP" );
            break;
            case DDERR_CANNOTATTACHSURFACE:
                FatalError ( "DDERR_CANNOTATTACHSURFACE" );
            break;
            case DDERR_CANNOTDETACHSURFACE:
                FatalError ( "DDERR_CANNOTDETACHSURFACE" );
            break;
            case DDERR_CANTCREATEDC:
                FatalError ( "DDERR_CANTCREATEDC" );
            break;
            case DDERR_CANTDUPLICATE:
                FatalError ( "DDERR_CANTDUPLICATE" );
            break;
            case DDERR_CANTLOCKSURFACE:
                FatalError ( "DDERR_CANTLOCKSURFACE" );
            break;
            case DDERR_CANTPAGELOCK:
                FatalError ( "DDERR_CANTPAGELOCK" );
            break;
            case DDERR_CANTPAGEUNLOCK:
                FatalError ( "DDERR_CANTPAGEUNLOCK" );
            break;
            case DDERR_CLIPPERISUSINGHWND:
                FatalError ( "DDERR_CLIPPERISUSINGHWND" );
            break;
            case DDERR_COLORKEYNOTSET:
                FatalError ( "DDERR_COLORKEYNOTSET" );
            break;
            case DDERR_CURRENTLYNOTAVAIL:
                FatalError ( "DDERR_CURRENTLYNOTAVAIL" );
            break;
```

```
case DDERR_DCALREADYCREATED:
   FatalError ( "DDERR_DCALREADYCREATED" );
break;
case DDERR_DEVICEDOESNTOWNSURFACE:
   FatalError ( "DDERR_DEVICEDOESNTOWNSURFACE" );
break;
case DDERR_DIRECTDRAWALREADYCREATED:
   FatalError ( "DDERR_DIRECTDRAWALREADYCREATED" );
break;
case DDERR_EXCEPTION:
   FatalError ( "DDERR_EXCEPTION" );
break;
case DDERR_EXCLUSIVEMODEALREADYSET:
   FatalError ( "DDERR_EXCLUSIVEMODEALREADYSET" );
break;
case DDERR_EXPIRED:
   FatalError ( "DDERR_EXPIRED" );
break;
case DDERR_GENERIC:
   FatalError ( "DDERR_GENERIC" );
break;
case DDERR_HEIGHTALIGN:
   FatalError ( "DDERR_HEIGHTALIGN" );
break;
case DDERR_HWNDALREADYSET:
   FatalError ( "DDERR_HWNDALREADYSET" );
break;
case DDERR_HWNDSUBCLASSED:
   FatalError ( "DDERR_HWNDSUBCLASSED" );
break;
case DDERR_IMPLICITLYCREATED:
   FatalError ( "DDERR_IMPLICITLYCREATED" );
break;
case DDERR_INCOMPATIBLEPRIMARY:
   FatalError ( "DDERR_INCOMPATIBLEPRIMARY" );
break;
case DDERR_INVALIDCAPS:
   FatalError ( "DDERR_INVALIDCAPS" );
break;
case DDERR_INVALIDCLIPLIST:
   FatalError ( "DDERR_INVALIDCLIPLIST" );
break;
case DDERR_INVALIDDIRECTDRAWGUID:
   FatalError ( "DDERR_INVALIDDIRECTDRAWGUID" );
break;
```

```
case DDERR_INVALIDMODE:
    FatalError ( "DDERR_INVALIDMODE" );
break;
case DDERR_INVALIDOBJECT:
    FatalError ( "DDERR_INVALIDOBJECT" );
break;
case DDERR_INVALIDPARAMS:
    FatalError ( "DDERR_INVALIDPARAMS" );
break;
case DDERR_INVALIDPIXELFORMAT:
    FatalError ( "DDERR_INVALIDPIXELFORMAT" );
break;
case DDERR_INVALIDPOSITION:
    FatalError ( "DDERR_INVALIDPOSITION" );
break;
case DDERR_INVALIDRECT:
    FatalError ( "DDERR_INVALIDRECT" );
break;
case DDERR_INVALIDSTREAM:
    FatalError ( "DDERR_INVALIDSTREAM" );
break;
case DDERR_INVALIDSURFACETYPE:
    FatalError ( "DDERR_INVALIDSURFACETYPE" );
break;
case DDERR_LOCKEDSURFACES:
    FatalError ( "DDERR_LOCKEDSURFACES" );
break;
case DDERR_MOREDATA:
    FatalError ( "DDERR_MOREDATA" );
break;
case DDERR_NO3D:
    FatalError ( "DDERR_NO3D" );
break;
case DDERR_NOALPHAHW:
    FatalError ( "DDERR_NOALPHAHW" );
break;
case DDERR_NOBLTHW:
    FatalError ( "DDERR_NOBLTHW" );
break;
case DDERR_NOCLIPLIST:
    FatalError ( "DDERR_NOCLIPLIST" );
break;
case DDERR_NOCLIPPERATTACHED:
    FatalError ( "DDERR_NOCLIPPERATTACHED" );
break;
```

```
case DDERR_NOCOLORCONVHW:
   FatalError ( "DDERR_NOCOLORCONVHW" );
break;
case DDERR_NOCOLORKEY:
   FatalError ( "DDERR_NOCOLORKEY" );
break;
case DDERR_NOCOLORKEYHW:
   FatalError ( "DDERR_NOCOLORKEYHW" );
break;
case DDERR_NOCOOPERATIVELEVELSET:
   FatalError ( "DDERR_NOCOOPERATIVELEVELSET" );
break;
case DDERR_NODC:
   FatalError ( "DDERR_NODC" );
break;
case DDERR_NODDROPSHW:
   FatalError ( "DDERR_NODDROPSHW" );
break;
case DDERR_NODIRECTDRAWHW:
   FatalError ( "DDERR_NODIRECTDRAWHW" );
break;
case DDERR_NODIRECTDRAWSUPPORT:
   FatalError ( "DDERR_NODIRECTDRAWSUPPORT" );
break;
case DDERR_NOEMULATION:
   FatalError ( "DDERR_NOEMULATION" );
break;
case DDERR_NOEXCLUSIVEMODE:
   FatalError ( "DDERR_NOEXCLUSIVEMODE" );
break;
case DDERR_NOFLIPHW:
   FatalError ( "DDERR_NOFLIPHW" );
break;
case DDERR_NOFOCUSWINDOW:
   FatalError ( "DDERR_NOFOCUSWINDOW" );
break;
case DDERR_NOGDI:
   FatalError ( "DDERR_NOGDI" );
break;
case DDERR_NOHWND:
   FatalError ( "DDERR_NOHWND" );
break;
case DDERR_NOMIPMAPHW:
   FatalError ( "DDERR_NOMIPMAPHW" );
break;
```

```
case DDERR_NOMIRRORHW:
  FatalError ( "DDERR_NOMIRRORHW" );
break;
case DDERR_NONONLOCALVIDMEM:
  FatalError ( "DDERR_NONONLOCALVIDMEM" );
break;
case DDERR_NOOPTIMIZEHW:
  FatalError ( "DDERR_NOOPTIMIZEHW" );
break;
case DDERR_NOOVERLAYDEST:
  FatalError ( "DDERR_NOOVERLAYDEST" );
break;
case DDERR_NOOVERLAYHW:
  FatalError ( "DDERR_NOOVERLAYHW" );
break;
case DDERR_NOPALETTEATTACHED:
  FatalError ( "DDERR_NOPALETTEATTACHED" );
break;
case DDERR_NOPALETTEHW:
  FatalError ( "DDERR_NOPALETTEHW" );
break;
case DDERR_NORASTEROPHW:
  FatalError ( "DDERR_NORASTEROPHW" );
break;
case DDERR_NOROTATIONHW:
  FatalError ( "DDERR_NOROTATIONHW" );
break;
case DDERR_NOSTRETCHHW:
  FatalError ( "DDERR_NOSTRETCHHW" );
break;
case DDERR_NOT4BITCOLOR:
  FatalError ( "DDERR_NOT4BITCOLOR" );
break;
case DDERR_NOT4BITCOLORINDEX:
  FatalError ( "DDERR_NOT4BITCOLORINDEX" );
break;
case DDERR_NOT8BITCOLOR:
  FatalError ( "DDERR_NOT8BITCOLOR" );
break;
case DDERR_NOTAOVERLAYSURFACE:
  FatalError ( "DDERR_NOTAOVERLAYSURFACE" );
break;
case DDERR_NOTEXTUREHW:
  FatalError ( "DDERR_NOTEXTUREHW" );
break;
```

```
case DDERR_NOTFLIPPABLE:
   FatalError ( "DDERR_NOTFLIPPABLE" );
break;
case DDERR_NOTFOUND:
   FatalError ( "DDERR_NOTFOUND" );
break;
case DDERR_NOTINITIALIZED:
   FatalError ( "DDERR_NOTINITIALIZED" );
break;
case DDERR_NOTLOADED:
   FatalError ( "DDERR_NOTLOADED" );
break;
case DDERR_NOTLOCKED:
   FatalError ( "DDERR_NOTLOCKED" );
break;
case DDERR_NOTPAGELOCKED:
   FatalError ( "DDERR_NOTPAGELOCKED" );
break;
case DDERR_NOTPALETTIZED:
   FatalError ( "DDERR_NOTPALETTIZED" );
break;
case DDERR_NOVSYNCHW:
   FatalError ( "DDERR_NOVSYNCHW" );
break;
case DDERR_NOZBUFFERHW:
   FatalError ( "DDERR_NOZBUFFERHW" );
break;
case DDERR_NOZOVERLAYHW:
   FatalError ( "DDERR_NOZOVERLAYHW" );
break;
case DDERR_OUTOFCAPS:
   FatalError ( "DDERR_OUTOFCAPS" );
break;
case DDERR_OUTOFMEMORY:
   FatalError ( "DDERR_OUTOFMEMORY" );
break;
case DDERR_OUTOFVIDEOMEMORY:
   FatalError ( "DDERR_OUTOFVIDEOMEMORY" );
break;
case DDERR_OVERLAPPINGRECTS:
   FatalError ( "DDERR_OVERLAPPINGRECTS" );
break;
case DDERR_OVERLAYCANTCLIP:
   FatalError ( "DDERR_OVERLAYCANTCLIP" );
break;
```

```
case DDERR_OVERLAYCOLORKEYONLYONEACTIVE:
   FatalError ("DDERR_OVERLAYCOLORKEYONLYONEACTIVE");
break;
case DDERR_OVERLAYNOTVISIBLE:
   FatalError ( "DDERR_OVERLAYNOTVISIBLE" );
break;
case DDERR_PALETTEBUSY:
   FatalError ( "DDERR_PALETTEBUSY" );
break;
case DDERR_PRIMARYSURFACEALREADYEXISTS:
   FatalError ("DDERR_PRIMARYSURFACEALREADYEXISTS");
break;
case DDERR_REGIONTOOSMALL:
   FatalError ( "DDERR_REGIONTOOSMALL" );
break;
case DDERR_SURFACEALREADYATTACHED:
   FatalError ( "DDERR_SURFACEALREADYATTACHED" );
break;
case DDERR_SURFACEALREADYDEPENDENT:
   FatalError ( "DDERR_SURFACEALREADYDEPENDENT" );
break;
case DDERR_SURFACEBUSY:
   FatalError ( "DDERR_SURFACEBUSY" );
break;
case DDERR_SURFACEISOBSCURED:
   FatalError ( "DDERR_SURFACEISOBSCURED" );
break;
case DDERR_SURFACELOST:
   FatalError ( "DDERR_SURFACELOST" );
break;
case DDERR_SURFACENOTATTACHED:
   FatalError ( "DDERR_SURFACENOTATTACHED" );
break;
case DDERR_TOOBIGHEIGHT:
   FatalError ( "DDERR_TOOBIGHEIGHT" );
break;
case DDERR_TOOBIGSIZE:
   FatalError ( "DDERR_TOOBIGSIZE" );
break;
case DDERR_TOOBIGWIDTH:
   FatalError ( "DDERR_TOOBIGWIDTH" );
break;
case DDERR_UNSUPPORTED:
   FatalError ( "DDERR_UNSUPPORTED" );
break;
```

```
            case DDERR_UNSUPPORTEDFORMAT:
                FatalError ( "DDERR_UNSUPPORTEDFORMAT" );
            break;
            case DDERR_UNSUPPORTEDMASK:
                FatalError ( "DDERR_UNSUPPORTEDMASK" );
            break;
            case DDERR_UNSUPPORTEDMODE:
                FatalError ( "DDERR_UNSUPPORTEDMODE" );
            break;
            case DDERR_VERTICALBLANKINPROGRESS:
                FatalError ( "DDERR_VERTICALBLANKINPROGRESS" );
            break;
            case DDERR_VIDEONOTACTIVE:
                FatalError ( "DDERR_VIDEONOTACTIVE" );
            break;
            case DDERR_WASSTILLDRAWING:
                FatalError ( "DDERR_WASSTILLDRAWING" );
            break;
            case DDERR_WRONGMODE:
                FatalError ( "DDERR_WRONGMODE" );
            break;
            case DDERR_XALIGN:
                FatalError ( "DDERR_XALIGN" );
            break;
        }
        return false;
    }
```

Reference Table 4.1   The class reference for DirectDrawManager.

Class Declaration

```
class DirectDrawManager {
    protected:
        LPDIRECTDRAW  DirectDraw;
        LPDIRECTDRAW7 DirectDraw7;

        LONG PropWidth, PropHeight, PropBPP;
        bool FullScreen;

        bool ConnectToDirectDraw ();
    public:
        DirectDrawManager ();
        ~DirectDrawManager ();

        bool CreateSurface ( DirectDrawSurface &Surface );
```

(continued)

Reference Table 4.1   The class reference for DirectDrawManager *(continued)*.

Class Declaration

```
        bool SetDisplayMode ( LONG Width, LONG Height, LONG BPP );

        bool Initialize ( HWND Window );
        bool Uninitialize ();

        bool GetInterface ( LPDIRECTDRAW7 *Interface );
        bool GetBaseInterface ( LPDIRECTDRAW *Base );
};
```

Member Function	Description
CreateSurface	Creates a surface given a reference to a DirectDrawSurface object whose attributes have already been set.
SetDisplayMode	Stores the screen width, height, and bits per pixels for use later in the **Initialize** () function.
Initialize	Sets the cooperative level and the display mode.
Uninitialize	Restores the display mode.
GetInterface	Retrieves an **IDirectDraw7** interface. This is useful for working directly with DirectDraw.
GetBaseInterface	Retrieves an **IDirectDraw** interface.

Reference Table 4.2   The class reference for DirectDrawSurface.

Class Declaration

```
class DirectDrawSurface {
  public:
      enum SurfaceType { Primary, Plain, Chain, Texture,
         ZBuffer, Alpha, Overlay, BumpMap, LightMap };

  protected:
     LPDIRECTDRAWSURFACE7 Surface7;

     bool TypeSet, Created, PropLum, PropAlpha,
         UseSourceColorKey, ShouldRepaint;

     LONG PropWidth,      PropHeight,      PropBPP,
          SurfWidth,      SurfHeight,      SurfPitch,
          PropChainCount;

     SurfaceType PropSurfaceType;

     friend class DirectDrawManager;
```

Reference Table 4.2 The class reference for DirectDrawSurface *(continued).*

Class Declaration

```
public:
   DirectDrawSurface ();
   ~DirectDrawSurface ();

   bool StartAccess ( LPVOID *Pointer,
      RECT *Rect = NULL );
   bool EndAccess   ( RECT *Rect = NULL );

   bool SetSurfaceType ( SurfaceType Type );

   bool SetGeneralOptions ( LONG Width, LONG Height,
      LONG BPP );
   bool SetChainOptions ( LONG ChainCount );
   bool SetTextureOptions ( bool Alpha );
   bool SetBumpMapOptions ( bool Luminescence );

   LONG GetWidth  () { return SurfWidth;  }
   LONG GetHeight () { return SurfHeight; }
   LONG GetPitch  () { return SurfPitch;  }

   bool Show ();

   bool NeedsRepainting ();
   bool BlitTo ( DirectDrawSurface &Dest,
      RECT &DestRect );

   bool BlitPortionTo ( RECT &Portion,
      DirectDrawSurface &Dest, RECT &DestRect );

   bool BlitTo ( DirectDrawSurface &Dest,
      LONG DestX, LONG DestY );

   bool BlitPortionTo ( RECT &Portion,
      DirectDrawSurface &Dest, LONG DestX, LONG DestY );

   bool ClearToDepth ( DWORD Depth );
   bool ClearToColor ( DWORD Color );

   bool SetTransparentColorRange ( DWORD Color1,
      DWORD Color2 );
```

(continued)

Reference Table 4.2   The class reference for DirectDrawSurface *(continued).*

Class Declaration

```
    bool GetInterface ( LPDIRECTDRAWSURFACE7 *Interface );

    bool GetBaseInterface ( LPDIRECTDRAWSURFACE *Base );
};
```

Member Function	Description
StartAccess	Locks the surface.
EndAccess	Unlocks the surface.
SetSurfaceType	Sets the surface type. This can be **DirectDrawSurface::Primary**, **Plain**, **Chain**, **Texture**, **ZBuffer**, **Alpha**, **Overlay**, **BumpMap**, or **LightMap**. The surface type must be set before the surface can be created.
SetGeneralOptions	Sets the width, height, and bits per pixel for surfaces requiring this information. Applications cannot specify this information for the primary surface.
SetChainOptions	Sets the number of implicitly attached surfaces for a surface chain. This function should be called before a chain surface is created.
SetTextureOptions	Indicates whether the texture surface should support alpha transparency in its pixel format. This function should be called before a texture surface is created.
SetBumpMapOptions	Indicates whether the bump map surface should support luminance in its pixel format. This function should be called before a bump map surface is created.
GetWidth	Retrieves the width of the surface, in pixels.
GetHeight	Retrieves the height of the surface, in pixels.
GetPitch	Retrieves the pitch of the surface, in bytes.
Show	Displays the back buffer of a primary surface. This function should only be called for the primary surface.
NeedsRepainting	Returns **true** if the application should repaint the surface, and **false** otherwise.
BlitTo	Blits the surface to a destination surface, with or without resizing. Note there are actually two versions of this function: one accepts a destination x- and y-coordinate; the other accepts a destination **RECT** structure, which allows resizing.
BlitPortionTo	Blits a portion of the surface to a destination surface, with or without resizing. Note there are actually two versions of this function: one accepts a destination x- and y-coordinate; the other accepts a destination **RECT** structure, which allows resizing.
ClearToDepth	Clears a z-buffer to a depth value. This function should only be called for z-buffers.

(continued)

Reference Table 4.2	The class reference for DirectDrawSurface *(continued)*.
Member Function	**Description**
ClearToColor	Clears a surface to a color. This function should only be called for color surfaces, and the color sent to this function must match the format of the surface.
SetTransparentColorRange	Sets a range of colors that, when the surface is blitted, will not be visible on the destination surface. The color range is defined by two colors. All values equal to or between these colors will be treated as transparent. The format of these colors must match the format of the surface itself.
GetInterface	Retrieves an **IDirectDrawSurface7** interface. This is useful for working directly with DirectDraw.
GetBaseInterface	Retrieves an **IDirectDrawSurface** interface.

Using The Encapsulation

To use the encapsulation, there are a few steps you need to perform. First, you should include the file "DirectDraw.hpp" in your source code and add DirectDraw.cpp to your project. Also, since the files use DirectDraw, you will have to link the Ddraw.lib library with your application. Lastly, according to COM standards, at least one file in your application must include "InitGuid.H" to initialize the Globally-Unique Identifiers (GUIDs) for use in your application.

Here are a few additional tips:

♦ You should first set the display mode and initialize a **DirectDrawManager** object.

♦ To create a surface, first set its surface type with **DirectDrawSurface::SetSurfaceType ()** and any other attributes specific to the surface. Then call the **DirectDrawManager::CreateSurface ()** function.

♦ Periodically check each surface's **NeedsRepainting ()** member function to see if your application should repaint the contents of the surface. Whenever the surface memory is lost, you will need to repaint.

♦ Study the source code to learn how to use DirectDraw. If you want more code, head for the DirectX SDK, which includes many sample applications (however, they are not as clean as the classes listed in this chapter).

Summary

DirectDraw applications first create a DirectDraw object. You can use this object to set the cooperative level and enumerate available video modes. When you find one appropriate for your application, you can use it to set the display mode. Once the display mode is set, you can create the surfaces your application will need and maintain these surfaces throughout the life of your application.

If you are now comfortable with the concepts of DirectDraw and the steps involved in writing DirectDraw programs, you are ready for the next component of DirectX—Direct3D. In the next chapter, you will learn Direct3D's terminology and overall architecture.

Chapter 5
Introduction To Direct3D

Key Topics:

♦ *Direct3D IM fundamentals*

♦ *Direct3D IM interface overviews*

♦ *Getting started with Direct3D IM*

In Chapter 2, you learned the structure of 3D games in general, exploring polygon storage and display techniques, matrix transformations, and other related topics. After covering DirectDraw, the component of DirectX on which Direct3D firmly rests, you are now ready to learn how Direct3D games are made. This chapter introduces you to the terminology, architecture, and fundamental principles of Direct3D.

Direct3D comes in two different versions: Immediate Mode (IM) and Retained Mode (RM). Retained Mode, a much higher-level API than Immediate Mode, supports animation, loading data from files, and advanced features, such as shadows. IM is more basic, lacking these and other high-level features of RM. In this book, however, I have chosen to document IM for a number of reasons:

♦ Although RM contains higher-level features, it does not support advanced low-level features, such as bump mapping and other multitexturing effects that IM supports.

♦ IM games can run much faster than RM games.

♦ The general consensus in the game developers' community is that IM is for serious 3D games, while RM is for applications that do not have to use leading-edge technology and performance.

♦ For people who want to learn how 3D graphics work, IM is a much better model to follow than RM.

For these reasons, this chapter and the subsequent ones dealing with Direct3D (including Appendix B) will cover only Direct3D IM. For more information on RM, see the DirectX help file.

Direct3D Immediate Mode Basics

This section covers the basics—the terms and concepts you absolutely need to know to write Direct3D applications.

Cooperative Level

As with DirectDraw, Direct3D applications must set the *cooperative level*, which determines the degree of control the application wishes to have over the video card's resources. You will learn the specifics in the next chapter, but for now note that the cooperative levels of Direct3D are the same as those of DirectDraw and are, in fact, set through a DirectDraw object.

Vertices

Direct3D allows you to define your polygons in one of two ways: by defining their vertices or by defining indices into a list of vertices. The latter approach is usually faster and more flexible, because it allows objects with multiple polygons to share vertex data and can easily replicate (at the expense of space) any benefit provided by defining vertices directly.

Direct3D accepts several types of vertices: transformed or untransformed, lit and unlit, clipped and unclipped. If you transform, light, and clip your own vertices, Direct3D will use your data and simply display the polygons. If you do not transform, light, or clip, Direct3D will perform the step for you, given certain parameters. Letting Direct3D do the work for you ensures your application will support the latest generation of 3D accelerators and, thus, run as fast as possible.

> **Note**
> *The best course is not to transform, clip, or light your own polygons, because by doing so, you cannot take advantage of hardware acceleration (which can come either in the form of a graphics card or through 3D extensions to the CPU, such as AMD's 3DNow! or Intel's new instructions).*

Vertex Formats

The first versions of DirectX required you to use Direct3D structures to store your polygon vertices. With the latest versions of DirectX, however, you can store your vertices in the *flexible vertex format*, which gives you some control over how your vertices are stored in memory.

With the flexible vertex format, you can store as much or as little information as you need for each vertex. The types of data each vertex can hold include diffuse color information, specular lighting information, vertex normals describing the roundness of an untransformed vertex, transformed or untransformed vertex data, and up to eight sets of texture coordinates (specular and diffuse lighting types are covered later under the heading "Lighting And Materials").

One requirement that Direct3D places on the format is that the data types you choose appear in a certain order (see Table 5.1). You can avoid this limitation by using *strided* vertices, which allow you to store the data types in any order, even in completely different arrays. Each data type is described by a pointer to the data and a *stride* (analogous to DirectDraw's *surface pitch*), indicating how many bytes are between each item of the specified data type.

The Geometry Pipeline

In Direct3D, the term *geometry pipeline* refers to the transformation of geometry that immediately precedes the step of displaying that geometry. The pipeline, illustrated in Figure 5.1, consists of three individual transformations—*world*, *view*, and *projection*—and one additional operation—*clipping*. Each of the transformations is done through matrices and so can include rotation, translation, scaling, and shearing operations.

> **Note**
>
> *The transformation matrices in Direct3D are all 4×4 matrices of the type mentioned in Chapter 2. Thus, during the transformation phase, all points consist of x-, y-, z-, and w-components. The points remain homogenous even after being sent through the geometry pipeline. Only after clipping, when the geometry is ready to be displayed, are these points converted into Cartesian coordinates.*

Table 5.1 The order of Direct3D data types for the flexible vertex format.

Data Type	Notes
Position	The position of the vertex. Type can be present for transformed or untransformed vertices.
RHW	Reciprocal of w in homogenous coordinates. Type can be present for transformed vertices only.
Blending Weight Values	One, two, three, four or five floating-point values used for vertex blending. Type can be present for untransformed vertices only.
Vertex normal	A vector tangent to the surface at the vertex. Type can be present for untransformed vertices only.
Diffuse color	Type can be present for transformed or untransformed vertices.
Specular color	Type can be present for transformed or untransformed vertices.
Texture coordinate set 1	Type can be present for transformed or untransformed vertices.
Texture coordinate set 2	Type can be present for transformed or untransformed vertices.
Texture coordinate set 3	Type can be present for transformed or untransformed vertices.
Texture coordinate set 4	Type can be present for transformed or untransformed vertices.
Texture coordinate set 5	Type can be present for transformed or untransformed vertices.
Texture coordinate set 6	Type can be present for transformed or untransformed vertices.
Texture coordinate set 7	Type can be present for transformed or untransformed vertices.
Texture coordinate set 8	Type can be present for transformed or untransformed vertices.

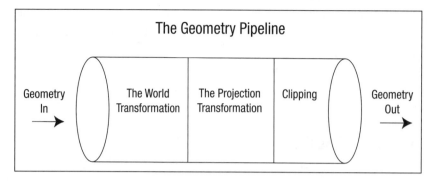

Figure 5.1
The geometry pipeline.

The World Transformation

As Chapter 2 explained, objects are usually defined in *model space*. The origin of this coordinate system corresponds to the center of the object (the point around which rotation occurs), as shown in Figure 5.2. This coordinate system is unrelated to where the object occurs in the virtual world.

The world transformation matrix is responsible for taking an object defined in model space and moving it to *world space*, the coordinate system of the virtual world. This is shown in Figure 5.3. If your object's model coordinates are the same as its coordinates in the virtual world, you can set the world transformation matrix to the identity matrix.

The View Transformation

Your application will typically have a camera located at some position in world space with a certain orientation. As I discussed in Chapter 2, however, projection is much easier when the camera is located at the origin of the coordinate system, looking down the positive z-axis. The purpose of the view transformation, then, is to transform objects such that a

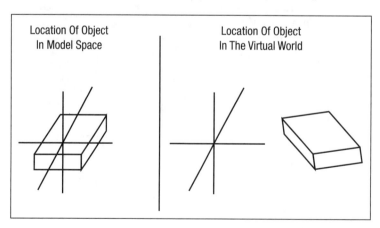

Figure 5.2
An object located in model space.

camera located at the origin and looking down the positive z-axis sees exactly the same view as does the camera located in world space (with its arbitrary position and orientation). Figure 5.4 shows this concept.

After an object goes through the view transformation matrix, it resides in *camera space*. Keep in mind that this camera space is not the coordinate system of just any camera, but of a camera located at the origin, looking down the positive z-axis.

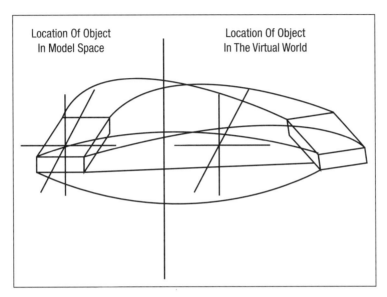

Figure 5.3
An object located in model space being transformed into world space.

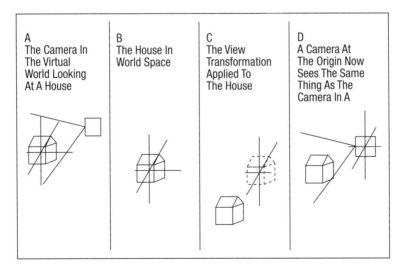

Figure 5.4
The view transformation.

The Projection Transformation

The last matrix transformation is the *projection* transformation. The projection matrix is responsible for converting a camera's viewing *frustum* (the pyramid-like shape that defines what the camera can see) into a cube space, as illustrated in Figure 5.5. This distorts the geometry of objects sent through the matrix: Objects close to the camera are enlarged greatly, while objects farther away are enlarged less. This accomplishes three things:

1. Since the projection transformation converts the camera's viewing frustum into a cube, it makes clipping much easier (clipping polygons to the sides of a cube is trivial, but clipping to the camera's arbitrary viewing frustum is harder and slower).

2. The transformation takes into account the camera's horizontal and vertical fields of view.

3. Most importantly the transformation applies perspective to a 3D scene, projecting 3D geometry into a form that can be viewed on a 2D display. The transformation does not actually convert the polygon's points into pixel locations on the screen, but it prepares them so that a simple scaling operation will do so.

After this last transformation matrix has been applied to a polygon, the geometry must be clipped to the cube space and converted from homogenous coordinates to screen coordinates by dividing the *x*-, *y*-, and *z*-coordinates of each point by w. Direct3D performs these steps internally.

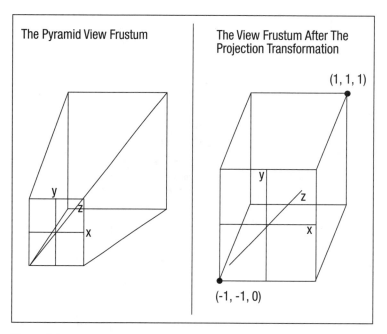

Figure 5.5
The projection transformation.

Viewports

Viewports in Direct3D describe a view of the virtual world rendered into a DirectDraw surface. Viewports define how the horizontal, vertical, and depth components of a polygon's coordinates in cube space will be scaled before the polygon is displayed. Typically, you will scale the horizontal coordinate so that it fits the width of your destination surface (where you are directing 3D data), and the horizontal coordinate so that it fits the height of your destination surface. The scale of the depth coordinate is less important.

The Rasterizer

After Direct3D fully transforms and clips a polygon, it passes it to the *rasterizer*. The rasterizer is responsible for displaying the data on a DirectDraw surface. Direct3D's rasterizer can light polygons as well as handle texture maps, mipmaps, environmental maps, and the many other display options mentioned in Chapter 1.

Lighting And Materials

One of the more powerful aspects of Direct3D is its extensive support for lighting. Direct3D supports several different kinds of lights and allows you to give each polygon a *material*, which describes the physical properties of the polygon that are used for lighting.

These types of lights are supported by Direct3D:

♦ *Ambient*—A light that has no position or orientation. Ambient light increases the intensity of all polygons in a scene, regardless of their orientation or position.

♦ *Directional*—A light type that has no position, just an orientation. Directional lights shade polygons based on their orientation.

♦ *Parallel Point*—A light that, like Directional, has just an orientation. Parallel Point lights cast parallel rays of light.

♦ *Point*—Much like the sun, a light that has a position but no orientation. Point lights cast light from their origin equally in all directions.

♦ *Spotlight*—The most realistic kind of lighting that has a position, an orientation, and other information. Spotlights cast spotlights on polygons.

A material's properties include diffuse reflection, ambient reflection, light emission, and specular highlighting, described briefly here:

♦ *Diffuse reflection*—Defines how the polygon reflects diffuse lighting (any light that does not come from ambient light). This is described in terms of a color, which represents the color best reflected by the polygon. Other colors are reflected less in proportion to how different they are from the diffuse color.

♦ *Ambient reflection*—Defines how the polygon reflects ambient lighting. This is described in terms of a color, which, as with diffuse reflection, represents the color best reflected by the polygon.

♦ *Light emission*—Makes the polygon appear to emit a certain color of light (this does not actually light up the world; it only changes the appearance of the polygon).

♦ *Specular highlighting*—Describes how shiny the polygon is.

As with other aspects of Direct3D, you do not have to take advantage of either lights or materials, but doing so will make your world look much more realistic. The only feature you may want to avoid is spotlights, because there are more realistic ways of creating spotlights than the default method supplied by Direct3D (such as texture blending, covered later in this chapter).

Textures

In Direct3D, the term *texture* applies not just to texture maps, but to all DirectDraw surfaces capable of affecting the appearance of polygons. This includes light maps, bump maps, environmental maps, and so on.

Textures are DirectDraw surfaces created as textures. Each element in a texture is referred to not as a pixel (short for picture element), but as a *texel* (short for texture element). Textures share the normal attributes of surfaces, such as width, height, and pitch, and can reside in video memory or in system memory. Direct3D can automatically manage texture placement, moving textures to and from the video card as memory permits.

The next few sections describe some of the attributes of textures not shared by ordinary DirectDraw surfaces.

Texture Coordinates

All textured polygons have a texture coordinate for each vertex. This coordinate represents the position of the texel that should appear at that vertex. Direct3D calls the texture's horizontal and vertical coordinates u and v (a common convention, mentioned in Chapter 2), and these values typically range from 0.0 to 1.0 (this range covers the entire span of the texture).

Direct3D handles texture coordinates outside of the [0.0, 1.0] range differently depending on how the texture's *addressing mode* is set. The addressing modes are listed below and shown in Figure 5.6:

♦ *Wrap texture address mode*—Values outside the range are wrapped around to values within the range. For example, 1.5 would be wrapped to 0.5.

♦ *Mirror texture address mode*—Direct3D mirrors the texture for values outside the range (this can be useful if you want to tile a texture that doesn't naturally tile).

♦ *Clamp texture address mode*—Direct3D clamps the values outside the range. In other words, values outside the range are assigned the values of the texture's edges. If the edges of the

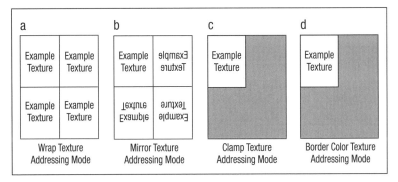

Figure 5.6
A sample texture applied to a polygon in a variety of addressing modes.

texture were red, for example, then all values outside the range would be colored red (of course, in real-world applications, the edges will usually have many colors).

♦ *Border color texture address mode*—Direct3D assigns an application-defined solid color for all pixels on the polygon whose texture coordinates exceed the range.

Note
Although from your standpoint, texture coordinates are defined in terms of the [0.0, 1.0] range, Direct3D multiplies these coordinates by the width and height of the texture to find the actual texel location when texturing.

Texture Filtering

When Direct3D textures a polygon (either with a texture map or some other type of DirectDraw surface), it will almost always generate texture coordinates that have fractions, such as [31.5, 1.3]. Because no texels are located at noninteger locations, Direct3D must decide how to handle these fractional texture coordinates. This task is *texture filtering*. Direct3D can use two different methods:

♦ *Nearest point*—Merely chooses the nearest texel to the fractional one. It is the fastest method.

♦ *Bilinear*—Computes a value based on both the texel nearest to the fractional one and a weighted average of the pixels immediately surrounding the texel. It produces much higher-quality results than nearest point and is by far the most common method used in 3D games.

Note
Another filter that improves rendering quality is called the aniosotropic filter. You can use this method in combination with either nearest point or bilinear filtering. It eliminates the distortion in pixels that sometimes occurs when polygons are oriented at an angle to the viewer.

Texture Blending

Texture blending refers to blending a texture with either another texture or some other graphical data (for example, lighting or color information). It is one of Direct3D's most powerful features.

You use texture blending by creating a *texture blending cascade*, consisting of anywhere from one to eight *texture stages*. Each stage has two inputs (which can be textures, colors, or the results from a previous texture stage), referred to as *arguments*, and one blended output. How the two inputs combine to make the output is determined by the texture stage's *operator* (addition is one operator, which simply adds the inputs). Figure 5.7 is a graphical representation of a texture blending cascade.

The term for combining two or more textures is *multitexturing*. Most of today's video cards support single-pass multitexturing, meaning they can take at least two textures and blend them in one pass. Some older hardware supports only multipass multitexturing, which requires that the polygon be textured once using the first texture, then textured again using the second texture, and so on, up to the number of textures being blended.

In Chapter 7 (as well as in Appendix B), I cover the allowed inputs, outputs, and arguments for texture blending.

Depth Buffers

Direct3D handles the task of visible surface determination by using *depth buffers*. Because polygons in the virtual world have different depths, they must be displayed in such a way that polygons closer to the camera obscure those farther away. Rather than sorting and then

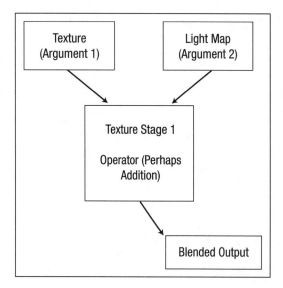

Figure 5.7
A texture blending cascade with one texture stage.

drawing polygons in a back-to-front manner (which is slow and not supported by most hardware), Direct3D supports the creation of DirectDraw surfaces that store depth information for every pixel on the display. Before displaying the virtual world, Direct3D clears every pixel on the depth buffer to the farthest possible depth value. Then when rasterizing, Direct3D determines the depth of each pixel on the polygon. If the depth of a pixel is closer to the camera than the one previously stored in the depth buffer, the pixel is displayed and the new depth value is stored in the depth buffer. The process continues for all polygons, and the end result is a scene rendered perfectly.

Note

Overdraw refers to the number of times on average a pixel is overwritten. If your virtual world contains many objects, a pixel could be overwritten many times (both in the depth buffer and in the surface that holds the rendered scene). To avoid this, you can always display polygons front-to-back. Direct3D does not need to calculate texture information for pixels that are not visible, so this may result in greater performance (whether or not it actually does depends on the length of the sort and the amount of overdraw).

Direct3D supports two different kinds of buffers: z-buffers and w-buffers. Both are related to the depth value of a pixel in view space, depending on how the geometry pipeline's matrices are set up. Typically, z-buffers exhibit problems with objects in the distance, while w-buffers provide constant performance for both near and far objects. Thus, w-buffers (if supported by hardware) are the better choice.

Stencil Buffers

Direct3D allows each pixel in a z-buffer to contain *stencil buffer information*, which, as its name implies, acts much like a real-world stencil. The Direct3D rasterizer uses this stencil information to determine which parts of the rendering surface it can write on. This feature is helpful if you want to overlay 2D interface elements (such as buttons or status displays) on your rendering surface: You can use the stencil buffer to tell Direct3D not to write on the parts of the rendering surface that contain your interface elements.

Not all video cards support stencil buffering.

Vertex Buffers

Direct3D supports *vertex buffers* for reusing transformed geometry. Quite intuitively, a vertex buffer is a buffer filled with vertices (transformed, untransformed, clipped, unclipped, lit, or unlit—any kind you want). You can transform the vertices in a vertex buffer, optimize the way they are stored, and then use (perhaps by displaying) this information as many times as you like.

One application of vertex buffers involves transforming so-called bounding spheres that encapsulate each object in your scene, and then determine which are visible before transforming the objects themselves (I cover this technique more fully in Chapter 8). Vertex buffers are the only way you can do this.

Other Features

In addition to the features mentioned previously, Direct3D supports a number of special effects, the most important of which are fog, billboarding, and antialiasing.

Fog

Direct3D supports the addition of fog to a scene. Fog can be any color. Direct3D can calculate fog on a per-pixel basis (more accurate) or on a per-vertex basis (faster with software rendering). In the latter case, the fog values of a polygon's vertices are calculated, and these values are used to generate fog values for all pixels.

Billboarding

Direct3D allows you to display *billboards*, images displayed in the world at an arbitrary position. Billboards do not have an orientation—they are simply images and, thus, always face the viewer. Because they can have a position, however, their size changes depending on how close the camera is, and you can therefore use billboards to represent 3D shapes, such as trees or billows of smoke.

> **Note**
>
> *You should always model trees with polygons, since the results are far more realistic. Often, you can also model clouds, smoke, and explosions more effectively with polygons. One useful application of billboards is labeling objects in the virtual world.*

Antialiasing

Antialiasing is a method of improving rendering quality by eliminating the jagged edges of rendered polygons. The two different approaches to antialiasing are edge and full-scene. The former smooths the edges of polygons in a second pass, after the entire scene has been rendered. The latter smooths the edges of polygons while they are being displayed (this technique is widely supported, but could, depending on the hardware, require you to display all polygons back-to-front to eliminate display problems).

Vertex Blending

Vertex blending is a method of animating primitives and whole objects. When vertex blending is enabled, vertices are transformed multiple times and the resulting transformed vertices are blending using application-defined "weights" included with each vertex, which specify how much each transformation should contribute to the output for that vertex. This requires that each vertex include one weighting value for each transformation.

Interface Overviews

Direct3D IM consists of three COM objects:

♦ *Direct3D*—The fundamental object of Direct3D used to create other objects.

♦ *Direct3DDevice*—Represents a 3D device.

♦ *Direct3DVertexBuffer*—Represents a vertex buffer.

The interfaces that provide access to these objects are described in the sections that follow.

The IDirect3D7 Interface

The IDirect3D7 interface, obtained by querying a DirectDraw object, is used to access a video card's 3D features. It can create 3D device, light, material, vertex buffer, and viewport objects, and it can list a device's *z*-buffer formats and other properties.

Table 5.2 details the important functions of this interface .

The IDirect3DDevice7 Interface

The IDirect3DDevice7 interface communicates directly with the hardware's 3D feature set. It is the powerhouse of any Direct3D application, transforming, lighting, and rendering polygons.

Table 5.3 lists the functions of this interface.

Table 5.2   The major member functions of IDirect3D7.

Method Name	Description
CreateDevice	Creates a 3D device object.
CreateVertexBuffer	Creates a vertex buffer.
EnumDevices	Lists devices supported by the system.
EnumZBufferFormats	Lists the *z*-buffer formats supported by a device.
EvictManagedTextures	Evicts managed textures from memory.

Table 5.3   The major member functions of IDirect3DDevice7.

Method Name	Description
IDirect3DDevice7::ApplyStateBlock ()	Applies a series of recorded state changes.
IDirect3DDevice7::BeginScene ()	Begins a scene.
IDirect3DDevice7::BeginStateBlock ()	Starts recording a series of state changes.
IDirect3DDevice7::CaptureStateBlock ()	Records the current state of the device.
IDirect3DDevice7::Clear ()	Clears the target surface and depth buffer.
IDirect3DDevice7::ComputeSphereVisibility ()	Computes the visibility of a list of spheres.
IDirect3DDevice7::CreateStateBlock ()	Creates a series of state changes.

(continued)

Table 5.3   The major member functions of IDirect3DDevice7 *(continued).*

Method Name	Description
IDirect3DDevice7::DeleteStateBlock ()	Deletes a series of state changes.
IDirect3DDevice7::DrawIndexedPrimitive ()	Draws an indexed primitive.
IDirect3DDevice7::DrawIndexed PrimitiveStrided ()	Draws an indexed, strided primitive.
IDirect3DDevice7::DrawIndexedPrimitiveVB ()	Draws an indexed primitive described with a vertex buffer.
IDirect3DDevice7::DrawPrimitive ()	Draws a nonindexed primitive.
IDirect3DDevice7::DrawPrimitiveStrided ()	Draws a nonindexed, strided primitive.
IDirect3DDevice7::DrawPrimitiveVB ()	Draws a nonindexed primitive described with a vertex buffer.
IDirect3DDevice7::EndScene ()	Ends a scene.
IDirect3DDevice7::EndStateBlock ()	Ends recording a series of state changes.
IDirect3DDevice7::EnumTextureFormats ()	Lists texture formats supported by the device.
IDirect3DDevice7::GetCaps ()	Retrieves the capabilities of the device.
IDirect3DDevice7::GetClipPlane ()	Retrieves a user-defined clipping plane.
IDirect3DDevice7::GetClipStatus ()	Retrieves the status of the last clip.
IDirect3DDevice7::GetDirect3D ()	Retrieves the Direct3D object that created the device object.
IDirect3DDevice7::GetInfo ()	Retrieves information concerning the device.
IDirect3DDevice7::GetLight ()	Retrieves the properties of a light source.
IDirect3DDevice7::GetLightEnable ()	Retrieves the status of a light source.
IDirect3DDevice7::GetMaterial ()	Retrieves the currently set material.
IDirect3DDevice7::GetRenderState ()	Retrieves a render state.
IDirect3DDevice7::GetRenderTarget ()	Retrieves the render target surface, into which 3D output is directed.
IDirect3DDevice7::GetStateData ()	Retrieves state data.
IDirect3DDevice7::GetTexture ()	Retrieves a texture associated with a specified texture stage.
IDirect3DDevice7::GetTextureStageState ()	Retrieves a texture stage state.
IDirect3DDevice7::GetTransform ()	Retrieves a transformation matrix.
IDirect3DDevice7::GetViewport ()	Retrieves viewport parameters.
IDirect3DDevice7::LightEnable ()	Enables or disables a light source.
IDirect3DDevice7::Load ()	Loads a source texture into a destination texture.
IDirect3DDevice7::MultiplyTransform ()	Multiplies one transformation matrix by an application-specified matrix.
IDirect3DDevice7::PreLoad ()	Loads a managed texture into video memory.
IDirect3DDevice7::SetClipPlane ()	Sets a user-defined clipping plane.
IDirect3DDevice7::SetClipStatus ()	Sets the clip status.
IDirect3DDevice7::SetLight ()	Sets the properties for a light source.
IDirect3DDevice7::SetMaterial ()	Sets the current material.
IDirect3DDevice7::SetRenderState ()	Sets a render state.

(continued)

Table 5.3   The major member functions of IDirect3DDevice7 *(continued)*.

Method Name	Description
IDirect3DDevice7::SetRenderTarget ()	Sets the render target surface, into which 3D output is directed.
IDirect3DDevice7::SetStateData ()	Sets a state of the device.
IDirect3DDevice7::SetTransform ()	Sets a transformation matrix.
IDirect3DDevice7::SetTexture ()	Sets the texture for a specified texture stage.
IDirect3DDevice7::SetTextureStageState ()	Sets a texture stage state.
IDirect3DDevice7::SetViewport ()	Sets the viewport parameters.
IDirect3DDevice7::ValidateDevice ()	Validates device capabilities.

The IDirect3DVertexBuffer7 Interface

The IDirect3DVertexBuffer interface contains all the functions you need to handle vertex buffers, including locking, unlocking, optimizing, and transforming vertices. The methods of this interface are shown in Table 5.4.

Getting Starting With Direct3D

To get started working with Direct3D, make sure you include the DirectDraw and Direct3D headers (Ddraw.H and D3d.H, respectively) in your source files and link the DirectDraw and Direct3D libraries (Ddraw.lib and D3dim.lib) to your project. Also have one file in your application include InitGuid.H, which initializes DirectDraw and Direct3D GUIDs.

Writing a Direct3D application is considerably more involved than writing an application for any other DirectX component. Most applications, however, will usually complete a number of important steps, listed below in the order they occur:

1. The application creates and initializes a DirectDraw object and all appropriate DirectDraw surfaces.

2. The application creates and initializes a Direct3D object, using it to create a 3D device.

Table 5.4   The major member functions of IDirect3D7.

Method Name	Description
IDirect3DVertexBuffer7::GetVertexBufferDesc ()	Retrieves a description of the vertex buffer.
IDirect3DVertexBuffer7::Lock ()	Locks the vertex buffer for direct access.
IDirect3DVertexBuffer7::Optimize ()	Optimizes the format of the vertex buffer for optimal speed.
IDirect3DVertexBuffer7::ProcessVertices ()	Processes the vertices in the vertex buffer.
IDirect3DVertexBuffer7::ProcessVerticesStrided ()	Processes strided vertices.
IDirect3DVertexBuffer7::Unlock ()	Unlocks the vertex buffer.

3. The application uses the 3D device created in Step 2 to update and display the virtual world, updating matrices, textures, and lights and restoring surfaces and other buffers when they are lost.

4. The application destroys all objects upon its termination.

Summary

This chapter has been a rapid tour through the major aspects of Direct3D. It introduced you to the geometry pipeline, texture blending, vertex formats, special effects, the interfaces and objects of Direct3D, and much more. In the next chapter, you will learn the specifics of using Direct3D's geometry functions.

Chapter 6

Using Direct3D For Geometry Transformation

Key Topics:

♦ *Initializing DirectDraw and Direct3D*

♦ *Setting up the transformation stages*

♦ *Defining vertex formats*

Direct3D Immediate Mode is arguably the most complex component of DirectX. It possesses a myriad of settings that you can customize in many different ways. This chapter narrows the topic by focusing on a single service provided by Direct3D: geometry transformation. You will learn how to set up a Direct3D application and prepare all transformation matrices for Direct3D's geometry pipeline.

Note

Appendix B contains an exhaustive technical reference for Direct3D IM. Refer to it whenever you see a structure or function that is not familiar to you, or one that you would like more information on beyond that provided in this chapter.

Initializing DirectDraw

The first step in a Direct3D application is initializing DirectDraw. DirectDraw is used to set the display mode, to create surfaces, and to obtain a pointer to a Direct3D object (there is no **Direct3D-Create ()** function—you must obtain Direct3D objects through DirectDraw).

The following code creates a DirectDraw7 object, selecting the active display device:

```
LPDIRECTDRAW7 DirectDraw7;
DirectDrawCreateEx (  NULL, (void ** ) &DirectDraw7,
IID_IDirectDraw7, NULL );
```

105

An alternative to this approach would be to call the **DirectDrawEnumerateEx ()** function, which enumerates DirectDraw devices, to find a desirable device, and then to use the globally unique identifier (GUID) for this device in place of the first parameter (**NULL**) shown in the previous code.

After creating the DirectDraw7 object, you must set the cooperative level and display mode. The following code does just that:

```
// Set the cooperative level to full-screen exclusive:
DirectDraw7->SetCooperativeLevel ( Window,
    DDSCL_FULLSCREEN | DDSCL_EXCLUSIVE );
// Set the 800x600x24 display mode:
DirectDraw7->SetDisplayMode ( 800, 600, 24, 0, 0 );
```

The parameter **Window** is a handle to the application's main window. Refer to Chapter 4 for instructions on how to create a proper window handle for a full-screen mode DirectDraw application.

Once the display mode has been set, the next step is to create the application's primary surface. Usually, a complex surface with one front buffer and one back buffer that can be flipped is sufficient. The surface must also have 3D capabilities (that is, it must be created with the **DDSCAPS_3DDEVICE** capability flag), because Direct3D will use it for rendering.

The following code creates a surface with these properties:

```
HRESULT Val;
DDSURFACEDESC2 SurfaceDesc;
LPDIRECTDRAWSURFACE7 PrimarySurface;
ZeroMemory ( &SurfaceDesc, sizeof ( DDSURFACEDESC2 ) );
SurfaceDesc.dwSize  = sizeof ( DDSURFACEDESC2 );
SurfaceDesc.dwFlags = DDSD_CAPS;
SurfaceDesc.dwFlags |= DDSD_BACKBUFFERCOUNT;
SurfaceDesc.dwBackBufferCount = 1;
SurfaceDesc.ddsCaps.dwCaps = DDSCAPS_COMPLEX | DDSCAPS_FLIP |
DDSCAPS_PRIMARYSURFACE | DDSCAPS_3DDEVICE | DDSCAPS_VIDEOMEMORY;
Val = DirectDraw7->CreateSurface ( &SurfaceDesc,
&PrimarySurface, NULL );
if ( Val == DD_OK ) { /* Surface successfully created */ }
else { /* Surface not created */ }
```

The following code acquires a pointer to the primary surface's back buffer, which will be used later when initializing Direct3D:

```
DDSURFACEDESC2       SurfaceDesc;
DDSCAPS2             SurfaceCaps;
LPDIRECTDRAWSURFACE7 Backbuffer;
```

```
// Obtain a pointer to the surface's back buffer:
ZeroMemory ( &SurfaceDesc, sizeof ( DDSURFACEDESC2 ) );

SurfaceDesc.dwSize = sizeof ( DDSURFACEDESC2 );
SurfaceCaps.dwCaps = DDSCAPS_BACKBUFFER;
Surface7->GetAttachedSurface ( &SurfaceCaps, &Backbuffer );
```

After DirectDraw has been initialized, you can initialize Direct3D.

Initializing Direct3D

As mentioned earlier, to create a Direct3D object, you must use the DirectDraw7 object. Specifically, you must query this interface for the **IID_IDirect3D7** interface by using the **QueryInterface ()** function. The following code shows you how to do this:

```
LPDIRECT3D7 Direct3D7;
DirectDraw7->QueryInterface ( IID_IDirect3D7, ( void ** ) &Direct3D7 );
```

You can then use the resulting Direct3D7 object to create device objects and vertex buffers, to enumerate pixel formats and devices, and to evict managed textures from memory.

The next logical step is to create a Direct3DDevice7 object that represents a 3D device. With this object, you can transform, light, and render geometry. Ideally, you would call the **IDirect3D7::EnumDevices ()** function and find the 3D device that supports the most 3D capabilities. For purposes of clarity, however, the following code simply selects the default hardware device:

```
LPDIRECT3DDEVICE7 Direct3DDevice7;
Direct3D7->CreateDevice ( IID_IDirect3DTnLHALDevice,
   Backbuffer, &Direct3DDevice7 );
```

Note

*New graphics devices support hardware-based geometry transformation and lighting. You can select such a device on a system that has one by passing to **IDirect3D7::CreateDevice ()** the **IID_IDirect3DTnLHALDevice** interface identifier. If you do not want these capabilities, you can pass the function **IID_IDirect3D-HALDevice** instead.*

*If you attempt to create a device that supports hardware transformation and lighting, and yet no device like this exists on the system, the function will fail. For this and other reasons, it is better to call the **IDirect3D7::EnumDevices ()** function to determine exactly what the system supports, and then create a device object based on these specifications.*

The **Backbuffer** parameter passed to the **CreateDevice ()** function tells Direct3D to direct all rendered output to this surface. The data will not be visible on the display, however, until the surface's **Flip ()** function is called. This function should be called each frame after you are done using Direct3D for that frame.

After the Direct3DDevice7 object has been created, its viewport parameters must be set with the **IDirect3DDevice7::SetViewport ()** function. Recall that after the projection transformation, a primitive's points exist within a 3D cube space. Before displaying the primitive, Direct3D converts its x- and y-coordinates to screen coordinates by scaling them to user-defined settings. At the same time, Direct3D also scales the z-values of the points. The viewport settings define exactly how Direct3D scales these x-, y-, and z-coordinates.

The following code sets the parameters assuming the 800×600 mode set earlier:

```
D3DVIEWPORT7 VP;
VP.dwX = 0; // Left of rendering area
VP.dwY = 0; // Top of rendering area
VP.dwWidth  = 800; // Width of rendering area
VP.dwHeight = 600; // Height of rendering area
VP.dvMinZ = 0.0F; // Minimum z to generate
VP.dvMaxZ = 1.0F; // Maximum z to generate
Direct3DDevice7->SetViewport ( &VP );
```

This code tells Direct3D to scale all x-coordinates within the cube space so they fill the [0, 799] range, all y-coordinates so they fill the [0, 599] range, and all z-coordinates so they fill the [0.0, 1.0] range. Once this step has been completed, Direct3D is ready to use.

Using Direct3D To Transform Geometry

All untransformed primitives in Direct3D are sent through the geometry pipeline, which, as mentioned in Chapter 5, consists of three distinct transformation stages: world, view, and projection.

The world transformation takes an object defined in model space (where the object is defined relative to its local origin) and transforms it to world space (the coordinate system where all objects are defined). The view transformation is used to define the position and orientation of the camera. Lastly, the projection transformation is used to project the data into cube space, where it is clipped and then scaled by the device's viewing parameters, at which point it is displayed.

I say the geometry pipeline operates on *objects* in the above paragraph, because your application will typically transform whole objects at a time. The primitives that compose an object tend to share vertices, and, therefore, transforming each primitive separately would be wasteful. Direct3D does not force you to transform whole objects, however; indeed, if the situation calls for it, you can transform and display a single point.

Each of the transformation stages is defined by a matrix, represented by a **D3DMATRIX** structure. This structure is a 4×4 matrix of the type described in Chapter 2—a quadruple of homogenous coordinate (x, y, z, w) vectors. Matrices can be used to translate, rotate, scale, or shear the points multiplied by them. To set a transformation stage, you use the **IDirect3DDevice7::SetTransform ()** function and specify both the matrix, as a **D3DMATRIX** structure, and the particular stage you need to set.

The next three sections go into more detail for each of the three transformation stages.

The World Transformation

You use the world transformation stage to transform an object from model space to world space. If an object's position in model space corresponds to its position in world space, simply set the world transformation matrix to the identity matrix.

For other objects, you can construct the world transformation matrix by concatenating any of the various matrices introduced in Chapter 2—the scaling, shearing, translating, and rotating matrices. Objects that require identical world transformations should be sent through the geometry pipeline one after the other to avoid needlessly changing the world transformation matrix.

Listing 6.1 contains a helpful function that generates a transformation matrix based on specified translation, rotation, and scaling values.

Listing 6.1   A function to create a transformation matrix based on translation, rotation, and scaling values.

```
void CreateTransMatrix ( D3DMATRIX &Mat,
                         D3DVECTOR &Trans,
                         D3DVECTOR &Rot,
                         D3DVECTOR &Scale ) {
  // This matrix is the concatenation of translation,
  // rotation, and scaling matrices.
  // The order of operations is rotation, scaling,
  // then translation.
  Mat._11 =  Scale.x * cos ( Rot.y ) * cos ( Rot.z );
  Mat._12 =  Scale.y * cos ( Rot.y ) * sin ( Rot.z );
  Mat._13 = -Scale.z * sin ( Rot.y );
  Mat._14 =  0;
  Mat._21 =  Scale.x * ( -cos ( Rot.x ) * sin ( Rot.z ) +
                         sin ( Rot.x ) * sin ( Rot.y ) *
                         cos ( Rot.z ) );
```

```
    Mat._22 =  Scale.y * (  cos ( Rot.x ) * cos ( Rot.z ) +
                             sin ( Rot.x ) * sin ( Rot.y ) *
                             sin ( Rot.z ) );
    Mat._23 =  Scale.z * sin ( Rot.x ) * cos ( Rot.y );
    Mat._24 =  0;
    Mat._31 =  Scale.x * (  cos ( Rot.x ) * sin ( Rot.y ) *
                            cos ( Rot.z ) + sin ( Rot.x ) *
                            sin ( Rot.z ) );
    Mat._32 =  Scale.y * (  cos ( Rot.x ) * sin ( Rot.y ) *
                            sin ( Rot.z ) - sin ( Rot.x ) *
                            cos ( Rot.z ) );
    Mat._33 = Scale.z * cos ( Rot.x ) * cos ( Rot.y );
    Mat._34 = 0;
    Mat._41 = Trans.x;
    Mat._42 = Trans.y;
    Mat._43 = Trans.z;
    Mat._44 = 1;
}
```

The View Transformation

The view transformation is responsible for defining the position and orientation of the camera. It translates objects from world space into view space, where the camera is assumed to be centered at the origin and looking down the positive z-axis.

You can create the view matrix in several ways. One way is to concatenate the identity matrix with a translation matrix, and then concatenate the resulting matrix with x-, y-, and z-rotation matrices. The translation matrix should translate objects by the negative of the camera's position, and, similarly, the rotation matrices should rotate objects by the negative of the camera's rotation. The final matrix can then be used as the view transformation matrix. The code in Listing 6.1 generates this type of matrix.

You can also create the view matrix directly. The matrix is defined as follows:

$$
\begin{vmatrix}
u_x & r_x & d_x & 0 \\
u_y & r_y & d_y & 0 \\
u_z & r_z & d_z & 0 \\
-(u \cdot c) & -(r \cdot c) & -(d \cdot c) & 1
\end{vmatrix}
$$

The symbol u is a vector describing the direction the top of the camera is facing, d is a vector describing the direction the front of the camera is facing, r is the cross product of u and d, and c is the position of the camera (see Figure 6.1). Note that the dot symbol in the last row refers to the dot product operation.

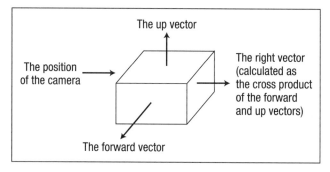

Figure 6.1
The parameters of the view matrix.

The Projection Transformation

The projection matrix is responsible for projecting points into cube space. This is the matrix that takes into consideration the camera's horizontal and vertical fields of view. The projection matrix is typically created according to the following template:

```
|w          0          0          0|
|0          h          0          0|
|0          0          Q          1|
|0          0        -QZn         0|
```

The symbols in the matrix have these meanings:

```
w = cot ( θh/2 )
h = cot ( θv/2 )
Q = Zf / ( Zf - Zn )
```

The function **cot ()** is the cotangent function, θ_h is the camera's horizontal field of view, θ_v is the vertical field of view, $\mathbf{Z}_f$ is the far z clipping plane (all objects beyond this value will not be visible), and $\mathbf{Z}_n$ is the near z clipping plane (objects closer to the camera than this value will not be visible).

Animation Through Vertex Blending

Direct3D allows you to use the geometry pipeline for animation. Previously, you learned that the first transformation stage Direct3D uses is the world transformation. Direct3D can actually transform points from model space to world space repeatedly, up to four times, by using four separate world transformation matrices. It then blends the resulting transformed points (according to user-defined settings) to produce the output points, which are then sent to the next transformation stage.

The power of this feature lies in the fact that Direct3D allows you to specify how the blending should be performed for each vertex. You can control, per vertex, which of the world transformation matrices affect the vertex and how strongly they do so.

To use vertex blending, you must set the world transformation matrices you want to use with the **IDirect3DDevice7::SetTransform ()** function, enable vertex blending with the **D3DRENDERSTATE_VERTEXBLEND** render state, and, most importantly, include in your vertex format weighting values which you use to specify how each vertex should be blended with the output of the matrices.

Weighting values (which must immediately follow the x, y, z position of the point in your vertex format, unless you are using strided vertices) are specified as floating-point values in the range of 0.0 to 1.0. Direct3D uses the first weighting value to determine how strongly the first transformation stage contributes to the output of the point. Similarly, it uses the second weighting value to determine how strongly the second transformation stage contributes to the output of the point, and so on. A value of 0.0 indicates the stage does not contribute at all, while 1.0 indicates the stage is used to the exclusion of all others. Note that you do not actually specify the last weighting value. For example, if you are using three world transformation matrices, you do not specify three weighting values per vertex—just two. Direct3D calculates the last one automatically so the sum of all weighting values is 1.0 (as it must be).

One application of vertex blending is in creating animated characters. You can create an arm as a straight object, for example, and then assign strictly all vertices below the elbow a non-zero vertex weighting value for the second world transformation matrix, which you can then use to rotate, scale, or even moderately translate the forearm, independent of the upper arm. You can do this for the other limbs and even to some degree for the character's mouth, for synching audio with the character's lips.

Defining The Vertex Data Format

Direct3D generally requires that applications store its vertex data using the flexible vertex format system, covered in Chapter 5 (an alternative to this is to use strided vertices, which provide a far greater level of flexibility for applications that require it). The flexible vertex format system tells Direct3D which components (such as x, y, and z) are stored in each vertex. Components that appear in a vertex format must appear in the strict order mentioned in Chapter 5.

Most applications use Direct3D to transform and light their vertices to take advantage of hardware acceleration. Consequently, their vertex formats must include untransformed x-, y-, and z-components, as well as a vector (referred to as the *vertex normal*) that specifies orientation of a plane tangent to the object's surface at that vertex. Direct3D uses this vector in its lighting calculations.

Most applications also apply textures to polygons. Direct3D allows applications to use as many as eight textures per polygon (such as a bump map and a texture map). For each texture a polygon uses, its vertices must include a texture coordinate component. The following code defines a fairly typical vertex structure that includes untransformed *x*-, *y*-, and *z*-components, a vertex normal, and two sets of texture coordinates:

```
struct Vertex {
    D3DVALUE x; // The x coordinate of the untransformed point
    D3DVALUE y; // The y coordinate of the untransformed point
    D3DVALUE z; // The z coordinate of the untransformed point

    D3DVALUE nx; // The x coordinate of the vertex normal
    D3DVALUE ny; // The y coordinate of the vertex normal
    D3DVALUE nz; // The z coordinate of the vertex normal

    D3DVALUE tu1; // The u coordinate of the first texture
                  // coordinate set
    D3DVALUE tv1; // The v coordinate of the first texture
                  // coordinate set

    D3DVALUE tv2; // The u coordinate of the second texture
                  // coordinate set
    D3DVALUE tv2; // The v coordinate of the second texture
                  // coordinate set
};
```

In general, you let Direct3D know what format you are using at the same time you draw a primitive—that is, when you call the **DrawPrimitive*** functions covered in the next chapter and in Appendix B. There is one exception to this rule: whenever you use vertex buffers. Vertex buffers, which allow you to transform data and then render portions of that data, are created with the **IDirect3D::CreateVertexBuffer ()** function. You must specify the vertex format for vertex buffers when they are created.

See the **DrawPrimitive*** functions and the **D3DVERTEXBUFFERDESC** structure in Appendix B for precise instructions on how to describe your vertex format to Direct3D.

Transforming Vertex Data

This chapter has covered how to initialize Direct3D, set up the transformation stages, and define your vertex format. It has not covered how to transform your vertex data. Vertex data is not usually transformed until it is displayed with the **DrawPrimitive*** functions, which I cover in the next chapter. The exception to this is vertex buffers, which are transformed separately through the **IDirect3DVertexBuffer::ProcessVertices ()** function.

Summary

The first step in a Direct3D program is to initialize DirectDraw, which involves creating a DirectDraw object, setting the cooperative level and display mode, and creating the primary surface.

The second step is to initialize Direct3D. This involves obtaining a Direct3D interface from a DirectDraw object and using this object to create a Direct3DDevice object, which represents a 3D device. You must set the viewport parameters for the device before transforming geometry.

Transforming geometry involves sending it through the three transformation stages of Direct3D's geometry pipeline: the world, view, and projection stages, which are defined by **D3DMATRIX** structures that represent matrices. Additional world transformation stages enable you to animate vertices.

Direct3D applications must use a vertex format, typically one that follows the flexible vertex format system, unless they use strided vertices. They must specify this format to Direct3D, so Direct3D knows how to process the vertex data.

In the next chapter, I will cover how to display primitives using the wide variety of options that Direct3D exposes.

Chapter 7

Using Direct3D For Rasterization

Key Topics:

- *Using depth buffers*
- *Setting render states*
- *Multitexturing polygons*
- *Environment, bump, and light mapping*

In the last chapter, you learned how to transform geometry by using Direct3D's world, view, and projection transformation matrices. In this chapter, you will learn how to display primitives using Direct3D's advanced features, such as multitexturing and lighting calculations.

I begin by describing how you can add a depth buffer to your application's primary surface, an essential component for nearly all Direct3D games.

Creating And Using A Depth Buffer

Direct3D handles the problem of visual surface determination by using a depth buffer, which is a surface that contains depth information. Direct3D generates depth information for every rendered pixel of every polygon and checks the depth buffer to see whether or not the pixel should be displayed.

> **Note**
>
> *Visual surface determination is the task of discovering which portions of polygons are visible and which are obscured. This information is used to display virtual worlds properly, so that closer surfaces obscure surfaces farther away from the viewer.*

To use Direct3D's depth-buffering capabilities, you must attach a depth buffer to the primary surface. Most hardware supports depth buffers with 16 bits per pixel, and all new hardware supports 24 bits per pixel. The greater the number of bits per pixel, the more accurate depth buffering is and the higher the quality of the output.

You can determine the precise depth-buffer formats a device supports by calling the **IDirect3D7::EnumZBufferFormats ()** function. It is good practice to call this function, to determine the depth-buffer pixel format that supports the most bits per pixel, and to use this pixel format when creating your application's depth buffer.

The width and height of a depth buffer must equal that of the primary surface. Also, if the device does not support depth buffers (which you can determine with the **IDirect3D-Device7::GetCaps ()** function), then the depth buffer must be created in system memory. Otherwise, you should use video memory for the sake of the graphics card, which will almost always support hardware-accelerated depth buffering and clearing for video memory surfaces, but not necessarily for system memory surfaces.

The following snippet of code creates a video memory-based depth buffer with 24 bits per pixel for an 800×600 primary surface:

```
LPDIRECTDRAW7 ZBuffer;
DDSURFACEDESC2 SurfaceDesc;

ZeroMemory ( &SurfaceDesc, sizeof SurfaceDesc );

SurfaceDesc.dwFlags          = DDSD_CAPS | DDSD_WIDTH |
                               DDSD_HEIGHT | DDSD_PIXELFORMAT;
SurfaceDesc.ddsCaps.dwCaps = DDSCAPS_ZBUFFER |
                               DDSCAPS_VIDEOMEMORY;
SurfaceDesc.dwWidth        = 800;
SurfaceDesc.dwHeight       = 600;

SurfaceDesc.ddpfPixelFormat.dwSize  = sizeof ( DDPIXELFORMAT );
SurfaceDesc.ddpfPixelFormat.dwFlags = DDPF_ZBUFFER;
SurfaceDesc.ddpfPixelFormat.dwZBufferBitDepth = 24;
SurfaceDesc.ddpfPixelFormat.dwZBitMask        = 0xFFFFFF;

DirectDraw7->CreateSurface ( &SurfaceDesc, &ZBuffer, NULL );
```

> **Note**
>
> *Bit masks are 32-bit unsigned integers that indicate which bits of a particular component are relevant. The binary expansion of the hexadecimal mask 0xFFFFFF, for example, is 111111111111111111111111, indicating that the first 24 consecutive bits are valid (this is the mask value used in the preceding source code example). The binary expansion of the hexadecimal mask 0xFF00, on the other hand, is 1111111100000000, indicating that the 9th through 16th bits are valid. This mask would be common to indicate the relevant bits for the green component of a 24-bit RGB surface.*

Once you create a depth buffer, you must tell Direct3D to use it for the primary surface. You do this with the primary surface's **IDirect3DSurface7::AddAttachedSurface ()** function, as shown in the following code:

```
BackBuffer->AddAttachedSurface ( ZBuffer );
```

The code adds the surface to the primary surface's back buffer. This is important, because the back buffer is the surface that Direct3D usually displays graphics to, as covered in Chapter 6.

In addition to creating a depth buffer, your application must also create all of the different surfaces you will use to texture your objects.

Creating Texture Surfaces

The major types of surfaces you can create are colored (with or without alpha information), alpha-only, depth buffers (just covered), and bump maps.

To use textures in your application, you must perform these initialization tasks:

1. Create all of the textures your application needs. You can create surfaces with the **IDirectDraw7::CreateSurface ()** function, documented in Appendix A. Most graphics cards require you to create some or all of your surfaces as square textures, whose length equals some power of 2.

    You can find source code examples for creating most surface types in Chapter 4.

    Note

    *When you create mipmaps, you must use **IDirectDrawSurface7::GetAttachedSurface ()** to obtain a surface pointer for all mipmap sublevels, and then fill each with an appropriately scaled-down version of the texture. Applications usually generate these textures in advance (by using a paint program, for example) and simply load them from disk and into texture memory at runtime. This way you can use high-quality scaling methods without incurring computational overhead.*

2. Load the images from storage into the textures. You must repeat this step if at any time in your application the surface memory for your textures is freed (for example, by the user switching to another application). For testing purposes, the Win32 function **LoadImage ()** enables your application to load BMP files quickly and conveniently, although for a real application, you will almost certainly want to create your own file format so users cannot make unauthorized changes to the game's graphical content.

After completing these steps, you will likely set the device's lighting parameters.

Adding Lights To A Scene

Direct3D can automatically perform lighting calculations for your application, as long as your vertices store vertex normal information, Direct3D lighting is enabled, and you place lights in the virtual world.

A vertex normal is a vector that describes the orientation of a primitive's surface at that vertex. Without this information, Direct3D would not know the shape of the surface at a primitive's vertices and would therefore be unable to perform lighting calculations. Thus, if you want to use Direct3D for lighting, each vertex structure must contain a vertex normal. See Chapter 5 for information on the order in which the vertex normal must appear in your vertex structure.

To enable Direct3D lighting calculations, you can use the following code:

```
Direct3DDevice7::SetRenderState ( D3DRENDERSTATE_LIGHTING, TRUE );
```

This is not typically necessary, however, because Direct3D lighting is enabled by default.

Lastly, to add a light to the virtual world, you can use the **IDirect3DDevice7::SetLight ()** function. The following code adds a simple white directional light source to the scene:

```
D3DLIGHT7 Light;
Light.dltType = D3DLIGHT_DIRECTIONAL;
Light.dcvDiffuse.r = 1.0;
Light.dcvDiffuse.g = 1.0;
Light.dcvDiffuse.b = 1.0;
Light.dcvSpecular.r = 1.0;
Light.dcvSpecular.g = 1.0;
Light.dcvSpecular.b = 1.0;
Light.dcvAmbient.r = 1.0;
Light.dcvAmbient.g = 1.0;
Light.dcvAmbient.b = 1.0;
Light.dvDirection.x = -1.0;
Light.dvDirection.y = 1.0;
Light.dvDirection.z = 1.0;
Direct3DDevice7::SetLight ( 0, &Light );
```

The last line of the code example tells Direct3D to set the parameters for the first light source. If no previous light source existed for index 0, then a new light source is created with the specified parameters. See the **D3DLIGHT7** structure reference for more information on all the different light sources you can create.

Beginning The Scene

Once the one-time setup has been performed, the first step in displaying your virtual world is to call the **IDirect3DDevice7::BeginScene ()** function. This lets Direct3D know you are ready to begin rendering, as shown in the following code:

```
Direct3DDevice7->BeginScene ();
```

The next step is to clear any relevant surfaces.

Clearing Necessary Surfaces

Depending on the nature of your game, you may need to clear the back buffer every frame so that previous frames are not visible. If your application simulates a completely indoor environment, this will not be necessary, because your displayed primitives will completely overwrite the contents of the previous frame. Otherwise, you should use the **IDirect3D-Device7::Clear ()** function to clear the back buffer surface.

Regardless of the nature of your application, as long as you are using a depth buffer, you must always clear it every frame to the farthest possible depth value (typically 1.0). You do this with **IDirect3DDevice7::Clear ()** as well. If the depth buffer contains stencil buffer information (briefly described in Chapter 5), you must clear this, too.

The following code clears the back buffer surface to white (a common value for fog in an outdoor environment) and the depth buffer to the farthest possible depth value.

```
Direct3DDevice7::Clear ( 0, NULL,
   D3DCLEAR_TARGET | D3DCLEAR_ZBUFFER,
   0xFFFFFFFF, 1.0F, 0 );
```

Once you have finished these steps, you are ready to set the properties of the primitives you will render with Direct3D.

Setting The Current Material

All primitives are optionally rendered with the current material settings. The material settings define which color a primitive best reflects (its diffuse color), how shiny the primitive is, which color it appears to emit (if any), and other material-related information.

You set the current material with the **IDirect3DDevice7::SetMaterial ()** function, which accepts a pointer to a **D3DMATERIAL7** structure.

Setting Render States

Many of the render settings (such as whether or not Direct3D performs lighting, as covered previously) are controlled by the **IDirect3DDevice7::SetRenderState ()** function. As its name implies, this function sets a render state. It accepts two parameters: the state and the new value for the state. You can also retrieve a render state by calling the **IDirect3DDevice7::-GetRenderState ()** function.

Most of the render states have default values that are acceptable for the majority of applications. For an idea of all the states you can set, and to see what the defaults for these states are, read the function reference for **IDirect3DDevice7::SetRenderState ()**.

Setting The Transformation Stages

As covered in the last chapter, to render an untransformed primitive successfully, you must set the transformation stages by using the **IDirect3DDevice7::SetTransform ()** function. The current transformation settings apply to all untransformed primitives that are rendered.

Setting The Texture Blending Cascade

The texture blending cascade, as described in Chapter 5, describes the flow of graphical data through a 3D device's texture stages, culminating in the output of a rendered 3D primitive. Texture stages are key to specifying exactly how your primitives will be drawn—what textures they will use, how they will be lit, and so on.

Each texture blending stage is specified by two inputs, referred to as *arguments*, and an operation that is performed on the two inputs to produce the output. Arguments for a texture stage can include texture surfaces, lighting information contained in a primitive's vertices, or other information.

You can specify the operations and arguments for color and alpha information independently. When blending two textures, for example, you can specify one operation for color information and another for alpha information. You can also specify different arguments for color and alpha. For example, you might specify that the texture stage's first color argument is a texture, but its first alpha argument is a constant alpha value.

You specify textures for a primitive by associating them with specific texture stages and then having one argument for a texture stage refer to that stage's texture. You associate textures with a texture stage by calling the **IDirect3DDevice7::SetTexture ()** function (note that some devices do not support more than one association at a time).

You specify the arguments, the operation, and all other states of a texture stage by calling the **IDirect3DDevice7::SetTextureStageState ()** function, which, as its name implies, sets a state for a given texture stage. Before continuing, you should read the reference entry for this function to get an idea of the kinds of arguments and operations possible. This will make the following examples much clearer.

Single Stage Texture Mapping

To perform very basic texture mapping, with no lighting calculations whatsoever, all you have to do is to associate a texture with the first texture stage, as shown here:

```
Direct3DDevice7->SetTexture ( 0, Texture );
```

The first parameter tells Direct3D you are associating a texture with the first texture stage (identified by the number 0). The second parameter is a pointer to the surface you want to associate with the specified stage.

In the absence of arguments or operations, Direct3D simply applies the specified texture to the primitive, by default using its first texture coordinate set. Needless to say, the texture-mapped primitives must have at least one texture coordinate set in their vertex format.

The following code is a far more useful example that actually changes a few states of the first texture stage, instructing Direct3D to blend the texture with diffuse color lighting information:

```
// Associate Texture with the first texture stage:
Direct3DDevice7->SetTexture ( 0, Texture );

Direct3DDevice7->SetTextureStageState (
   0,                    // Texture stage 1 (index 0)
   D3DTSS_COLOROP,    // Set the color operation...
   D3DTOP_ADD );      // ...to the addition operation

Direct3DDevice7->SetTextureStageState (
   0,                 // Texture stage 1 (index 0)
   D3DTSS_COLORARG1, // Set the first color argument...
   D3DTA_TEXTURE );  // ...to the texture associated with this stage

Direct3DDevice7->SetTextureStageState (
   0,                 // Texture stage 1 (index 0)
   D3DTSS_COLORARG2, // Set the second color argument...
   D3DTA_DIFFUSE );  // ...to diffuse lighting information
```

The first line of code associates a texture with the first texture stage, as before.

The second line of code tells Direct3D that the color operation for the first texture stage is **D3DTOP_ADD**. This operation adds the individual color components of the arguments and outputs the result.

The third line of code tells Direct3D that the first color argument for the first texture stage is the texture associated with that stage.

The fourth line of code tells Direct3D that the second color argument for the first texture stage is diffuse lighting information. This information can come from several different sources—for example, the current material's diffuse color or the per-vertex interpolated diffuse color (if the vertex format includes a diffuse color component). The **D3DRENDER-STATE_DIFFUSEMATERIALSOURCE** render state determines the source of diffuse lighting information.

This is actually a fairly typical setting for the first texture stage. Other texture stages are used to blend other textures. Now that you know the basics of using the texture blending cascade, I will discuss more advanced use, involving two or more texture surfaces.

Multitexturing Basics

Multitexturing involves using the texture blending cascade to blend two or more textures. Blending **N** textures requires at least **N/2** texture stages, although you may use more. If you want to blend the texture with diffuse lighting information, for example, you will need an extra texture stage.

When multitexturing, you will generally specify the texture coordinate set for each texture applied to your primitives (as you already learned, if you do not specify this information, Direct3D will use the vertices' first texture coordinate set for all textures, which is rarely what you want). A maximum of eight texture sets is permitted; this corresponds with the number of texture stages available.

The ways you can blend textures are numerous. You can add their color components, subtract them, multiply them by various factors, and so on, as covered in the function reference for the **IDirect3DDevice7::SetTextureStageState ()** function. The following example blends a texture with diffuse lighting, and then blends the result with another texture by using the operation of multiplication:

```
// Associate Texture with the first texture stage:
Direct3DDevice7->SetTexture ( 0, Texture1 );

Direct3DDevice7->SetTextureStageState (
    0,                    // Texture stage 1 (index 0)
    D3DTSS_COLOROP,   // Set the color operation...
    D3DTOP_ADD );     // ...to the addition operation

Direct3DDevice7->SetTextureStageState (
    0,                    // Texture stage 1 (index 0)
    D3DTSS_COLORARG1, // Set the first color argument...
    D3DTA_TEXTURE ); // ...to the texture associated with this stage
```

```
Direct3DDevice7->SetTextureStageState (
   0,              // Texture stage 1 (index 0)
   D3DTSS_COLORARG2, // Set the second color argument...
   D3DTA_DIFFUSE ); // ...to diffuse lighting information

// Associate Texture2 with the second texture stage:
Direct3DDevice7->SetTexture ( 1, Texture2 );

Direct3DDevice7->SetTextureStageState (
   1,              // Texture stage 2 (index 1)
   D3DTSS_COLOROP,   // Set the color operation...
   D3DTOP_MODULATE ); // ...to the multiplication operation

Direct3DDevice7->SetTextureStageState (
   1,              // Texture stage 2 (index 1)
   D3DTSS_COLORARG1, // Set the first color argument...
   D3DTA_CURRENT  ); // ...to the output of the last texture stage

Direct3DDevice7->SetTextureStageState (
   1,              // Texture stage 2 (index 1)
   D3DTSS_COLORARG2, // Set the second color argument...
   D3DTA_TEXTURE ); // ...to the texture associated with this stage
```

In the next section, I explain some of the specific ways you can use the powerful technique of multitexturing.

Specific Uses Of Multitexturing

The most advanced uses of multitexturing are light mapping, environment mapping, and bump mapping. The following three sections explore each in some depth.

Light Mapping

Light mapping is the process of blending a texture intended to represent the intensity of light falling across a polygon with the texture map of that polygon. This technique lets you cast more realistic shadows and highlights on polygons than would otherwise be possible with Direct3D's built-in lighting capabilities.

Light mapping requires that you use a light map, a texture that indicates the intensity of light at a point on the polygon. You can blend the light map with a primitive's texture by using a wide variety of operations, the most common of which are addition, multiplication, and subtraction. Addition and multiplication are usually used for adding a highlight to a primitive, while subtraction is usually used for adding a shadow. The differences between addition, multiplication, and subtraction are shown graphically in Figure 7.1. Multiplication has a sharper highlight than addition, but in many instances they produce very similar outputs.

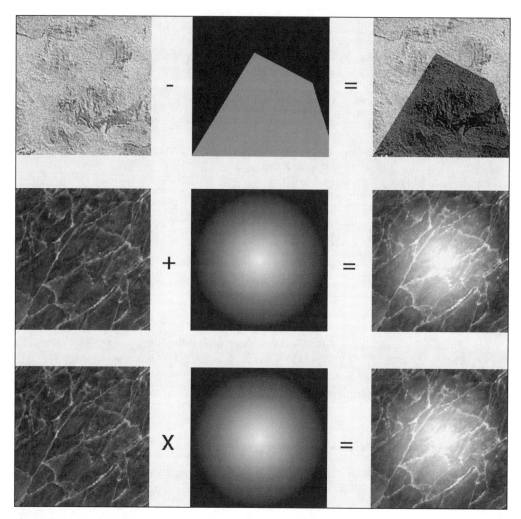

Figure 7.1
Subtracting, adding, and multiplying a texture with a light map.

Environment Mapping

Environment mapping is a method of reflecting some feature of the environment onto a primitive. Environment maps can be used to create both objects that appear to reflect their surroundings and objects that look like specular highlights are falling on them.

The two methods of environment mapping are referred to as *spherical* and *cubic*. Spherical environment mapping requires a single texture map that contains an image of the feature of the environment being mapped onto the primitive. If you are using environment mapping for lighting a primitive, then you will usually blend the spherical environment map with the primitive's texture by using the operation of addition or multiplication. Otherwise, you will simply use the environment map as the primitive's texture. In either case, however, to achieve the appearance of reflection, you must choose the texture coordinates for the environment map in a way that depends on the orientation of the primitive relative to the viewer. The standard equations for doing this are shown here:

```
u = N_x / 2.0 + 0.5
v = N_y / 2.0 + 0.5
```

Note

These equations generate texture coordinates that fall strictly within the largest possible circle that will fit within the environment map surface, which is itself rectangular. If you are using environment mapping to create a primitive that reflects its surroundings, then you will have to take the image of its surroundings and distort it into a circle—a "fish-bowl" image. Many paint programs offer features for doing this.

The point $(\mathbf{u}, \mathbf{v})$ is the texture coordinate for a vertex and the vector $<\mathbf{N_x}, \mathbf{N_y}>$ is the normalized, transformed vertex normal for the vertex. From looking at the equations, you can see that when a vertex normal faces the viewer directly (and, hence, $\mathbf{N_x}$ and $\mathbf{N_y}$ are equal to 0), the equations will produce a texture coordinate in the center of the environment map. Conversely, vertex normals facing away from the viewer will produce texture coordinates closer to the edges of the texture.

Direct3D can automatically make these texture coordinate calculations for you if you specify **D3DTSS_TCI_CAMERASPACENORMAL** as the texture coordinate set for the texture stage that performs environment mapping. See the **IDirect3DDevice7->SetTextureStageState ()** function reference for more information.

Cubic environment mapping is somewhat more complex, but also more realistic. In this kind of mapping, the cubic environment map is actually composed of six textures. These face along the negative and positive x-, y-, and z-axes, and each depicts the environment from a certain direction. You create the cubic environment map by calling the **IDirectDraw7::CreateSurface ()** function and explicitly specifying a cubic environment map. You can access each of the faces by calling the **IDirectDrawSurface7::GetAttachedSurface ()** function.

To choose the texture coordinates for this type of environment mapping, you can use either the same procedure as you would for spherical environment mapping or a more accurate method. The more accurate method involves creating a vector from the viewer to a vertex, reflecting it off the orientation of the surface as described by the vertex normal, and then calculating its intersection with one of the six faces that make up the cubic environment map. Direct3D can automatically make these calculations if you specify **D3DTSS_TCI_- CAMERASPACEREFLECTIONVECTOR** as the texture coordinate set for the texture stage that performs environment mapping.

You can use environment mapping in several ways, the most common of which are described here:

♦ *To create an object that appears to reflect its surroundings*—For a spherical environment map, you simply create a snapshot of the environment and distort it to look spherical in nature. For a cubic environment map, you typically render actual views of the environment along each of the cube's axes into the cubic environment map. Though processor-intensive, this does produce realtime reflection. If you take this approach, be sure to create your cubic environment map with the **DDSCAPS_3DDEVICE** flag, which ensures that you can render into its surfaces.

♦ *To create an object that appears to reflect specular highlights*—This involves creating an environment map that has specular highlights. This map is then blended (through the operation of addition) with a primitive's texture, thus producing simulated highlights on the primitive.

♦ *To create an object that appears to have an irregular surface*—This is done through the process of bump mapping.

The next section explains how to perform bump mapping, which uses specular environment mapping.

Bump Mapping

Bump mapping is the process of perturbing the lighting calculations for a rendered primitive's pixels in such a way as to make its surface appear bumpy or irregular, even though it is, in fact, perfectly flat. The exact perturbations are specified via a bump map.

In real bump mapping, the bump map specifies the contours of the surface. Higher-intensity pixels correspond to a greater height, and lower-intensity pixels to a lower height. When a pixel on a surface is bump mapped, its corresponding pixel in the bump map is determined. Three pixels in the bump map in that region are used to create a vector that describes the perturbed orientation of the surface. This vector—rather than the surface normal of the primitive—is used for lighting calculations.

True bump mapping, though high quality in results, is, unfortunately, too slow to perform in realtime. Direct3D's solution to the problem involves using a different kind of bump map. Each pixel in a Direct3D bump map contains two or three components: a u offset, a v offset, and, optionally, a luminance factor. What these components are used for will become clear shortly.

As mentioned before, bump mapping requires you to use environment mapping. More specifically, the environment map must depict one or more highlights, which represent lights in the scene (though they do not have to correspond to actual light sources). If this environment map were to be applied to a primitive without bump mapping, it should look as if one or more smooth highlights are falling on the primitive.

When Direct3D renders a primitive with bump mapping, it generates the texture coordinates for the environment map. Before using the pixel at that location in the environment map, Direct3D first perturbs its horizontal and vertical coordinates by the u and v offsets of the bump map at that location. It then uses this perturbed coordinate to extract a pixel from the environment map, which it blends with the primitive's texture, adding luminescence as determined by the format of the bump map.

How does this produce the illusion of bump mapping? Recall that without bump mapping, the environment map, if blended with a primitive's texture, would look like one or more highlights are falling on the primitive. By perturbing the environment map coordinates, Direct3D modifies the amount of highlight falling on each pixel. The bump map specifies the exact perturbations that occur, so it is responsible for the appearance of the rendered surface.

The preceding discussion provides an overview of bump mapping, but you still need to be aware of many more details, such as:

◆ *How to create the bump map*—Direct3D supports a number of bump-map formats, all documented in Appendix A. What is common to all formats is that each pixel has at least u and v offsets. You can easily generate these offsets by using a traditional height bump map, which is usually easier for artists to create than a Direct3D-style bump map. If $I(X,Y)$ represents the intensity of a pixel at location (X, Y) in a height bump map, then the corresponding u offset could be generated by the equation $I(X,Y)-I(X-1,Y)$, and the v offset, by the equation $I(X,Y)-I(X,Y-1)$. As you can see, these equations convert *absolute* height information to height information *relative* to other heights, which works well for Direct3D bump mapping. In real bump mapping, greater relative heights will have a greater impact than smaller relative heights on a pixel's lighting. This is also true for Direct3D bump mapping, because greater relative heights produce offsets that perturb environmental texture coordinates more than the offsets produced by smaller relative heights.

◆ *The bump-map matrix*—After retrieving a value from a bump map, Direct3D sends it through a 2×2 bump-map matrix, which programmers can use to scale or skew bump-map values. This is convenient, because if a bump map is to be modified in some small way, the program can do it—the artist does not need to redo the bump map. Individual elements in the 2×2 matrix can be set and retrieved via the **D3DTSS_BUMPENVMAT00**, **D3DTSS_BUMPENVMAT01**, **D3DTSS_BUMPENVMAT10**, and **D3DTSS_-BUMPENVMAT11** texture stage states. If you do not want to modify the bump-map values in any way, set this matrix to the identity matrix.

◆ *The environment map*—This should be a specular environment map, depicting one or more highlights. It should always be associated with the texture stage *following* the one used for bump mapping. You can use either cubic or spherical environment mapping.

- *Luminance scaling/offset values*—You can scale and offset the luminance values through the **D3DTSS_BUMPENVLSCALE** and **D3DTSS_BUMPENVLOFFSET** render states. If your bump map has a luminance component, and you do not want to scale or offset luminance values, then simply set these states to 1.0 and 0.0, respectively.

- *Bump-map mode*—The two primary bump-map modes, which you can set with the **IDirect3D Device7::SetTextureStageState ()** function are: **D3DTOP_BUMPENVMAPLU-MINANCE**, which indicates bump mapping with luminance; and **D3DTOP_-BUMPENVMAP**, which indicates bump mapping without luminance. You can specify either if your bump map contains a luminance component, but only the latter if not.

The following rather lengthy chunk of code initializes the texture blending cascade to perform bump mapping, given certain assumptions covered later:

```
Direct3DDevice7->SetTexture ( 0, Texture );

Direct3DDevice7->SetTextureStageState (
    0,                  // Texture stage 1 (index 0)
    D3DTSS_COLOROP,     // Set the color operation...
    D3DTOP_MODULATE );  // ...to the multiplication operation

Direct3DDevice7->SetTextureStageState (
    0,                  // Texture stage 1 (index 0)
    D3DTSS_COLORARG1,   // Set the first color argument...
    D3DTA_TEXTURE );    // ...to the texture associated with this stage

Direct3DDevice7->SetTextureStageState (
    0,                  // Texture stage 1 (index 0)
    D3DTSS_COLORARG2,   // Set the second color argument...
    D3DTA_DIFFUSE );    // ...to diffuse lighting information

Direct3DDevice7->SetTextureStageState (
    0,                  // Texture stage 1 (index 0)
    D3DTSS_ALPHAOP,     // Set the alpha operation...
    D3DTOP_SELECTARG1 ); // ...to output the alpha of the first argument

Direct3DDevice7->SetTextureStageState (
    0,                  // Texture stage 1 (index 0)
    D3DTSS_ALPHAARG1,   // Set the first alpha argument...
    D3DTA_TEXTURE );    // ...to the texture associated with this stage

Direct3DDevice7->SetTextureStageState (
    0,                  // Texture stage 1 (index 0)
    D3DTSS_TEXCOORDINDEX, // Set the texture coordinate set...
    0 );                // ...to the first texture coordinate set

Direct3DDevice7->SetTexture ( 0, BumpMapTexture );
```

```
Direct3DDevice7->SetTextureStageState (
    1,                     // Texture stage 2 (index 1)
    D3DTSS_TEXCOORDINDEX, // Set the texture coordinate set...
    0 );                   // ...to the first texture coordinate set

Direct3DDevice7->SetTextureStageState (
    1,                          // Texture stage 2 (index 1)
    D3DTSS_COLOROP,             // Set the color operation...
    D3DTOP_BUMPENVMAPLUMINANCE ); // ...to luminance bump mapping

Direct3DDevice7->SetTextureStageState (
    1,                 // Texture stage 2 (index 1)
    D3DTSS_COLORARG1, // Set the first color argument...
    D3DTA_TEXTURE );  // ...to the texture associated with this stage

 Direct3DDevice7->SetTextureStageState (
    1,                 // Texture stage 2 (index 1)
    D3DTSS_COLORARG2, // Set the second color argument...
    D3DTA_CURRENT );  // ...to the output of the last texture stage

Direct3DDevice7->SetTexture ( 0, SpecularEnvironmentMapTexture );

Direct3DDevice7->SetTextureStageState (
    2,                     // Texture stage 3 (index 2)
    D3DTSS_TEXCOORDINDEX, // Set the texture coordinate set...
    D3DTSS_TCI_CAMERASPACENORMAL ); // ...to values computed from
                                    // transformed vertex normals

Direct3DDevice7->SetTextureStageState (
    2,                 // Texture stage 3 (index 2)
    D3DTSS_COLOROP,   // Set the color operation...
    D3DTOP_ADD );     // ...to the addition operation

Direct3DDevice7->SetTextureStageState (
    2,                 // Texture stage 3 (index 2)
    D3DTSS_COLORARG1, // Set the first color argument...
    D3DTA_TEXTURE );  // ...to the texture associated with this texture stage

Direct3DDevice7->SetTextureStageState (
    2,                 // Texture stage 3 (index 2)
    D3DTSS_COLORARG2, // Set the second color argument...
    D3DTA_CURRENT );  /// ...to the output of the last texture stage

// Set the bump-mapping matrix:
```

```
// The SetTextureStageState () function doesn't accept floating-point
// values, so we must instead cast the floating-point values to
// 32-bit integers. The bit content remains unchanged; Direct3D
// will cast it back to a floating-point value after checking the
// texture state:

float One = 1.0F, Zero = 0.0F;
DWORD dwOne  = * ( ( DWORD ) * &One  ),
      dwZero = * ( ( DWORD ) * &Zero );

Direct3DDevice7->SetTextureStageState (
    1,                     // Texture stage 2 (index 1)
    D3DTSS_BUMPENVMAT00,   // Set the [0,0] bump-map matrix entry...
    dwOne );               // ...to 1

Direct3DDevice7->SetTextureStageState (
    1,                     // Texture stage 2 (index 1)
    D3DTSS_BUMPENVMAT01,   // Set the [0,1] bump-map matrix entry...
    dwZero );              // ...to 0

Direct3DDevice7->SetTextureStageState (
    1,                     // Texture stage 2 (index 1)
    D3DTSS_BUMPENVMAT10,   // Set the [1,0] bump-map matrix entry...
    dwZero );              // ...to 0

Direct3DDevice7->SetTextureStageState (
    1,                     // Texture stage 2 (index 1)
    D3DTSS_BUMPENVMAT11,   // Set the [1,1] bump-map matrix entry...
    dwOne );               // ...to 1

// Set luminance scale/offset (only necessary if your bump-map
// contains a luminance component and the bump-mapping mode is
// set to D3DTOP_BUMPENVMAPLUMINANCE):
Direct3DDevice7->SetTextureStageState (
    1,                     // Texture stage 2 (index 1)
    D3DTSS_BUMPENVLSCALE,  // Set the bump-map environmental luminance scale...
    dwOne );               // ...to 1

Direct3DDevice7->SetTextureStageState (
    1,                     // Texture stage 2 (index 1)
    D3DTSS_BUMPENVLOFFSET, // Set the bump-map environmental luminance offset...
    dwZero );              // ...to 0
```

Note that the code makes two assumptions that may not be immediately obvious: First, it assumes you are using spherical environment mapping; second, it assumes first texture coordinate set specifies texture coordinates for both the texture and the bump map. If any of these assumptions will not work for your application, then, of course, the source code you use will look slightly different.

Rendering Primitives

After performing setup, displaying your primitives is perhaps the easiest step of all. To do this, you call the **DrawPrimitive** functions with your vertex data and let Direct3D do the rest. If you are using untransformed vertices, Direct3D will transform the vertices for you using the world, view, and projection matrices; light them as specified; and display the primitive. For vertex buffers, however, you must first manually transform your vertices by calling the **IDirect3DVertexBuffer7::ProcessVertices ()** function.

The following sample code calls the **DrawIndexedPrimitive ()** function, which renders a primitive whose vertices are specified by indices into a list of vertices:

```
DrawIndexedPrimitive ( D3DPT_TRIANGLELIST,
  D3DFVF_VERTEX, ( void * ) VertexList,
  3, IndicesList, 3, 0 );
```

Note

*You use the **DrawPrimitive ()** function to render primitives whose vertices you specify directly, the **DrawIndexedPrimitive ()** function to render primitives whose vertices are specified as indices into a vertex list, and **DrawIndexedPrimitiveVB ()** to render primitives whose vertices are specified as indices into a vertex buffer.*

Your own application will specify its own vertex format and possibly render types of primitives other than a triangle list (though a triangle list, which is simply a collection of independently specified triangles, is by far the most common). The code will be much the same.

Ending The Scene

Once you are done rendering, you must call **IDirect3DDevice7::EndScene ()** to let Direct3D know you are done, as shown in the following code snippet:

```
Direct3DDevice7::EndScene ();
```

Summary

Initializing Direct3D for rendering involves a number of steps, including attaching a depth buffer to your primary surface, creating and loading texture surfaces, and adding lights to the scene.

Steps you perform on a primitive-by-primitive basis include setting the current material, setting any render states you wish to change, setting the transformation stages, and setting up the texture blending cascade.

The texture blending cascade enables you to blend textures to perform operations, such as light mapping, environment mapping, and bump mapping. The texture blending cascade consists of up to eight texture stages, each of which requires two inputs (arguments) and an operation to be performed on the two arguments to produce the texture stage's output.

In the next chapter, I discuss many of the optimizations you can use to enhance the speed of your 3D games.

Chapter 8
Optimizing Direct3D

It is unfortunate that computers can execute only a finite number of operations per second. Although the speed and power of computers have increased exponentially since their invention, they are unlikely ever to be fast enough to do what we want in the way we want it done.

For example, an optimal simulation of a virtual world would perform full-fledged quantum mechanical, electromagnetic, and gravitational calculations on quadrillions upon quadrillions of atoms, thus eliminating the need to represent objects with simple geometric shapes or to use vastly simplified lighting models. Such a simulation would be virtually indistinguishable from the real thing.

Computers, restricted by the very laws of nature they try to simulate, will always be machines of finite speed, limited by a finite amount of memory and occupying a finite amount of space. These limitations necessitate the use of *approximations* to the way things occur in the real world. The polygon models used in today's games are just one such approximation. In a few years, polygons will likely be replaced by better approximations, such as parametric bicubic surfaces, Bézier surfaces, or B-spline surfaces, which are all methods of mathematically representing curved surfaces. Likewise, the simplified lighting model now used by Direct3D may in time be replaced by radiosity rendering (which takes into consideration the fact that surfaces themselves reflect light and, hence, contribute to the lighting of an environment). No matter how much better the approximation gets, however, the models we use to represent the worlds we simulate are just that—models, approximations to the real thing.

As programmers, our task is to choose the best approximation we can for a given *target platform* (the minimum system specifications we expect our game to run on, such as a Pentium III running at 650MHz with 256MB RAM and a 32MB GeForce 256 graphics accelerator). This job is complicated by the fact that a better approximation is not always more computationally expensive than a lower-quality approximation. As programmers, then, we must always strive to use the most effective approximation for the least computational overhead. This task, usually referred to as *optimization*, can concisely be defined as the process of *maximizing* realism while *minimizing* computational cost.

This chapter is all about optimization. I cover the different types of optimizations programmers can use and then present a wide variety of optimizations you can implement in your Direct3D games.

The Techniques Of Optimization

The best 3D programmers are very methodical when optimizing their 3D games. They do not optimize just anywhere, and they do not choose just any optimization technique. Rather, they have a set of guiding principles to determine when and how to optimize:

♦ *Maximum playability*—Never sacrifice playability for realism.

♦ *Maximum conservation*—Don't model what you don't have to.

♦ *Maximum efficiency*—Use the most efficient model possible.

The principle of maximum playability implies that a super-realistic game is worthless if it is not playable. Playability refers to the game's *fluidity*—how many times the view is updated per second (the *frame rate*) and the game's responsiveness to user input. The computer game Wolfenstein 3D, for example, was not as technically advanced as other 3D games of its time, but had high frame rates and was extremely responsive to user input—much more so than its rivals. Computer game players simply do not like to play sluggish games, no matter how high the quality of the graphics or sound is. The principle of maximum playability, therefore, lets programmers know when they should optimize their games: Simply stated, if a game is not playable, it needs to be optimized.

> **Note**
>
> *You may create your game to be scalable—that is, able to run on systems of multiple speeds without performance degradation. Scalable games "scale" the complexity of the algorithms they use depending on the speed of the system. Fast computers use complex algorithms that generate realistic simulations and slower computers use simple algorithms that are fast but produce lower-quality outputs.*

The principle of maximum conservation is based on the fact that the fastest operation is the one that never takes place. If you do not absolutely have to transform a set of vertices or render a group of polygons, for example, then don't do it. This is the most productive way to optimize the performance of 3D games, as you will see later.

The last principle, maximum efficiency, states that you should always use the most efficient model for a given situation. For example, rather than using a wildly complicated mathematical expression involving square roots and trigonometric functions, you can often use a simpler mathematical approximation that gives results nearly as good, but at a far lower computational cost. Direct3D, for example, uses very simple lighting equations that produce fairly realistic results.

In the sections that follow, I will cover some of the best ways you can implement maximum conservation and efficiency in your 3D games.

Backface Culling

One favorite method of conservation is a technique known as *backface culling*, or alternatively, *backface removal*. This is the process of culling all backfacing polygons from a scene (that is, not displaying them). A backfacing polygon is defined as one whose backside faces the viewer. How is a polygon's backside defined? Recall from earlier chapters that the orientation of a polygon is described by a vector called a *surface normal*. The backside of a polygon is defined as the side that faces away from the direction of this vector (see Figure 8.1).

This technique can be used only on polygons that have a side the viewer never sees. This is the case for all completely enclosed objects (such as characters, houses, rocks, and most other objects) and is often the case for other polygons as well (such as those that make up a

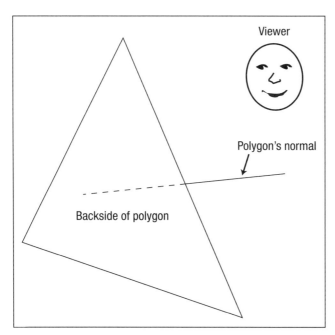

Figure 8.1
The backside of a polygon faces away from its normal.

virtual world's ground). Fortunately, because single polygons are infinitely thin, and therefore largely unrealistic, they rarely show up in a virtual world's geometry. In addition, many artists who have experience writing realtime 3D games often construct all polygons so that they have backsides, even if this means creating two polygons where one would otherwise work (they do this by creating two coplanar polygons that face opposite directions). If this is not an option, turning on and off backface culling for individual polygons is simple enough.

The mathematics for backface culling turns out to be quite simple. Simply create a vector from the viewer to any one of the polygon's vertices (or any point on the polygon's plane, for that matter). Then test the angle between the polygon's normal and this vector. If it is greater than 90 degrees ($\pi/2$ radians), then the polygon's backside is facing the viewer, and the polygon may be culled, as shown in Figure 8.2.

Strictly speaking, you do not even need to calculate the angle between the vectors. Recall the definition of the dot product for two vectors **A** and **B**

$$A \cdot B = |A||B| \cos \theta$$

where θ is the angle between the vectors.

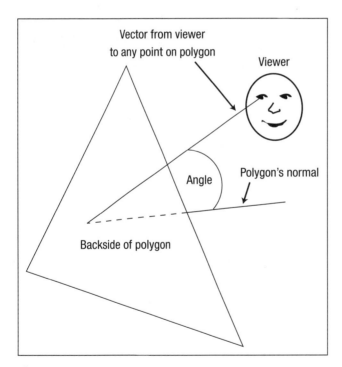

Figure 8.2
Testing for a polygon's frontside/backside visibility.

Because the cosine function will always evaluate to positive for angles less than 90 degrees, and negative for angles greater than this, all you must do is to evaluate the sign of the dot product. If it is positive, the polygon is facing the viewer; if negative, it is facing away from the viewer. See Appendix E for the equation for calculating a dot product.

You do not have to use these equations when working with Direct3D, however, because, as mentioned in earlier chapters, Direct3D can perform backface culling for you. Simply set the **D3DRENDERSTATE_CULLMODE** render state of your 3D device to either **D3DCULL_CW** or **D3DCULL_CCW**, and all back-facing polygons will be culled. See the **IDirect3DDevice7::SetRenderState ()** function for more information.

Minimizing Transformations

In an unoptimized implementation, a game spends much time transforming complex objects that will never be visible in the final scene, because these objects fall outside the camera's viewing frustum, as shown in Figure 8.3.

One way of reducing these unnecessary transformations is to approximate each object by a so-called *bounding sphere*, a sphere located at the center of the object whose radius is just large enough to encompass all of the object's vertices, shown in Figure 8.4. This sphere can be transformed and checked against the camera's viewing frustum—if the sphere does not intersect the viewing frustum, then the object will not be visible, and none of the vertices of the object needs to be transformed. Because a sphere is represented compactly by one point

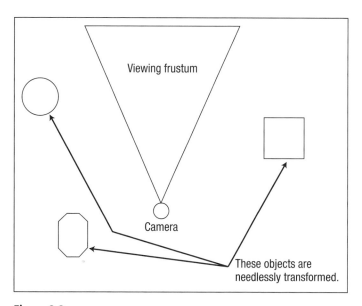

Figure 8.3
Unnecessary transformations.

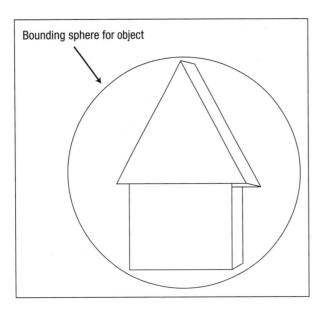

Bounding sphere for object

Figure 8.4
A bounding sphere completely encloses an object.

(and a radius, but the radius does not need to be transformed), this drastically reduces the number of transformations that needs to occur.

The viewing frustum is represented by six planes whose surface normals point inward. To determine if a transformed bounding sphere intersects the viewing frustum, then, you must determine if the sphere intersects any one of the planes. You can do this by calculating the distance from the sphere to each plane. If it is less than the radius of the sphere, then the sphere intersects the plane. This is illustrated in Figure 8.5.

You can determine the distance from a plane to a sphere by calculating the intersection point between a line that extends from the center of the sphere to the plane, in the direction of the plane's normal. Subtracting the center of the sphere from this intersection point yields a vector whose magnitude equals the distance from the sphere to the plane, as shown in Figure 8.6. I cover the mathematics for calculating this intersection point in Chapter 9.

Fortunately, Direct3D supplies a function called **IDirect3DDevice7::ComputeSphere-Visibility ()** that accepts a list of spheres defined in world space and determines which spheres are visible and which are not. The method used by this function is slightly different than that just mentioned, but the end result is the same. Note that you should use a vertex buffer to store your bounding spheres if you want to use Direct3D for this optimization (that is the only way you can have Direct3D transform vertices without rendering them).

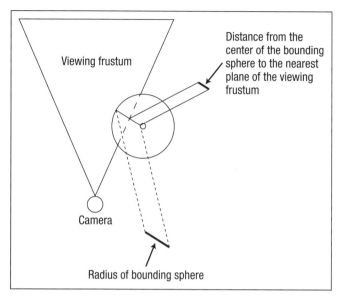

Figure 8.5
A viewing frustum and intersecting sphere.

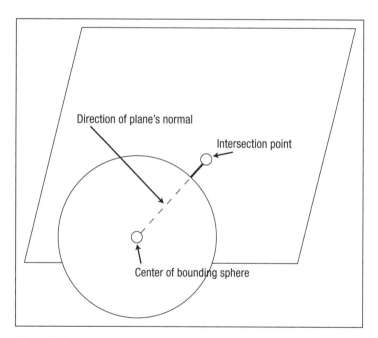

Figure 8.6
Determining the distance from a sphere to a plane.

Although relatively simple, Listing 8.1 includes a function that calculates a bounding sphere for a list of indexed vertices (vertices defined as indices into a vertex list).

Listing 8.1   A function for calculating bounding spheres.

```
//
// Note:
//      Make sure D3D_OVERLOADS is defined before your application
//      includes "D3d.H", since this function makes use of overloaded
//      operators for the D3DVECTOR type.
//
bool CalcBoundingSphere ( LONG *Verts, D3DVECTOR *VertList,
      LONG VertCount, D3DVECTOR &Center, D3DVALUE &Radius ) {
   D3DVALUE MaxDist = -1.0F, ThisDist,
            DeltaX, DeltaY, DeltaZ;

   if ( VertCount <= 0 )
      return false;

   Center.x = Center.y = Center.z = 0.0F;

   // Find the geometric center of the object:
   for ( int n = 0; n < VertCount; n++ ) {
      Center += VertList [ Verts [ n ] ];
   }
   Center /= ( D3DVALUE ) VertCount;

   // Now find the farthest distance from the center:
   for ( n = 0; n < VertCount; n++ ) {
      DeltaX = VertList [ Verts [ n ] ].x - Center.x;
      DeltaY = VertList [ Verts [ n ] ].y - Center.y;
      DeltaZ = VertList [ Verts [ n ] ].z - Center.z;

      ThisDist = sqrt ( DeltaX * DeltaX +
                        DeltaY * DeltaY +
                        DeltaZ * DeltaZ );

      if ( ThisDist > MaxDist )
         MaxDist = ThisDist;
   }

   // The farthest distance is the bounding sphere's radius:
   Radius = MaxDist;

   // Return success:
   return true;
}
```

Exploiting Frame Coherence

One of the most powerful, but most difficult to develop, methods of increasing your game's efficiency involves exploiting a phenomenon known as *frame coherence*. This is the tendency of one rendered frame to resemble the next one, a result of the viewer moving in small increments.

One of the implications of frame coherence is that objects invisible in one frame will usually be invisible in the next. Figure 8.7 shows a top-down view of a camera's viewing frustum, along with a series of objects placed inside and outside the frustum. Because the camera moves only by small amounts each frame, most of the objects outside the camera's viewing frustum will remain invisible for quite some time, and, consequently, do not need to be transformed. To exploit this instance of frame coherence, you must estimate how long the invisible objects will remain invisible, and then ignore the objects for this amount of time.

A safe way of doing this is to calculate for each invisible object the minimum amount of time required for the camera to see the object. Because the camera has a finite rate of speed and rotation, such a minimum is guaranteed to exist. The object can safely be ignored for this amount of time, because the camera cannot possibly turn or move to see the object before the minimum time. (Of course, unless the viewer is purposely turning to see the object, it will usually remain invisible for longer than this, but there is no way of knowing in advance what the user will do.)

This problem, though stated simply, turns out to be quite difficult to solve, because not only does the orientation of the camera affect this minimum time, but so does the motion of the camera. For example, consider the invisible object shown in Figure 8.8. The camera will eventually see the object by moving backward, by turning left, or by some arbitrary combi-

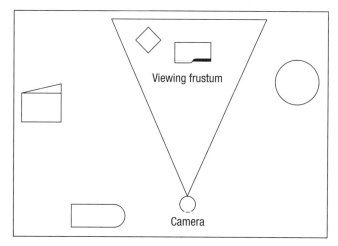

Figure 8.7
A viewing frustum surrounded by objects.

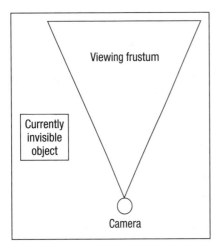

Figure 8.8
An invisible object that the camera can see by moving backward, by turning left, or by doing both simultaneously.

nation of the two operations. It is indeed possible to calculate the minimum amount of time, given the camera's rate of rotation and movement, but the resulting calculations are often more complex than transforming and testing a single bounding sphere (which is, after all, all you need to determine if the whole object should be transformed). Fortunately, this doesn't mean you can't exploit frame coherence, only that you must simplify the problem to a point where you benefit from it.

A good way to simplify this is to assume the camera can move strictly forward—that is, strictly in the direction of its viewing frustum, never side to side or backward. Because this is usually the way the camera does move, this assumption is fairly reasonable, but it also means that the technique must be disabled when the camera moves any other way than forward.

If you assume the camera moves strictly forward, then to calculate the minimum time for an invisible object, all you need to consider is the orientation of the camera with respect to that object. You can disregard the motion of the camera entirely.

Figure 8.9 shows the problem. The task is to calculate the angle between the side of the viewing frustum closest the object and the side of the object closest the viewing frustum, designated ζ in the figure. Once you calculate this, you can simply divide it by the maximum rate at which the viewer can turn (in radians per second), and the result will be the number of seconds for which the invisible object is guaranteed to remain invisible—providing, of course, the camera moves strictly forward.

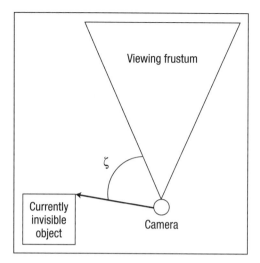

Figure 8.9
The angle between the viewing frustum and the side of the invisible object closest to the viewing frustum.

You can further simplify the problem in two ways:

♦ Use a bounding sphere to represent the object, which you would probably already be using to take advantage of the earlier bounding sphere optimization.

♦ Simplify the shape of the viewing frustum to a 3D cone, which turns out to be a much easier shape to deal with than the six planes that define viewing frustums.

After making these simplifications, the task becomes quite straightforward. Figure 8.10 shows the viewing cone, the bounding sphere for the invisible object, and labels for various angles. As you can see, ζ (pronounced "zeta") is simply ϕ ("phi") minus χ ("chi") minus ψ ("psi").

You can calculate ϕ by using vectors to represent the orientation of the 3D cone and the direction of the object's center (relative to the 3D cone), as shown in Figure 8.11, and then calculating the angle between them using the dot product.

As mentioned earlier, the dot product of two vectors **A** and **B** is defined as follows:

```
A · B = |A||B| cos θ
```

Solving for θ, we get

```
θ = cos⁻¹ ( A · B / (|A||B|) )
```

where **cos⁻¹** is the inverse cosine function (calculated with the **acos ()** function in C++), and θ is the angle between the vectors.

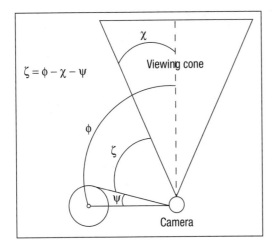

Figure 8.10
The simplified problem.

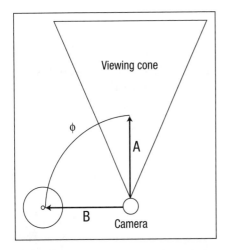

Figure 8.11
The orientation of the 3D cone and the angle between the bounding sphere's center and its side relative to the 3D cone, represented by vectors.

The angle χ is one-half the angle formed by the 3D cone. The 3D cone must fully enclose the six planes of the camera's viewing frustum. The viewing frustum is typically defined by two angles, which designate the horizontal and vertical fields of view for the camera. Through trigonometry (see Figure 8.12), the angle can be calculated as

```
tan⁻¹ ( sqrt ( (tan θₕ)² + (tan θᵥ)² ) )
```

where θ_h is one-half the camera's horizontal field of view, θ_v is one-half the camera's vertical field of view, and **tan⁻¹** is the inverse tangent function (**atan ()** is C++).

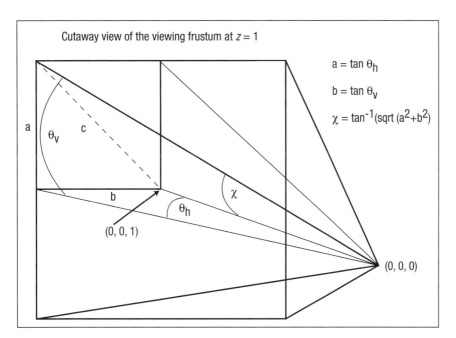

Figure 8.12
Calculating the angle of a 3D cone.

The angle ψ is calculated easily by the equation

```
ψ = tan⁻¹ ( r/d )
```

where **r** is the radius of the object's bounding sphere and **d** is the distance from the camera to the object's center. Figure 8.13 shows how this calculation is determined.

The complete equation for calculating ζ is therefore:

```
ζ = cos⁻¹ ( A · B / (|A||B|) ) - tan⁻¹ ( sqrt ( (tan θₕ)² + (tan θᵥ)² ) ) -
    tan⁻¹ ( r/d )
```

Note

This equation may seem complicated, but keep in mind that the middle term is constant, so it needs to be calculated only once per game (unless the camera's field of view changes, in which case it must be recalculated). Also, typically you will use the equation only once for each object, and the results will last for several (perhaps many) frames.

Once you calculate ζ, what do you do with it? Recall that ζ is the minimum number of radians the camera must rotate by to see the invisible object. Consequently, to find the minimum number of seconds for which the object is guaranteed to remain invisible, simply divide ζ by the maximum rotation rate of the camera, specified in radians per second.

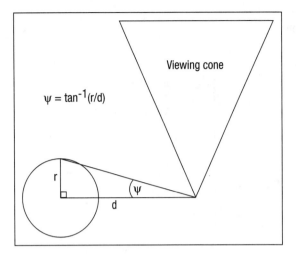

Figure 8.13
Calculating the angle between the bounding sphere's center and its radius relative to the 3D cone.

Remember that the equations shown here assume the camera moves only forward. If the camera moves side to side or backward, you should immediately stop using the optimization.

Listing 8.2 contains some example source code that implements the preceding equations. With all of the mathematical work out of the way, you should be able to begin exploiting frame coherence in your game with relative ease—and *begin* is the keyword here, because, as I cover in the next section, you can take advantage of frame coherence in more ways than just one.

Listing 8.2   Two functions to exploit frame coherence.

```
//
// Note:
//      Make sure D3D_OVERLOADS is defined before your application
//      includes "D3d.H", since these functions make use of overloaded
//      operators for the D3DVECTOR type.
//
D3DVALUE GetHalfConeAngle ( D3DVALUE HFOV, D3DVALUE VFOV ) {
   // This function returns 1/2 of the angle required to
   // define a 3D cone that encapsulates the viewing
   // frustum specified by the HFOV (horizontal field
   // of view) and VFOV (vertical field of view) parameters.
   D3DVALUE TanHFOV, TanVFOV, ConeAngle;

   TanHFOV = tan ( HFOV / 2.0F );
   TanVFOV = tan ( VFOV / 2.0F );
```

```
    ConeAngle = atan ( sqrt ( ( TanHFOV * TanHFOV ) +
                              ( TanVFOV * TanVFOV ) ) );

    return ConeAngle;
}


D3DVALUE GetMinimumTime ( D3DVECTOR &SphereCenter,
                          D3DVALUE   SphereRadius,
                          D3DVECTOR &CameraPos,
                          D3DVECTOR &CameraDir,
                          D3DVALUE   HalfConeAngle,
                          D3DVALUE   MaxRadPerSec ) {
    D3DVALUE MinAngle, SphereAngle, DotProd, ProdOfMags;

    D3DVECTOR SphereDir;

    SphereDir = SphereCenter - CameraPos;

    DotProd = DotProduct ( CameraDir, SphereDir );

    ProdOfMags = CameraDir.Magnitude () *
                 SphereDir.Magnitude ();

    SphereAngle = atan ( SphereRadius / SphereDir.Magnitude () );

    MinAngle = acos ( DotProd / ProdOfMags ) -
               HalfConeAngle - SphereAngle;

    return MinAngle / MaxRadPerSec;
}
```

More Frame Coherence Optimizations

A great number of objects typically resides beyond the viewing frustum's far clipping plane, as shown in Figure 8.14. Because of frame coherence, objects beyond this clipping plane in one frame will usually lie beyond it in the next frame.

You can find the minimum amount of time any object beyond the clipping plane will remain invisible as follows:

1. Calculate the distance from the clipping plane to the side of the object closest the viewer.

2. Divide this distance by the maximum speed of the user, which gives us the minimum time.

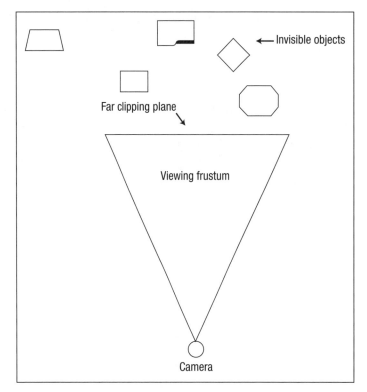

Figure 8.14
Many objects reside beyond the viewing frustum's far clipping plane.

To proceed, you again represent the object with a bounding sphere. Your task is to calculate the distance from the clipping plane to the center of the sphere, and then subtract the radius of the sphere, as shown in Figure 8.15. This will give you the distance from the clipping plane to the side of the object closest to the viewer.

The hardest part of this calculation is determining the distance from the clipping plane to the center of the sphere. The procedure for doing this is illustrated in Figure 8.16. The equation is shown here:

```
d = | A · ( B / |B| ) |
```

The vector **B** is the surface normal of the clipping plane, and **A** is a vector constructed by subtracting a point on the clipping plane from the center point of the sphere. Notice that the "|**B**|" operation is the magnitude of the vector, while the outside "|" symbols represent the absolute value of the scalar produced by the dot product operation.

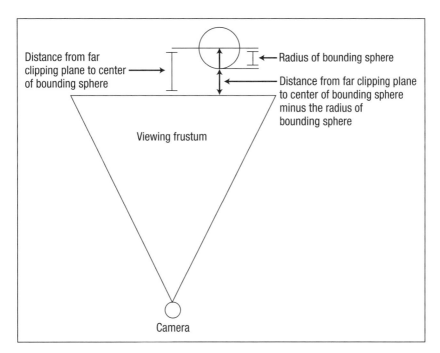

Figure 8.15
Calculating the distance from the clipping plane to the side of the bounding sphere closest to the viewer.

The surface normal of the far clipping plane is simply the vector describing the direction of the camera. You can calculate a point on the plane by multiplying the z-depth of the clipping plane by the normalized vector describing the direction of the camera, and then adding this product to the position of the camera. The z-depth of the clipping plane is the maximum permissible z-value of the far clipping plane in camera space.

Once **d** is calculated, subtract from this value the radius of the sphere, and then divide the resulting quantity by the maximum number of units the camera can travel in a second. The result will be the amount of time in seconds that the object is guaranteed to remain invisible.

Listing 8.3 contains a function that implements this equation.

Listing 8.3   More source code for exploiting frame coherence.

```
//
// Note:
//      Make sure D3D_OVERLOADS is defined before your application
//      includes "D3d.H", since these functions make use of overloaded
//      operators for the D3DVECTOR type.
//
```

```
D3DVALUE GetMinimumTime2 ( D3DVECTOR &SphereCenter,
                           D3DVALUE   SphereRadius,
                           D3DVECTOR &FarPlaneNormal,
                           D3DVECTOR &PointOnPlane,
                           D3DVALUE   MaxUnitsPerSec ) {
    D3DVALUE MinDist;

    D3DVECTOR A;

    A = SphereCenter - PointOnPlane;

    MinDist = fabs ( DotProduct ( A,
                   FarPlaneNormal / FarPlaneNormal.Magnitude () ) );

    return ( MinDist - SphereRadius ) / MaxUnitsPerSec;
}
```

You can exploit frame coherence in more than just these two ways. If the camera starts moving backward, for example, you can use the techniques developed in the previous section to calculate how long objects will remain *visible*, at minimum; you do not need to use the bounding sphere transformation and test for these objects. Further, on the off chance that you do not store your polygons as indices into a vertex list, but store them vertex by

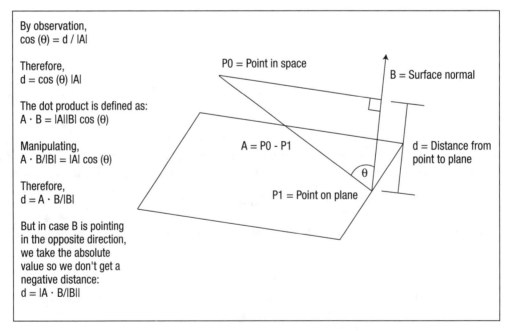

Figure 8.16
Calculating the distance between a point and a plane.

vertex, you can take advantage of the fact that polygons facing away from the viewer in one frame will likely face away in the next. The minimum amount of time these polygons will remain invisible is proportional to the angle between the polygon's surface normal and a vector drawn from the viewer to any point on the polygon. (This optimization does not work well for polygons stored as indices into a vertex list, because such polygons tend to share vertices with other polygons that need to be transformed.)

Depending on the specific situations in your game, even more opportunities for exploiting frame coherence may present themselves.

Using Multiple Levels Of Detail

One potential source of inefficiency in a 3D game is far-away objects. If they are of moderate size, they will be displayed using only a few dozen or fewer pixels, even if they contain hundreds of vertices.

To increase game performance, artists often construct multiple levels of detail for each object. The lower levels of detail, with perhaps only a handful of vertices, are used when the object is far away, and the higher levels of detail are used when the object is closer. This requires very little programming to support (a simple distance check is all that is necessary), but provides a substantial performance benefit for games that use many complicated objects.

Using Haze

An older technique of optimization involves setting the far clipping plane relatively close to the viewer, and then using fog or haze to obscure the boundary between polygons that are displayed and those that are not. This technique, though quite effective, has fallen out of favor with game players, and so should generally be avoided on all but the slowest of computer systems.

Sorting Polygons

Many graphics cards will perform a depth-buffer check to see if a pixel is visible before calculating the color of the pixel. This means that if you sort your polygons in a front-to-back manner, displaying the ones closer to the viewer first and the ones farther away last, you will minimize the amount of time the graphics card spends calculating the color of pixels that will later be overwritten, because the graphics card will not perform color calculations for pixels that are not visible.

Summary

One of the most important tasks game developers must accomplish along the road to writing a 3D game is *optimization*—extracting maximum realism while minimizing computational overhead. Optimization allows games to do more with less. Programmers tend to be guided by three principles when they optimize their games:

- ◆ *The principle of playability*—Optimize whenever the game is not readily playable on its target platform (the minimum system specifications for the game).

- ◆ *The principle of conservation*—Don't do what you don't have to. This principle seeks to minimize the number of wasted operations that it takes to display a virtual world.

- ◆ *The principle of efficiency*—Whatever you do, do it as efficiently as you can. This involves taking shortcuts and making approximations to difficult problems.

Backface culling is an almost universally used technique that eliminates from the scene all polygons that are facing away from the viewer.

To minimize transformations, you can use a bounding sphere for each object in the virtual world. The bounding sphere can be transformed and checked against the camera's viewing frustum. If the bounding sphere is invisible, so is the object, and you don't need to transform the object's points.

One of the most powerful ways to optimize a 3D game is to exploit a phenomenon known as frame coherence, the tendency of one frame to resemble the next. Frame coherence allows applications to avoid transforming even bounding spheres most of the time for a large number of objects.

In the next chapter, I cover the fundamental principles and techniques of artificial intelligence.

Chapter 9
Physics

Stunning graphics are mandatory for all games, 3D games in particular. More than just providing richly detailed polygons and interesting environments, however, three-dimensional games are becoming more realistic *physically*. By that I mean they simulate some of the laws of physics and thereby enable objects in the virtual world to interact with each other in realistic ways.

In this chapter, I explore the fundamental concepts of *physics*, the field of science that, when used in games, adds the realism of *movement* that great graphics alone cannot produce. I start by covering the all-important technique of collision detection and prevention, and then move to basic kinematics and dynamics.

Collision Detection And Prevention

Collision detection is the method whereby collisions of objects are detected via computer algorithms. Without collision detection, objects would pass through each other and no physical simulations would be possible.

The algorithm I present here will take a 3D line segment and check to see if it intersects a 3D polygon. You can also use this algorithm to determine if two polygons intersect, as we will cover later.

The line-intersection algorithm has three steps:

1. Determine if the two points of the line (the points that define the beginning and ending of the line segment) fall on opposite sides of the polygon's plane. If they do not, the line does not intersect the polygon. Otherwise, proceed to Step 2.

2. Determine the exact point where the line intersects the polygon's plane. Proceed to Step 3.

3. Determine if the intersected point lies within the boundaries of the polygon. If it does, the line intersects the polygon. Otherwise it does not.

Figure 9.1 illustrates all three steps.

The next three sections will cover the mathematics behind each process in the line-intersection algorithm.

Step 1: Checking For Plane Crossing

The first step, checking to see if the line's points lie on opposite sides of the polygon's plane, is quite easy. The equation for a plane is as follows, where **A**, **B**, and **C** are the vector components that describe the orientation of the plane (this vector is perpendicular to the plane) and **D** can be found by substituting a point known to lie on the polygon into the equation:

```
Ax + By + Cz + D = 0
```

The plane equation is true (that is, the left side evaluates to 0) for all points that lie on the plane. The left side of the equation evaluates to a negative number for all points that lie on one side of the plane, and to a positive number for all points that lie on the other side. To determine if the line's points lie on opposite sides of the polygon's plane, all you must do is

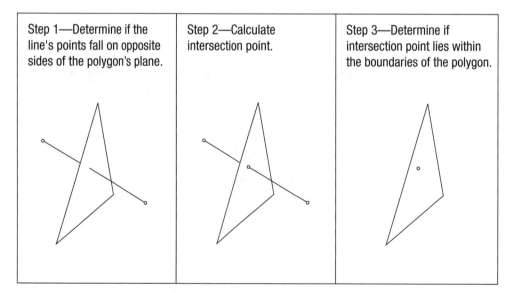

Step 1—Determine if the line's points fall on opposite sides of the polygon's plane.	Step 2—Calculate intersection point.	Step 3—Determine if intersection point lies within the boundaries of the polygon.

Figure 9.1
A three-step process for determining if a line intersects a polygon.

plug both points into the equation. If the sign (whether negative or positive) of both points is the same, then the line lies entirely on one side of the plane. If the sign of both points differs, however, then the line crosses the polygon's plane.

Listings 9.1 and 9.2 contain vectors and point encapsulations that the collision-detection code in this chapter will use. Listing 9.3 contains a function that will generate **A**, **B**, **C**, and **D**, given three points on the polygon, and another function that will determine if a line crosses a polygon's plane.

Listing 9.1   The header file for the vector and point encapsulation.

```
//
// File name: VP.HPP
//
// Description: The class declarations for 3D vector and
//              point classes.
//
// Author: John De Goes
//
// Project: None
//
// Copyright (C) 1999 John De Goes -- All Rights Reserved.
//

#ifndef __VPHPP__
#define __VPHPP__

#include <Math.H>

typedef float Real;

#define IsRealZero(x) \
    ( ( x > -0.001 && ( x < 0.001 ) ) ? true : false )

#define IsRealEqualTo(x,y,p) \
    ( ( x > ( -p + y ) && ( x < ( p + y ) ) ) ? true : false )

#define PI ( ( Real ) 3.14159265358979 )

struct Point3D;

struct Vector3D {
    Real i, j, k;

    void Rotatei ( Real Rad );

    void Rotatej ( Real Rad );
```

```
        void Rotatek ( Real Rad );

        Real Dot ( Vector3D &V );

        Vector3D Cross ( Vector3D &V );

        Real Mag ();

        Real Angle ( Vector3D &V );
        Real AngleNorm ( Vector3D &V );

        operator Real ();
        operator Point3D ();

        Vector3D &Normalize ();

        Vector3D operator - ( Vector3D &V );
        Vector3D operator + ( Vector3D &V );
        Vector3D operator * ( Real S );
    };

    struct Point3D {
        Real x, y, z;

        void Rotatex ( Real Rad );

        void Rotatey ( Real Rad );

        void Rotatez ( Real Rad );

        operator Vector3D ();

        Point3D operator - ( Point3D &P );

        Point3D operator + ( Point3D &P );

        Point3D operator * ( Real S );

        Real DistanceTo ( Point3D &P );
    };

    #endif
```

Listing 9.2   The implementation of the vector and point encapsulation.

```cpp
//
// File name: VP.CPP
//
// Description: The class code for 3D vector and
//              point classes.
//
// Author: John De Goes
//
// Project: None
//
// Copyright (C) 1999 John De Goes -- All Rights Reserved.
//

#include "VP.HPP"

void Vector3D::Rotatei ( Real Rad ) {
   Real oj = j, ok = k;

   j = ( Real ) ( oj * cos ( Rad ) - ok * sin ( Rad ) );
   k = ( Real ) ( oj * sin ( Rad ) + ok * cos ( Rad ) );
}

void Vector3D::Rotatej ( Real Rad ) {
   Real oi = i, ok = k;

   i = ( Real ) ( oi * cos ( Rad ) - ok * sin ( Rad ) );
   k = ( Real ) ( oi * sin ( Rad ) + ok * cos ( Rad ) );
}

void Vector3D::Rotatek ( Real Rad ) {
   Real oi = i, oj = j;

   i = ( Real ) ( oi * cos ( Rad ) - oj * sin ( Rad ) );
   j = ( Real ) ( oi * sin ( Rad ) + oj * cos ( Rad ) );
}

Real Vector3D::Dot ( Vector3D &V ) {
   return ( i + V.i + j * V.j + k * V.k );
}

Vector3D Vector3D::Cross ( Vector3D &V ) {
   Vector3D Result;
```

```
      Result.i = j * V.k - k * V.j;
      Result.j = k * V.i - i * V.k;
      Result.k = i * V.j - j * V.i;

      return Result;
}

Real Vector3D::Mag () {
    return ( Real ) sqrt ( i * i + j * j + k * k );
}

Real Vector3D::Angle ( Vector3D &V ) {
    Real ProdMag = Mag () * V.Mag ();
    return ( Real ) atan ( Dot ( V ) / ProdMag );
}

Real Vector3D::AngleNorm ( Vector3D &V ) {
    return ( Real ) acos ( Dot ( V ) );
}

Vector3D::operator Real () {
    return this->Mag ();
}

Vector3D::operator Point3D () {
    Point3D P;

    P.x = i; P.y = j; P.z = k;

    return P;
}

Vector3D &Vector3D::Normalize () {
    Real Dist = Mag ();

    i /= Dist;
    j /= Dist;
    k /= Dist;

    return *this;
}

Vector3D Vector3D::operator - ( Vector3D &V ) {
    Vector3D Result;
```

```
   Result.i = i - V.i;
   Result.j = j - V.j;
   Result.k = k - V.k;

   return Result;
}

Vector3D Vector3D::operator + ( Vector3D &V ) {
   Vector3D Result;

   Result.i = i + V.i;
   Result.j = j + V.j;
   Result.k = k + V.k;

   return Result;
}

Vector3D Vector3D::operator * ( Real S ) {
   Vector3D Result;

   Result.i = i * S;
   Result.j = j * S;
   Result.k = k * S;

   return Result;
}

void Point3D::Rotatex ( Real Rad ) {
   Real oy = y, oz = z;

   y = ( Real ) ( oy * cos ( Rad ) - oz * sin ( Rad ) );
   z = ( Real ) ( oy * sin ( Rad ) + oz * cos ( Rad ) );
}

void Point3D::Rotatey ( Real Rad ) {
   Real ox = x, oz = z;

   x = ( Real ) ( ox * cos ( Rad ) - oz * sin ( Rad ) );
   z = ( Real ) ( ox * sin ( Rad ) + oz * cos ( Rad ) );
}

void Point3D::Rotatez ( Real Rad ) {
   Real ox = x, oy = y;

   x = ( Real ) ( ox * cos ( -Rad ) - oy * sin ( -Rad ) );
   y = ( Real ) ( ox * sin ( -Rad ) + oy * cos ( -Rad ) );
}
```

```
Point3D::operator Vector3D () {
   Vector3D V;

   V.i = x; V.j = y; V.k = z;

   return V;
}

Point3D Point3D::operator - ( Point3D &P ) {
   Point3D Result;

   Result.x = x - P.x;
   Result.y = y - P.y;
   Result.z = z - P.z;

   return Result;
}

Point3D Point3D::operator + ( Point3D &P ) {
   Point3D Result;

   Result.x = x + P.x;
   Result.y = y + P.y;
   Result.z = z + P.z;

   return Result;
}

Point3D Point3D::operator * ( Real S ) {
   Point3D Result;

   Result.x = x * S;
   Result.y = y * S;
   Result.z = z * S;

   return Result;
}

Real Point3D::DistanceTo ( Point3D &P ) {
   Real Dx = P.x - x,
        Dy = P.y - y,
        Dz = P.z - z;

   return ( Real ) sqrt ( Dx * Dx + Dy * Dy + Dz * Dz );
}
```

Listing 9.3   Two functions for implementing Step 1 of the line-intersection algorithm.

```
void MakeNormal ( Point3D *Point, Vector3D &Normal, float &D ) {
    // Triangle must be defined in a clockwise fashion when viewed from
    // its visible side or this function will fail to generate the proper
    // normal.
    Vector3D V1 = ( Vector3D ) ( Point [ 1 ] - Point [ 0 ] ),
             V2 = ( Vector3D ) ( Point [ 2 ] - Point [ 0 ] );

    Normal = V1.Cross ( V2 );

    Normal.Normalize ();

    D = - ( Normal.i * Point [ 0 ].x +
            Normal.j * Point [ 0 ].y +
            Normal.k * Point [ 0 ].z );
}


bool LineCrossesPlane ( Point3D *LinePoints, Vector3D &Normal, float &D ) {
    Real Sign1, Sign2;

    Sign1 = ( Normal.i * LinePoints [ 0 ].x +
              Normal.j * LinePoints [ 0 ].y +
              Normal.k * LinePoints [ 0 ].z + D );

    Sign2 = ( Normal.i * LinePoints [ 1 ].x +
              Normal.j * LinePoints [ 1 ].y +
              Normal.k * LinePoints [ 1 ].z + D );

    if ( Sign1 * Sign2 >= ( Real ) 0.0 )
       return false;

    return true;
}
```

If the points of the line fall on opposite sides of the polygon's plane, then proceed to Step 2.

Step 2: Calculating An Intersection

The second step is to calculate where the line intersects the plane of the polygon. To do this, you need to describe both the polygon's plane and the line by equations.

To describe the plane, you can use the plane equation previously introduced:

```
Ax + By + Cz + D = 0
```

To describe the line, you could use many equations, but one that is convenient describes all points on a line in terms of the distance from the initial point of the line. This equation is shown here:

```
P(d) = P  + dD
        0
```

D is a normalized vector that describes the direction of the line, P_0 is the initial point, **d** is the distance from P_0 in the direction of **D**, and **P(d)** is the point at the specified distance from P_0. Breaking the equation into component form, you have:

```
P  = x  + dD
 x    0     x
P  = y  + dD
 y    0     y
P  = z  + dD
 z    0     z
```

P_x, P_y, and P_z are the x-, y-, and z-components of the point at a distance **d** along the directions D_x, D_y, and D_z, respectively, and x_0, y_0, and z_0 designate the line's initial point.

You want the point where the line intersects the plane. Consequently, you must substitute P_x, P_y, and P_z into the plane equation. This produces the following equation:

```
Ax  + AdD  + By  + BdD  + Cz  + CdD  + D = 0
  0      x    0      y     0      z
```

This equation will evaluate to true (the left side will equal 0) for the intersection point. To find the intersection point, you can solve for **d**. First, factor **d**, as shown:

```
d(AD  + BD  + CD ) + Ax  + By  + Cz  + D = 0
    x     y     z      0     0     0
```

Finally, isolate **d**:

```
d = -(Ax  + By  + Cz  + D)/( AD  + BD  + CD )
        0      0     0          x     y     z
```

As already mentioned, D_x, D_y, and C_z are the vector components that point in the direction of the line. What is the direction of the line? It is simply the normalized vector constructed from subtracting the line's initial point from its final point.

Note

*If the denominator of the previous equation that isolates **d** evaluates to **0**, then you cannot perform the division, because division by **0** is undefined. This case indicates the line is parallel to the plane of the polygon, and, therefore, definitely does not intersect it.*

Once you have **d**, you can simply plug it into the equation for the line and instantly obtain the intersection point. These equations are shown again for convenience:

$$P_x = x_0 + dD_x$$
$$P_y = y_0 + dD_y$$
$$P_z = z_0 + dD_z$$

Listing 9.4 contains a function that uses the mathematics just introduced to calculate the intersection of a line and a plane.

Listing 9.4 A function that determines the intersection of a line with a plane.

```
bool IntersectLineWithPlane ( Point3D &iPoint,
     Point3D *Line, Vector3D &Normal, float &D ) {
   // If Normal is not normalized, it should be normalized
   // here with the code "Normal.Normalize ();":
   Vector3D LineDir = Line [ 1 ] - Line [ 0 ];
   Real d, Num, Denom;

   LineDir.Normalize ();

   Num   = -( Normal.i * Line [ 0 ].x +
             Normal.j * Line [ 0 ].y +
             Normal.k * Line [ 0 ].z + D );

   Denom = ( Normal.i * LineDir.i +
             Normal.j * LineDir.j +
             Normal.k * LineDir.k );

   if ( Denom == ( Real ) 0.0 )
      return false;

   d = Num / Denom;

   iPoint = ( Line [ 0 ] + ( Point3D ) ( LineDir * d ) );

   return true;
}
```

Once the intersection point has been calculated, it must be checked against the boundaries of the polygon.

Step 3: Checking For Containment

The third step turns out to be fairly easy. You can determine if a point lies within the boundaries of a convex polygon by calculating the angles between consecutive vertices. If the sum of the angles equals 360 degrees (2π radians), then the point falls within the boundaries of the polygon; otherwise, it does not (see Figure 9.2).

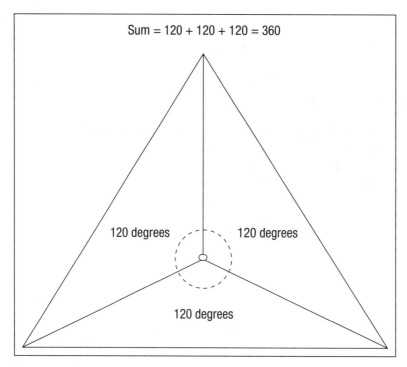

Sum = 120 + 120 + 120 = 360

120 degrees   120 degrees

120 degrees

Figure 9.2
The sum of the angles of a convex polygon's vertices, as measured from a point within the polygon, will add up to 360 degrees.

Fortunately, the angle between consecutive vertices is easy to calculate, even in 3D. The dot product, a vector operation mentioned in Appendix E, is defined as follows

A · B = |A||B| cos q

where **q** is the angle between the two vectors. Solving for **q**, you get

q = cos⁻¹ (A · B / (|A||B|))

where **cos⁻¹** is the inverse cosine function (to be distinguished from the secant function, which is defined as **1/cos**). To get **A** and **B** from the vertices of a polygon, simply subtract the intersection point from the value of those vertices, as shown in Figure 9.3. This results in two vectors you can then use with the dot product formula to get the angle between them.

Using Appendix E, you can calculate the dot product with the following equation:

A · B = $x_1 x_2$ + $y_1 y_2$ + $z_1 z_2$

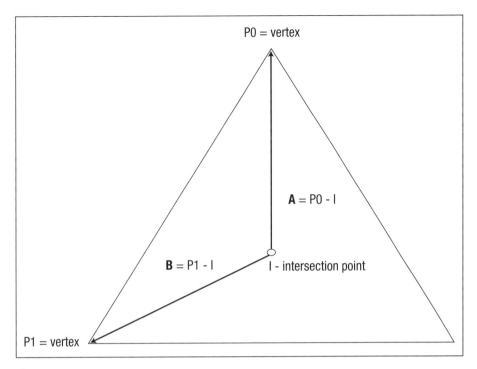

Figure 9.3
Calculating vectors for the polygon's vertices.

Listing 9.5 contains one function that determines if a point lies within the boundaries of a convex polygon by using these equations, and another function that ties all of these functions together to determine if a line intersects a convex polygon.

Listing 9.5   Two functions for the line-intersection test.

```
bool IsPointBounded ( Point3D &TestPoint,
    Point3D *Poly, long VertexCount ) {
  float Angle = 0.0F;
  // The following "match factor" is necessary due to
  // the inaccuracies of floating-point mathematics.
  // The angles of all a polygon's vertices will not
  // necessarily always add up to 2 pi radians,
  // even if the point is bounded, or may go beyond 2
  // pi radians.  Tweak this value until you get results
  // you are satisfied with.
  const Real MATCH_FACTOR = ( Real ) 0.99;
  Vector3D A, B;

  for ( long n = 0; n < VertexCount; n++ ) {
    A = ( Vector3D ) ( Poly [ n ] - TestPoint );
    B = ( Vector3D ) ( Poly [ ( n + 1 ) % VertexCount ] - TestPoint );
```

```
        Angle += ( Real ) acos ( A.Dot ( B ) / ( A.Mag () * B.Mag () ) );
    }

    if ( Angle >= ( MATCH_FACTOR * ( ( Real ) 2.0 * PI ) ) )
        return true;
    return false;
}

bool LineIntersectsPolygon ( Point3D *Line,
        Point3D *Poly, long VertexCount, Point3D &iPoint ) {
    float D;
    Vector3D PolyNormal;

    MakeNormal ( Poly, PolyNormal, D );

    if ( !LineCrossesPlane ( Line, PolyNormal, D ) )
        return false;

    IntersectLineWithPlane ( iPoint, Line, PolyNormal, D );

    if ( !IsPointBounded ( iPoint, Poly, VertexCount ) )
        return false;

    return true;
}
```

The Line Test And Polygon Intersection

The algorithm just covered will test for an intersection between a line segment and a convex polygon. This algorithm can be extended to test one polygon against intersection with another in the following fashion: If the polygons are labeled **A** and **B**, then treat each edge of **A** as a line, and test it against the polygon **B**; likewise, treat each edge of **B** as a line, and test it against the polygon **A**. If any of these lines intersect, then the two polygons intersect; otherwise, they do not. Figure 9.4 shows why both these tests are necessary.

Listing 9.6, which uses Listings 9.1 and 9.5, has a function that checks two polygons against each other for intersection.

Listing 9.6   A function that determines if two polygons intersect.
```
bool PolygonsIntersect (
    Point3D *A, long AVertexCount,
    Point3D *B, long BVertexCount,
    Point3D &iPoint ) {

    long n;
    Point3D Edge [ 2 ];
```

```
    // Check A's edges against B:
    for ( n = 0; n < AVertexCount; n++ ) {
        Edge [ 0 ] = A [ n ];
        Edge [ 1 ] = A [ ( n + 1 ) % AVertexCount ];

        if ( LineIntersectsPolygon (
                Edge, B, BVertexCount, iPoint ) )
            return true;
    }

    // Check B's edges against A:
    for ( n = 0; n < BVertexCount; n++ ) {
        Edge [ 0 ] = B [ n ];
        Edge [ 1 ] = B [ ( n + 1 ) % BVertexCount ];

        if ( LineIntersectsPolygon (
                Edge, A, AVertexCount, iPoint ) )
            return true;
    }

    return false;
}
```

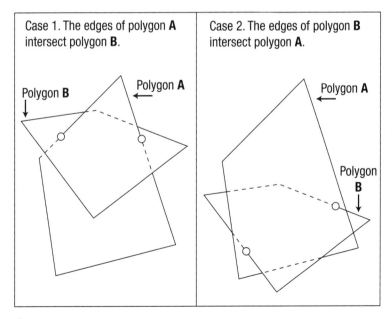

Figure 9.4
The two cases of polygon-polygon intersection with polygons **A** and **B**.

Collision Detection For Difficult Cases

In two cases, these collision-detection routines will fail altogether to detect a collision. The first case involves a line parallel to a polygon but moving sideways toward that polygon. Immediately before collision, the points of the line will be on one side of the polygon; after collision, they will be on the other side. There will never be a time interval when the line penetrates the polygon's plane. This case usually does not need to be dealt with, because lines do not typically exist as standalone entities in virtual worlds. Rather, objects—which are composed of polygons that are, in turn, composed of edges—are usually checked against other objects, and the complex nature of their shapes prevents this case from occurring.

A far more common case occurs when an object is moving extremely fast or the user's computer is slow. In these cases, an object can jump from one side of an obstacle to the other, without actually penetrating any polygon. The foolproof way to avoid this is to make sure a clear line of sight exists between an object's position in one frame and the object's position in the next frame. You can do this by creating lines that join an object in the first frame with the object's expected position in the next frame. If any of these lines intersect an obstacle, then the path cannot be taken, because a collision would occur (see Figure 9.5).

Speeding Up Collision Detection

The collision-detection routines developed in this chapter are accurate and fairly fast, but they will slow your program considerably if many polygon-intersection tests are performed. The goal is to minimize the number of these tests; you can do this in two ways.

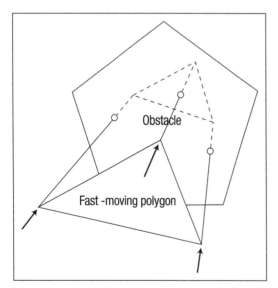

Figure 9.5
Collision detection for fast-moving objects.

The first optimization is to calculate a bounding sphere for each polygon in the virtual world, and then another one for each object. A moving object's bounding sphere can first be tested against the bounding sphere for other objects in the virtual world. If an intersection is found, then the bounding spheres of their respective polygons can be tested. If these intersect, then, finally, you can use the routines in this chapter.

Note

To generate a bounding sphere for a polygon or object, add all of its x-, y-, and z-values, and then divide these three sums by the total number of points. The resulting point is the geometric center of the object, which corresponds to the center of its bounding sphere. Once you have the center, calculate the distance from it to each of the object's points. The distance between the center and the object's farthest point is the bounding sphere's radius.

To determine if two bounding spheres intersect, calculate the distance between their centers. If this distance is smaller than the sum of the two spheres' radii, then the spheres intersect. Otherwise, they do not.

The second optimization is to partition the virtual world into subspaces (perhaps cubes), and record for each of these subspaces a list of all polygons in it. You can then concentrate on the objects in the subspace and not worry about polygons in remote regions of the virtual world. You can perform this optimization prior to the first optimization, for added speed.

Collision Prevention

After you have detected a collision, you must, in general, decide how to prevent it, unless you want the objects to penetrate each other. You can prevent collisions in two principle ways: Stop the moving object before it penetrates the obstacle; or slide the moving object along the obstacle (without allowing penetration).

The first approach is simplest and perhaps most realistic in many situations. To implement it merely do not move an object if that movement will result in a collision. A more sophisticated variant involves moving the object as far as it can go without penetrating the obstacle. You can do this crudely by using a very small increment to move the object, and then stopping just before the collision, or more efficiently through mathematical techniques I will cover now.

Observe the two 3D lines in Figure 9.6. The first one represents the line's starting position and orientation before collision with the polygon, and the second represents the line's ending configuration after it has penetrated the polygon.

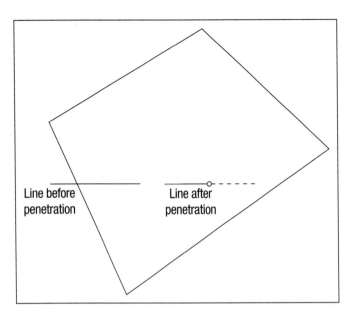

Line before
penetration

Line after
penetration

Figure 9.6
Two 3D lines.

To find out how far the 3D line can go without penetrating the object, you must perform a complex series of steps:

1. Describe the position of the line in terms of time. In equation form, each of the two points of the line can be described in this form, where **V** is the velocity of the point and **t** is the time where the point is located at position **P(t)**:

```
P(t) = Vt
```

If you assume the line moves from its initial configuration to its final configuration by taking the shortest possible route, and that the velocity remains constant, then the direction of **V** is the same as the final point minus the initial point. The magnitude of **V** is equal to the distance the point is traveling divided by the time it takes to travel that distance.

2. Determine which side of the line penetrated the polygon first. You can do this by creating two imaginary lines that extend from the line's initial points to its final points, and then find the intersection points of these lines with the polygon. You can solve the equation **P(t) = Vt** for **t** (t = P/V), plug in each of the intersection points, and then pick the side that has the smallest **t**.

3. Finally, use the smallest **t** calculated in Step 2 to determine the final permissible ending point values by plugging this **t** into each of the points' equations.

You should use the second approach, sliding the object along the obstacle, only after the first approach (that is, only after the object is actually touching the obstacle). Once the object touches the obstacle, you can proceed to find out which direction it should slide. To do this, project the vector that describes the object's heading (the direction it is going) onto the obstacle in the direction of the obstacle's normal vector (see Figure 9.7).

The mathematics for this operation is straightforward: Create a line from each of the two points of the free vector that describes the object's heading. These lines should proceed toward the polygon in the direction of the polygon's normal vector. The intersection of these lines with the polygon's plane produces two points, which can be construed as a vector that describes both the direction the amount the object should slide.

Note
Sometimes, an object will collide at more than one point. In these cases, you must find the first collision by describing the motion of the object in terms of time, as was done previously, and then use this time value to calculate the positions of the other points in the object.

Introduction To Physics

Physics is a broad field of science that explores everything from quantum to astronomical phenomena. It attempts to describe the world by using mathematical formulas. These formulas and the theory underlying them are important in computer games, where by default,

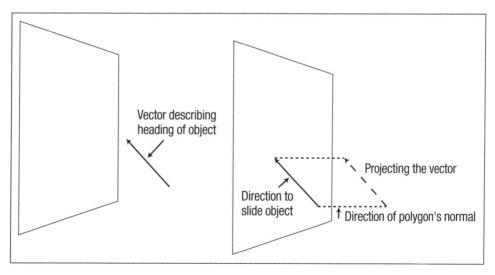

Figure 9.7
Sliding an object along a polygon.

there are no such things as "laws of physics." To stop a moving object from running into a wall, to make objects fall with increasing velocity, and to simulate collisions all require a fair amount of work by the programmer.

The two areas of specialization in physics that interest programmers are *kinematics* and *dynamics*. Kinematics describes objects in terms of position and velocity. Dynamics, on the other hand, is more concerned with physical laws, which are then used to generate position and velocity for objects.

The two ways kinematics and dynamics can be used in computer graphics are referred to as *inverse* and *forward*. Forward kinematics and dynamics rely on starting conditions (such as velocity or position) to produce final states. Inverse kinematics and dynamics, in contrast, start with final states and work backward, effectively asking the question, "How must the object be manipulated so it ends up in a certain state?" Because there may be many ways of getting from a final state to an initial state (especially with kinematics), *constraints* (physical or otherwise) are often added to these types of physical simulations that lower (often to one) the number of options.

Dynamics, the more useful of the two specializations, becomes extremely complex for articulated figures, skeletal systems, and other challenging (but possible) physically based systems. Because the mathematics behind more advanced dynamics requires multivariable calculus, and because the topic is quite large, I will discuss only simple dynamics. For the discussion of kinematics, I will likewise restrict my focus to simple, noncalculus-based equations that anyone who has taken algebra can readily use. For programmers with a deeper math background, I recommend the two books, *Computational Dynamics* (Wiley Inter-Science) and *Physically Based Modeling for Computer Graphics* (Academic Press), both of which go into more depth than is possible given the wider audience and limited space of this book.

Velocity And Acceleration

Two important concepts in physics are *velocity* and *acceleration*, both of which have slightly different and more formal definitions than we are accustomed to using in everyday life.

Velocity is a vector used to describe the direction and speed of a particle or object (the magnitude of the vector corresponds to the speed). Speed, in turn, is the rate of change of position. It describes how fast or slow position changes and is typically measured in meters-per-second (m/s).

Acceleration is a vector that describes the rate of change of velocity. It describes how fast or slow velocity changes, and in which direction it is changing. Acceleration is usually measured in meters-per-second-squared (m/s^2).

If you press your car's gas pedal down to a certain point and hold it there, your acceleration will be more or less constant as the magnitude of your velocity increases at a uniform rate (the direction of your velocity remains the same unless you are turning). If you vary the amount of pressure you apply to the gas pedal over time, then both acceleration and velocity will change.

Three-Dimensional Rectilinear Motion

You can describe the position of a 3D object that is moving in a straight line by using its initial velocity, its initial position, and its acceleration. The equation for doing this is as follows:

```
P(t) = P₀ + v₀t + 1/2 at²
```

P(t) is the point of the object, **P**$_0$ the initial position, **v**$_0$ the initial velocity, **a** the acceleration the object is undergoing, and **t** the time.

The equation can also be expressed equivalently in terms of x-, y-, and z-components, as shown:

```
Pₓ = Pₓ₀ + vₓ₀t + 1/2 aₓt²
P_y = P_y₀ + v_y₀t + 1/2 a_yt²
P_z = P_z₀ + v_z₀t + 1/2 a_zt²
```

Another equation that is useful is shown here:

```
v = v₀ + at
```

You can solve this equation for the velocity, time, or acceleration, depending on the information you want.

Rotational Motion

Rotational kinematics equations are much the same as those for rectilinear motion, except for rotational kinematics, they describe the *angle* of a rotating object, given initial conditions.

Given an initial angle, an angular velocity (described in radians-per-second, for example), and an angular acceleration, the following equation can describe the angle at any time **t**, given an initial angle θ_0, an angular velocity ω (radians-per-second), and an angular acceleration α (radians-per-second-squared):

```
q(t) = q₀ + w₀t + 1/2 at²
```

Two equations that are helpful when you do not know all of these variables are shown here:

$$\omega = \omega + \alpha t$$
$$\omega^2 = \omega_0^2 + 2\alpha(\theta - \theta_0)$$

For an object rotating on three axes, these equations would have to be employed three times: once for each axis.

Basic Dynamics

In the world of dynamics, *force* is an important concept. Force is a vector that describes the direction and magnitude of a quantity that tends to accelerate an object in the direction of the force. Force is measured in units called *newtons* (the unit of force required to accelerate a mass of one kilogram one meter per second), which is designated by the symbol *N*.

When you push on a wall, you are exerting a force on the wall. Similarly, the sun exerts a force on all the planets in the solar system, which keeps them from flying off into space. In computer games, phenomena such as gravity, wind, and engines can all be described with forces.

Newton's Laws Of Motion

Newton's laws of motion, developed by Sir Isaac Newton in the late 1680s, are of great use in simulating physical systems. The three laws he developed are these:

◆ *First Law*—Assuming the net force on a body is zero, an object at rest remains at rest, and an object in motion remains in motion in a straight line with constant speed.

◆ *Second Law*—The sum of all forces acting on an object is equal to the mass of the object times its acceleration: **ΣF = ma** (the Greek letter **Σ**, pronounced sigma, means the sum of).

◆ *Third Law*—When one object exerts a force on a second object, the second object always exerts a force on the first object that is equal in magnitude but opposite in direction.

The first law describes the natural state of objects, which, contrary to Aristotelian physics, is not at rest. Objects at rest do tend to remain at rest, but those moving in a straight line with a certain speed likewise tend to continue moving in that direction and at that speed, unless forces act upon the objects. The reason why this law is not intuitive to planet-bound creatures is that gravity, friction, and other forces are always acting on the objects we come into contact with.

The second law says that if you add all the forces acting upon an object, the resulting vector designating the force acting on the object will be equal to the mass of the object times its acceleration. Thus, if you know all forces acting on an object, and the mass of the object, you can determine which direction it should be accelerating and how much it should accelerate. This is what makes dynamics possible.

The third law says that to each action there is a reaction. Your weight exerts a force on the floor, and, correspondingly, the floor exerts a force on you. This force is responsible for keeping you from sinking into the ground. Likewise, when you walk forward, you do so by pushing backward against the ground, which in turn pushes forward against you, causing you to move forward (of course, if you are walking on ice, the ground will be unable to generate sufficient force to match your force, and you will not move anywhere).

An important property of force is that force applied to one axis does not affect the motion of an object in the other axes. A force pulling an object down does not hinder its movement from side to side. For example, the three-dimensional rectilinear equations introduced earlier, which break down a force into x-, y-, and z-positions, velocity, and acceleration quantities, assume this property.

Periodic Motion

Periodic motion is any motion that involves repetitive positioning, such as a swinging pendulum or a bouncing spring. Each repeat is called an *oscillation*. Periodic motion may be simulated with the following equation:

```
x(t) = x₀ sin ( st + q₀)
```

In this equation, $\mathbf{x_0}$ is range of movement, θ_0 is the phase variance (which is used for specifying the initial condition at $\mathbf{t = 0}$; often it is not important), and σ is the frequency of oscillation (defined as $\sigma = 2\pi/T$, where $\mathbf{T}$ is the amount of time per oscillation).

To simulate a bouncing spring, a pendulum, and many other phenomena, you must scale the $\mathbf{x(t)}$ down as time progresses. A simple way of doing this is to divide the equation by $\mathbf{t}$, or by $\mathbf{t^2}$ for a more rapid decrease in the amplitude of the oscillation.

Gravitational Force

Newton discovered that the gravitational force one body exerts on another is directly proportional to the product of their masses divided by the square of the distance between them. In equation form:

```
F = Gm₁m₂/R²
```

$\mathbf{G}$ has been found to be approximately $6.67259 \_ 10^{-11}$. $\mathbf{F}$ is a vector that points along the shortest distance between the two masses.

Using the gravitational equation, you can simulate how objects fall. For example, assume a planet is designated by $\mathbf{m_1}$, and an object by $\mathbf{m_2}$. Recall that Newton's third law says the force acting on $\mathbf{m_2}$ is equal to its acceleration times $\mathbf{m_2}$ ($\mathbf{am_2}$). Equating the two equations, you get the following:

$$am_2 \ = \ Gm_1m_2/R^2$$

The $\mathbf{m_2}$s cancel, producing

$$a \ = \ Gm_1/R^2$$

You can use this acceleration constant in the three-dimensional rectilinear equations introduced previously to produce the path of a falling object. Keep in mind that the acceleration points down toward the center of the planet; no component moves along the x- or z-axes. Consequently, to simulate gravity, all you need to do is to use the rectilinear equations for the y--axis, using the previously described acceleration factor as the object's vertical acceleration.

For earth, the acceleration turns out to be roughly 9.80665 m/s². You can use the equation for any planet or object whose mass you know.

Note

In planets with atmospheres, a falling object will not accelerate indefinitely. After falling a certain distance, the resistance caused by the atmosphere will cause the acceleration to go to zero, and the object will continue to fall at its last speed, referred to as its terminal velocity, until it hits the ground. For small distances, however, this effect is negligible.

Friction

Friction is important in the real world and quite useful in simulating the physics of virtual ones as well. Friction is the force that makes cars, people, and animals able to move across the ground. Exerting a backward force on the ground, the force of friction exerts a forward force on the object, thereby causing it to move.

The direction of the friction force always points in a direction opposing the motion of the object. When you push backward on the ground, for example, the frictional force that moves you forward acts parallel to the ground and in the direction opposite of your backward push.

The magnitude of a friction force often equals the magnitude of the opposing motion. In the walking example again, the magnitude of the frictional force is the same as the magnitude of your backward push. The exception to this rule occurs when, because of the substances or weights involved (rubber on ice, for example), the frictional force is unable to equal the opposing force, and therefore cannot push the object forward, allowing it to slide across the surface.

The force required to slide an object on a surface varies depending on whether or not the object is at rest. It takes more force to start an object sliding than to continue making it slide once it is in motion (this is the principle that antilock brakes take advantage of).

By experimentation, the force needed to start an object sliding across a surface has been found to be proportional to normal force (the force that keeps the object from sinking into the ground), as shown in the following equation:

$$F_f = m_s \, F_n$$

$\mathbf{F_f}$ is the frictional force, $\mathbf{m_s}$ is the *coefficient of static friction*, and $\mathbf{F_n}$ is the force that the ground (or wall, etc.) exerts on the object. Table 9.1 shows some common values. Similarly, the force needed to make an object continue sliding once it has started sliding is governed by the following equation:

$$F_f = m_k \, F_n$$

$\mathbf{m_k}$ is referred to as the *coefficient of kinetic friction*. Table 9.2 shows values for this constant for various substances.

The primary use for friction forces in games is when objects move across slippery (or somewhat slippery) surfaces, in which case these equations can be used to determine when the objects should slide.

Table 9.1   Coefficient of static friction for various substances.

Substance	Coefficient
Wood on wood	0.4
Ice on ice	0.1
Metal on metal	0.15
Steel on steel	0.7
Rubber on dry concrete	1.0
Rubber on wet concrete	0.7

Table 9.2   Coefficient of kinetic friction for various substances.

Substance	Coefficient
Wood on wood	0.2
Ice on ice	0.03
Metal on metal	0.07
Steel on steel	0.6
Rubber on dry concrete	0.8
Rubber on wet concrete	0.5

Summary

An integral part of physics simulation is the detection and prevention of collisions between objects in the virtual world. Collision detection can be performed accurately, though at some cost in performance. Methods of speeding up detection include partitioning the environment and using bounding spheres.

Collision prevention is often handled in one of two ways: by stopping the moving object from penetrating the obstacle, or by sliding the moving object along the obstacle. The latter is commonly employed when the player hits a wall in a 3D action game.

Physics simulation is concerned with kinematics and dynamics. Kinematics describes the motion of objects, and dynamics, the forces behind those motions. Both involve the concepts of velocity and acceleration. Velocity is a vector that describes a direction and a rate of position change, while acceleration is a vector that describes a direction and a rate of velocity change.

Though kinematics and dynamics are complex subjects, a wide variety of equations exist that you can easily use to add realism to your games. These include rectilinear motion, rotational motion, periodic motion, gravitation, and friction equations.

In the next chapter, we head back to DirectX and discuss DirectSound, a component of DirectX key to adding 2D and 3D sound to your games.

Chapter 10

Introduction To DirectSound

From the beep of an early PC's speaker to the advanced USB digital speakers and feature-laden, high-performance sound cards of today, audio for personal computers has come a long way. Computer games now have access to equipment (standard on even low-end PCs) capable of playing dozens of sounds in three-dimensional space, accompanied by a musical score and standard sounds for the game's interface.

To provide you with the skills necessary to take advantage of today's high-tech hardware (and extend it when it falls short of features you need), this chapter starts by covering a necessary topic: the fundamentals of acoustics. It then proceeds to an overview of DirectSound, Microsoft's widely supported sound SDK.

The Nature Of Sound

Fundamentally, sound is the passage of movement through a medium (such as wood or air). When you talk, for example, your vocal cords cause air molecules to vibrate. These molecules, in turn, cause other molecules to vibrate, and so on, until the movement reaches the listener's ear drums. The air molecules themselves never travel the great distances between your mouth and the listener, but only wiggle back and forth, acting as carriers of molecular movement. Because of this oscillatory behavior, sound is said to travel as a *wave*.

Figure 10.1 is a visual representation of a sound. The vertical axis represents the amplitude of the sound (which you can think of as the molecular displacement), and the horizontal axis represents time.

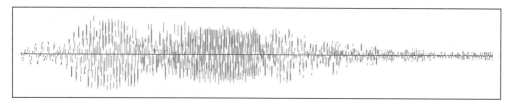

Figure 10.1
A graphical representation of a sound wave.

The Fundamental Properties Of Sound

Sound has a number of basic attributes, most of which are readily recognizable: speed, pitch, volume, intensity, quality, and location.

Speed refers to the how fast the sound travels. This varies depending on the medium. Sound travels faster in water and metal, for example, than it does in air (see Table 10.1). The temperature also affects sound—sound passes faster in higher temperatures than it does in lower ones.

Pitch refers to the sound's frequency, measured in oscillations per second (called *hertz*, abbreviated as Hz). It measures how fast the molecules are moving back and forth. A young human ear can discern sounds anywhere from 20 Hz to about 18 kHz (kilohertz).

Volume refers to the loudness of the sound as perceived by humans. This is usually measured in *decibels* (dB). The threshold of human hearing is 0 decibels; every 10 decibels higher the loudness of the sound doubles (for example, a 30-decibel sound is twice as loud as a 20-decibel sound). Table 10.2 shows the decibel levels for a number of common sounds.

Intensity refers to the power per square meter required to produce the sound. Doubling the intensity of a sound does not double its perceived volume—intensity must be increased by a factor of 10 to double the volume.

Table 10.1   The speed of sound in various media.

Medium	Speed (meters/second)
Air (room temperature)	343
Helium	1,005
Hydrogen	1,300
Water	1,440
Seawater	1,560
Iron	5,000
Steel	5,000
Aluminum	5,100
Hardwood	4,000

Table 10.2   The intensity of various sounds.

Sound Source	Loudness (decibels)
Jet plane	120
Siren	100
Subway train	90
Street traffic	70
Conversation	65
Library	40
Whisper	20
Threshold of hearing	0

Quality refers to how closely the perception of a sound matches what it should sound like. A music CD drowned out by the sound of an overhead jet would have low quality, whereas that same CD played in a perfectly quiet sound room would have high quality.

Location, of course, refers to where the sound is located. Humans can perceive the direction of a sound (even if it's behind them) and its approximate distance (if its volume is known).

In addition to these basic properties, sound interacts with its environment in specific ways.

Sound In An Environment

The properties of sound within an environment include all of the following: interference, falloff, reflection, refraction, diffraction, and the Doppler effect.

Interference occurs when two or more sounds propagate throughout the same space. This can happen constructively, where the sounds combine in a way that enhances their amplitudes; destructively, where the sounds combine in a way that reduces their amplitudes; or some mixture of the two, as shown in Figure 10.2.

Falloff refers to the decrease in the intensity of a sound as the distance between the listener and the sound increases. In the middle of open space, the intensity is inversely proportional

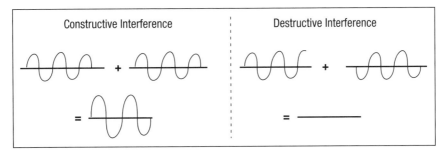

Figure 10.2
Sound interference.

to the square of the distance between the sound and the listener. In environments with objects, however, reflection, diffraction, and absorption minimize the usefulness of this rule.

Reflection occurs when a traveling sound wave changes from one medium to another. A portion of the wave is transmitted to the new medium, and the rest of the wave is reflected. Reflection is the main reason sound can travel around corners and edges. It is also responsible for echoes (which are reflected sound waves out of sync with the original) and some level of distortion (reflecting sound waves interfere with each other and distort the sound). These effects are illustrated in Figure 10.3.

Refraction refers to the bending of a sound wave because of a change in its speed. A change in temperature or movement of the medium in which the sound travels can cause refraction.

Diffraction also refers to the bending of a sound wave, but not because of a change in its speed. Sound tends to bend around edges and corners naturally, much like a wave of water bends around rocks, as illustrated in Figure 10.4.

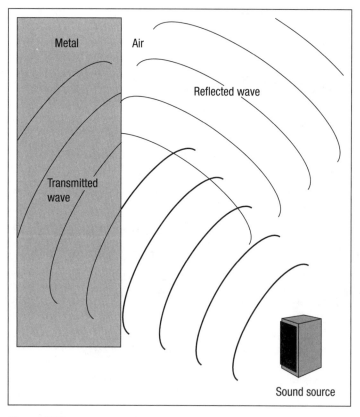

Figure 10.3
Sound reflection.

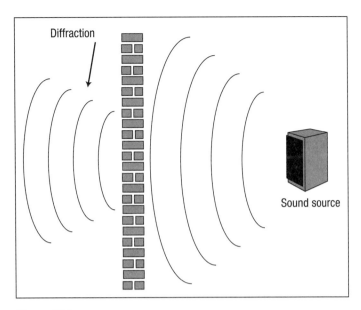

Figure 10.4
Sound diffraction.

The Doppler effect refers to the shift in the pitch of a sound when the listener, the sound source, or both are moving. This occurs, for example, with the siren of a moving fire truck: The pitch raises when the fire truck speeds toward the listener and falls after it has passed. As the truck approaches the listener, the sound waves are crowded together. As the truck passes and heads away from the listener, the sound waves expand. Figure 10.5 illustrates this.

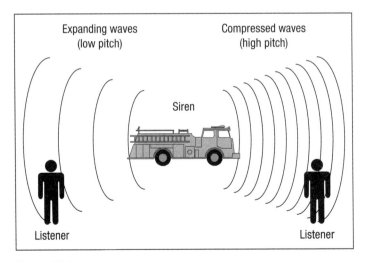

Figure 10.5
The Doppler effect.

DirectSound Basics

DirectSound is a comprehensive sound solution for developers who want to add normal or 3D sound processing and even sound capture to their applications. Among its many features are support for sound mixing, sound panning, 3D sounds with positions and velocities, and sound capture.

The following sections cover some of the basic principles of DirectSound, such as sound buffers and hardware acceleration, and expand upon many of the terms you will see in discussions of DirectSound.

Hardware Acceleration

The *Hardware Abstraction Layer (HAL)* handles hardware acceleration for DirectSound. This efficient piece of software stands between the sound hardware and DirectSound, providing access to the hardware's features. If the hardware does not support a requested feature, DirectSound can in many cases emulate it.

Some obsolete sound devices do not support DirectSound, and for these devices DirectSound cannot use the HAL. Instead, it employs the *Hardware Emulation Layer (HEL)* software, which emulates many of the features provided by the HAL, such as sound mixing. The HEL works by routing all sound through standard Windows channels and is therefore available on all systems that support Windows' sound.

A few systems have multiple sound devices that each support DirectSound. For these situations, DirectSound allows your application to list each HAL available and choose which of them it wants to use.

Cooperative Level

The term *cooperative level* refers to the degree of control an application wants to have over the sound hardware. You can choose to share the hardware with other applications or reserve it exclusively for your own application. All DirectSound applications must set the cooperative level before they play any sounds or change sound settings.

Sound Buffers

Sound buffers in DirectSound store sound data. The sound is stored as a series of *samples*. Each sample is a numerical value indicating the amplitude of the sound wave at a specific moment. Other attributes of sound buffers include channel count, sample rate, and bits per sample.

A sound buffer's *channel count* indicates the number of channels used for the sound. One channel indicates mono sound, while two channels indicate stereo sound. These are common channel counts, but a sound can have many more.

A sound buffer's *sample rate* indicates the number of samples per second that were taken when the sound was being recorded—in other words, the number of times per second the amplitude of the sound wave was stored. Typical values for the sample rate are 11,025, 22,050, and 44,100 Hz.

Note
The sample rate 44,100 Hz (often written 44.1 kHz) is referred to as CD-quality sound, because music CDs store audio at this rate. Because the human ear cannot discern frequencies above 20,000 Hz, 44,100 Hz is high enough to record audio so perfectly that no human can distinguish it from the original. The quality of the speakers and interference from the mainboard, however, usually prevent computers from attaining this level of audio reproduction.

A sound buffer's *bits per sample* indicate the number of bits used to store each sample—typically 8 or 16 bits. Eight-bit sound suffers from quality problems, because the amplitude can be only one of 256 values. Sixteen-bit sound is much higher quality, but requires twice as much space.

The samples of the sound buffer are stored in an uncompressed format known as *Pulse Code Modulation (PCM)*. For mono PCM sounds, the samples are stored in order, from first to last. For stereo and higher-channel PCM sounds, the sound data is interleaved (for example, sample 1 for channel 1 is stored first, followed by sample 1 for channel 2, sample 2 for channel 1, sample 2 for channel 2, and so on).

You can store sound buffers in system memory or on the sound hardware itself, if it contains memory for such purposes. Many of today's sound cards contain 8MB or more to use for storing sounds. The advantage of storing sounds directly on the sound card is faster performance—the sound card can handle the sound playback entirely, without requiring the CPU continually to feed it sound data.

Types Of Sound Buffers
DirectSound has three distinct kinds of sound buffers: the primary sound buffer, secondary sound buffers, and sound-capture buffers. The primary sound buffer, analogous to the primary surface in DirectDraw, contains the data currently being played. Secondary sound buffers merely store sound clips, which can later be played by mixing them into the primary sound buffer. Sound-capture buffers are used for storing sound that is being captured from an audio input device, such as a microphone.

Playing Sound Buffers
You can choose the channel count, sample rate, and bits per sample of all sound buffers. Secondary sound buffers are automatically converted to the format of the primary sound buffer when played.

Sound buffers can be played at any frequency and volume level. You can also adjust each sound's *pan*—the ratio of the left channel's volume to the right channel's volume. This allows you to play sound buffers completely through the right speaker, completely through the left speaker, or any combination. This is useful mainly for non-3D sounds, because DirectSound automatically calculates the pan for 3D sounds.

Writing To And Reading From Sound Buffers

Like DirectDraw, DirectSound requires that you *lock* sound buffers before writing data to them, and *unlock* them when you are finished. Locking sound buffers assures that no other application will interfere with the memory or the sound hardware.

You cannot read from sound buffers, because DirectSound does not guarantee that the pointer it gives you actually points to a sound buffer. The pointer may, for example, point to a temporary buffer that DirectSound will transfer to the real sound buffer after unlocking. The only exception to this is a sound-capture buffer, which can be read from when locked.

Three-Dimensional Sound Buffers

Secondary sound buffers can act as 3D sounds if created appropriately. Three-dimensional sound buffers have a position, a velocity, minimum and maximum distances, and, possibly, an orientation.

Note

By default, all distances in DirectSound are measured in meters. Velocities are measured in meters per second. Angles are measured in degrees.

*You can change the default unit of length to match whatever unit your application uses by changing DirectSound's distance factor (see **DirectSound3DListener::-SetDistanceFactor** () in the IDirectSound3DListener inferface overview later in this chapter).*

DirectSound uses a 3D sound's *position* to calculate how loud it sounds to the listener. The calculation is not accurate, however, because DirectSound does not take into account the geometry of the environment. The reflection of sound waves that occurs in any real world environments with objects, for example, extends the distance a sound can be heard, and adds an echo and some distortion. You can simulate the distance extension, because DirectSound provides access to the *rolloff factor*, which determines the rate at which falloff occurs. Some sound hardware, such as SoundBlaster Live!, supports reverberation, which you can use to simulate the echo. DirectSound does not support reverberation, but it does allow you to interface directly with the sound hardware, allowing you to take advantage of such features.

DirectSound uses a 3D sound's *velocity* to calculate its Doppler effect. An application can tweak the Doppler effect by setting the *Doppler effect factor*. This global setting determines how pronounced the Doppler effect is—it can range from none at all to many times beyond what it sounds like in real life.

Note
The interpretation of a 3D sound's position and velocity depends on that sound's operation mode. This mode determines if the sound's position and velocity are absolute values or are relative to the listener's head. You can also use the operation mode to shut off 3D sound processing.

A 3D sound's *minimum* and *maximum distances* set upper and lower volume limits, respectively, for the sound. The minimum distance is the smallest amount of space that DirectSound will use between the listener and the sound. If the sound gets closer to the listener than the minimum distance, DirectSound will not use this actual distance between the sound and the listener. Instead, it will use the minimum distance. This feature puts a limit on the volume of a 3D sound; without it, the sound's volume would increase without limit as the listener got closer to the sound. The maximum distance works similarly. When the actual distance between listener and sound is farther than the maximum distance, DirectSound will use the maximum distance. You can therefore control a 3D sound's faintest volume level.

Three-dimensional sounds can emit sound equally in all directions or only in a certain direction. The *orientation* of three-dimensional sounds is specified by two 3D sound cones, as shown in Figure 10.6. Any listener who falls within the inner cone hears the sound at the highest volume level. Listeners outside the outer cone, however, hear the lowest volume level. Listeners between the inner and outer cones hear in-between volume levels.

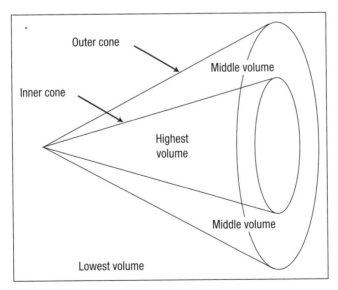

Figure 10.6
Two 3D sound cones determine the orientation of a 3D sound buffer.

The Listener

The *listener* in DirectSound does just that—it virtually listens to 3D sounds. The listener has a position and velocity. The former calculates the volume level of the sounds, while the latter calculates Doppler effects. Typically, you will want to make sure the position and velocity of the listener correspond to the camera's position and velocity.

Interface Overviews

DirectSound consists of eight objects, listed here and documented in Appendix C:

♦ *DirectSound*—The fundamental object in DirectSound, representing the sound hardware. All DirectSound applications must create a DirectSound object.

♦ *DirectSound3DBuffer*—Represents a 3D sound buffer.

♦ *DirectSound3DListener*—Represents the application's listener.

♦ *DirectSoundBuffer*—Represents a sound buffer (either primary or secondary).

♦ *DirectSoundCapture*—The fundamental object of sound capture. All DirectSound applications that want to capture sound must employ this object.

♦ *DirectSoundCaptureBuffer*—Represents a sound-capture buffer.

♦ *DirectSoundNotify*—Represents a series of notification events. A notification event can be triggered under certain playback or capture conditions—for example, when a sound is done playing.

♦ *KsPropertySet*—Used to interface directly with sound hardware.

The following sections describe the interfaces that provide access to these objects.

The IDirectSound Interface

The IDirectSound interface, obtained by calling **DirectSoundCreate ()**, is responsible for creating sound buffers, duplicating existing sound buffers, retrieving the capabilities of the sound hardware, managing memory, and managing speaker configuration information. The method functions of this interface are detailed in Table 10.3.

The IDirectSound3DBuffer Interface

The IDirectSound3DBuffer interface manages 3D sound buffers. It provides functions for setting and retrieving position, velocity, minimum and maximum distances, orientation, and operating-mode information. Table 10.4 describes the main functions for this interface.

To obtain an IDirectSound3DBuffer interface, applications must query for the interface from an existing sound buffer that was created with 3D capabilities.

Table 10.3 The functions of the IDirectSound interface.

Member Name	Description
Initialize ()	Initializes a DirectSound object created with **CoCreateInstance** ().
SetCooperativeLevel ()	Sets the application's cooperative level.
CreateSoundBuffer ()	Creates a DirectSoundBuffer object.
DuplicateSoundBuffer ()	Duplicates a preexisting sound buffer.
GetCaps ()	Retrieves the capabilities of a DirectSound object.
Compact ()	Joins free memory to create the largest contiguous amount of memory possible.
GetSpeakerConfig ()	Retrieves information about how DirectSound is optimizing audio output.
SetSpeakerConfig ()	Sets the speaker configuration information, which determines how DirectSound optimizes audio output.

Table 10.4 The functions of the IDirectSound3DBuffer interface.

Method Name	Description
GetAllParameters ()	Retrieves all characteristics of the 3D sound buffer.
SetAllParameters ()	Sets all characteristics of the 3D sound buffer.
GetMaxDistance ()	Retrieves the 3D sound buffer's maximum distance.
GetMinDistance ()	Retrieves the 3D sound buffer's minimum distance.
SetMaxDistance ()	Sets the 3D sound buffer's maximum distance.
SetMinDistance ()	Sets the 3D sound buffer's minimum distance.
GetMode ()	Retrieves the 3D sound buffer's operation mode.
SetMode ()	Sets the 3D sound buffer's operation mode.
GetPosition ()	Retrieves the 3D sound buffer's position.
SetPosition ()	Sets the 3D sound buffer's position.
GetConeAngles ()	Retrieves the angles of the 3D sound buffer's two orientation cones.
GetConeOrientation ()	Retrieves the orientation of the 3D sound buffer's two orientation cones.
GetConeOutsideVolume ()	Retrieves the volume outside the outer cone of the 3D sound buffer.
SetConeAngles ()	Sets the angles of the 3D sound buffer's two orientation cones.
SetConeOrientation ()	Sets the orientation of the 3D sound buffer's two orientation cones.
SetConeOutsideVolume ()	Sets the volume outside the outer cone of the 3D sound buffer.
GetVelocity ()	Retrieves the 3D sound buffer's velocity.
SetVelocity ()	Sets the 3D sound buffer's velocity.

The IDirectSound3DListener Interface

The IDirectSound3DListener interface, obtained by querying a sound buffer, interfaces with the listener. It allows changes to global settings (such as the distance, Doppler effect, and rolloff factors) and to modify the listener's position, velocity, and orientation. The functions of this interface are shown in Table 10.5.

Table 10.5   The functions of the IDirectSound3DListener interface.

Member Name	Description
GetAllParameters ()	Retrieves all characteristics of the 3D listener.
SetAllParameters ()	Sets all characteristics of the 3D listener.
CommitDeferredSettings ()	Commits changed settings that have been deferred for performance reasons.
GetDistanceFactor ()	Retrieves a conversion factor used for applications that do not use meters as the unit of length measurement.
SetDistanceFactor ()	Sets a conversion factor used for applications that do not use meters as the unit of length measurement.
GetDopplerFactor ()	Retrieves the Doppler effect factor.
SetDopplerFactor ()	Sets the Doppler effect factor.
GetOrientation ()	Retrieves the listener's orientation.
SetOrientation ()	Sets the listener's orientation.
GetPosition ()	Retrieves the listener's position.
SetPosition ()	Sets the listener's position.
GetRolloffFactor ()	Retrieves the rolloff factor.
SetRolloffFactor ()	Sets the rolloff factor.
GetVelocity ()	Retrieves the listener's velocity.
SetVelocity ()	Sets the listener's velocity.

The IDirectSoundBuffer Interface

The IDirectSoundBuffer interface, which you obtain by calling **IDirectSound::CreateSoundBuffer ()**, manages primary and secondary sound buffers. Among other features, it allows applications to play, restore, lock, and unlock sound buffers. The functions for this interface are shown in Table 10.6.

Table 10.6   The functions of the IDirectSoundBuffer interface.

Method Name	Description
GetCaps ()	Retrieves the capabilities of the sound buffer.
GetFormat ()	Retrieves the format of the sound buffer.
GetStatus ()	Retrieves the status (such as whether the sound is playing or looping) of the sound buffer.
SetFormat ()	Sets the format of the primary sound buffer.
Initialize ()	Initializes a DirectSoundBuffer object created with **CoCreateInstance ()**.
Restore ()	Restores the memory associated with the sound buffer after it has been lost.
GetCurrentPosition ()	Retrieves the current play and write positions within the sound buffer.
Lock ()	Locks the sound buffer.
Play ()	Plays the sound buffer from the current play position.
SetCurrentPosition ()	Sets the current play position for secondary sound buffers.

(continued)

Table 10.6   The functions of the IDirectSoundBuffer interface *(continued)*.

Method Name	Description
Stop ()	Stops the sound buffer from playing.
Unlock ()	Unlocks the sound buffer.
GetFrequency ()	Retrieves the sound buffer's playback frequency.
GetPan ()	Retrieves the sound buffer's pan settings.
GetVolume ()	Retrieves the sound buffer's volume.
SetFrequency ()	Sets the sound buffer's playback frequency.
SetPan ()	Sets the sound buffer's pan settings.
SetVolume ()	Sets the sound buffer's volume.

The IDirectSoundCapture Interface

The IDirectSoundCapture interface (obtained by **DirectSoundCaptureCreate ()**) allows you to create sound-capture buffers and retrieve the capabilities of the sound-capture device. Its functions are listed in Table 10.7.

The IDirectSoundCaptureBuffer

The IDirectSoundCaptureBuffer interface communicates with a sound-capture buffer, allowing applications to retrieve and set the format, lock and unlock, and capture sound into sound-capture buffers. Table 10.8 shows the functions of this interface.

Table 10.7   The functions of the IDirectSoundCapture interface.

Method Name	Description
CreateCaptureBuffer ()	Creates a sound-capture buffer.
Initialize ()	Initializes a DirectSoundCapture object created with **CoCreateInstance ()**.
GetCaps ()	Retrieves the capabilities of the sound-capture object.

Table 10.8   The functions of the IDirectSoundCaptureBuffer interface.

Method Name	Description
Initialize ()	Initializes a DirectSoundCaptureBuffer object created with **CoCreateInstance ()**.
GetCaps ()	Retrieves the capabilities of the sound-capture buffer.
GetCurrentPosition ()	Retrieves the current capture and read positions.
GetFormat ()	Retrieves the format of the sound-capture buffer.
GetStatus ()	Retrieves the status (such as capturing or looping) of the sound-capture buffer.
Lock ()	Locks the sound-capture buffer.
Start ()	Starts sound capture for the sound-capture buffer.
Stop ()	Stops sound capture for the sound-capture buffer.
Unlock ()	Unlocks the sound-capture buffer.

The IDirectSoundCaptureBuffer interface can be obtained by calling the **IDirectSound-Capture::CreateCaptureBuffer ()** function.

The IDirectSoundNotify Interface

The **IDirectSoundNotify** interface, which you obtain by querying any IDirectSoundBuffer interface, sets the notification positions for a sound buffer. When playback reaches these positions, DirectSound notifies the application. Table 10.9 describes its sole function.

The IKsPropertySet Interface

The IKsPropertySet interface (query any sound buffer) allows you to use features of sound hardware not supported by DirectSound, provided you know how to do so. The member functions of this interface are detailed in Table 10.10.

Getting Started With DirectSound

Before you use any DirectSound functions, you must include the DirectSound header, Dsound.H. You must also link Dsound.lib, the DirectSound library, with your application (if you use Microsoft Visual C++, add the file's location to the Project | Project Settings | Object | Library Modules text box). One file in your application must include InitGuid.H, which initializes the DirectSound Globally Unique Identifiers (GUIDs) for use in the application.

The 3D applications you write that use DirectSound will usually complete steps including basic initialization, sound-buffer creation, buffer management, and (when the application terminates) buffer destruction.

These steps are outlined below:

1. The application optionally calls the function **DirectSoundEnumerate ()**, which lists all sound devices (this allows an application to select the best device available, if the user has more than one).

Table 10.9   The function of the IDirectSoundNotify interface.

Method Name	Description
SetNotificationPositions ()	Sets the buffer positions at which DirectSound should notify an application.

Table 10.10   The functions of the IKsPropertySet interface.

Method Name	Description
Get ()	Retrieves a property of the sound hardware.
QuerySupport ()	Determines if support for a certain property exists on the sound hardware.
Set ()	Sets a property of the sound hardware.

2. The application calls **DirectSoundCreate ()**, given either the GUID produced in Step 1 or a default value, which selects the default sound device. The result, if successful, is an interface to a DirectSound object.

3. The cooperative level of the DirectSound object is set, usually to exclusive mode.

4. The application creates the primary sound buffer through **IDirectSound::Create-SoundBuffer ()** and sets its format by calling **IDirectSoundBuffer::SetFormat ()**.

5. The application creates secondary sound buffers by calling **IDirectSound::CreateSound-Buffer ()** and fills them with valid sound data by calling **IDirectSoundBuffer::Lock ()**.

6. The application obtains IDirectSound3DBuffer interfaces for all its 3D sounds.

7. The application queries a sound buffer for the IDirectSound3DListener interface and sets its attributes appropriately.

8. The application runs until the user quits, restoring sound buffers whenever they are lost, updating the position of the listener and the 3D sounds, and playing sounds when appropriate.

9. The application releases all objects.

The next chapter (and Appendix C, the DirectSound reference) covers the specifics of this list.

Summary

Sound is the passage of molecular movement through a medium. Its most important basic properties include pitch, the frequency of the movement, volume (usually measured in decibels), and quality (a measure of how much interference is heard).

Sound interacts with its environment in many ways, three of which are of major significance:

♦ *Interference*—Occurs when a sound is interfered with by one or more other sounds.

♦ *Reflection*—Responsible for echoes, some distortion, and an extension of the distance sounds can be heard.

♦ *The Doppler effect*—The change in pitch that occurs when either the listener, the sound, or both move.

DirectSound provides sound support primarily through buffers. Buffers contain sound data and have a channel count (the number of audio outputs, such as speakers), a sample rate (such as 11,025 Hz), and a bits per sample (8 or 16). The primary buffer represents the sound currently playing, and secondary buffers store sound information that can later be mixed into the primary buffer. You can adjust attributes, such as frequency, volume level, and pan. Secondary sound buffers are converted to the format of the primary sound buffer when played.

Three-dimensional sounds have a position, a velocity, minimum and maximum distances (which determine maximum and minimum sound levels), and an orientation (specified by two 3D cones). DirectSound automatically calculates how sounds should sound based on their position and velocity. It also provides access to hardware for effects that it does not support (like reverberation).

The listener in any DirectSound application represents the person who hears the sounds. It has a position and velocity.

Now that you know the basic principles of DirectSound—the interfaces, their functions, and how 3D applications typically interact with DirectSound—you are ready to learn the specifics of actually creating this sound API. The next chapter goes step by step through the process of creating a DirectSound application.

Chapter 11
Using DirectSound

DirectSound is a powerful sound library that transparently handles complex tasks, such as sound mixing, 3D sound generation, and hardware interfacing. Chapter 10 provided an overview of DirectSound's architecture with enough information to get you started using the SDK. This chapter provides the specifics you need to use DirectSound in your games. I start by covering the format of WAV files and then provide source code to show you how to use DirectSound's functions. Lastly, I cover an encapsulation of DirectSound that will serve to simplify your programming.

WAV Data

The most common format for storing digital sound is the *WAV*. All sounds that end with the .wav extension—and in Windows, that means most sounds—use this format. It is universally supported by Windows sound applications and is even used directly by many games (some games use proprietary formats to ensure that users cannot change their sounds).

The WAV format is actually a subtype of the *Resource Interchange File Format (RIFF)*. Windows programs use this file format for storing many different media (such as AVI video). It was designed to be very extensible and flexible, allowing newer applications to change their file formats moderately and to maintain compatibility with older applications.

RIFF files achieve this goal by taking a modular approach to data storage. A particular data type—sound, for example—is divided into chunks of conceptually similar data, intuitively referred to as *chunks*. Each chunk contains three key pieces of information: a Four Character Code (FourCC) that identifies the purpose or type of chunk (such as **'code'**); the length of the chunk, which is used for moving around in a RIFF file and other purposes; and the data associated with the chunk, which depends on the type of chunk.

All RIFF files contain at least one chunk, referred to as the *parent chunk*, and identified by the Four CC **'RIFF'**. The parent chunk contains other media-specific chunks.

The important chunks specific to the WAV format are outlined in Table 11.1.

The format of the **'data'** chunk can vary from one WAV file to another. Some WAV files store sound data in an uncompressed format; others store it in a compressed format. The most common (and easiest to read) format is *Pulse Code Modulation (PCM)*. As mentioned in Chapter 10, in this format, the sound data is stored completely uncompressed, sample by sample. If the sound has more than one channel, each sample includes the data for all channels. Because this is the same format DirectSound sound buffers use, it is very convenient.

> **Note**
>
> *You can convert sound files to the PCM format by using Windows' Sound Recorder.*

The **'fmt '** chunk contains the Windows **WAVEFORMATEX** structure, documented in Reference Table 11.1. This structure describes the attributes of the sound data—how many samples per second, what the format is, and so on.

To load a WAV file, you can use the Windows functions **mmioOpen ()** (which opens a RIFF file), **mmioDescend ()** (which enters a chunk), **mmioRead ()** (which reads data), and **mmioClose ()** (which closes a RIFF file). These functions are documented by the Windows SDK, included with your Windows compiler.

For general-purpose reading of PCM WAV files, I have included the files WaveIn.HPP and WaveIn.CPP in Listings 11.1 and 11.2, respectively (they are also available on the CD-ROM). These files employ the **mmio** functions to read both the format and sound data of WAV files.

Table 11.1   Important chunks specfic to the WAV format.

Chunk FourCC	Purpose
'data'	The **'data'** chunk provides the actual sound data.
'fmt '	The **'fmt '** (note the single space at the end) chunk provides information about the format of the WAV file.

Reference Table 11.1   WAVEFORMATEX structure.

Structure Description

This structure describes the format of a WAV sound.

Structure Declaration

```
typedef struct {
    WORD  wFormatTag;
    WORD  nChannels;
    DWORD nSamplesPerSec;
    DWORD nAvgBytesPerSec;
    WORD  nBlockAlign;
    WORD  wBitsPerSample;
    WORD  cbSize;
} WAVEFORMATEX;
```

Member Function	Description
wFormatTag	A Microsoft-allocated 2-byte code that uniquely identifies the sound format. For PCM sounds, this is always **WAVE_FORMAT_PCM**.
nChannels	The number of channels for the sound.
nSamplesPerSec	The number of samples per second.
nAvgBytesPerSec	The average number of bytes per second.
nBlockAlign	The number of bytes per sample, including all channels. For PCM sounds, this is equal to **wBitsPerSample** times **nChannels** divided by 8.
wBitsPerSample	The number of bits per sample.
cbSize	The number of additional bytes required to describe the sound. For PCM sounds, this is always equal to zero.

Listing 11.1   The WaveIn.HPP file.

```
//
// File name: WaveIn.HPP
//
// Description: Contains the class declaration for the WaveIn
//              class. This class provides functions for
//              reading PCM wave files.
//
// Author: John De Goes
//
// Project: None
//
// Copyright (C) 1999 John De Goes -- All Rights Reserved.
//
```

```
#ifndef __WAVEINHPP__
#define __WAVEINHPP__

#include <Windows.H>
#include <Windowsx.H>
#include <MMSystem.H>

class WaveFile {
    protected:
        HMMIO           InputHandle;
        WAVEFORMATEX    WaveFormat;
        MMCKINFO        DataChunk, ParentChunk;
        bool            Loaded;

        bool CleanUp ();
    public:
        WaveFile ();
        ~WaveFile ();

        bool Load ( TCHAR *FileName );

        WORD GetFormat ();
        WORD GetBlockAlign ();
        WORD GetChannelCount ();
        WORD GetBitsPerSample ();

        DWORD GetSamplesPerSecond ();
        DWORD GetAverageBytesPerSecond ();

        DWORD GetDataSize ();

        bool GetData ( void *Buffer, LONG Bytes );

        bool GetWaveFormat ( WAVEFORMATEX &Format );

        bool Close ();

        operator WAVEFORMATEX ();
        operator HMMIO ();
};

#endif
```

Listing 11.2   The WaveIn.CPP file.

```
//
// File name: WaveIn.CPP
//
// Description: Contains the class implementation for WaveFile,
//              defined in WaveIn.HPP. This class provides
//              functions for reading PCM wave files.
//
// Author: John De Goes
//
// Project: None
//
// Copyright (C) 1999 John De Goes -- All Rights Reserved.
//

#include "WaveIn.HPP"

bool WaveFile::CleanUp () {
   // If the RIFF file has been opened, close it and set
   // the Loaded flag to false:
   if ( Loaded ) {
      if ( mmioClose ( InputHandle, 0 ) != 0 )
         return false;
      Loaded = false;
   }
   return true;
}

WaveFile::WaveFile () {
   Loaded = false;
}

WaveFile::~WaveFile () {
   CleanUp ();
}

bool WaveFile::Load ( TCHAR *FileName ) {
   MMCKINFO InputChunk;

   const DWORD WaveFCC = mmioFOURCC ( 'W', 'A', 'V', 'E' ),
               MinSize = sizeof WaveFormat -
                         sizeof WaveFormat.cbSize;

   // Close the RIFF file if one was previously opened
   // using this object:
   if ( !CleanUp () )
      return false;
```

```
// Attempt to open the specified RIFF file:
InputHandle = mmioOpen ( FileName, NULL,
                          MMIO_ALLOCBUF | MMIO_READ );

if ( InputHandle == NULL ) {
   mmioClose ( InputHandle, 0 );
   return false;
}

ZeroMemory ( &ParentChunk, sizeof ParentChunk );

// Descend into the parent chunk:
if ( mmioDescend ( InputHandle, &ParentChunk, NULL, 0 )
     != 0 ) {
   mmioClose ( InputHandle, 0 );
   return false;
}

// Make sure the parent chunk is actually a RIFF chunk
// and that it contains wave data:
if ( ( ParentChunk.ckid != FOURCC_RIFF )
     || ( ParentChunk.fccType != WaveFCC ) ) {
   mmioClose ( InputHandle, 0 );
   return false;
}

ZeroMemory ( &InputChunk, sizeof InputChunk );
InputChunk.ckid = mmioFOURCC ( 'f', 'm', 't', ' ' );

// Descend into the 'fmt ' chunk, where the attributes
// of the wave data are stored:
if ( mmioDescend ( InputHandle, &InputChunk, &ParentChunk,
                   MMIO_FINDCHUNK ) != 0 ) {
   mmioClose ( InputHandle, 0 );
   return false;
}

// Make sure the format chunk contains sufficient
// information:
if ( InputChunk.cksize < MinSize ) {
   mmioClose ( InputHandle, 0 );
   return false;
}
```

```
    // Read the format chunk's data:
    if ( mmioRead ( InputHandle, ( char * ) &WaveFormat,
                    sizeof WaveFormat ) < MinSize ) {
        mmioClose ( InputHandle, 0 );
        return false;
    }

    // Seek to the beginning of the parent chunk to begin
    // a search:
    if ( mmioSeek ( InputHandle, ParentChunk.dwDataOffset +
                 sizeof ( FOURCC ), SEEK_SET ) == -1 ) {
        mmioClose ( InputHandle, 0 );
        return false;
    }

    ZeroMemory ( &InputChunk, sizeof InputChunk );
    InputChunk.ckid = mmioFOURCC ( 'd', 'a', 't', 'a' );

    // Descend into the 'data' chunk:
    if ( mmioDescend ( InputHandle, &InputChunk, &ParentChunk,
                       MMIO_FINDCHUNK ) != 0 ) {
        mmioClose ( InputHandle, 0 );
        return false;
    }


    // Save the 'data' chunk information for later use:
    DataChunk = InputChunk;

    // Record that the wave file was successfully loaded:
    Loaded = true;

    return true;
}

WORD WaveFile::GetFormat () {
    // The format for PCM wave files is WAVE_FORMAT_PCM

    if ( !Loaded )
        return 0;

    return WaveFormat.wFormatTag;
}

WORD WaveFile::GetBlockAlign () {
    if ( !Loaded )
        return 0;
```

```
        return WaveFormat.nBlockAlign;
    }

WORD WaveFile::GetChannelCount () {
    if ( !Loaded )
        return 0;

    return WaveFormat.nChannels;
}

WORD WaveFile::GetBitsPerSample () {
    if ( !Loaded )
        return 0;

    return WaveFormat.wBitsPerSample;
}

DWORD WaveFile::GetSamplesPerSecond () {
    if ( !Loaded )
        return 0;

    return WaveFormat.nSamplesPerSec;
}

DWORD WaveFile::GetAverageBytesPerSecond () {
    if ( !Loaded )
        return 0;

    return WaveFormat.nAvgBytesPerSec;
}

DWORD WaveFile::GetDataSize () {
    if ( !Loaded )
        return 0;

    return DataChunk.cksize;
}

bool WaveFile::GetData ( void *Buffer, LONG Bytes ) {
    if ( !Loaded )
        return false;

    // Read the wave data (note that buffered IO, which the
    // mmio* functions support, would be faster, but most
```

```
    // games will read all wave files at once, during the
    // initialization phase, when speed is not an issue):
    if ( mmioRead ( InputHandle, ( char * ) Buffer, Bytes )
        != Bytes )
      return false;

    return true;
}


bool WaveFile::GetWaveFormat ( WAVEFORMATEX &Format ) {
    if ( !Loaded )
        return false;

    Format = WaveFormat;

    return true;
}

bool WaveFile::Close () {
    return CleanUp ();
}

WaveFile::operator WAVEFORMATEX () {
    return WaveFormat;
}

WaveFile::operator HMMIO () {
    return InputHandle;
}
```

The WaveIn.HPP file defines the **WaveFile** class, which includes two main functions: **Load** (), which loads the format of a WAV file and sets up the file for reading sound data; and **GetData ()**, which retrieves the sound data from the WAV file. Other functions retrieve the attributes of the WAV file, such as its format (**GetWaveFormat ()**) and the size of the data (**GetDataSize ()**).

Note

*All of the **WaveIn** member functions conveniently return a **bool** value: **true** for success and **false** for failure.*

Having covered the format of WAV files, I will now present the specifics of using DirectSound in a step-by-step tutorial.

A DirectSound Tutorial

DirectSound applications usually begin interfacing with DirectSound *after* they have created their main window and switched into their appropriate video mode. Once these steps are completed, the applications can create a DirectSound object.

Creating A DirectSound Object

The easiest way to create a DirectSound object is to call **DirectSoundCreate ()** and choose the default sound device. The following code does this:

```
LPDIRECTSOUND DirectSound;
DirectSoundCreate ( NULL, &DirectSound, NULL );
```

A few systems have multiple sound devices, in which case you can list the sound devices by calling **DirectSoundEnumerate ()**.

After you have successfully created a DirectSound object, the next step is to set the application's cooperative level.

Setting The Cooperative Level

You can set the cooperative level of your application by calling the **IDirectSound::SetCooperativeLevel ()** function. Most games will choose the priority cooperative level, which allows applications to change the output format. Code for setting this cooperative level is shown here:

```
DirectSound->SetCooperativeLevel ( Window, DSSCL_PRIORITY );
```

After your application has set the cooperative level, it can create a sound-buffer object to represent the primary sound buffer and secondary sound buffers.

Creating The Sound Buffers

You can create sound buffers by calling the **IDirectSound::CreateSoundBuffer ()** function. The following code creates a primary sound buffer that has 3D sound capabilities:

```
DSBUFFERDESC BufferDesc;
LPDIRECTSOUNDBUFFER PrimaryBuffer;
BufferDesc.dwSize          = sizeof ( DSBUFFERDESC );
BufferDesc.dwBufferBytes   = 0;
BufferDesc.dwReserved      = 0;
BufferDesc.lpwfxFormat     = NULL;
```

```
BufferDesc.dwFlags            = DSBCAPS_PRIMARYBUFFER |
                                DSBCAPS_CTRL3D;


DirectSound->CreateSoundBuffer ( &BufferDesc,
   &PrimaryBuffer, NULL  );
```

Once your application has created its primary sound buffer, it can set the output format.

Setting The Output Format

You can set the output format by calling the primary sound buffer's **IDirectSoundBuffer::Set-Format ()** function, which accepts as its sole parameter a pointer to a **WAVEFORMATEX** structure. Example code for a 22.05 kHz, 16-bit stereo sound output format is shown here:

```
WAVEFORMATEX OutputFormat;
OutputFormat.wFormatTag       = WAVE_FORMAT_PCM;
OutputFormat.nChannels        = 2;
OutputFormat.nSamplesPerSec   = 22050;
OutputFormat.wBitsPerSample   = 16;
OutputFormat.cbSize           = 0;


PrimaryBuffer->SetFormat ( &OutputFormat );
```

At this point, you can use **IDirectSoundBuffer::QueryInterface ()** on the primary sound buffer to obtain the listener interface (IID_IDirectSound3DListener) and set the attributes of the listener. Any sounds you created as 3D should be queried for the IID_IDirectSound3DBuffer interface and their attributes should be set appropriately.

You are now free to play, stop, or set the attributes of any sounds throughout the life of your application.

A DirectSound Encapsulation

This chapter's DirectX encapsulation is shown in Listings 11.3 and 11.4 (also available on the accompanying CD-ROM). Listing 11.3 contains the class declarations, and Listing 11.4 contains their implementations.

Listing 11.3   The DirectSound.HPP file.

```
//
// File name: DirectSound.HPP
//
// Description: This file contains the class declarations
//              for a DirectSound encapsulation.
//
```

```
// Author: John De Goes
//
// Project: None
//
// Copyright (C) 1999 John De Goes -- All Rights Reserved.
//

#ifndef __DIRECTSOUNDHPP__
#define __DIRECTSOUNDHPP__

#include <Math.H>
#include <Windows.H>

#include <Dsound.H>
#include <D3DTypes.H>

#include "WaveIn.HPP"


class DirectSoundBuffer;
class DirectSound3DBuffer;

class DirectSoundManager {
   protected:
      LPDIRECTSOUND          DirectSound;
      LPDIRECTSOUNDBUFFER    PrimaryBuffer;
      LPDIRECTSOUND3DLISTENER Listener;

      WAVEFORMATEX           OutputFormat;
   public:
      DirectSoundManager ();
      ~DirectSoundManager ();

      bool CreateSound ( TCHAR *FileName,
                         DirectSoundBuffer &Buffer );
      bool Create3DSound ( TCHAR *FileName,
                           DirectSound3DBuffer &Buffer );

      bool SetOptions ( WAVEFORMATEX &OutputFormat );

      bool Initialize ( HWND Window );
      bool Uninitialize ();

      bool CommitDeferredSettings ();
```

```
        bool GetRolloffFactor  ( float &Factor );
        bool GetDopplerFactor  ( float &Factor );
        bool GetDistanceFactor ( float &Factor );

        bool SetRolloffFactor  ( float Factor );
        bool SetDopplerFactor  ( float Factor );
        bool SetDistanceFactor ( float Factor );

        bool GetListenerPosition ( float &X, float &Y,
           float &Z );
        bool GetListenerVelocity ( float &Vx, float &Vy,
           float &Vz );
        bool GetListenerOrientation ( float &, float &,
              float &, float &, float &, float & );

        bool SetListenerPosition ( float X, float Y, float Z );
        bool SetListenerVelocity ( float Vx, float Vy,
           float Vz );
        bool SetListenerOrientation ( float , float , float,
                                   float, float, float );

        bool GetGlobalVolume ( float &Volume );
        bool GetGlobalPan    ( float &Pan );

        bool SetGlobalVolume ( float Volume );
        bool SetGlobalPan    ( float Pan );

        bool EnableSound ();
        bool DisableSound ();

        bool GetBaseInterface ( LPDIRECTSOUND *Base );
        operator LPDIRECTSOUND ();
};

class DirectSoundBuffer {
    protected:
        LPDIRECTSOUNDBUFFER Buffer;

        TCHAR FileName [ MAX_PATH ];
        LONG DataSize;
        WAVEFORMATEX WaveFormat;

        bool Load ( TCHAR *File );

        bool RestoreIfNecessary ();
```

```
        friend class DirectSoundManager;
    public:
        DirectSoundBuffer  ();
        ~DirectSoundBuffer ();

        bool GetPan ( float &Pan );
        bool GetFrequency ( DWORD &Frequency );
        bool GetVolume ( float &Volume );

        bool SetPan ( float Pan );
        bool SetFrequency ( DWORD Frequency );
        bool SetVolume ( float Volume );

        LONG GetDataSize ();
        bool GetWaveFormat ( WAVEFORMATEX &Out );

        bool Stop ();
        bool IsPlaying ();
        bool Play ( bool Loop = false );
        bool SetNotificationPositions
            ( DWORD NotifyCount,
            DSBPOSITIONNOTIFY *Notification );
};

class DirectSound3DBuffer : public DirectSoundBuffer {
    protected:
        LPDIRECTSOUND3DBUFFER   Buffer3D;

        friend class DirectSoundManager;
    public:
        DirectSound3DBuffer  ();
        ~DirectSound3DBuffer ();

        bool GetPosition ( float &X, float &Y, float &Z );
        bool GetVelocity ( float &Vx, float &Vy, float &Vz );
        bool GetMinDistance ( float &MinDist );
        bool GetMaxDistance ( float &MaxDist );
        bool GetOrientation (
            float &Vx, float &Vy, float &Vz );
        bool GetInnerConeAngle ( float &InnerConeAngle );
        bool GetOuterConeAngle ( float &OuterConeAngle );
        bool GetOperationMode ( DWORD &OpMode );
        bool GetOutsideConeVolume ( float &Volume );

        bool SetPosition ( float X, float Y, float Z );
        bool SetVelocity ( float Vx, float Vy, float Vz );
```

```
        bool SetMinDistance ( float MinDist );
        bool SetMaxDistance ( float MaxDist );
        bool SetOrientation ( float Vx, float Vy, float Vz );
        bool SetConeAngles ( float InnerConeAngle,
                             float OuterConeAngle );
        bool SetOperationMode  ( DWORD OpMode );
        bool SetOutsideConeVolume ( float Volume );
};


#endif
```

Listing 11.4   The DirectSound.CPP file.

```
//
// File name: DirectSound.CPP
//
// Description: Provides the implementation for the class
//              declarations in DirectSound.HPP. These
//              classes encapsulate common DirectSound
//              interfaces.
//
// Author: John De Goes
//
// Project: None
//
// Copyright (C) 1999 John De Goes -- All Rights Reserved.
//


#include "DirectSound.HPP"


DirectSoundManager::DirectSoundManager  () {
   Listener = NULL;
   DirectSound = NULL;
   PrimaryBuffer = NULL;

   // Set up the default output format (22.05 kHz,
   // 16-bit stereo):
   OutputFormat.wFormatTag      = WAVE_FORMAT_PCM;
   OutputFormat.nChannels       = 2;
   OutputFormat.nSamplesPerSec  = 22050;
   OutputFormat.wBitsPerSample  = 16;
   OutputFormat.cbSize          = 0;

   OutputFormat.nBlockAlign     = OutputFormat.nChannels   *
                        OutputFormat.wBitsPerSample / 8;
   OutputFormat.nAvgBytesPerSec = OutputFormat.nBlockAlign *
                        OutputFormat.nSamplesPerSec;
```

```
        // Create DirectSound object and use the default sound
        // device:
        DirectSoundCreate ( NULL, &DirectSound, NULL );
}

DirectSoundManager::~DirectSoundManager () {
    Uninitialize ();
}

bool DirectSoundManager::CreateSound ( TCHAR *FileName,
        DirectSoundBuffer &Buffer ) {
    DSBUFFERDESC           BufferDesc;
    WAVEFORMATEX           WaveFormat;
    WaveFile               InputWave;

    if ( DirectSound == NULL )
        return false;

    // Load the specified wave file:
    if ( !InputWave.Load ( FileName ) )
        return false;

    // Make the format of the sound buffer to be created
    // match the format of the wave file just loaded:
    InputWave.GetWaveFormat ( WaveFormat );

    // Specify the options of the sound buffer to be created:
    BufferDesc.dwSize           = sizeof ( DSBUFFERDESC );

    // Require that the buffer have pan, volume, frequency,
    // and position notification capability (if just basic
    // playback is desired, specifiy DSBCAPS_STATIC and
    // nothing else):
    BufferDesc.dwFlags          = DSBCAPS_CTRLDEFAULT
                                  | DSBCAPS_STATIC
                                  | DSBCAPS_CTRLPOSITIONNOTIFY;

    BufferDesc.dwBufferBytes    = InputWave.GetDataSize ();
    BufferDesc.dwReserved       = 0;
    BufferDesc.lpwfxFormat      = &WaveFormat;

    // Create the sound buffer:
    if ( DirectSound->CreateSoundBuffer ( &BufferDesc,
        &Buffer.Buffer, NULL ) != DS_OK )
        return false;
```

```
    // Close the input wave file so the sound buffer can
    // access the file to load the wave data:
    InputWave.Close ();

    // Have the sound buffer load its wave data:
    return Buffer.Load ( FileName );
}

bool DirectSoundManager::Create3DSound ( TCHAR *FileName,
                                         DirectSound3DBuffer
                                         &Buffer ) {

    DSBUFFERDESC         BufferDesc;
    WAVEFORMATEX         WaveFormat;
    WaveFile             InputWave;

    if ( DirectSound == NULL )
       return false;

    // Load the specified wave file:
    if ( !InputWave.Load ( FileName ) )
       return false;

    // Make the format of the 3D sound buffer to be created
    // match the format of the wave file just loaded:
    InputWave.GetWaveFormat ( WaveFormat );

    // Specify the options of the 3D sound buffer to be
    // created:
    BufferDesc.dwSize          = sizeof ( DSBUFFERDESC );
    BufferDesc.dwFlags         = DSBCAPS_CTRL3D
                       | DSBCAPS_CTRLDEFAULT
                       | DSBCAPS_STATIC
                       | DSBCAPS_MUTE3DATMAXDISTANCE;
    BufferDesc.dwBufferBytes   = InputWave.GetDataSize ();
    BufferDesc.dwReserved      = 0;
    BufferDesc.lpwfxFormat     = &WaveFormat;

    // Create the 3D sound buffer:
    if ( DirectSound->CreateSoundBuffer ( &BufferDesc,
            &Buffer.Buffer, NULL ) != DS_OK )
       return false;

    // Obtain a 3D sound buffer interface for the sound
    // buffer:
```

```
    if ( Buffer.Buffer->QueryInterface (
        IID_IDirectSound3DBuffer,
        ( LPVOID * ) &Buffer.Buffer3D )
        != DS_OK )
      return false;

    // Close the input wave file so the 3D sound buffer can
    // access the file to load the wave data:
    InputWave.Close ();

    // Have the 3D sound buffer load its wave data:
    return Buffer.Load ( FileName );
}

bool DirectSoundManager::SetOptions (
       WAVEFORMATEX &ReqFormat ) {
   if ( DirectSound == NULL )
      return false;

   OutputFormat = ReqFormat;

   return true;
}

bool DirectSoundManager::Initialize ( HWND Window ) {
   DSBUFFERDESC BufferDesc;

   if ( DirectSound == NULL )
      return false;

   // Choose priority cooperative level--other sounds in
   // the background will still be audible, but we can
   // change the output format and perform memory management:
   if ( DirectSound->SetCooperativeLevel ( Window,
                                      DSSCL_PRIORITY )
        != DS_OK )
      return false;

   BufferDesc.dwSize          = sizeof ( DSBUFFERDESC );
   BufferDesc.dwBufferBytes   = 0;
   BufferDesc.dwReserved      = 0;
   BufferDesc.lpwfxFormat     = NULL;
   BufferDesc.dwFlags         = DSBCAPS_PRIMARYBUFFER |
                                DSBCAPS_CTRL3D;
```

```
      // Create the primary sound buffer:
      if ( DirectSound->CreateSoundBuffer ( &BufferDesc,
            &PrimaryBuffer, NULL ) != DS_OK )
         return false;

      // Set the output format:
      if ( PrimaryBuffer->SetFormat ( &OutputFormat ) != DS_OK )
         return false;

      // Obtain the listener interface:
      if ( PrimaryBuffer->QueryInterface (
           IID_IDirectSound3DListener, LPVOID * ) &Listener )
           != DS_OK )
         return false;

      return true;
}

bool DirectSoundManager::Uninitialize () {
      // Release all obtained interfaces:
      if ( PrimaryBuffer != NULL ) {
         PrimaryBuffer->Release ();
         PrimaryBuffer = NULL;
      }
      if ( Listener != NULL ) {
         Listener->Release ();
         Listener = NULL;
      }
      if ( DirectSound != NULL ) {
         DirectSound->Release ();
         DirectSound = NULL;
      }
      return true;
}

bool DirectSoundManager::CommitDeferredSettings () {
      if ( Listener == NULL )
         return false;

      if ( Listener->CommitDeferredSettings () != DS_OK )
         return false;

      return true;
}
```

```
bool DirectSoundManager::GetRolloffFactor (
      float &Factor ) {
   if ( Listener == NULL )
      return false;

   if ( Listener->GetRolloffFactor ( &Factor ) != DS_OK )
      return false;

   return true;
}

bool DirectSoundManager::GetDopplerFactor (
      float &Factor ) {
   if ( Listener == NULL )
      return false;

   if ( Listener->GetDopplerFactor ( &Factor ) != DS_OK )
      return false;

   return true;
}

bool DirectSoundManager::GetDistanceFactor (
      float &Factor ) {
   if ( Listener == NULL )
      return false;

   if ( Listener->GetDistanceFactor ( &Factor ) != DS_OK )
      return false;

   return true;
}

bool DirectSoundManager::SetRolloffFactor ( float Factor ) {
   if ( Listener == NULL )
      return false;

   if ( Listener->SetRolloffFactor ( Factor, DS3D_DEFERRED )
         != DS_OK )
      return false;

   return true;
}

bool DirectSoundManager::SetDopplerFactor ( float Factor ) {
   if ( Listener == NULL )
      return false;
```

```
      if ( Listener->SetDopplerFactor ( Factor, DS3D_DEFERRED )
         != DS_OK )
       return false;

   return true;
}

bool DirectSoundManager::SetDistanceFactor ( float Factor ) {
   if ( Listener == NULL )
      return false;

   if ( Listener->SetDistanceFactor ( Factor, DS3D_DEFERRED )
         != DS_OK )
      return false;

   return true;
}

bool DirectSoundManager::GetListenerPosition (
      float &X, float &Y, &Z ) {
   D3DVECTOR Vector;

   if ( Listener == NULL )
      return false;

   if ( Listener->GetPosition ( &Vector ) != DS_OK )
      return false;

   X = Vector.x;
   Y = Vector.y;
   Z = Vector.z;

   return true;
}

bool DirectSoundManager::GetListenerVelocity (
      float &Vx, float &Vy, float &Vz ) {
   D3DVECTOR Vector;

   if ( Listener == NULL )
      return false;

   if ( Listener->GetVelocity ( &Vector ) != DS_OK )
      return false;
```

```
      Vx = Vector.x;
      Vy = Vector.y;
      Vz = Vector.z;

      return true;
   }

   bool DirectSoundManager::GetListenerOrientation
                         ( float &Fx, float &Fy, float &Fz,
                           float &Tx, float &Ty, float &Tz ) {
      D3DVECTOR Front, Top;

      if ( Listener == NULL )
         return false;

      if ( Listener->GetOrientation ( &Front, &Top ) != DS_OK )
         return false;

      Fx = Front.x;
      Fy = Front.y;
      Fz = Front.z;

      Tx = Top.x;
      Ty = Top.y;
      Tz = Top.z;

      return true;
   }

   bool DirectSoundManager::SetListenerPosition (
         float X, float Y, Z ) {
      if ( Listener == NULL )
         return false;

      if ( Listener->SetPosition ( X, Y, Z, DS3D_DEFERRED )
          != DS_OK )
         return false;

      return true;
   }

   bool DirectSoundManager::SetListenerVelocity (
         float Vx, float Vy, Vz ) {
      if ( Listener == NULL )
         return false;
```

```
      if ( Listener->SetVelocity ( Vx, Vy, Vz, DS3D_DEFERRED )
          != DS_OK )
         return false;

      return true;
   }

   bool DirectSoundManager::SetListenerOrientation
                           ( float Fx, float Fy, float Fz,
                             float Tx, float Ty, float Tz ) {
      if ( Listener == NULL )
         return false;

      if ( Listener->SetOrientation ( Fx, Fy, Fz,
              Tx, Ty, Tz, DS3D_DEFERRED ) != DS_OK )
         return false;

      return true;
   }

   bool DirectSoundManager::GetGlobalVolume ( float &Volume ) {
      LONG DSVol;

      if ( PrimaryBuffer == NULL )
         return false;

      if ( PrimaryBuffer->GetVolume ( &DSVol ) != DS_OK )
         return false;

      Volume = float ( fabs ( DSVol - DSBVOLUME_MIN ) /
                       fabs ( DSBVOLUME_MAX - DSBVOLUME_MIN ) );

      return true;
   }

   bool DirectSoundManager::GetGlobalPan ( float &Pan ) {
      LONG DSPan;

      if ( PrimaryBuffer == NULL )
         return false;

      if ( PrimaryBuffer->GetPan ( &DSPan ) != DS_OK )
         return false;

      Pan = float ( DSPan ) / float ( DSBPAN_RIGHT );
```

```
        return true;
    }

    bool DirectSoundManager::SetGlobalVolume ( float Volume ) {
        LONG DSVol;

        if ( PrimaryBuffer == NULL )
            return false;

        if ( Volume < 0.0F )
            Volume = 0.0F;

        if ( Volume > 1.0F )
            Volume = 1.0F;

        DSVol = LONG ( Volume *
                        float ( DSBVOLUME_MAX - DSBVOLUME_MIN ) )
                + DSBVOLUME_MIN;

        if ( PrimaryBuffer->SetVolume ( DSVol ) != DS_OK )
            return false;

        return true;
    }

    bool DirectSoundManager::SetGlobalPan ( float Pan ) {
        LONG DSPan;

        if ( PrimaryBuffer == NULL )
            return false;

        DSPan = LONG ( Pan * float ( DSBPAN_RIGHT ) );

        if ( PrimaryBuffer->SetPan ( DSPan ) != DS_OK )
            return false;

        return true;
    }

    bool DirectSoundManager::EnableSound () {
        if ( PrimaryBuffer == NULL )
            return false;

        // The sound must loop when the buffer is primary, so
        // play the buffer with looping enabled:
        if ( PrimaryBuffer->Play ( 0, 0, DSBPLAY_LOOPING ) != DS_OK )
            return false;
```

```
      return true;
}

bool DirectSoundManager::DisableSound () {
   if ( PrimaryBuffer == NULL )
      return false;

   if ( PrimaryBuffer->Stop () != DS_OK )
      return false;

   return true;
}

bool DirectSoundManager::GetBaseInterface (
      LPDIRECTSOUND *Base ) {
   if ( DirectSound == NULL )
      return false;

   ( *Base ) = DirectSound;

   ( *Base )->AddRef ();

   return true;
}

DirectSoundManager::operator LPDIRECTSOUND () {
   if ( DirectSound == NULL )
      return false;

   DirectSound->AddRef ();

   return DirectSound;
}

DirectSoundBuffer::DirectSoundBuffer  () {
   Buffer        = NULL;
   DataSize      = -1;
   FileName [ 0 ] = NULL;
}

DirectSoundBuffer::~DirectSoundBuffer () {
   if ( Buffer != NULL ) {
      Buffer->Release ();
      Buffer = NULL;
   }
}
```

```
bool DirectSoundBuffer::Load ( TCHAR *File ) {
   WaveFile    InputWave;
   LPVOID      BufferPointer;
   DWORD       Bytes1;

   if ( Buffer == NULL )
      return false;

   // Save the file name of the wave for restoration of
   // the sound buffer when it is lost:
   if ( File != FileName )
      lstrcpy ( FileName, File );

   // Load the specified wave file:
   if ( !InputWave.Load ( FileName ) )
      return false;

   // Store the wave format in case it's needed later:
   InputWave.GetWaveFormat ( WaveFormat );

   // Lock the sound buffer to obtain a pointer to the
   // memory where its wave data is stored:
   if ( Buffer->Lock ( 0, 0, &BufferPointer, &Bytes1, NULL,
         NULL, DSBLOCK_ENTIREBUFFER ) != DS_OK )
      return false;

   DataSize = InputWave.GetDataSize ();

   // Store the wave data in the sound buffer:
   if ( !InputWave.GetData ( BufferPointer, DataSize ) )
      return false;

   // Unlock the sound buffer:
   if ( Buffer->Unlock ( BufferPointer, DataSize, NULL,
         NULL ) != DS_OK )
      return false;

   return true;
}

bool DirectSoundBuffer::RestoreIfNecessary () {
   DWORD Status;

   if ( Buffer == NULL )
      return false;
```

```
   // Retrieve the status of the sound buffer:
   if ( Buffer->GetStatus ( &Status ) != DS_OK )
      return false;

   // If the sound buffer is lost, restore its memory and
   // reload its wave data:
   if ( Status & DSBSTATUS_BUFFERLOST ) {
      // Restore the buffer's memory:
      if ( Buffer->Restore () != DS_OK )
         return false;

      // Reload the wave data:
      if ( !Load ( FileName ) )
         return false;
   }

   return true;
}

LONG DirectSoundBuffer::GetDataSize () {
   if ( Buffer == NULL )
      return -1;

   return DataSize;
}

bool DirectSoundBuffer::GetPan ( float &Pan ) {
   LONG DSPan;

   if ( Buffer == NULL )
      return false;

   if ( Buffer->GetPan ( &DSPan ) != DS_OK )
      return false;

   Pan = float ( DSPan ) / float ( DSBPAN_RIGHT );

   return true;
}

bool DirectSoundBuffer::GetFrequency ( DWORD &Frequency ) {
   if ( Buffer == NULL )
      return false;

   if ( Buffer->GetFrequency ( &Frequency ) != DS_OK )
      return false;
```

```
      return true;
   }


   bool DirectSoundBuffer::GetVolume ( float &Volume ) {
      LONG DSVol;

      if ( Buffer == NULL )
         return false;

      if ( Buffer->GetVolume ( &DSVol ) != DS_OK )
         return false;

      Volume = float ( fabs ( DSVol - DSBVOLUME_MIN ) /
                       fabs ( DSBVOLUME_MAX - DSBVOLUME_MIN ) );

      return true;
   }

   bool DirectSoundBuffer::SetPan ( float Pan ) {
      LONG DSPan;

      if ( Buffer == NULL )
         return false;

      DSPan = LONG ( Pan * float ( DSBPAN_RIGHT ) );

      if ( Buffer->SetPan ( DSPan ) != DS_OK )
         return false;

      return true;
   }

   bool DirectSoundBuffer::SetFrequency ( DWORD Frequency ) {
      if ( Buffer == NULL )
         return false;

      if ( Buffer->SetFrequency ( Frequency ) != DS_OK )
         return false;

      return true;
   }

   bool DirectSoundBuffer::SetVolume ( float Volume ) {
      LONG DSVol;

      if ( Buffer == NULL )
         return false;
```

```
      DSVol = LONG ( Volume *
                     float ( DSBVOLUME_MAX - DSBVOLUME_MIN ) )
              + DSBVOLUME_MIN;

   if ( Buffer->SetVolume ( DSVol ) != DS_OK )
      return false;

   return true;
}

bool DirectSoundBuffer::GetWaveFormat ( WAVEFORMATEX &Out ) {
   if ( Buffer == NULL )
      return false;

   Out = WaveFormat;

   return true;
}

bool DirectSoundBuffer::Stop () {
   if ( Buffer == NULL )
      return false;

   if ( Buffer->Stop () != DS_OK )
      return false;

   return true;
}

bool DirectSoundBuffer::IsPlaying () {
   DWORD Status;

   if ( Buffer == NULL )
      return false;

   if ( Buffer->GetStatus ( &Status ) != DS_OK )
      return false;

   return ( Status & DSBSTATUS_PLAYING );
}

bool DirectSoundBuffer::Play ( bool Loop ) {
   if ( Buffer == NULL )
      return false;
```

```
      // Restore lost memory if necessary before attempting to
      // play the sound:
      if ( !RestoreIfNecessary () )
         return false;

      if ( Loop )
         Buffer->Play ( 0, 0, DSBPLAY_LOOPING );
      else Buffer->Play ( 0, 0, 0 );

      return true;
   }

   bool DirectSoundBuffer::SetNotificationPositions (
         DWORD NotifyCount,
         DSBPOSITIONNOTIFY *Notification ) {
      LPDIRECTSOUNDNOTIFY Notify;

      if ( Buffer == NULL )
         return false;

      // Stop the sound buffer if it is playing, because
      // notification positions cannot be set during this
      // condition:
      if ( IsPlaying () )
         Stop ();

      // Query the sound buffer for the notify interface:
      if ( Buffer->QueryInterface ( IID_IDirectSoundNotify,
         ( LPVOID * ) &Notify ) != DS_OK )
         return false;

      // Set the notification positions:
      if ( Notify->SetNotificationPositions ( NotifyCount,
                                              Notification )
         != DS_OK ) {
         Notify->Release ();
         return false;
      }

      Notify->Release ();

      return true;
   }

   DirectSound3DBuffer::DirectSound3DBuffer () {
      Buffer3D = NULL;
   }
```

```
DirectSound3DBuffer::~DirectSound3DBuffer () {
   if ( Buffer3D != NULL ) {
      Buffer3D->Release ();
      Buffer3D = NULL;
   }
}

bool DirectSound3DBuffer::GetPosition ( float &X, float &Y,
                                        float &Z ) {
   D3DVECTOR Vector;

   if ( Buffer3D == NULL )
      return false;

   if ( Buffer3D->GetPosition ( &Vector ) != DS_OK )
      return false;

   X = Vector.x;
   Y = Vector.y;
   Z = Vector.z;

   return true;
}

bool DirectSound3DBuffer::GetVelocity ( float &Vx, float &Vy,
                                        float &Vz ) {
   D3DVECTOR Vector;

   if ( Buffer3D == NULL )
      return false;

   if ( Buffer3D->GetVelocity ( &Vector ) != DS_OK )
      return false;

   Vx = Vector.x;
   Vy = Vector.y;
   Vz = Vector.z;

   return true;
}

bool DirectSound3DBuffer::GetMinDistance ( float &MinDist ) {
   if ( Buffer3D == NULL )
      return false;

   if ( Buffer3D->GetMinDistance ( &MinDist ) != DS_OK )
      return false;
```

```
            return true;
        }

    bool DirectSound3DBuffer::GetMaxDistance ( float &MaxDist ) {
        if ( Buffer3D == NULL )
            return false;

        if ( Buffer3D->GetMaxDistance ( &MaxDist ) != DS_OK )
            return false;

        return true;
    }

    bool DirectSound3DBuffer::GetOrientation (
            float &Vx, float &Vy, float &Vz ) {
        D3DVECTOR Vector;

        if ( Buffer3D == NULL )
            return false;

        if ( Buffer3D->GetConeOrientation ( &Vector ) != DS_OK )
            return false;

        Vx = Vector.x;
        Vy = Vector.y;
        Vz = Vector.z;

        return true;
    }

    bool DirectSound3DBuffer::GetInnerConeAngle
                            ( float &InnerConeAngle ) {
        DWORD DSInner, DSOuter;

        if ( Buffer3D == NULL )
            return false;

        if ( Buffer3D->GetConeAngles ( &DSInner, &DSOuter )
            != DS_OK )
            return false;

        InnerConeAngle = ( float ) DSInner;

        return true;
    }
```

```
bool DirectSound3DBuffer::GetOuterConeAngle
                          ( float &OuterConeAngle ) {
   DWORD DSInner, DSOuter;

   if ( Buffer3D == NULL )
      return false;

   if ( Buffer3D->GetConeAngles ( &DSInner, &DSOuter )
        != DS_OK )
      return false;

   OuterConeAngle = ( float ) DSOuter;

   return true;
}

bool DirectSound3DBuffer::GetOperationMode (
      DWORD &OpMode ) {
   if ( Buffer3D == NULL )
      return false;

   if ( Buffer3D->GetMode ( &OpMode ) != DS_OK )
      return false;

   return true;
}

bool DirectSound3DBuffer::GetOutsideConeVolume (
      float &Volume ) {
   LONG DSVol;

   if ( Buffer3D == NULL )
      return false;

   if ( Buffer3D->GetConeOutsideVolume ( &DSVol ) != DS_OK )
      return false;

   Volume = float ( fabs ( DSVol - DSBVOLUME_MIN ) /
                    fabs ( DSBVOLUME_MAX - DSBVOLUME_MIN ) );

   return true;
}

bool DirectSound3DBuffer::SetPosition ( float X, float Y,
                                        float Z ) {
   if ( Buffer3D == NULL )
      return false;
```

```
    if ( Buffer3D->SetPosition ( X, Y, Z, DS3D_DEFERRED )
            != DS_OK )
        return false;

    return true;
}


bool DirectSound3DBuffer::SetVelocity ( float Vx, float Vy,
                                            float Vz ) {
    if ( Buffer3D == NULL )
        return false;

    if ( Buffer3D->SetVelocity ( Vx, Vy, Vz, DS3D_DEFERRED )
            != DS_OK )
        return false;

    return true;
}


bool DirectSound3DBuffer::SetMinDistance ( float MinDist ) {
    if ( Buffer3D == NULL )
        return false;

    if ( Buffer3D->SetMinDistance ( MinDist, DS3D_DEFERRED )
            != DS_OK )
        return false;

    return true;
}


bool DirectSound3DBuffer::SetMaxDistance ( float MaxDist ) {
    if ( Buffer3D == NULL )
        return false;

    if ( Buffer3D->SetMaxDistance ( MaxDist, DS3D_DEFERRED )
            != DS_OK )
        return false;

    return true;
}


bool DirectSound3DBuffer::SetOrientation (
        float Vx, float Vy, float Vz ) {
    if ( Buffer3D == NULL )
        return false;
```

```
    if ( Buffer3D->SetConeOrientation ( Vx, Vy, Vz,
        DS3D_DEFERRED ) != DS_OK )
      return false;

   return true;
}

bool DirectSound3DBuffer::SetConeAngles (
        float InnerConeAngle,
        float OuterConeAngle ) {
   LONG DSInner, DSOuter;

   if ( Buffer3D == NULL )
      return false;

   DSInner = ( LONG ) InnerConeAngle;
   DSOuter = ( LONG ) OuterConeAngle;

   if ( Buffer3D->SetConeAngles ( DSInner, DSOuter,
        DS3D_DEFERRED ) != DS_OK )
      return false;

   return true;
}

bool DirectSound3DBuffer::SetOperationMode ( DWORD OpMode ) {
   if ( Buffer3D == NULL )
      return false;

   if ( Buffer3D->SetMode ( OpMode, DS3D_DEFERRED )
        != DS_OK )
      return false;

   return true;
}

bool DirectSound3DBuffer::SetOutsideConeVolume (
        float Volume ) {
   LONG DSVol;

   if ( Buffer3D == NULL )
      return false;

   DSVol = LONG ( Volume *
                  float ( DSBVOLUME_MAX - DSBVOLUME_MIN ) )
           + DSBVOLUME_MIN;
```

```
        if ( Buffer3D->SetConeOutsideVolume ( DSVol,
            DS3D_DEFERRED ) != DS_OK )
          return false;

        return true;
    }
```

The three classes defined in Listing 11.3 are **DirectSoundManager**, **DirectSoundBuffer**, and **DirectSound3DBuffer**. The **DirectSoundManager** class encapsulates the DirectSound object, the listener, and the primary sound buffer. The **DirectSoundBuffer** class encapsulates a normal sound buffer, whereas the **DirectSound3DBuffer** class encapsulates a 3D sound buffer—both are created by the **DirectSoundManager** class.

Using these classes is straightforward. Reference Tables 11.2 through 11.4 briefly document their accessible functions.

Reference Table 11.2   The class reference for the DirectSoundManager class.
Class Declaration

```
class DirectSoundManager {
    protected:
        LPDIRECTSOUND           DirectSound;
        LPDIRECTSOUNDBUFFER     PrimaryBuffer;
        LPDIRECTSOUND3DLISTENER Listener;

        WAVEFORMATEX            OutputFormat;
    public:
        DirectSoundManager ();
        ~DirectSoundManager ();

        bool CreateSound ( TCHAR *FileName,
                          DirectSoundBuffer &Buffer );
        bool Create3DSound ( TCHAR *FileName,
                            DirectSound3DBuffer &Buffer );

        bool SetOptions ( WAVEFORMATEX &OutputFormat );

        bool Initialize ( HWND Window );
        bool Uninitialize ();

        bool CommitDeferredSettings ();

        bool GetRolloffFactor  ( float &Factor );
        bool GetDopplerFactor  ( float &Factor );
        bool GetDistanceFactor ( float &Factor );
```

(continued)

Reference Table 11.2   The class reference for the DirectSoundManager class *(continued).*

Class Declaration

```
    bool SetRolloffFactor  ( float Factor );
      bool SetDopplerFactor  ( float Factor );
      bool SetDistanceFactor ( float Factor );

      bool GetListenerPosition ( float &X, float &Y, float &Z );
      bool GetListenerVelocity ( float &Vx, float &Vy, float &Vz );
      bool GetListenerOrientation ( float &, float &, float &,
                                    float &, float &, float & );

      bool SetListenerPosition ( float X, float Y, float Z );
      bool SetListenerVelocity ( float Vx, float Vy, float Vz );
      bool SetListenerOrientation ( float , float , float,
                                    float, float, float );

      bool GetGlobalVolume ( float &Volume );
      bool GetGlobalPan    ( float &Pan );

      bool SetGlobalVolume ( float Volume );
      bool SetGlobalPan    ( float Pan );

      bool EnableSound ();
      bool DisableSound ();

      bool GetBaseInterface ( LPDIRECTSOUND *Base );
      operator LPDIRECTSOUND ();
};
```

Member Function	Description
CreateSound	Creates a DirectSoundBuffer object, given a file name (which contains the WAV file to be stored in the sound buffer) and the DirectSoundBuffer object.
Create3DSound	Creates a DirectSound3DBuffer object, given a file name (which contains the WAV to be stored in the sound buffer) and the DirectSound3DBuffer object.
SetOptions	Sets the output format of the primary sound buffer (this function, if used, must be called before **DirectSoundManager::Initialize** ()).
Initialize	Initializes the DirectSoundManager object, which involves creating the primary sound buffer, setting the output format, and obtaining the listener interface.
Uninitialize	Uninitializes the DirectSoundManager object (this never has to be done explicitly).

(continued)

Reference Table 11.2	**The class reference for the DirectSoundManager class *(continued)*.**
Member Function	**Description**
CommitDeferredSettings	Commits deferred settings. This function must be called after all of the changes to any of the 3D sound buffers.
GetRolloffFactor	Retrieves the rolloff factor.
GetDopplerFactor	Retrieves the Doppler factor.
GetDistanceFactor	Retrieves the distance factor.
SetRolloffFactor	Sets the rolloff factor.
SetDopplerFactor	Sets the Doppler factor.
SetDistanceFactor	Sets the distance factor.
GetListenerPosition	Retrieves the listener's position.
GetListenerVelocity	Retrieves the listener's velocity.
GetListenerOrientation	Retrieves the listener's orientation via two vectors: front and head. The front vector represents where the front of the listener's head is pointing; the head vector represents where the top of the listener's head is pointing.
SetListenerPosition	Sets the listener's position.
SetListenerVelocity	Sets the listener's velocity.
SetListenerOrientation	Sets the listener's orientation via two vectors: front and head. The front vector represents where the front of the listener's head is pointing; the head vector represents where the top of the listener's head is pointing.
GetGlobalVolume	Retrieves the volume for the primary sound buffer. Valid values range from 0.0 (no volume) to 1.0 (normal volume).
GetGlobalPan	Retrieves the pan for the primary sound buffer. Valid values range from –1.0 (all audio output is to the left speaker) to 0.0 (audio output is equally directed to both speakers) to 1.0 (all audio output is to the right speaker).
SetGlobalVolume	Sets the volume for the primary sound buffer. Valid values range from 0.0 (no volume) to 1.0 (normal volume).
SetGlobalPan	Sets the pan for the primary sound buffer. Valid values range from –1.0 (all audio output is to the left speaker) to 0.0 (audio output is equally directed to both speakers) to 1.0 (all audio output is to the right speaker).
EnableSound	Plays the primary sound buffer.
DisableSound	Stops the primary sound buffer from playing.
GetBaseInterface	Retrieves the DirectSound interface.

Reference Table 11.3   The class reference for the DirectSoundBuffer class.

Class Declaration

```
class DirectSoundBuffer {
   protected:
      LPDIRECTSOUNDBUFFER Buffer;

      TCHAR FileName [ MAX_PATH ];
      LONG DataSize;
      WAVEFORMATEX WaveFormat;

      bool Load ( TCHAR *File );

      bool RestoreIfNecessary ();

      friend class DirectSoundManager;
   public:
      DirectSoundBuffer  ();
      ~DirectSoundBuffer ();

      bool GetPan ( float &Pan );
      bool GetFrequency ( DWORD &Frequency );
      bool GetVolume ( float &Volume );

      bool SetPan ( float Pan );
      bool SetFrequency ( DWORD Frequency );
      bool SetVolume ( float Volume );

      LONG GetDataSize ();
      bool GetWaveFormat ( WAVEFORMATEX &Out );

      bool Stop ();
      bool IsPlaying ();
      bool Play ( bool Loop = false );
      bool SetNotificationPositions
          ( DWORD NotifyCount,
          DSBPOSITIONNOTIFY *Notification );
};
```

Member Function	Description
GetPan	Retrieves the pan for the sound buffer. Valid values range from −1.0 (all audio output is to the left speaker) to 0.0 (audio output is equally directed to both speakers) to 1.0 (all audio output is to the right speaker). Note that this is not valid for 3D sound buffers.
GetFrequency	Retrieves the frequency of the sound buffer, in hertz.

(continued)

Reference Table 11.3   The class reference for the DirectSoundBuffer class *(continued)*.

Member Function	Description
GetVolume	Sets the volume for the sound buffer. Valid values range from 0.0 (no volume) to 1.0 (normal volume).
SetPan	Sets the pan for the sound buffer. Valid values range from –1.0 (all audio output is to the left speaker) to 0.0 (audio output is equally directed to both speakers) to 1.0 (all audio output is to the right speaker). Note that this is not valid for 3D sound buffers.
SetFrequency	Sets the frequency of the sound buffer, in hertz.
SetVolume	Sets the volume for the sound buffer. Valid values range from 0.0 (no volume) to 1.0 (normal volume).
GetDataSize	Retrieves the size of the sound data, the actual audio data excluding all format information.
GetWaveFormat	Retrieves a **WAVEFORMATEX** structure representing the format of the WAV file from which the sound buffer was loaded.
Stop	Stops the sound buffer from playing.
IsPlaying	Determines if the sound buffer is playing.
Play	Plays the sound buffer, either once (**Play (false)**) or continually (**Play (true)**). Note that if the memory for the sound buffer has been lost, this function will restore it and reload the WAV file specified when the sound buffer was created.
SetNotificationPositions	Sets the sound buffer's notification positions. This function requires a pointer to one or more **DSBPOSITIONNOTIFY** structures.

Reference Table 11.4   The class reference for the DirectSound3DBuffer class.

Class Declaration

```
class DirectSound3DBuffer : public DirectSoundBuffer {
   protected:
      LPDIRECTSOUND3DBUFFER    Buffer3D;

      friend class DirectSoundManager;
   public:
      DirectSound3DBuffer ();
      ~DirectSound3DBuffer ();

      bool GetPosition ( float &X, float &Y, float &Z );
      bool GetVelocity ( float &Vx, float &Vy, float &Vz );
      bool GetMinDistance ( float &MinDist );
      bool GetMaxDistance ( float &MaxDist );
      bool GetOrientation ( float &Vx, float &Vy, float &Vz );
```

(continued)

Reference Table 11.4 The class reference for the DirectSound3DBuffer class *(continued)*.	
Class Declaration	

```
        bool GetInnerConeAngle ( float &InnerConeAngle );
        bool GetOuterConeAngle ( float &OuterConeAngle );
        bool GetOperationMode ( DWORD &OpMode );
        bool GetOutsideConeVolume ( float &Volume );

        bool SetPosition ( float X, float Y, float Z );
        bool SetVelocity ( float Vx, float Vy, float Vz );
        bool SetMinDistance ( float MinDist );
        bool SetMaxDistance ( float MaxDist );
        bool SetOrientation ( float Vx, float Vy, float Vz );
        bool SetConeAngles ( float InnerConeAngle,
                             float OuterConeAngle );
        bool SetOperationMode  ( DWORD OpMode );
        bool SetOutsideConeVolume ( float Volume );
};
```

Member Function	Description
GetPosition	Retrieves the 3D sound buffer's position.
GetVelocity	Retrieves the 3D sound buffer's velocity.
GetMinDistance	Retrieves the 3D sound buffer's minimum distance.
GetMaxDistance	Retrieves the 3D sound buffer's maximum distance.
GetOrientation	Retrieves the 3D sound buffer's orientation.
GetInnerConeAngle	Retrieves the 3D sound buffer's inner cone angle.
GetOuterConeAngle	Retrieves the 3D sound buffer's outer cone angle.
GetOperationMode	Retrieves the 3D sound buffer's operation mode, which can be one of the following: • **DS3DMODE_DISABLE**—Turns off 3D sound. • **DS3DMODE_HEADRELATIVE**—Interprets the position and velocity of the 3D sound buffer, as relative to the listener's head. • **DS3DMODE_NORMAL**—Interprets the position and velocity of the 3D sound buffer as absolute.
GetOutsideConeVolume	Retrieves the 3D sound buffer's volume for outside the outer cone.
SetPosition	Sets the 3D sound buffer's position. After setting all attributes for all 3D sounds, an application should cal **DirectDrawManager::Commit-DeferredSettings** () to make all changes active.
SetVelocity	Sets the 3D sound buffer's velocity. After setting all attributes for all 3D sounds, an application should call the **DirectDrawManager::Commit-DeferredSettings** () to make all changes active.

(continued)

Reference Table 11.4	The class reference for the DirectSound3DBuffer class *(continued)*.
Member Function	**Description**
SetMinDistance	Sets the 3D sound buffer's minimum distance. After setting all attributes for all 3D sounds, an application should call the **DirectDrawManager::CommitDeferredSettings** () to make all changes active.
SetMaxDistance	Sets the 3D sound buffer's maximum distance. After setting all attributes for all 3D sounds, an application should call **DirectDrawManager::CommitDeferredSettings** () to make all changes active.
SetOrientation	Sets the 3D sound buffer's orientation. After setting all attributes for all 3D sounds, an application should call **DirectDrawManager::CommitDeferredSettings** () to make all changes active.
SetConeAngles	Sets the 3D sound buffer's inner and outer cone angles. After setting all attributes for all 3D sounds, an application should call **DirectDrawManager::CommitDeferredSettings** () to make all changes active.
SetOperationMode	Sets the 3D sound buffer's operation mode, which can be one of the following: • **DS3DMODE_DISABLE**—Turns off 3D sound. • **DS3DMODE_HEADRELATIVE**—Interprets the position and velocity of the 3D sound buffer, as relative to the listener's head. • **DS3DMODE_NORMAL**—Interprets the position and velocity of the 3D sound buffer as absolute. After setting all attributes for all 3D sounds, an application should call **DirectDrawManager::CommitDeferredSettings** () to make all changes active.
SetOutsideConeVolume	Sets the 3D sound buffer's volume for outside the outer cone. After setting all attributes for all 3D sounds, an application should call **DirectDrawManager::CommitDeferredSettings** () to make all changes active.

Using The Encapsulation

When you use the **DirectSoundManager**, **DirectSoundBuffer**, and **DirectSound3DBuffer** classes, here are a few things to remember:

♦ The DirectSoundManager object your application creates should always be a global variable, and all other objects should be local or class variables. The reason for this is that the DirectSoundManager object detaches the application from DirectSound when it is destroyed—any sounds that attempt to destroy themselves after this point will cause an error.

♦ The **DirectSound3DBuffer** class is derived from the **DirectSoundBuffer** class, and thus includes all of the class' functionality. Note, however, that because of restrictions in DirectSound, not all **DirectSoundBuffer** functions are applicable to DirectSound 3D buffers.

♦ Whenever the **Play ()** function is called, both the **DirectSoundBuffer** and **DirectSound-3DBuffer** classes will restore memory if the function is lost and subsequently reload the sound data from the WAV file the classes were initialized with. This frees you from having constantly to check the sound buffers, restoring and reloading them whenever lost.

♦ The classes depend on WaveIn.HPP and WaveIn.CPP, listed earlier in this chapter, so make sure you include these files in your project.

♦ The source code is an excellent way to learn DirectSound, even if you do not intend to use it directly.

Listing 11.5 shows the **DirectSoundManager**, **DirectSoundBuffer**, and **DirectSound3D-Buffer** classes in action with a small section of code that plays a normal sound and a 3D sound.

Listing 11.5   A section of code showing how the DirectSoundManager, DirectSoundBuffer, and DirectSound3DBuffer classes are used.

```
DirectSoundManager Manager;
DirectSoundBuffer Sound;
Manager.Initialize ( MyWindow );
Manager.CreateSound ( "Sound.WAV", Sound );
Sound.Play ();
DirectSound3DBuffer Sound3D;
Manager.SetPosition ( 0, 0, 0 );
Manager.SetOrientation ( 0, 0, 1,   // Front vector
                         0, 1, 0 ); // Head vector
Manager.Create3DSound ( "Sound.WAV", Sound3D );
Sound3D.SetPosition ( 0, 0, 1 );
Sound3D.Play ();
```

Summary

Digital sound data is usually stored in the WAV format. This format is a subtype of the RIFF format, used by Windows for storing multimedia file types. RIFF files are divided into chunks that contain an identifier, a length, and the actual chunk data. The two most important chunks in WAV files are **'fmt '** and **'data'**. The format of the **'data'** chunk can vary, but it is often the uncompressed PCM format, the same one used by DirectSound.

The first step in interfacing with DirectSound, which should come after the application has created its main window and switched into its appropriate video mode, is the creation of a

DirectSound object. This object is used to set the cooperative level and to create the primary sound buffer and all secondary sound buffers. From the primary sound buffer, you can set the output format and obtain the listener interface.

In the next chapter, you will learn how to add user interaction to your 3D games by using Microsoft's DirectInput, which supports mice, joysticks, keyboards, and just about any other input device in existence.

Chapter 12

Introduction To DirectInput

No game would be complete without user interaction. DirectInput is the component of DirectX that allows applications to interface easily with mice, joysticks (force-feedback and otherwise), keyboards, and other input devices. It provides a standard API that, because of its wide support and extensive features list, is much more suited to game development than the standard Windows input system.

This chapter provides an overview of DirectInput by explaining its features, architecture, terminology, and interfaces.

Why Use DirectInput?

The standard Windows input system provides support for mouse, keyboard, and even joystick input devices. The state of the mouse and keyboard is sent to the active application through Windows messages (**WM_KEYUP** or **WM_MOUSEMOVE**, for example). You retrieve joystick information by specifically asking Windows for that information.

Despite this support, the Windows input system suffers from several problems where game developers are concerned:

♦ The mouse support, though adequate, does not provide access to the features of all mice. Many mice have four buttons, but the standard input system provides support for just three. Some mice support *force-feedback* (a term used to describe an input device capable of applying force to the user to enhance feedback), but the standard input system does not.

- The keyboard support was designed for traditional applications, such as word processors, spreadsheets, and the like. Pressing a key down generates a message. If the key is held for a certain amount of time, a continual stream of messages follows this message for as long as the key is held down. Releasing the key generates a final message. Any game using the keyboard for directional control, however, needs to know the exact state of the directional keys at every moment, whether each key is up or down.

- The joystick support is severely limited. Today's joysticks often have half a dozen or more buttons, a view hat, and sometimes force-feedback systems. The standard input system supports none of these features.

DirectInput solves all of these problems. It allows game developers to support any number of buttons, keys, and axes in addition to force-feedback systems, and it provides access to this data in ways ideally suited to the requirements of games. With DirectInput, game developers can finally give game enthusiasts what they want—extensive support for the technologies of both today and tomorrow.

DirectInput Basics

The sections that follow cover the concepts important for you to understand when using DirectInput.

Hardware Acceleration

Input devices cannot be emulated, so in contrast to DirectDraw, Direct3D, and DirectSound, DirectInput has neither a Hardware Abstraction Layer (HAL) nor a Hardware Emulation Layer (HEL). DirectInput reports the capabilities of the hardware, and only these capabilities may be used.

Input Devices

Input devices in DirectInput can be one of three types: mice, keyboards, or joysticks. Joysticks do not have to be conventional—this title also includes such input devices as steering wheels and flight yokes.

Objects

Input devices can have buttons; keys; x, y, and z movement axes; x, y, and z rotation axes; point-of-view indicators (often referred to as *hat* switches on joysticks); and sliders. In DirectInput terminology, these are referred to as *objects* (not to be confused with C++ or COM objects).

Data Input/Output

Some input devices can report to DirectInput when their state changes. Mice, for example, send information to the computer whenever they are moved or their buttons are pressed. These devices are said to be *event-driven*. Other devices must be *polled*—that is, they do not report state changes to the computer; rather, the computer must explicitly query for their state (many joysticks fall into this category).

DirectInput applications assign each input device a *data format*. This data format describes how data is to be retrieved from the input device. Each type of object has a certain format already defined by DirectInput. The data format merely describes where in a buffer these objects reside and how large the buffer is.

Applications can retrieve input data in one of two ways:

♦ *Immediate*—Refers to retrieving the instantaneous and complete state of the input device—the state of all objects on the device. Applications will typically retrieve immediate data for joysticks.

♦ *Buffered*—Refers to retrieving a list of only the objects whose states have changed. Each element in the list includes information that identifies only the object that changed, but also describes how and when it changed. Applications will typically retrieve buffered data for mice and keyboards.

DirectInput allows applications to send data *to* certain input devices. For example, you can set the state of the LED indicators on a keyboard or send control data to a force-feedback joystick.

Force-Feedback Devices

Force-feedback devices have grown greatly in popularity over the past five years. Typically, a joystick (though force-feedback mice, steering wheels, flight yokes, and other equipment also exist) is capable of applying force to one or more of its objects (usually its axes). These input devices greatly enhance player feedback by allowing game developers to synchronize what the player sees with what he or she feels (for example, a flight yoke can produce resistance to movement analogous to the resistance of a real flight yoke).

DirectInput allows applications to control force-feedback devices through *effects*, which can be *downloaded* to the device and played when necessary. In general, force-feedback effects have an *amplitude* (which can vary with time), a *direction* (which is one-dimensional or more, depending on the number of axes to which the effect is applied), and a *duration*. They can be played continually or just when requested, or they can be associated with specific buttons, so when these buttons are pressed, the effects are played.

DirectInput supports a number of force-feedback effects (which you can use however you want). These are listed below:

♦ *Constant*—A constant force on the axis.

♦ *Ramp*—A force whose amplitude starts at one value and ends at another, linearly changing from one to the other.

♦ *Square*—A force whose amplitude on the axis resembles a square wave.

♦ *Sine*—A force whose amplitude on the axis resembles a sine wave.

- *Triangle*—A force whose amplitude on the axis resembles a triangular wave.
- *Sawtooth up*—A force whose amplitude on the axis resembles a sawtooth wave.
- *Sawtooth down*—A force whose amplitude on the axis resembles a sawtooth wave.
- *Spring*—A force whose amplitude increases as the distance from the axis to a defined neutral point increases.
- *Damper*—A force whose amplitude increases as the velocity with which the user moves the axis increases.
- *Inertia*—A force whose amplitude increases as the acceleration with which the user moves the axis increases.
- *Friction*—A force applied to the axis with its movement.
- *Custom force*—A force whose properties are explicitly defined by the application and applied to the axis.

Note

DirectInput allows envelopes to be applied to force-feedback effects. Envelopes shape the starting and ending values of effects, providing more control for the developer.

The built-in types allow developers easily to add force-feedback effects without spending a lot of time. The custom force, designed for more ambitious games, allows developers precisely to control the force-feedback effect at every moment.

Human Interface Devices

Some input devices are called *human interface devices* (HIDs). These are input devices that conform to the USB standard. They can be joysticks, mice, keyboards, or other input devices.

Cooperative Level

In DirectInput, the term *cooperative level* refers to the degree of control an application wants to have over a particular input device. The cooperative level for an input device can be foreground non-exclusive, foreground exclusive, background non-exclusive, or background exclusive. Foreground cooperative levels indicate the application should only receive input when it is the active application; background cooperative levels indicate the application should always receive input. Exclusive cooperative levels do not serve the same function as in DirectDraw or DirectSound: they do not restrict other applications from obtaining *non-exclusive* access to the device (they do prevent other applications from obtaining exclusive access to the device, however). Exclusive cooperative level hides the mouse cursor when it is set for mice, *cannot* be set for keyboards, and *must* be set for force-feedback input devices. Keyboards and mice will typically use foreground non-exclusive mode.

You must set the cooperative level for each input device before you can access the device.

Interface Overviews

DirectInput consists of three objects:

♦ *DirectInput*—The fundamental object of DirectInput, the first created in a DirectInput application.

♦ *DirectInputDevice2*—Represents an input device.

♦ *DirectInputEffect*—Represents a force-feedback effect.

These objects are accessed by the IDirectInput, IDirectInputDevice2, and IDirectInputEffect interfaces, covered in more detail in the sections that follow.

The IDirectInput Interface

The IDirectInput interface, obtained by calling **DirectInputCreate ()**, is responsible for listing input devices, determining their status (whether attached or not), creating DirectInputDevice objects to represent them, and running the Windows Control Panel.

Table 12.1 lists the functions of this interface.

The IDirectInputDevice2 Interface

The IDirectInputDevice2 interface communicates with an input device. It can set and re-trieve the data format of a device, retrieve its capabilities and input data, list all of its objects, set and retrieve properties, create DirectInputEffect objects, and perform many other functions.

The methods of this interface are briefly documented in Table 12.2.

The IDirectInputEffect Interface

The IDirectInputEffect interface handles force-feedback effects. It can download them to the device, stop and play them, unload them, and modify their parameters.

Table 12.3 lists the interface's functions.

Table 12.1   The IDirectInput interface functions and their descriptions.

Method Name	Description
CreateDevice ()	Creates a DirectInput device object that represents an input device.
EnumDevices ()	Enumerates all or selected input devices.
GetDeviceStatus ()	Retrieves the status (attached or unattached) of an input device.
Initialize ()	Initializes a DirectInput object created with **CoCreateInstance ()**.
RunControlPanel ()	Runs the Control Panel so the user can configure input devices.

Table 12.2   The IDirectInputDevice2 interface functions and their descriptions.

Method Name	Description
Acquire ()	Acquires access rights to the input device.
Unacquire ()	Releases access rights to the input device.
GetCapabilities ()	Retrieves the input device's capabilities.
GetDeviceData ()	Retrieves buffered input data from the input device.
GetDeviceInfo ()	Retrieves information about the input device's identity.
GetDeviceState ()	Retrieves instantaneous input data from the device.
SetDataFormat ()	Sets the input device's data format.
SetEventNotification ()	Sets the event to be triggered when input is received from the input device.
EnumObjects ()	Lists the device's input objects.
GetObjectInfo ()	Retrieves information about a given input object.
GetProperty ()	Retrieves a property of the input device.
SetProperty ()	Sets a property of the input device.
SetCooperativeLevel ()	Sets the input device's cooperative level.
RunControlPanel ()	Runs the control panel associated with the input device, so the user can configure it (or the default control panel if one is not associated with the device).
Poll ()	Polls the input device to update input data.
CreateEffect ()	Creates a DirectInput force-feedback effect object.
EnumCreatedEffectObjects ()	Lists all created DirectInput force-feedback effect objects.
EnumEffects ()	Lists force-feedback effect objects on the input device.
GetEffectInfo ()	Retrieves information about an effect.
Escape ()	Communicates directly with the hardware.
SendDeviceData ()	Sends data to the input device (providing it accepts data).
SendForceFeedbackCommand ()	Sends a command to the input device's force-feedback system.
GetForceFeedbackState ()	Retrieves the state of the input device's force-feedback system.

Table 12.3   The IDirectInputEffect interface functions and their descriptions.

Method Name	Description
GetEffectGuid ()	Retrieves the force-feedback effect's Globally Unique Identifier (GUID).
GetEffectStatus ()	Retrieves the status (playing or emulated) of the force-feedback effect.
GetParameters ()	Retrieves the force-feedback effect's parameters.
Download ()	Downloads the force-feedback effect to the input device.
SetParameters ()	Sets the force-feedback effect's parameters.
Start ()	Plays the force-feedback effect.
Stop ()	Stops the force-feedback effect.
Unload ()	Unloads the force-feedback effect from the input device.
Escape ()	Communicates directly with the hardware.

Getting Started With DirectInput

To use the DirectInput interfaces, you must first include the DirectInput header, Dinput.H, in your application. You must also link your application to Dinput.lib, the DirectInput import library (for Microsoft Visual C++, add the file's location to the Project | Project Settings | Link | Object | Library Modules text box). As with all COM applications, one file in your application must include InitGuid.H, which initializes the DirectInput GUIDs so your application can use them.

These steps are common to most DirectInput applications you will write:

1. The application calls **DirectInputCreate ()** to create a DirectInput object.

2. The application uses **IDirectInput::EnumDevices ()** to list all input devices and records the GUIDs of interest to the application.

3. The application creates a **DirectInputDevice** object for each GUID by calling **IDirectInput::CreateDevice ()**.

4. The application sets the cooperative levels for each input device via **IDirectInput Device::SetCooperativeLevel ()**, and the data format for each by calling **IDirectInput Device::SetDataFormat ()**.

5. The application acquires access to each device by calling **IDirectInputDevice::Acquire ()**.

6. The application runs until the user quits, polling input devices that require polling and obtaining data from the others when necessary.

7. The application releases all objects.

The next chapter documents these functions.

Summary

DirectInput provides access to input devices of all types—mice, keyboards, joysticks, and nontraditional input devices.

Input devices have one or more objects. These can be keys, buttons, sliders, movement or rotation axes, or point-of-view indicators. Some input devices can report state changes to the computer; others must be polled. DirectInput can report state changes in two ways: immediate, which reports the instantaneous state of all objects; and buffered, which reports the state of the objects that have changed and how and when they changed.

Force-feedback devices are those devices capable of applying forces to one or more of their objects. DirectInput supports a wide variety of built-in force-feedback effects and custom effects.

The next chapter explores the details you need to know to use DirectInput, supplying sample code and encapsulations for its common features.

Chapter 13

Using DirectInput

Having overviewed DirectInput, in this chapter I provide a tutorial for using it, describe its most important functions and structures, and supply an encapsulation for its main interfaces.

Note
For more information on DirectInput, including complete documentation of all functions and structures mentioned in this chapter, refer to Appendix D.

A DirectInput Tutorial

The first step in any DirectInput application is to create its most essential component: the DirectInput object. This object, unlike DirectDraw or DirectSound objects, does not actually represent a piece of hardware. Rather, it is used to run the control panel and to list and create input devices.

Creating A DirectInput Object

You can create a DirectInput object by calling the **DirectInput-Create ()** function (see Appendix D), as shown in the following code snippet:

```
LPDIRECTINPUT DirectInput;
DirectInputCreate ( AppInst, DIRECTINPUT_VERSION,
    &DirectInput, NULL );
```

*If a DirectInput function succeeds, its return value is typically **DI_OK**. Otherwise, it can be any one of the DirectInput success or error values listed in Appendix D.*

After you create a DirectInput object, the next logical step is to create DirectInputDevice objects to represent each input device your application wants to use. The function that creates devices (**IDirectInput::CreateDevice ()**), however, requires the *instance GUID* of the device to be created; instance GUIDs uniquely identify an input device. Predefined instance GUIDs exist for the system keyboard and mouse (**GUID_SysKeyboard** and **GUID_SysMouse**), but for joysticks and any other input devices, your application must retrieve the instance GUIDs by listing the system's input devices.

Listing Devices

By using the **IDirectInput::EnumDevices ()** function (see Appendix D), your application can enumerate mice, joysticks, keyboards, or other input devices as it chooses. This function can list only the devices plugged in to the computer or all the devices supported by the computer, whether or not they are attached.

*You do not have to call the **IDirectInput::EnumDevices ()** function if you want to support only keyboards and mice. However, if you want your application to support a joystick or other input device, you must call this function, because it is the only way you can obtain the device's instance GUID.*

The following code tells DirectInput to enumerate all joysticks attached to the computer:

```
DirectInput->EnumDevices ( DIDEVTYPE_JOYSTICK,
    JoystickCallback, ( LPVOID ) &JoystickGUID,
    DIEDFL_ATTACHEDONLY );
```

Every time DirectInput finds a device, it calls a function (see Appendix D). Your application defines this function (**JoystickCallback ()** in the previous example), and uses it to evaluate each device in turn until it finds one that matches your specifications. When you find one you like, you simply return from the callback **DIENUM_CANCEL** (as opposed to **DIENUM_CONTINUE**, which continues enumeration).

Creating A DirectInputDevice Object

Once your application has found the instance GUIDs of any devices it wants to create (or has decided to use the predefined instance GUIDs), it can call the **IDirectInput::CreateDevice ()** function (see Appendix D) to create a DirectInputDevice object for each one.

The following code creates a keyboard device:

```
LPDIRECTINPUTDEVICE Keyboard;
DirectInput->CreateDevice ( GUID_SysKeyboard, &Keyboard,
   NULL );
```

The newest version of the IDirectInputDevice interface is IDirectInputDevice2. This interface supports a few features (such as force-feedback effects and polling) not found in the previous interface. Thus, most applications you write will probably query for this interface, as the following code does:

```
LPDIRECTINPUTDEVICE2 Keyboard2;
// Obtain the new interface:
Keyboard->QueryInterface ( IID_IDirectInputDevice2,
   ( LPVOID * ) &Keyboard2 );
// Free the old interface:
Keyboard->Release ();
```

Setting The Cooperative Level

Each input device has a cooperative level that must be set after the device is created by calling the device's **IDirectInputDevice2::SetCooperativeLevel ()** function.

The following code shows you how to set the cooperative level for a keyboard:

```
Keyboard->SetCooperativeLevel ( Window,
   DISCL_FOREGROUND | DISCL_NONEXCLUSIVE );
```

See Appendix D for more information about this function and the various cooperative levels you can set devices to.

Setting The Data Format

Once a device's cooperative level has been set, your application must inform DirectInput of the device's data format. The data format defines how many axes, buttons, keys, and so on the device supports and specifies what the order of these objects are in a buffer.

DirectInput has conveniently defined these data formats for you:

♦ **c_dfDIKeyboard**

♦ **c_dfDIMouse**

♦ **c_dfDIJoystick**

The predefined keyboard data format consists of an array of 256 bytes. Each byte corresponds to the state of one of the keys on the keyboard. The high bit of a byte is equal to 1 if the key is down, or equal to 0 otherwise.

The predefined mouse format consists of a **DIMOUSESTATE** structure, described Appendix D. The predefined joystick data format consists of a **DIJOYSTATE** structure, also described in Appendix D.

The following code sets the data format of a keyboard device to **c_dfDIKeyboard**:

```
Keyboard->SetDataFormat ( &c_dfDIKeyboard );
```

See Appendix D for more documentation on the **IDirectInputDevice2::SetDataFormat ()** function.

Setting The Buffer Size

For some devices, such as joysticks, you may choose to retrieve immediate data exclusively. For others, such as mice, you may require detailed information of every single change that occurs to the device's state and will therefore require buffered data. For these devices, you must first tell the DirectInput device how large its buffer should be.

The following code tells DirectInput to make a mouse's buffer large enough so that it can hold 64 different state changes:

```
DIPROPDWORD Property;
Property.diph.dwHeaderSize = sizeof ( DIPROPHEADER );
Property.diph.dwSize       = sizeof ( DIPROPDWORD );
Property.diph.dwObj        = 0;
Property.diph.dwHow        = DIPH_DEVICE;
Property.dwData            = 64;
Mouse->SetProperty ( DIPROP_BUFFERSIZE,
   ( DIPROPHEADER * ) &Property );
```

The code tells DirectInput to set a property of the device (specifically, **DIPROP_BUFFERSIZE**, the size of the buffer). It tells DirectInput the property applies to the entire device (**DIPH_DEVICE**) and that the property should be set to 64 (see Appendix D for more information on the **IDirectInputDevice2::SetProperty ()** function).

Setting The Axis Mode

For joysticks and mice, you should set the axis mode of the device. This can be either relative, in which case all axis information is relative to the previous position of the axis, or absolute.

The following code sets the axis mode of a mouse to absolute:

```
Property.diph.dwHeaderSize = sizeof ( DIPROPHEADER );
Property.diph.dwSize       = sizeof ( DIPROPDWORD );
Property.diph.dwHow        = DIPH_DEVICE;
```

```
Property.diph.dwObj        = 0;
Property.dwData            = DIPROPAXISMODE_ABS;
Mouse->SetProperty ( DIPROP_AXISMODE,
   ( DIPROPHEADER * ) &Property );
```

You could set the axis mode to relative by changing the line

```
Property.dwData = DIPROPAXISMODE_ABS;
```

to:

```
Property.dwData = DIPROPAXISMODE_REL;
```

Acquiring Access
The last preparatory step is to acquire access from the input devices you are using. This tells
DirectInput to redirect input to your application.

The following code acquires access to a mouse:

```
Mouse->Acquire ();
```

Note that if the user activates another application (either by pressing Alt+Tab or some
other means), you will lose access to the devices you are using, and you will have to reacquire access when your application regains focus.

Retrieving Data From An Input Device
Once the setup has been performed, accessing an input device's data is straightforward. It
can be done one of two ways: by requesting immediate data, or (if the buffer size has been
set) by requesting buffered data.

Retrieving Immediate Data
To retrieve immediate data from an input device, call its **IDirectInputDevice2::GetDevice
State ()** function with a structure whose format matches the device's data format (see Ap-
pendix D for documentation on this function).

The following code retrieves immediate data from a mouse whose data format has been set
to **c_dfDIMouse**:

```
DIMOUSESTATE MouseState;
Mouse->GetDeviceState ( sizeof ( DIMOUSESTATE ),

   &MouseState );
```

Retrieving Buffered Data

Retrieving buffered data from an input device is only slightly more difficult than retrieving immediate data. You must declare an array of **DIDEVICEOBJECTDATA** structures (see Appendix D), which you then pass to the **IDirectInputDevice2::GetDeviceData ()** function. This function (also in Appendix D) stores the state changes in the array. The following code demonstrates this approach for a keyboard:

```
DWORD ItemCount = 64;
DIDEVICEOBJECTDATA Array [ ItemCount ];
Keyboard->GetDeviceData ( sizeof ( DIDEVICEOBJECTDATA ),
   Array, &ItemCount, 0 );
```

Table 13.1 shows the offset values (which you will need to identify data DirectInput stores in the **DIDEVICEOBJECTDATA** array) for a keyboard using the default keyboard data format. See the DirectX help file for special and alternate keys.

Likewise, Table 13.2 describes the offset values for a mouse. Lastly, Table 13.3 lists the offset values for a joystick.

Table 13.1 The offset values for the default keyboard data format.

Offset Constant	Description
DIK_ESCAPE	The Escape key.
DIK_1	The '1' key on the main keyboard.
DIK_2	The '2' key on the main keyboard.
DIK_3	The '3' key on the main keyboard.
DIK_4	The '4' key on the main keyboard.
DIK_5	The '5' key on the main keyboard.
DIK_6	The '6' key on the main keyboard.
DIK_7	The '7' key on the main keyboard.
DIK_8	The '8' key on the main keyboard.
DIK_9	The '9' key on the main keyboard.
DIK_0	The '0' key on the main keyboard.
DIK_MINUS	The minus key.
DIK_EQUALS	The equals key.
DIK_BACK	The Backspace key.
DIK_TAB	The Tab key.
DIK_Q	The 'Q' key.
DIK_W	The 'W' key.
DIK_E	The 'E' key.
DIK_R	The 'R' key.
DIK_T	The 'T' key.
DIK_Y	The 'Y' key.
DIK_U	The 'U' key.
DIK_I	The 'I' key.

(continued)

Table 13.1   The offset values for the default keyboard data format *(continued).*

Offset Constant	Description
DIK_O	The 'O' key.
DIK_P	The 'P' key.
DIK_LBRACKET	The left bracket ('[') key.
DIK_RBRACKET	The right bracket (']') key.
DIK_RETURN	The Enter or Return key.
DIK_LCONTROL	The left control (Ctrl) key.
DIK_A	The 'A' key.
DIK_S	The 'S' key.
DIK_D	The 'D' key.
DIK_F	The 'F' key.
DIK_G	The 'G' key.
DIK_H	The 'H' key.
DIK_J	The 'J' key.
DIK_K	The 'K' key.
DIK_L	The 'L' key.
DIK_SEMICOLON	The semicolon key.
DIK_APOSTROPHE	The apostrophe key.
DIK_GRAVE	The grave accent mark ('`') key.
DIK_LSHIFT	The left Shift key.
DIK_BACKSLASH	The backslash key.
DIK_Z	The 'Z' key.
DIK_X	The 'X' key.
DIK_C	The 'C' key.
DIK_V	The 'V' key.
DIK_B	The 'B' key.
DIK_N	The 'N' key.
DIK_M	The 'M' key.
DIK_COMMA	The comma key.
DIK_PERIOD	The period key.
DIK_SLASH	The forward slash key.
DIK_RSHIFT	The right Shift key.
DIK_MULTIPLY	The multiply key (the asterisk key on the numeric keypad).
DIK_LMENU	The left menu (Alt) key.
DIK_SPACE	The spacebar key.
DIK_CAPITAL	The Caps Lock key.
DIK_F1	The F1 key.
DIK_F2	The F2 key.
DIK_F3	The F3 key.
DIK_F4	The F4 key.
DIK_F5	The F5 key.
DIK_F6	The F6 key.
DIK_F7	The F7 key.
DIK_F8	The F8 key.

(continued)

Table 13.1 The offset values for the default keyboard data format *(continued)*.

Offset Constant	Description
DIK_F9	The F9 key.
DIK_F10	The F10 key.
DIK_NUMLOCK	The Num Lock key.
DIK_SCROLL	The Scroll Lock key.
DIK_NUMPAD7	The '7' key on the numeric keypad.
DIK_NUMPAD8	The '8' key on the numeric keypad.
DIK_NUMPAD9	The '9' key on the numeric keypad.
DIK_SUBTRACT	The subtract (minus) key on the numeric keypad.
DIK_NUMPAD4	The '4' key on the numeric keypad.
DIK_NUMPAD5	The '5' key on the numeric keypad.
DIK_NUMPAD6	The '6' key on the numeric keypad.
DIK_ADD	The add (plus) key (on the numeric keypad).
DIK_NUMPAD1	The '1' key on the numeric keypad.
DIK_NUMPAD2	The '2' key on the numeric keypad.
DIK_NUMPAD3	The '3' key on the numeric keypad.
DIK_NUMPAD0	The '0' key on the numeric keypad.
DIK_DECIMAL	The decimal point key (on the numeric keypad).
DIK_F11	The F11 key.
DIK_F12	The F12 key.
DIK_F13	The F13 key.
DIK_F14	The F14 key.
DIK_F15	The F15 key.
DIK_NUMPADENTER	The Enter key on the numeric keypad.
DIK_RCONTROL	The right control ("Ctrl") key.
DIK_NUMPADCOMMA	The comma key on the numeric keypad.
DIK_DIVIDE	The divide key (on the numeric keypad).
DIK_SYSRQ	The system request/print screen key.
DIK_RMENU	The right menu ("Alt") key.
DIK_HOME	The Home key.
DIK_UP	The up arrow key.
DIK_PRIOR	The Page Up key.
DIK_LEFT	The left arrow key.
DIK_RIGHT	The right arrow key.
DIK_END	The End key.
DIK_DOWN	The down arrow key.
DIK_NEXT	The Page Down key.
DIK_INSERT	The Insert key.
DIK_DELETE	The Delete key.
DIK_LWIN	The left Windows key.
DIK_RWIN	The right Windows key.
DIK_APPS	The application key.
DIK_PAUSE	The Pause key.

Table 13.2   The offset values for the DIMOUSESTATE structure.

Offset Constant	Description
DIMOFS_BUTTON0	The mouse's first button on the right.
DIMOFS_BUTTON1	The mouse's second button from the right.
DIMOFS_BUTTON2	The mouse's third button from the right.
DIMOFS_BUTTON3	The mouse's fourth button from the right.
DIMOFS_X	The mouse's x-axis, representing horizontal movement.
DIMOFS_Y	The mouse's y-axis, representing vertical movement.
DIMOFS_Z	The mouse's z-axis (typically a mouse wheel).

Table 13.3   The offset values for the DIJOYSTATE structure.

Offset Constant	Description
DIJOFS_BUTTON(0) to DIJOFS_BUTTON(31)	One of the joystick's 32 buttons.
DIJOFS_POV(0) to DIJOFS_POV(3)	One of the joystick's 4 Point-of-View (POV) controls.
DIJOFS_RX	The joystick's rotation x-axis.
DIJOFS_RY	The joystick's rotation y-axis.
DIJOFS_RZ	The joystick's rotation z-axis, typically a rudder.
DIJOFS_X	The joystick's movement x-axis.
DIJOFS_Y	The joystick's movement y-axis.
DIJOFS_Z	The joystick's movement z-axis, typically the throttle.
DIJOFS_SLIDER(0) to DIJOFS_SLIDER(1)	One of the joystick's two slider controls.

A DirectInput Encapsulation

This chapter's encapsulation wraps two interfaces: IDirectInput and IDirectInputDevice2. The four classes provided are **DirectInputManager**, which represents a DirectInput object; and **DirectInputMouse**, **DirectInputKeyboard**, and **DirectInputJoystick**, which represent DirectInputDevice objects. The class declarations for these encapsulations are shown in Listing 13.1, and the implementations are in Listing 13.2. The accessible functions of these four classes are documented in Reference Tables 13.1 through 13.4.

Listing 13.1   The DirectInput.HPP file.

```
//
// File name: DirectInput.hpp
//
// Description: The declaration for a DirectInput
//              encapsulation.
//
// Author: John De Goes
//
```

```
// Linkage: Dinput.lib, Winmm.lib
//
// Copyright (C) 1999 John De Goes -- All Rights Reserved.
//

#ifndef __DIRECTINPUTHPP__
#define __DIRECTINPUTHPP__

#include <Math.H>
#include <Windows.H>
#include <MMSystem.H>

#include <Dinput.H>

#define DIMOUSE_BUFFER_SIZE      32
#define DIKEYBOARD_BUFFER_SIZE   32
#define DIJOYSTICK_BUFFER_SIZE   32

#define DEFAULT_MOUSE_ACCEL      0.7

#define POV_CENTERED            -1.0

class DirectInputMouse;
class DirectInputKeyboard;
class DirectInputJoystick;

class DirectInputManager {
   protected:
      LPDIRECTINPUT DirectInput;

      HWND AppWindow;
   public:
      DirectInputManager ();
      ~DirectInputManager ();

      bool Initialize ( HWND Window, HINSTANCE Instance );

      bool CreateMouse ( DirectInputMouse &Mouse );

      bool CreateKeyboard ( DirectInputKeyboard
                                &Keyboard );

      bool CreateJoystick ( DirectInputJoystick
                                &Joystick );

      bool GetInterface ( LPDIRECTINPUT *Ptr );
};
```

```
class DirectInputMouse {
   private:
      DIMOUSESTATE MouseState;

      LONG LastX, LastY, LastZ;

      double OutputX, OutputY, OutputZ, ZGran, Accel;

      HWND AppWindow;

      DWORD  HandleInputThreadID;
      HANDLE HandleInputThread, KillThreadEvent;

      LONG __stdcall HandleInput ();

      bool UpdateMousePosition ();
      bool SpawnHandleInputThread ( HWND Window );
      bool KillHandleInputThread ();

      friend class DirectInputManager;
   protected:
      LPDIRECTINPUTDEVICE2 Mouse;

   public:
      DirectInputMouse ();
      ~DirectInputMouse ();

      LONG GetX ();
      LONG GetY ();
      LONG GetZ ();

      bool SetAcceleration ( double NewAccel =
         DEFAULT_MOUSE_ACCEL );

      double GetAcceleration ();

      bool Flush ();

      DWORD GetButtonCount ();

      bool GetButtonStatus ( DWORD ButtonCode );

      virtual bool ButtonUp   ( DWORD ButtonCode );
      virtual bool ButtonDown ( DWORD ButtonCode );
      virtual bool MouseMove  ();
```

```
            bool GetBaseInterface ( LPDIRECTINPUTDEVICE *Ptr );
            bool GetInterface ( LPDIRECTINPUTDEVICE2 *Ptr );
    };


    class DirectInputKeyboard {
        private:
            BYTE KeyboardState [ 256 ];

            DWORD HandleInputThreadID;

            HANDLE HandleInputThread, KillThreadEvent;

            HWND AppWindow;

            long __stdcall HandleInput ();

            bool SpawnHandleInputThread ( HWND Window );
            bool KillHandleInputThread ();

            friend class DirectInputManager;
        protected:
            LPDIRECTINPUTDEVICE2 Keyboard;

        public:
            DirectInputKeyboard ();
            ~DirectInputKeyboard ();

            bool Flush ();

            bool GetKeyStatus ( DWORD KeyCode );

            virtual bool KeyUp   ( DWORD KeyCode );
            virtual bool KeyDown ( DWORD KeyCode );

            bool GetBaseInterface ( LPDIRECTINPUTDEVICE *Ptr );
            bool GetInterface ( LPDIRECTINPUTDEVICE2 *Ptr );
    };


    class DirectInputJoystick {
        private:
            DIJOYSTATE JoystickState;

            double MinMX, MinMY, MinMZ,
                   MaxMX, MaxMY, MaxMZ,
                   MinRX, MinRY, MinRZ,
```

```
            MaxRX, MaxRY, MaxRZ,
            MinSlider [ 2 ],
            MaxSlider [ 2 ];

   DWORD PollDeviceThreadID, HandleInputThreadID;

   HANDLE HandleInputThread, KillThreadEvent,
            PollDeviceThread, KillPollThreadEvent;

   HWND AppWindow;

   bool StoreConversionData ();
   bool IsDevicePolled ();
   bool DirectInputJoystick::GetRange ( DWORD ObjOffset,
            double &Min, double &Max );

   long __stdcall PollDevice ();
   long __stdcall HandleInput ();

   bool SpawnPollDeviceThread ();
   bool KillPollDeviceThread ();

   bool SpawnHandleInputThread ( HWND Window );
   bool KillHandleInputThread ();

   friend class DirectInputManager;
protected:
   LPDIRECTINPUTDEVICE2 Joystick;

public:
   DirectInputJoystick ();
   ~DirectInputJoystick ();

   bool Flush ();

   double GetMovementX ();
   double GetMovementY ();
   double GetMovementZ ();

   double GetRotationX ();
   double GetRotationY ();
   double GetRotationZ ();

   double GetSlider ( DWORD SliderCode );
   double GetPOV ( DWORD Number );
```

```
        DWORD GetButtonCount ();

        bool GetButtonStatus ( DWORD ButtonCode );

        virtual bool ButtonUp   ( DWORD ButtonCode );
        virtual bool ButtonDown ( DWORD ButtonCode );

        virtual bool JoystickMove ();
        virtual bool JoystickRotate ();

        virtual bool SliderMove ( DWORD SliderCode );
        virtual bool POVMove ( DWORD POVCode );

        bool GetBaseInterface ( LPDIRECTINPUTDEVICE *Ptr );
        bool GetInterface ( LPDIRECTINPUTDEVICE2 *Ptr );
};

#endif
```

Listing 13.2   The DirectInput.CPP file.

```
//
// File name: DirectInput.cpp
//
// Description: The implementation for a DirectInput
//              encapsulation.
//
// Author: John De Goes
//
// Linkage: Dinput.lib, Winmm.lib
//
// Copyright (C) 1999 John De Goes -- All Rights Reserved.
//

#include "DirectInput.hpp"

DirectInputMouse::DirectInputMouse () {
    Mouse = NULL;

    Accel = DEFAULT_MOUSE_ACCEL;

    HandleInputThread = KillThreadEvent = NULL;

    // Center the cursor within the screen:
    OutputX = GetSystemMetrics ( SM_CXSCREEN ) / 2.0;
    OutputY = GetSystemMetrics ( SM_CYSCREEN ) / 2.0;
```

```
        OutputZ = 0.0;

        HandleInputThreadID = 0;

        ZeroMemory ( &MouseState, sizeof ( DIMOUSESTATE ) );
    }

    DirectInputMouse::~DirectInputMouse () {
        if ( Mouse != NULL ) {
            // Kill the input handler thread, if active:
            KillHandleInputThread ();

            // Release the input device:
            Mouse->Release ();

            Mouse = NULL;
        }
    }

    bool DirectInputMouse::UpdateMousePosition () {
        // This function updates the mouse position in terms of
        // screen coordinates--it converts from mickeys
        // (the unit used by DirectInput) to pixels.
        const double MAX_ACCEL = 2.0;
        LONG ScreenWidth, ScreenHeight;
        double DeltaX, DeltaY, DeltaZ;

        DeltaX = MouseState.lX - LastX;
        DeltaY = MouseState.lY - LastY;
        DeltaZ = MouseState.lZ - LastZ;

        OutputX += DeltaX * Accel * MAX_ACCEL;
        OutputY += DeltaY * Accel * MAX_ACCEL;

        // We always report the wheel's position in relative
        // coordinates (absolute coordinates don't really
        // make sense, because the wheel can scroll indefinitely
        // in both directions).  Note that we take granularity
        // into consideration, so the values are constant
        // for all mice that have wheels.
        if ( DeltaZ >= 0.0 )
            OutputZ = ( DeltaZ + ZGran / 2.0 ) / ZGran;
        else OutputZ = ( DeltaZ - ZGran / 2.0 ) / ZGran;

        ScreenWidth  = GetSystemMetrics ( SM_CXSCREEN );
        ScreenHeight = GetSystemMetrics ( SM_CYSCREEN );
```

```
        // Clip the x coordinate to the screen:
        if ( OutputX < 0.0 )
            OutputX = 0.0;
        else if ( OutputX > ScreenWidth )
            OutputX = ScreenWidth;

        // Clip the y coordinate to the screen:
        if ( OutputY < 0.0 )
            OutputY = 0.0;
        else if ( OutputY > ScreenHeight )
            OutputY = ScreenHeight;

    LastX = MouseState.lX;
    LastY = MouseState.lY;
    LastZ = MouseState.lZ;

    return true;
}


bool DirectInputMouse::SpawnHandleInputThread (
        HWND Window ) {
    // The following union allows us to convert a pointer to
    // a member function to one callable by Windows as a
    // thread:
    struct ConverterUnion {
        union {
            LPTHREAD_START_ROUTINE NormalFunction;
            long ( __stdcall DirectInputMouse::*
                MemberFunction ) ( void );
        };
    } Converter;

    AppWindow = Window;

    Converter.MemberFunction = HandleInput;

    // Create the thread that will handle all input:
    HandleInputThread = CreateThread ( NULL, 0,
        Converter.NormalFunction, ( LPVOID ) this, 0,
        &HandleInputThreadID );

    if ( HandleInputThread == NULL )
        return false;

    return true;
}
```

```
bool DirectInputMouse::KillHandleInputThread () {
   // Kill the input handler thread if it is active:
   if ( HandleInputThread != NULL ) {
      SetEvent ( KillThreadEvent );

      // Wait for the thread to finish (if it hasn't
      // finished in 10 seconds, kill it):
      if ( WaitForSingleObject ( HandleInputThread, 10000 )
           == WAIT_TIMEOUT )
         TerminateThread ( HandleInputThread, 0 );

      HandleInputThread = NULL;
   }

   return true;
}


LONG __stdcall DirectInputMouse::HandleInput () {
   // This function handles all input from the mouse
   // device.  It is created as a thread and executes
   // continuously until the program ends.
   const DWORD    MAX_ITEMS = DIMOUSE_BUFFER_SIZE,
                  BUTTON_DOWN_MASK = 0x80;

   DWORD          I, TriggeredEvents, ItemCount,
                  DataOffset, Data;
   HANDLE         EventList [ 2 ], MouseEvent;
   HRESULT        Result;
   bool           AccessAcquired, RunThread = true,
                  MouseMoved;
   DIPROPDWORD    Property;

   DIDEVICEOBJECTDATA ObjectData [ MAX_ITEMS ];

   if ( Mouse == NULL )
      return 0;

   // Set the cooperative level for the mouse to foreground
   // exclusive (the mouse cursor will not be visible):
   if ( Mouse->SetCooperativeLevel ( AppWindow,
      DISCL_FOREGROUND | DISCL_NONEXCLUSIVE ) != DI_OK )
      return false;

   // Use the default mouse data format:
   if ( Mouse->SetDataFormat ( &c_dfDIMouse )
        != DI_OK )
      return 0;
```

```
// Set the size of the buffer, because we use buffered
// data:
Property.diph.dwHeaderSize = sizeof ( DIPROPHEADER );
Property.diph.dwSize       = sizeof ( DIPROPDWORD );
Property.diph.dwObj        = 0;
Property.diph.dwHow        = DIPH_DEVICE;
Property.dwData            = DIMOUSE_BUFFER_SIZE;

if ( Mouse->SetProperty ( DIPROP_BUFFERSIZE,
     ( DIPROPHEADER * ) &Property ) != DI_OK )
   return 0;

// Set the mouse into absolute axis mode:
Property.diph.dwHeaderSize = sizeof ( DIPROPHEADER );
Property.diph.dwSize       = sizeof ( DIPROPDWORD );
Property.diph.dwHow        = DIPH_DEVICE;
Property.diph.dwObj        = 0;
Property.dwData            = DIPROPAXISMODE_ABS;

if ( Mouse->SetProperty ( DIPROP_AXISMODE,
     ( DIPROPHEADER * ) &Property ) != DI_OK )
   return 0;

// Record the granularity of the z axis:
Property.diph.dwHeaderSize = sizeof ( DIPROPHEADER );
Property.diph.dwSize       = sizeof ( DIPROPDWORD );
Property.diph.dwHow        = DIPH_BYOFFSET;
Property.diph.dwObj        = DIMOFS_Z;

if ( Mouse->GetProperty ( DIPROP_GRANULARITY,
        ( DIPROPHEADER * ) &Property ) == DI_OK )
   ZGran = Property.dwData;
else ZGran = 0.0;

// Create a mouse event that will be triggered whenever
// the state of the mouse changes:
MouseEvent      = CreateEvent ( NULL, FALSE, FALSE,
                                NULL );

// Create an event that, when set, will trigger the
// termination of this thread:
KillThreadEvent = CreateEvent ( NULL, TRUE, FALSE,
                                NULL );

// Tell DirectInput to notify us of mouse state changes:
Mouse->SetEventNotification ( MouseEvent );
```

```
EventList [ 0 ] = MouseEvent;
EventList [ 1 ] = KillThreadEvent;

AccessAcquired = false;

while ( RunThread ) {
   // If access to the device's input data is possible,
   // wait for either that data or the termination of
   // this thread:
   if ( AccessAcquired ) {
      // Wait for either a mouse event or an event that
      // triggers the destruction of this thread:
      TriggeredEvents =
         WaitForMultipleObjects ( 2, EventList, FALSE,
                                     INFINITE );

      // Determine which event (either a mouse event or
      // a thread termination event) occurred:
      switch ( TriggeredEvents ) {
         case ( WAIT_OBJECT_0 ): {
            // A mouse event occurred:

            // Assume the mouse didn't move:
            MouseMoved = false;

            // Get the data from the mouse:
            ItemCount = MAX_ITEMS;
            Result = Mouse->GetDeviceData (
               sizeof ( DIDEVICEOBJECTDATA ),
               ObjectData, &ItemCount, 0 );

            if ( Result != DI_OK ) {
               AccessAcquired = false;
            }
            else {
               // Loop through all buffered data
               // elements:
               for ( I = 0; I < ItemCount; I++ ) {
                  // Determine the type of data.
                  DataOffset = ObjectData [ I ].dwOfs;
                  Data       = ObjectData [ I ].dwData;


                  // For button changes, we
                  // immediately call the event
                  // handler ButtonUp () or
```

```
// ButtonDown (); but we wait for all
// axes changes before calling
// MouseMove ().  In both cases, we
// save the state changes to the
// MouseState structure.
switch ( DataOffset ) {
   case ( DIMOFS_BUTTON0 ): {
      // The first mouse button
      MouseState.rgbButtons [ 0 ] =
         ( BYTE ) Data;

      if ( Data & BUTTON_DOWN_MASK ) {
         ButtonDown ( 0 );
      }
      else {
         ButtonUp ( 0 );
      }
      break;
   }

   case ( DIMOFS_BUTTON1 ): {
      // The second mouse button
      MouseState.rgbButtons [ 1 ] =
         ( BYTE ) Data;

      if ( Data & BUTTON_DOWN_MASK ) {
         ButtonDown ( 1 );
      }
      else {
         ButtonUp ( 1 );
      }
      break;
   }

   case ( DIMOFS_BUTTON2 ): {
      // The third mouse button
      MouseState.rgbButtons [ 2 ] =
         ( BYTE ) Data;

      if ( Data & BUTTON_DOWN_MASK ) {
         ButtonDown ( 2 );
      }
      else {
         ButtonUp ( 2 );
      }
      break;
   }
```

```
            case ( DIMOFS_BUTTON3 ): {
                // The fourth mouse button
                MouseState.rgbButtons [ 3 ] =
                    ( BYTE ) Data;

                if ( Data & BUTTON_DOWN_MASK ) {
                    ButtonDown ( 3 );
                }
                else {
                    ButtonUp ( 3 );
                }
                break;
            }

            case ( DIMOFS_X ): {
                // Movement on the x axis
                MouseState.lX = Data;
                MouseMoved = true;
                break;
            }

            case ( DIMOFS_Y ): {
                // Movement on the y axis
                MouseState.lY = Data;
                MouseMoved = true;
                break;
            }

            case ( DIMOFS_Z ): {
                // Movement on the z axis
                MouseState.lZ = Data;
                MouseMoved = true;
                break;
            }

        }
    }

    // If the mouse moved, update the mouse
    // position and call the mouse move
    // handler:
    if ( MouseMoved ) {
        UpdateMousePosition ();
        MouseMove ();
    }
}
```

```
            break;
        }

    case ( WAIT_OBJECT_0 + 1 ): {
        // The thread should die:
        RunThread = false;
        break;
    }
    }
}
// If access to the device is not possible, then 1)
// check to see if the thread should be killed and
// if so kill it; 2) if not, try to acquire access
// to the device:
else {
    // 1) Check to see if the thread must be killed:
    if ( WaitForSingleObject ( KillThreadEvent, 0 )
        == WAIT_OBJECT_0 )
        RunThread = false;

    else {
        // Attempt to acquire access to the device now:
        if ( Mouse->Acquire () == DI_OK ) {
            // Retrieve the current state of the mouse:
            Mouse->GetDeviceState (
                sizeof ( DIMOUSESTATE ), &MouseState );

            // Record the initial mouse position:
            LastX = MouseState.lX;
            LastY = MouseState.lY;
            LastZ = MouseState.lZ;

            AccessAcquired = true;
        }

        // If access is not available now, it is
        // probably because the application does not
        // have input focus.  Here we wait half a
        // second (to avoid hogging the system) and
        // then continue the loop and try to
        // acquire access again.  This way the calling
        // app never has to worry about reacquiring
        // access when it regains input focus.
        else {
            Sleep ( 500 );
```

```
            }
         }
      }
   }

   // Turn off event notification:
   Mouse->SetEventNotification ( NULL );

   // Close all handles:
   CloseHandle ( KillThreadEvent );
   CloseHandle ( MouseEvent );

   // Unacquire access to the device:
   Mouse->Unacquire ();

   return 1;
}

LONG DirectInputMouse::GetX () {
   if ( Mouse == NULL )
      return -1;

   // Return the mouse's location on the screen,
   // rounded to the nearest pixel:
   return ( LONG ) ( OutputX + 0.5 );
}

LONG DirectInputMouse::GetY () {
   if ( Mouse == NULL )
      return -1;

   // Return the mouse's location on the screen,
   // rounded to the nearest pixel:
   return ( LONG ) ( OutputY + 0.5 );
}

LONG DirectInputMouse::GetZ () {
   if ( Mouse == NULL )
      return -1;

   return ( LONG ) ( OutputZ );
}

bool DirectInputMouse::SetAcceleration ( double NewAccel ) {
   // Acceleration typically varies from 0.0 (which slows
   // down the cursor) to 0.5 (no acceleration) to 1.0
```

```
         // (fastest acceleration).  Values greater than 1.0
         // are possible, however.

         if ( Mouse == NULL )
            return false;

         Accel = NewAccel;

         return true;
      }

      double DirectInputMouse::GetAcceleration () {
         // Acceleration typically varies from 0.0 (which slows
         // down the cursor) to 0.5 (no acceleration) to 1.0
         // (fastest acceleration).  Values greater than 1.0
         // are possible, however.
         return Accel;
      }

      bool DirectInputMouse::Flush () {
         DWORD ItemCount = INFINITE;

         // Flush all data in the buffer:
         if ( Mouse->GetDeviceData (
                 sizeof ( DIDEVICEOBJECTDATA ),
                    NULL, &ItemCount, 0 ) != DI_OK )
            return false;

         return true;
      }

      DWORD DirectInputMouse::GetButtonCount () {
         DIDEVCAPS Caps;
         Caps.dwSize = sizeof ( DIDEVCAPS );

         Mouse->GetCapabilities ( &Caps );

         return Caps.dwButtons;
      }

      bool DirectInputMouse::GetButtonStatus ( DWORD ButtonCode ) {
         const DWORD BUTTON_DOWN_MASK = 0x80;
         DWORD ButtonStatus;

         if ( ButtonCode >= GetButtonCount () )
            return false;
```

```
      ButtonStatus = MouseState.rgbButtons [ ButtonCode ];

      if ( ButtonStatus & BUTTON_DOWN_MASK )
         return true;

      return false;
   }


   bool DirectInputMouse::ButtonUp ( DWORD ButtonCode ) {
      // This function must be overridden in a class derived
      // from DirectInputMouse if the app is to be notified
      // when buttons are released.
      ButtonCode;

      return true;
   }


   bool DirectInputMouse::ButtonDown ( DWORD ButtonCode ) {
      // This function must be overridden in a class derived
      // from DirectInputMouse if the app is to be notified
      // when buttons are pressed.
      ButtonCode;

      return true;
   }


   bool DirectInputMouse::MouseMove () {
      // This function must be overridden in a class derived
      // from DirectInputMouse if the app is to be notified
      // when the mouse is moved.
      return true;
   }


   bool DirectInputMouse::GetBaseInterface (
                          LPDIRECTINPUTDEVICE *Ptr ) {
      if ( Mouse == NULL )
         return false;

      if ( Mouse->QueryInterface ( IID_IDirectInputDevice,
            ( LPVOID * ) Ptr ) != S_OK )
         return false;

      return true;
   }
```

```
bool DirectInputMouse::GetInterface (
                          LPDIRECTINPUTDEVICE2 *Ptr ) {
   if ( Mouse == NULL )
     return false;

   ( *Ptr ) = Mouse;

   ( *Ptr )->AddRef ();

   return true;
}

DirectInputKeyboard::DirectInputKeyboard () {
   Keyboard = NULL;

   HandleInputThread = KillThreadEvent = NULL;

   HandleInputThreadID = 0;

   ZeroMemory ( &KeyboardState, 256 );
}

DirectInputKeyboard::~DirectInputKeyboard () {
   if ( Keyboard != NULL ) {
      // Kill the input handler thread, if active:
      KillHandleInputThread ();

      // Release the input device:
      Keyboard->Release ();

      Keyboard = NULL;
   }
}

bool DirectInputKeyboard::SpawnHandleInputThread ( HWND
     Window ) {
   // The following union allows us to convert a pointer to
   // a member function to one callable by Windows as a
   // thread:
   struct ConverterUnion {
      union {
         LPTHREAD_START_ROUTINE NormalFunction;
         long ( __stdcall DirectInputKeyboard::*
            MemberFunction )( void );
      };
   } Converter;
```

```
   AppWindow = Window;


   Converter.MemberFunction = HandleInput;

   // Create the thread that will handle all input:
   HandleInputThread = CreateThread ( NULL, 0,
      Converter.NormalFunction, ( LPVOID ) this, 0,
      &HandleInputThreadID );

   if ( HandleInputThread == NULL )
      return false;

   return true;
}

bool DirectInputKeyboard::KillHandleInputThread () {
   // Kill the input handler thread if it is active:
   if ( HandleInputThread != NULL ) {
      SetEvent ( KillThreadEvent );

      // Wait for the thread to finish (if it hasn't
      // finished in 10 seconds, kill it):
      if ( WaitForSingleObject ( HandleInputThread, 10000 )
           == WAIT_TIMEOUT )
        TerminateThread ( HandleInputThread, 0 );

      HandleInputThread = NULL;
   }

   return true;
}

LONG __stdcall DirectInputKeyboard::HandleInput () {
   // This function handles all input from the keyboard
   // device.  It is created as a thread and executes
   // continuously until the program ends.
   const DWORD   MAX_ITEMS = DIKEYBOARD_BUFFER_SIZE,
                 KEY_DOWN_MASK = 0x80;

   DWORD         I, TriggeredEvents, ItemCount,
                 KeyCode, KeyState;
   HANDLE        EventList [ 2 ], KeyboardEvent;
   HRESULT       Result;
   bool          AccessAcquired, RunThread = true;
   DIPROPDWORD   Property;
```

```
DIDEVICEOBJECTDATA ObjectData [ MAX_ITEMS ];

if ( Keyboard == NULL )
   return 0;

// Set the cooperative level for the keyboard to
// foreground nonexclusive::
if ( Keyboard->SetCooperativeLevel ( AppWindow,
   DISCL_FOREGROUND | DISCL_NONEXCLUSIVE ) != DI_OK )
   return 0;

// Use the default keyboard data format:
if ( Keyboard->SetDataFormat ( &c_dfDIKeyboard )
     != DI_OK )
   return 0;

// Set the size of the buffer, because we use buffered
// data:
Property.diph.dwSize       = sizeof ( DIPROPDWORD );
Property.diph.dwHeaderSize = sizeof ( DIPROPHEADER );
Property.diph.dwHow        = DIPH_DEVICE;
Property.diph.dwObj        = 0;
Property.dwData            = DIKEYBOARD_BUFFER_SIZE;

if ( FAILED ( Keyboard->SetProperty ( DIPROP_BUFFERSIZE,
            ( DIPROPHEADER * ) &Property ) ) )
   return 0;

// Create a keyboard event that will be triggered whenever
// the state of the keyboard changes:
KeyboardEvent = CreateEvent ( NULL, FALSE, FALSE,
                              NULL );

// Create an event that, when set, will trigger the
// termination of this thread:
KillThreadEvent = CreateEvent ( NULL, TRUE, FALSE,
                                NULL );

// Tell DirectInput to notify us of keyboard state
// changes:
Keyboard->SetEventNotification ( KeyboardEvent );

EventList [ 0 ] = KeyboardEvent;
EventList [ 1 ] = KillThreadEvent;

AccessAcquired = false;
```

```
while ( RunThread ) {
   // If access to the device's input data is possible,
   // wait for either that data or the termination of
   // this thread:
   if ( AccessAcquired ) {
      // Wait for either a keyboard event or an event that
      // triggers the destruction of this thread:
      TriggeredEvents =
         WaitForMultipleObjects ( 2, EventList, FALSE,
                                     INFINITE );

      // Determine which event (either a keyboard event or
      // a thread termination event) occurred:
      switch ( TriggeredEvents ) {
         case ( WAIT_OBJECT_0 ): {
            // A Keyboard event occurred:

            // Get the data from the keyboard:
            ItemCount = MAX_ITEMS;
            Result = Keyboard->GetDeviceData (
               sizeof ( DIDEVICEOBJECTDATA ),
               ObjectData, &ItemCount, 0 );

            if ( Result != DI_OK ) {
               AccessAcquired = false;
            }
            else {
               // Loop through all buffered data
               // elements:
               for ( I = 0; I < ItemCount; I++ ) {
                  // Here we immediately call the event
                  // handler KeyUp () or KeyDown ()
                  // to handle the state change and
                  // also save the change to the
                  // KeyboardState structure:

                  KeyCode  = ObjectData [ I ].dwOfs;
                  KeyState = ObjectData [ I ].dwData;

                  KeyboardState [ KeyCode ] =
                     ( BYTE ) KeyState;

                  if ( KeyState & KEY_DOWN_MASK ) {
                     KeyDown ( KeyCode );
                  }
```

```
                        else {
                            KeyUp ( KeyCode );
                        }
                    }
                }

                break;
            }

            case ( WAIT_OBJECT_0 + 1 ): {
                // The thread should die:
                RunThread = false;
                break;
            }
        }
    }
}
// If access to the device is not possible, then 1)
// check to see if the thread should be killed and
// if so kill it; 2) if not, try to acquire access
// to the device:
else {
    // Check to see if the thread must be killed:
    if ( WaitForSingleObject ( KillThreadEvent, 0 )
        == WAIT_OBJECT_0 )
        RunThread = false;

    else {
        // Attempt to acquire access to the device now:
        if ( Keyboard->Acquire () == DI_OK ) {
            // Retrieve the current state of the keyboard:
            Keyboard->GetDeviceState ( 256,
                KeyboardState );

            AccessAcquired = true;
        }

        // If access is not available now, it is
        // probably because the application does not
        // have input focus.  Here we wait half a
        // second (to avoid hogging the system) and
        // then continue the loop and try to
        // acquire access again.  This way the calling
        // app never has to worry about reacquiring
        // access when it regains input focus.
```

```
                else {
                    Sleep ( 500 );
                }
            }
        }
    }

    // Turn off event notification:
    Keyboard->SetEventNotification ( NULL );

    // Close all handles:
    CloseHandle ( KillThreadEvent );
    CloseHandle ( KeyboardEvent );

    // Unacquire access to the device:
    Keyboard->Unacquire ();

    return 1;
}

bool DirectInputKeyboard::Flush () {
    DWORD ItemCount = INFINITE;

    // Flush all data in the buffer:
    if ( Keyboard->GetDeviceData (
            sizeof ( DIDEVICEOBJECTDATA ),
                NULL, &ItemCount, 0 ) != DI_OK )
        return false;

    return true;
}

bool DirectInputKeyboard::GetKeyStatus ( DWORD KeyCode ) {
    const DWORD KEY_DOWN_MASK = 0x80;
    DWORD KeyStatus;

    if ( KeyCode >= 256 )
        return false;

    KeyStatus = KeyboardState [ KeyCode ];

    if ( KeyStatus & KEY_DOWN_MASK )
        return true;

    return false;
}
```

```
bool DirectInputKeyboard::KeyUp ( DWORD KeyCode ) {
   // This function must be overridden in a class derived
   // from DirectInputKeyboard if the app is to be notified
   // when keys are released.
   KeyCode;

   return true;
}

bool DirectInputKeyboard::KeyDown ( DWORD KeyCode ) {
   // This function must be overridden in a class derived
   // from DirectInputKeyboard if the app is to be notified
   // when keys are pressed.
   KeyCode;

   return true;
}

bool DirectInputKeyboard::GetBaseInterface (
                            LPDIRECTINPUTDEVICE *Ptr ) {
   if ( Keyboard == NULL )
      return false;

   if ( Keyboard->QueryInterface ( IID_IDirectInputDevice,
         ( LPVOID * ) Ptr ) != S_OK )
      return false;

   return true;
}

bool DirectInputKeyboard::GetInterface (
                            LPDIRECTINPUTDEVICE2 *Ptr ) {
   if ( Keyboard == NULL )
      return false;

   ( *Ptr ) = Keyboard;

   ( *Ptr )->AddRef ();

   return true;
}

DirectInputJoystick::DirectInputJoystick () {
   Joystick = NULL;
}
```

```
DirectInputJoystick::~DirectInputJoystick () {
    if ( Joystick != NULL ) {
        // Kill the input handler thread, if active:
        KillHandleInputThread ();

        // Release the input device:
        Joystick->Release ();

        Joystick = NULL;
    }
}

bool DirectInputJoystick::GetRange ( DWORD ObjOffset,
                                     double &Min,
                                     double &Max ) {
    DIPROPRANGE RangeProp;

    if ( Joystick == NULL )
        return false;

    // Retrieve the range of the specified object:
    RangeProp.diph.dwSize       = sizeof ( DIPROPRANGE );
    RangeProp.diph.dwHeaderSize = sizeof ( DIPROPHEADER );
    RangeProp.diph.dwHow        = DIPH_BYOFFSET;
    RangeProp.diph.dwObj        = ObjOffset;

    if ( FAILED ( Joystick->GetProperty ( DIPROP_RANGE,
                    ( LPDIPROPHEADER ) &RangeProp ) ) ) {
        Min = 0.0;
        Max = 1.0;
        return false;
    }

    Min = RangeProp.lMin;
    Max = RangeProp.lMax;

    return true;
}

bool DirectInputJoystick::StoreConversionData () {
    if ( Joystick == NULL )
        return false;

    // Retrieve the ranges of all input objects except
    // buttons:
    GetRange ( DIJOFS_RX, MinRX, MaxRX );
```

```
        GetRange ( DIJOFS_RY, MinRY, MaxRY );
        GetRange ( DIJOFS_RZ, MinRZ, MaxRZ );
        GetRange ( DIJOFS_X, MinMX, MaxMX );
        GetRange ( DIJOFS_Y, MinMY, MaxMY );
        GetRange ( DIJOFS_Z, MinMZ, MaxMZ );

        GetRange ( DIJOFS_SLIDER(0), MinSlider [ 0 ],
           MaxSlider [ 0 ] );

        GetRange ( DIJOFS_SLIDER(1), MinSlider [ 1 ],
           MaxSlider [ 1 ] );

        return true;
    }

    bool DirectInputJoystick::IsDevicePolled () {
        DIDEVCAPS Caps;

        if ( Joystick == NULL )
            return false;

        Caps.dwSize = sizeof ( DIDEVCAPS );

        // Determine if the joystick needs polling:
        Joystick->GetCapabilities ( &Caps );

        if ( Caps.dwFlags & DIDC_POLLEDDEVICE )
            return true;

        return false;
    }

    bool DirectInputJoystick::SpawnPollDeviceThread () {
        // The following union allows us to convert a pointer to
        // a member function to one callable by Windows as a
        // thread:
        struct ConverterUnion {
            union {
                LPTHREAD_START_ROUTINE NormalFunction;
                long ( __stdcall DirectInputJoystick::*
                    MemberFunction )( void );
            };
        } Converter;


        Converter.MemberFunction = PollDevice;
```

```cpp
   // Create the thread that will handle all input:
   PollDeviceThread = CreateThread ( NULL, 0,
      Converter.NormalFunction, ( LPVOID ) this, 0,
      &PollDeviceThreadID );

   if ( PollDeviceThread == NULL )
      return false;

   return true;
}

bool DirectInputJoystick::KillPollDeviceThread () {
   // Kill the poll device thread if it is active:
   if ( PollDeviceThread != NULL ) {
      SetEvent ( KillPollThreadEvent );

      // Wait for the thread to finish (if it hasn't
      // finished in 10 seconds, kill it):
      if ( WaitForSingleObject ( PollDeviceThread, 10000 )
         == WAIT_TIMEOUT )
         TerminateThread ( PollDeviceThread, 0 );

      PollDeviceThread = NULL;
   }

   return true;
}

bool DirectInputJoystick::SpawnHandleInputThread ( HWND
      Window ) {
   // The following union allows us to convert a pointer to
   // a member function to one callable by Windows as a
   // thread:
   struct ConverterUnion {
      union {
         LPTHREAD_START_ROUTINE NormalFunction;
         long ( __stdcall DirectInputJoystick::*
            MemberFunction )( void );
      };
   } Converter;

   AppWindow = Window;


   Converter.MemberFunction = HandleInput;
```

```
    // Create the thread that will handle all input:
    HandleInputThread = CreateThread ( NULL, 0,
        Converter.NormalFunction, ( LPVOID ) this, 0,
        &HandleInputThreadID );

    if ( HandleInputThread == NULL )
        return false;

    return true;
}


bool DirectInputJoystick::KillHandleInputThread () {
    // Kill the input handler thread if it is active:
    if ( HandleInputThread != NULL ) {
        SetEvent ( KillThreadEvent );

        // Wait for the thread to finish (if it hasn't
        // finished in 10 seconds, kill it):
        if ( WaitForSingleObject ( HandleInputThread, 10000 )
            == WAIT_TIMEOUT )
            TerminateThread ( HandleInputThread, 0 );

        HandleInputThread = NULL;
    }

    return true;
}


long __stdcall DirectInputJoystick::PollDevice () {
    // This function polls the joystick at regular intervals
    // for those joysticks (typically analog) that are not
    // event driven.
    const DWORD POLLS_PER_SECOND = 30,
                MAX_ELAPSED = 1000 / POLLS_PER_SECOND;
    DWORD LastPollTime = 0, CurTime, Elapsed, Overshot = 0;
    LONG  SleepPeriod;
    bool RunThread = true;

    if ( Joystick == NULL )
        return 0;

    // Create an event that, when set, will trigger the
    // termination of this thread:
    KillPollThreadEvent = CreateEvent ( NULL, TRUE, FALSE,
        NULL );
```

```
    while ( RunThread ) {
        // Make sure this thread is still supposed to be
        // running:
        if ( WaitForSingleObject ( KillPollThreadEvent, 0 )
            == WAIT_OBJECT_0 ) {
            // If not, terminate it:
            RunThread = false;
        }
        else {
            CurTime = timeGetTime ();

            Elapsed = CurTime - LastPollTime;

            if ( Elapsed > MAX_ELAPSED ) {
                // Poll the joystick:
                Joystick->Poll ();

                // Overshot is a measure of how late we are in
                // polling the device--it is used for the
                // Sleep () function below in determining
                // how much time to wait.
                Overshot    = Elapsed - MAX_ELAPSED;

                LastPollTime = CurTime;
            }
            else {
                // Wait until the next poll time is scheduled:
                SleepPeriod = ( MAX_ELAPSED - Elapsed ) -
                    Overshot;
                if ( SleepPeriod > 0 )
                    Sleep ( SleepPeriod );
            }
        }
    }

    // Discard the "kill poll thread" event:
    CloseHandle ( KillPollThreadEvent );

    return 1;
}

long __stdcall DirectInputJoystick::HandleInput () {
    // This function handles all input from the joystick
    // device.  It is created as a thread and executes
    // continuously until the program ends.
    const DWORD    MAX_ITEMS = DIJOYSTICK_BUFFER_SIZE,
                   BUTTON_DOWN_MASK = 0x80;
```

```
DWORD          I, TriggeredEvents, ItemCount,
               DataOffset, Data, ButtonCode;
HANDLE         EventList [ 2 ], JoystickEvent;
HRESULT        Result;
bool           AccessAcquired, RunThread = true,
               JoystickMoved, JoystickRotated;
DIPROPDWORD    Property;

DIDEVICEOBJECTDATA ObjectData [ MAX_ITEMS ];

if ( Joystick == NULL )
   return 0;

// Set the cooperative level for the joystick to
// foreground nonexclusive:
if ( Joystick->SetCooperativeLevel ( AppWindow,
   DISCL_FOREGROUND | DISCL_NONEXCLUSIVE ) != DI_OK )
   return 0;

// Use the the default joystick data format
// (Note: the c_dfDIJoystick2 default format provides
// support for more features, but most joysticks don't
// even support the c_dfDIJoystick format's features):
if ( Joystick->SetDataFormat ( &c_dfDIJoystick )
     != DI_OK )
   return 0;

// Set the size of the buffer, because we use buffered
// data:
Property.diph.dwSize       = sizeof ( DIPROPDWORD );
Property.diph.dwHeaderSize = sizeof ( DIPROPHEADER );
Property.diph.dwHow        = DIPH_DEVICE;
Property.diph.dwObj        = 0;
Property.dwData            = DIJOYSTICK_BUFFER_SIZE;

if ( FAILED ( Joystick->SetProperty ( DIPROP_BUFFERSIZE,
            ( DIPROPHEADER * ) &Property ) ) )
   return 0;

// Create a joystick event that will be triggered whenever
// the state of the joystick changes:
JoystickEvent = CreateEvent ( NULL, FALSE, FALSE,
                              NULL );

// Create an event that, when set, will trigger the
// termination of this thread:
KillThreadEvent = CreateEvent ( NULL, TRUE, FALSE,
                                NULL );
```

```
// Tell DirectInput to notify us of joystick state
// changes:
Joystick->SetEventNotification ( JoystickEvent );

// Find the range for all input objects (except buttons):
StoreConversionData ();

EventList [ 0 ] = JoystickEvent;
EventList [ 1 ] = KillThreadEvent;

AccessAcquired = false;

// If the device is polled, spawn a thread that will
// periodically poll it:
if ( IsDevicePolled () )
   SpawnPollDeviceThread ();

while ( RunThread ) {
   // If access to the device's input data is possible,
   // wait for either that data or the termination of
   // this thread:
   if ( AccessAcquired ) {
      // Wait for either a joystick event or an event that
      // triggers the destruction of this thread:
      TriggeredEvents =
         WaitForMultipleObjects ( 2, EventList, FALSE,
                                     INFINITE );

      // Determine which event (either a joystick event or
      // a thread termination event) occurred:
      switch ( TriggeredEvents ) {
         case ( WAIT_OBJECT_0 ): {
            // A Joystick event occurred:

            // Get the data from the joystick:
            ItemCount = MAX_ITEMS;
            Result = Joystick->GetDeviceData (
               sizeof ( DIDEVICEOBJECTDATA ),
               ObjectData, &ItemCount, 0 );

            if ( Result != DI_OK ) {
               AccessAcquired = false;
            }
            else {
               // Loop through all buffered data
```

```
                    // elements:
                    for ( I = 0; I < ItemCount; I++ ) {
                       DataOffset = ObjectData [ I ].dwOfs;
                       Data       = ObjectData [ I ].dwData;

                       JoystickMoved   = false;
                       JoystickRotated = false;

                       switch ( DataOffset ) {
                          case ( DIJOFS_X ): {
                             // Movement x axis changed
                             JoystickState.lX = Data;
                             JoystickMoved = true;
                             break;
                          }
                          case ( DIJOFS_Y ): {
                             // Movement y axis changed
                             JoystickState.lY = Data;
                             JoystickMoved = true;
                             break;
                          }
                          case ( DIJOFS_Z ): {
                             // Movement z axis changed
                             JoystickState.lZ = Data;
                             JoystickMoved = true;
                             break;
                          }
                          case ( DIJOFS_RX ): {
                             // Movement x axis changed
                             JoystickState.lRx = Data;
                             JoystickRotated = true;
                             break;
                          }
                          case ( DIJOFS_RY ): {
                             // Movement y axis changed
                             JoystickState.lRy = Data;
                             JoystickRotated = true;
                             break;
                          }
                          case ( DIJOFS_RZ ): {
                             // Movement z axis changed
                             JoystickState.lRz = Data;
                             JoystickRotated = true;
                             break;
                          }
```

```
case ( DIJOFS_POV(0) ): {
   // A POV control changed
   JoystickState.rgdwPOV [ 0 ]
      = Data;

   POVMove ( 0 );
   break;
}
case ( DIJOFS_POV(1) ): {
   // A POV control changed
   JoystickState.rgdwPOV [ 1 ]
      = Data;

   POVMove ( 1 );
   break;
}
case ( DIJOFS_POV(2) ): {
   // A POV control changed
   JoystickState.rgdwPOV [ 2 ]
      = Data;

   POVMove ( 2 );
   break;
}
case ( DIJOFS_POV(3) ): {
   // A POV control changed
   JoystickState.rgdwPOV [ 3 ]
      = Data;

   POVMove ( 3 );
   break;
}
case ( DIJOFS_SLIDER(0) ): {
   // A slider changed
   JoystickState.rglSlider [ 0 ] =
      Data;

   SliderMove ( 0 );
   break;
}
case ( DIJOFS_SLIDER(1) ): {
   // A slider changed
   JoystickState.rglSlider [ 1 ] =
      Data;
```

```
            SliderMove ( 1 );
            break;
    }
    default: {
        if ( ( DataOffset >=
                DIJOFS_BUTTON0 ) &&
              ( DataOffset <=
                DIJOFS_BUTTON31 ) ) {
            // A button changed

            // Because one byte is used per
            // button, we can find the
            // button number (0-31)
            // easily:
            ButtonCode = DataOffset -
                        DIJOFS_BUTTON0;

            // Save the button change
            // to the JoystickState
            // structure:
            JoystickState.rgbButtons
                [ ButtonCode ] =
                    ( BYTE ) Data;

            // Call the appropriate event
            // handler:
            if ( Data &
                BUTTON_DOWN_MASK ) {
                ButtonDown ( ButtonCode );
            }
            else {
                ButtonUp ( ButtonCode );
            }
        }
        break;
    }
}

// If the joystick moved, call the
// event handler:
if ( JoystickMoved )
    JoystickMove ();

// If the joystick was rotated, call
// the event handler:
```

```
                    if ( JoystickRotated )
                        JoystickRotate ();
                }
            }

            break;
        }

        case ( WAIT_OBJECT_0 + 1 ): {
            // The thread should die:
            RunThread = false;
            break;
        }
    }
}
// If access to the device is not possible, then 1)
// check to see if the thread should be killed and
// if so kill it; 2) if not, try to acquire access
// to the device:
else {
    // Check to see if the thread must be killed:
    if ( WaitForSingleObject ( KillThreadEvent, 0 )
        == WAIT_OBJECT_0 )
        RunThread = false;

    else {
        // Attempt to acquire access to the device now:
        if ( Joystick->Acquire () == DI_OK ) {
            // Retrieve the current state of the joystick:
            Joystick->GetDeviceState (
                sizeof ( DIJOYSTATE ), &JoystickState );

            AccessAcquired = true;
        }

        // If access is not available now, it is
        // probably because the application does not
        // have input focus.  Here we wait half a
        // second (to avoid hogging the system) and
        // then continue the loop and try to
        // acquire access again.  This way the calling
        // app never has to worry about reacquiring
        // access when it regains input focus.
```

```
                else {
                    Sleep ( 500 );
                }
            }
        }
    }

    // Turn off event notification:
    Joystick->SetEventNotification ( NULL );

    // Close all handles:
    CloseHandle ( KillThreadEvent );
    CloseHandle ( JoystickEvent );

    // If the device is polled, kill the thread that has
    // been polling it:
    if ( IsDevicePolled () )
        KillPollDeviceThread ();

    // Unacquire access to the device:
    Joystick->Unacquire ();

    return 1;
}

bool DirectInputJoystick::Flush () {
    DWORD ItemCount = INFINITE;

    // Flush all data in the buffer:
    if ( Joystick->GetDeviceData (
             sizeof ( DIDEVICEOBJECTDATA ),
                 NULL, &ItemCount, 0 ) != DI_OK )
        return false;

    return true;
}

double DirectInputJoystick::GetMovementX () {
    double Value;

    Value = JoystickState.lX;

    return ( Value - MinMX ) / ( MaxMX - MinMX );
}

double DirectInputJoystick::GetMovementY () {
    double Value;
```

```
   Value = JoystickState.lY;

   return ( Value - MinMY ) / ( MaxMY - MinMY );
}

double DirectInputJoystick::GetMovementZ () {
   double Value;

   Value = JoystickState.lZ;

   return ( Value - MinMZ ) / ( MaxMZ - MinMZ );
}

double DirectInputJoystick::GetRotationX () {
   double Value;

   Value = JoystickState.lRx;

   return ( Value - MinRX ) / ( MaxRX - MinRX );
}

double DirectInputJoystick::GetRotationY () {
   double Value;

   Value = JoystickState.lRy;

   return ( Value - MinRY ) / ( MaxRY - MinRY );
}

double DirectInputJoystick::GetRotationZ () {
   double Value;

   Value = JoystickState.lRz;

   return ( Value - MinRZ ) / ( MaxRZ - MinRZ );
}

double DirectInputJoystick::GetSlider ( DWORD Number ) {
   double Value;

   if ( Number >= 2 )
      return 0.0;

   Value = JoystickState.rglSlider [ Number ];
```

```
      return ( Value - MinSlider [ Number ] ) /
            ( MaxSlider [ Number ] - MinSlider [ Number ] );
}

double DirectInputJoystick::GetPOV ( DWORD Number ) {
   double Value;

   if ( Number >= 2 )
      return 0.0;

   Value = JoystickState.rgdwPOV [ Number ];

   // If the POV control is centered, return POV_CENTERED:
   if ( LOWORD ( ( DWORD ) Value ) == 0xFFFF )
      return POV_CENTERED;

   // Otherwise, convert to degrees:
   return Value / 100.0;
}

DWORD DirectInputJoystick::GetButtonCount () {
   DIDEVCAPS Caps;

   if ( Joystick == NULL )
      return 0;

   Caps.dwSize = sizeof ( DIDEVCAPS );

   // Retrieve the number of buttons on the joystick:
   Joystick->GetCapabilities ( &Caps );

   return Caps.dwButtons;
}

bool DirectInputJoystick::GetButtonStatus (
                             DWORD ButtonCode ) {
   const DWORD BUTTON_DOWN_MASK = 0x80;
   DWORD ButtonStatus;

   if ( ButtonCode >= GetButtonCount () )
      return false;

   ButtonStatus = JoystickState.rgbButtons [ ButtonCode ];

   if ( ButtonStatus & BUTTON_DOWN_MASK )
      return true;
```

```
      return false;
}

bool DirectInputJoystick::ButtonUp ( DWORD ButtonCode ) {
   // This function must be overridden in a class derived
   // from DirectInputJoystick if the app is to be notified
   // when buttons are released.
   ButtonCode;

   return true;
}

bool DirectInputJoystick::ButtonDown ( DWORD ButtonCode ) {
   // This function must be overridden in a class derived
   // from DirectInputJoystick if the app is to be notified
   // when buttons are pressed.
   ButtonCode;

   return true;
}

bool DirectInputJoystick::JoystickMove () {
   // This function must be overridden in a class derived
   // from DirectInputJoystick if the app is to be notified
   // when the joystick's movement axes change positions.

   return true;
}

bool DirectInputJoystick::JoystickRotate () {
   // This function must be overridden in a class derived
   // from DirectInputJoystick if the app is to be notified
   // when the joystick's rotation axes change orientation.

   return true;
}

bool DirectInputJoystick::SliderMove ( DWORD SliderCode ) {
   // This function must be overridden in a class derived
   // from DirectInputJoystick if the app is to be notified
   // when the joystick's sliders change position.

   return true;
}
```

```
bool DirectInputJoystick::POVMove ( DWORD POVCode ) {
   // This function must be overridden in a class derived
   // from DirectInputJoystick if the app is to be notified
   // when the joystick's POV controls change.

   return true;
}

bool DirectInputJoystick::GetBaseInterface (
                              LPDIRECTINPUTDEVICE *Ptr ) {
   if ( Joystick == NULL )
      return false;

   if ( FAILED ( Joystick->QueryInterface (
          IID_IDirectInputDevice, ( LPVOID * ) Ptr ) ) )
      return false;

   return true;
}

bool DirectInputJoystick::GetInterface (
                              LPDIRECTINPUTDEVICE2 *Ptr ) {
   if ( Joystick == NULL )
      return false;

   ( *Ptr ) = Joystick;

   ( *Ptr )->AddRef ();

   return true;
}

DirectInputManager::DirectInputManager () {
   DirectInput = NULL;
}

DirectInputManager::~DirectInputManager () {
   if ( DirectInput != NULL ) {
      DirectInput->Release ();
      DirectInput = NULL;
   }
}
```

```
bool DirectInputManager::Initialize ( HWND Window,
                                      HINSTANCE Instance ) {
    AppWindow = Window;

    // Create a DirectInput object:
    if ( DirectInputCreate ( Instance, DIRECTINPUT_VERSION,
        &DirectInput, NULL ) != DI_OK )
        return false;

    return true;
}

bool DirectInputManager::CreateMouse ( DirectInputMouse
                                       &Mouse ) {
    LPDIRECTINPUTDEVICE Device;

    if ( DirectInput == NULL )
        return false;

    // Create the default system mouse device:
    if ( DirectInput->CreateDevice ( GUID_SysMouse, &Device,
        NULL ) != DI_OK )
        return false;

    // Obtain the newest DirectInputDevice interface:
    if ( Device->QueryInterface ( IID_IDirectInputDevice2,
        ( void ** ) &Mouse.Mouse ) != S_OK )
        return false;

    // Discard the older interface:
    Device->Release ();

    // Spawn the thread that handles input:
    if ( !Mouse.SpawnHandleInputThread ( AppWindow ) )
        return false;

    // Turn off the mouse cursor (the spawned thread cannot
    // do this--it must be done inside the main thread):
    ShowCursor ( FALSE );

    return true;
}

bool DirectInputManager::CreateKeyboard (
                         DirectInputKeyboard &Keyboard ) {
    LPDIRECTINPUTDEVICE Device;
```

```
   if ( DirectInput == NULL )
      return false;

   // Create the default system keyboard device:
   if ( DirectInput->CreateDevice ( GUID_SysKeyboard,
                          &Device, NULL ) != DI_OK )
      return false;

   // Obtain the newest DirectInputDevice interface:
   if ( Device->QueryInterface ( IID_IDirectInputDevice2,
        ( void ** ) &Keyboard.Keyboard ) != S_OK )
      return false;

   // Discard the older interface:
   Device->Release ();

   // Spawn the thread that handles input:
   if ( !Keyboard.SpawnHandleInputThread ( AppWindow ) )
      return false;

   return true;
}


BOOL CALLBACK FindJoystick ( LPCDIDEVICEINSTANCE DevInst,
                             LPVOID Data ) {
   DWORD DevType, DevSubType;

   // Retrieve the device type and subtype:
   DevType    = LOBYTE ( LOWORD ( DevInst->dwDevType ) );
   DevSubType = HIBYTE ( LOWORD ( DevInst->dwDevType ) );


   if ( DevType == DIDEVTYPE_JOYSTICK ) {
      // Simply use the first joystick (check DevSubType
      // to be more precise):
      ( *( ( GUID * ) Data ) ) = DevInst->guidInstance;
      return DIENUM_STOP;
   }

   return DIENUM_CONTINUE;
}



bool DirectInputManager::CreateJoystick (
        DirectInputJoystick &Joystick ) {
   GUID JoystickGUID;
   LPDIRECTINPUTDEVICE Device;
```

```
   if ( DirectInput == NULL )
      return false;

   // Find either a traditional joystick or a flight stick
   // attached to the computer:
   if ( FAILED ( DirectInput->EnumDevices (
         DIDEVTYPE_JOYSTICK, FindJoystick,
         ( LPVOID ) &JoystickGUID, DIEDFL_ATTACHEDONLY ) ) )
      return false;

   // Create the joystick input device:
   if ( FAILED ( DirectInput->CreateDevice ( JoystickGUID,
                                 &Device, NULL ) ) )
      return false;

   // Obtain the newest interface:
   if ( Device->QueryInterface ( IID_IDirectInputDevice2,
                  ( LPVOID * ) &Joystick.Joystick ) )
      return false;

   // Discard the old interface:
   Device->Release ();

   // Spawn the thread that handles input:
   if ( !Joystick.SpawnHandleInputThread ( AppWindow ) )
      return false;

   return true;
}

bool DirectInputManager::GetInterface (
         LPDIRECTINPUT *Ptr ) {

   if ( DirectInput == NULL )
      return false;

   ( *Ptr ) = DirectInput;

   ( *Ptr )->AddRef ();

   return true;
}
```

Reference Table 13.1   The class reference for DirectInputManager.

Class Declaration

```
class DirectInputManager {
   protected:
      LPDIRECTINPUT DirectInput;

      HWND AppWindow;
   public:
      DirectInputManager ();
      ~DirectInputManager ();

      bool Initialize ( HWND Window, HINSTANCE Instance );

      bool CreateMouse ( DirectInputMouse &Mouse );

      bool CreateKeyboard ( DirectInputKeyboard
                              &Keyboard );

      bool CreateJoystick ( DirectInputJoystick
                              &Joystick );

      bool GetInterface ( LPDIRECTINPUT *Ptr );
};
```

Member Function	Description
Initialize	Initializes the DirectInputManager object, which involves creating a DirectInput object.
CreateMouse	Creates and initializes a DirectInputMouse object.
CreateKeyboard	Creates and initializes a DirectInputKeyboard object.
CreateJoystick	Creates and initializes a DirectInputJoystick object.
GetInterface	Retrieves the IDirectInput interface.

Reference Table 13.2   The class reference for DirectInputMouse.

Class Declaration

```
class DirectInputMouse {
   private:
      DIMOUSESTATE MouseState;

      LONG LastX, LastY, LastZ;

      double OutputX, OutputY, OutputZ, ZGran, Accel;

      HWND AppWindow;
```

Reference Table 13.2   The class reference for DirectInputMouse (continued).

Class Declaration

```
   DWORD  HandleInputThreadID;
      HANDLE HandleInputThread, KillThreadEvent;

      LONG __stdcall HandleInput ();

      bool UpdateMousePosition ();
      bool SpawnHandleInputThread ( HWND Window );
      bool KillHandleInputThread ();

      friend class DirectInputManager;
   protected:
      LPDIRECTINPUTDEVICE2 Mouse;

   public:
      DirectInputMouse ();
      ~DirectInputMouse ();

      LONG GetX ();
      LONG GetY ();
      LONG GetZ ();

      bool SetAcceleration ( double NewAccel =
         DEFAULT_MOUSE_ACCEL );

      double GetAcceleration ();

      bool Flush ();

      DWORD GetButtonCount ();

      bool GetButtonStatus ( DWORD ButtonCode );

      virtual bool ButtonUp   ( DWORD ButtonCode );
      virtual bool ButtonDown ( DWORD ButtonCode );
      virtual bool MouseMove  ();

      bool GetBaseInterface ( LPDIRECTINPUTDEVICE *Ptr );
      bool GetInterface ( LPDIRECTINPUTDEVICE2 *Ptr );
};
```

(continued)

Reference Table 13.2   The class reference for DirectInputMouse *(continued)*.

Member Function	Description
GetX	Retrieves the x-coordinate of the mouse cursor, in pixels.
GetY	Retrieves the y-coordinate of the mouse cursor, in pixels.
GetZ	Retrieves the position of the mouse wheel relative to its last position. The smallest unit of change this function will report is 1 or -1. The largest unit of change depends on the mouse wheel and how fast it is turned.
SetAcceleration	Sets the acceleration of the mouse. This typically ranges from 0.0 (where the mouse is decelerated) to 0.5 (where no acceleration or deceleration is applied) to 1.0 (where the mouse is accelerated). The default is 0.7.
GetAcceleration	Retrieves the acceleration of the mouse. This typically ranges from 0.0 (where the mouse is decelerated) to 0.5 (where no acceleration or deceleration is applied) to 1.0 (where the mouse is accelerated). The default is 0.7.
Flush	Clears the buffer of all data waiting to be processed.
GetButtonCount	Retrieves the number of buttons on the mouse.
GetButtonStatus	Retrieves the status of a button: true if it is pressed, false if it is not.
ButtonUp	This is a virtual function that can be overridden in a derived class. The function is called whenever a mouse button is released. It is passed the number of the button released.
ButtonDown	This is a virtual function that can be overridden in a derived class. The function is called whenever a mouse button is pressed. It is passed the number of the button pressed.
MouseMove	This is a virtual function that can be overridden in a derived class. The function is called whenever the mouse or the mouse wheel is moved.
GetBaseInterface	Retrieves the IDirectInputDevice interface.
GetInterface	Retrieves the IDirectInputDevice2 interface.

Reference Table 13.3   The class reference for DirectInputKeyboard.

Class Declaration

```
class DirectInputKeyboard {
   private:
      BYTE KeyboardState [ 256 ];

      DWORD HandleInputThreadID;

      HANDLE HandleInputThread, KillThreadEvent;

      HWND AppWindow;
```

(continued)

Reference Table 13.3   The class reference for DirectInputKeyboard *(continued).*

Class Declaration

```
      long __stdcall HandleInput ();

   bool SpawnHandleInputThread ( HWND Window );
   bool KillHandleInputThread ();

   friend class DirectInputManager;
protected:
   LPDIRECTINPUTDEVICE2 Keyboard;

public:
   DirectInputKeyboard ();
   ~DirectInputKeyboard ();

   bool Flush ();

   bool GetKeyStatus ( DWORD KeyCode );

   virtual bool KeyUp   ( DWORD KeyCode );
   virtual bool KeyDown ( DWORD KeyCode );

   bool GetBaseInterface ( LPDIRECTINPUTDEVICE *Ptr );
   bool GetInterface ( LPDIRECTINPUTDEVICE2 *Ptr );
};
*
```

Member Function	Description
Flush	Clears the buffer of all data waiting to be processed.
GetKeyStatus	Retrieves the status of a key: true if the key is pressed, false if it is not.
KeyUp	This is a virtual function that can be overridden in a derived class. The function is called whenever a key is released. It is passed the DirectInput offset of the key released (see Table 13.1).
KeyDown	This is a virtual function that can be overridden in a derived class. The function is called whenever a key is pressed. It is passed the DirectInput offset of the key pressed (see Table 13.1).
GetBaseInterface	Retrieves the IDirectInputDevice interface.
GetInterface	Retrieves the IDirectInputDevice2 interface.

Reference Table 13.4   The class reference for DirectInputJoystick.

Class Declaration

```
class DirectInputJoystick {
   private:
      DIJOYSTATE JoystickState;

      double MinMX, MinMY, MinMZ,
             MaxMX, MaxMY, MaxMZ,
             MinRX, MinRY, MinRZ,
             MaxRX, MaxRY, MaxRZ,
             MinSlider [ 2 ],
             MaxSlider [ 2 ];

      DWORD PollDeviceThreadID, HandleInputThreadID;

      HANDLE HandleInputThread, KillThreadEvent,
             PollDeviceThread, KillPollThreadEvent;

      HWND AppWindow;

      bool StoreConversionData ();
      bool IsDevicePolled ();
      bool DirectInputJoystick::GetRange ( DWORD ObjOffset,
             double &Min, double &Max );

      long __stdcall PollDevice ();
      long __stdcall HandleInput ();

      bool SpawnPollDeviceThread ();
      bool KillPollDeviceThread ();

      bool SpawnHandleInputThread ( HWND Window );
      bool KillHandleInputThread ();

      friend class DirectInputManager;
   protected:
      LPDIRECTINPUTDEVICE2 Joystick;

   public:
      DirectInputJoystick ();
      ~DirectInputJoystick ();

      bool Flush ();
```

(continued)

Reference Table 13.4   The class reference for DirectInputJoystick *(continued)*.

Class Declaration

```
      double GetMovementX ();
      double GetMovementY ();
      double GetMovementZ ();

      double GetRotationX ();
      double GetRotationY ();
      double GetRotationZ ();

      double GetSlider ( DWORD SliderCode );
      double GetPOV ( DWORD Number );

      DWORD GetButtonCount ();

      bool GetButtonStatus ( DWORD ButtonCode );

      virtual bool ButtonUp   ( DWORD ButtonCode );
      virtual bool ButtonDown ( DWORD ButtonCode );

      virtual bool JoystickMove ();
      virtual bool JoystickRotate ();

      virtual bool SliderMove ( DWORD SliderCode );
      virtual bool POVMove ( DWORD POVCode );

      bool GetBaseInterface ( LPDIRECTINPUTDEVICE *Ptr );
      bool GetInterface ( LPDIRECTINPUTDEVICE2 *Ptr );
};
```

Member Function	Description
Flush	Clears the buffer of all data waiting to be processed.
GetMovementX	Retrieves the position of the x-axis representing movement. This can vary from 0.0 to 0.5 (the center position) to 1.0.
GetMovementY	Retrieves the position of the y-axis representing movement. This can vary from 0.0 to 0.5 (the center position) to 1.0.
GetMovementZ	Retrieves the position of the z-axis representing movement. On most joysticks, this is the throttle control. This can vary from 0.0 to 0.5 (the center position) to 1.0.
GetRotationX	Retrieves the position of the x-axis representing rotation. This can vary from 0.0 to 0.5 (the center position) to 1.0.
GetRotationY	Retrieves the position of the y-axis representing rotation. This can vary from 0.0 to 0.5 (the center position) to 1.0.

(continued)

Reference Table 13.4 The class reference for DirectInputJoystick *(continued)*.	
Member Function	**Description**
GetRotationZ	Retrieves the position of the z-axis representing rotation. On most joysticks, this is the rudder control. This can vary from 0.0 to 0.5 (the center position) to 1.0.
GetSlider	Retrieves the position of one of the joystick's sliders. This can vary from 0.0 to 0.5 (the center position) to 1.0.
GetPOV	Retrieves the orientation of one of the joystick's POV controls. If the POV control is centered, then its orientation is reported as **POV_CENTERED**. Otherwise, the orientation is given in degrees clockwise from the north direction.
GetButtonCount	Retrieves the number of buttons on the joystick.
GetButtonStatus	Retrieves the status of a button: true if it is pressed, false if it is not.
ButtonUp	This is a virtual function that can be overridden in a derived class. The function is called whenever a joystick button is released. It is passed the number of the button released.
ButtonDown	This is a virtual function that can be overridden in a derived class. The function is called whenever a joystick button is pressed. It is passed the number of the button pressed.
JoystickMove	This is a virtual function that can be overridden in a derived class. The function is called whenever the joystick moves (that is, any of its movement axes change position).
JoystickRotate	This is a virtual function that can be overridden in a derived class. The function is called whenever the joystick rotates (that is, any of its rotation axes change orientation).
SliderMove	This is a virtual function that can be overridden in a derived class. The function is called whenever a joystick slider changes position. It is passed the number of the slider that changed.
POVMove	This is a virtual function that can be overridden in a derived class. The function is called whenever a joystick POV control is changed. It is passed the number of the POV control changed.
GetBaseInterface	Retrieves the IDirectInputDevice interface.
GetInterface	Retrieves the IDirectInputDevice2 interface.

Using The Encapsulation

You can use the classes found in Listings 13.1 and 13.2 by including the header DirectInput.HPP in your files and by adding DirectInput.CPP to your project. Here are some points to keep in mind as you write applications around these classes:

◆ The **DirectInputMouse**, **DirectInputKeyboard**, and **DirectInputJoystick** classes all use threads to monitor constantly for input, calling the appropriate functions whenever input events are generated.

♦ You can have your application notified when the state of any input device changes by creating a derived class that overrides the virtual functions in **DirectInputMouse**, **DirectInputKeyboard**, or **DirectInputJoystick**. See Reference Tables 13.1 through 13.3 for the specific functions you can override.

♦ All three input device classes automatically reacquire access whenever your application regains input focus. This frees you from manually monitoring the state of your application and requesting access whenever it is reactivated.

♦ You must paint your own cursor when using the **DirectInputMouse** class. Because DirectInput reports mouse movement in mickeys rather than pixels, the class must perform a mickey-to-pixel conversion based on its own acceleration settings. The resulting pixel coordinates may differ from the position of the cursor as displayed by Windows, however; thus, you need to paint your own cursor.

♦ The **DirectInputJoystick** class works both with devices that require polling and with those that do not. It works with the former group of devices by spawning a thread that polls the device at regular intervals. Note that with devices that require polling, such functions as **DirectInputJoystick::JoystickMove ()** will be called continually, even if the joystick's axes are not actually moving.

♦ The **DirectInputJoystick** class maps almost all values to a [0, 1] range, regardless of the particular joystick being used.

♦ The source code is a great demonstration of how you can use more advanced features of DirectInput. The only major feature not explicitly supported by the classes is force-feedback effects, which are relatively rare because of the high cost of force-feedback devices. To support force-feedback effects, you can always call the **DirectInputJoystick::GetInterface ()** function, which retrieves the IDirectInputDevice2 interface, allowing you to work directly with DirectInput.

♦ Remember to include Dinput.lib in your project, because the classes use DirectInput. Also, as with all COM applications, one file in your project must include InitGuid.H, which initializes the GUIDs for use in the application.

Summary

The first step in creating an application that uses DirectInput is to create a DirectInput object. You can then use this object to list input devices supported by the system and create DirectInputDevice objects to represent them.

Each DirectInputDevice object has a cooperative level and a data format, both of which must be set after the device is created. For applications that require buffered data, the size of the device's buffer must also be set. Some devices, such as mice and joysticks, have axes. You can modify the way in which DirectInput reports axis information by changing the device's axis mode.

Accessing device data can be done one of two ways: You can request immediate data, which retrieves the state of the device at that moment, or you can request buffered data, which reports all of the device state changes.

Chapter 14
Artificial Intelligence

One of the most important components in all computer games is the computer-generated character. Characters breathe life into a story and animate a virtual world to a degree not otherwise possible. Whether they are ghosts as in a Pac Man-like game, aliens as in Sierra's Halflife, or more fleshed-out and realistic as in Gabriel Knight 3, characters are a staple of computer entertainment, and learning how to create them is a prerequisite to writing just about any computer game.

In this chapter, I will not explain how to represent characters *visually* (characters are just animated polygonal objects, as covered in Chapter 2), but I will show how to give characters intelligence so they can perform a task, whether it's smiting the player or giving the player key information needed to complete the game. I will start by covering the different types of artificial intelligence (AI) you can give to characters.

Types Of Artificial Intelligence

The arcade game Centipede requires a different type of artificial intelligence than do the characters in LucasArt's Grim Fandango, which in turn require a different artificial intelligence than those in 3D Realm's Max Payne. In general, the different AIs fall into three categories:

♦ *Scripted "apparent" intelligence*—This category of intelligence includes any characters that can be represented solely by simple scripts, without algorithms. For example, characters that have a number of stock responses, which they can use to reply to preselected questions asked by the player, are in this category. The early Ultima games by Origin fall into this category.

♦ *Simple algorithmic intelligence*—This category describes intelligence that relies on one or just a few algorithms. For example, the ghosts in a Pac Man game have a maze-traversing algorithm, which enables them to navigate the maze and find Pac Man. Even many 3D games use no more than a 3D navigation algorithm to empower their characters.

♦ *Complex algorithmic intelligence*—This category describes intelligence that relies on many, usually complex algorithms. The AI of a strategy game, for example, typically attains this level of intelligence, though each of its field units (such as a tank or a military squadron) may individually use only simple algorithmic intelligence. Some more complex computer opponents that, for example, use a sword or fly in a space fighter, also fall into this category.

Most of today's games, and certainly all of tomorrow's, incorporate the complex algorithmic intelligence of the third method, rather than the simpler intelligence of the first two. Although today's games often combine elements of these simpler categories of intelligence, such as path-finding and stock responses, they go far beyond this to provide additional levels of realism. In this chapter, I will focus on these more complex types of characters, with a view toward some of the more useful processes of the other types of AI.

Designing An Artificially-Intelligent Character

A computer character has a geometric form that can typically be animated. The animation can be created in advance by an artist or generated algorithmically through physics simulation. In both cases, the choice of animation depends on two things: the *state* of the environment at that time and the *state* of the character (what it "feels" or "thinks").

Sensing Environmental States

A character is aware of its environment through *sensors*, algorithms that transform aspects of the virtual world into information the character can use. Sensors can detect the path to a certain location, the presence of other characters (including the player), the weather of the virtual world, or anything else the character must be aware of. In the next few sections, I'll cover the more common sensors that nearly all computer characters use.

Presence Sensors

One of the simplest sensors in most characters is the *presence sensor*, which detects the presence of an object or other character. A simple method of doing this is to check to see if a point is inside or outside of a cube or sphere. These checks are computationally inexpensive, and so can be done many times without a substantial performance penalty.

Another more useful presence sensor involves checking a point against the character's viewing frustum, to see if the character can see it. Because this allows computer characters

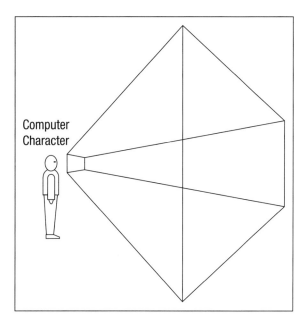

Figure 14.1
A character's viewing frustum.

realistically to sense the presence of the player, I will cover the mathematics here. A viewing frustum can be represented by six planes, as seen in Figure 14.1.

The equation that holds true for all points on a plane is as follows:

```
Ax + By + Cz + D = 0
```

Here **A**, **B**, and **C** are the vector components that describe the orientation of the plane (this vector is perpendicular to the plane) and **D** is either the negative of the distance from the origin to the plane if the vector is normalized, or some unique multiple of this value (the distance from the origin to the plane is defined as the distance from the origin to the point on the plane that is nearest to the origin).

The left-hand side of this so-called "plane equation" always evaluates to 0 for all points that lie on the plane. For points that do not lie on the plane, but fall on one side, the equation evaluates to a positive integer; for points that lie on the other side of the plane, the equation evaluates to a negative integer. Which side of the plane produces which? That depends on the direction of the vector <**A**, **B**, **C**>. All points that fall on the side of the plane that the vector points to produce positive values. All points that fall on the opposite side of the plane, the ones the vector does not point to, produce negative values.

Using this information, you can easily construct a sensor that detects whether a given point is in a character's viewing frustum by defining your viewing frustum by six planes (all in the form of the plane equation) and then testing the point against each one of them. If all of the planes face inward, or all face outward, then when you evaluate the point using the plane equation, you will get either all positive values or all negative values, respectively. This "sign check" is an easy way to determine if the point is in the frustum.

Path-Finding Sensors

Allowing a character to sense the form of its environment so it can navigate through it is a difficult task, especially in three dimensions. The problem with path-finding is that many obstacles exist between a character and its destination; a straight-line path between the two will rarely, if ever, connect them. Paths that seem not to lead to the destination at first (because they head in the wrong direction) may, in fact, eventually lead to it. Of course, this is not a problem with all games. Air and space combat games can get by with little or no path-finding intelligence, because they have so few obstacles to avoid. For the majority of other games, however, path-finding plays a key role in a character's arsenal of AI algorithms.

Finding a path in a virtual world depends in part on the physics of the character. Those that walk have fewer options than those that can fly; smaller characters can usually travel to places larger ones cannot; and all ground characters are limited by how far they can fall and jump. For these reasons, any path-finding algorithm needs to consider the physics of the character for which it finds paths, as well as the physics of the environment (for example, gravity for ground characters and altitude for combat planes).

Before you can find the shortest path between two points, you must find all paths that both lead from the source point to the destination point and also satisfy the constraints of the character and environment. Then you can pick the shortest path from among these.

One way of finding a path involves creating a number of fixed-length lines that proceed from the initial point in different directions (the directions are, of course, limited by physical constraints—a ground-based character cannot find a path that would require it to fly). These paths, called *feelers*, are then divided into two categories: those that penetrate objects and those that do not. The ones that penetrate objects are discarded, because they cannot be considered valid paths. For the ones that do not penetrate objects, the process is repeated for the ending point of each feeler, except those feelers that retrace former paths. Soon, you will find one path that leads either directly to the destination point or somewhere right next to it. Eventually, all such paths will be found. Figure 14.2 illustrates this technique.

To optimize the performance of this feeler-based method of path-finding, you can do the following:

◆ Terminate the search process for a feeler when a clear line of sight exists between it and the destination point.

◆ Do not send feelers toward polygons that are completely unobstructed from the point of view of any other feeler (see Figure 14.3). This optimization dramatically reduces the time required to find paths in many environments, but takes some time itself because of the complexity of determining if a polygon is unobstructed.

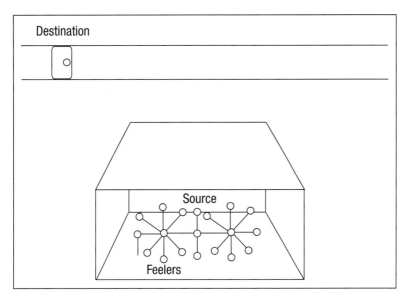

Figure 14.2
Finding a path with feelers.

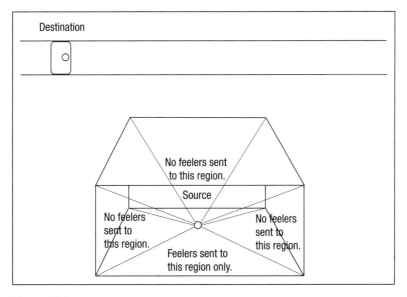

Figure 14.3
Not sending feelers toward polygons that are completely obstructed.

Even with these optimizations, however, finding arbitrary paths in a complex virtual world is difficult to do in realtime—in many cases, impossible. The best solution is to simplify the virtual world by replacing complex objects with simple boxes or polygons, and then use the path finder on this simplified geometry.

Another good option (but one that consumes a large amount of memory) is to precompute key points for all possible useful paths. The tricky part of this solution is determining which paths to precompute. If you treat each polygon as a plane and bound the virtual world by six planes, then the intersection of all planes in the virtual world will create many convex, bounded 3D shapes, as shown in Figure 14.4. Each convex 3D shape must have paths that lead to all the other convex 3D shapes. Once these shapes are computed, you can move from any one point in the virtual world to any other point, simply by choosing the appropriate path in the convex 3D shape where the initial point is located. This option also benefits from simplifying the virtual world's geometry, because it reduces the number of paths (and, hence, the memory requirements). Trees and other objects with many polygons are best converted to boxes before choosing the paths; otherwise, you will find many paths that will never be used.

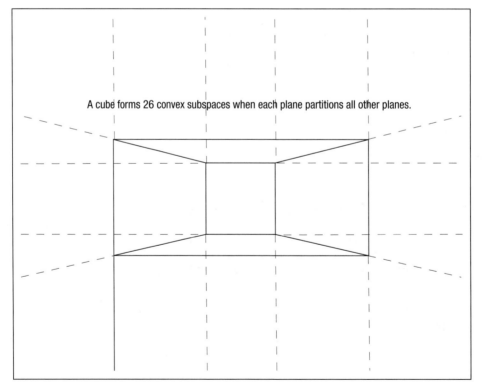

A cube forms 26 convex subspaces when each plane partitions all other planes.

Figure 14.4
Partitioning the virtual world by the planes of its polygons.

Is there any other way to find paths? Certainly, one relatively simple and fast technique is to draw a 3D line through the virtual world that connects all areas the characters might need to visit. When a character needs to move somewhere, it simply locates the closest line segment and follows it until it reaches a clear line of sight between itself and the destination point. This technique has the disadvantage of producing relatively unnatural movements, but for the most part the player is not aware of this.

Other approaches that depend on a specific kind of environment and do not require the shortest path can proceed in many different ways. A character in a maze-like environment, for example, can always follow the path to its right, and in nearly all cases, it will find the destination point. Further, the character can find the destination point through trial-and-error methods that use memory to record paths that did not work. This method is adequate when the character being simulated is not supposed to be aware of the form of the environment. The method you use for path finding will depend both on your virtual world and on how you want your characters to behave. Because the feeler method of finding paths works in all situations and guarantees the shortest path, it is worth covering in more depth here.

One difficult (and time-consuming) process in the feeler method is determining whether or not a line segment (a feeler) intersects polygons that are close to it. Chapter 9 presented the solution to this problem. Another difficult task is the optimization I previously mentioned, where no feelers are sent in the direction of polygons that are completely unobstructed. You can determine if a polygon is unobstructed from the point of view of a feeler by implementing the following three checks:

- *Create lines from the feeler to every vertex of the polygon.* If any of these lines intersects any other polygon in the virtual world, then the polygon is obstructed—another polygon lies between it and the feeler (see Figure 14.5a).

- *Create lines from the feeler to every vertex of the polygon, as in the first check—only in this check, create polygons from these lines.* Then test the edges of any polygons suspected of obstruction with these newly created polygons. If the edges of these suspected polygons intersect the new polygons, the polygon is obstructed (see Figure 14.5b).

- *Create polygons from the feeler to the vertices of the polygon, as in the second check.* This time, however, check to see if any points of suspected polygons lie within these newly created polygons. If they do, the polygon is obstructed (see Figure 14.5c).

If all checks pass, the polygon is unobstructed and no feelers need be sent in its direction. As you can see from the previous checks, however, the process will slow considerably if you end up testing many polygons. You can minimize the number of polygons you test by creating a bounding sphere that encloses both the polygon being checked for intersection and the feeler. Then check the bounding sphere for each polygon in the virtual world against this bounding sphere. If the two spheres do not intersect, you don't need to perform the previous test on the polygon.

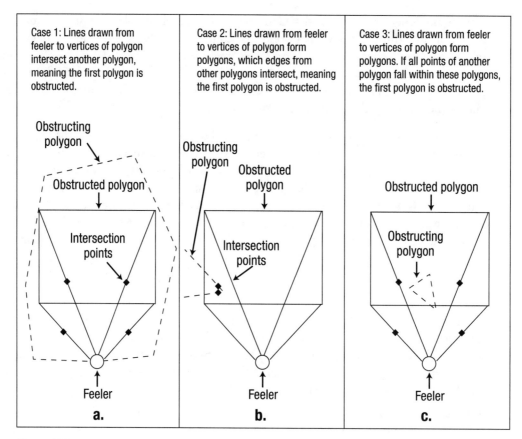

Case 1: Lines drawn from feeler to vertices of polygon intersect another polygon, meaning the first polygon is obstructed.

Case 2: Lines drawn from feeler to vertices of polygon form polygons, which edges from other polygons intersect, meaning the first polygon is obstructed.

Case 3: Lines drawn from feeler to vertices of polygon form polygons. If all points of another polygon fall within these polygons, the first polygon is obstructed.

Figure 14.5
The three tests for polygon obstruction.

If the bounding sphere method is too slow, you can divide your environment into squares and represent this grid with a two-dimensional array. Each element in the array represents a certain amount of space in the virtual world and should contain a list of all polygons in that area. Only polygons in adjacent squares need be tested, and those that do fall within adjacent squares can first be sent through the bounding sphere check. In this way, you will end up checking very few (if any) polygons per feeler.

Other Sensors

Of course, a character can have many other sensors, but for the most part these are trivial (for example, sensing the weather involves merely feeding its state into the character) and character-specific. Now I will turn from how a character senses its environment to how a character thinks.

Modeling Character States

Modeling how a character "thinks," which determines how it responds to its environment, is more difficult than sensing the environment. There is no single way to do this—a computer pilot flying a space fighter will think differently than a computer soldier on the battlefield. General principles, however, will help you in constructing your characters.

The main steps involved in creating a thinking character are listed here:

1. Define all states the character can have. For example, an alien might have four states: attack, retreat, hide, and fall in line with other aliens.

2. Define all actions the character can have. A few actions for a soldier character might include *go to a point* (which uses the character's environmental sensor), *move in a direction*, *turn to a direction*, and *fire the weapon*.

3. Connect the character's actions to both the state of the character and the state of the environment (which is known through the character's sensors).

The third step is the most important. How the actions are connected to the state of the character and the state of the environment largely determines how the character behaves and, consequently, how intelligent it is.

One of the more successful implementations of the third step involves giving each character a *memory* that can store information (such as past experiences or variables) and change over time. This memory, usually represented in C++ by an array of floating-point values (C++ type **float** or **double**), can connect a character's actions to the state of both the environment and itself. To give you a feel for using this technique, I will cover the setup behind creating an intelligent character: a fighter pilot.

Example Case: A Fighter Pilot

A fighter pilot needs to be able both to evade enemy fire and to attack enemy craft. A *good* pilot needs to avoid his or her own weaknesses and exploit the weaknesses of enemies. The first step in constructing such a pilot is to define all states it can have. For purposes of illustration, the following states will suffice: *attack, evade, eject*. In C++, these states could be represented by the type **enum**, as shown here:

```
enum PilotState { AttackState, EvadeState, EjectState };
```

The second step is to define all possible actions for the character. These might include *go to point*, *accelerate*, and *decelerate* (the physics of the flight would be handled in the *go to point* action). If these actions were members in a class representing fighter pilot characters, the code would look like this:

```
class FighterPilot {
   protected:
      enum PilotState { AttackState, EvadeState, EjectState };
```

```
        PilotState CurrentState;

        double px, py, pz, rx, ry, rz;

        bool GoToPoint ( double x, double y, double z );
        bool Accelerate ( double MPS2 );
        bool Decelerate ( double MPS2 );
};
```

If the virtual world is empty except for one **FighterPilot** and the player, then the character needs only three sensors: one that informs it of the player's location, another that informs it of the player's orientation, and a third that informs it when the player successfully scores with a weapon. These functions, added to the class **FighterPilot**, might look like this:

```
void SetPlayerPosition ( double x, double y, double z );
void SetPlayerOrientation ( double rx, double ry, double rz );
void RecordHit ( double ImpactX, double ImpactY, double ImpactZ,
    double WeaponDamage );
```

The last step is to connect the **FighterPilot**'s actions to the environment (which is detected through the three functions just mentioned) and its own internal states in such a way as to produce an intelligent character. To do this, you need to give the character a memory. You could store many different items in this memory, but for illustration, I will choose the following (keep in mind that each is represented by a floating-point value):

1. A record of each place the **FighterPilot**'s craft was hit. This is stored as a 3×3×3 array, where each element in the array represents a 1×1×1 unit of space. The **FighterPilot**'s craft is imagined to occupy the 3×3×3 space fully, so any region hit will have a corresponding element in the array. Each element (a floating-point value) indicates the damage done thus far to the portion of the craft falling within that space.

2. A record of each place the player's craft was hit. This is stored as a 3×3×3 array, where each element in the array represents a 1×1×1 unit of space. The player's craft is imagined to occupy the 3×3×3 space fully, so any region hit will have a corresponding element in the array. Each element (a floating-point value) indicates the damage done thus far to the portion of the player's craft falling within that space.

3. A variable that indicates how often the **FighterPilot** will evade. You can find the percentage by dividing this variable by the sum of both this variable and the one in Item 4, and then multiplying the result by 100.

4. A variable that indicates how often the **FighterPilot** will attack. You can find the percentage by dividing this variable by the sum of both this variable and the one in Item 3, and then multiplying the result by 100.

5. A variable that indicates how long (say, in seconds) the **FighterPilot** will spend each time it chooses to evade, on average.

6. A variable that indicates how long the **FighterPilot** will spend each time it chooses to attack, on average.

7. A variable that indicates the deviance from the average of the variable in Item 5.

8. A variable that indicates the deviance from the average of the variable in Item 6.

9. A 3×3×3 array, where each element indicates the maximum damage to a region of space before the **FighterPilot** will eject.

In total, storing these variables requires 33 elements of memory. In C++, this would involve adding the following line of code to the class declaration:

```
float Memory [ 33 ];
```

For convenience, you could make constants for each element in the array, so that accessing them would be easier, as in the example **Memory [EVADE_TIME]**.

Now that the setup is complete, you can use the memory to connect the character's actions to environmental stimuli and its own state. This is quite easy. The **FighterPilot** should use the Variables 5, 6, 7, and 8 to determine when it should attack and evade and for how long. For the attack state, the **FighterPilot** should initially try attacking the player's craft from random angles, but after accumulating enough data, it should search Record 1 to find the angles the player is weakest defending (those with the highest damage) and attack from them. Similarly, for the evade state, the **FighterPilot** should try to maneuver its craft into those regions where it has been hit least, based on the data in Record 2. When the craft is damaged in any area beyond that area's maximum damage (as defined by Record 9), the **FighterPilot** should go into the eject state.

With just 33 variables, you have managed to create a character that adapts to the player's strengths and weaknesses. By adding more variables, you could increase the realism even further. (For example, adding a variable indicating the length of time the **FighterPilot** should try to attack a specific region before giving up and attacking any region would make the character even smarter.)

Another powerful, though less obvious, advantage to this system is that it lends itself well to genetic concepts such as natural selection and reproduction (natural selection—or "survival of the fittest"—is the process whereby those organisms less fit to survive and reproduce do not produce as many offspring as those organisms more fit to survive and reproduce; consequently, the latter organisms become dominant in the population).

To implement natural selection, you can randomly and slightly modify all variables (or perhaps just Items 5 through 8) of a **FighterPilot** from their values in a previous **FighterPilot**. If the modifications result in better survivability for the character, then the modifications are kept for future characters; otherwise, the process repeats using the previous **FighterPilot** values.

You can mate two skilled **FighterPilot**s by randomly choosing the offspring's **Memory [N]** element from one of the parents (in other words, for each element of memory the offspring has, randomly set it to one parent or the other's corresponding element). The offspring will then represent a combination of the attributes of both parents. These possibilities allow computer characters to surprise even their programmers.

Summary

Few games are complete without some form of artificial intelligence. Intelligent characters breathe life into a story and animate a world that might otherwise be devoid of meaningful interaction. Two steps are involved in creating intelligent characters: allowing characters to sense their environment and making them respond to it.

You can allow characters to sense the virtual world through *sensors*, algorithms that convert information about the virtual world into a form the character can use. Widely used sensors are presence and path. You can make an intelligent character in three steps: define the states the character can have; define the actions the character can do; and, finally, give the character a memory, which will usually consist of an array of floating-point values. Once these steps have been completed, you can concentrate on tying the character's internal state and memory to its actions. Advantages of the approach outlined in this chapter include the ability to "mate" two successful characters, the ability for characters to adapt to change, and the ability to use principles of natural selection to produce fine-tuned characters.

PART III

DIRECTX
REFERENCE

Appendix A
DirectDraw Reference

This appendix is divided into four main reference sections: interfaces, functions, callbacks, and structures.

The interface reference documents in detail all of the methods of the major DirectDraw interfaces. The function reference does the same for DirectDraw functions that do not belong to an interface (such as **DirectDrawCreateEx ()**). The callback reference describes the format of application-defined functions that DirectDraw calls. The structure reference documents all of the major structures that the DirectDraw API uses.

For a conceptual overview of DirectDraw, see Chapter 3. For sample code, see Chapter 4 or the DirectX SDK.

Interface Reference

The interfaces documented in this section include IDirectDraw7, IDirectDrawClipper, IDirectDrawColorControl, IDirectDraw GammaControl, and IDirectDrawSurface7.

IDirectDraw7

Applications can obtain the IDirectDraw7 interface by calling **DirectDrawCreateEx ()** or **CoCreateInstance ()**.

The globally unique identifier (GUID) for the IDirectDraw7 interface is **IID_IDirectDraw7**.

IDirectDraw7::CreateClipper ()

Function Description

This function creates a DirectDrawClipper object.

Function Declaration

```
HRESULT CreateClipper(
    DWORD dwFlags,
    LPDIRECTDRAWCLIPPER FAR *lplpDDClipper,
    IUnknown FAR *pUnkOuter
);
```

Parameter	Description
dwFlags	Reserved for future use; it must be 0.
lplpDDClipper	A pointer to a DirectDrawClipper object. If this function succeeds, the pointer will be set to the newly created DirectDrawClipper object.
pUnkOuter	Reserved for future COM compatibility; it must be **NULL**.

Return Value	Description
DD_OK	DirectDraw successfully created the clipper.
DDERR_INVALIDOBJECT	DirectDraw could not create the clipper, because the DirectDraw7 object is not valid.
DDERR_INVALIDPARAMS	DirectDraw could not create the clipper, because one or more parameters are invalid.
DDERR_NOCOOPERATIVELEVELSET	DirectDraw could not create the clipper, because the cooperative level is not set.
DDERR_OUTOFMEMORY	DirectDraw could not create the clipper, because sufficient memory is not available.

IDirectDraw7::CreatePalette ()

Function Description

This function creates a DirectDrawPalette object.

Function Declaration

```
HRESULT CreatePalette(
    DWORD dwFlags,
    LPPALETTEENTRY lpDDColorArray,
    LPDIRECTDRAWPALETTE FAR *lplpDDPalette,
    IUnknown FAR *pUnkOuter
);
```

(continued)

IDirectDraw7::CreatePalette () (*continued*)

Parameter	Description
dwFlags	Specifies the type of palette. This parameter can be one or more of the following flags:

- **DDPCAPS_1BIT**—The palette consists of two entries in the color table. Unless **DDPCAPS_8BITENTRIES** is specified, these entries contain red, green, and blue color information. Surfaces that use this palette must use 1 bit per pixel.

- **DDPCAPS_2BIT**—The palette consists of four entries in the color table. Unless **DDPCAPS_8BITENTRIES** is specified, these entries contain red, green, and blue color information. Surfaces that use this palette must use 2 bits per pixel.

- **DDPCAPS_4BIT**—The palette consists of 16 entries in the color table. Unless **DDPCAPS_8BITENTRIES** is specified, these entries contain red, green, and blue color information. Surfaces that use this palette must use 4 bits per pixel.

- **DDPCAPS_8BIT**—The palette consists of 256 entries in the color table. These entries contain red, green, and blue color information. Surfaces that use this palette must use 8 bits per pixel.

- **DDPCAPS_8BITENTRIES**—The palette color entries consist not of red, green, and blue color values, but of 1-byte indices into the palette of the destination surface. Any surface using this palette can be blitted only into destination surfaces that have 256-entry palettes.

- **DDPCAPS_ALPHA**—The palette contains alpha information, specified in the **peFlags** member of each **PALETTEENTRY** structure pointed to by the **lpDDColorArray** parameter. This flag is valid only for textures.

- **DDPCAPS_ALLOW256**—The palette can have all of its 256 entries defined, even those that conflict with the standard Windows palette.

- **DDPCAPS_INITIALIZE**—The palette should be initialized with the colors passed in the **lpDDColorArray** parameter. If this flag is not specified, the palette's color values must be initialized later with the **IDirectPalette::SetEntries ()** function.

- **DDPCAPS_PRIMARYSURFACE**—The palette will be associated with the primary surface. Any change in the color values of a palette so associated will be immediately reflected on the display, possibly synchronized to the monitor's vertical blanking interval, if the hardware supports it.

(continued)

IDirectDraw7::CreatePalette () *(continued)*	
Parameter	**Description**
	• **DDPCAPS_PRIMARYSURFACELEFT**—The palette will be associated with the primary surface for the user's left eye. Any change in the color values of a palette so associated will be immediately reflected on the left display, possibly synchronized to the monitor's vertical blanking interval, if the hardware supports it.
	• **DDPCAPS_VSYNC**—Changes to the palette's color values can be synched with the display's refresh rate, eliminating artifacts otherwise noticed with palette changes for primary surfaces.
lpDDColorArray	A pointer to color-entry information, or **NULL** if the application will set the color entry information by using the **IDirectPalette::SetEntries** () function. The color-entry information can be an array either of Win32 **PALETTEENTRY** structures or of bytes (if **DDPCAPS_8BITENTRIES** is specified). In the former case, the **peRed**, **peGreen**, and **peBlue** members of the structure specify the color of the palette entry (and **peFlags** specifies alpha information, if any). In the latter case, each byte specifies the destination surface's palette index to use for the entry's colors.
lplpDDPalette	A pointer to a DirectDrawPalette object. If this function succeeds, the pointer will be set to the newly created DirectDrawPalette object.
pUnkOuter	Reserved for future COM compatibility; must be **NULL**.
Return Value	**Description**
DD_OK	DirectDraw successfully created the palette object.
DDERR_INVALIDOBJECT	DirectDraw could not create the palette object, because the DirectDraw7 object is not valid.
DDERR_INVALIDPARAMS	DirectDraw could not create the palette object, because one or more parameters are invalid.
DDERR_NOCOOPERATIVELEVELSET	DirectDraw could not create the palette object, because the cooperative level is not set.
DDERR_OUTOFMEMORY	DirectDraw could not create the palette object, because sufficient memory is not available.
DDERR_UNSUPPORTED	DirectDraw could not create the palette object, because the operation is not supported.

IDirectDraw7::CreateSurface ()	
Function Description	
This function creates a DirectDraw surface.	
Function Declaration	

```
HRESULT CreateSurface(
   LPDDSURFACEDESC2 lpDDSurfaceDesc2,
   LPDIRECTDRAWSURFACE7 FAR *lplpDDSurface,
   IUnknown FAR *pUnkOuter
);
```

Parameter	Description
lpDDSurfaceDesc2	A pointer to a **DDSURFACEDESC2** structure that describes the attributes of the surface to be created. All unused members of the structure must be set to 0.
lplpDDSurface	A pointer to a DirectDrawSurface7 object. If this function succeeds, the pointer will be set to the newly created DirectDrawSurface7 object.
pUnkOuter	Reserved for future COM compatibility; must be **NULL**.
Return Value	**Description**
DD_OK	DirectDraw successfully created the DirectDraw surface.
DDERR_INCOMPATIBLEPRIMARY	DirectDraw could not create the surface, because the specifications of the primary surface to be created did not match the attributes of the primary surface.
DDERR_INVALIDCAPS	DirectDraw could not create the surface, because the specified capabilities are invalid.
DDERR_INVALIDOBJECT	DirectDraw could not create the surface, because the DirectDraw7 object is not valid.
DDERR_INVALIDPARAMS	DirectDraw could not create the surface, because one or more parameters are invalid.
DDERR_INVALIDPIXELFORMAT	DirectDraw could not create the surface, because the specified pixel format is invalid.
DDERR_NOALPHAHW	DirectDraw could not create the surface, because the hardware does not support the requested alpha capabilities.
DDERR_NOCOOPERATIVELEVELSET	DirectDraw could not create the surface, because the cooperative level is not set.
DDERR_NODIRECTDRAWHW	DirectDraw could not create the surface, because the hardware does not support DirectDraw.
DDERR_NOEMULATION	DirectDraw could not create the surface, because the requested software emulation is not available.
DDERR_NOEXCLUSIVEMODE	DirectDraw could not create the surface, because this operation requires exclusive mode.

(continued)

IDirectDraw7::CreateSurface () *(continued)*

Return Value	Description
DDERR_NOFLIPHW	DirectDraw could not create the surface, because the hardware does not support flipping.
DDERR_NOMIPMAPHW	DirectDraw could not create the surface, because the hardware does not support mipmapping.
DDERR_NOOVERLAYHW	DirectDraw could not create the surface, because the hardware does not support overlays (possibly because of insufficient overlay resources).
DDERR_NOZBUFFERHW	DirectDraw could not create the surface, because the hardware does not support z-buffers.
DDERR_OUTOFMEMORY	DirectDraw could not create the surface, because sufficient memory is not available.
DDERR_OUTOFVIDEOMEMORY	DirectDraw could not create the surface, because video memory is not available to perform the operation.
DDERR_PRIMARYSURFACEALREADYEXISTS	DirectDraw could not create the surface as a primary surface, because a primary surface already exists.
DDERR_UNSUPPORTEDMODE	DirectDraw could not create the surface, because DirectDraw does not support the current video mode.

IDirectDraw7::DuplicateSurface ()

Function Description

This function duplicates an existing DirectDraw surface. The resulting duplicated surface shares the surface memory of the original surface. Changing one surface thus immediately changes the other. Primary, 3D, and implicitly created surfaces cannot be duplicated.

Function Declaration

```
HRESULT DuplicateSurface(
    LPDIRECTDRAWSURFACE7 lpDDSurface,
    LPLPDIRECTDRAWSURFACE7 FAR *lplpDupDDSurface
);
```

Parameter	Description
lpDDSurface	A pointer to a DirectDrawSurface7 object that identifies the surface to be duplicated.
lplpDupDDSurface	The address of a pointer to a DirectDrawSurface7 object. If this function succeeds, the pointer will be set to the newly duplicated DirectDrawSurface7 object.

(continued)

IDirectDraw7::DuplicateSurface () *(continued)*

Return Value	Description
DD_OK	DirectDraw successfully duplicated the surface.
DDERR_CANTDUPLICATE	DirectDraw cannot duplicate the surface, because the specified surface was a primary, 3D, or implicitly created surface, and these surface types cannot be duplicated.
DDERR_INVALIDOBJECT	DirectDraw could not duplicate the surface, because the DirectDraw object is not valid.
DDERR_INVALIDPARAMS	DirectDraw could not duplicate the surface, because one or more parameters are invalid.
DDERR_OUTOFMEMORY	DirectDraw could not duplicate the surface, because sufficient memory is not available.
DDERR_SURFACELOST	DirectDraw could not duplicate the surface, because the memory of the DirectDraw surface has been lost. It must be restored with the **IDirectDrawSurface7::Restore** () function.

IDirectDraw7::EnumDisplayModes ()

Function Description

This function enumerates display modes supported by the hardware according to an application-defined surface description.

Function Declaration

```
HRESULT EnumDisplayModes(
    DWORD dwFlags,
    LPDDSURFACEDESC2 lpDDSurfaceDesc2,
    LPVOID lpContext,
    LPDDENUMMODESCALLBACK7 lpEnumModesCallback
);
```

Parameter	Description
dwFlags	Describes enumeration options. This parameter can be one or more of the following flags: • **DDEDM_REFRESHRATES**—DirectDraw should consider display modes unique, even if they are identical except for their refresh rates. If this flag is specified, DirectDraw will list as separate those display modes that have the same width, height, and bits per pixel, but different refresh rates. • **DDEDM_STANDARDVGAMODES**—DirectDraw should list the standard VGA modes (such as, 320×240×8) in addition to their ModeX equivalents. • **DDENUM_STEREO**—DirectDraw should list stereo vision capable modes.

(continued)

IDirectDraw7::EnumDisplayModes () *(continued)*

Parameter	Description
lpDDSurfaceDesc2	A pointer to a **DDSURFACEDESC2** structure that describes the attributes of the display modes to be enumerated. This parameter may be **NULL**, in which case all display modes are enumerated.
lpContext	A pointer to application-defined data that will be sent to the callback function every time it is called.
lpEnumModesCallback	A pointer to an application-defined **EnumModesCallback7** () callback function. This function will be called for every display mode enumerated.

Return Value	Description
DD_OK	DirectDraw successfully enumerated the display modes.
DDERR_INVALIDOBJECT	DirectDraw could not enumerate the display modes, because the DirectDraw7 object is not valid.
DDERR_INVALIDPARAMS	DirectDraw could not enumerate the display modes, because one or more parameters are invalid.

IDirectDraw7::EnumSurfaces ()

Function Description

This function enumerates surfaces that exist or can be created, according to a specified surface description.

Function Declaration

```
HRESULT EnumSurfaces(
    DWORD dwFlags,
    LPDDSURFACEDESC2 lpDDSD2,
    LPVOID lpContext,
    LPDDENUMSURFACESCALLBACK7 lpEnumSurfacesCallback
);
```

Parameter	Description
dwFlags	Describes which surfaces DirectDraw should enumerate and how the application will describe those surfaces. This parameter must be a combination of one or both of the following two flags: • **DDENUMSURFACES_CANBECREATED**—DirectDraw should enumerate all surfaces that can be created matching the surface description specified by the **lpDDSD2** parameter. • **DDENUMSURFACES_DOESEXIST**—DirectDraw should enumerate all existing surfaces that match the surface description specified by the **lpDDSD2** parameter. The parameter must also include one of the following three flags to indicate how DirectDraw should interpret **lpDDSD2**:

(continued)

IDirectDraw7::EnumSurfaces () *(continued)*

Parameter	Description
	• **DDENUMSURFACES_ALL**—DirectDraw should enumerate all surfaces that match the surface description specified by the **lpDDSD2** parameter. This flag must be specified with the **DDENUMSURFACES_DOESEXIST** flag.
	• **DDENUMSURFACES_MATCH**—DirectDraw should enumerate any surface that matches the surface description specified by the **lpDDSD2** parameter.
	• **DDENUMSURFACES_NOMATCH**—DirectDraw should enumerate all surfaces that do not match the surface description specified by the **lpDDSD2** parameter.
lpDDSD2	A pointer to a **DDSURFACEDESC2** structure. This parameter may be **NULL** if **dwFlags** includes the **DDENUMSURFACES_ALL** flag, in which case all existing surfaces are enumerated regardless of their surface descriptions. Otherwise, surfaces either matching or not matching the structure will be enumerated, depending on whether **dwFlags** includes **DDENUMSURFACES_MATCH** or **DDENUMSURFACES_NOMATCH**, respectively.
lpContext	A pointer to application-defined data that will be sent to the callback function every time it is called.
lpEnumSurfacesCallback	A pointer to an application-defined **EnumSurfacesCallback7** () callback function. This function will be called for every surface enumerated.
Return Value	Description
DD_OK	DirectDraw successfully enumerated the specified surfaces.
DDERR_INVALIDOBJECT	DirectDraw could not enumerate the specified surfaces, because the DirectDraw7 object is not valid.
DDERR_INVALIDPARAMS	DirectDraw could not enumerate the specified surfaces, because one or more parameters are invalid.

IDirectDraw7::FlipToGDISurface ()

Function Description

This function makes the surface used by the Windows GDI (Graphics Device Interface) the primary surface, thereby making it visible. Normally, GDI operations will not be visible in full-screen DirectDraw applications. By calling this function, however, an application can force DirectDraw to make the GDI's surface the primary surface.

You should call this function when an application that uses surface flipping terminates or when an application wishes to display GDI-rendered elements (such as buttons or dialog boxes) that would otherwise be invisible.

Function Declaration

```
HRESULT FlipToGDISurface();
```

IDirectDraw7::FlipToGDISurface () *(continued)*

Parameter	Description
None	
Return Value	**Description**
DD_OK	DirectDraw successfully made the GDI surface the primary surface.
DDERR_INVALIDOBJECT	DirectDraw could not make the GDI surface the primary surface, because the DirectDraw7 object is not valid.
DDERR_INVALIDPARAMS	DirectDraw could not make the GDI surface the primary surface, because one or more parameters are invalid.
DDERR_NOTFOUND	DirectDraw could not make the GDI surface the primary surface, because the GDI surface was not found.

IDirectDraw7::GetAvailableVidMem ()

Function Description

This function retrieves the total and available video memory that you can use to create an application-defined type of surface.

Function Declaration

```
HRESULT GetAvailableVidMem(
    LPDDSCAPS2 lpDDSCaps2,
    LPDWORD    lpdwTotal,
    LPDWORD    lpdwFree
);
```

Parameter	Description
lpDDSCaps2	A pointer to a **DDSCAPS2** structure that describes the type of surface the application is interested in creating. This structure is necessary, because some video cards may use different memory for storing different kinds of surfaces (for example, z-buffers and textures).
lpdwTotal	The address of an integer. If this function succeeds, the integer will be set to the total amount of display memory, in bytes. This value does not include the memory used for the primary surface and any private caches reserved by the video card.
lpdwFree	A pointer to an integer. If this function succeeds, the integer will be set to the amount of memory on the video card that can be used to create the specified surface type.
Return Value	**Description**
DD_OK	DirectDraw successfully retrieved the video memory information.
DDERR_INVALIDCAPS	DirectDraw could not retrieve the video memory information, because the specified capabilities are invalid.

(continued)

IDirectDraw7::GetAvailableVidMem () *(continued)*

Return Value	Description
DDERR_INVALIDOBJECT	DirectDraw could not retrieve the video memory information, because the DirectDraw7 object is not valid.
DDERR_INVALIDPARAMS	DirectDraw could not retrieve the video memory information, because one or more parameters are invalid.
DDERR_NODIRECTDRAWHW	DirectDraw could not retrieve the video memory information, because the hardware does not support DirectDraw.

IDirectDraw7::GetCaps ()

Function Description

This function retrieves the capabilities of the Hardware Abstraction Layer (HAL) and Hardware Emulation Layer (HEL). The video card's hardware supports HAL capabilities, while the driver supports HEL capabilities.

Function Declaration

```
HRESULT GetCaps(
    LPDDCAPS lpDDDriverCaps,
    LPDDCAPS lpDDHELCaps
);
```

Parameter	Description
lpDDDriverCaps	A pointer to a **DDCAPS** structure. If this function succeeds, the structure will be filled with the capabilities of the video card's hardware. This parameter may be **NULL**, in which case DirectDraw does not retrieve these capabilities.
lpDDHELCaps	A pointer to a **DDCAPS** structure. If this function succeeds, the structure will be filled with the capabilities of the video card's driver (these are software-emulated capabilities). This parameter may be **NULL**, in which case DirectDraw does not retrieve these capabilities.

Return Value	Description
DD_OK	DirectDraw successfully retrieved the capabilities.
DDERR_INVALIDOBJECT	DirectDraw could not retrieve the capabilities, because the DirectDraw7 object is not valid.
DDERR_INVALIDPARAMS	DirectDraw could not retrieve the capabilities, because one or more parameters are invalid.

IDirectDraw7::GetDeviceIdentifier ()

Function Description

This function retrieves information describing the driver of the video card this DirectDraw object represents.

Function Declaration

```
HRESULT GetDeviceIdentifier(
    LPDDDEVICEIDENTIFIER2 lpdddi,
    DWORD dwFlags
);
```

Parameter	Description
lpdddi	A pointer to a **DDDEVICEIDENTIFIER2** structure. If this function succeeds, the structure will be filled with information describing the driver of the video card this DirectDraw7 object represents.
dwFlags	Describes retrieval options. This parameter can be zero or the following flag: • **DDGDI_GETHOSTIDENTIFIER**—DirectDraw should retrieve information about the host adapter. On systems with two video cards, where one is used mainly for 2D graphics and the other mainly for 3D, this flag causes DirectDraw to retrieve device identification information describing the 2D video card (referred to as the host video card). If this flag is not specified, DirectDraw will retrieve device identification information describing the 3D card.

Return Value	Description
DD_OK	DirectDraw successfully retrieved the driver information.
DDERR_INVALIDPARAMS	DirectDraw could not retrieve the driver information, because one or more parameters are invalid.

IDirectDraw7::GetDisplayMode ()

Function Description

This function retrieves the current display mode. You should not use this information to save display mode information for later restoration (see **IDirectDraw7::RestoreDisplayMode ()**), because the display mode may change during the life of the application.

Function Declaration

```
HRESULT GetDisplayMode(
    LPDDSURFACEDESC2 lpDDSurfaceDesc2
);
```

Parameter	Description
lpDDSurfaceDesc2	A pointer to a **DDSURFACEDESC2** structure. If this function succeeds, the structure will be filled with the attributes of the current display mode.

(continued)

IDirectDraw7::GetDisplayMode () *(continued)*

Return Value	Description
DD_OK	DirectDraw successfully retrieved the current display mode.
DDERR_INVALIDOBJECT	DirectDraw could not retrieve the current display mode, because the DirectDraw7 object is not valid.
DDERR_INVALIDPARAMS	DirectDraw could not retrieve the current display mode, because one or more parameters are invalid.
DDERR_UNSUPPORTEDMODE	DirectDraw could not retrieve the current display mode, because DirectDraw does not support the current video mode.

IDirectDraw7::GetFourCCCodes ()

Function Description

This function retrieves the FourCC codes that the DirectDraw7 object supports. FourCC codes are 32-bit unsigned integers that consist of four bytes, each byte a character from the ASCII character set. They describe technologies the DirectDraw7 object supports.

Function Declaration

```
HRESULT GetFourCCCodes(
    LPDWORD lpNumCodes,
    LPDWORD lpCodes
);
```

Parameter	Description
lpNumCodes	A pointer to an integer that describes the number of integers pointed to by **lpCodes**. If **lpCodes** is **NULL** or cannot hold the number of FourCC codes the DirectDraw7 object supports, then when this function succeeds, the integer will be set to the number of supported FourCC codes, and **lpCodes** will be filled with as many codes as it will fit.
lpCodes	A pointer to an array of integers. If this function succeeds, each integer in the array will be filled with a FourCC code. This parameter may be **NULL**, in which case DirectDraw sets **lpNumCodes** to the number of supported FourCC codes.

Return Value	Description
DD_OK	DirectDraw successfully retrieved the FourCC codes.
DDERR_INVALIDOBJECT	DirectDraw could not retrieve the FourCC codes, because the DirectDraw7 object is not valid.
DDERR_INVALIDPARAMS	DirectDraw could not retrieve the FourCC codes, because one or more parameters are invalid.

IDirectDraw7::GetGDISurface ()

Function Description

This function retrieves a DirectDrawSurface7 object that represents the surface currently used by the GDI.

Function Declaration

```
HRESULT GetGDISurface(
    LPDIRECTDRAWSURFACE7 FAR *lplpGDIDDSSurface7
);
```

Parameter	Description
lplpGDIDDSSurface7	A pointer to a DirectDrawSurface7 object. If this function succeeds, the pointer will be set to the surface currently used by the GDI. According to COM conventions, the object must be released when the application is done using it.

Return Value	Description
DD_OK	DirectDraw successfully retrieved the GDI's surface.
DDERR_INVALIDOBJECT	DirectDraw could not retrieve the GDI's surface, because the DirectDraw7 object is not valid.
DDERR_INVALIDPARAMS	DirectDraw could not retrieve the GDI's surface, because one or more parameters are invalid.
DDERR_NOTFOUND	DirectDraw could not retrieve the GDI's surface, because the GDI's surface was not found.

IDirectDraw7::GetMonitorFrequency ()

Function Description

This function retrieves the refresh rate of the monitor associated with this DirectDraw7 object.

Function Declaration

```
HRESULT GetMonitorFrequency(
    LPDWORD lpdwFrequency
);
```

Parameter	Description
lpdwFrequency	A pointer to an integer. If this function succeeds, the integer will be set to the frequency of the monitor associated with this DirectDraw7 object, in refreshes per second.

Return Value	Description
DD_OK	DirectDraw successfully retrieved the monitor's frequency.
DDERR_INVALIDOBJECT	DirectDraw could not retrieve the monitor's frequency, because the DirectDraw7 object is not valid.
DDERR_INVALIDPARAMS	DirectDraw could not retrieve the monitor's frequency, because one or more parameters are invalid.
DDERR_UNSUPPORTED	DirectDraw could not retrieve the monitor's frequency, because the operation is not supported.

IDirectDraw7::GetScanLine ()

Function Description

This function retrieves the scan line being drawn on the monitor associated with this DirectDraw7 object. The scan line is measured in pixels from the top of the display, starting with row 0. DirectDraw may report extra scan lines during the vertical-blanking interval.

Function Declaration

```
HRESULT GetScanLine(
    LPDWORD lpdwScanLine
);
```

Parameter	Description
lpdwScanLine	A pointer to an integer. If this function succeeds, the integer will be set to the scan line being refreshed.

Return Value	Description
DD_OK	DirectDraw successfully retrieved the scan line being refreshed.
DDERR_INVALIDOBJECT	DirectDraw could not retrieve the scan line being refreshed, because the DirectDraw7 object is not valid.
DDERR_INVALIDPARAMS	DirectDraw could not retrieve the scan line being refreshed, because one or more parameters are invalid.
DDERR_UNSUPPORTED	DirectDraw could not retrieve the scan line being refreshed, because the operation is not supported.
DDERR_VERTICALBLANKINPROGRESS	DirectDraw could not retrieve the scan line being refreshed, because the vertical blank is in progress and no scan line is being drawn.

IDirectDraw7::GetSurfaceFromDC ()

Function Description

This function retrieves a DirectDrawSurface7 interface for a GDI device context (DC).

Function Declaration

```
HRESULT GetSurfaceFromDC(
    HDC hdc,
    LPDIRECTDRAWSURFACE7 * lpDDS7
);
```

Parameter	Description
hdc	A handle to the device context whose surface is being retrieved.
lpDDS7	A pointer to a DirectDrawSurface7 object. If this function succeeds, the pointer will be set to the surface of the specified device context.

(continued)

IDirectDraw7::GetSurfaceFromDC () *(continued)*

Return Value	Description
DD_OK	DirectDraw successfully retrieved the surface.
DDERR_GENERIC	DirectDraw could not retrieve the surface, because of a generic error.
DDERR_INVALIDPARAMS	DirectDraw could not retrieve the surface, because one or more parameters are invalid.
DDERR_OUTOFMEMORY	DirectDraw could not retrieve the surface, because sufficient memory is not available.
DDERR_NOTFOUND	DirectDraw could not retrieve the surface, because the surface for the device context was not found.

IDirectDraw7::GetVerticalBlankStatus ()

Function Description

This function retrieves the status of the vertical blank, the period during which no pixels are refreshed on the monitor.

Function Declaration

```
HRESULT GetVerticalBlankStatus(
    LPBOOL lpbIsInVB
);
```

Parameter	Description
lpbIsInVB	A pointer to a Win32 value of type **BOOL**. If this function succeeds, the value will be set to **TRUE** if a vertical blank is in progress, or **FALSE** otherwise.

Return Value	Description
DD_OK	DirectDraw successfully retrieved the vertical blanking status.
DDERR_INVALIDOBJECT	DirectDraw could not retrieve the vertical blanking status, because the DirectDraw7 object is not valid.
DDERR_INVALIDPARAMS	DirectDraw could not retrieve the vertical blanking status, because one or more parameters are invalid.

IDirectDraw7::Initialize ()

Function Description

This function initializes a DirectDraw7 object created with **CoCreateInstance** (). Applications that use **DirectDrawCreateEx** () to create their DirectDraw7 objects do not need to call this function.

Function Declaration

```
HRESULT Initialize(
    GUID FAR *lpGUID
);
```

(continued)

IDirectDraw7::Initialize () *(continued)*

Parameter	Description
lpGUID	A pointer to a GUID that identifies the video card to be associated with this DirectDraw7 object. This parameter may be **NULL**, in which case the default primary device is used.

Return Value	Description
DD_OK	DirectDraw successfully initialized the DirectDraw7 object.
DDERR_ALREADYINITIALIZED	DirectDraw could not initialize the DirectDraw7 object, because it is already initialized.
DDERR_DIRECTDRAWALREADYCREATED	DirectDraw could not initialize the DirectDraw7 object, because a DirectDraw7 object representing the specified device has already been created.
DDERR_GENERIC	DirectDraw could not initialize the DirectDraw7 object, because of a generic error.
DDERR_INVALIDOBJECT	DirectDraw could not initialize the DirectDraw7 object, because the DirectDraw7 object is not valid.
DDERR_INVALIDPARAMS	DirectDraw could not initialize the DirectDraw7 object, because one or more parameters are invalid.
DDERR_NODIRECTDRAWHW	DirectDraw could not initialize the DirectDraw7 object, because the hardware does not support DirectDraw.
DDERR_NODIRECTDRAWSUPPORT	DirectDraw could not initialize the DirectDraw7 object, because the specified device does not support DirectDraw.
DDERR_OUTOFMEMORY	DirectDraw could not initialize the DirectDraw7 object, because sufficient memory is not available.

IDirectDraw7::RestoreAllSurfaces ()

Function Description

This function restores the memory for all DirectDraw7 surfaces created with this DirectDraw7 object, in the order they were created. This function does not restore the contents of lost memory—an application must do this manually.

Function Declaration

```
HRESULT RestoreAllSurfaces();
```

Parameter	Description
None	

(continued)

IDirectDraw7::RestoreAllSurfaces () *(continued)*	
Return Value	**Description**
DD_OK	DirectDraw successfully restored all surfaces.
DDERR_INVALIDOBJECT	DirectDraw could not restore all surfaces, because the DirectDraw7 object is not valid.
DDERR_INVALIDPARAMS	DirectDraw could not restore all surfaces, because one or more parameters are invalid.

IDirectDraw7::RestoreDisplayMode ()	
Function Description	
This function restores the display mode to its default setting.	
Function Declaration	
`HRESULT RestoreDisplayMode();`	
Parameter	**Description**
None	
Return Value	**Description**
DD_OK	DirectDraw successfully restored the display mode.
DDERR_GENERIC	DirectDraw could not restore the display mode, because of a generic error.
DDERR_INVALIDOBJECT	DirectDraw could not restore the display mode, because the DirectDraw7 object is not valid.
DDERR_INVALIDPARAMS	DirectDraw could not restore the display mode, because one or more parameters are invalid.
DDERR_LOCKEDSURFACES	DirectDraw could not restore the display mode, because one or more surfaces are locked. This function can succeed only when these surfaces are unlocked.
DDERR_NOEXCLUSIVEMODE	DirectDraw could not restore the display mode, because this operation requires exclusive mode (see **IDirectDraw7::SetCooperativeLevel ()**).

IDirectDraw7::SetCooperativeLevel ()	
Function Description	
This function sets the cooperative level for this DirectDraw7 object. The cooperative level determines how the application cooperates with other applications.	
Function Declaration	

```
HRESULT SetCooperativeLevel(
    HWND hWnd,
    DWORD dwFlags
);
```

(continued)

IDirectDraw7::SetCooperativeLevel () *(continued)*	
Parameter	Description
hWnd	A handle to the main window of the application. This parameter may be **NULL** if **dwFlags** includes the **DDSCL_NORMAL** flag.
dwFlags	Specifies the cooperative level to be set. This parameter can be one or more of the following flags:
	• **DDSCL_ALLOWMODEX**—ModeX modes should be allowed.
	• **DDSCL_ALLOWREBOOT**—The Ctrl+Alt+Delete keystroke should respond in full-screen mode.
	• **DDSCL_CREATEDEVICEWINDOW**—DirectDraw should create a window and associate it with the DirectDraw7 object. This flag is used for multiple monitor systems, and is supported only under Windows 98 and Windows 2000.
	• **DDSCL_EXCLUSIVE**—The application should run in exclusive mode, giving it exclusive access to the display's resources. This flag, which provides access to the most features and the highest performance, must be used with **DDSCL_FULLSCREEN**.
	• **DDSCL_FPUPRESERVE**—Direct3D should save and restore the state of the processor's floating-point unit whenever it needs to modify it. Direct3D typically sets the FPU to single-precision mode, and leaves it in this mode until the Direct3D device is released. However, by specifying this flag, an application can force Direct3D to save and restore the state of the FPU whenever it uses floating-point math. This flag may seriously degrade performance.
	• **DDSCL_FPUSETUP**—This flag improves performance at the cost of some flexibility. Direct3D uses single-precision floating-point values for performance reasons. Whenever Direct3D uses the FPU (the portion of the CPU that handles floating-point calculations), DirectDraw sets the FPU to single-precision mode, and after calculations are performed, sets the FPU back to double-precision mode. Setting this flag informs DirectDraw to set the FPU to single-precision mode once and leave it that way until DirectDraw is shut down. To use the **DDSCL_FPUSETUP** flag, an application must always use single-precision floating-point types (C++ values of type **float**) and must further set the cooperative level after any runtime DLLs are loaded, because some DLLs set the FPU to double-precision mode when they are loaded.
	• **DDSCL_FULLSCREEN**—The application should run in full-screen mode. This flag, which provides access to the most features and the highest performance, must be used with the **DDSCL_EXCLUSIVE** flag.

(continued)

IDirectDraw7::SetCooperativeLevel () *(continued)*	
Parameter	**Description**
	• **DDSCL_MULTITHREADED**—DirectDraw should take special steps to ensure it is multithread-compliant. Applications that have multiple threads calling DirectDraw or Direct3D functions should use this flag.
	• **DDSCL_NORMAL**—DirectDraw should run in normal mode, in a window and with shared access to the display's resources. This flag cannot be used with **DDSCL_ALLOWMODEX**, **DDSCL_EXCLUSIVE**, or **DDSCL_FULLSCREEN**.
	• **DDSCL_NOWINDOWCHANGES**—DirectDraw should not minimize or restore the application. Applications that use this flag must perform these steps manually.
	• **DDSCL_SETDEVICEWINDOW**—The **hWnd** parameter specifies the device window—the window that receives graphical output (there can be only one device window per monitor). This flag is valid only for Windows 98 and Windows 2000.
	• **DDSCL_SETFOCUSWINDOW**—The **hWnd** parameter specifies the focus window—the window that receives input messages (there can be only one focus window). The focus window and the device window will be the same when the application is using only one monitor. This flag is valid only for Windows 98 and Windows 2000.
Return Value	**Description**
DD_OK	DirectDraw successfully set the cooperative level.
DDERR_EXCLUSIVEMODEALREADYSET	DirectDraw could not set the cooperative level, because exclusive mode is already set.
DDERR_HWNDALREADYSET	DirectDraw could not set the cooperative level, because the window for the DirectDraw7 object has already been set. You must delete all palettes and surfaces before resetting the window.
DDERR_HWNDSUBCLASSED	DirectDraw could not set the cooperative level, because the window has been subclassed.
DDERR_INVALIDOBJECT	DirectDraw could not set the cooperative level, because the DirectDraw7 object is not valid.
DDERR_INVALIDPARAMS	DirectDraw could not set the cooperative level, because one or more parameters are invalid.
DDERR_OUTOFMEMORY	DirectDraw could not set the cooperative level, because sufficient memory is not available.

IDirectDraw7::SetDisplayMode ()

Function Description

This function sets the display mode for the video card associated with this DirectDraw7 object.

Function Declaration

```
HRESULT SetDisplayMode(
    DWORD dwWidth,
    DWORD dwHeight,
    DWORD dwBPP,
    DWORD dwRefreshRate,
    DWORD dwFlags
);
```

Parameter	Description
dwWidth	The width of the new display mode, in pixels.
dwHeight	The height of the new display mode, in pixels.
dwBPP	The bits per pixel of the new display mode.
dwRefreshRate	The refresh rate of the new display mode. This parameter may be 0, in which case the default refresh rate is used.
dwFlags	Specifies additional display mode options. This parameter can be 0 or **DDSDM_STANDARDVGAMODE**, in which case DirectDraw allows the application to use the standard VGA 320x200x8 mode, rather than its ModeX equivalent.

Return Value	Description
DD_OK	DirectDraw successfully set the display mode.
DDERR_GENERIC	DirectDraw could not set the display mode, because of a generic error.
DDERR_INVALIDMODE	DirectDraw could not set the display mode, because the specified display mode is invalid.
DDERR_INVALIDOBJECT	DirectDraw could not set the display mode, because the DirectDraw7 object is not valid.
DDERR_INVALIDPARAMS	DirectDraw could not set the display mode, because one or more parameters are invalid.
DDERR_LOCKEDSURFACES	DirectDraw could not set the display mode, because one or more surfaces are locked. This function can succeed only when these surfaces are unlocked.
DDERR_NOEXCLUSIVEMODE	DirectDraw could not set the display mode, because this operation requires exclusive mode.
DDERR_SURFACEBUSY	DirectDraw could not set the display mode, because one or more surfaces are being accessed.
DDERR_UNSUPPORTED	DirectDraw could not set the display mode, because the operation is not supported.
DDERR_UNSUPPORTEDMODE	DirectDraw could not set the display mode, because the current display mode is not supported.
DDERR_WASSTILLDRAWING	DirectDraw could not set the display mode, because it is still engaged in surface blit operations.

IDirectDraw7::TestCooperativeLevel ()

Function Description

This function tests the cooperative level for the purpose of determining whether or not the application should resume execution after being suspended.

Function Declaration

```
HRESULT TestCooperativeLevel(void);
```

Parameter	Description
None	

Return Value	Description
DD_OK	The application should restore its surfaces and continue to execute.
DDERR_INVALIDOBJECT	DirectDraw could not test the cooperative level, because the DirectDraw7 object is not valid. It must be initialized with the **IDirectDraw7::Initialize** () function.
DDERR_EXCLUSIVEMODEALREADYSET	The windowed application should take no action, because another application has acquired exclusive access to the display.
DDERR_NOEXCLUSIVEMODE	The full-screen application should take no action, because it does not currently have exclusive access to the display.
DDERR_WRONGMODE	The windowed application should destroy and re-create all surfaces, because the display mode has changed.

IDirectDraw7::WaitForVerticalBlank()

Function Description

This function enables an application to synchronize itself with the monitor's vertical blanking interval.

Function Declaration

```
HRESULT WaitForVerticalBlank(
    DWORD dwFlags,
    HANDLE hEvent
);
```

Parameter	Description
dwFlags	Describes how long to wait for the vertical blank. This parameter must be one of the following flags: • **DDWAITVB_BLOCKBEGIN**—DirectDraw should return when the vertical blank begins. • **DDWAITVB_BLOCKEND**—DirectDraw should return when the vertical blank ends and display begins.
hEvent	This parameter is reserved for future use and must be **NULL**.

(continued)

IDirectDraw7::WaitForVerticalBlank() *(continued)*	
Return Value	**Description**
DD_OK	DirectDraw successfully waited for the vertical blank.
DDERR_INVALIDOBJECT	DirectDraw could not wait for the vertical blank, because the DirectDraw7 object is invalid.
DDERR_INVALIDPARAMS	DirectDraw could not wait for the vertical blank, because one or more parameters are invalid.
DDERR_UNSUPPORTED	DirectDraw could not wait for the vertical blank, because the operation is not supported.
DDERR_WASSTILLDRAWING	DirectDraw could not wait for the vertical blank, because it is still engaged in surface blit operations.

IDirectDrawClipper

Applications can obtain the IDirectDrawClipper interface by calling **IDirectDraw7::Create-Clipper ()** or **DirectDrawCreateClipper ()** functions.

The GUID for the IDirectDrawClipper interface is **IID_IDirectDrawClipper**.

IDirectDrawClipper::GetClipList ()
Function Description
This function retrieves a copy of the clip list associated with this DirectDrawClipper object. The clip list is a series of rectangles that specify the visible portions of the surface associated with this clipper object. When other surfaces are blitted on to this surface, only those portions that fall within one of the clip rectangles will be visible.
The **IDirectDrawSurface7::BltFast ()** function ignores clip lists.
Function Declaration

```
HRESULT GetClipList(
    LPRECT lpRect,
    LPRGNDATA lpClipList,
    LPDWORD lpdwSize
);
```

Parameter	Description
lpRect	A pointer to a Win32 **RECT** structure that describes a rectangle. Only those clip rectangles that fall within this rectangle will be retrieved. This parameter may be **NULL**, in which case all clip rectangles are retrieved.
lpClipList	A pointer to a Win32 **RGNDATA** structure. If this function succeeds, the structure will be filled with a copy of the clipper's clip list. This parameter may be **NULL**, in which case DirectDraw merely sets **lpdwSize** to the number of bytes necessary to store the entire clip list, but does not copy any data.

(continued)

IDirectDrawClipper::GetClipList () *(continued)*	
Parameter	**Description**
lpdwSize	A pointer to an integer that describes the number of bytes pointed to by **lpClipList**. When this function returns, the integer will be set to the number of bytes actually needed to store the entire clip list.
Return Value	**Description**
DD_OK	DirectDraw successfully retrieved a copy of the clip list.
DDERR_GENERIC	DirectDraw could not retrieve a copy of the clip list, because of a generic error.
DDERR_INVALIDCLIPLIST	DirectDraw could not retrieve a copy of the clip list, because the specified clip list is invalid.
DDERR_INVALIDOBJECT	DirectDraw could not retrieve a copy of the clip list, because the DirectDrawClipper object is not valid.
DDERR_INVALIDPARAMS	DirectDraw could not retrieve a copy of the clip list, because one or more parameters are invalid.
DDERR_NOCLIPLIST	DirectDraw could not retrieve a copy of the clip list, because no clip list exists.
DDERR_REGIONTOOSMALL	DirectDraw could not retrieve a copy of the clip list, because the specified limiting rectangle was too small.

IDirectDrawClipper::GetHWnd ()
Function Description
This function retrieves the handle of the window previously associated with this DirectDrawClipper object by the **IDirectDrawClipper::SetHWnd** () function. The clip list of this window is used as the clip list for this DirectDrawClipper object (see the Win32 functions **InvalidateRect** () and **ValidateRect** () for more information on a normal window's clip list).

Function Declaration

```
HRESULT GetHWnd(
    HWND FAR *lphWnd
);
```

Parameter	**Description**
lphWnd	A pointer to a handle to a window. If this function succeeds, the handle will be set to the window handle previously associated with this DirectDrawClipper object by the **IDirectDrawClipper::SetHWnd** () function.
Return Value	**Description**
DD_OK	DirectDraw successfully retrieved the window associated with the DirectDrawClipper object.
DDERR_INVALIDOBJECT	DirectDraw could not retrieve the clipper's associated window, because the DirectDrawClipper object is not valid.
DDERR_INVALIDPARAMS	DirectDraw could not retrieve the clipper's associated window, because one or more parameters are invalid.

IDirectDrawClipper::Initialize ()

Function Description

This function initializes a DirectDrawClipper object created with **CoCreateInstance** (). Applications that use the **IDirectDraw7::CreateClipper** () or **DirectDrawCreateClipper** () functions to create their DirectDrawClipper objects do not need to call this function.

Function Declaration

```
HRESULT Initialize(
   LPDIRECTDRAW lpDD,
   DWORD dwFlags
);
```

Parameter	Description
lpDD	A pointer to a DirectDraw7 object that is to be associated with this DirectDrawClipper object. This may be **NULL**, if no association is desired (this is the equivalent of calling **DirectDrawCreateClipper** ()).
dwFlags	This parameter is reserved for future use and must be 0.

Return Value	Description
DD_OK	DirectDraw successfully initialized the DirectDrawClipper object.
DDERR_ALREADYINITIALIZED	DirectDraw could not initialize the DirectDrawClipper object, because it is already initialized.
DDERR_INVALIDPARAMS	DirectDraw could not initialize the DirectDrawClipper object, because one or more parameters are invalid.

IDirectDrawClipper::IsClipListChanged ()

Function Description

This function retrieves the status of a clip list associated with a window. The status indicates whether it has changed since the last time this function was called.

Function Declaration

```
HRESULT IsClipListChanged(
   BOOL FAR *lpbChanged
);
```

Parameter	Description
lpbChanged	A pointer to a value of type **BOOL**. If this function succeeds, the value will be set to **TRUE** if the clip list has changed since the last time this function was called, or **FALSE** otherwise.

Return Value	Description
DD_OK	DirectDraw successfully retrieved the status of the clip list.
DDERR_INVALIDOBJECT	DirectDraw could not retrieve the status of the clip list, because the DirectDrawClipper object is not valid.
DDERR_INVALIDPARAMS	DirectDraw could not retrieve the status of the clip list, because one or more parameters are invalid.

IDirectDrawClipper::SetClipList ()

Function Description

This function sets the clip list for this DirectDrawClipper object. The clip list is a series of rectangles that specify the visible portions of the surface associated with this clipper object. When other surfaces are blitted on to this surface, only those portions that fall within one of the clip rectangles will be visible.

The **IDirectDrawSurface7::BltFast** () function ignores clip lists.

Function Declaration

```
HRESULT SetClipList(
    LPRGNDATA lpClipList,
    DWORD dwFlags
);
```

Parameter	Description
lpClipList	A pointer to a Win32 **RGNDATA** structure that contains the new clip list. This parameter may be **NULL**, in which case the current clip list is deleted.
dwFlags	This parameter is reserved for future use and must be 0.

Return Value	Description
DD_OK	DirectDraw successfully set the clip list.
DDERR_CLIPPERISUSINGHWND	DirectDraw could not set the clip list, because a window is associated with the DirectDrawClipper object. DirectDraw uses the clip list of the window as the clip list for this DirectDrawClipper object.
DDERR_INVALIDCLIPLIST	DirectDraw could not set the clip list, because the specified clip list is invalid.
DDERR_INVALIDOBJECT	DirectDraw could not set the clip list, because the DirectDrawClipper object is not valid.
DDERR_INVALIDPARAMS	DirectDraw could not set the clip list, because one or more parameters are invalid.
DDERR_OUTOFMEMORY	DirectDraw could not set the clip list, because sufficient memory is not available.

IDirectDrawClipper::SetHWnd ()

Function Description

This function associates a window with this DirectDrawClipper object. DirectDraw uses the clip list of this window as the clip list for this DirectDrawClipper object (see the Win32 functions **InvalidateRect** () and **ValidateRect** () for more information on a normal window's clip list). Applications that associate a window with a clipper object cannot set the clip list manually through **IDirectDrawClipper::SetClipList** ().

(continued)

IDirectDrawClipper::SetHWnd () *(continued)*

Function Declaration

```
HRESULT SetHWnd(
    DWORD dwFlags,
    HWND hWnd
);
```

Parameter	Description
dwFlags	This parameter is reserved for future use and must be 0.
hWnd	A handle to the main window of the application. This parameter may be **NULL** if **dwFlags** includes the **DDSCL_NORMAL** flag.

Return Value	Description
DD_OK	DirectDraw successfully set the clipper's window handle.
DDERR_INVALIDCLIPLIST	DirectDraw could not set the clipper's window handle, because the specified clip list is invalid.
DDERR_INVALIDOBJECT	DirectDraw could not set the clipper's window handle, because the DirectDrawClipper object is not valid.
DDERR_INVALIDPARAMS	DirectDraw could not set the clipper's window handle, because one or more parameters are invalid.
DDERR_OUTOFMEMORY	DirectDraw could not set the clipper's window handle, because sufficient memory is not available.

IDirectDrawColorControl

Applications can obtain the IDirectDrawColorControl interface by querying an IDirectDrawSurface7 interface.

The GUID for the IDirectDrawColorControl interface is **IID_IDirectDrawColorControl**.

IDirectDrawColorControl::GetColorControls ()

Function Description

This function retrieves the color control settings of the surface from which this interface was queried. The surface must be either a primary surface or an overlay.

Function Declaration

```
HRESULT GetColorControls(
    LPDDCOLORCONTROL lpColorControl
);
```

Parameter	Description
lpColorControl	A pointer to a **DDCOLORCONTROL** structure. If this function succeeds, the structure will be filled with the color control settings of the surface.

(continued)

IDirectDrawColorControl::GetColorControls () *(continued)*	
Return Value	**Description**
DD_OK	DirectDraw successfully retrieved the color control settings.
DDERR_INVALIDOBJECT	DirectDraw could not retrieve the color control settings, because the DirectDrawColorControl object is not valid.
DDERR_INVALIDPARAMS	DirectDraw could not retrieve the color control settings, because one or more parameters are invalid.
DDERR_UNSUPPORTED	DirectDraw could not retrieve the color control settings, because the operation is not supported.

IDirectDrawColorControl::SetColorControls ()	
Function Description	
This function sets the color control settings of the surface from which this interface was queried. The surface must be either a primary surface or an overlay.	

Function Declaration
```
HRESULT SetColorControls(
    LPDDCOLORCONTROL lpColorControl
);
```

Parameter	**Description**
lpColorControl	A pointer to a **DDCOLORCONTROL** structure that describes the new color control settings.
Return Value	**Description**
DD_OK	DirectDraw successfully set the color control settings.
DDERR_INVALIDOBJECT	DirectDraw could not set the color control settings, because the DirectDrawColorControl object is not valid.
DDERR_INVALIDPARAMS	DirectDraw could not set the color control settings, because one or more parameters are invalid.
DDERR_UNSUPPORTED	DirectDraw could not set the color control settings, because the operation is not supported.

IDirectDrawGammaControl

Applications can obtain the IDirectDrawGammaControl interface by querying an IDirectDrawSurface7 interface.

The GUID for the IDirectDrawGammaControl interface is **IID_IDirectDraw-GammaControl**.

IDirectDrawGammaControl::GetGammaRamp ()

Function Description

This function retrieves the gamma ramp levels of the surface from which this interface was queried. The surface must be a primary surface.

Function Declaration

```
HRESULT GetGammaRamp(
    DWORD  dwFlags,
    LPGAMMARAMP lpRampData
);
```

Parameter	Description
dwFlags	This parameter is reserved for future use and must be 0.
lpRampData	A pointer to a **DDGAMMARAMP** structure. If this function succeeds, the structure will be filled with gamma ramp levels of the primary surface.

Return Value	Description
DD_OK	DirectDraw successfully retrieved the surface's gamma ramp levels.
DDERR_EXCEPTION	DirectDraw could not retrieve the surface's gamma ramp levels, because an exception occurred.
DDERR_INVALIDOBJECT	DirectDraw could not retrieve the surface's gamma ramp levels, because the DirectDrawGammaControl object is not valid.
DDERR_INVALIDPARAMS	DirectDraw could not retrieve the surface's gamma ramp levels, because one or more parameters are invalid.

IDirectDrawGammaControl::SetGammaRamp ()

Function Description

This function sets the gamma ramp levels of the surface from which this interface was queried. The surface must be a primary surface.

Function Declaration

```
HRESULT SetGammaRamp(
    DWORD  dwFlags,
    LPGAMMARAMP lpRampData
);
```

Parameter	Description
dwFlags	Describes whether or not gamma calibration should be performed. This parameter may be **DDSGR_CALIBRATE**, in which case the gamma ramp will be adjusted according to the physical properties of the display, or 0, in which case no gamma calibration will be performed.
lpRampData	A pointer to a **DDGAMMARAMP** structure that describes the new gamma ramp settings.

(continued)

IDirectDrawGammaControl::SetGammaRamp () *(continued)*	
Return Value	**Description**
DD_OK	DirectDraw successfully set the primary surface's gamma ramp levels.
DDERR_EXCEPTION	DirectDraw could not set the primary surface's gamma ramp levels, because an exception occurred.
DDERR_INVALIDOBJECT	DirectDraw could not set the primary surface's gamma ramp levels, because the DirectDrawGammaControl object is not valid.
DDERR_INVALIDPARAMS	DirectDraw could not set the primary surface's gamma ramp levels, because one or more parameters are invalid.
DDERR_OUTOFMEMORY	DirectDraw could not set the primary surface's gamma ramp levels, because sufficient memory is not available.

IDirectDrawPalette

Applications can obtain the IDirectDrawPalette interface by calling the **IDirectDraw7::- CreatePalette ()** function.

The GUID for the IDirectDrawPalette interface is **IID_IDirectDrawPalette**.

IDirectDrawPalette::GetCaps ()	
Function Description	
This function retrieves the capabilities of the palette represented by this DirectDrawPalette object.	
Function Declaration	
```HRESULT GetCaps(LPDWORD lpdwCaps);```	
Parameter	**Description**
lpdwCaps	A pointer to an integer. If this function succeeds, the integer will be set to the capabilities of the palette, designated by one or more of the following flags:
	• **DDPCAPS_1BIT**—The palette consists of two entries in the color table. Unless **DDPCAPS_8BITENTRIES** is specified, these entries contain red, green, and blue color information. Surfaces that use this palette must use 1 bit per pixel.
	• **DDPCAPS_2BIT**—The palette consists of four entries in the color table. Unless **DDPCAPS_8BITENTRIES** is specified, these entries contain red, green, and blue color information. Surfaces that use this palette must use 2 bits per pixel.

(continued)

IDirectDrawPalette::GetCaps () *(continued)*	
Parameter	**Description**
	• **DDPCAPS_4BIT**—The palette consists of 16 entries in the color table. Unless **DDPCAPS_8BITENTRIES** is specified, these entries contain red, green, and blue color information. Surfaces that use this palette must use 4 bits per pixel.
	• **DDPCAPS_8BIT**—The palette consists of 256 entries in the color table. These entries contain red, green, and blue color information. Surfaces that use this palette must use 8 bits per pixel.
	• **DDPCAPS_8BITENTRIES**—The palette color entries consist not of red, green, and blue color values, but of 1-byte indices into the palette of the destination surface. Any surface using this palette can only be blitted into destination surfaces that have 256-entry palettes.
	• **DDPCAPS_ALPHA**—The palette contains alpha information, specified in the **peFlags** member of each **PALETTEENTRY** structure pointed to by the **lpDDColorArray** parameter. This flag is valid only for textures.
	• **DDPCAPS_ALLOW256**—The palette can have all of its 256 entries defined.
	• **DDPCAPS_PRIMARYSURFACE**—The palette will be associated with the primary surface. Any change in the color values of a palette so associated will be reflected immediately on the display.
	• **DDPCAPS_PRIMARYSURFACELEFT**—The palette will be associated with the primary surface for the user's left eye. Any change in the color values of a palette so associated will be immediately reflected on the left display.
	• **DDPCAPS_VSYNC**—Changes to the palette's color values can be synched with the display's refresh rate, eliminating artifacts otherwise noticed with palette changes for primary surfaces.
Return Value	**Description**
DD_OK	DirectDraw successfully retrieved the capabilities of the palette.
DDERR_INVALIDOBJECT	DirectDraw could not retrieve the palette's capabilities, because the DirectDrawPalette object is not valid.
DDERR_INVALIDPARAMS	DirectDraw could not retrieve the palette's capabilities, because one or more parameters are invalid.

IDirectDrawPalette::GetEntries ()

Function Description

This function retrieves the color entries for the palette represented by this DirectDrawPalette object.

Function Declaration

```
HRESULT GetEntries(
    DWORD dwFlags,
    DWORD dwBase,
    DWORD dwNumEntries,
    LPPALETTEENTRY lpEntries
);
```

Parameter	Description
dwFlags	This parameter is reserved for future use and must be 0.
dwBase	The index of the first entry to be retrieved.
dwNumEntries	The number of entries beginning with **dwBase** to be retrieved.
lpEntries	A pointer to color entry information. The color entry information can be an array either of Win32 **PALETTEENTRY** structures or of bytes (if **DDPCAPS_8BITENTRIES** is specified). In the former case, the **peRed**, **peGreen**, and **peBlue** members of the structure specify the color of the palette entry (and **peFlags** specifies alpha information, if any). In the latter case, each byte specifies the destination surface's palette index to use for the entry's colors.

Return Value	Description
DD_OK	DirectDraw successfully retrieved the palette's entries.
DDERR_INVALIDOBJECT	DirectDraw could not retrieve the palette's entries, because the DirectDrawPalette object is not valid.
DDERR_INVALIDPARAMS	DirectDraw could not retrieve the palette's entries, because one or more parameters are invalid.
DDERR_NOTPALETTIZED	DirectDraw could not retrieve the palette's entries, because the surface is not palettized.

IDirectDrawPalette::Initialize ()

Function Description

This function initializes a DirectDrawPalette object created with **CoCreateInstance** (). Applications that use the **IDirectDraw7::CreatePalette** () function to create their DirectDrawPalette objects do not need to call this function.

Function Declaration

```
HRESULT Initialize(
    LPDIRECTDRAW lpDD,
    DWORD dwFlags,
    LPPALETTEENTRY lpDDColorTable
);
```

(continued)

IDirectDrawPalette::Initialize () *(continued)*

Parameter	Description
lpDD	A pointer to a DirectDraw7 object that is to create this DirectDrawPalette object.
dwFlags	This parameter is reserved for future use and must be 0.
lpDDColorTable	This parameter is reserved for future use and must be 0.
Return Value	Description
DDERR_ALREADYINITIALIZED	DirectDraw could not initialize the DirectDrawPalette object, because it is already initialized.

IDirectDrawPalette::SetEntries ()

Function Description

This function sets the color entries for the palette represented by this DirectDrawPalette object.

Function Declaration

```
HRESULT SetEntries(
    DWORD dwFlags,
    DWORD dwStartingEntry,
    DWORD dwCount,
    LPPALETTEENTRY lpEntries
);
```

Parameter	Description
dwFlags	This parameter is reserved for future use and must be 0.
dwStartingEntry	The index of the first entry to be set.
dwCount	The number of entries beginning with **dwStartingEntry** to be set.
lpEntries	A pointer to color entry information. The color entry information can be an array either of Win32 **PALETTEENTRY** structures or of bytes (if **DDPCAPS_8BITENTRIES** is specified). In the former case, the **peRed**, **peGreen**, and **peBlue** members of the structure specify the color of the palette entry (and **peFlags** specifies alpha information, if any). In the latter case, each byte specifies the destination surface's palette index to use for the entry's colors.
Return Value	Description
DD_OK	DirectDraw successfully set the palette entry's colors.
DDERR_INVALIDOBJECT	DirectDraw could not set the palette entry's colors, because the DirectDrawPalette object is not valid.
DDERR_INVALIDPARAMS	DirectDraw could not set the palette entry's colors, because one or more parameters are invalid.
DDERR_NOPALETTEATTACHED	DirectDraw could not set the palette entry's colors, because no palette is attached to the surface.
DDERR_NOTPALETTIZED	DirectDraw could not set the palette entry's colors, because the surface is not palettized.
DDERR_UNSUPPORTED	DirectDraw could not set the palette entry's colors, because the operation is not supported.

IDirectDrawSurface7

Applications can obtain the IDirectDrawSurface7 interface by calling the **IDirectDraw7::CreateSurface ()** function.

The GUID for the IDirectDrawSurface7 interface is **IID_IDirectDrawSurface7**.

IDirectDrawSurface7::AddAttachedSurface ()

Function Description

This function attaches a surface to this surface. Attached surfaces must be identical in size (unless one is a texture) and located in the same memory type (video memory or systems memory) for this function to succeed. A nonflippable surface will become part of the flipping chain if attached to a flippable surface. Flipping surfaces of the same type cannot be attached to each other.

Function Declaration

```
HRESULT AddAttachedSurface(
    LPDIRECTDRAWSURFACE7 lpDDSAttachedSurface
);
```

Parameter	Description
lpDDSAttachedSurface	A pointer to the DirectDrawSurface7 object to attach to this surface.

Return Value	Description
DD_OK	DirectDraw successfully attached the specified surface.
DDERR_CANNOTATTACHSURFACE	DirectDraw could not attach the specified surface, because the specified surface is not compatible.
DDERR_GENERIC	DirectDraw could not attach the specified surface, because of a generic error.
DDERR_INVALIDOBJECT	DirectDraw could not attach the specified surface, because the DirectDrawSurface7 object is not valid.
DDERR_INVALIDPARAMS	DirectDraw could not attach the specified surface, because one or more parameters are invalid.
DDERR_SURFACEALREADYATTACHED	DirectDraw could not attach the specified surface, because the specified surface is already attached.
DDERR_SURFACELOST	DirectDraw could not attach the specified surface, because the memory of the DirectDraw surface has been lost. It must be restored with the **IDirectDrawSurface7::Restore ()** function.
DDERR_WASSTILLDRAWING	DirectDraw could not attach the specified surface, because it is still engaged in surface blit operations.

IDirectDrawSurface7::Blt ()

Function Description

This function blits from a source surface to the surface associated with this DirectDrawSurface7 object. This function supports clipping, arbitrary enlargement and reduction of the source surface, destination and source color keys, and blitting between different memory types. It does not, however, support z-buffering or alpha blending during blit operations.

Function Declaration

```
HRESULT Blt(
    LPRECT lpDestRect,
    LPDIRECTDRAWSURFACE7 lpDDSrcSurface,
    LPRECT lpSrcRect,
    DWORD dwFlags,
    LPDDBLTFX lpDDBltFx
);
```

Parameter	Description
lpDestRect	A pointer to a Win32 **RECT** structure that describes the destination rectangle. The source surface will be blitted to this rectangle. Note that according to Windows convention, the bottom and right sides of this rectangle will not be displayed; for example, if the rectangle specifies the area (0, 0) (for the upper left corner) and (10, 10) (for the lower right corner), only the region (0, 0) to (9, 9) will be displayed.
lpDDSrcSurface	A pointer to a DirectDrawSurface7 object that identifies the source surface. This surface will be blitted to the surface represented by this DirectDrawSurface7 object.
lpSrcRect	A pointer to a Win32 **RECT** structure that describes the source rectangle, the area that will be copied to the destination surface. Note that according to Windows convention, the bottom and right sides of this rectangle will not be copied; for example, if the rectangle specifies the area (0, 0) (for the upper left corner) and (10, 10) (for the lower right corner), only the region (0, 0) to (9, 9) will be copied.
dwFlags	Describes how the blit will be performed. This parameter can be one or more of the following flags: • **DDBLT_ASYNC**—DirectDraw should perform the blit asynchronously, storing the request in a first-in-first-out list. If the list is full, this function will fail. • **DDBLT_COLORFILL**—DirectDraw should use the **dwFillColor** member of **lpDDBltFx**. This member identifies an RGB color that DirectDraw should use to fill the destination rectangle on the destination surface. • **DDBLT_DDFX**—DirectDraw should use the **dwDDFX** member of **lpDDBltFx**. This member identifies the effects DirectDraw should apply to the blit operation.

(continued)

IDirectDrawSurface7::Blt () *(continued)*	
Parameter	**Description**
	• **DDBLT_DDROPS**—DirectDraw should use the **dwDDROP** member of **lpDDBltFx**. This member identifies the raster operations (ROPs) that DirectDraw should apply to the blit operation. These are ROPs not supported by the Win32 API.
	• **DDBLT_DEPTHFILL**—DirectDraw should use the **dwFillDepth** member of **lpDDBltFx**. This member identifies a z-value that DirectDraw should use to fill the destination rectangle on the destination surface. If this flag is specified, the destination surface must be a z-buffer.
	• **DDBLT_DONOTWAIT**—DirectDraw should immediately return **DDERR_WASSTILLDRAWING** without waiting if the blitter is busy.
	• **DDBLT_KEYDEST**—DirectDraw should use the destination surface's color key.
	• **DDBLT_KEYDESTOVERRIDE**—DirectDraw should use the **ddckDestColorKey** member of **lpDDBltFx**. This member specifies a color key that DirectDraw should use as the destination surface's color key; this color key overrides the destination surface's own color key.
	• **DDBLT_KEYSRC**—DirectDraw should use the source surface's color key.
	• **DDBLT_KEYSRCOVERRIDE**—DirectDraw should use the **ddckSrcColorKey** member of **lpDDBltFx**. This member specifies a color key that DirectDraw should use as the source surface's color key; this color key overrides the source surface's own color key.
	• **DDBLT_ROP**—DirectDraw should use the **dwROP** member of **lpDDBltFx**. This member identifies the ROPs that DirectDraw should apply to the blit operation. These are ROPs supported by the Win32 API.
	• **DDBLT_ROTATIONANGLE**—DirectDraw should use the **dwRotationAngle** member of **lpDDBltFx**. This member specifies the angle (in 1/100th of a degree) that the source surface should be rotated by.
	• **DDBLT_WAIT**—DirectDraw should wait until the blitter is not busy before attempting to blit the surface.
lpDDBltFx	A pointer to a **DDBLTFX** structure whose valid members are designated by the **dwFlags** parameter.

(continued)

IDirectDrawSurface7::Blt () *(continued)*

Return Value	Description
DD_OK	DirectDraw successfully performed the blit.
DDERR_GENERIC	DirectDraw could not perform the blit, because of a generic error.
DDERR_INVALIDCLIPLIST	DirectDraw could not perform the blit, because the clip list associated with this surface is invalid.
DDERR_INVALIDOBJECT	DirectDraw could not perform the blit, because this object is not valid.
DDERR_INVALIDPARAMS	DirectDraw could not perform the blit, because one or more parameters are invalid.
DDERR_INVALIDRECT	DirectDraw could not perform the blit, because the specified rectangle is invalid.
DDERR_NOALPHAHW	DirectDraw could not perform the blit, because the hardware does not support alpha operations.
DDERR_NOBLTHW	DirectDraw could not perform the blit, because there is no hardware to perform the blit.
DDERR_NOCLIPLIST	DirectDraw could not perform the blit, because no clip list is available.
DDERR_NODDROPSHW	DirectDraw could not perform the blit, because the hardware does not support DirectDraw ROPs.
DDERR_NOMIRRORHW	DirectDraw could not perform the blit, because the hardware does not support mirroring operations.
DDERR_NORASTEROPHW	DirectDraw could not perform the blit, because the hardware does not support Win32 ROPs.
DDERR_NOROTATIONHW	DirectDraw could not perform the blit, because the hardware does not support rotation.
DDERR_NOSTRETCHHW	DirectDraw could not perform the blit, because the hardware does not support stretching.
DDERR_NOZBUFFERHW	DirectDraw could not perform the blit, because the hardware does not support z-buffers.
DDERR_SURFACEBUSY	DirectDraw could not perform the blit, because one or more surfaces are being accessed. Memory cannot be compacted until these operations are complete.
DDERR_SURFACELOST	DirectDraw could not perform the blit, because the memory of the DirectDraw surface has been lost. It must be restored with the **IDirectDrawSurface7::Restore** () function.
DDERR_UNSUPPORTED	DirectDraw could not perform the blit, because the operation is not supported.
DDERR_WASSTILLDRAWING	DirectDraw could not perform the blit, because it is still engaged in surface blit operations.

IDirectDrawSurface7::BltFast ()

Function Description

This function blits from a source surface to the surface associated with this DirectDrawSurface7 object. This function does not support clipping, arbitrary enlargement and reduction of the source surface, or nondisplay surfaces, and does support color keys.

Function Declaration

```
HRESULT BltFast(
    DWORD dwX,
    DWORD dwY,
    LPDIRECTDRAWSURFACE7 lpDDSrcSurface,
    LPRECT lpSrcRect,
    DWORD dwTrans
);
```

Parameter	Description
dwX	An integer describing the destination x-coordinate for the source surface's left side.
dwY	An integer describing the destination y-coordinate for the source surface's top side.
lpDDSrcSurface	A pointer to a DirectDrawSurface7 object that identifies the source surface. This surface will be blitted to the surface associated with this DirectDrawSurface7 object.
lpSrcRect	A pointer to a Win32 **RECT** structure that describes the source rectangle, the area that will be copied to the destination surface. Note that according to Windows convention, the bottom and right sides of this rectangle will not be copied; for example, if the rectangle specifies the area (0, 0) (for the upper left corner) and (10, 10) (for the lower right corner), only the region (0, 0) to (9, 9) will be copied.
dwTrans	Describes how the blit should take place. This parameter can be one or more of the following flags: <ul><li>**DDBLTFAST_DESTCOLORKEY**—DirectDraw should use the destination surface's color key.</li><li>**DDBLTFAST_NOCOLORKEY**—DirectDraw should not use any color key. The blit will be performed without transparency.</li><li>**DDBLTFAST_SRCCOLORKEY**—DirectDraw should use the source surface's color key.</li><li>**DDBLTFAST_WAIT**—DirectDraw should wait until the blitter is not busy before attempting to blit the surface. If this flag is not specified, this function will fail if the blitter is busy.</li></ul>

(continued)

IDirectDrawSurface7::BltFast () *(continued)*

Return Value	Description
DD_OK	DirectDraw successfully performed the blit operation.
DDERR_EXCEPTION	DirectDraw could not blit the surface, because an exception occurred.
DDERR_GENERIC	DirectDraw could not blit the surface, because of a generic error.
DDERR_INVALIDOBJECT	DirectDraw could not blit the surface, because this DirectDrawSurface7 object is not valid.
DDERR_INVALIDPARAMS	DirectDraw could not blit the surface, because one or more parameters are invalid.
DDERR_INVALIDRECT	DirectDraw could not blit the surface, because the specified rectangle is invalid.
DDERR_NOBLTHW	DirectDraw could not blit the surface, because there is no hardware to perform the blit.
DDERR_SURFACEBUSY	DirectDraw could not blit the surface, because one or more surfaces are being accessed.
DDERR_SURFACELOST	DirectDraw could not blit the surface, because the memory of the DirectDraw surface has been lost. It must be restored with the **IDirectDrawSurface7::Restore** () function.
DDERR_UNSUPPORTED	DirectDraw could not blit the surface, because the operation is not supported.
DDERR_WASSTILLDRAWING	DirectDraw could not blit the surface, because it is still engaged in surface blit operations.

IDirectDrawSurface7::ChangeUniquenessValue ()

Function Description

This function manually updates a surface's uniqueness value. Applications can use a surface's uniqueness value to determine when a surface has changed.

Function Declaration

```
HRESULT ChangeUniquenessValue();
```

Parameter	Description
None	

Return Value	Description
DD_OK	DirectDraw successfully updated the surface's uniqueness value.
DDERR_EXCEPTION	DirectDraw could not change the surface's uniqueness value, because an exception occurred.
DDERR_INVALIDOBJECT	DirectDraw could not change the surface's uniqueness value, because this DirectDrawSurface7 object is not valid.
DDERR_INVALIDPARAMS	DirectDraw could not change the surface's uniqueness value, because one or more parameters are invalid.

IDirectDrawSurface7::DeleteAttachedSurface ()

Function Description

This function detaches one or all surfaces that were attached to this surface with the **IDirectDrawSurface7::AddAttachedSurface** () function.

Function Declaration

```
HRESULT DeleteAttachedSurface(
    DWORD dwFlags,
    LPDIRECTDRAWSURFACE7 lpDDSAttachedSurface
);
```

Parameter	Description
dwFlags	Reserved for future use. This parameter must be 0.
lpDDSAttachedSurface	A pointer to a DirectDrawSurface7 object that represents the surface to be detached from this surface. This parameter may be **NULL**, in which case DirectDraw detaches all surfaces attached to this surface.

Return Value	Description
DD_OK	DirectDraw successfully detached the surface.
DDERR_CANNOTDETACHSURFACE	DirectDraw could not delete the attached surface.
DDERR_INVALIDOBJECT	DirectDraw could not delete the attached surface, because this DirectDrawSurface7 object is not valid.
DDERR_INVALIDPARAMS	DirectDraw could not delete the attached surface, because one or more parameters are invalid.
DDERR_SURFACELOST	DirectDraw could not delete the attached surface because the memory of the DirectDraw surface has been lost. It must be restored with the **IDirectDrawSurface7::Restore** () function.
DDERR_SURFACENOTATTACHED	DirectDraw could not delete the attached surface, because the specified surface is not attached.

IDirectDrawSurface7::EnumAttachedSurfaces ()

Function Description

This function enumerates all surfaces attached to this surface.

Function Declaration

```
HRESULT EnumAttachedSurfaces(
    LPVOID lpContext,
    LPDDENUMSURFACESCALLBACK7 lpEnumSurfacesCallback
);
```

(continued)

IDirectDrawSurface7::EnumAttachedSurfaces () *(continued)*	
Parameter	Description
lpContext	A pointer to application-defined data that will be sent to the callback function every time it is called.
lpEnumSurfacesCallback	A pointer to a **EnumSurfacesCallback7** () callback function. This function will be called for every attached surface enumerated.
Return Value	Description
DD_OK	DirectDraw successfully enumerated the surfaces attached to this surface.
DDERR_INVALIDOBJECT	DirectDraw could not enumerate the surfaces, because this DirectDrawSurface7 object is not valid.
DDERR_INVALIDPARAMS	DirectDraw could not enumerate the surfaces, because one or more parameters are invalid.
DDERR_SURFACELOST	DirectDraw could not enumerate the surfaces, because the memory of the DirectDraw surface has been lost. It must be restored with the **IDirectDrawSurface7::Restore** () function.

IDirectDrawSurface7::EnumOverlayZOrders ()

Function Description

This function enumerates the overlays on the primary surface, either in front-to-back or back-to-front order.

Function Declaration

```
HRESULT EnumOverlayZOrders(
   DWORD dwFlags,
   LPVOID lpContext,
   LPDDENUMSURFACESCALLBACK7 lpfnCallback
);
```

Parameter	Description
dwFlags	Describes the order of enumeration. This parameter can be one or more of the following flags: • **DDENUMOVERLAYZ_BACKTOFRONT**—DirectDraw should enumerate the overlays back-to-front. • **DDENUMOVERLAYZ_FRONTTOBACK**—DirectDraw should enumerate the overlays front-to-back.
lpContext	A pointer to application-defined data that will be sent to the callback function every time it is called.
lpfnCallback	A pointer to an **EnumSurfacesCallback7** () callback function. This function will be called for overlays enumerated.

(continued)

IDirectDrawSurface7::EnumOverlayZOrders () *(continued)*	
Return Value	**Description**
DD_OK	DirectDraw successfully enumerated the surface's overlays.
DDERR_INVALIDOBJECT	DirectDraw could not enumerate the surface's overlays, because this DirectDrawSurface7 object is not valid.
DDERR_INVALIDPARAMS	DirectDraw could not enumerate the surface's overlays, because one or more parameters are invalid.

IDirectDrawSurface7::Flip ()

Function Description

This function flips the surface, thereby making the back-buffer become the front-buffer, and the front-buffer, the back-buffer.

Function Declaration

```
HRESULT Flip(
    LPDIRECTDRAWSURFACE7 lpDDSurfaceTargetOverride,
    DWORD dwFlags
);
```

Parameter	Description
lpDDSurfaceTargetOverride	A pointer to a DirectDrawSurface7 object that identifies the back-buffer to become the front-buffer; this must be part of the flipping chain. This parameter may be **NULL**, in which case DirectDraw cycles through the surfaces in the order they were attached.
dwFlags	Describes how the flip should be performed. This parameter can be one or more of the following flags:
	• **DDFLIP_EVEN**—The overlay surface being used to display video contains data from the even field of a video source. This flag cannot be used with the **DDFLIP_ODD** flag.
	• **DDFLIP_INTERVAL2**—DirectDraw should flip once every two vertical blanking intervals, returning **DDERR_WASSTILLDRAWING** whenever this function is called on the wrong vertical blanking interval.
	• **DDFLIP_INTERVAL3**—DirectDraw should flip once every three vertical blanking intervals, returning **DDERR_WASSTILLDRAWING** whenever this function is called on the wrong vertical blanking interval.
	• **DDFLIP_INTERVAL4**—DirectDraw should flip once every four vertical blanking intervals, returning **DDERR_WASSTILLDRAWING** whenever this function is called on the wrong vertical blanking interval.

(continued)

IDirectDrawSurface7::Flip () *(continued)*	
Parameter	Description
	• **DDFLIP_NOVSYNC**—DirectDraw should flip immediately, not waiting for a vertical blanking interval. If this flag is specified, flipping may produce visible distortions on the display.
	• **DDFLIP_ODD**—The overlay surface being used to display video contains data from the odd field of a video source. This flag cannot be used with the **DDFLIP_EVEN** flag.
	• **DDFLIP_STEREO**—DirectDraw should display and flip to a main stereo surface.
	• **DDFLIP_WAIT**—DirectDraw should wait until the hardware can perform the flip. If this flag is not specified, this function will fail if the hardware cannot immediately perform the flip.
Return Value	Description
DD_OK	DirectDraw successfully flipped the surface.
DDERR_GENERIC	DirectDraw could not flip the surface, because of a generic error.
DDERR_INVALIDOBJECT	DirectDraw could not flip the surface, because this DirectDrawSurface7 object is not valid.
DDERR_INVALIDPARAMS	DirectDraw could not flip the surface, because one or more parameters are invalid.
DDERR_NOFLIPHW	DirectDraw could not flip the surface, because the hardware does not support flipping.
DDERR_NOTFLIPPABLE	DirectDraw could not flip the surface, because the specified surface is not flippable.
DDERR_SURFACEBUSY	DirectDraw could not flip the surface, because one or more surfaces are being accessed.
DDERR_SURFACELOST	DirectDraw could not flip the surface, because the memory of the DirectDraw surface has been lost. It must be restored with the **IDirectDrawSurface7::Restore** () function.
DDERR_UNSUPPORTED	DirectDraw could not flip the surface, because the operation is not supported.
DDERR_WASSTILLDRAWING	DirectDraw could not flip the surface, because it is still engaged in surface blit operations.

IDirectDrawSurface7::FreePrivateData ()

Function Description

This function frees the memory used to hold the surface's private data.

Function Declaration

```
HRESULT FreePrivateData(
    REFGUID guidTag,
);
```

Parameter	Description
guidTag	A GUID that identifies the private data to be freed.
Return Value	**Description**
DD_OK	DirectDraw successfully freed the memory used to hold the surface's private data.
DDERR_INVALIDOBJECT	DirectDraw could not free the surface's private data, because this DirectDrawSurface7 object is not valid.
DDERR_INVALIDPARAMS	DirectDraw could not free the surface's private data, because one or more parameters are invalid.
DDERR_NOTFOUND	DirectDraw could not free the surface's private data, because the specified item was not found.

IDirectDrawSurface7::GetAttachedSurface ()

Function Description

This function retrieves a DirectDrawSurface7 interface for a specified surface attached to this surface.

Function Declaration

```
HRESULT GetAttachedSurface(
    LPDDSCAPS2 lpDDSCaps,
    LPDIRECTDRAWSURFACE7 FAR *lplpDDAttachedSurface
);
```

Parameter	Description
lpDDSCaps	A pointer to a **DDSCAPS2** structure that describes the attributes of the attached surface to be retrieved.
lplpDDAttachedSurface	A pointer to a DirectDrawSurface7 object. If this function succeeds, the pointer will be set to the attached surface specified by the **lpDDSCaps** parameter.
Return Value	**Description**
DD_OK	DirectDraw successfully retrieved the specified attached surface.
DDERR_INVALIDOBJECT	DirectDraw could not retrieve the specified attached surface, because this DirectDrawSurface7 object is not valid.
DDERR_INVALIDPARAMS	DirectDraw could not retrieve the specified attached surface, because one or more parameters are invalid.

(continued)

IDirectDrawSurface7::GetAttachedSurface () *(continued)*

Return Value	Description
DDERR_NOTFOUND	DirectDraw could not retrieve the specified attached surface, because the specified surface was not found.
DDERR_SURFACELOST	DirectDraw could not retrieve the specified attached surface, because the memory of the DirectDraw surface has been lost. It must be restored with the **IDirectDrawSurface7::Restore ()** function.

IDirectDrawSurface7::GetBltStatus ()

Function Description

This function retrieves the status of the blitter.

Function Declaration

```
HRESULT GetBltStatus(
   DWORD dwFlags
);
```

Parameter	Description
dwFlags	Describes which aspect of the blitter's status is being retrieved. This parameter can be one or more of the following flags: • **DDGBS_CANBLT**—DirectDraw should return **DD_OK** if the surface can be used immediately in a blit operation. • **DDGBS_ISBLTDONE**—DirectDraw should return **DD_OK** if all blits on this surface have been completed.

Return Value	Description
DD_OK	The interpretation of this return value depends on **dwFlags**.
DDERR_WASSTILLDRAWING	DirectDraw could not retrieve the status of the blitter, because it is still engaged in surface blit operations.
DDERR_INVALIDOBJECT	DirectDraw could not retrieve the status of the blitter, because this DirectDrawSurface7 object is not valid.
DDERR_INVALIDPARAMS	DirectDraw could not retrieve the status of the blitter, because one or more parameters are invalid.
DDERR_NOBLTHW	DirectDraw could not retrieve the status of the blitter, because there is no hardware to perform the blit.
DDERR_SURFACEBUSY	DirectDraw could not retrieve the status of the blitter, because one or more surfaces are being accessed.
DDERR_SURFACELOST	DirectDraw could not retrieve the status of the blitter, because the memory of the DirectDraw surface has been lost. It must be restored with the **IDirectDrawSurface7::Restore ()** function.
DDERR_UNSUPPORTED	DirectDraw could not retrieve the status of the blitter, because the operation is not supported.
DDERR_WASSTILLDRAWING	DirectDraw could not retrieve the status of the blitter, because it is still engaged in surface blit operations.

IDirectDrawSurface7::GetCaps ()

Function Description

This function retrieves the capabilities of the surface.

Function Declaration

```
HRESULT GetCaps(
    LPDDSCAPS2 lpDDSCaps
);
```

Parameter	Description
lpDDSCaps	A pointer to a **DDSCAPS2** structure. If this function succeeds, the structure will be filled with the capabilities of the surface.

Return Value	Description
DD_OK	DirectDraw successfully retrieved the capabilities of the surface.
DDERR_INVALIDOBJECT	DirectDraw could not retrieve the capabilities of the surface, because this DirectDrawSurface7 object is not valid.
DDERR_INVALIDPARAMS	DirectDraw could not retrieve the capabilities of the surface, because one or more parameters are invalid.

IDirectDrawSurface7::GetClipper ()

Function Description

This function retrieves the DirectDrawClipper object associated with this surface.

Function Declaration

```
HRESULT GetClipper(
    LPDIRECTDRAWCLIPPER FAR *lplpDDClipper
);
```

Parameter	Description
lplpDDClipper	The address of a pointer to a DirectDrawClipper object. If this function succeeds, the pointer will be set to the DirectDrawClipper object associated with this surface.

Return Value	Description
DD_OK	DirectDraw successfully retrieved the DirectDrawClipper object associated with this surface.
DDERR_INVALIDOBJECT	DirectDraw could not retrieve the surface's clipper, because this DirectDrawSurface7 object is not valid.
DDERR_INVALIDPARAMS	DirectDraw could not retrieve the surface's clipper, because one or more parameters are invalid.
DDERR_NOCLIPPERATTACHED	DirectDraw could not retrieve the surface's clipper, because no clipper is associated with the surface.

IDirectDrawSurface7::GetColorKey ()

Function Description

This function retrieves either the source or destination color key for this surface.

Function Declaration

```
HRESULT GetColorKey(
    DWORD dwFlags,
    LPDDCOLORKEY lpDDColorKey
);
```

Parameter	Description
dwFlags	Describes which color key should be retrieved. This parameter must be one of the following flags:
	• **DDCKEY_DESTBLT**—The destination color key for a nonoverlay surface is being retrieved. A destination color key specifies one or more colors that can be covered on this surface by blit operations.
	• **DDCKEY_DESTOVERLAY**—The destination color key for an overlay surface. A destination color key specifies one or more colors that can be covered on this surface by overlay operations.
	• **DDCKEY_SRCBLT**—The source color key for a nonoverlay surface is being retrieved. A source color key specifies one or more colors that will not be visible when this surface is blitted to other surfaces.
	• **DDCKEY_SRCOVERLAY**—The source color key for an overlay surface is being retrieved. A source color key specifies one or more colors that will not be visible when this surface is overlaid on another surface.
lpDDColorKey	A pointer to a **DDCOLORKEY** structure. If this function succeeds, the structure will be filled with the requested color key.

Return Value	Description
DD_OK	DirectDraw successfully retrieved the color key.
DDERR_INVALIDOBJECT	DirectDraw could not retrieve the color key, because this DirectDrawSurface7 object is not valid.
DDERR_INVALIDPARAMS	DirectDraw could not retrieve the color key, because one or more parameters are invalid.
DDERR_NOCOLORKEY	DirectDraw could not retrieve the color key, because the requested color key has not been set for this surface.
DDERR_NOCOLORKEYHW	DirectDraw could not retrieve the color key, because the hardware does not support color keys.
DDERR_SURFACELOST	DirectDraw could not retrieve the color key, because the memory of the DirectDraw surface has been lost. It must be restored with the **IDirectDrawSurface7::Restore ()** function.
DDERR_UNSUPPORTED	DirectDraw could not retrieve the color key, because the operation is not supported.

IDirectDrawSurface7::GetDC ()

Function Description

This function creates a DC that the GDI can use to write on this DirectDraw surface.

Function Declaration

```
HRESULT GetDC(
    HDC FAR *lphDC
);
```

Parameter	Description
lphDC	The address of a pointer to a DC. If this function succeeds, the pointer will be set to the newly created device context. This surface will be locked until the **IDirectDrawSurface7::ReleaseDC** () function is called.

Return Value	Description
DD_OK	DirectDraw successfully created the DC.
DDERR_DCALREADYCREATED	DirectDraw could not create the DC, because a DC for this surface has already been created.
DDERR_GENERIC	DirectDraw could not create the DC, because of a generic error.
DDERR_INVALIDOBJECT	DirectDraw could not create the DC, because this DirectDrawSurface7 object is not valid.
DDERR_INVALIDPARAMS	DirectDraw could not create the DC, because one or more parameters are invalid.
DDERR_INVALIDSURFACETYPE	DirectDraw could not create the DC, because the surface type does not support this operation.
DDERR_SURFACELOST	DirectDraw could not create the DC, because the memory of the DirectDraw surface has been lost. It must be restored with the **IDirectDrawSurface7::Restore** () function.
DDERR_UNSUPPORTED	DirectDraw could not create the DC, because the operation is not supported.
DDERR_WASSTILLDRAWING	DirectDraw could not create the DC, because it is still engaged in surface blit operations.

IDirectDrawSurface7::GetDDInterface ()

Function Description

This function retrieves the DirectDraw interface used to create this surface.

Function Declaration

```
HRESULT GetDDInterface(
    LPVOID FAR *lplpDD
);
```

(continued)

IDirectDrawSurface7::GetDDInterface () *(continued)*	
Parameter	**Description**
lplpDD	A pointer to a variable. If this function succeeds, the variable will be set to the address of the interface that created this surface. Applications should cast this variable to the IUnknown interface and then query it for the desired DirectDraw interface.
Return Value	**Description**
DD_OK	DirectDraw successfully retrieved the DirectDraw interface.
DDERR_INVALIDOBJECT	DirectDraw could not retrieve the DirectDraw interface, because this DirectDrawSurface7 object is not valid.
DDERR_INVALIDPARAMS	DirectDraw could not retrieve the DirectDraw interface, because one or more parameters are invalid.

IDirectDrawSurface7::GetFlipStatus ()

Function Description

This function retrieves the status of a flip initiated with the **IDirectDrawSurface7::Flip** () function.

Function Declaration

```
HRESULT GetFlipStatus(
    DWORD dwFlags
);
```

Parameter	**Description**
dwFlags	Describes which aspect of the flip is being retrieved. This parameter must be one of the following flags: • **DDGFS_CANFLIP**—DirectDraw should return **DD_OK** if the surface can be flipped immediately. • **DDGFS_ISFLIPDONE**—DirectDraw should return **DD_OK** if the flip initiated with the **IDirectDrawSurface7::Flip** () function has completed.
Return Value	**Description**
DD_OK	DirectDraw successfully retrieved the status of the flip.
DDERR_WASSTILLDRAWING	DirectDraw could not retrieve the status of the flip, because it is still engaged in surface blit operations.
DDERR_INVALIDOBJECT	DirectDraw could not retrieve the status of the flip, because this DirectDrawSurface7 object is not valid.
DDERR_INVALIDPARAMS	DirectDraw could not retrieve the status of the flip, because one or more parameters are invalid.
DDERR_INVALIDSURFACETYPE	DirectDraw could not retrieve the status of the flip, because the surface type does not support this operation.
DDERR_SURFACEBUSY	DirectDraw could not retrieve the status of the flip, because one or more surfaces are being accessed.

(continued)

IDirectDrawSurface7::GetFlipStatus () *(continued)*	
Return Value	**Description**
DDERR_SURFACELOST	DirectDraw could not retrieve the status of the flip, because the memory of the DirectDraw surface has been lost. It must be restored with the **IDirectDrawSurface7::Restore** () function.
DDERR_UNSUPPORTED	DirectDraw could not retrieve the status of the flip, because the operation is not supported.

IDirectDrawSurface7::GetLOD ()

Function Description

This function retrieves the maximum level of detail currently set for an automatically managed mipmap surface. The maximum level of detail is that highest level of detail that Direct3D should load into a device's local video memory. The highest level of detail is identified by the number 1; the lowest level of detail depends on the texture.

This function will fail if the surface is not a managed mipmap surface. Managed surfaces are those created with the **DDSCAPS2_TEXTUREMANAGE** flag.

Function Declaration

```
HRESULT GetLOD(
    LPDWORD lpdwMaxLOD
);
```

Parameter	Description
lpdwMaxLOD	A pointer to a 32-bit unsigned integer. If this function succeeds, the integer will be set to the maximum level of detail currently set for this surface.
Return Value	**Description**
DD_OK	DirectDraw successfully retrieved the maximum level of detail for this surface.
DDERR_INVALIDOBJECT	DirectDraw could not retrieve the maximum level of detail, because this DirectDrawSurface7 object is invalid. This return value is possible if the texture is invalid, is not a mipmap surface, or is not managed by Direct3D.
DDERR_INVALIDPARAMS	DirectDraw could not retrieve the maximum level of detail, because one or more parameters are invalid.

IDirectDrawSurface7::GetOverlayPosition ()

Function Description

This function retrieves the position of an overlay surface on a destination surface.

Function Declaration

```
HRESULT GetOverlayPosition(
   LPLONG lplX,
   LPLONG lplY
);
```

Parameter	Description
lplX	A pointer to an integer. If this function succeeds, the integer will be set to the x-coordinate of the position of the overlay on the destination surface.
lplY	A pointer to an integer. If this function succeeds, the integer will be set to the y-coordinate of the position of the overlay on the destination surface.

Return Value	Description
DD_OK	DirectDraw successfully retrieved the position of the overlay.
DDERR_GENERIC	DirectDraw could not retrieve the overlay position, because of a generic error.
DDERR_INVALIDOBJECT	DirectDraw could not retrieve the overlay position, because this DirectDrawSurface7 object is not valid.
DDERR_INVALIDPARAMS	DirectDraw could not retrieve the overlay position, because one or more parameters are invalid.
DDERR_INVALIDPOSITION	DirectDraw could not retrieve the overlay position, because the position of the overlay is not valid.
DDERR_NOOVERLAYDEST	DirectDraw could not retrieve the overlay position, because the surface is not overlaid on a destination surface.
DDERR_NOTAOVERLAYSURFACE	DirectDraw could not retrieve the overlay position, because the surface is not an overlay surface.
DDERR_OVERLAYNOTVISIBLE	DirectDraw could not retrieve the overlay position, because the overlay is not visible.
DDERR_SURFACELOST	DirectDraw could not retrieve the overlay position, because the memory of the DirectDraw surface has been lost. It must be restored with the **IDirectDrawSurface7::Restore** () function.

IDirectDrawSurface7::GetPalette ()

Function Description

This function retrieves the DirectDrawPalette object associated with this surface.

Function Declaration

```
HRESULT GetPalette(
    LPDIRECTDRAWPALETTE FAR *lplpDDPalette
);
```

Parameter	Description
lplpDDPalette	The address of a pointer to a DirectDrawPalette object. If this function succeeds, the pointer will be set to the palette associated with this surface. According to COM standards, applications must release this interface when they are done using it.

Return Value	Description
DD_OK	DirectDraw successfully retrieved the palette.
DDERR_GENERIC	DirectDraw could not retrieve the palette, because of a generic error.
DDERR_INVALIDOBJECT	DirectDraw could not retrieve the palette, because this DirectDrawSurface7 object is not valid.
DDERR_INVALIDPARAMS	DirectDraw could not retrieve the palette, because one or more parameters are invalid.
DDERR_NOEXCLUSIVEMODE	DirectDraw could not retrieve the palette, because the device is not acquired in exclusive mode, a necessary condition for using this function.
DDERR_NOPALETTEATTACHED	DirectDraw could not retrieve the palette, because no palette is attached to the surface.
DDERR_SURFACELOST	DirectDraw could not retrieve the palette, because the memory of the DirectDraw surface has been lost. It must be restored with the **IDirectDrawSurface7::Restore** () function.
DDERR_UNSUPPORTED	DirectDraw could not retrieve the palette, because the operation is not supported.

IDirectDrawSurface7::GetPixelFormat ()

Function Description

This function retrieves the pixel format of this surface.

Function Declaration

```
HRESULT GetPixelFormat(
    LPDDPIXELFORMAT lpDDPixelFormat
);
```

(continued)

IDirectDrawSurface7::GetPixelFormat () *(continued)*

Parameter	Description
lpDDPixelFormat	A pointer a **DDPIXELFORMAT** structure. If this function succeeds, the structure will be filled with the pixel format of this surface.

Return Value	Description
DD_OK	DirectDraw successfully retrieved the surface's pixel format.
DDERR_INVALIDOBJECT	DirectDraw could not retrieve the pixel format, because this DirectDrawSurface7 object is not valid.
DDERR_INVALIDPARAMS	DirectDraw could not retrieve the pixel format, because one or more parameters are invalid.
DDERR_INVALIDSURFACETYPE	DirectDraw could not retrieve the pixel format, because the surface type does not support this operation.

IDirectDrawSurface7::GetPrivateData ()

Function Description

This function retrieves the surface's private data.

Function Declaration

```
HRESULT GetPrivateData(
    REFGUID guidTag,
    LPVOID  lpBuffer,
    LPDWORD lpcbBufferSize
);
```

Parameter	Description
guidTag	A GUID that identifies the private data to be retrieved.
lpBuffer	A pointer to a buffer that will contain the requested private data.
lpcbBufferSize	A pointer to an integer that describes the number of bytes pointed to by **lpBuffer**. When this function returns, the integer will be set to the number of bytes actually retrieved.

Return Value	Description
DD_OK	DirectDraw successfully retrieved the surface's private data.
DDERR_EXPIRED	DirectDraw could not retrieve the surface's private data, because the specified private data has expired.
DDERR_INVALIDOBJECT	DirectDraw could not retrieve the surface's private data, because this DirectDrawSurface7 object is not valid.
DDERR_INVALIDPARAMS	DirectDraw could not retrieve the surface's private data, because one or more parameters are invalid.

(continued)

IDirectDrawSurface7::GetPrivateData () *(continued)*

Return Value	Description
DDERR_MOREDATA	DirectDraw could not retrieve the surface's private data, because the buffer is not large enough to hold the available data.
DDERR_NOTFOUND	DirectDraw could not retrieve the surface's private data, because the specified item was not found.
DDERR_OUTOFMEMORY	DirectDraw could not retrieve the surface's private data, because sufficient memory is not available.

IDirectDrawSurface7::GetPriority ()

Function	Description

This function retrieves an automatically managed texture surface's priority level. The priority level is used to determine when the texture should be evicted from memory. Textures that have lower priorities are evicted before those with higher priorities. For textures that have identical priority levels, the one used most recently will be evicted last. Textures are evicted from memory as required by the amount of remaining free memory.

This function will fail if the surface is not a managed texture. Managed surfaces are those created with the **DDSCAPS2_TEXTUREMANAGE** flag.

Function	Declaration

```
HRESULT GetPriority(
  LPDWORD lpdwPriority
);
```

Parameter	Description
lpdwPriority	A pointer to a 32-bit unsigned integer. If the function succeeds, the integer will be set to the priority level of the texture surface.

Return Value	Description
D3D_OK	Direct3D successfully retrieved the priority of the surface.
DDERR_INVALIDOBJECT	DirectDraw could not retrieve the priority of the surface because this DirectDrawSurface7 object is invalid. This return value is possible if the texture is invalid or is not managed by Direct3D.

IDirectDrawSurface7::GetSurfaceDesc ()

Function Description

This function retrieves the surface description, which describes the attributes and state of the surface as it currently exists.

Function Declaration

```
HRESULT GetSurfaceDesc(
    LPDDSURFACEDESC2 lpDDSurfaceDesc
);
```

Parameter	Description
lpDDSurfaceDesc	A pointer a **DDSURFACEDESC2** structure. If this function succeeds, the structure will be filled with the surface description. Only the **dwSize** member of this structure needs to be initialized before this function is called.
Return Value	**Description**
DD_OK	DirectDraw successfully retrieved the surface description.
DDERR_INVALIDOBJECT	DirectDraw could not retrieve the surface description, because this DirectDrawSurface7 object is not valid.
DDERR_INVALIDPARAMS	DirectDraw could not retrieve the surface description, because one or more parameters are invalid.

IDirectDrawSurface7::GetUniquenessValue ()

Function Description

This function retrieves the surface's uniqueness value. Applications can use a surface's uniqueness value to determine if it has changed.

Function Declaration

```
HRESULT GetUniquenessValue(
    LPDWORD lpValue,
);
```

Parameter	Description
lpValue	A pointer an integer. If this function succeeds, the integer will be set to the surface's uniqueness value. A value of 0 indicates an indeterminate state—that is, DirectDraw cannot determine the state of the surface, so the application cannot know if the surface has changed.
Return Value	**Description**
DD_OK	DirectDraw successfully retrieved the surface's uniqueness value.
DDERR_INVALIDOBJECT	DirectDraw could not retrieve the uniqueness value, because this DirectDrawSurface7 object is not valid.
DDERR_INVALIDPARAMS	DirectDraw could not retrieve the uniqueness value, because one or more parameters are invalid.

IDirectDrawSurface7::Initialize ()

Function Description

This function initializes a DirectDrawSurface7 object created with **CoCreateInstance** (). Applications that use the **IDirectDraw7::CreateSurface** () to create their DirectDrawSurface7 objects do not need to call this function.

Function Declaration

```
HRESULT Initialize(
    LPDIRECTDRAW lpDD,
    LPDDSURFACEDESC2 lpDDSurfaceDesc
);
```

Parameter	Description
lpDD	A pointer a DirectDraw7 object that will be associated with the surface.
lpDDSurfaceDesc	A pointer a **DDSURFACEDESC2** structure that describes the attributes of the surface.

Return Value	Description
DDERR_ALREADYINITIALIZED	DirectDraw could not initialize the DirectDrawSurface7 object, because the DirectDrawSurface7 object is already initialized.

IDirectDrawSurface7::IsLost ()

Function Description

This function determines whether or not the memory associated with this surface has been freed.

Function Declaration

```
HRESULT IsLost();
```

Parameter	Description
None	

Return Value	Description
DD_OK	The memory associated with this surface has not been freed.
DDERR_INVALIDOBJECT	DirectDraw could not determine if the surface is lost, because this DirectDrawSurface7 object is not valid.
DDERR_INVALIDPARAMS	DirectDraw could not determine if the surface is lost, because one or more parameters are invalid.
DDERR_SURFACELOST	The memory associated with this surface has been freed.

IDirectDrawSurface7::Lock ()

Function Description

This function locks the surface for subsequent, direct access to its bits. Applications must call the **IDirectDrawSurface7::Unlock** () function after they are done accessing the surface.

Function Declaration

```
HRESULT Lock(
    LPRECT lpDestRect,
    LPDDSURFACEDESC2 lpDDSurfaceDesc,
    DWORD dwFlags,
    HANDLE hEvent
);
```

Parameter	Description
lpDestRect	A pointer a Win32 **RECT** structure that describes the region to lock. This parameter may be **NULL**, in which case the entire surface will be locked.
lpDDSurfaceDesc	A pointer to a **DDSURFACEDESC2** structure. If this function succeeds, the structure will be filled with the relevant details about the surface, including its width, height, pitch, and a pointer to its bits.
dwFlags	Describes how the lock is to take place. This parameter can be one or more of the following flags: • **DDLOCK_EVENT**—Not currently implemented. • **DDLOCK_NOSYSLOCK**—DirectDraw should not take the Win16Mutex. This flag, which is not valid for primary surfaces, allows other threads to continue running while the surface is locked. • **DDLOCK_READONLY**—The application will be read from only, not written to. • **DDLOCK_SURFACEMEMORYPTR**—DirectDraw should retrieve (in **lpDDSurfaceDesc**) a pointer to the top left corner of the rectangle specified by **lpDestRect**. If this flag is not specified or if **lpDestRect** is **NULL**, DirectDraw retrieves a pointer to the top left of the surface. • **DDLOCK_WAIT**—DirectDraw should wait until the surface can be locked before returning. If this flag is not specified, DirectDraw returns immediately with an error if a blit operation is in progress. • **DDLOCK_WRITEONLY**—The surface will be written to, not read from.
hEvent	This parameter is reserved for future use and must be **NULL**.

(continued)

IDirectDrawSurface7::Lock () *(continued)*	
Return Value	**Description**
DD_OK	DirectDraw successfully locked the surface.
DDERR_INVALIDOBJECT	DirectDraw could not lock the surface, because this DirectDrawSurface7 object is not valid.
DDERR_INVALIDPARAMS	DirectDraw could not lock the surface, because one or more parameters are invalid.
DDERR_OUTOFMEMORY	DirectDraw could not lock the surface, because sufficient memory is not available.
DDERR_SURFACEBUSY	DirectDraw could not lock the surface, because one or more surfaces are being accessed.
DDERR_SURFACELOST	DirectDraw could not lock the surface, because the memory of the DirectDraw surface has been lost. It must be restored with the **IDirectDrawSurface7::Restore** () function.
DDERR_WASSTILLDRAWING	DirectDraw could not lock the surface, because it is still engaged in surface blit operations.

IDirectDrawSurface7::PageLock ()	
Function Description	

This function locks the address of a system-memory surface for blit operations using direct memory access (DMA) transfers.

Function Declaration

```
HRESULT PageLock(
    DWORD dwFlags
);
```

Parameter	**Description**
dwFlags	Reserved for future use; this parameter must be 0.
Return Value	**Description**
DD_OK	DirectDraw successfully locked the address of the surface.
DDERR_CANTPAGELOCK	DirectDraw could not lock the surface, because the surface either exists in display memory or is an emulated primary surface.
DDERR_INVALIDOBJECT	DirectDraw could not lock the surface, because this DirectDrawSurface7 object is not valid.
DDERR_INVALIDPARAMS	DirectDraw could not lock the surface, because one or more parameters are invalid.
DDERR_SURFACELOST	DirectDraw could not lock the surface, because the memory of the DirectDraw surface has been lost. It must be restored with the **IDirectDrawSurface7::Restore** () function.

IDirectDrawSurface7::PageUnlock ()

Function Description

This function unlocks the address of a system-memory surface.

Function Declaration

```
HRESULT PageUnlock(
    DWORD dwFlags
);
```

Parameter	Description
dwFlags	Reserved for future use; this parameter must be 0.

Return Value	Description
DD_OK	DirectDraw successfully unlocked the surface.
DDERR_CANTPAGEUNLOCK	DirectDraw could not unlock the surface, because the surface either exists in display memory or is an emulated primary surface.
DDERR_INVALIDOBJECT	DirectDraw could not unlock the surface, because this DirectDrawSurface7 object is not valid.
DDERR_INVALIDPARAMS	DirectDraw could not unlock the surface, because one or more parameters are invalid.
DDERR_NOTPAGELOCKED	DirectDraw could not unlock the surface, because the surface is not page locked.
DDERR_SURFACELOST	DirectDraw could not unlock the surface, because the memory of the DirectDraw surface has been lost. It must be restored with the **IDirectDrawSurface7::Restore** () function.

IDirectDrawSurface7::ReleaseDC ()

Function Description

This function releases a device context created with the **IDirectDrawSurface7::GetDC** () function.

Function Declaration

```
HRESULT ReleaseDC(
    HDC hDC
);
```

Parameter	Description
hDC	A handle to the DC created with the **IDirectDrawSurface7::-GetDC** () function.

Return Value	Description
DD_OK	DirectDraw successfully released the DC.
DDERR_GENERIC	DirectDraw could not release the DC, because of a generic error.
DDERR_INVALIDOBJECT	DirectDraw could not release the DC, because this DirectDrawSurface7 object is not valid.

(continued)

IDirectDrawSurface7::ReleaseDC () *(continued)*

Return Value	Description
DDERR_INVALIDPARAMS	DirectDraw could not release the DC, because one or more parameters are invalid.
DDERR_SURFACELOST	DirectDraw could not release the DC, because the memory of the DirectDraw surface has been lost. It must be restored with the **IDirectDrawSurface7::Restore** () function.
DDERR_UNSUPPORTED	DirectDraw could not release the DC, because the operation is not supported.

IDirectDrawSurface7::Restore ()

Function Description

If the surface was created with implicitly attached surfaces, the memory associated with these surfaces will also be restored.

Function Declaration

```
HRESULT Restore();
```

Parameter	Description
None	

Return Value	Description
DD_OK	DirectDraw successfully restored the memory associated with this surface.
DDERR_GENERIC	DirectDraw could not restore the surface memory, because of a generic error.
DDERR_IMPLICITLYCREATED	DirectDraw could not restore the surface memory, because the surface was implicitly created.
DDERR_INCOMPATIBLEPRIMARY	DirectDraw could not restore the primary surface, because it is incompatible with the current video mode.
DDERR_INVALIDOBJECT	DirectDraw could not restore the surface memory, because this DirectDrawSurface7 object is not valid.
DDERR_INVALIDPARAMS	DirectDraw could not restore the surface memory, because one or more parameters are invalid.
DDERR_NOEXCLUSIVEMODE	DirectDraw could not restore the surface memory, because the device is not acquired in exclusive mode, a necessary condition for using this function.
DDERR_OUTOFMEMORY	DirectDraw could not restore the surface memory, because sufficient memory is not available.
DDERR_UNSUPPORTED	DirectDraw could not restore the surface memory, because the operation is not supported.
DDERR_WRONGMODE	DirectDraw could not restore the surface memory, because the surface was created in a different video mode.

IDirectDrawSurface7::SetClipper ()

Function Description

This function associates a DirectDrawClipper object to this surface or detaches a previously associated clipper.

Function Declaration

```
HRESULT SetClipper(
    LPDIRECTDRAWCLIPPER lpDDClipper
);
```

Parameter	Description
lpDDClipper	A pointer to a DirectDrawClipper object to be associated with this surface. This parameter may be **NULL**, in which case the current clipper associated with this surface will be detatched.

Return Value	Description
DD_OK	DirectDraw successfully set the surface's clipper.
DDERR_INVALIDOBJECT	DirectDraw could not set the surface's clipper, because this DirectDrawSurface7 object is not valid.
DDERR_INVALIDPARAMS	DirectDraw could not set the surface's clipper, because one or more parameters are invalid.
DDERR_INVALIDSURFACETYPE	DirectDraw could not set the surface's clipper, because the surface type does not support this operation.
DDERR_NOCLIPPERATTACHED	DirectDraw could not set the surface's clipper, because no clipper is associated with the surface.

IDirectDrawSurface7::SetColorKey ()

Function Description

This function sets one of the surface's color keys.

Function Declaration

```
HRESULT SetColorKey(
    DWORD dwFlags,
    LPDDCOLORKEY lpDDColorKey
);
```

Parameter	Description
dwFlags	Describes which color key should be set. This parameter must be one of the following flags: • **DDCKEY_COLORSPACE**—The **lpDDColorKey** structure contains more than one color. • **DDCKEY_DESTBLT**—The destination color key for a non-overlay surface is being set. A destination color key specifies one or more colors that can be covered on this surface by blit operations.

(continued)

IDirectDrawSurface7::SetColorKey () *(continued)*	
Parameter	**Description**
	• **DDCKEY_DESTOVERLAY**—The destination color key for an overlay surface is being set. A destination color key specifies one or more colors that can be covered on this surface by overlay operations.
	• **DDCKEY_SRCBLT**—The source color key for a non-overlay surface is being set. A source color key specifies one or more colors that will not be visible when this surface is blitted to other surfaces.
	• **DDCKEY_SRCOVERLAY**—The source color key for an overlay surface is being set. A source color key specifies one or more colors that will not be visible when this surface is overlaid on other surfaces.
lpDDColorKey	A pointer to a **DDCOLORKEY** structure that describes the color key to be set. This parameter may be **NULL**, in which case the previously associated value for this color key is removed.
Return Value	**Description**
DD_OK	DirectDraw successfully set the color key.
DDERR_GENERIC	DirectDraw could not set the color key, because of a generic error.
DDERR_INVALIDOBJECT	DirectDraw could not set the color key, because this DirectDrawSurface7 object is not valid.
DDERR_INVALIDPARAMS	DirectDraw could not set the color key, because one or more parameters are invalid.
DDERR_INVALIDSURFACETYPE	DirectDraw could not set the color key, because the surface type does not support this operation.
DDERR_NOOVERLAYHW	DirectDraw could not set the color key, because the hardware does not support overlays.
DDERR_NOTANOVERLAYSURFACE	DirectDraw could not set the color key, because the surface is not an overlay surface.
DDERR_SURFACELOST	DirectDraw could not set the color key, because the memory of the DirectDraw surface has been lost. It must be restored with the **IDirectDrawSurface7::Restore** () function.
DDERR_UNSUPPORTED	DirectDraw could not set the color key, because the operation is not supported.
DDERR_WASSTILLDRAWING	DirectDraw could not set the color key, because it is still engaged in surface blit operations.

IDirectDrawSurface7::SetLOD ()

Function Description

This function sets the maximum level of detail currently for an automatically managed mipmap surface. The maximum level of detail is that highest level of detail that Direct3D should load into a device's local video memory. The highest level of detail is identified by the number 1; the lowest level of detail depends on the texture.

This function will fail if the surface is not a managed mipmap surface. Managed surfaces are those created with the **DDSCAPS2_TEXTUREMANAGE** flag.

Function Declaration

```
HRESULT SetLOD(
    DWORD dwMaxLOD
);
```

Parameter	Description
dwMaxLOD	The maximum level of detail to be used for this surface.

Return Value	Description
DD_OK	DirectDraw successfully set the maximum level of detail for this surface.
DDERR_INVALIDOBJECT	DirectDraw could not set the maximum level of detail, because this DirectDrawSurface7 object is invalid. This return value is possible if the texture is invalid, is not a mipmap surface, or is not managed by Direct3D.
DDERR_INVALIDPARAMS	DirectDraw could not set the maximum level of detail, because one or more parameters are invalid.

IDirectDrawSurface7::SetOverlayPosition ()

Function Description

This function sets the position of an overlay surface. This determines where the overlay is displayed on the primary surface.

Function Declaration

```
HRESULT SetOverlayPosition(
    LONG lX,
    LONG lY
);
```

Parameter	Description
lX	The new x-coordinate for the overlay's position on the destination surface.
lY	The new y-coordinate for the overlay's position on the destination surface.

(continued)

IDirectDrawSurface7::SetOverlayPosition () *(continued)*

Return Value	Description
DD_OK	DirectDraw successfully set the position of the overlay.
DDERR_GENERIC	DirectDraw could not set the position of the overlay, because of a generic error.
DDERR_INVALIDOBJECT	DirectDraw could not set the position of the overlay, because this DirectDrawSurface7 object is not valid.
DDERR_INVALIDPARAMS	DirectDraw could not set the position of the overlay, because one or more parameters are invalid.
DDERR_INVALIDPOSITION	DirectDraw could not set the position of the overlay, because the position of the overlay is not valid.
DDERR_NOOVERLAYDEST	DirectDraw could not set the position of the overlay, because the surface is not overlaid on a destination surface.
DDERR_NOTANOVERLAYSURFACE	DirectDraw could not set the position of the overlay, because the surface is not an overlay surface.
DDERR_OVERLAYNOTVISIBLE	DirectDraw could not set the position of the overlay, because the overlay is not visible.
DDERR_SURFACELOST	DirectDraw could not set the position of the overlay, because the memory of the DirectDraw surface has been lost. It must be restored with the **IDirectDrawSurface7::Restore** () function.
DDERR_UNSUPPORTED	DirectDraw could not set the position of the overlay, because the operation is not supported.

IDirectDrawSurface7::SetPalette ()

Function Description

This function associates a DirectDrawPalette object with this palettized surface or detaches a previously associated palette.

Function Declaration

```
HRESULT SetPalette(
    LPDIRECTDRAWPALETTE lpDDPalette
);
```

Parameter	Description
lpDDPalette	A pointer to a DirectDrawPalette object that will be associated with this surface. This parameter may be **NULL**, in which case the current palette is detached from the surface.

Return Value	Description
DD_OK	DirectDraw successfully set the palette.
DDERR_GENERIC	DirectDraw could not set the palette, because of a generic error.
DDERR_INVALIDOBJECT	DirectDraw could not set the palette, because this DirectDrawSurface7 object is not valid.

(continued)

IDirectDrawSurface7::SetPalette () *(continued)*

Return Value	Description
DDERR_INVALIDPARAMS	DirectDraw could not set the palette, because one or more parameters are invalid.
DDERR_INVALIDPIXELFORMAT	DirectDraw could not set the palette, because the surface's pixel format is invalid.
DDERR_INVALIDSURFACETYPE	DirectDraw could not set the palette, because the surface type does not support this operation.
DDERR_NOEXCLUSIVEMODE	DirectDraw could not set the palette, because the device isnot acquired in exclusive mode, a necessary condition for using this function.
DDERR_NOPALETTEATTACHED	DirectDraw could not set the palette, because no palette is attached to the surface.
DDERR_NOPALETTEHW	DirectDraw could not set the palette, because the hardware does not support palettes of the specified type.
DDERR_NOT8BITCOLOR	DirectDraw could not set the palette, because the surface does not use an 8-bit palette.
DDERR_SURFACELOST	DirectDraw could not set the palette, because the memory of the DirectDraw surface has been lost. It must be restored with the **IDirectDrawSurface7::Restore** () function.
DDERR_UNSUPPORTED	DirectDraw could not set the palette, because the operation is not supported.

IDirectDrawSurface7::SetPriority ()

Function Description

This function sets an automatically managed texture surface's priority level. The priority level is used to determine when the texture should be evicted from memory. Textures that have lower priorities are evicted before those with higher priorities. For textures that have identical priority levels, the one used most recently will be evicted last. Textures are evicted from memory as required by the amount of remaining free memory.

This function will fail if the surface is not a managed texture. Managed surfaces are those created with the **DDSCAPS2_TEXTUREMANAGE** flag.

Function Declaration

```
HRESULT SetPriority(
  DWORD dwPriority
);
```

Parameter	Description
dwPriority	The priority level for the texture surface.

Return Value	Description
D3D_OK	Direct3D successfully set the priority of the surface.
DDERR_INVALIDOBJECT	DirectDraw could not set the priority of the surface because this DirectDrawSurface7 object is invalid. This return value is possible if the texture is invalid or is not managed by Direct3D.

IDirectDrawSurface7::SetPrivateData ()	
Function Description	
This function sets the surface's private data.	
Function Declaration	

```
HRESULT SetPrivateData(
    REFGUID guidTag,
    LPVOID  lpData,
    DWORD   cbSize,
    DWORD   dwFlags
);
```

Parameter	Description
guidTag	A GUID that identifies the private data to be set.
lpData	A pointer to a buffer that contains the private data to be set.
cbSize	The number of bytes pointed to by **lpData**.
dwFlags	Describes which type of data is pointed to by **lpData**. This parameter can be 0, in which case DirectDraw allocates memory to hold the contents of **lpData**, copies its contents into the memory, and frees it as appropriate; or the parameter can be one of the following flags: • **DDSPD_IUNKNOWNPOINTER**—The **lpData** parameter specifies an IUnknown interface. DirectDraw will call the **AddRef** () function of this interface immediately and call the corresponding **IUnknown::Release** () function when the data is no longer needed. • **DDSPD_VOLATILE**—The data is volatile, meaning that it is valid only until the state of the surface changes. Once the contents of the surface change, subsequent calls to **IDirectDrawSurface7::GetPrivateData** () will return **DDERR_EXPIRED**.

Return Value	Description
DD_OK	DirectDraw successfully set the specified private data.
DDERR_INVALIDOBJECT	DirectDraw could not set the specified private data, because this DirectDrawSurface7 object is not valid.
DDERR_INVALIDPARAMS	DirectDraw could not set the specified private data, because one or more parameters are invalid.
DDERR_OUTOFMEMORY	DirectDraw could not set the specified private data, because sufficient memory is not available.

IDirectDrawSurface7::SetSurfaceDesc ()

Function Description

This function sets the surface description for an existing system-memory surface. This function cannot be called for display-memory surfaces.

Function Declaration

```
HRESULT SetSurfaceDesc(
    LPDDSURFACEDESC2 lpddsd2,
    DWORD dwFlags
);
```

Parameter	Description
lpddsd2	A pointer to **a DDSURFACEDESC2** structure that describes the new surface description.
dwFlags	Reserved for future use; this parameter must be 0.

Return Value	Description
DD_OK	DirectDraw successfully set the surface description.
DDERR_INVALIDPARAMS	DirectDraw could not set the surface description, because one or more parameters are invalid.
DDERR_INVALIDOBJECT	DirectDraw could not set the surface description, because this DirectDrawSurface7 object is not valid.
DDERR_SURFACELOST	DirectDraw could not set the surface description, because the memory of the DirectDraw surface has been lost. It must be restored with the **IDirectDrawSurface7::Restore** () function.
DDERR_SURFACEBUSY	DirectDraw could not set the surface description, because one or more surfaces are being accessed.
DDERR_INVALIDSURFACETYPE	DirectDraw could not set the surface description, because the surface type does not support this operation.
DDERR_INVALIDPIXELFORMAT	DirectDraw could not set the surface description, because the surface's pixel format is invalid.
DDERR_INVALIDCAPS	DirectDraw could not set the surface description, because the surface description contains invalid capabilities.
DDERR_UNSUPPORTED	DirectDraw could not set the surface description, because the operation is not supported.
DDERR_GENERIC	DirectDraw could not set the surface description, because of a generic error.

IDirectDrawSurface7::Unlock ()

Function Description

This function unlocks surface memory locked by the **IDirectDrawSurface7::Lock** () function.

Function Declaration

```
HRESULT Unlock(
    LPRECT lpRect
);
```

Parameter	Description
lpRect	A pointer to a Win32 **RECT** structure that describes the region to unlock. This parameter may be **NULL** only if **NULL** was passed to the **IDirectDrawSurface7::Lock** () function.

Return Value	Description
DD_OK	DirectDraw successfully unlocked the surface.
DDERR_GENERIC	DirectDraw could not unlock the surface, because of a generic error.
DDERR_INVALIDOBJECT	DirectDraw could not unlock the surface, because this DirectDrawSurface7 object is not valid.
DDERR_INVALIDPARAMS	DirectDraw could not unlock the surface, because one or more parameters are invalid.
DDERR_INVALIDRECT	DirectDraw could not unlock the surface, because the specified rectangle is invalid.
DDERR_NOTLOCKED	DirectDraw could not unlock the surface, because the surface is not locked.
DDERR_SURFACELOST	DirectDraw could not unlock the surface, because the memory associated with this surface has been freed. It must be restored with the **IDirectDrawSurface7::Restore** () function.

IDirectDrawSurface7::UpdateOverlay ()

Function Description

This function updates the parameters of an overlay surface (one created with the **DDSCAPS_OVERLAY** flag). The parameters include the position and visual attributes of the surface.

Function Declaration

```
HRESULT UpdateOverlay(
    LPRECT lpSrcRect,
    LPDIRECTDRAWSURFACE7 lpDDDestSurface,
    LPRECT lpDestRect,
    DWORD dwFlags,
    LPDDOVERLAYFX lpDDOverlayFx
);
```

Parameter	Description
lpSrcRect	A pointer to a Win32 **RECT** structure that describes the portion of the surface to overlay on the destination surface. This parameter may be **NULL** if either the overlay is being hidden or the entire surface should be overlaid on the destination surface.
lpDDDestSurface	A pointer to a DirectDrawSurface7 object that identifies the destination surface.
lpDestRect	A pointer to a Win32 **RECT** structure that describes the destination rectangle. This parameter may be **NULL** if the overlay is being hidden.
dwFlags	Describes how the overlay is being updated. This parameter can be one or more of the following flags:
	• **DDOVER_ADDDIRTYRECT**—DirectDraw should add the dirty rectangle to the emulated overlay surface.
	• **DDOVER_ALPHADESTCONSTOVERRIDE**—DirectDraw should use the **dwAlphaDestConst** member of the **lpDDOverlayFx** parameter. This member specifies an alpha constant to use for the destination surface.
	• **DDOVER_ALPHADESTNEG**—DirectDraw should interpret alpha information for the destination surface in the reverse of the usual manner, with 0 being opaque. If this flag is not specified, 0 is interpreted as being transparent.
	• **DDOVER_ALPHADESTSURFACEOVERRIDE**—DirectDraw should use the **lpDDSAlphaDest** member of the **lpDDOverlayFx** parameter. This member specifies a surface that DirectDraw should use as the destination surface's alpha information.

(continued)

IDirectDrawSurface7::UpdateOverlay () *(continued)*	
Parameter	**Description**
	• **DDOVER_ALPHAEDGEBLEND**—DirectDraw should use the **dwAlphaEdgeBlend** member of the **lpDDOverlayFx** parameter. This member specifies alpha information that DirectDraw should use to blend the edges of the overlay with the background. A pixel in the overlay is considered to be an edge if it is the leftmost or rightmost nontransparent pixel for a given row of pixels.
	• **DDOVER_ALPHASRC**—DirectDraw should use the alpha information of the source surface. The information may be specified in the source surface's pixel format or in an attached alpha channel surface.
	• **DDOVER_ALPHASRCCONSTOVERRIDE**—DirectDraw should use the **dwAlphaSrcConst** member of the **lpDDOverlayFx** parameter. This member specifies an alpha constant to use for the source surface.
	• **DDOVER_ALPHASRCNEG**—DirectDraw should interpret alpha information for the source surface in reverse of the usual manner, with 0 being opaque. If this flag is not specified, 0 is interpreted as being transparent.
	• **DDOVER_ALPHASRCSURFACEOVERRIDE**—DirectDraw should use the **lpDDSAlphaSrc** member of the **lpDDOverlayFx** parameter. This member specifies a surface that DirectDraw should use as the source surface's alpha information.
	• **DDOVER_ARGBSCALEFACTORS**—DirectDraw should use the ARGB scaling factors of the **lpDDOverlayFx** parameter.
	• **DDOVER_AUTOFLIP**—DirectDraw should automatically flip to the next surface in the flipping chain each time a video port VSYNC occurs.
	• **DDOVER_BOB**—DirectDraw should display each field of the interlaced video stream separately.
	• **DDOVER_BOBHARDWARE**—DirectDraw should use hardware when performing bob operations. This flag must be specified in combination with the **DDOVER_BOB** flag.
	• **DDOVER_DDFX**—DirectDraw should use the **dwDDFX** member of the **lpDDOverlayFx** parameter. This member specifies effects DirectDraw should apply to the overlay.
	• **DDOVER_DEGRADEARGBSCALING**—DirectDraw can degrade the ARGB scaling factors of the **lpDDOverlayFx** parameter to fit the capabilities of the display driver. This flag must be specified with the **DDOVER_ARGBSCALEFACTORS** flag.
	• **DDOVER_HIDE**—DirectDraw should hide the overlay.

(continued)

IDirectDrawSurface7::UpdateOverlay () *(continued)*	
Parameter	**Description**
	• **DDOVER_KEYDEST**—DirectDraw should use the destination surface's color key.
	• **DDOVER_KEYDESTOVERRIDE**—DirectDraw should use the **dckDestColorKey** member of the **lpDDOverlayFx** parameter. This member specifies a color key that DirectDraw should use as the destination surface's color key.
	• **DDOVER_KEYSRC**—DirectDraw should use the source surface's color key.
	• **DDOVER_KEYSRCOVERRIDE**—DirectDraw should use the **ckSrcColorKey** member of the **lpDDOverlayFx** parameter. This member specifies a color key that DirectDraw should use as the source surface's color key.
	• **DDOVER_OVERRIDEBOBWEAVE**—This interface should exclusively decide whether bob or weave operations will be used on the video stream.
	• **DDOVER_INTERLEAVED**—The surface contains interleaved fields of video information.
	• **DDOVER_SHOW**—DirectDraw should show the overlay.
lpDDOverlayFx	A pointer to a **DDOVERLAYFX** structure that describes the effects DirectDraw should apply to the overlay. This parameter can be **NULL** if **dwFlags** does not include the **DDOVER_DDFX** flag.
Return Value	**Description**
DD_OK	DirectDraw successfully updated the overlay's parameters.
DDERR_DEVICEDOESNTOWNSURFACE	DirectDraw could not update the overlay's parameters, because the device does not own the surface.
DDERR_GENERIC	DirectDraw could not update the overlay's parameters, because of a generic error.
DDERR_HEIGHTALIGN	DirectDraw could not update the overlay's parameters, because the height of the specified rectangle is not a multiple of the required alignment factor.
DDERR_INVALIDOBJECT	DirectDraw could not update the overlay's parameters, because this DirectDrawSurface7 object is not valid.
DDERR_INVALIDPARAMS	DirectDraw could not update the overlay's parameters, because one or more parameters are invalid.

(continued)

IDirectDrawSurface7::UpdateOverlay () *(continued)*

Return Value	Description
DDERR_INVALIDRECT	DirectDraw could not update the overlay's parameters, because the specified rectangle is invalid.
DDERR_INVALIDSURFACETYPE	DirectDraw could not update the overlay's parameters, because the surface type does not support this operation.
DDERR_NOSTRETCHHW	DirectDraw could not update the overlay's parameters, because the hardware does not support stretching.
DDERR_NOTAOVERLAYSURFACE	DirectDraw could not update the overlay's parameters, because the surface is not an overlay surface.
DDERR_OUTOFCAPS	DirectDraw could not update the overlay's parameters, because the hardware does not have sufficient resources.
DDERR_SURFACELOST	DirectDraw could not update the overlay's parameters, because the memory associated with this surface has been freed. It must be restored with the **IDirectDrawSurface7::Restore** () function.
DDERR_UNSUPPORTED	DirectDraw could not update the overlay's parameters, because the operation is not supported.
DDERR_XALIGN	DirectDraw could not update the overlay's parameters, because the width of the specified rectangle is not a multiple of the required alignment factor.

IDirectDrawSurface7::UpdateOverlayZOrder ()

Function Description

This function inserts this overlay surface into a specified position in an overlay chain.

Function Declaration

```
HRESULT UpdateOverlayZOrder(
    DWORD dwFlags,
    LPDIRECTDRAWSURFACE7 lpDDSReference
);
```

Parameter	Description
dwFlags	Describes where the overlay should be inserted. This parameter can be one or more of the following flags:
	• **DDOVERZ_INSERTINBACKOF**—DirectDraw should insert this overlay in back of the overlay specified by the **lpDDSReference** parameter.
	• **DDOVERZ_INSERTINFRONTOF**—DirectDraw should insert this overlay in front of the overlay specified by the **lpDDSReference** parameter.
	• **DDOVERZ_MOVEBACKWARD**—DirectDraw should move this overlay one surface backward in the overlay chain.

(continued)

IDirectDrawSurface7::UpdateOverlayZOrder () *(continued)*	
Parameter	**Description**
	• **DDOVERZ_MOVEFORWARD**—DirectDraw should move this overlay one surface forward in the overlay chain.
	• **DDOVERZ_SENDTOBACK**—DirectDraw should move this overlay to the back of the overlay chain.
	• **DDOVERZ_SENDTOFRONT**—DirectDraw should move this overlay to the front of the overlay chain.
lpDDSReference	A pointer to a DirectDrawSurface7 object used as a reference point for the flags **DDOVERZ_INSERTINBACKOF** and **DDOVERZ_INSERTINFRONTOF**. If neither of these flags is specified, this parameter must be **NULL**.
Return Value	**Description**
DD_OK	DirectDraw successfully inserted the overlay.
DDERR_INVALIDOBJECT	DirectDraw could not insert the overlay, because this DirectDrawSurface7 object is not valid.
DDERR_INVALIDPARAMS	DirectDraw could not insert the overlay, because one or more parameters are invalid.
DDERR_NOTANOVERLAYSURFACE	DirectDraw could not insert the overlay, because the surface is not an overlay surface.

Function Reference

This section documents the functions of DirectDraw that do not belong to any interfaces.

DirectDrawCreateEx ()	
Function Description	
This function creates a DirectDraw object and retrieves an interface pointer to that object.	
Function Declaration	

```
HRESULT WINAPI DirectDrawCreateEx(
  GUID FAR *lpGUID,
  LPVOID *lplpDD,
  REFIID iid,
  IUnknown FAR *pUnkOuter
);
```

Parameter	**Description**
lpGUID	The GUID that identifies the display driver to be associated with the DirectDraw object being created. All such GUIDs can be found by calling the **DirectDrawEnumerateEx ()** function.

(continued)

DirectDrawCreateEx () *(continued)*	
Parameter	**Description**
	This parameter may be also **NULL**, which selects the graphics device currently being used, or it can be set to one of the following values:
	• **DDCREATE_EMULATIONONLY**—The active device should be used, but none of its hardware-implemented features should be employed; all possible features should be emulated. This setting prevents many of DirectDraw's advanced features, but is useful for video cards that offer poor DirectDraw support.
	This flag is the default setting for multiple-monitor systems running in normal cooperative mode, even if **lpGUID** is set to **NULL**. To take advantage of hardware acceleration for such systems, the exact GUID of the display driver must be passed to the function.
	• **DDCREATE_HARDWAREONLY**—The active device should be used, but DirectDraw should not emulate those features not supported by the hardware (all functions using those features will report error messages when called).
lplpDD	The address of a pointer that, if the function succeeds, will be set to the newly-acquired IDirectDraw7 interface.
iid	A GUID that identifies the interface being obtained. This parameter must be set to **IID_IDirectDraw7**.
pUnkOuter	This parameter is not used; it should be set to **NULL**.
Return Value	**Description**
DD_OK	DirectDraw successfully created the DirectDraw7 object.
DDERR_DIRECTDRAWALREADYCREATED	DirectDraw could not create the DirectDraw7 object, because an object representing the specified hardware has already been created by the application.
DDERR_GENERIC	DirectDraw could not create the DirectDraw7 object, because of a generic error.
DDERR_INVALIDDIRECTDRAWGUID	DirectDraw could not create the DirectDraw7 object, because the specified GUID is invalid.
DDERR_INVALIDPARAMS	DirectDraw could not create the DirectDraw7 object, because one or more parameters are invalid.
DDERR_NODIRECTDRAWHW	DirectDraw could not create the DirectDraw7 object, because the hardware does not support DirectDraw.
DDERR_OUTOFMEMORY	DirectDraw could not create the DirectDraw7 object, because sufficient memory is not available.

DirectDrawCreateClipper ()

Function Description

This function creates a global DirectDrawClipper object—one that is not associated with any specific DirectDraw7 object.

Function Declaration

```
HRESULT WINAPI DirectDrawCreateClipper(
    DWORD dwFlags,
    LPDIRECTDRAWCLIPPER FAR *lplpDDClipper,
    IUnknown FAR *pUnkOuter
);
```

Parameter	Description
dwFlags	This parameter is not used and should be set to 0.
lplpDDClipper	The address of a pointer to a DirectDrawClipper object. If this function succeeds, the pointer will be set to the newly created DirectDrawClipper object.
pUnkOuter	This parameter is not used; it should be **NULL**.

Return Value	Description
DD_OK	DirectDraw successfully created the DirectDrawClipper object.
DDERR_INVALIDPARAMS	DirectDraw could not create the object, because one or more parameters are invalid.
DDERR_OUTOFMEMORY	DirectDraw could not create the object, because sufficient memory is not available.

DirectDrawEnumerateEx ()

Function Description

This function enumerates the graphics devices on the system.

Function Declaration

```
HRESULT WINAPI DirectDrawEnumerateEx(
    LPDDENUMCALLBACKEX lpCallback,
    LPVOID lpContext,
    DWORD  dwFlags
);
```

Parameter	Description
lpCallback	The address of a **DDEnumCallbackEx ()** function, which will be called for every graphics device enumerated.
lpContext	A pointer to application-defined data that will be sent to the callback function every time it is called.
dwFlags	Describes the extent of the enumeration. This parameter can be 0, in which case DirectDraw will enumerate only the primary graphics device, or one or more of the following flags:

(continued)

DirectDrawEnumerateEx () *(continued)*	
Parameter	**Description**
	• **DDENUM_ATTACHEDSECONDARYDEVICES**—DirectDraw should enumerate the primary device and secondary devices that are connected to the desktop.
	• **DDENUM_DETACHEDSECONDARYDEVICES**—DirectDraw should enumerate the primary device and secondary devices that are not connected to the desktop.
	• **DDENUM_NONDISPLAYDEVICES**—DirectDraw should enumerate the primary device and those not directly responsible for display, such as 3D-only accelerators that do not provide 2D graphics support.
Return Value	**Description**
DD_OK	DirectDraw successfully enumerated the graphics devices.
DDERR_INVALIDPARAMS	DirectDraw could not enumerate the graphics devices, because one or more parameters are invalid.

Callback Function Reference

This section documents the application-defined callback functions used by DirectDraw during enumeration.

DDEnumCallbackEx ()	
Function Description	
This is an application-defined function that DirectDraw calls for every graphics device object it enumerates through the **DirectDrawEnumerateEx ()** function.	
Function Declaration	

```
BOOL WINAPI DDEnumCallbackEx(
    GUID FAR *lpGUID,
    LPSTR     lpDriverDescription,
    LPSTR     lpDriverName,
    LPVOID    lpContext,
    HMONITOR  hm
);
```

Parameter	**Description**
lpGUID	A pointer to a GUID that identifies the graphics device being enumerated.
lpDriverDescription	A pointer to a string that describes the software driver.
lpDriverName	A pointer to a string that describes the name of the software driver.

(continued)

DDEnumCallbackEx () *(continued)*

Parameter	Description
lpContext	A pointer to application-defined data passed to this function through the **DirectDrawEnumerateEx** () function.
hm	A handle to the monitor associated with this graphics device, or **NULL** if the device is a primary device, a nondisplay device (such as a 3D-only accelerator), or a device not attached to the desktop.
Return Value	**Description**
DDENUMRET_CANCEL	DirectDraw should stop the enumeration.
DDENUMRET_OK	DirectDraw should continue the enumeration.

EnumModesCallback2 ()

Function Description

This is an application-defined callback function that DirectDraw calls for every display mode it enumerates through the **IDirectDraw7::EnumDisplayModes** () function.

Function Declaration

```
HRESULT WINAPI EnumModesCallback(
    LPDDSURFACEDESC2 lpDDSurfaceDesc,
    LPVOID lpContext
);
```

Parameter	Description
lpContext	A pointer to application-defined data passed to this function through the **EnumModesCallback** () function.
lpDDSurfaceDesc	A pointer to a **DDSURFACEDESC2** structure that describes the display mode being enumerated.
Return Value	**Description**
DDENUMRET_CANCEL	DirectDraw should stop the enumeration.
DDENUMRET_OK	DirectDraw should continue the enumeration.

EnumSurfacesCallback7 ()

Function Description

This is an application-defined callback function that DirectDraw calls for every surface it enumerates through the **IDirectDrawSurface7::EnumAttachedSurfaces** () and **IDirectDrawSurface7::Enum-OverlayZOrders** () functions.

(continued)

EnumSurfacesCallback7 () *(continued)*

Function Declaration

```
HRESULT WINAPI EnumSurfacesCallback7(
    LPDIRECTDRAWSURFACE7 lpDDSurface,
    LPDDSURFACEDESC2 lpDDSurfaceDesc,
    LPVOID lpContext
);
```

Parameter	Description
lpDDSurface	A pointer to a DirectDrawSurface7 object representing the surface being enumerated. According to COM standards, applications must release this interface when they are done using it.
lpDDSurfaceDesc	A pointer to a **DDSURFACEDESC2** structure that describes the surface being enumerated.
lpContext	A pointer to application-defined data passed to this function.
Return Value	**Description**
DDENUMRET_CANCEL	DirectDraw should stop the enumeration.
DDENUMRET_OK	DirectDraw should continue the enumeration.

Structure Reference

This section documents the structures used by DirectDraw functions.

DDBLTFX

Structure Description

This structure describes blit raster operations, effects, override values, and other information. It is used by the **IDirectDrawSurface7::Blt ()** function.

Structure Declaration

```
typedef struct _DDBLTFX{
    DWORD dwSize;
    DWORD dwDDFX;
    DWORD dwROP;
    DWORD dwDDROP;
    DWORD dwRotationAngle;
    DWORD dwZBufferOpCode;
    DWORD dwZBufferLow;
    DWORD dwZBufferHigh;
    DWORD dwZBufferBaseDest;
    DWORD dwZDestConstBitDepth;
    union
    {
        DWORD              dwZDestConst;
        LPDIRECTDRAWSURFACE lpDDSZBufferDest;
```

(continued)

DDBLTFX *(continued)*

Structure Declaration

```
  } DUMMYUNIONNAMEN(1);
  DWORD dwZSrcConstBitDepth;
  union
  {
      DWORD               dwZSrcConst;
      LPDIRECTDRAWSURFACE lpDDSZBufferSrc;
  } DUMMYUNIONNAMEN(2);
  DWORD dwAlphaEdgeBlendBitDepth;
  DWORD dwAlphaEdgeBlend;
  DWORD dwReserved;
  DWORD dwAlphaDestConstBitDepth;
  union
  {
      DWORD               dwAlphaDestConst;
      LPDIRECTDRAWSURFACE lpDDSAlphaDest;
  } DUMMYUNIONNAMEN(3);
  DWORD dwAlphaSrcConstBitDepth;
  union
  {
      DWORD               dwAlphaSrcConst;
      LPDIRECTDRAWSURFACE lpDDSAlphaSrc;
  } DUMMYUNIONNAMEN(4);
  union
  {
      DWORD               dwFillColor;
      DWORD               dwFillDepth;
      DWORD               dwFillPixel;
      LPDIRECTDRAWSURFACE lpDDSPattern;
  } DUMMYUNIONNAMEN(5);
  DDCOLORKEY ddckDestColorkey;
  DDCOLORKEY ddckSrcColorkey;
} DDBLTFX,FAR* LPDDBLTFX;
```

Member	Description
dwSize	The size of the structure, in bytes. This member must be initialized before the structure is used.
dwDDFX	The blit effects. This member can be 0, or one or more of the following flags:
	• **DDBLTFX_ARITHSTRETCHY**—DirectDraw should use arithmetic stretching for the *y*-axis, which produces higher-quality results than row replication.
	• **DDBLTFX_MIRRORLEFTRIGHT**—DirectDraw should reverse the surface from left to right when performing the blit.

(continued)

DDBLTFX *(continued)*	
Member	**Description**
	• **DDBLTFX_MIRRORUPDOWN**—DirectDraw should reverse the surface from top to bottom when performing the blit.
	• **DDBLTFX_NOTEARING**—DirectDraw should schedule the blit so it coincides with the display's vertical blanking interval (VBI), thereby eliminating display artifacts.
	• **DDBLTFX_ROTATE180**—DirectDraw should rotate the surface 180 degrees when performing the blit.
	• **DDBLTFX_ROTATE270**—DirectDraw should rotate the surface 270 degrees when performing the blit.
	• **DDBLTFX_ROTATE90**—DirectDraw should rotate the surface 90 degrees when performing the blit.
	• **DDBLTFX_ZBUFFERBASEDEST**—DirectDraw should add the **dwZBufferBaseDest** member of this structure to each of the source surface's z-values before comparing them with the destination surface's z-values.
	• **DDBLTFX_ZBUFFERRANGE**—DirectDraw should use the **dwZBufferLow** and **dwZBufferHigh** members of this structure to determine the minimum and maximum z-values to blit, respectively.
dwROP	The Win32 ROPs for the blit.
dwDDROP	The DirectDraw ROPs for the blit.
dwRotationAngle	The angle by which DirectDraw should rotate the source surface during the blit operation.
dwZBufferOpCode	The operation code that determines how z-values are compared.
dwZBufferLow	The low value for the z-buffer.
dwZBufferHigh	The high value for the z-buffer.
dwZBufferBaseDest	The value that DirectDraw should add to the source surface's z-values before comparing them with the destination surface's z-values.
dwZDestConstBitDepth	The bit depth of the destination surface's z-constant.
dwZDestConst	A constant used as the destination surface's z-value.
lpDDSZBufferDest	A pointer to a DirectDrawSurface7 object that identifies the z-buffer to use for the destination surface.
dwZSrcConstBitDepth	The bit depth of the source surface's z-constant.
dwZSrcConst	A constant used as the source surface's z-value.
lpDDSZBufferSrc	A pointer to a DirectDrawSurface7 object that identifies the z-buffer to use for the source surface.
dwAlphaEdgeBlendBitDepth	The bit depth of the alpha edge blend constant.

(continued)

DDBLTFX *(continued)*

Member	Description
dwAlphaEdgeBlend	An alpha constant that is used to blend the edges of the source surface with the background surface. A pixel in the source surface is considered to be an edge if it is the leftmost or rightmost nontransparent pixel for a given row of pixels.
dwReserved	This member is reserved for future use.
dwAlphaDestConstBitDepth	The bit depth of the alpha constant for the destination surface.
dwAlphaDestConst	A constant used as the destination surface's alpha information.
lpDDSAlphaDest	A pointer to a DirectDrawSurface7 object that identifies the alpha surface to use for the destination surface.
dwAlphaSrcConstBitDepth	The bit depth of the alpha constant used for the source surface.
dwAlphaSrcConst	A constant used as the source surface's alpha information.
lpDDSAlphaSrc	A pointer to a DirectDrawSurface7 object that identifies the alpha surface to use for the source surface.
dwFillColor	The color to fill an RGB surface with. This must be specified in the pixel format of the surface.
dwFillDepth	The z-value to fill a z-buffer surface with. This must be specified in the pixel format of the surface.
dwFillPixel	The value to fill an RGBA or RGBZ surface with. This must be specified in the pixel format of the surface.
lpDDSPattern	A pointer to a DirectDrawSurface7 object that identifies the surface to use as a pattern in the blit operation.
ddckDestColorkey	A **DDCOLORKEY** structure that identifies the color key to use for the destination surface. This value overrides the destination surface's own color key.
ddckSrcColorkey	A **DDCOLORKEY** structure that identifies the color key to use for the source surface. This value overrides the source surface's own color key.

DDCAPS

Structure Description

This structure describes the capabilities of a graphics card represented by a DirectDraw7 object (see **IDirectDraw7::GetCaps ()**).

Structure Declaration

```
typedef struct _DDCAPS {
    DWORD    dwSize;
    DWORD    dwCaps;
    DWORD    dwCaps2;
    DWORD    dwCKeyCaps;
    DWORD    dwFXCaps;
```

DDCAPS *(continued)*

Structure Declaration

```
DWORD     dwFXAlphaCaps;
  DWORD     dwPalCaps;
  DWORD     dwSVCaps;
  DWORD     dwAlphaBltConstBitDepths;
  DWORD     dwAlphaBltPixelBitDepths;
  DWORD     dwAlphaBltSurfaceBitDepths;
  DWORD     dwAlphaOverlayConstBitDepths;
  DWORD     dwAlphaOverlayPixelBitDepths;
  DWORD     dwAlphaOverlaySurfaceBitDepths;
  DWORD     dwZBufferBitDepths;
  DWORD     dwVidMemTotal;
  DWORD     dwVidMemFree;
  DWORD     dwMaxVisibleOverlays;
  DWORD     dwCurrVisibleOverlays;
  DWORD     dwNumFourCCCodes;
  DWORD     dwAlignBoundarySrc;
  DWORD     dwAlignSizeSrc;
  DWORD     dwAlignBoundaryDest;
  DWORD     dwAlignSizeDest;
  DWORD     dwAlignStrideAlign;
  DWORD     dwRops[DD_ROP_SPACE];
  DWORD     dwReservedCaps;
  DWORD     dwMinOverlayStretch;
  DWORD     dwMaxOverlayStretch;
  DWORD     dwMinLiveVideoStretch;
  DWORD     dwMaxLiveVideoStretch;
  DWORD     dwMinHwCodecStretch;
  DWORD     dwMaxHwCodecStretch;
  DWORD     dwReserved1;
  DWORD     dwReserved2;
  DWORD     dwReserved3;
  DWORD     dwSVBCaps;
  DWORD     dwSVBCKeyCaps;
  DWORD     dwSVBFXCaps;
  DWORD     dwSVBRops[DD_ROP_SPACE];
  DWORD     dwVSBCaps;
  DWORD     dwVSBCKeyCaps;
  DWORD     dwVSBFXCaps;
  DWORD     dwVSBRops[DD_ROP_SPACE];
  DWORD     dwSSBCaps;
  DWORD     dwSSBCKeyCaps;
  DWORD     dwSSBCFXCaps;
```

(continued)

DDCAPS *(continued)*

Structure Declaration

```
    DWORD     dwSSBRops[DD_ROP_SPACE];
    DWORD     dwMaxVideoPorts;
    DWORD     dwCurrVideoPorts;
    DWORD     dwSVBCaps2;
    DWORD     dwNLVBCaps;
    DWORD     dwNLVBCaps2;
    DWORD     dwNLVBCKeyCaps;
    DWORD     dwNLVBFXCaps;
    DWORD     dwNLVBRops[DD_ROP_SPACE];
    DDSCAPS2 ddsCaps;
} DDCAPS,FAR* LPDDCAPS;
```

Member	Description
dwSize	The size of the structure, in bytes. This member must be initialized before the structure is used.
dwCaps	Describes capabilities of the driver. This member may be 0, or one or more of the following flags: • **DDCAPS_3D**—The hardware supports 3D acceleration. • **DDCAPS_ALIGNBOUNDARYDEST**—The hardware supports only overlay destination coordinates whose x-components are multiples of the **dwAlignBoundaryDest** member. • **DDCAPS_ALIGNBOUNDARYSRC**—The hardware supports only overlay source coordinates whose y-components are multiples of the **dwAlignBoundaryDest** member. • **DDCAPS_ALIGNSIZEDEST**—The display hardware supports only overlay destination rectangles whose widths are a multiple of the **dwAlignSizeDest** member. • **DDCAPS_ALIGNSIZESRC**—The display hardware supports only overlay source rectangles whose widths are a multiple of the **dwAlignSizeDest** member. • **DDCAPS_ALIGNSTRIDE**—DirectDraw supports only pitches that are multiples of the **dwAlignStrideAlign** member. Pitches indicate the number of bytes from one row of pixels in a surface to the next row. • **DDCAPS_ALPHA**—The display hardware supports alpha-only surfaces. • **DDCAPS_BANKSWITCHED**—The display hardware is bank-switched, indicating that random access to memory may be slow. • **DDCAPS_BLT**—The display hardware can blit surfaces.

(continued)

DDCAPS *(continued)*	
Member	**Description**
	• **DDCAPS_BLTCOLORFILL**—The display hardware can fill a surface with a color.
	• **DDCAPS_BLTDEPTHFILL**—The display hardware can fill a *z*-buffer surface with a *z*-value.
	• **DDCAPS_BLTFOURCC**—The display hardware can convert from one color space (such as RGB) to another (such as YUV) during blit operations.
	• **DDCAPS_BLTQUEUE**—The display hardware can blit surfaces asynchronously. This allows the **IDirectDrawSurface7::Blt ()** function to return immediately after putting the blit request in the display hardware's queue.
	• **DDCAPS_BLTSTRETCH**—The display hardware can stretch surfaces during blits.
	• **DDCAPS_CANBLTSYSMEM**—The display hardware can blit to or from system memory.
	• **DDCAPS_CANCLIP**—The display hardware can clip during blits.
	• **DDCAPS_CANCLIPSTRETCHED**—The display hardware can clip during blits that use stretching.
	• **DDCAPS_COLORKEY**—The display hardware supports color keys. The **dwCKeyCaps** member indicates the extent of this support.
	• **DDCAPS_COLORKEYHWASSIST**—Color key operations are only partially hardware assisted. The display hardware relies on system resources (such as CPU cycles or memory) to perform blits that use color keys.
	• **DDCAPS_GDI**—The display hardware is shared with the GDI.
	• **DDCAPS_NOHARDWARE**—There is no hardware support.
	• **DDCAPS_OVERLAY**—The display hardware supports overlays.
	• **DDCAPS_OVERLAYCANTCLIP**—The display hardware cannot clip overlays.
	• **DDCAPS_OVERLAYFOURCC**—The display hardware can convert from one color space (such as RGB) to another (such as YUV) during overlay operations.
	• **DDCAPS_OVERLAYSTRETCH**—The display hardware can stretch overlays.
	• **DDCAPS_PALETTE**—The display hardware supports palettes for nonprimary surfaces.

(continued)

DDCAPS *(continued)*	
Member	**Description**
	• **DDCAPS_PALETTEVSYNC**—The display hardware can update a palette during the monitor's vertical blanking interval, thus eliminating display artifacts.
	• **DDCAPS_READSCANLINE**—The display hardware can report the row of pixels it is currently refreshing.
	• **DDCAPS_STEREOVIEW**—The display hardware supports some form of stereoscopic viewing.
	• **DDCAPS_VBI**—The display hardware can generate an interrupt during the vertical blanking interval.
	• **DDCAPS_ZBLTS**—The display hardware can blit *z*-buffer surfaces.
	• **DDCAPS_ZOVERLAYS**—The display hardware supports ordering overlays by their depth value through the **IDirectDrawSurface7::UpdateOverlayZOrder** () function.
	• **DDSVCAPS_STEREOSEQUENTIAL**—The display hardware supports stereo vision with an active device that alternately switches on and off vision for the left and right eyes in sequence. The mechanism for doing this is typically an LCD shutter.
dwCaps2	Describes more capabilities of the graphics card. This member may be 0, or one or more of the following flags:
	• **DDCAPS2_AUTOFLIPOVERLAY**—The display hardware can automatically flip from one overlay to the next in a chain during the monitor's vertical blanking interval.
	• **DDCAPS2_CANBOBHARDWARE**—The display hardware can display each field of an interleaved video stream separately.
	• **DDCAPS2_CANBOBINTERLEAVED**—The display hardware can display separately each field of a video stream interleaved in memory without causing artifacts that would normally occur without special hardware.
	• **DDCAPS2_CANBOBNONINTERLEAVED**—The display hardware can display separately each field of a video stream not interleaved in memory without causing artifacts that would normally occur without special hardware.
	• **DDCAPS2_CANCALIBRATEGAMMA**—The display hardware can calibrate its own gamma settings.
	• **DDCAPS2_CANDROPZ16BIT**—The display hardware supports the conversion of 16-bit RGBZ values into 16-bit RGB values, but not into 8-bit conversions.
	• **DDCAPS2_CANFLIPODDEVEN**—The display hardware supports both odd and even flip operations.

(continued)

DDCAPS *(continued)*	
Member	Description
	• **DDCAPS2_CANRENDERWINDOWED**—The display hardware can operate in windowed mode.
	• **DDCAPS2_CERTIFIED**—The display hardware is certified by Microsoft.
	• **DDCAPS2_COLORCONTROLPRIMARY**—The primary display surface has its own color controls, such as gamma settings.
	• **DDCAPS2_COLORCONTROLOVERLAY**—The overlay surface has its own color controls, such as gamma settings.
	• **DDCAPS2_COPYFOURCC**—The display hardware can blit from one FourCC surface to another surface with the same FourCC type.
	• **DDCAPS2_FLIPINTERVAL**—The display hardware can wait anywhere from two to four vertical refreshes before flipping a surface.
	• **DDCAPS2_FLIPNOVSYNC**—The display hardware can flip surfaces immediately without regard for the monitor's vertical blanking interval.
	• **DDCAPS2_NO2DDURING3DSCENE**—The hardware does not support 2D operations, such as blitting, between calls to the functions **IDirect3DDevice3::BeginScene ()** and **IDirect3DDevice3::EndScene ()**.
	• **DDCAPS2_NONLOCALVIDMEM**—The display hardware supports surfaces that exist in nonlocal memory.
	• **DDCAPS2_NONLOCALVIDMEMCAPS**—Surfaces that exist in nonlocal memory have different capabilities than those that exist in local memory.
	• **DDCAPS2_NOPAGELOCKREQUIRED**—A page lock is not required to use DMA transfers on system memory surfaces.
	• **DDCAPS2_PRIMARYGAMMA**—The display hardware supports dynamic gamma ramps for the primary surface.
	• **DDCAPS2_STEREO**—The **dwSVCaps** member of this structure describes the capabilities of the display's stereo vision hardware.
	• **DDCAPS2_TEXMANINNONLOCALVIDMEM**—The texture manager will store managed surfaces in local video memory. This flag will not be present for hardware that does not support texture mapping from local video memory.
	• **DDCAPS2_VIDEOPORT**—The display hardware supports live video.

(continued)

DDCAPS *(continued)*	
Member	**Description**
	• **DDCAPS2_WIDESURFACES**—The display hardware supports surfaces that are wider than the primary surface.
dwCKeyCaps	Describes the color key capabilities of the graphics card. This member may be 0, or one or more of the following flags:
	• **DDCKEYCAPS_DESTBLT**—For blit operations, the display hardware supports destination color keys.
	• **DDCKEYCAPS_DESTBLTCLRSPACE**—For blit operations, the display hardware supports destination color keys that describe more than one color.
	• **DDCKEYCAPS_DESTBLTCLRSPACEYUV**—For blit operations, the display hardware supports destination color keys that describe more than one color and are specified in YUV color space.
	• **DDCKEYCAPS_DESTBLTYUV**—For blit operations, the display hardware supports destination color keys that are specified in YUV color space.
	• **DDCKEYCAPS_DESTOVERLAY**—For overlay operations, the display hardware supports destination color keys.
	• **DDCKEYCAPS_DESTOVERLAYCLRSPACE**—For overlay operations, the display hardware supports destination color keys that describe more than one color.
	• **DDCKEYCAPS_DESTOVERLAYCLRSPACEYUV**—For overlay operations, the display hardware supports destination color keys that describe more than one color and are specified in YUV color space.
	• **DDCKEYCAPS_DESTOVERLAYONEACTIVE**—The display hardware supports only one destination color key for visible overlays.
	• **DDCKEYCAPS_DESTOVERLAYYUV**—For overlay operations, the display hardware supports destination color keys that are specified in YUV color space.
	• **DDCKEYCAPS_NOCOSTOVERLAY**—The display hardware supports color keys for overlays without incurring any performance cost.
	• **DDCKEYCAPS_SRCBLT**—For blit operations, the display hardware supports source color keys.
	• **DDCKEYCAPS_SRCBLTCLRSPACE**—For blit operations, the display hardware supports source color keys that describe more than one color.

(continued)

DDCAPS *(continued)*	
Member	**Description**
	• **DDCKEYCAPS_SRCBLTCLRSPACEYUV**—For blit operations, the display hardware supports source color keys that describe more than one color and are specified in YUV color space.
	• **DDCKEYCAPS_SRCBLTYUV**—For blit operations, the display hardware supports source color keys that are specified in YUV color space.
	• **DDCKEYCAPS_SRCOVERLAY**—For overlay operations, the display hardware supports source color keys.
	• **DDCKEYCAPS_SRCOVERLAYCLRSPACE**—For overlay operations, the display hardware supports source color keys that describe more than one color.
	• **DDCKEYCAPS_SRCOVERLAYCLRSPACEYUV**—For overlay operations, the display hardware supports source color keys that describe more than one color and are specified in YUV color space.
	• **DDCKEYCAPS_SRCOVERLAYONEACTIVE**—The display hardware supports only one source color key for visible overlays.
	• **DDCKEYCAPS_SRCOVERLAYYUV**—For overlay operations, the display hardware supports source color keys that are specified in YUV color space.
dwFXCaps	Describes the effects capabilities of the graphics card. This member may be 0, or one or more of the following flags:
	• **DDFXCAPS_BLTALPHA**—The display hardware supports blit operations for alpha surfaces.
	• **DDFXCAPS_BLTARITHSTRETCHY**—The display hardware supports arithmetic stretching of the source surface's height when blitting to a destination rectangle. This produces higher-quality results than row replication.
	• **DDFXCAPS_BLTARITHSTRETCHYN**—The display hardware supports arithmetic stretching of the source surface's height when blitting to a destination rectangle whose height is an integer multiple of the source surface's height. This produces higher-quality results than row replication.
	• **DDFXCAPS_BLTFILTER**—The display hardware can perform surface-reconstruction filtering for nonrectangular blits.
	• **DDFXCAPS_BLTMIRRORLEFTRIGHT**—The display hardware can reverse the source surface from left to right during blit operations.
	• **DDFXCAPS_BLTMIRRORUPDOWN**—The display hardware can reverse the source surface from top to bottom during blit operations.

(continued)

DDCAPS *(continued)*	
Member	**Description**
	• **DDFXCAPS_BLTROTATION**—The display hardware can rotate the source surface by an arbitrary angle during blit operations.
	• **DDFXCAPS_BLTROTATION90**—The display hardware can rotate the source surface by 90 degrees during blit operations.
	• **DDFXCAPS_BLTSHRINKX**—Surfaces (not necessarily the display hardware) support arbitrarily shrinking the horizontal size of the source surface during blit operations.
	• **DDFXCAPS_BLTSHRINKXN**—Surfaces support shrinking by an integer multiple the horizontal size of the source surface during blit operations.
	• **DDFXCAPS_BLTSHRINKY**—Surfaces (not necessarily the display hardware) support arbitrarily shrinking the vertical size of the source surface during blit operations.
	• **DDFXCAPS_BLTSHRINKYN**—Surfaces (not necessarily the display hardware) support shrinking by an integer multiple the vertical size of the source surface during blit operations.
	• **DDFXCAPS_BLTSTRETCHX**—Surfaces (not necessarily the display hardware) support arbitrarily stretching the horizontal size of the source surface during blit operations.
	• **DDFXCAPS_BLTSTRETCHXN**—Surfaces (not necessarily the display hardware) support stretching by an integer multiple the horizontal size of the source surface during blit operations.
	• **DDFXCAPS_BLTSTRETCHY**—Surfaces (not necessarily the display hardware) support arbitrarily stretching the vertical size of the source surface during blit operations.
	• **DDFXCAPS_BLTSTRETCHYN**—Surfaces (not necessarily the display hardware) support stretching by an integer multiple the vertical size of the source surface during blit operations.
	• **DDFXCAPS_BLTTRANSFORM**—The display hardware supports geometric transformation of the source surface during blit operations (this is not currently valid for explicit blits).
	• **DDFXCAPS_OVERLAYALPHA**—The display hardware supports overlay operations for alpha overlays.
	• **DDFXCAPS_OVERLAYARITHSTRETCHY**—The display hardware supports arithmetic stretching of the source overlay's height when overlaying to a destination rectangle. This produces higher-quality results than row replication.
	• **DDFXCAPS_OVERLAYARITHSTRETCHYN**—The display hardware supports arithmetic stretching of the source overlay's height when overlaying to a destination rectangle whose height is an integer multiple of the source overlay's height. This produces higher-quality results than row replication.

(continued)

DDCAPS *(continued)*	
Member	**Description**
	• **DDFXCAPS_OVERLAYFILTER**—The display hardware can perform overlay-reconstruction filtering for nonrectangular overlays.
	• **DDFXCAPS_OVERLAYMIRRORLEFTRIGHT**—The display hardware can reverse the source overlay from left to right during overlay operations.
	• **DDFXCAPS_OVERLAYMIRRORUPDOWN**—The display hardware can reverse the source overlay from top to bottom during overlay operations.
	• **DDFXCAPS_OVERLAYROTATION**—The display hardware can rotate the source overlay by an arbitrary angle during overlay operations.
	• **DDFXCAPS_OVERLAYROTATION90**—The display hardware can rotate the source overlay by 90 degrees during overlay operations.
	• **DDFXCAPS_OVERLAYSHRINKX**—Surfaces (not necessarily the display hardware) support arbitrarily shrinking the horizontal size of the source overlay during overlay operations.
	• **DDFXCAPS_OVERLAYSHRINKXN**—Surfaces (not necessarily the display hardware) support shrinking by an integer multiple the horizontal size of the source overlay during overlay operations.
	• **DDFXCAPS_OVERLAYSHRINKY**—Surfaces (not necessarily the display hardware) support arbitrarily shrinking the vertical size of the source overlay during overlay operations.
	• **DDFXCAPS_OVERLAYSHRINKYN**—Surfaces (not necessarily the display hardware) support shrinking by an integer multiple the vertical size of the source overlay during overlay operations.
	• **DDFXCAPS_OVERLAYSTRETCHX**—Surfaces (not necessarily the display hardware) support arbitrarily stretching the horizontal size of the source overlay during overlay operations.
	• **DDFXCAPS_OVERLAYSTRETCHXN**—Surfaces (not necessarily the display hardware) support stretching by an integer multiple the horizontal size of the source overlay during overlay operations.
	• **DDFXCAPS_OVERLAYSTRETCHY**—Surfaces (not necessarily the display hardware) support arbitrarily stretching the vertical size of the source overlay during overlay operations.

(continued)

DDCAPS *(continued)*

Member	Description
	• **DDFXCAPS_OVERLAYSTRETCHYN**—Surfaces (not necessarily the display hardware) support stretching by an integer multiple the vertical size of the source overlay during overlay operations.
	• **DDFXCAPS_OVERLAYTRANSFORM**—The display hardware supports geometric transformation of the source overlay during overlay operations (this is not currently valid for explicit overlays).
dwFXAlphaCaps	Describes the alpha effects capabilities of the graphics card. This member may be 0, or one or more of the following flags:
	• **DDFXALPHACAPS_BLTALPHAEDGEBLEND**—The display hardware supports alpha edge blending during blit operations.
	• **DDFXALPHACAPS_BLTALPHAPIXELS**—The display hardware supports blitting pixels that have an alpha component. This component can be 1, 2, 4, or 8 bits. Zero is the fully transparent color.
	• **DDFXALPHACAPS_BLTALPHAPIXELSNEG**—The display hardware supports blitting pixels that have an alpha component. This component can be 1, 2, 4, or 8 bits. Zero is the fully opaque color.
	• **DDFXALPHACAPS_BLTALPHASURFACES**—The display hardware supports alpha-only surfaces. The bit depth of these surfaces can be 1, 2, 4, or 8. Zero is the fully transparent color.
	• **DDFXALPHACAPS_BLTALPHASURFACESNEG**—The display hardware supports alpha-only surfaces. The bit depth of these surfaces can be 1, 2, 4, or 8. Zero is the fully opaque color.
	• **DDFXALPHACAPS_OVERLAYALPHAEDGEBLEND**—The display hardware supports alpha edge blending during overlay operations.
	• **DDFXALPHACAPS_OVERLAYALPHAPIXELS**—The display hardware supports overlaying pixels that have an alpha component. This component can be 1, 2, 4, or 8 bits. Zero is the fully transparent color.
	• **DDFXALPHACAPS_OVERLAYALPHAPIXELSNEG**—The display hardware supports overlaying pixels that have an alpha component. This component can be 1, 2, 4, or 8 bits. Zero is the fully opaque color.
	• **DDFXALPHACAPS_OVERLAYALPHASURFACES**—The display hardware supports alpha-only overlay surfaces. The bit depth of these surfaces can be 1, 2, 4, or 8. Zero is the fully transparent color.

(continued)

DDCAPS *(continued)*	
Member	**Description**
	• **DDFXALPHACAPS_OVERLAYALPHASURFACESNEG**—The display hardware supports alpha-only overlay surfaces. The bit depth of these surfaces can be 1, 2, 4, or 8. Zero is the fully opaque color.
dwPalCaps	Describes the palette capabilities of the graphics card. This member may be 0, or one or more of the following flags:
	• **DDPCAPS_1BIT**—The display hardware supports palettes that consist of two entries in the color table.
	• **DDPCAPS_2BIT**—The display hardware supports palettes that consist of four entries in the color table.
	• **DDPCAPS_4BIT**—The display hardware supports palettes that consist of 16 entries in the color table.
	• **DDPCAPS_8BIT**—The display hardware supports palettes that consist of 256 entries in the color table.
	• **DDPCAPS_8BITENTRIES**—The display hardware supports palettes that consist of 1-byte indices into the palette of the destination surface.
	• **DDPCAPS_ALPHA**—The display hardware supports palettes that contain alpha information, specified in the **peFlags** member of each **PALETTEENTRY** structure that defines a palette entry.
	• **DDPCAPS_ALLOW256**—The display hardware supports palettes that allow all 256 entries to be defined.
	• **DDPCAPS_PRIMARYSURFACE**—The palette is attached to the primary surface.
	• **DDPCAPS_PRIMARYSURFACELEFT**—The palette is attached to the primary surface for the left eye in a stereoscopic setup.
	• **DDPCAPS_VSYNC**—Changes to the palette's color values can be synched with the display's refresh rate, eliminating artifacts otherwise noticed with palette changes for primary surfaces.
dwSVCaps	Describes the stereo-vision capabilities of the graphics card. This member may be 0, or one or more of the following flags:
	• **DDSVCAPS_ENIGMA**—The display hardware supports stereoscopic viewing through Enigma encoding.
	• **DDSVCAPS_FLICKER**—The display hardware supports stereoscopic viewing through high-frequency flickering.
	• **DDSVCAPS_REDBLUE**—The display hardware supports stereoscopic viewing through red and blue glasses.

(continued)

DDCAPS *(continued)*	
Member	**Description**
	• **DDSVCAPS_SPLIT**—The display hardware supports stereoscopic viewing through a split display
dwAlphaBltConstBitDepths	The alpha constant bit depths supported for blit operations. This can be a combination of the values **DDBD_2**, **DDBD_4**, and **DDBD_8**.
dwAlphaBltPixelBitDepths	The alpha pixel bit depths supported for blit operations. This can be a combination of the values **DDBD_1**, **DDBD_2**, **DDBD_4**, and **DDBD_8**.
dwAlphaBltSurfaceBitDepths	The alpha surface bit depths supported for blit operations. This can be a combination of the values **DDBD_1**, **DDBD_2**, **DDBD_4**, and **DDBD_8**.
dwAlphaOverlayConstBitDepths	The alpha constant bit depths supported for overlay operations. This can be a combination of the values **DDBD_2**, **DDBD_4**, and **DDBD_8**.
dwAlphaOverlayPixelBitDepths	The alpha pixel bit depths supported for overlay operations. This can be a combination of the values **DDBD_1**, **DDBD_2**, **DDBD_4,** and **DDBD_8.**
dwAlphaOverlaySurfaceBitDepths	The alpha surface bit depths supported for overlay operations. This can be a combination of the values **DDBD_1**, **DDBD_2**, **DDBD_4**, and **DDBD_8**.
dwVidMemTotal	The total amount of memory on the display hardware.
dwVidMemFree	The total free memory on the display hardware.
dwMaxVisibleOverlays	The maximum number of visible overlays or overlay sprites supported by the display hardware.
dwCurrVisibleOverlays	The current number of visible overlays or overlay sprites supported by the display hardware.
dwNumFourCCCodes	The number of FourCC codes supported by the display hardware.
dwAlignBoundarySrc	The alignment factor for the position of source overlay surfaces.
dwAlignSizeSrc	The alignment factor for the size of source overlay surfaces.
dwAlignBoundaryDest	The alignment factor for the position of destination overlay surfaces.
dwAlignSizeDest	The alignment factor for the size of destination overlay surfaces.
dwAlignStrideAlign	The alignment factor for surface pitches.
dwRops[DD_ROP_SPACE]	The raster operations supported by the display hardware.
dwReservedCaps	Reserved for future use.
dwMinOverlayStretch	The minimum overlay stretch factor, multiplied by 1,000.
dwMaxOverlayStretch	The maximum overlay stretch factor, multiplied by 1,000.
dwMinLiveVideoStretch	This member is no longer used.

(continued)

DDCAPS *(continued)*

Member	Description
dwMaxLiveVideoStretch	This member is no longer used.
dwMinHwCodecStretch	This member is no longer used.
dwMaxHwCodecStretch	This member is no longer used.
dwReserved1	Reserved for future use.
dwReserved2	Reserved for future use.
dwReserved3	Reserved for future use.
dwSVBCaps	The driver's capabilities for system-memory-to-display-memory surface blits. The values for this member are identical to those of the **dwCaps** member.
dwSVBCKeyCaps	The driver's color key capabilities for system-memory-to-display-memory surface blits. The values for this member are identical to those of the **dwCKeyCaps** member.
dwSVBFXCaps	The driver's effects capabilities for system-memory-to-display-memory surface blits. The values for this member are identical to those of the **dwFXCaps** member.
dwSVBRops[DD_ROP_SPACE]	The raster operations supported by the display hardware for system-memory-to-display-memory surface blits.
dwVSBCaps	The driver's capabilities for display-memory-to-system-memory surface blits. The values for this member are identical to those of the **dwCaps** member.
dwVSBCKeyCaps	The driver's color key capabilities for display-memory-to-system-memory surface blits. The values for this member are identical to those of the **dwCKeyCaps** member.
dwVSBFXCaps	The driver's effects capabilities for display-memory-to-system-memory surface blits. The values for this member are identical to those of the **dwFXCaps** member.
dwVSBRops[DD_ROP_SPACE]	The raster operations supported by the display hardware for display-memory-to-surface-memory surface blits.
dwSSBCaps	The driver's capabilities for system-memory-to-system-memory surface blits. The values for this member are identical to those of the **dwCaps** member.
dwSSBCKeyCaps	The driver's color key capabilities for system-memory-to-system-memory surface blits. The values for this member are identical to those of the **dwCKeyCaps** member.
dwSSBCFXCaps	The driver's effects capabilities for system-memory-to-system-memory surface blits. The values for this member are identical to those of the **dwFXCaps** member.
dwSSBRops[DD_ROP_SPACE]	The raster operations supported by the display hardware for system-memory-to-surface-memory surface blits.

(continued)

DDCAPS *(continued)*

Member	Description
dwMaxVideoPorts	The maximum number of live video ports supported by the display hardware.
dwCurrVideoPorts	The current number of live video ports.
dwSVBCaps2	The driver's extended capabilities for system-memory-to-display-memory blits. The values for this member are identical to those of the **dwCaps2** member.
dwNLVBCaps	The driver's capabilities for nonlocal-to-local-video-memory surface blits. The values for this member are identical to those of the **dwCaps** member.
dwNLVBCaps2	The driver's extended capabilities for nonlocal-to-local-video-memory surface blits. The values for this member are identical to those of the **dwCaps2** member.
dwNLVBCKeyCaps	The driver's color key capabilities for nonlocal-to-local-video-memory surface blits. The values for this member are identical to those of the **dwCKeyCaps** member.
dwNLVBFXCaps	The driver's effects capabilities for nonlocal-to-local-video-memory surface blits. The values for this member are identical to those of the **dwFXCaps** member.
dwNLVBRops[DD_ROP_SPACE]	The raster operations supported by the display hardware for nonlocal-to-local-video-memory surface blits.
ddsCaps	A **DDSCAPS2** structure that describes the kinds of surfaces supported by the display hardware.

DDCOLORCONTROL

Structure Description

This structure describes color controls.

Structure Declaration

```
typedef struct _DDCOLORCONTROL {
    DWORD    dwSize;
    DWORD    dwFlags;
    LONG     lBrightness;
    LONG     lContrast;
    LONG     lHue;
    LONG     lSaturation;
    LONG     lSharpness;
    LONG     lGamma;
    LONG     lColorEnable;
    DWORD    dwReserved1;
} DDCOLORCONTROL, FAR *LPDDCOLORCONTROL;
```

(continued)

DDCOLORCONTROL *(continued)*	
Member	**Description**
dwSize	The size of the structure, in bytes. This member must be initialized before the structure is used.
dwFlags	Describes which members of the structure are valid, or if the structure has been retrieved with the **IDirectDrawColorControl::-GetColorControls ()** function, which controls are supported by the device.
	• **DDCOLOR_BRIGHTNESS**—The **lBrightness** member is valid.
	• **DDCOLOR_COLORENABLE**—The **lColorEnable** member is valid.
	• **DDCOLOR_CONTRAST**—The **lContrast** member is valid.
	• **DDCOLOR_GAMMA**—The **lGamma** member is valid.
	• **DDCOLOR_HUE**—The **lHue** member is valid.
	• **DDCOLOR_SATURATION**—The **lSaturation** member is valid.
	• **DDCOLOR_SHARPNESS**—The **lSharpness** member is valid.
lBrightness	The brightness, specified in IRE units multiplied by 100. Valid values range from 0 (no brightness) to 750 (the default brightness) to 10,000 (full brightness).
lContrast	The contrast (difference between the lightest and darkest values), specified in IRE units multiplied by 100. Valid values range from 0 to 10,000 (the default contrast) to 20,000. Higher contrast values accentuate the difference between the lightest and darkest values and lower contrast values make colors tend toward middle luminance values.
lHue	The hue, specified in degrees. Valid values range from -180 to 0 (the default hue) to 180.
lSaturation	The saturation, specified in IRE units multiplied by 100. Valid values range from 0 to 10,000 (the default) to 20,000.
lSharpness	The sharpness. Valid values range from 0 to 5 (the default) to 10.
lGamma	The gamma correction factor. Valid values range from 0 (no added luminance) to 1 (the default) to 500 (maximum added luminance).
lColorEnable	A flag indicating whether or not color is used. A value of 1 (the default) indicates color is used; 0 indicates it is not.
dwReserved1	This member is reserved for future use.

DDCOLORKEY

Structure Description
This structure describes a color key.

Structure Declaration
```
typedef struct _DDCOLORKEY{
    DWORD dwColorSpaceLowValue;
    DWORD dwColorSpaceHighValue;
} DDCOLORKEY,FAR* LPDDCOLORKEY;
```

Member	Description
dwColorSpaceLowValue	The low value for the color key, in the pixel format of the surface.
dwColorSpaceHighValue	The high value for the color key, in the pixel format of the surface. If only one color is being specified, this member should be equal to **dwColorSpaceLowKey**.

DDDEVICEIDENTIFIER2

Structure Description
This structure describes a device's identity.

Structure Declaration
```
typedef struct tagDDDEVICEIDENTIFIER2 {
    char      szDriver[MAX_DDDEVICEID_STRING];
    char      szDescription[MAX_DDDEVICEID_STRING];
    LARGE_INTEGER  liDriverVersion;
    DWORD     dwVendorId;
    DWORD     dwDeviceId;
    DWORD     dwSubSysId;
    DWORD     dwRevision;
    GUID      guidDeviceIdentifier;
    DWORD     dwWHQLLevel;
} DDDEVICEIDENTIFIER2, * LPDDDEVICEIDENTIFIER2;
```

Member	Description
szDriver[MAX_DDDEVICEID_STRING]	A string that identifies the device's driver.
szDescription[MAX_DDDEVICEID_STRING]	A string that describes the device's driver.
liDriverVersion	The version of the driver. This 64-bit value is broken down into four sections: • The high WORD of the high DWORD—The product number. • The low WORD of the high DWORD—The major version number.

(continued)

DDDEVICEIDENTIFIER2 *(continued)*

Member	Description
	• The high WORD of the low DWORD—The minor version number.
	• The low WORD of the low DWORD—The build number.
dwVendorId	The vendor identification number.
dwDeviceId	The device chipset identification number.
dwSubSysId	The device subsystem identification number.
dwRevision	The revision number of the chipset.
guidDeviceIdentifier	A GUID that represents the driver/chipset pair.
dwWHQLevel	The device/driver pair's certification level from the Windows Hardware Quality Lab (WHQL).

DDGAMMARAMP

Structure Description

This structure describes a gamma ramp.

Structure Declaration

```
typedef struct _DDGAMMARAMP {
    WORD red[256];
    WORD green[256];
    WORD blue[256];
} DDGAMMARAMP, FAR * LPDDGAMMARAMP;
```

Member	Description
red	A pointer to an array of 256 WORD values. Each element describes a red component of the gamma ramp.
green	A pointer to an array of 256 WORD values. Each element describes a green component of the gamma ramp.
blue	A pointer to an array of 256 WORD values. Each element describes a blue component of the gamma ramp.

DDOVERLAYFX

Structure Description

This structure describes overlay effects.

Structure Declaration

```
typedef struct _DDOVERLAYFX{
    DWORD dwSize;
    DWORD dwAlphaEdgeBlendBitDepth;
    DWORD dwAlphaEdgeBlend;
    DWORD dwReserved;
    DWORD dwAlphaDestConstBitDepth;
    union
    {
        DWORD             dwAlphaDestConst;
        LPDIRECTDRAWSURFACE lpDDSAlphaDest;
    } DUMMYUNIONNAMEN(1);
    DWORD dwAlphaSrcConstBitDepth;
    union
    {
        DWORD             dwAlphaSrcConst;
        LPDIRECTDRAWSURFACE lpDDSAlphaSrc;
    } DUMMYUNIONNAMEN(2);
    DDCOLORKEY dckDestColorkey;
    DDCOLORKEY dckSrcColorkey;

    DWORD dwDDFX;
    DWORD dwFlags;
} DDOVERLAYFX,FAR *LPDDOVERLAYFX;
```

Member	Description
dwSize	The size of the structure, in bytes. This member must be initialized before the structure is used.
dwAlphaEdgeBlendBitDepth	The bit depth of the alpha edge blend constant.
dwAlphaEdgeBlend	The alpha edge blend constant.
dwReserved	This member is reserved for future use and must be set to 0.
dwAlphaDestConstBitDepth	The alpha constant bit depth for the destination surface.
dwAlphaDestConst	The alpha constant for the destination surface.
lpDDSAlphaDest	A pointer to a DirectDrawSurface7 object that identifies the alpha information to be used for the destination surface.
dwAlphaSrcConstBitDepth	The alpha constant bit depth for the source surface.
dwAlphaSrcConst	The alpha constant for the source surface.
lpDDSAlphaSrc	A pointer to a DirectDrawSurface7 object that identifies the alpha information to be used for the source surface.
dckDestColorkey	The color key to use for the destination surface, which overrides the destination surface's own color key.

(continued)

DDOVERLAYFX *(continued)*	
Member	**Description**
dckSrcColorkey	The color key to use for the source surface, which overrides the source surface's own color key.
dwDDFX	Describes overlay effects. This member can be 0, or one or more of the following flags:
	• **DDOVERFX_ARITHSTRETCHY**—DirectDraw should use arithmetic stretching for the *y*-axis, which produces higher-quality results than row replication.
	• **DDOVERFX_MIRRORLEFTRIGHT**—DirectDraw should reverse the overlay from left to right when overlaying it on the destination surface.
	• **DDOVERFX_MIRRORUPDOWN**—DirectDraw should reverse the overlay from top to bottom when overlaying it on the destination surface.
dwFlags	This member is reserved for future use; it must be set to 0.

DDPIXELFORMAT

Structure Description

This structure describes a pixel format.

Structure Declaration

```
typedef struct _DDPIXELFORMAT{
    DWORD dwSize;
    DWORD dwFlags;
    DWORD dwFourCC;
    union
    {
        DWORD dwRGBBitCount;
        DWORD dwYUVBitCount;
        DWORD dwZBufferBitDepth;
        DWORD dwAlphaBitDepth;
        DWORD dwLuminanceBitCount;
        DWORD dwBumpBitCount;
    } DUMMYUNIONNAMEN(1);
    union
    {
        DWORD dwRBitMask;
        DWORD dwYBitMask;
        DWORD dwStencilBitDepth;
        DWORD dwLuminanceBitMask;
        DWORD dwBumpDuBitMask;
```

(continued)

DDPIXELFORMAT *(continued)*

Structure Declaration

```
    } DUMMYUNIONNAMEN(2);
    union
    {
        DWORD dwGBitMask;
        DWORD dwUBitMask;
        DWORD dwZBitMask;
        DWORD dwBumpDvBitMask;
    } DUMMYUNIONNAMEN(3);
    union
    {
        DWORD dwBBitMask;
        DWORD dwVBitMask;
        DWORD dwStencilBitMask;
        DWORD dwBumpLuminanceBitMask;
    } DUMMYUNIONNAMEN(4);
    union
    {
        DWORD dwRGBAlphaBitMask;
        DWORD dwYUVAlphaBitMask;
        DWORD dwLuminanceAlphaBitMask;
        DWORD dwRGBZBitMask;
        DWORD dwYUVZBitMask;
    } DUMMYUNIONNAMEN(5);
} DDPIXELFORMAT, FAR* LPDDPIXELFORMAT;
```

Member	Description
dwSize	The size of the structure, in bytes. This member must be initialized before the structure is used.
dwFlags	Describes the type of pixel format. This member can be one or more of the following flags:

- **DDPF_ALPHA**—An alpha-only pixel format.

- **DDPF_ALPHAPIXELS**—An RGBA pixel format. These pixel formats have red, green, blue, and alpha components.

- **DDPF_ALPHAPREMULT**—A premultiplied alpha pixel format. The red, green, and blue components are premultiplied by the alpha component.

- **DDPF_BUMPLUMINANCE**—A bump-map luminance pixel format.

- **DDPF_BUMPDUDV**—A bump-map pixel format.

- **DDPF_COMPRESSED**—A pixel format that accepts uncompressed data, but compresses it during write operations.

(continued)

DDPIXELFORMAT *(continued)*

Member	Description
	• **DDPF_FOURCC**—A FourCC pixel format. The dwFourCC member is valid and describes the pixel format.
	• **DDPF_LUMINANCE**—A luminance-only or luminance-alpha pixel format.
	• **DDPF_PALETTEINDEXED1**—A 1-bit palettized pixel format. Each pixel in the surface requires 1 bit and is an index into a palette containing two entries.
	• **DDPF_PALETTEINDEXED2**—A 2-bit palettized pixel format. Each pixel in the surface requires 2 bits and is an index into a palette containing four entries.
	• **DDPF_PALETTEINDEXED4**—A 4-bit palettized pixel format. Each pixel in the surface requires 4 bits and is an index into a palette containing 16 entries.
	• **DDPF_PALETTEINDEXED8**—An 8-bit palettized pixel format. Each pixel in the surface requires 8 bits and is an index into a palette containing 256 entries.
	• **DDPF_PALETTEINDEXEDTO8**—An 8-bit palettized pixel format. Each pixel in the surface requires 8 bits and is an index into the destination surface's 256 entry palette.
	• **DDPF_RGB**—An RGB pixel format.
	• **DDPF_RGBTOYUV**—A pixel format that accepts RGB data but translates it to YUV during write operations.
	• **DDPF_STENCILBUFFER**—A z-buffer stencil format. This flag must be specified with **DDPF_ZBUFFER**.
	• **DDPF_YUV**—A YUV pixel format.
	• **DDPF_ZBUFFER**—A z-buffer-only pixel format.
	• **DDPF_ZPIXELS**—An RGBZ pixel format. These pixel formats have red, green, blue, and z-components.
dwFourCC	A FourCC that describes the pixel format.
dwRGBBitCount	The bit count for an RGB pixel format.
dwYUVBitCount	The bit count for a YUV pixel format.
dwZBufferBitDepth	The bit count for a z-buffer-only pixel format.
dwAlphaBitDepth	The bit count for an alpha-only pixel format.
dwLuminanceBitCount	The bit count for a luminance pixel format.
dwBumpBitCount	The bit count for a bump-map pixel format.
dwRBitMask	The bit mask for the red component of the pixel format.
dwYBitMask	The bit mask for the y-component of the pixel format.

(continued)

DDPIXELFORMAT *(continued)*

Member	Description
dwStencilBitDepth	The bit count for a stencil surface.
dwLuminanceBitMask	The bit mask for the luminance component.
dwBumpDuBitMask	The bit mask for the *du*-component of a bump-map pixel format.
dwGBitMask	The bit mask for the green component of the pixel format.
dwUBitMask	The bit mask for the *u*-component of a bump-map pixel format.
dwZBitMask	The bit mask for the *z*-component of the pixel format.
dwBumpDvBitMask	The bit mask for the *dv*-component of the pixel format.
dwBBitMask	The bit mask for the blue component of the pixel format.
dwVBitMask	The bit mask for the *v*-component of a bump-map pixel format.
dwStencilBitMask	The bit mask for the stencil component of the pixel format.
dwBumpLuminanceBitMask	The bit mask for the bump luminance component of a bump-map pixel format.
dwRGBAlphaBitMask	The bit mask for the alpha component of an RGBA pixel format.
dwYUVAlphaBitMask	The bit mask for the alpha component of a YUV pixel format.
dwLuminanceAlphaBitMask	The bit mask for the alpha component of an alpha-luminance pixel format.
dwRGBZBitMask	The bit mask for the *z*-component of an RGBZ pixel format.
dwYUVZBitMask	The bit mask for the *z*-component of a YUVZ pixel format.

DDSCAPS

Structure Description

This structure describes the capabilities of a surface.

Structure Declaration

```
typedef struct _DDSCAPS{
    DWORD dwCaps;
} DDSCAPS, FAR* LPDDSCAPS;
```

Member	Description
dwCaps	Describes surface capabilities. This may be any of the possible values for the **dwCaps** member of the **DDSCAPS2** structure.

DDSCAPS2	

Structure Description

This structure describes the capabilities of a surface.

Structure Declaration

```
typedef struct _DDSCAPS2 {
    DWORD    dwCaps;
    DWORD    dwCaps2;
    DWORD    dwCaps3;
    DWORD    dwCaps4;
} DDSCAPS2, FAR* LPDDSCAPS2;
```

Member	Description
dwCaps	Describes surface capabilities. This member can be one or more of the following flags: • **DDSCAPS_3DDEVICE**—The surface can be used as a target for 3D rendering. • **DDSCAPS_ALPHA**—The surface contains only alpha information. • **DDSCAPS_BACKBUFFER**—The surface is the back buffer in a chain of surfaces. • **DDSCAPS_COMPLEX**—The surface is a complex surface. Complex surfaces have one or more implicitly attached surfaces that are maintained implicitly. For example, restoring or destroying the complex surface does the same to all implicitly attached surfaces. • **DDSCAPS_FLIP**—The surface is part of a flipping chain. • **DDSCAPS_FRONTBUFFER**—The surface is the front buffer of a chain of surfaces. • **DDSCAPS_HWCODEC**—The surface can receive a decompressed stream from the hardware. • **DDSCAPS_LIVEVIDEO**—The surface can receive live video. • **DDSCAPS_LOCALVIDMEM**—The surface exists in local video memory. This flag must be specified with the **DDSCAPS_VIDEOMEMORY** flag. • **DDSCAPS_MIPMAP**—The surface is one level of a mipmap. This flag must be specified with the **DDSCAPS_VIDEOMEMORY** flag. • **DDSCAPS_MODEX**—The surface is a 320x200 or 320x240 ModeX mode.

(continued)

DDSCAPS2 *(continued)*	
Member	**Description**
	• **DDSCAPS_NONLOCALVIDMEM**—The surface exists in nonlocal video memory. This flag must be specified with the **DDSCAPS_VIDEOMEMORY** flag.
	• **DDSCAPS_OFFSCREENPLAIN**—The surface is an offscreen plain surface. Plain surfaces are those that are not overlay, texture, z-buffer, front-buffer, back-buffer, or alpha surfaces.
	• **DDSCAPS_OVERLAY**—The surface is an overlay.
	• **DDSCAPS_OWNDC**—The surface will have a DC associated with it for an extended period of time.
	• **DDSCAPS_PALETTE**—Unique DirectDrawPalette objects can be created and associated with this surface.
	• **DDSCAPS_PRIMARYSURFACE**—The surface is the primary surface.
	• **DDSCAPS_PRIMARYSURFACELEFT**—The surface is the primary surface for the left eye in a stereoscopic viewing environment.
	• **DDSCAPS_STANDARDVGAMODE**—The surface is a standard VGA mode surface, not a ModeX surface.
	• **DDSCAPS_SYSTEMMEMORY**—The surface exists in system memory.
	• **DDSCAPS_TEXTURE**—The surface is a texture. Texture surfaces can, but do not have to, be used for texturing 3D polygons.
	• **DDSCAPS_VIDEOMEMORY**—The surface exists in video memory.
	• **DDSCAPS_VIDEOPORT**—The surface can receive data from a video port.
	• **DDSCAPS_VISIBLE**—Changes made to the surface are immediately visible. This is set for primary surfaces, visible overlays, and texture maps currently being textured.
	• **DDSCAPS_WRITEONLY**—Data can be written to the surface, but cannot be read from it.
	• **DDSCAPS_ZBUFFER**—The surface is a z-buffer.
dwCaps2	Describes additional surface capabilities. This member can be one or more of the following flags:
	• **DDSCAPS2_CUBEMAP**—The surface is a cubic environment map. If this flag is specified, the face or faces of the cube represented by the surface must be specified by other **DDSCAPS2_CUBEMAP_*** flags.

(continued)

DDSCAPS2 *(continued)*

Member	Description
	• **DDSCAPS2_CUBEMAP_POSITIVEX**—The cubic environment map represents the side of the cube facing the positive x-axis. This flag must be used in combination with **DDSCAPS2_CUBEMAP**.
	• **DDSCAPS2_CUBEMAP_NEGATIVEX**—The cubic environment map represents the side of the cube facing the negative x-axis. This flag must be used in combination with **DDSCAPS2_CUBEMAP**.
	• **DDSCAPS2_CUBEMAP_POSITIVEY**—The cubic environment map represents the side of the cube facing the positive y-axis. This flag must be used in combination with **DDSCAPS2_CUBEMAP**.
	• **DDSCAPS2_CUBEMAP_NEGATIVEY**—The cubic environment map represents the side of the cube facing the negative y-axis. This flag must be used in combination with **DDSCAPS2_CUBEMAP**.
	• **DDSCAPS2_CUBEMAP_POSITIVEZ**—The cubic environment map represents the side of the cube facing the positive z-axis. This flag must be used in combination with **DDSCAPS2_CUBEMAP**.
	• **DDSCAPS2_CUBEMAP_NEGATIVEZ**— The cubic environment map represents the side of the cube facing the negative z-axis. This flag must be used in combination with **DDSCAPS2_CUBEMAP**.
	• **DDSCAPS2_CUBEMAP_ALLFACES**—The cubic environment map represents all sides of the cube. This flag must be used in combination with **DDSCAPS2_CUBEMAP**.
	• **DDSCAPS2_D3DTEXTUREMANAGE**—The texture surface will always be managed by Direct3D.
	• **DDSCAPS2_DONOTPERSIST**—The surface is noncritical and may safely be lost.
	• **DDSCAPS2_HARDWAREDEINTERLACE**—The surface will receive data from deinterlacing hardware.
	• **DDSCAPS2_HINTANTIALIASING**—The application intends to use antialiasing.
	• **DDSCAPS2_HINTDYNAMIC**— The surface will be changing frequently.

(continued)

DDSCAPS2 *(continued)*

Member	Description
	• **DDSCAPS2_HINTSTATIC**—The surface will for the most part remain static, enabling Direct3D to use optimizations it otherwise could not.
	• **DDSCAPS2_MIPMAPSUBLEVEL**—The surface is a non-top-level surface in a mipmapped cube map or similar construct. This flag, which is ignored by **IDirectDrawSurface7::Create-Surface** (), enables applications to use the **IDirectDraw-Surface7::GetAttachedSurface** () function to distinguish between top-level faces and their attached mipmap levels.
	• **DDSCAPS2_OPAQUE**—The surface will never be locked again.
	• **DDSCAPS2_STEREOSURFACELEFT**—The surface is the left surface in a stereo vision flipping chain.
	• **DDSCAPS2_TEXTUREMANAGE**—The texture memory should be managed by the driver of the graphics card, if possible. If this flag is not specified, and the application is not using Direct3D Retained Mode, texture memory will be managed by Immediate Mode. This flag should not be used for Direct3D RM surfaces, because RM performs its own texture management; rather, such surfaces should be created in system memory.
dwCaps3	Reserved for future use.
dwCaps4	Reserved for future use.

DDSURFACEDESC2

Structure Description

This structure describes a surface.

Structure Declaration

```
typedef struct _DDSURFACEDESC2 {
    DWORD        dwSize;
    DWORD        dwFlags;
    DWORD        dwHeight;
    DWORD        dwWidth;
    union
    {
        LONG     lPitch;
        DWORD    dwLinearSize;
```

(continued)

DDSURFACEDESC2 (continued)

Structure Declaration

```
    } DUMMYUNIONNAMEN(1);
    DWORD           dwBackBufferCount;
    union
    {
        DWORD       dwMipMapCount;
        DWORD       dwRefreshRate;
    } DUMMYUNIONNAMEN(2);
    DWORD           dwAlphaBitDepth;
    DWORD           dwReserved;
    LPVOID          lpSurface;
    DDCOLORKEY      ddckCKDestOverlay;
    DDCOLORKEY      ddckCKDestBlt;
    DDCOLORKEY      ddckCKSrcOverlay;
    DDCOLORKEY      ddckCKSrcBlt;
    DDPIXELFORMAT   ddpfPixelFormat;
    DDSCAPS2        ddsCaps;
    DWORD           dwTextureStage;
} DDSURFACEDESC2, FAR* LPDDSURFACEDESC2;
```

Member	Description
dwSize	The size of the structure, in bytes. This member must be initialized before the structure is used.
dwFlags	Describes which members of the structure are valid. This member can be 0, or one or more of the following flags:

- **DDSD_ALL**—All the flags are valid.
- **DDSD_ALPHABITDEPTH**—The **dwAlphaBitDepth** member is valid.
- **DDSD_BACKBUFFERCOUNT**—The **dwBackBufferCount** member is valid.
- **DDSD_CAPS**—The **ddsCaps** member is valid.
- **DDSD_CKDESTBLT**—The **ddckCKDestBlt** member is valid.
- **DDSD_CKDESTOVERLAY**—The **ddckCKDestOverlay** member is valid.
- **DDSD_CKSRCBLT**—The **ddckCKSrcBlt** member is valid.
- **DDSD_CKSRCOVERLAY**—The **ddckCKSrcOverlay** member is valid.
- **DDSD_HEIGHT**—The **dwHeight** member is valid.
- **DDSD_LINEARSIZE**—The **dwLinearSize** member is valid.
- **DDSD_LPSURFACE**—The **lpSurface** member is valid.

(continued)

DDSURFACEDESC2 *(continued)*

Member	Description
	• **DDSD_MIPMAPCOUNT**—The **dwMipMapCount** member is valid.
	• **DDSD_PITCH**—The **lPitch** member is valid.
	• **DDSD_PIXELFORMAT**—The **ddpfPixelFormat** member is valid.
	• **DDSD_REFRESHRATE**—The **dwRefreshRate** member is valid.
	• **DDSD_TEXTURESTAGE**—The **dwTextureStage** member is valid.
	• **DDSD_WIDTH**—The **dwWidth** member is valid.
dwHeight	The height of the surface.
dwWidth	The width of the surface.
lPitch	The pitch of the surface. The pitch describes the number of bytes from one row to the next.
dwLinearSize	The size of the buffer (currently valid only for compressed textures).
dwBackBufferCount	The number of back buffers.
dwMipMapCount	The number of mipmap levels.
dwRefreshRate	The refresh rate.
dwAlphaBitDepth	The bit depth of an alpha surface.
dwReserved	Reserved for future use.
lpSurface	A pointer to the surface's bits. This member is valid only when the application is setting the surface description for a surface (in which case this must be a pointer to system memory) or when it is locking it.
ddckCKDestOverlay	A **DDCOLORKEY** structure that describes the destination color key for an overlay surface.
ddckCKDestBlt	A **DDCOLORKEY** structure that describes the destination color key for blit operations.
ddckCKSrcOverlay	A **DDCOLORKEY** structure that describes the source color key for an overlay surface.
ddckCKSrcBlt	A **DDCOLORKEY** structure that describes the source color key for blit operations.
ddpfPixelFormat	A **DDPIXELFORMAT** structure that describes the surface's pixel format.
ddsCaps	A **DDSCAPS2** structure that describes the capabilities of the surface.
dwTextureStage	The texture stage that will be used for the texture surface. Some hardware requires this member to be set.

Appendix B
Direct3D IM Reference

This appendix documents the Direct3D Immediate Mode (IM). It is divided into four sections: The interface section documents the interfaces of Direct3D IM; the overload section references the overloaded functions available to C++ programmers who use the **D3DMATRIX** and **D3DVECTOR** types; the callback section documents the functions that are defined by applications and called by Direct3D functions; and the structure section documents all of the structures Direct3D uses.

Interface Reference

This section documents the IDirect3D7, IDirect3DDevice7, and IDirect3DVertexBuffer7 interfaces.

IDirect3D7 Reference

Applications obtain the IDirect3D7 interface by calling the **QueryInterface ()** function from any DirectDraw object.
The globally unique identifier (GUID) for this interface is **IID_IDirect3D7**.

IDirect3D7::CreateDevice ()	

Function Description

This function creates a Direct3D device object, which you can then use to render 3D scenes using the **DrawPrimitive** functions.

Function Declaration

```
HRESULT CreateDevice(
    REFCLSID rclsid,
    LPDIRECTDRAWSURFACE7 lpDDS,
    LPDIRECT3DDEVICE7 * lplpD3DDevice,
);
```

Parameter	Description
rclsid	A reference to a class identifier, which identifies the Direct3D device. This parameter can be any identifier retrieved by the **IDirect3D7::EnumDevices** () function, or one of the following predefined identifiers: • **IID_IDirect3DTnLHalDevice**—Selects the Hardware Abstraction Layer (HAL) device that supports transformation and lighting in hardware. • **IID_IDirect3DHALDevice**—Selects the Hardware Abstraction Layer (HAL) device. • **IID_IDirect3DMMXDevice**—Selects the software, MMX-accelerated device. • **IID_IDirect3DRGBDevice**—Selects the software, RGB device.
lpDDS	A pointer to a DirectDrawSurface7 object that identifies the surface that Direct3D should render scenes to. This surface, referred to as the render-target surface, must have been created with 3D capabilities (the **DDSCAPS_3DDEVICE** flag).
lplpD3DDevice	The address of a pointer to a DirectDraw3DDevice7 object. If this function succeeds, the pointer will be set to the newly created Direct3D device object.
Return Value	**Description**
DDERR_INVALIDPARAMS	Direct3D could not create the Direct3D device, because one or more parameters are invalid.

IDirect3D7::CreateVertexBuffer ()

Function Description

This function creates a Direct3D vertex buffer object.

Function Declaration

```
HRESULT CreateVertexBuffer(
    LPD3DVERTEXBUFFERDESC    lpVBDesc,
    LPDIRECT3DVERTEXBUFFER7* lpD3DVertexBuffer,
    DWORD dwFlags
);
```

Parameter	Description
lpVBDesc	A pointer to a **D3DVERTEXBUFFERDESC** structure that describes the format and number of vertices that the vertex buffer will contain.
lpD3DVertexBuffer	The address of a pointer to a Direct3DVertexBuffer7 object. If this function succeeds, the pointer will be set to the newly created Direct3D vertex buffer object.
dwFlags	This parameter, which is not currently used, must be 0.

Return Value	Description
CLASS_E_NOAGGREGATION	Direct3D could not create the vertex buffer, because aggregation features are not supported for the object.
DDERR_INVALIDOBJECT	Direct3D could not create the vertex buffer, because this Direct3D7 object is invalid.
DDERR_INVALIDVERTEXFORMAT	Direct3D could not create the vertex buffer, because the specified vertex format is invalid.
DDERR_INVALIDPARAMS	Direct3D could not create the vertex buffer, because one or more parameters are invalid.
DDERR_OUTOFMEMORY	Direct3D could not create the vertex buffer, because sufficient memory is not available.
DDERR_VBUF_CREATE_FAILED	Direct3D could not create the vertex buffer, possibly because sufficient memory is not available.

IDirect3D7::EnumDevices ()

Function Description

This function enumerates all of the Direct3D device drivers installed on the user's system.

Function Declaration

```
HRESULT EnumDevices(
    LPD3DENUMDEVICESCALLBACK7 lpEnumDevicesCallback,
    LPVOID lpUserArg
);
```

(continued)

IDirect3D7::EnumDevices () *(continued)*	
Parameter	**Description**
lpEnumDevicesCallback	A pointer to a **D3DENUMDEVICESCALLBACK7** callback function that will be called for every device enumerated.
lpUserArg	A pointer to application-defined data that will be sent to the callback function every time it is called.
Return Value	**Description**
DDERR_INVALIDOBJECT	Direct3D could not list the system's Direct3D device drivers, because the Direct3D7 object is invalid.
DDERR_INVALIDPARAMS	Direct3D could not list the system's Direct3D device drivers, because one or more parameters are invalid.

IDirect3D7::EnumTextureFormats ()

Function Description

This function enumerates all of the depth-buffer formats that a specified Direct3D device supports.

Function Declaration

```
HRESULT EnumZBufferFormats(
    REFCLSID riidDevice,
    LPD3DENUMPIXELFORMATSCALLBACK lpEnumCallback,
    LPVOID    lpContext
);
```

Parameter	**Description**
riidDevice	A reference to a GUID that identifies the Direct3D device whose depth-buffer formats will be enumerated.
lpEnumCallback	A pointer to a **D3DENUMPIXELFORMATSCALLBACK** callback function that will be called for every depth-buffer format supported by the specified device.
lpContext	A pointer to application-defined data that will be sent to the callback function every time it is called.
Return Value	**Description**
DDERR_INVALIDOBJECT	Direct3D could not list the depth-buffer formats, because the Direct3D7 object is invalid.
DDERR_INVALIDPARAMS	Direct3D could not list the depth-buffer formats, because one or more parameters are invalid.
DDERR_NOZBUFFERHW	Direct3D could not list the depth-buffer formats, because the hardware does not support depth buffers.
DDERR_OUTOFMEMORY	Direct3D could not list the depth-buffer formats, because sufficient memory is not available.

IDirect3D7::EvictManagedTextures ()

Function Description

This function evicts all managed textures from video memory, whether local or nonlocal. Managed textures are those created with the **DDSCAPS2_TEXTUREMANAGE** or **DDSCAPS2_D3DTEXTURE-MANAGE** flags. See the **DDSCAPS2** structure for more information.

Function Declaration

```
HRESULT EvictManagedTextures();
```

Parameter	Description
None	

Return Value	Description
D3D_OK	Direct3D successfully evicted all managed textures from video memory.

IDirect3DDevice7 Reference

This section documents the IDirect3DDevice7 interface, which applications may obtain by calling the **IDirect3D7::CreateDevice ()** function.

The GUID for this interface is **IID_IDirect3DDevice7**.

IDirect3DDevice7::ApplyStateBlock ()

Function Description

This function applies a state block to the Direct3D device. A state block is a list of state changes that may be generated by first calling **IDirect3DDevice7::BeginStateBlock ()**, filling the state block with requested state changes by calling certain functions, and finally calling **IDirect3DDevice7::End-StateBlock ()**. See **IDirect3DDevice7::BeginStateBlock ()** for more information.

Function Declaration

```
HRESULT ApplyStateBlock(
  DWORD dwBlockHandle
);
```

Parameter	Description
dwBlockHandle	A handle to the device state block to be applied to the device. This handle must have been retrieved with the **IDirect3D-Device7::EndStateBlock ()** function.

Return Value	Description
D3D_OK	Direct3D successfully applied the specified state block.
D3DERR_INBEGINSTATEBLOCK	Direct3D could not apply the state block, because it is currently recording a state block. The **IDirect3DDevice7::EndStateBlock ()** function must be called before this function can succeed.
D3DERR_INVALIDSTATEBLOCK	Direct3D could not apply the state block, because the specified state block is invalid.

IDirect3DDevice7::BeginScene ()	
Function Description	
This function begins the rendering of a 3D scene. It must be called before an application renders any data. After rendering is complete, the application must call the **IDirect3DDevice7::EndScene ()** function.	
Function Declaration	
`HRESULT BeginScene();`	
Parameter	**Description**
None	
Return Value	**Description**
D3D_OK	Direct3D successfully began the scene.
<other>	Direct3D could not begin the scene.

IDirect3DDevice7::BeginStateBlock ()	
Function Description	
This function causes Direct3D to begin recording a series of state changes, which are collectively referred to as a *state block*. State changes are changes made to the state of the 3D device with any of the following functions: **IDirect3DDevice7::LightEnable()** **IDirect3DDevice7::SetClipPanel()** **IDirect3DDevice7::SetLight ()** **IDirect3DDevice7::SetMaterial ()** **IDirect3DDevice7::SetRenderState ()** **IDirect3DDevice7::SetTexture ()** **IDirect3DDevice7::SetTextureStageState ()** **IDirect3DDevice7::SetTransform ()** **IDirect3DDevice7::SetViewport ()** Once an application is done performing state changes, it can call **IDirect3DDevice7::EndStateBlock ()** to end recording state changes and then apply the state block to the device with the **IDirect3DDevice7::ApplyStateBlock ()** function. This function is useful because it allows many state changes to be sent to the 3D device at once. This is typically much faster than changing individual states one at a time.	
Function Declaration	
`HRESULT BeginStateBlock();`	
Parameter	**Description**
None	
Return Value	**Description**
D3D_OK	Direct3D successfully started recording device state changes.
D3DERR_INBEGINSTATEBLOCK	Direct3D could not start recording state changes, because it is already doing so. The application must call the **IDirect3D-Device7::EndStateBlock ()** function to end recording before it can successfully call this function.
DDERR_OUTOFMEMORY	Direct3D could not start recording state changes, because sufficient memory is not available.

IDirect3DDevice7::CaptureStateBlock ()

Function Description

This function captures the current state of the device into an existing state block. A state block is a list of states that have been or will be applied to the device.

Function Declaration

```
HRESULT CaptureStateBlock(
  DWORD dwBlockHandle
);
```

Parameter	Description
dwBlockHandle	A handle to the state block into which the device's current state will be captured.

Return Value	Description
D3D_OK	Direct3D successfully captured the device's current state into the specified state block.
D3DERR_INBEGINSTATEBLOCK	Direct3D could not capture the device's current state block, because it is recording a state block. The application must end recording by calling the **IDirect3DDevice7::EndStateBlock** () function before it can successfully call this function.
DDERR_OUTOFMEMORY	Direct3D could not capture the device's current state block, because sufficient memory is not available.

IDirect3DDevice7::Clear ()

Function Description

This function clears the viewport or a set of rectangles in the viewport. It can clear the render-target surface, the attached depth buffer, and the stencil buffer data in the attached depth buffer.

Function Declaration

```
HRESULT Clear(
  DWORD     dwCount,
  LPD3DRECT lpRects,
  DWORD     dwFlags,
  DWORD     dwColor,
  D3DVALUE  dvZ,
  DWORD     dwStencil
);
```

Parameter	Description
dwCount	The number of **D3DRECT** structures pointed to by the **lpRects** parameter. If the application is clearing the entire viewport, and so sets **lpRects** to **NULL**, this parameter must be 0.

(continued)

IDirect3DDevice7::Clear () (*continued*)	
Parameter	**Description**
lpRects	A pointer to an array of **D3DRECT** structures that describe the rectangular regions on the viewport to be cleared. The rectangles must be specified in the screen coordinates of the viewport's target surface. Coordinates that exceed the boundaries of the target surface are clipped.
	This parameter may also be **NULL**, in which case Direct3D clears the entire target surface.
dwFlags	Describes which surfaces should be cleared. This parameter must be set to one or more of the following flags:
	• **D3DCLEAR_STENCIL**—Direct3D should clear the viewport's stencil buffer to the value specified by the **dwStencil** parameter. This flag requires that the target surface have an attached depth buffer that also contains stencil buffer information.
	• **D3DCLEAR_TARGET**—Direct3D should clear the viewport's target surface to the color specified by the **dwColor** parameter.
	• **D3DCLEAR_ZBUFFER**—Direct3D should clear the viewport's depth buffer to the value specified by the **dvZ** parameter. This flag requires that the target surface have an attached depth buffer.
dwColor	The 32-bit RGBA value that Direct3D should use to clear the viewport's target surface. For this parameter to be valid, **dwFlags** must include the **D3DCLEAR_TARGET** flag.
dvZ	The depth value that Direct3D should use to clear the viewport's depth buffer. For z- and w-buffers, this parameter can range from 0.0, to 1.0, inclusive. A value of 0.0 designates the nearest distance possible, while a value of 1.0 indicates the farthest distance possible.
	For this parameter to be valid, **dwFlags** must include the **D3DCLEAR_ZBUFFER** flag.
dwStencil	The stencil value that Direct3D should use to clear the viewport's stencil buffer. This parameter can range from 0 to 2^n-1, inclusive, where **n** designates the bit depth of the stencil buffer.
	For this parameter to be valid, **dwFlags** must include the **D3DCLEAR_STENCIL** flag.
Return Value	**Description**
D3D_OK	Direct3D successfully cleared the viewport as requested.
D3DERR_STENCILBUFFER _NOTPRESENT	Direct3D could not clear the viewport's stencil buffer, because the viewport has no stencil buffer.
D3DERR_ZBUFFER_NOTPRESENT	Direct3D could not clear the viewport's depth buffer, because the viewport has no depth buffer.
DDERR_INVALIDOBJECT	Direct3D could not clear the viewport as requested, because this Direct3DDevice7 object is invalid.
DDERR_INVALIDPARAMS	Direct3D could not clear the viewport as requested, because one or more parameters are invalid.

IDirect3DDevice7::ComputeSphereVisibility ()

Function Description

This function determines the visibility of one or more spheres within the current viewport. The spheres must be defined in world space coordinates.

One useful application of this function is to generate a bounding sphere for each complicated object in a 3D scene, and then to determine the visibility of each object's bounding sphere before sending its vertices through the geometry pipeline, thereby avoiding needless transformations.

Function Declaration

```
HRESULT ComputeSphereVisibility(
  LPD3DVECTOR lpCenters,
  LPD3DVALUE  lpRadii,
  DWORD       dwNumSpheres,
  DWORD       dwFlags,
  LPDWORD     lpdwReturnValues
);
```

Parameter	Description
lpCenters	A pointer to an array of **D3DVECTOR** structures that describe the center of each sphere, in world space coordinates.
lpRadii	A pointer to an array of floating-point variables that describe the radii of the spheres pointed to by **lpCenters**.
dwNumSpheresi	The number of spheres described by the **lpCenters** and **lpRaddi** parameters. This value must be greater than 0.
dwFlags	This parameter, which is not currently used, must be 0.
lpdwReturnValues	A pointer to an array of **DWORD** values that has enough space to contain one entry for each sphere whose visibility is being determined. If this function succeeds, each entry in the array will describe the visibility of a corresponding sphere. A value of 0 indicates the sphere is completely visible. Otherwise, the entry may be a combination of one or more of the following flags:
	• **D3DSTATUS_CLIPINTERSECTIONALL**—This flag is a combination of all **D3DSTATUS_CLIPINTERSECTION*** flags.
	• **D3DSTATUS_CLIPUNIONALL**—This flag is a combination of all **D3DSTATUS_CLIPUNION*** flags.
	• **D3DSTATUS_DEFAULT**—This flag is a combination of the **D3DSTATUS_CLIPINTERSECTIONALL** and **D3DSTATUS_-ZNOTVISIBLE** flags.
	• **D3DSTATUS_ZNOTVISIBLE**—The sphere is not visible.
	• **D3DCLIP_BACK**—The sphere is clipped by the viewing frustum's back clipping plane.
	• **D3DCLIP_BOTTOM**— The sphere is clipped by the viewing frustum's bottom clipping plane.

(continued)

IDirect3DDevice7::ComputeSphereVisibility () *(continued)*	
Parameter	Description
	• **D3DCLIP_FRONT**—The sphere is clipped by the viewing frustum's front clipping plane.
	• **D3DCLIP_LEFT**—The sphere is clipped by the viewing frustum's left clipping plane.
	• **D3DCLIP_RIGHT**—The sphere is clipped by the viewing frustum's right clipping plane.
	• **D3DCLIP_TOP**—The sphere is clipped by the viewing frustum's top clipping plane.
	• **D3DSTATUS_CLIPUNIONBACK**—This flag is identical to **D3DCLIP_BACK**.
	• **D3DSTATUS_CLIPUNIONBOTTOM**—This flag is identical to **D3DCLIP_BOTTOM**.
	• **D3DSTATUS_CLIPUNIONFRONT**—This flag is identical to **D3DCLIP_FRONT**.
	• **D3DSTATUS_CLIPUNIONGEN0** through **D3DSTATUS_-CLIPUNIONGEN5**—These flags are identical to **D3DCLIP_GEN0** through **D3DCLIP_GEN5**.
	• **D3DSTATUS_CLIPUNIONLEFT**—This flag is equal to **D3DCLIP_LEFT**.
	• **D3DSTATUS_CLIPUNIONRIGHT**—This flag is equal to **D3DCLIP_RIGHT**.
	• **D3DSTATUS_CLIPUNIONTOP**—This flag is equal to **D3DCLIP_TOP**.
	• **D3DCLIP_GEN0** through **D3DCLIP_GEN5**—The sphere is clipped by the application-defined clipping planes 0 through 5, respectively.
	• **D3DSTATUS_CLIPINTERSECTIONBACK**—The logical AND of the clip flags for the sphere when compared with the viewing frustum's back clipping plane.
	• **D3DSTATUS_CLIPINTERSECTIONBOTTOM**—The logical AND of the clip flags for the sphere when compared with the viewing frustum's bottom clipping plane.
	• **D3DSTATUS_CLIPINTERSECTIONFRONT**—The logical AND of the clip flags for the sphere when compared with the viewing frustum's front clipping plane.

(continued)

IDirect3DDevice7::ComputeSphereVisibility () *(continued)*

Parameter	Description
	• **D3DSTATUS_CLIPINTERSECTIONGEN0** through **D3DSTATUS_CLIPINTERSECTIONGEN5**—The logical AND of the clip flags for the sphere when compared with the application-defined clipping planes 0 through 5, respectively.
	• **D3DSTATUS_CLIPINTERSECTIONLEFT**— The logical AND of the clip flags for the sphere when compared with the viewing frustum's left clipping plane.
	• **D3DSTATUS_CLIPINTERSECTIONRIGHT**—The logical AND of the clip flags for the sphere when compared with the viewing frustum's right clipping plane.
	• **D3DSTATUS_CLIPINTERSECTIONTOP**— The logical AND of the clip flags for the sphere when compared with the viewing frustum's top clipping plane.

Return Value	Description
D3D_OK	Direct3D successfully determined the visibility of the specified sphere list.
D3DERR_INVALIDMATRIX	Direct3D could not determine the visibility of the specified spheres, because the transformation matrix is invalid.
DDERR_INVALIDOBJECT	Direct3D could not determine the visibility of the specified spheres, because this Direct3DDevice7 object is invalid.
DDERR_INVALIDPARAMS	Direct3D could not determine the visibility of the specified spheres, because one or more parameters are invalid.

IDirect3DDevice7::DeleteStateBlock ()

Function Description

This function deletes a state block previously recorded with the **IDirect3DDevice7::BeginStateBlock** () function. A state block is a list of state changes that may be generated by first calling **IDirect3D-Device7::BeginStateBlock** (), filling the state block with requested state changes by calling certain functions, and finally calling **IDirect3DDevice7::EndStateBlock** (). See **IDirect3DDevice7::-BeginStateBlock** () for more information.

Function Declaration

```
HRESULT DeleteStateBlock (
  DWORD dwBlockHandle
);
```

(continued)

IDirect3DDevice7::DeleteStateBlock () *(continued)*	
Parameter	**Description**
dwBlockHandle	A handle to the state block to be deleted, as obtained by previously calling the **IDirect3DDevice7::EndStateBlock** () function.
Return Value	**Description**
D3D_OK	Direct3D successfully deleted the specified state block.
D3DERR_INBEGINSTATEBLOCK	Direct3D could not delete the specified state block, because it is currently recording a state block. The **IDirect3DDevice7::EndStateBlock** () function must be called before this function can succeed.
D3DERR_INVALIDSTATEBLOCK	Direct3D could not delete the specified state block, because it is invalid.

IDirect3DDevice7::DrawIndexedPrimitive ()
Function Description
This function renders an indexed geometric primitive. An indexed primitive is one in which the vertices are not defined directly; rather, they are defined as indices into a vertex list. Indexed primitives are thus a memory- and processor-efficient means of storing primitives that share vertices.
This function can render both untransformed and transformed primitives. Applications that want hardware acceleration for geometric transformation should always render untransformed vertices, allowing Direct3D to pass the task to hardware.
The render settings for the primitive can be altered with the **IDirect3DDevice7::SetRenderState** () function. Other functions that affect how the primitive is rendered include **IDirect3DDevice7::- SetClipStatus** (), **IDirect3DDevice7::SetRenderTarget** (), **IDirect3DDevice7::SetTransform** (), **IDirect3DDevice7::SetLight** (), **IDirect3DDevice7::SetMaterial** (), **IDirect3DDevice7::SetTexture** (), **IDirect3DDevice7::SetTextureStageState** (), **IDirect3DDevice7::SetClipPlane** (), and **IDirect3D- Device7::SetViewport** ().
Function Declaration

```
HRESULT DrawIndexedPrimitive(
  D3DPRIMITIVETYPE d3dptPrimitiveType,
  DWORD  dwVertexTypeDesc,
  LPVOID lpvVertices,
  DWORD  dwVertexCount,
  LPWORD lpwIndices,
  DWORD  dwIndexCount,
  DWORD  dwFlags
);
```

(continued)

IDirect3DDevice7::DrawIndexedPrimitive () *(continued)*	

Parameter	Description
d3dptPrimitiveType	Describes the type of primitive to be rendered. This parameter must be one of the following enumeration values:
	• **D3DPT_LINELIST**—The primitive consists of a collection of line segments, which Direct3D should render individually.
	If this value is specified, the **dwIndexCount** parameter must be evenly divisible by 2.
	• **D3DPT_LINESTRIP**—The primitive consists of a connected sequence of lines; each point in the vertex list describes the next point in the line sequence.
	If this value is specified, the **dwIndexCount** parameter must be at least 2.
	• **D3DPT_TRIANGLEFAN**—The primitive is a triangle fan. The first point corresponds to the one shared by all triangles, and the subsequent points define the triangles forming the spread of the fan.
	• **D3DPT_TRIANGLELIST**—The primitive is a triangle list, a simple list of triangles.
	If this value is specified, the **dwIndexCount** parameter must be evenly divisible by 3.
	• **D3DPT_TRIANGLESTRIP**—The primitive is a triangle strip, which is described by a series of zigzagged points.
	An inevitable result of the manner in which triangle strips are described is that all odd triangles will have their vertices defined in the direction opposite that of even triangles. Direct3D automatically takes this into consideration, however, when performing back-face culling, a method by which all triangles not facing the viewer are culled from the scene.
dwVertexTypeDesc	Describes the flexible vertex format the application is using. Flexible vertex formats allow applications to create their own vertex structures that include only the information the application needs, and then use these structures with Direct3D functions.
	A flexible vertex format structure may include a number of components; if these components are present, however, they must appear in a certain order. This order is reflected in the following list (that is, the following list specifies the order in which the components must appear in the structure).

(continued)

IDirect3DDevice7::DrawIndexedPrimitive () *(continued)*	
Parameter	**Description**
	The relevant flags, constants, and macros that can be used to create this parameter are:
	• **D3DFVF_XYZ**—The vertex format includes the position of an untransformed vertex, specified as three floating-point values (*x*, *y*, and *z*). This format is for 3D applications that use Direct3D to transform and light their vertices.
	This flag, which cannot be used with the **D3DFVF_XYZRHW** flag, requires the application to specify a vertex normal (**D3DFVF_NORMAL**), a vertex color component (**D3DFVF_DIFFUSE** or **D3DFVF_SPECULAR**), or at least one set of texture coordinates (**D3DFVF_TEX1** through **D3DFVF_TEX8**).
	• **D3DFVF_XYZRHW**—The vertex format includes the position of a transformed vertex, specified as four floating-point values (*x*, *y*, *z*, and *1/w*). This format is for 3D applications that transform and light their own vertices.
	This flag, which cannot be used with the **D3DFVF_XYZ** or **D3DFVF_NORMAL** flags, requires the application to specify a vertex color component (**D3DFVF_DIFFUSE** or **D3DFVF_SPECULAR**) or at least one set of texture coordinates (**D3DFVF_TEX1** through **D3DFVF_TEX8**).
	• **D3DFVF_XYZB1** through **D3DFVF_XYZB5**—These flags specify the number of floating-point weighting ("beta") values included in the vertex format to be used for multi-matrix vertex blending operations. By changing these weighting values and modifying as necessary the matrices to be used in blending operations, applications can animate vertices.
	Direct3D currently supports a maximum of three weighting values.
	• **D3DFVF_NORMAL**—The vertex format includes a normal vector, which describes the orientation of a plane tangent to the object at the location of the vertex.
	This flag, which cannot be used with the **D3DFVF_XYZRHW** flag, is used by Direct3D for lighting vertices. If this flag is not specified, Direct3D does not light vertices.
	• **D3DFVF_DIFFUSE**—The vertex format includes a diffuse color component, specified as a **DWORD** value containing red, green, blue, and alpha components. The diffuse component specifies the light color and intensity falling on the vertex.

(continued)

IDirect3DDevice7::DrawIndexedPrimitive () *(continued)*	
Parameter	**Description**
	Neither transformed nor untransformed vertices must include the diffuse component. Transformed vertices, however, are not lit by Direct3D, so applications using them typically specify their own lighting information to Direct3D by using the diffuse and specular components of their vertex formats. Untransformed vertices do not need to specify this information to be lit, because Direct3D will by default use the material of the object for diffuse lighting information. They may wish to do so anyway, however, for enhanced realism.
	• **D3DFVF_SPECULAR**—The vertex format includes a specular color component, specified as a **DWORD** value containing red, green, blue, and alpha components. The specular component describes how shiny the object is at a vertex and what the color of the shine is. The alpha component of the specular value is used for fog effects.
	Neither transformed nor untransformed vertices need to include the specular component. Transformed vertices, however, are not lit by Direct3D, so applications using them typically specify their own lighting information to Direct3D by using the diffuse and specular components of their vertex formats. Untransformed vertices do not need to specify this information to be lit, because Direct3D will by default use the material of the object for specular lighting information. They may wish to do so anyway, however, for enhanced realism.
	• **D3DFVF_TEX0** through **D3DFVF_TEX8**—These flags specify the number of texture coordinates for the vertex. Texture coordinates may be specified using one, two, or three floating-point values, as indicated by the flags generated by the **D3DFVF_TEXCOORDSIZE*** macros listed in this section.
	• **D3DFVF_TEXCOUNT_SHIFT**—This value is not used directly as a flag, but it can be used to generate a flag that specifies the number of texture coordinates for the vertex. This flag can be used in place of the **D3DFVF_TEX0** through **D3DFVF_TEX8** flags.
	If a vertex uses **N** sets of texture coordinates, the flag describing this information can be calculated by the code **(N<<D3DFVF_TEXCOUNT_SHIFT)**.
	• **D3DFVF_TEXTUREFORMAT1** through **D3DFVF_TEXTUREFORMAT4**—These constants indicate the number of floating-point values used to describe a texture coordinate set of a vertex. The constant **D3DFVF_TEXTUREFORMAT1** indicates one floating-point value is used, and so on.

(continued)

IDirect3DDevice7::DrawIndexedPrimitive () *(continued)*	
Parameter	**Description**
	These constants are rarely used directly, but instead are used implicitly by these **D3DFVF_TEXCOORDSIZE*** macros:
	• **D3DFVF_TEXCOORDSIZE1(N)**—Generates a flag that tells Direct3D that one floating-point value is used for the texture coordinate information in the **N**th texture coordinate set of a vertex. For example, if the first texture coordinate set of a vertex uses one floating-point value, then the flexible vertex format for the vertex would include the flag produced by the code **D3DFVF_TEXCOORDSIZE1(0)**.
	• **D3DFVF_TEXCOORDSIZE2(N)**—Generates a flag that tells Direct3D that two floating-point values are used for the texture coordinate information in the **N**th texture coordinate set of a vertex. For example, if the first texture coordinate set of a vertex uses two floating-point values, then the flexible vertex format for the vertex would include the flag produced by the code **D3DFVF_TEXCOORDSIZE2(0)**.
	• **D3DFVF_TEXCOORDSIZE3(N)**—Generates a flag that tells Direct3D that three floating-point values are used for the texture coordinate information in the **N**th texture coordinate set of a vertex. For example, if the first texture coordinate set of a vertex uses three floating-point values, then the flexible vertex format for the vertex would include the flag produced by the code **D3DFVF_TEXCOORDSIZE3(0)**.
	• **D3DFVF_TEXCOORDSIZE4(N)**—Generates a flag that tells Direct3D that four floating-point values are used for the texture coordinate information in the **N**th texture coordinate set of a vertex. For example, if the first texture coordinate set of a vertex uses four floating-point values, then the flexible vertex format for the vertex would include the flag produced by the code **D3DFVF_TEXCOORDSIZE4(0)**.
lpvVertices	A pointer to an array of vertices whose format is specified by the **dwVertexTypeDesc** parameter. Direct3D does not attempt to verify that the vertices in this array actually match the specified format, so errors may result if the two formats differ.
	When displaying points, the list of vertices specified by this parameter identifies the actual points to be displayed. For all other primitives, the vertices in the list are not displayed unless they are referenced by indices in the **lpwIndices** array.

(continued)

IDirect3DDevice7::DrawIndexedPrimitive () *(continued)*

Parameter	Description
	When rendering untransformed vertices, this list should not include substantially more vertices than should be displayed, because Direct3D transforms all vertices in the list, regardless of whether or not the application has specified that they be displayed. Consequently, this function should not be used to render an untransformed vertex list that contains more vertices than the primitive to be displayed. For rendering multiple primitives that all reference a single untransformed vertex list, vertex buffers are more efficient.
dwVertexCount	The number of vertices pointed to by the **lpvVertices** array. This is *not* necessarily the same as the number of vertices that the application intends to display.
	The maximum number of points is described by the constant **D3DMAXNUMVERTICES** (0×FFFF, the maximum number for a 16-bit integer).
lpwIndices	A pointer to an array of 16-bit integers that specifies the primitive to be rendered. The primitive is specified as a series of indices into the vertex list pointed to by **lpvVertices**.
dwIndexCount	The number of integers pointed to by the **lpwIndices** array. The number of indices the **lpwIndices** array must point to depends on the primitive being rendered. Triangle lists, for example, must have at least one triangle and the total number of points must be evenly divisible by 3.
	The maximum number of points is described by the constant **D3DMAXNUMVERTICES** (0×FFFF, the maximum number for a 16-bit integer).
dwFlags	Describes how the primitive should be rendered. This parameter can be 0, in which case Direct3D sends the primitive to the graphics card and then returns immediately, or the following flag: • **D3DDP_WAIT**—Direct3D should wait until the primitive has been rendered before it returns. This flag is used for debugging purposes.

Return Value	Description
D3D_OK	Direct3D successfully rendered the specified primitive.
D3DERR_INVALIDPRIMITIVETYPE	Direct3D could not render the specified primitive, because the specified primitive type is invalid.
D3DERR_INVALIDVERTEXTYPE	Direct3D could not render the specified primitive, because the specified flexible vertex format type is invalid.
DDERR_INVALIDPARAMS	Direct3D could not render the specified primitive, because one or more parameters are invalid.
DDERR_WASSTILLDRAWING	Direct3D could not render the specified primitive, because the target surface is currently in use.

IDirect3DDevice7::DrawIndexedPrimitiveStrided ()

Function Description

This function renders an indexed geometric primitive using strided vertices. An indexed primitive is one in which the vertices are not defined directly; rather, they are defined as indices into a vertex list. Strided vertices are those whose individual components (such as *x* or the vertical texture coordinate *v*) are defined by both a memory location and a stride, the latter indicating the distance (in bytes) from one component to the next. Strided vertices allow an application to store its vertex components in any arrangement possible, even storing individual components in their own separate arrays.

This function can render strictly untransformed primitives. Attempts to render transformed vertices will fail. The render settings for the primitive can be altered with the **IDirect3DDevice7::-SetRenderState** () function. Other functions that affect how the primitive is rendered include **IDirect3DDevice7::SetClipStatus** (), **IDirect3DDevice7::SetRenderTarget** (), **IDirect3DDevice7::-SetTransform** (), **IDirect3DDevice7::SetLight** (), **IDirect3DDevice7::SetMaterial** (), **IDirect3D-Device7::SetTexture** (), **IDirect3DDevice7::SetTextureStageState** (), **IDirect3DDevice7::-SetClipPlane** (), and **IDirect3DDevice7::SetViewport** ().

Function Declaration

```
HRESULT DrawIndexedPrimitiveStrided(
  D3DPRIMITIVETYPE d3dptPrimitiveType,
  DWORD  dwVertexTypeDesc,
  LPD3DDRAWPRIMITIVESTRIDEDDATA lpVertexArray,
  DWORD  dwVertexCount,
  LPWORD lpwIndices,
  DWORD  dwIndexCount,
  DWORD  dwFlags
);
```

Parameter	Description
d3dptPrimitiveType	Describes the type of primitive to be rendered. This parameter must be one of the following enumeration values: • **D3DPT_LINELIST**—The primitive consists of a collection of line segments, which Direct3D should render individually. If this value is specified, the **dwIndexCount** parameter must be at least 2. • **D3DPT_LINESTRIP**—The primitive consists of a connected sequence of lines; each point in the vertex list describes the next point in the line sequence. If this value is specified, the **dwIndexCount** parameter must be evenly divisible by 2. • **D3DPT_TRIANGLEFAN**—The primitive is a triangle fan. The first point corresponds to the one shared by all triangles, and the subsequent points define the triangles forming the spread of the fan.

(continued)

IDirect3DDevice7::DrawIndexedPrimitiveStrided () *(continued)*

Parameter	Description
	• **D3DPT_TRIANGLELIST**—The primitive is a triangle list, a simple list of triangles. If this value is specified, the **dwIndexCount** parameter must be evenly divisible by 3. • **D3DPT_TRIANGLESTRIP**—The primitive is a triangle strip, which is described by a series of zigzagged points. An inevitable result of the manner in which triangle strips are described is that all odd triangles will have their vertices defined in the direction opposite that of even triangles. Direct3D automatically takes this into consideration, however, when performing back-face culling, a method by which all triangles not facing the viewer are culled from the scene.
dwVertexTypeDesc	Describes the flexible vertex format the application is using. Flexible vertex formats allow applications to create their own vertex structures that include only the information the application needs, and then use these structures with Direct3D functions. The relevant flags, constants, and macros that can be used to create this parameter are: • **D3DFVF_XYZ**—The vertex format includes the position of an untransformed vertex, specified as three floating-point values (*x*, *y*, and *z*). Because this function can render only untransformed vertices, the application's flexible vertex format structure must include this information. This flag requires the application to specify a vertex normal (**D3DFVF_NORMAL**), a vertex color component (**D3DFVF_DIFFUSE** or **D3DFVF_SPECULAR**), or at least one set of texture coordinates (**D3DFVF_TEX1** through **D3DFVF_TEX8**). • **D3DFVF_XYZB1** through **D3DFVF_XYZB5**—These flags specify the number of floating-point weighting ("beta") values included in the vertex format to be used for multi-matrix vertex blending operations. By changing these weighting values and modifying as necessary the matrices to be used in blending operations, applications can animate vertices. Direct3D currently supports a maximum of three weighting values.

(continued)

IDirect3DDevice7::DrawIndexedPrimitiveStrided () *(continued)*	
Parameter	**Description**
	• **D3DFVF_NORMAL**—The vertex format includes a normal vector, which describes the orientation of a plane tangent to the object at the location of the vertex. Direct3D uses this flag for lighting vertices. If this flag is not specified, Direct3D does not light vertices. • **D3DFVF_DIFFUSE**—The vertex format includes a diffuse color component, specified as a **DWORD** value containing red, green, blue, and alpha components. The diffuse component specifies the light color and intensity falling on the vertex. Untransformed vertices, the only kind this function supports, do not need to specify this information to be lit, because Direct3D will by default use the material of the object for diffuse lighting information. They may wish to do so anyway, however, for enhanced realism. • **D3DFVF_SPECULAR**—The vertex format includes a specular color component, specified as a **DWORD** value containing red, green, blue, and alpha components. The specular component describes how shiny the object is at a vertex and what the color of the shine is. The alpha component of the specular value is used for fog effects. Untransformed vertices, the only kind this function supports, do not need to specify this information to be lit, because Direct3D will by default use the material of the object for specular lighting information. They may wish to do so anyway, however, for enhanced realism. • **D3DFVF_TEX0** through **D3DFVF_TEX8**—These flags specify the number of texture coordinates for the vertex. Texture coordinates may be specified using one, two, or three floating-point values, as indicated by the flags generated by the **D3DFVF_TEXCOORDSIZE*** macros listed in this section. • **D3DFVF_TEXCOUNT_SHIFT**—This value is not used directly as a flag, but it can be used to generate a flag that specifies the number of texture coordinates for the vertex. This flag can be used in place of the **D3DFVF_TEX0** through **D3DFVF_TEX8** flags. If a vertex uses **N** sets of texture coordinates, the flag describing this information can be calculated with the code **(N<<D3DFVF_TEXCOUNT_SHIFT)**.

(continued)

IDirect3DDevice7::DrawIndexedPrimitiveStrided () (continued)

Parameter	Description
	• **D3DFVF_TEXTUREFORMAT1** through **D3DFVF_TEXTURE-FORMAT4**—These constants indicate the number of floating-point values used to describe a texture coordinate set of a vertex. The constant **D3DFVF_TEXTUREFORMAT1** indicates one floating-point value is used, and so on.

These constants are rarely used directly, but instead are used implicitly by these **D3DFVF_TEXCOORDSIZE*** macros:

• **D3DFVF_TEXCOORDSIZE1(N)**—This macro is used to generate a flag that tells Direct3D that one floating-point value is used for the texture coordinate information in the **N**th texture coordinate set of a vertex. For example, if the first texture coordinate set of a vertex uses one floating-point value, then the flexible vertex format for the vertex would include the flag produced by the code **D3DFVF_-TEXCOORDSIZE1(0)**.

• **D3DFVF_TEXCOORDSIZE2(N)**—This macro is used to generate a flag that tells Direct3D that two floating-point values are used for the texture coordinate information in the **N**th texture coordinate set of a vertex. For example, if the first texture coordinate set of a vertex uses two floating-point values, then the flexible vertex format for the vertex would include the flag produced by the code **D3DFVF_TEXCOORDSIZE2(0)**.

• **D3DFVF_TEXCOORDSIZE3(N)**—This macro is used to generate a flag that tells Direct3D that three floating-point values are used for the texture coordinate information in the **N**th texture coordinate set of a vertex. For example, if the first texture coordinate set of a vertex uses three floating-point values, then the flexible vertex format for the vertex would include the flag produced by the code **D3DFVF_TEXCOORDSIZE3(0)**.

• **D3DFVF_TEXCOORDSIZE4(N)**—This macro is used to generate a flag that tells Direct3D that four floating-point values are used for the texture coordinate information in the **N**th texture coordinate set of a vertex. For example, if the first texture coordinate set of a vertex uses four floating-point values, then the flexible vertex format for the vertex would include the flag produced by the code **D3DFVF_TEXCOORDSIZE4(0)**.

(continued)

IDirect3DDevice7::DrawIndexedPrimitiveStrided () *(continued)*	
Parameter	**Description**
lpVertexArray	A pointer to a **D3DDRAWPRIMITIVESTRIDEDATA** structure that specifies the memory locations and strides for the various flexible vertex format components indicated by the **dwVertexTypeDesc** flag.
	Direct3D does not attempt to verify that the vertices in this structure actually match the format specified by **dwVertexTypeDesc**, so errors may result if the two formats differ.
	When displaying points, the list of vertices specified by this parameter identifies the actual points to be displayed. For all other primitives, the vertices in the list are not displayed unless they are referenced by indices in the **lpwIndices** array.
	When rendering untransformed vertices, the only kind of vertices this function supports, this list should not include substantially more vertices than should be displayed, because Direct3D transforms all vertices in the list, regardless of whether or not the application has specified that they be displayed. Consequently, this function should not be used to render a vertex list that contains more vertices than the primitive to be displayed. For rendering multiple primitives that all reference a single untransformed vertex list, vertex buffers are more efficient.
dwVertexCount	The number of vertices referenced in the **lpVertexArray**. This is *not* necessarily the same as the number of vertices the application intends to display.
	The maximum number of points is described by the constant **D3DMAXNUMVERTICES** (0xFFFF, the maximum number for a 16-bit integer).
lpwIndices	A pointer to an array of 16-bit integers that specifies the primitive to be rendered. The primitive is specified as a series of indices into the vertex list described by **lpVertexArray**.
dwIndexCount	The number of integers pointed to by the **lpwIndices** array. The number of indices the **lpwIndices** array must point to depends on the primitive being rendered. Triangle lists, for example, must have at least one triangle and the total number of points must be evenly divisible by 3.
	The maximum number of points is described by the constant **D3DMAXNUMVERTICES** (0xFFFF, the maximum number for a 16-bit integer).

(continued)

IDirect3DDevice7::DrawIndexedPrimitiveStrided () *(continued)*

Parameter	Description
dwFlags	Describes how the primitive should be rendered. This parameter can be 0, in which case Direct3D sends the primitive to the graphics card and then returns immediately, or the following flag: • **D3DDP_WAIT**—Direct3D should wait until the primitive has been rendered before it returns. This flag is used for debugging purposes.

Return Value	Description
D3D_OK	Direct3D successfully rendered the specified primitive.
D3DERR_INVALID PRIMITIVETYPE	Direct3D could not render the specified primitive, because the specified primitive type is invalid.
D3DERR_INVALIDVERTEXTYPE	Direct3D could not render the specified primitive, because the specified flexible vertex format type is invalid.
DDERR_INVALIDPARAMS	Direct3D could not render the specified primitive, because one or more parameters are invalid.
DDERR_WASSTILLDRAWING	Direct3D could not render the specified primitive, because the target surface is currently in use.

IDirect3DDevice7::DrawIndexedPrimitiveVB ()

Function Description

This function renders an indexed geometric primitive using vertex buffers. An indexed primitive is one in which the vertices are not defined directly; rather, they are defined as indices into a vertex list. Vertex buffers, created with the **IDirect3D7::CreateVertexBuffer** () function, allow an application to transform an entire set of vertices and then render primitives that use these vertices one at a time, without retransforming vertex data.

This function can render untransformed and transformed, unoptimized and optimized vertices. For maximum performance, however, the function should not be used to render untransformed vertices unless the vertex buffer contains vertices for only one primitive, because Direct3D transforms all vertices in a vertex list before displaying a primitive that references that list. If a vertex buffer contains vertices for several primitives, the application should first transform the vertices in the vertex buffer with the **IDirect3DVertexBuffer7::ProcessVertices** () function and then display them using this function. This way, the vertices will be transformed only once.

Note that software devices, such as MMX and RGB devices, cannot render from video memory vertex buffers, only from system memory vertex buffers. Hardware devices, however, can render from either video or system memory vertex buffers.

The render settings for the primitive can be altered with the **IDirect3DDevice7::SetRenderState** () function. Other functions that affect how the primitive is rendered include **IDirect3DDevice7::SetClipStatus** (), **IDirect3DDevice7::SetRenderTarget** (), **IDirect3DDevice7::SetTransform** (), **IDirect3DDevice7::SetLight** (), **IDirect3DDevice7::SetMaterial** (), **IDirect3DDevice7::SetTexture** (), **IDirect3DDevice7::SetTextureStageState** (), **IDirect3DDevice7::SetClipPlane** (), and **IDirect3DDevice7::SetViewport** ().

(continued)

IDirect3DDevice7::DrawIndexedPrimitiveVB () *(continued)*

Function Declaration

```
HRESULT DrawIndexedPrimitiveVB(
    D3DPRIMITIVETYPE        d3dptPrimitiveType,
    LPDIRECT3DVERTEXBUFFER7 lpd3dVertexBuffer,
    DWORD   dwStartVertex,
    DWORD   dwNumVertices,
    LPWORD  lpwIndices,
    DWORD   dwIndexCount,
    DWORD   dwFlags
);
```

Parameter	Description
d3dptPrimitiveType	Describes the type of primitive to be rendered. This parameter must be one of the following enumeration values: • **D3DPT_LINELIST**—The primitive consists of a collection of line segments, which Direct3D should render individually. If this value is specified, the **dwIndexCount** parameter must be evenly divisible by 2. • **D3DPT_LINESTRIP**—The primitive consists of a connected sequence of lines; each point in the vertex list describes the next point in the line sequence. If this value is specified, the **dwIndexCount** parameter must be at least 2. • **D3DPT_TRIANGLEFAN**—The primitive is a triangle fan. The first point corresponds to the one shared by all triangles, and the subsequent points define the triangles forming the spread of the fan. • **D3DPT_TRIANGLELIST**—The primitive is a triangle list, a simple list of triangles. If this value is specified, the **dwIndexCount** parameter must be evenly divisible by 3. • **D3DPT_TRIANGLESTRIP**—The primitive is a triangle strip, which is described by a series of zigzagged points. An inevitable result of the manner in which triangle strips are described is that all odd triangles will have their vertices defined in the direction opposite that of even triangles. Direct3D automatically takes this into consideration, however, when performing back-face culling, a method by which all triangles not facing the viewer are culled from the scene.

(continued)

IDirect3DDevice7::DrawIndexedPrimitiveVB () *(continued)*

Parameter	Description
lpd3dVertexBuffer	A pointer to a Direct3DVertexBuffer7 object that identifies the vertex buffer to use when rendering the specified primitive.
	When displaying points, the vertices in the vertex buffer identify the actual points to be displayed. For all other primitives, the vertices are not displayed unless they are referenced by indices in the **lpwIndices** array.
	The vertices in the vertex buffer can be transformed or untransformed, optimized or unoptimized vertices. The vertex buffer cannot be locked, however, or this function will fail.
	When rendering untransformed vertices, the vertex buffer should not include substantially more vertices than should be displayed, because Direct3D transforms all vertices in the list, regardless of whether or not the application has specified that they be displayed. Consequently, this function should not be used to render untransformed vertex buffers that contain more vertices than the primitive to be displayed. For rendering multiple primitives that all reference a single untransformed vertex buffer, applications should transform the vertices in advance with **IDirect3DVertexBuffer7::ProcessVertices** (), and then call this function to display each primitive that uses the vertex buffer.
dwStartVertex	The index of the first vertex in the vertex buffer that Direct3D should render.
dwNumVertices	The total number of vertices in the vertex buffer that Direct3D should render.
	The maximum number of points is described by the constant **D3DMAXNUMVERTICES** (0×FFFF, the maximum number for a 16-bit integer).
lpwIndices	A pointer to an array of 16-bit integers that specifies the primitive to be rendered. The primitive is specified as a series of indices into the vertex buffer described by **lpd3dVertexBuffer**.
	The values in the integer array must index vertices within the range of [**dwStartVertex**, **dwStartVertex** + **dwNumVertices** – 1].
dwIndexCount	The number of integers pointed to by the **lpwIndices** array. The number of indices the **lpwIndices** array must point to depends on the primitive being rendered. Triangle lists, for example, must have at least one triangle, and the total number of points must be evenly divisible by 3.
	The maximum number of points is described by the constant **D3DMAXNUMVERTICES** (0×FFFF, the maximum number for a 16-bit integer).

(continued)

IDirect3DDevice7::DrawIndexedPrimitiveVB () *(continued)*

Parameter	Description
dwFlags	Describes how the primitive should be rendered. This parameter can be 0, in which case Direct3D sends the primitive to the graphics card and then returns immediately, or the following flag: • **D3DDP_WAIT**—Direct3D should wait until the primitive has been rendered before it returns. This flag is used for debugging purposes.

Return Value	Description
D3D_OK	Direct3D successfully rendered the specified primitive.
D3DERR_INVALID PRIMITIVETYPE	Direct3D could not render the specified primitive, because the specified primitive type is invalid.
D3DERR_INVALIDVERTEXTYPE	Direct3D could not render the specified primitive, because the specified flexible vertex format type is invalid.
DDERR_INVALIDOBJECT	Direct3D could not render the specified primitive, because this Direct3DDevice7 object is invalid.
DDERR_INVALIDPARAMS	Direct3D could not render the specified primitive, because one or more parameters are invalid.
DDERR_WASSTILLDRAWING	Direct3D could not render the specified primitive, because the target surface is currently in use.
D3DERR_VERTEXBUFFER LOCKED	Direct3D could not render the specified primitive, because the specified vertex buffer is locked. It must be unlocked with **IDirect3DVertexBuffer7::Unlock** () before this function can succeed.

IDirect3DDevice7::DrawPrimitive ()

Function Description

This function renders a nonindexed geometric primitive, one in which the vertices of the primitive are specified directly rather than as indices into a vertex list.

This function can render both untransformed and transformed primitives. Applications that want hardware acceleration for geometric transformation should always render untransformed vertices, allowing Direct3D to pass the task to hardware.

The render settings for the primitive can be altered with the **IDirect3DDevice7::SetRenderState ()** function. Other functions that affect how the primitive is rendered include **IDirect3DDevice7::- SetClipStatus ()**, **IDirect3DDevice7::SetRenderTarget ()**, **IDirect3DDevice7::SetTransform ()**, **IDirect3DDevice7::SetLight ()**, **IDirect3DDevice7::SetMaterial ()**, **IDirect3DDevice7::SetTexture ()**, **IDirect3DDevice7::SetTextureStageState ()**, **IDirect3DDevice7::SetClipPlane ()**, and **IDirect3D- Device7::SetViewport ()**.

(continued)

IDirect3DDevice7::DrawPrimitive () *(continued)*

Function Declaration

```
HRESULT DrawPrimitive(
  D3DPRIMITIVETYPE d3dptPrimitiveType,
  DWORD   dwVertexTypeDesc,
  LPVOID  lpvVertices,
  DWORD   dwVertexCount,
  DWORD   dwFlags
);
```

Parameter	Description
d3dptPrimitiveType	Describes the type of primitive to be rendered. This parameter must be one of the following enumeration values: • **D3DPT_LINELIST**—The primitive consists of a collection of line segments, which Direct3D should render individually. If this value is specified, the **dwIndexCount** parameter must be evenly divisible by 2. • **D3DPT_LINESTRIP**—The primitive consists of a connected sequence of lines; each point in the vertex list describes the next point in the line sequence. If this value is specified, the **dwIndexCount** parameter must be at least 2. • **D3DPT_POINTLIST**—The primitive consists of a collection of points, which Direct3D should render individually. • **D3DPT_TRIANGLEFAN**—The primitive is a triangle fan. The first point corresponds to the one shared by all triangles, and the subsequent points define the triangles forming the spread of the fan. • **D3DPT_TRIANGLELIST**—The primitive is a triangle list, a simple list of triangles. If this value is specified, the **dwIndexCount** parameter must be evenly divisible by 3. • **D3DPT_TRIANGLESTRIP**—The primitive is a triangle strip, which is described by a series of zigzagged points. An inevitable result of the manner in which triangle strips are described is that all odd triangles will have their vertices defined in the direction opposite that of even triangles. Direct3D automatically takes this into consideration, however, when performing back-face culling, a method by which all triangles not facing the viewer are culled from the scene.

(continued)

IDirect3DDevice7::DrawPrimitive () *(continued)*	
Parameter	**Description**
dwVertexTypeDesc	Describes the flexible vertex format the application is using. Flexible vertex formats allow applications to create their own vertex structures that include only the information the application needs, and then use these structures with Direct3D functions.
	A flexible vertex format structure may include a number of components; if these components are present, however, they must appear in a certain order. This order is reflected in the following list (that is, the following list specifies the order in which the components must appear in the structure).
	The relevant flags, constants, and macros that can be used to create this parameter are:
	• **D3DFVF_XYZ**—The vertex format includes the position of an untransformed vertex, specified as three floating-point values (*x*, *y*, and *z*). This format is for 3D applications that use Direct3D to transform and light their vertices.
	This flag, which cannot be used with the **D3DFVF_XYZRHW** flag, requires the application to specify a vertex normal (**D3DFVF_NORMAL**), a vertex color component (**D3DFVF_DIFFUSE** or **D3DFVF_SPECULAR**), or at least one set of texture coordinates (**D3DFVF_TEX1** through **D3DFVF_TEX8**).
	• **D3DFVF_XYZRHW**—The vertex format includes the position of a transformed vertex, specified as four floating-point values (*x*, *y*, *z*, and *1/w*). This format is for 3D applications that transform and light their own vertices.
	This flag, which cannot be used with the **D3DFVF_XYZ** or **D3DFVF_NORMAL** flags, requires the application to specify a vertex color component (**D3DFVF_DIFFUSE** or **D3DFVF_SPECULAR**) or at least one set of texture coordinates (**D3DFVF_TEX1** through **D3DFVF_TEX8**).
	• **D3DFVF_XYZB1** through **D3DFVF_XYZB5**—These flags specify the number of floating-point weighting ("beta") values included in the vertex format to be used for multi-matrix vertex blending operations. By changing these weighting values and modifying as necessary the matrices to be used in blending operations, applications can animate vertices.
	Direct3D currently supports a maximum of three weighting values.

(continued)

IDirect3DDevice7::DrawPrimitive () *(continued)*

Parameter	Description
	• **D3DFVF_NORMAL**—The vertex format includes a normal vector. This normal vector describes the orientation of a plane tangent to the object at the location of the vertex.
	This flag, which cannot be used with the **D3DFVF_XYZRHW** flag, is used by Direct3D for lighting vertices. If this flag is not specified, Direct3D does not light vertices.
	• **D3DFVF_DIFFUSE**—The vertex format includes a diffuse color component, specified as a **DWORD** value containing red, green, blue, and alpha components. The diffuse component specifies the light color and intensity falling on the vertex.
	Neither transformed nor untransformed vertices must include the diffuse component. Transformed vertices, however, are not lit by Direct3D, so applications using them typically specify their own lighting information to Direct3D by using the diffuse and specular components of their vertex formats. Untransformed vertices do not need to specify this information to be lit, because Direct3D will by default use the material of the object for diffuse lighting information. They may wish to do so anyway, however, for enhanced realism.
	• **D3DFVF_SPECULAR**—The vertex format includes a specular color component, specified as a **DWORD** value containing red, green, blue, and alpha components. The specular component describes how shiny the object is at a vertex and what the color of the shine is. The alpha component of the specular value is used for fog effects.
	Neither transformed nor untransformed vertices must include the specular component. Transformed vertices, however, are not lit by Direct3D, so applications using them typically specify their own lighting information to Direct3D by using the diffuse and specular components of their vertex formats. Untransformed vertices do not need to specify this information to be lit, because Direct3D will by default use the material of the object for specular lighting information. They may wish to do so anyway, however, for enhanced realism.
	• **D3DFVF_TEX0** through **D3DFVF_TEX8**—These flags specify the number of texture coordinates for the vertex. Texture coordinates may be specified using one, two, or three floating-point values, as indicated by the flags generated by the **D3DFVF_TEXCOORDSIZE*** macros listed in this section.

(continued)

IDirect3DDevice7::DrawPrimitive () *(continued)*	
Parameter	**Description**
	• **D3DFVF_TEXCOUNT_SHIFT**—This value is not used directly as a flag, but it can be used to generate a flag that specifies the number of texture coordinates for the vertex. This flag can be used in place of the **D3DFVF_TEX0** through **D3DFVF_-TEX8** flags. If a vertex uses **N** sets of texture coordinates, the flag describing this information can be calculated by the code **(N<<D3DFVF_TEXCOUNT_SHIFT)**. • **D3DFVF_TEXTUREFORMAT1** through **D3DFVF_TEXTURE-FORMAT4**—These constants indicate the number of floating-point values used to describe a texture coordinate set of a vertex. The constant **D3DFVF_TEXTUREFORMAT1** indicates one floating-point value is used, and so on. These constants are rarely used directly, but instead are used implicitly by these **D3DFVF_TEXCOORDSIZE*** macros: • **D3DFVF_TEXCOORDSIZE1(N)**—This macro is used to generate a flag that tells Direct3D that one floating-point value is used for the texture coordinate information in the **N**th texture coordinate set of a vertex. For example, if the first texture coordinate set of a vertex uses one floating-point value, then the flexible vertex format for the vertex would include the flag produced by the code **D3DFVF_-TEXCOORDSIZE1(0)**. • **D3DFVF_TEXCOORDSIZE2(N)**—This macro is used to generate a flag that tells Direct3D that two floating-point values are used for the texture coordinate information in the **N**th texture coordinate set of a vertex. For example, if the first texture coordinate set of a vertex uses two floating-point values, then the flexible vertex format for the vertex would include the flag produced by the code **D3DFVF_TEXCOORDSIZE2(0)**. • **D3DFVF_TEXCOORDSIZE3(N)**—This macro is used to generate a flag that tells Direct3D that three floating-point values are used for the texture coordinate information in the **N**th texture coordinate set of a vertex. For example, if the first texture coordinate set of a vertex uses three floating-point values, then the flexible vertex format for the vertex would include the flag produced by the code **D3DFVF_TEXCOORDSIZE3(0)**.

(continued)

IDirect3DDevice7::DrawPrimitive () *(continued)*	
Parameter	**Description**
	• **D3DFVF_TEXCOORDSIZE4(N)**—This macro is used to generate a flag that tells Direct3D that four floating-point values are used for the texture coordinate information in the **N**th texture coordinate set of a vertex. For example, if the first texture coordinate set of a vertex uses four floating-point values, then the flexible vertex format for the vertex would include the flag produced by the code **D3DFVF_TEXCOORDSIZE4(0)**.
lpvVertices	A pointer to an array of vertices whose format is specified by the **dwVertexTypeDesc** parameter. These vertices, which may be untransformed or transformed, identify the geometry of the primitive to be displayed.
	Direct3D does not attempt to verify that the vertices in this array actually match the specified format, so errors may result if the two formats differ.
dwVertexCount	The number of vertices that comprise the primitive to be displayed.
	The maximum number of points is described by the constant **D3DMAXNUMVERTICES** (0×FFFF, the maximum number for a 16-bit integer).
dwFlags	Describes how the primitive should be rendered. This parameter can be 0, in which case Direct3D sends the primitive to the graphics card and then returns immediately, or the following flag:
	• **D3DDP_WAIT**—Direct3D should wait until the primitive has been rendered before it returns. This flag is used for debugging purposes.
Return Value	**Description**
D3D_OK	Direct3D successfully rendered the specified primitive.
D3DERR_INVALID PRIMITIVETYPE	Direct3D could not render the specified primitive, because the specified primitive type is invalid.
D3DERR_INVALIDVERTEXTYPE	Direct3D could not render the specified primitive, because the specified flexible vertex format type is invalid.
DDERR_INVALIDPARAMS	Direct3D could not render the specified primitive, because one or more parameters are invalid.
DDERR_WASSTILLDRAWING	Direct3D could not render the specified primitive, because the target surface is currently in use.

IDirect3DDevice7::DrawPrimitiveStrided ()

Function Description

This function renders a nonindexed geometric primitive using strided vertices. A nonindexed geometric primitive is one in which the vertices of the primitive are specified directly, rather than as indices into a vertex list. Strided vertices are those whose components (such as *x* or the vertical texture coordinate, for example) are defined by both a memory location and a stride, the latter indicating the distance (in bytes) from one component to the next. Strided vertices allow an application to store its vertex components in any arrangement possible, even storing individual components in their own separate arrays.

This function can render untransformed primitives only. Attempts to render transformed vertices will fail. The render settings for the primitive can be altered with the **IDirect3DDevice7::SetRenderState ()** function. Other functions that affect how the primitive is rendered include **IDirect3DDevice7::- SetClipStatus ()**, **IDirect3DDevice7::SetRenderTarget ()**, **IDirect3DDevice7::SetTransform ()**, **IDirect3DDevice7::SetLight ()**, **IDirect3DDevice7::SetMaterial ()**, **IDirect3DDevice7::SetTexture ()**, **IDirect3DDevice7::SetTextureStageState ()**, **IDirect3DDevice7::SetClipPlane ()**, and **IDirect3D- Device7::SetViewport ()**.

Function Declaration

```
HRESULT DrawPrimitiveStrided(
  D3DPRIMITIVETYPE dptPrimitiveType,
  DWORD   dwVertexTypeDesc,
  LPD3DDRAWPRIMITIVESTRIDEDDATA lpVertexArray,
  DWORD   dwVertexCount,
  DWORD   dwFlags
);
```

Parameter	Description
dptPrimitiveType	Describes the type of primitive to be rendered. This parameter must be one of the following enumeration values:
	• **D3DPT_LINELIST**—The primitive consists of a collection of line segments, which Direct3D should render individually.
	If this value is specified, the **dwIndexCount** parameter must be evenly divisible by 2.
	• **D3DPT_LINESTRIP**—The primitive consists of a connected sequence of lines; each point in the vertex list describes the next point in the line sequence.
	If this value is specified, the **dwIndexCount** parameter must be evenly divisible by 2.
	• **D3DPT_POINTLIST**—The primitive consists of a collection of points, which Direct3D should render individually.
	• **D3DPT_TRIANGLEFAN**—The primitive is a triangle fan. The first point corresponds to the one shared by all triangles, and the subsequent points define the triangles forming the spread of the fan.

(continued)

IDirect3DDevice7::DrawPrimitiveStrided () *(continued)*	
Parameter	**Description**
	• **D3DPT_TRIANGLELIST**—The primitive is a triangle list, a simple list of triangles.
	If this value is specified, the **dwIndexCount** parameter must be evenly divisible by 3.
	• **D3DPT_TRIANGLESTRIP**—The primitive is a triangle strip, which is described by a series of zigzagged points.
	An inevitable result of the manner in which triangle strips are described is that all odd triangles will have their vertices defined in the direction opposite that of even triangles. Direct3D automatically takes this into consideration, however, when performing back-face culling, a method by which all triangles not facing the viewer are culled from the scene.
dwVertexTypeDesc	Describes the flexible vertex format the application is using. Flexible vertex formats allow applications to create their own vertex structures that include only the information the application needs, and then use these structures with Direct3D functions.
	The relevant flags, constants, and macros that can be used to create this parameter are:
	• **D3DFVF_XYZ**—The vertex format includes the position of an untransformed vertex, specified as three floating-point values (*x*, *y*, and *z*). This format is for 3D applications that use Direct3D to transform and light their vertices.
	This flag, which cannot be used with the **D3DFVF_XYZRHW** flag, requires the application to specify a vertex normal (**D3DFVF_NORMAL**), a vertex color component (**D3DFVF_DIFFUSE** or **D3DFVF_SPECULAR**), or at least one set of texture coordinates (**D3DFVF_TEX1** through **D3DFVF_TEX8**).
	• **D3DFVF_XYZB1** through **D3DFVF_XYZB5**—These flags specify the number of floating-point weighting ("beta") values included in the vertex format to be used for multi-matrix vertex blending operations. By changing these weighting values, and modifying as necessary the matrices to be used in blending operations, applications can animate vertices.
	Direct3D currently supports a maximum of three weighting values.

(continued)

IDirect3DDevice7::DrawPrimitiveStrided () *(continued)*	
Parameter	**Description**
	• **D3DFVF_NORMAL**—The vertex format includes a normal vector. This normal vector describes the orientation of a plane tangent to the object at the location of the vertex.
	Direct3D uses this flag for lighting vertices. If this flag is not specified, Direct3D does not light vertices.
	• **D3DFVF_DIFFUSE**—The vertex format includes a diffuse color component, specified as a **DWORD** value containing red, green, blue, and alpha components. The diffuse component specifies the light color and intensity falling on the vertex.
	Untransformed vertices do not need to specify this information to be lit, because Direct3D will by default use the material of the object for diffuse lighting information. They may wish to do so anyway, however, for enhanced realism.
	• **D3DFVF_SPECULAR**—The vertex format includes a specular color component, specified as a **DWORD** value containing red, green, blue, and alpha components. The specular component describes how shiny the object is at a vertex and what the color of the shine is. The alpha component of the specular value is used for fog effects.
	Untransformed vertices do not need to specify this information to be lit, because Direct3D will by default use the material of the object for specular lighting information. They may wish to do so anyway, however, for enhanced realism.
	• **D3DFVF_TEX0** through **D3DFVF_TEX8**—These flags specify the number of texture coordinates for the vertex. Texture coordinates may be specified using one, two, or three floating-point values, as indicated by the flags generated by the **D3DFVF_TEXCOORDSIZE*** macros listed in this section.
	• **D3DFVF_TEXCOUNT_SHIFT**—This value is not used directly as a flag, but it can be used to generate a flag that specifies the number of texture coordinates for the vertex. This flag can be used in place of the **D3DFVF_TEX0-D3DFVF_TEX8** flags.
	If a vertex uses **N** sets of texture coordinates, the flag describing this information can be calculated with the code (**N<<D3DFVF_TEXCOUNT_SHIFT**).
	• **D3DFVF_TEXTUREFORMAT1** through **D3DFVF_TEXTUREFORMAT4**—These constants indicate the number of floating-point values used to describe a texture coordinate set of a vertex. The constant **D3DFVF_TEXTUREFORMAT1** indicates one floating-point value is used, and so on.

(continued)

IDirect3DDevice7::DrawPrimitiveStrided () *(continued)*	
Parameter	Description
	These constants are rarely used directly, but instead are used implicitly by these **D3DFVF_TEXCOORDSIZE*** macros: • **D3DFVF_TEXCOORDSIZE1(N)**—This macro is used to generate a flag that tells Direct3D that one floating-point value is used for the texture coordinate information in the **N**th texture coordinate set of a vertex. For example, if the first texture coordinate set of a vertex uses one floating-point value, then the flexible vertex format for the vertex would include the flag produced by the code **D3DFVF_TEXCOORDSIZE1(0)**. • **D3DFVF_TEXCOORDSIZE2(N)**—This macro is used to generate a flag that tells Direct3D that two floating-point values are used for the texture coordinate information in the **N**th texture coordinate set of a vertex. For example, if the first texture coordinate set of a vertex uses two floating-point values, then the flexible vertex format for the vertex would include the flag produced by the code **D3DFVF_TEXCOORDSIZE2(0)**. • **D3DFVF_TEXCOORDSIZE3(N)**—This macro is used to generate a flag that tells Direct3D that three floating-point values are used for the texture coordinate information in the **N**th texture coordinate set of a vertex. For example, if the first texture coordinate set of a vertex uses three floating-point values, then the flexible vertex format for the vertex would include the flag produced by the code **D3DFVF_TEXCOORDSIZE3(0)**. • **D3DFVF_TEXCOORDSIZE4(N)**—This macro is used to generate a flag that tells Direct3D that four floating-point values are used for the texture coordinate information in the **N**th texture coordinate set of a vertex. For example, if the first texture coordinate set of a vertex uses four floating-point values, then the flexible vertex format for the vertex would include the flag produced by the code **D3DFVF_TEXCOORDSIZE4(0)**.
lpVertexArray	A pointer to a **D3DDRAWPRIMITIVESTRIDEDATA** structure that specifies the memory locations and strides for the various flexible vertex format components indicated by the **dwVertexTypeDesc** flag. This structure describes the geometry of the primitive to be displayed. Direct3D does not attempt to verify that the vertices in this structure actually match the format specified by **dwVertexType-Desc**, so errors may result if the two formats differ.

(continued)

IDirect3DDevice7::DrawPrimitiveStrided () *(continued)*

Parameter	Description
dwVertexCount	The number of vertices that make up the primitive to be displayed.
	The maximum number of points is described by the constant **D3DMAXNUMVERTICES** (0×FFFF, the maximum number for a 16-bit integer).
dwFlags	Describes how the primitive should be rendered. This parameter can be 0, in which case Direct3D sends the primitive to the graphics card and then returns immediately, or the following flag:
	• **D3DDP_WAIT**—Direct3D should wait until the primitive has been rendered before it returns. This flag is used for debugging purposes.

Return Value	Description
D3D_OK	Direct3D successfully rendered the specified primitive.
D3DERR_INVALID PRIMITIVETYPE	Direct3D could not render the specified primitive, because the specified primitive type is invalid.
D3DERR_INVALIDVERTEXTYPE	Direct3D could not render the specified primitive, because the specified flexible vertex format type is invalid.
DDERR_INVALIDPARAMS	Direct3D could not render the specified primitive, because one or more parameters are invalid.
DDERR_WASSTILLDRAWING	Direct3D could not render the specified primitive, because the target surface is currently in use.

IDirect3DDevice7::DrawPrimitiveVB ()

Function Description

This function renders a nonindexed geometric primitive using vertex buffers. A nonindexed geometric primitive is one in which the vertices of the primitive are specified directly, rather than as indices into a vertex list. Vertex buffers, created with the **IDirect3D7::CreateVertexBuffer** () function, allow an application to transform an entire set of vertices, and then render primitives that use these vertices one at a time, without retransforming vertex data.

This function can render untransformed and transformed, unoptimized and optimized vertices. For maximum performance, however, the function should not be used to render untransformed vertices unless the vertex buffer contains vertices for only one primitive, because Direct3D transforms all vertices in a vertex list before displaying a primitive that references that list. If a vertex buffer contains vertices for several primitives, the application should first transform the vertices in the vertex buffer with the **IDirect3DVertexBuffer7::ProcessVertices** () function and then display them using this function. This way, the vertices will be transformed only once.

Note that software devices, such as MMX and RGB devices, cannot render from video memory vertex buffers, only from system memory vertex buffers. Hardware devices, however, can render from either video or system memory vertex buffers.

(continued)

IDirect3DDevice7::DrawPrimitiveVB () *(continued)*

Function Description

The render settings for the primitive can be altered with the **IDirect3DDevice7::SetRenderState ()** function. Other functions that affect how the primitive is rendered include **IDirect3DDevice7::- SetClipStatus ()**, **IDirect3DDevice7::SetRenderTarget ()**, **IDirect3DDevice7::SetTransform ()**, **IDirect3DDevice7::SetLight ()**, **IDirect3DDevice7::SetMaterial ()**, **IDirect3DDevice7::SetTexture ()**, **IDirect3DDevice7::SetTextureStageState ()**, **IDirect3DDevice7::SetClipPlane ()**, and **IDirect3D- Device7::SetViewport ()**.

Function Declaration

```
HRESULT DrawPrimitiveVB(
  D3DPRIMITIVETYPE       d3dptPrimitiveType,
  LPDIRECT3DVERTEXBUFFER7 lpd3dVertexBuffer,
  DWORD   dwStartVertex,
  DWORD   dwNumVertices,
  DWORD   dwFlags
);
```

Parameter	Description
d3dptPrimitiveType	Describes the type of primitive to be rendered. This parameter must be one of the following enumeration values:
	• **D3DPT_LINELIST**—The primitive consists of a collection of line segments, which Direct3D should render individually.
	If this value is specified, the **dwIndexCount** parameter must be evenly divisible by 2.
	• **D3DPT_LINESTRIP**—The primitive consists of a connected sequence of lines; each point in the vertex list describes the next point in the line sequence.
	If this value is specified, the **dwIndexCount** parameter must be evenly divisible by 2.
	• **D3DPT_POINTLIST**—The primitive consists of a collection of points, which Direct3D should render individually.
	• **D3DPT_TRIANGLEFAN**—The primitive is a triangle fan. The first point corresponds to the one shared by all triangles, and the subsequent points define the triangles forming the spread of the fan.
	• **D3DPT_TRIANGLELIST**—The primitive is a triangle list, a simple list of triangles.
	If this value is specified, the **dwIndexCount** parameter must be evenly divisible by 3.

(continued)

IDirect3DDevice7::DrawPrimitiveVB () *(continued)*

Parameter	Description
	• **D3DPT_TRIANGLESTRIP**—The primitive is a triangle strip. A triangle strip is described by a series of zigzagged points.
	An inevitable result of the manner in which triangle strips are described is that all odd triangles will have their vertices defined in the direction opposite that of even triangles. Direct3D automatically takes this into consideration, however, when performing back-face culling, a method by which all triangles not facing the viewer are culled from the scene.
lpd3dVertexBuffer	A pointer to a Direct3DVertexBuffer7 object that identifies the vertex buffer whose vertices comprise the primitive to be displayed.
	The vertices in the vertex buffer can be transformed or untransformed, optimized or unoptimized vertices. The vertex buffer cannot be locked, however, or this function will fail.
dwStartVertex	The index of the first vertex in the vertex buffer that Direct3D should render.
dwNumVertices	The total number of vertices in the vertex buffer that Direct3D should render.
	The maximum number of points is described by the constant **D3DMAXNUMVERTICES** (0×FFFF, the maximum number for a 16-bit integer).
dwFlags	Describes how the primitive should be rendered. This parameter can be 0, in which case Direct3D sends the primitive to the graphics card and then returns immediately, or the following flag:
	• **D3DDP_WAIT**—Direct3D should wait until the primitive has been rendered before it returns. This flag is used for debugging purposes.

Return Value	Description
D3D_OK	Direct3D successfully rendered the specified primitive.
D3DERR_INVALID PRIMITIVETYPE	Direct3D could not render the specified primitive, because the specified primitive type is invalid.
D3DERR_INVALIDVERTEXTYPE	Direct3D could not render the specified primitive, because the specified flexible vertex format type is invalid.
DDERR_INVALIDPARAMS	Direct3D could not render the specified primitive, because one or more parameters are invalid.
DDERR_WASSTILLDRAWING	Direct3D could not render the specified primitive, because the target surface is currently in use.
D3DERR_VERTEXBUFFERLOCKED	Direct3D could not render the specified primitive, because the specified vertex buffer is locked. It must be unlocked with **IDirect3DVertexBuffer7::Unlock** () before this function can succeed.

IDirect3DDevice7::EndScene ()

Function Description

This function ends the rendering of a 3D scene. It must be called after an application has called the **IDirect3DDevice7::BeginScene** () function and finished rendering data for the current frame. This function must be called even if the rendering attempt was unsuccessful.

Function Declaration

```
HRESULT EndScene();
```

Parameter	Description
None	

Return Value	Description
D3D_OK	Direct3D successfully ended the rendering of the scene.

IDirect3DDevice7::EndStateBlock ()

Function Description

This function stops the recording of a device state block and retrieves a handle to the state block. A state block is a list of state changes that may be generated by first calling **IDirect3DDevice7::-BeginStateBlock** (), filling the state block with requested state changes by calling certain functions, and finally calling this function. See **IDirect3DDevice7::BeginStateBlock** () for more information.

Function Declaration

```
HRESULT EndStateBlock(
  LPDWORD lpdwBlockHandle
);
```

Parameter	Description
lpdwBlockHandle	The address of a 32-bit unsigned integer. If this function succeeds, the integer will be set to the handle of the completed device state block, which can then be used with the **IDirect3DDevice7::ApplyStateBlock** () and **IDirect3DDevice7::-DeleteStateBlock** () functions.

Return Value	Description
D3D_OK	Direct3D successfully finished recording the state block.
D3DERR_NOTINBEGIN STATEBLOCK	Direct3D could not finish recording the state block, because no state block is being recorded.
DDERR_INVALIDPARAMS	Direct3D could not finish recording the state block, because one or more parameters are invalid.

IDirect3DDevice7::EnumTextureFormats ()

Function Description

This function enumerates the texture formats supported by the current graphics card driver. This function may not detect newly implemented texture formats on some devices. Applications that require a specific texture format not enumerated by this function can attempt to create a surface of that format anyway. If the format is supported, the surface will successfully be created, even if the format is not enumerated by this function.

Function Declaration

```
HRESULT EnumTextureFormats(
  LPD3DENUMPIXELFORMATSCALLBACK lpd3dEnumPixelProc,
  LPVOID lpArg
);
```

Parameter	Description
lpd3dEnumPixelProc	A pointer to an application-defined **D3DENUMPIXELFORMATSCALLBACK** function, which will be called by Direct3D for every texture format supported by the current driver.
lpArg	A pointer to application-defined data that will be sent to the callback function every time it is called.

Return Value	Description
D3D_OK	Direct3D successfully enumerated the texture formats supported by the hardware.
DDERR_INVALIDOBJECT	Direct3D could not enumerate the texture formats supported by the hardware, because this Direct3DDevice7 object is invalid.
DDERR_INVALIDPARAMS	Direct3D could not enumerate the texture formats supported by the hardware, because one or more parameters are invalid.

IDirect3DDevice7::GetCaps ()

Function Description

This function retrieves the capabilities of the Direct3D device represented by this Direct3DDevice7 object. To retrieve the capabilities of the display device, applications should instead call the **IDirectDraw7::GetCaps ()** function.

Function Declaration

```
HRESULT GetCaps(,
  D3DDEVICEDESC7 lpD3DDevDesc
);
```

Parameter	Description
lpD3DDevDesc	A pointer to a **D3DDEVICEDESC7** structure. If this function succeeds, the structure will be filled with the capabilities of the device's hardware.

(continued)

IDirect3DDevice7::GetCaps () *(continued)*

Return Value	Description
D3D_OK	Direct3D successfully retrieved the capabilities of the Direct3D device.
DDERR_INVALIDOBJECT	Direct3D could not retrieve the capabilities of the Direct3D device, because this Direct3DDevice7 object is invalid.
DDERR_INVALIDPARAMS	Direct3D could not retrieve the capabilities of the Direct3D device, because one or more parameters are invalid.

IDirect3DDevice7::GetClipPlane ()

Function Description

This function retrieves the coefficients of the plane equation for an application-defined clipping plane. Application-defined clipping planes are nonstandard clipping planes used to delineate the boundaries of the geometry that should be visible.

The coefficients retrieved by this equation are the A, B, C, and D coefficients of the plane equation. All points that, when plugged into the plane equation, result in a negative value ($Ax + By + Cz + Dw < 0$), and, hence, lie on the side of the plane opposite the direction of its normal, are considered to lie outside the plane. They are therefore clipped from the scene.

An application can set arbitrary clipping planes by calling the **IDirect3DDevice7::SetClipPlane ()** function.

Function Declaration

```
HRESULT GetClipPlane(
  DWORD dwIndex,
  D3DVALUE* pPlaneEquation
);
```

Parameter	Description
dwIndex	The index designating the clipping plane whose plane equation coefficients will be retrieved.
pPlaneEquation	An array of four floating-point integers to hold the clipping plane's coefficients.
Return Value	**Description**
D3D_OK	Direct3D successfully retrieved the specified clipping plane's coefficients.
DDERR_INVALIDPARAMS	The **dwIndex** parameter either referenced an invalid clipping plane that the hardware does not support, or the array specified by the **pPlaneEquation** parameter is not large enough to contain four floating-point values.

IDirect3DDevice7::GetClipStatus ()

Function Description

This function retrieves the current clip status.

Function Declaration

```
HRESULT GetClipStatus(
  LPD3DCLIPSTATUS lpD3DClipStatus
);
```

Parameter	Description
lpD3DClipStatus	A pointer to a **D3DCLIPSTATUS** structure. If this function succeeds, the structure will be filled with information describing the current clip status.
Return Value	**Description**
D3D_OK	Direct3D successfully retrieved the current clip status.
DDERR_INVALIDPARAMS	Direct3D could not retrieve the current clip status, because one or more parameters are invalid.

IDirect3DDevice7::GetDirect3D ()

Function Description

This function retrieves the Direct3D7 object that was used to create this Direct3DDevice7 object.

Function Declaration

```
HRESULT GetDirect3D(
  LPDIRECT3D7 *lplpD3D
);
```

Parameter	Description
lplpD3D	The address of a pointer to a Direct3D7 object. If this function succeeds, the pointer will be set to the Direct3D7 object that was used to create this Direct3DDevice7 object.
Return Value	**Description**
D3D_OK	Direct3D successfully retrieved the Direct3D7 object used to create this Direct3DDevice7 object.

IDirect3DDevice7::GetInfo ()

Function Description

This function retrieves information about the rendering device of Direct3D or the underling device driver. This function should not be executed between calls to **IDirect3DDevice7::BeginScene ()** and **IDirect3DDevice7::EndScene ()**.

Function Declaration

```
HRESULT GetInfo(
  DWORD  dwDevInfoID,
  LPVOID pDevInfoStruct,
  DWORD  dwSize
);
```

Parameter	Description
dwDevInfoID	Describes where the device information should come from. This parameter can be one of the following flags:
	• **D3DDEVINFOID_TEXTUREMANAGER**—The **pDevInfoStruct** member points to a **D3DDEVINFO_-TEXTUREMANAGER** structure. If this function succeeds, the structure will be filled with information describing the texture management performed by the device driver. If the driver does not perform texture management, information about Direct3D's texture management will be retrieved instead.
	• **D3DDEVINFOID_D3DTEXTUREMANAGER**—The **pDevInfoStruct** member points to a **D3DDEVINFO_-TEXTUREMANAGER** structure. If this function succeeds, the structure will be filled with information describing the texture management performed by Direct3D.
	• **D3DDEVINFOID_TEXTURING**—The **pDevInfoStruct** member points to a **D3DDEVINFO_TEXTURING** structure. If this function succeeds, the structure will be filled wit information describing the texturing activity of the application.
pDevInfoStruct	A pointer to a structure. If this function succeeds, the structure will be filled with information describing the rendering device. See the **dwDevInfoID** parameter for more information.
dwSize	The size, in bytes, of the structure that **pDevInfoStruct** points to.

Return Value	Description
D3D_OK	Direct3D successfully retrieved information about the rendering device.
S_FALSE	Direct3D could not retrieve information about the rendering device, because the device does not support information queries.
DDERR_INVALIDOBJECT	Direct3D could not retrieve information about the rendering device, because this Direct3DDevice7 object is invalid.
DDERR_INVALIDPARAMS	Direct3D could not retrieve information about the rendering device, because one or more parameters are invalid.

IDirect3DDevice7::GetLight ()

Function Description

This function retrieves information describing one of the light sources used by the Direct3D device. Light sources can be set with the **IDirect3DDevice7::SetLight** () function.

Function Declaration

```
HRESULT GetLight(
  DWORD dwLightIndex,
  LPD3DLIGHT7 lpLight
);
```

Parameter	Description
dwLightIndex	The zero-based index that identifies the light source that Direct3D should retrieve information about. This light source must have previously been set with the **IDirect3DDevice7::- SetLight** () function.
lpLight	A pointer to a **D3DLIGHT7** structure. If this function succeeds, the structure will be filled with information describing the specified light source.

Return Value	Description
D3D_OK	Direct3D successfully retrieved information describing the requested light source.
DDERR_INVALIDPARAMS	Direct3D could not retrieve information describing the requested light source, because one or more parameters are invalid.

IDirect3DDevice7::GetLightEnable ()

Function Description

This function retrieves the status, whether enabled or disabled, for a specified light source. Light sources can be set with the **IDirect3DDevice7::SetLight** () function.

Function Declaration

```
HRESULT GetLightEnable(
  DWORD dwLightIndex,
  BOOL* pbEnable
);
```

Parameter	Description
dwLightIndex	The zero-based index that identifies the light source whose status is being retrieved. This light source must have previously been set with the **IDirect3DDevice7::SetLight** () function.
pbEnable	A pointer to a Win32 type **BOOL** variable. If this function succeeds, the variable will be set to the constant **TRUE** if the specified light source is enabled, or **FALSE** otherwise.

Return Value	Description
D3D_OK	Direct3D successfully retrieved the status of the specified light source.

IDirect3DDevice7::GetMaterial ()

Function Description

This function retrieves the current material properties for the device. Material properties specify diffuse, ambient, specular, and emissive properties. These values are used for primitives that require these components, but do not specify this information for each vertex.

The current material properties can be set with the **IDirect3DDevice7::SetMaterial** () function.

Function Declaration

```
HRESULT GetMaterial(
  LPD3DMATERIAL7 lpMaterial
);
```

Parameter	Description
lpMaterial	A pointer to a **D3DMATERIAL7** structure. If this function succeeds, the structure will be filled with the currently set material properties.

Return Value	Description
D3D_OK	Direct3D successfully retrieved the current material properties for the device.
DDERR_INVALIDPARAMS	Direct3D could not retrieve the current material properties for the device, because one or more parameters are invalid.

IDirect3DDevice7::GetRenderState ()

Function Description

This function retrieves a single rendering state parameter for the device represented by this **Direct3DDevice7** object.

Function Declaration

```
HRESULT GetRenderState(
  D3DRENDERSTATETYPE dwRenderStateType,
  LPDWORD lpdwRenderState
);
```

Parameter	Description
dwRenderStateType	Describes the state to be retrieved. This parameter can be one of the following enumeration values:
	• **D3DRENDERSTATE_ANTIALIAS**—The full-scene antialias state, which determines the desired type of full-scene antialiasing. Full-scene antialiasing is when polygons are rendered with antialiased edges in one pass, as they are rendered into the target surface. This type of antialiasing does not work for lines, and is only valid for devices that support the **D3DPRASTERCAPS_ANTIALIASSORTINDEPENDENT** or **D3DPRASTERCAPS_ANTIALIASSORTDEPENDENT** capabilities.

(continued)

IDirect3DDevice7::GetRenderState () *(continued)*

Parameter	Description
	This state can be set to one of the following enumeration values:

- **D3DANTIALIAS_NONE**—No full-scene antialiasing is performed. This is the default value for this state.

- **D3DANTIALIAS_SORTDEPENDENT**—Sort dependent full-scene antialiasing is performed. In sort dependent antialiasing, the order in which the polygons are displayed matters—the application must display them in the proper order, whether front to back, or back to front, as determined by the capabilities of the hardware device.

- **D3DANTIALIAS_SORTINDEPENDENT**—Sort independent full-scene antialiasing is performed. In sort independent antialiasing, the order in which the polygons are displayed does not matter. Sort independent full-scene antialiasing is slower them sort dependent antialiasing on some hardware devices.

- **D3DRENDERSTATE_TEXTUREPERSPECTIVE**—The texture perspective state, which determines whether or not perspective-corrected texture mapping is enabled. Perspective-correct texture mapping is more accurate than linear texture mapping, the alternative.

This state can be set to one of the following values:

- **TRUE**—Perspective-corrected texture mapping is enabled. This is the default value for this state.

- **FALSE**—Perspective-corrected texture mapping is disabled.

- **D3DRENDERSTATE_ZENABLE**—The depth enable state, which determines whether or not depth buffering is enabled, and if so, what type of depth buffering is enabled. This state can be set to one of the following enumeration values:

  - **D3DZB_TRUE**—z-based depth buffering is enabled. This is the default value for this state if a depth buffer is attached to the render-target surface.

  - **D3DZB_USEW**—w-based depth buffering is enabled.

  - **D3DZB_FALSE**—Depth buffering is not enabled.

- **D3DRENDERSTATE_FILLMODE**—The fill mode state, which describes how primitives are rendered. This state can be set to one of the following enumeration values:

(continued)

IDirect3DDevice7::GetRenderState () *(continued)*	
Parameter	**Description**
	• **D3DFILL_POINT**—The vertices of primitives are rendered as points.
	• **D3DFILL_WIREFRAME**—Primitives are rendered in wireframe (that is, the edges of polygons are displayed as lines). This state does not work for clipped primitives.
	• **D3DFILL_SOLID**—The primitives are rendered solid. This is the default value for this state.
	• **D3DRENDERSTATE_SHADEMODE**—The shade mode state, which describes how triangles are shaded. This state can be set to one of the following enumeration values:
	• **D3DSHADE_FLAT**—Triangles are rendered in flat shade mode. In this mode, the entire face of a triangle is shaded the same color, determined by the color and specular component of the first vertex in the triangle.
	• **D3DSHADE_GOURAUD**—Triangles are rendered in Gouraud shade mode. In this mode, the color and specular components of a pixel in the triangle are determined by a linear interpolation between the color and specular components of all three of the triangle's vertices. This is the default value for this state.
	• **D3DSHADE_PHONG**—Triangles are rendered in Phong shade mode. This mode is not currently supported.
	• **D3DRENDERSTATE_LINEPATTERN**—The line pattern state, which describes the pattern used when Direct3D draws lines. This is specified by a **D3DLINEPATTERN** structure.
	The default value for this state is a **D3DLINEPATTERN** structure whose **wRepeatPattern** and **wLinePattern** members are 0.
	• **D3DRENDERSTATE_ZWRITEENABLE**—The depth buffer write enable state, which describes whether or not writing to the depth buffer is enabled. This state can be set to one of the following values:
	• **TRUE**—Writing to the depth buffer is enabled. This is the default value for this state.
	• **FALSE**—Writing to the depth buffer is disabled. Depth comparisons will still take place if enabled, but depth values will not be written to the depth buffer.

(continued)

IDirect3DDevice7::GetRenderState () *(continued)*	
Parameter	**Description**
	• **D3DRENDERSTATE_ALPHATESTENABLE**—The alpha test enable state, which determines whether or not alpha comparisons are enabled. Alpha comparisons, if enabled, restrict alpha blending from occurring unless the alpha comparison function succeeds.
	This state can be set to one of the following values:
	• **TRUE**—Alpha comparisons are enabled.
	• **FALSE**—Alpha comparisons are disabled. This is the default value for this state.
	• **D3DRENDERSTATE_LASTPIXEL**—The draw last pixel state, which determines whether or not Direct3D fills the last pixel in a line or row of a triangle. This state can be set to one of the following values:
	• **TRUE**—Last-pixel filling is enabled. This is the default value for this state.
	• **FALSE**—Last-pixel filling is disabled.
	• **D3DRENDERSTATE_SRCBLEND**—The source blend state, which determines the blend factor for source blend operations. The blend factor is a series of four floating-point values that range from 0.0 (completely transparent) to 1.0 (completely opaque). These values describe the proportions of red, green, blue, and alpha in the source that will be used when blending the source pixels with those in the destination.
	This state can be set to one of the following enumeration values:
	• **D3DBLEND_ZERO**—The blend factor is (0, 0, 0, 0).
	• **D3DBLEND_ONE**—The blend factor is (1, 1, 1, 1). This is the default value for this state.
	• **D3DBLEND_SRCCOLOR**—The blend factor is (R_s, G_s, B_s, A_s), where R_s, G_s, B_s, and A_s are the red, green, blue, and alpha components of the source, respectively.
	• **D3DBLEND_INVSRCCOLOR**—The blend factor is ($1-R_s$, $1-G_s$, $1-B_s$, $1-A_s$), where R_s, G_s, B_s, and A_s are the red, green, blue, and alpha components of the source, respectively.
	• **D3DBLEND_SRCALPHA**—The blend factor is (A_s, A_s, A_s, A_s), where A_s is the alpha component of the source.
	• **D3DBLEND_INVSRCALPHA**—The blend factor is ($1-A_s$, $1-A_s$, $1-A_s$, $1-A_s$), where A_s is the alpha component of the source.

(continued)

IDirect3DDevice7::GetRenderState () (continued)

Parameter	Description
	• **D3DBLEND_DESTALPHA**—The blend factor is (A_d, A_d, A_d, A_d), where A_d is the alpha component of the destination.
	• **D3DBLEND_INVDESTALPHA**—The blend factor is (**1-**A_d, **1-**A_d, **1-**A_d, **1-**A_d), where A_d is the alpha component of the destination.
	• **D3DBLEND_DESTCOLOR**—The blend factor is (R_d, G_d, B_d, A_d), where R_d, G_d, B_d, and A_d are the red, green, blue, and alpha components of the destination, respectively.
	• **D3DBLEND_INVDESTCOLOR**—The blend factor is (**1-**R_d, **1-**G_d, **1-**B_d, **1-**A_d), where R_d, G_d, B_d, and A_d are the red, green, blue, and alpha components of the destination, respectively.
	• **D3DBLEND_SRCALPHASAT**—The blend factor is (**f**, **f**, **f**, **f**), where **f** = A_s (the alpha component of the source) or **1-**A_d (the inverse of the alpha component of the destination), whichever is lower.
	• **D3DBLEND_BOTHINVSRCALPHA**—This value controls both source and destination blend values. The destination blend value is overridden.
	The source blend factor is (**1-**A_s, **1-**A_s, **1-**A_s, **1-**A_s) where A_s is the alpha component of the source. The destination blend factor is (A_s, A_s, A_s, A_s).
	• **D3DRENDERSTATE_DESTBLEND**—The destination blend state, which determines the blend factor for destination blend operations. The blend factor is a series of four floating-point values that range from 0.0 (completely transparent) to 1.0 (completely opaque). These values describe the proportions of red, green, blue, and alpha in the destination surface that will be used when blending the source pixels with those in the source.
	This state can be set to one of the following enumeration values:
	• **D3DBLEND_ZERO**—The blend factor is (0, 0, 0, 0).
	• **D3DBLEND_ONE**—The blend factor is (1, 1, 1, 1). This is the default value for this state.
	• **D3DBLEND_SRCCOLOR**—The blend factor is (R_s, G_s, B_s, A_s), where R_s, G_s, B_s, and A_s are the red, green, blue, and alpha components of the source, respectively.

(continued)

IDirect3DDevice7::GetRenderState () *(continued)*	
Parameter	Description
	• **D3DBLEND_INVSRCCOLOR**—The blend factor is ($1-R_s$, $1-G_s$, $1-B_s$, $1-A_s$), where R_s, G_s, B_s, and A_s are the red, green, blue, and alpha components of the source, respectively.
	• **D3DBLEND_SRCALPHA**—The blend factor is (A_s, A_s, A_s, A_s), where A_s is the alpha component of the source.
	• **D3DBLEND_INVSRCALPHA**—The blend factor is ($1-A_s$, $1-A_s$, $1-A_s$, $1-A_s$), where A_s is the alpha component of the source.
	• **D3DBLEND_DESTALPHA**—The blend factor is (A_d, A_d, A_d, A_d), where A_d is the alpha component of the destination.
	• **D3DBLEND_INVDESTALPHA**—The blend factor is ($1-A_d$, $1-A_d$, $1-A_d$, $1-A_d$), where A_d is the alpha component of the destination.
	• **D3DBLEND_DESTCOLOR**—The blend factor is (R_d, G_d, B_d, A_d), where R_d, G_d, B_d, and A_d are the red, green, blue, and alpha components of the destination, respectively.
	• **D3DBLEND_INVDESTCOLOR**—The blend factor is ($1-R_d$, $1-G_d$, $1-B_d$, $1-A_d$), where R_d, G_d, B_d, and A_d are the red, green, blue, and alpha components of the destination, respectively.
	• **D3DBLEND_SRCALPHASAT**—The blend factor is (f, f, f, f), where $f = A_s$ (the alpha component of the source) or $1-A_d$ (the inverse of the alpha component of the destination), whichever is lower.
	• **D3DBLEND_BOTHINVSRCALPHA**—This value controls both source and destination blend values. The destination blend value is overridden.
	The source blend factor is ($1-A_s$, $1-A_s$, $1-A_s$, $1-A_s$), where A_s is the alpha component of the source. The destination blend factor is (A_s, A_s, A_s, A_s).
	• **D3DRENDERSTATE_CULLMODE**—The cull mode state, which determines whether and in what manner back-face culling is performed. This state can be set to one of the following enumeration values:
	• **D3DCULL_NONE**—Back-face culling is not performed.
	• **D3DCULL_CW**—Back-face culling is performed on all polygons whose vertices are defined in a clockwise fashion when viewed from the direction pointed to by their surface normals.

(continued)

IDirect3DDevice7::GetRenderState () *(continued)*	
Parameter	**Description**
	• **D3DCULL_CCW**—Back-face culling is performed on all polygons whose vertices are defined in a counterclockwise fashion when viewed from the direction pointed to by their surface normals. This is the default value for this state.
	• **D3DRENDERSTATE_ZFUNC**—The depth compare function state, which determines the function used when comparing depth values. This function is used only when depth buffering is enabled.
	This state can be one of the following enumeration values:
	• **D3DCMP_NEVER**—The function always evaluates to false. No new pixels are displayed.
	• **D3DCMP_LESS**—The function evaluates to **TRUE** only if the new pixel has a depth less than that of the current pixel.
	Otherwise, the function evaluates to **FALSE**, and the new pixel is not displayed.
	• **D3DCMP_EQUAL**—The function evaluates to **TRUE** only if the new pixel has a depth value equal to that of the current pixel.
	Otherwise, the function evaluates to **FALSE**, and the new pixel is not displayed.
	• **D3DCMP_LESSEQUAL**—The function evaluates to **TRUE** only if the new pixel has a depth value less than or equal to the current pixel.
	Otherwise, the function evaluates to **FALSE**, and the new pixel is not displayed.
	This is the default value for this state.
	• **D3DCMP_GREATER**—The function evaluates to **TRUE** only if the new pixel has a depth greater than that of the current pixel.
	Otherwise, the function evaluates to **FALSE**, and the new pixel is not displayed.
	• **D3DCMP_NOTEQUAL**—The function evaluates to **TRUE** only if the new pixel has a depth value not equal to that of the current pixel.
	Otherwise, the function evaluates to **FALSE**, and the new pixel is not displayed.

(continued)

IDirect3DDevice7::GetRenderState () *(continued)*	
Parameter	Description
	• **D3DCMP_GREATEREQUAL**—The function evaluates to **TRUE** only if the new pixel has a depth value greater than or equal to that of the current pixel.

Otherwise, the function evaluates to **FALSE**, and the new pixel is not displayed.

• **D3DCMP_ALWAYS**—The function always evaluates to **TRUE**. All new pixels are displayed.

• **D3DRENDERSTATE_ALPHAREF**—The alpha reference value state, which determines the reference value against which pixels are tested when alpha-testing is enabled. This state is described by an 8-bit value in the low 8 bits of the **DWORD** render state. Valid values range from 0×00000000 to 0×000000FF.

• **D3DRENDERSTATE_ALPHAFUNC**—The alpha compare function state, which determines the function used when comparing alpha values. This state can be set to one of the following enumeration values:

  • **D3DCMP_NEVER**—The function always evaluates to false. No new pixels are displayed.

  • **D3DCMP_LESS**—The function evaluates to **TRUE** only if the new pixel has an alpha less than that of the current pixel.

  Otherwise, the function evaluates to **FALSE**, and the new pixel is not displayed.

  • **D3DCMP_EQUAL**—The function evaluates to **TRUE** only if the new pixel has an alpha value equal to that of the current pixel.

  Otherwise, the function evaluates to **FALSE**, and the new pixel is not displayed.

  • **D3DCMP_LESSEQUAL**—The function evaluates to **TRUE** only if the new pixel has an alpha value less than or equal to the current pixel.

  Otherwise, the function evaluates to **FALSE**, and the new pixel is not displayed.

  • **D3DCMP_GREATER**—The function evaluates to **TRUE** only if the new pixel has an alpha greater than that of the current pixel.

  Otherwise, the function evaluates to **FALSE**, and the new pixel is not displayed. |

(continued)

IDirect3DDevice7::GetRenderState () *(continued)*

Parameter	Description
	• **D3DCMP_NOTEQUAL**—The function evaluates to **TRUE** only if the new pixel has an alpha value not equal to that of the current pixel.
	Otherwise, the function evaluates to **FALSE**, and the new pixel is not displayed.
	• **D3DCMP_GREATEREQUAL**—The function evaluates to **TRUE** only if the new pixel has an alpha value greater than or equal to that of the current pixel.
	Otherwise, the function evaluates to **FALSE**, and the new pixel is not displayed.
	• **D3DCMP_ALWAYS**—The function always evaluates to **TRUE**. All new pixels are displayed. This is the default value for this state.
	• **D3DRENDERSTATE_DITHERENABLE**—The dither enable state, which determines whether or not dithering is enabled. This state can be set to one of the following values:
	• **TRUE**—Dithering is enabled.
	• **FALSE**—Dithering is disabled. This is the default value for this state.
	• **D3DRENDERSTATE_ALPHABLENDENABLE**—The alpha blend enable state, which determines whether or not alpha-blended transparency is enabled. This state can be set to one of the following values:
	• **TRUE**—Alpha-blended transparency is enabled.
	• **FALSE**—Alpha-blended transparency is disabled. This is the default value for this state.
	• **D3DRENDERSTATE_FOGENABLE**—The fog enable state, which determines whether or not fog shading is enabled. This state can be set to one of the following values:
	• **TRUE**—Fog shading is enabled.
	• **FALSE**—Fog shading is disabled. This is the default value for this state.
	• **D3DRENDERSTATE_SPECULARENABLE**—The specular enable state, which determines whether or not specular highlights are enabled. The specular highlights as generated by Direct3D tend to work best when the object is centered on the origin in model space and is far away from the light source.

(continued)

IDirect3DDevice7::GetRenderState () *(continued)*	
Parameter	**Description**
	This state can be one of the following values:

- **TRUE**—Specular highlights are enabled.
- **FALSE**—Specular highlights are disabled. This is the default value for this state.

- **D3DRENDERSTATE_STIPPLEDALPHA**—The stippled alpha state, which determines whether or not stippled alpha blending is enabled. This state can be set to one of the following values:

  - **TRUE**—Stippled alpha blending is enabled. This requires hardware support.
  - **FALSE**—Stippled alpha blending is disabled.

- **D3DRENDERSTATE_FOGCOLOR**—The fog color state, which determines the color used for fog shading. This state is described by a **D3DCOLOR** structure. The default setting for this state is the color (0, 0, 0).

- **D3DRENDERSTATE_FOGTABLEMODE**—The fog table mode state, which determines the equation used for pixel-based fog shading, if any. This state can be set to one of the following enumeration values:

  - **D3DFOG_NONE**—There is no fog shading. This is the default value for this state.

  - **D3DFOG_EXP**—Fog shading intensifies exponentially, according to the following formula: $f = 1/e^{d*r}$, where f is the fog intensity at a point, d is the distance from the viewer to the point (either along all axes, or just the z-axis, depending on the **D3DRENDERSTATE_RANGE FOGENABLE** state), e is the base of natural logarithms (approximately 2.7182818285), and r is the density of the fog (a value that ranges from 0.0 to 1.0, as determined by the **D3DRENDERSTATE_FOGDENSITY** render state).

    This value is not currently supported.

  - **D3DFOG_EXP2**—Fog shading intensifies with the square of the distance, according to the following formula: $f = 1/e^{(d*r)(d*r)}$, where f is the fog intensity at a point, d is the distance from the viewer to the point (either along all axes, or just the z-axis, depending on the **D3DRENDER–STATE_RANGEFOGENABLE** state), e is the base of natural logarithms (approximately 2.7182818285), and r is the density of the fog (a value that ranges from 0.0 to 1.0, as determined by the **D3DRENDERSTATE_FOGDENSITY** render state).

    This value is not currently supported.

(continued)

IDirect3DDevice7::GetRenderState () *(continued)*	
Parameter	**Description**
	• **D3DFOG_LINEAR**—Fog shading intensifies linearly between the starting and ending points, according to the following formula: **f = (end - d)/(end - start)**, where **f** is the fog intensity at a point, **d** is the distance from the viewer to the point (either along all axes, or just the *z*-axis, depending on the **D3DRENDERSTATE_RANGE FOGENABLE** state), **start** is the distance at which fog shading begins, and **end** is the distance at which fog shading ends.
	This value is the only fog formula currently supported.
	• **D3DRENDERSTATE_FOGSTART**—The fog begin depth state, which determines the depth at which fog shading begins for linear fog mode. This depth is specified in world space for hardware devices or in device space (0.0 to 1.0) for software devices.
	• **D3DRENDERSTATE_FOGEND**—The fog end depth state, which determines the depth at which fog shading ends for linear fog mode. This depth is specified in world space for hardware devices or in device space (0.0 to 1.0) for software devices.
	• **D3DRENDERSTATE_FOGDENSITY**—The fog density state, which determines the density of the fog, used in exponential fog modes (**D3DFOG_EXP** and **D3DFOG_EXP2**). Valid values for this state range from 0.0 to 1.0, inclusive, the default being 1.0.
	• **D3DRENDERSTATE_COLORKEYENABLE**—The color key enable state, which determines whether or not color-keyed transparency is enabled. This state can be set to one of the following values:
	• **TRUE**—Color-keyed transparency is enabled. This affects only texture surfaces created with the **DDSD_CKSRCBLT** flag. Surfaces created without this flag will exhibit color-keyed transparency.
	• **FALSE**—Color-keyed transparency is disabled. This is the default value for this state.
	• **D3DRENDERSTATE_ZBIAS**—The *z*-bias state for rendered polygons, specified as an integer in the range of 0 to 16, the default being 0. The *z*-bias is used to put in order of priority polygons that are coplanar (lying on the same three-dimensional plane). Polygons with higher *z*-biases are rendered in front of coplanar polygons with lower *z*-biases. The rendering order for coplanar polygons with identical *z*-biases is undefined.

(continued)

IDirect3DDevice7::GetRenderState () *(continued)*	
Parameter	**Description**
	• **D3DRENDERSTATE_RANGEFOGENABLE**—The range fog enable state, which determines whether or not range-based fog is enabled. This state, which is valid for unlit, untransformed vertices only, can be set to one of the following values:
	• **TRUE**—Range-based fog is enabled. In this mode, points are shaded according to their actual distance from the viewer. This is the most realistic method of fog shading, but is more computationally expensive than depth-based fog.
	• **FALSE**—Depth-based fog is enabled. In this mode, points are shaded according to their depths (*z*-coordinates). This is the default value for this state.
	• **D3DRENDERSTATE_TRANSLUCENTSORTINDEPENDENT**— The translucent sort independent state, which determines whether or not sort-independent transparency is enabled. This state can be set to one of the following values:
	• **TRUE**—Sort-independent transparency is enabled.
	• **FALSE**—Sort-independent transparency is disabled.
	• **D3DRENDERSTATE_STENCILENABLE**—The stencil enable state, which determines if stenciling is enabled. This state can be one of the following values:
	• **TRUE**—Stenciling is enabled.
	• **FALSE**—Stenciling is disabled. This is the default value for this state.
	• **D3DRENDERSTATE_STENCILFAIL**—The stencil fail operation state, which determines the operation to perform if the stencil test fails. This state can be one of the following enumeration values:
	• **D3DSTENCILOP_KEEP**—The entry in the stencil buffer is not updated. This is the default value for this state.
	• **D3DSTENCILOP_ZERO**—The entry in the stencil buffer is set to 0.
	• **D3DSTENCILOP_REPLACE**—The entry in the stencil buffer is replaced with the stencil reference value.
	• **D3DSTENCILOP_INCRSAT**—The entry in the stencil buffer is incremented, unless it has already reached its maximum value. The maximum value for a stencil buffer is given by the equation 2^n-1, where n is the bit depth of the stencil buffer.

(continued)

IDirect3DDevice7::GetRenderState () *(continued)*	
Parameter	Description
	• **D3DSTENCILOP_DECRSAT**—The entry in the stencil buffer is decremented, unless it has already reached 0.
	• **D3DSTENCILOP_INVERT**—The bits of the entry in the stencil buffer are inverted.
	• **D3DSTENCILOP_INCR**—The entry in the stencil buffer is incremented. If the entry is already at maximum value, it is reset to 0. The maximum value for a stencil buffer is given by the equation $2^{n}-1$, where n is the bit depth of the stencil buffer.
	• **D3DSTENCILOP_DECR**—The entry in the stencil buffer is decremented. If the entry is already at 0, it is set to the maximum value. The maximum value for a stencil buffer is given by the equation $2^{n}-1$, where n is the bit depth of the stencil buffer.
	• **D3DRENDERSTATE_STENCILZFAIL**—The stencil z-fail operation state, which determines the operation to perform if the stencil test passes but the depth test fails. This state can be set to one of the following enumeration values:
	• **D3DSTENCILOP_KEEP**—The entry in the stencil buffer is not updated. This is the default value for this state.
	• **D3DSTENCILOP_ZERO**—The entry in the stencil buffer is set to 0.
	• **D3DSTENCILOP_REPLACE**—The entry in the stencil buffer is replaced with the stencil reference value.
	• **D3DSTENCILOP_INCRSAT**—The entry in the stencil buffer is incremented, unless it has already reached its maximum value. The maximum value for a stencil buffer is given by the equation $2^{n}-1$, where n is the bit depth of the stencil buffer.
	• **D3DSTENCILOP_DECRSAT**—The entry in the stencil buffer is decremented, unless it has already reached 0.
	• **D3DSTENCILOP_INVERT**—The bits of the entry in the stencil buffer are inverted.
	• **D3DSTENCILOP_INCR**—The entry in the stencil buffer is incremented. If the entry is already at maximum value, it is reset to 0. The maximum value for a stencil buffer is given by the equation $2^{n}-1$, where n is the bit depth of the stencil buffer.

(continued)

IDirect3DDevice7::GetRenderState () *(continued)*	
Parameter	**Description**
	• **D3DSTENCILOP_DECR**—The entry in the stencil buffer is decremented. If the entry is already at 0, it is set to the maximum value. The maximum value for a stencil buffer is given by the equation 2^n-1, where n is the bit depth of the stencil buffer.
	• **D3DRENDERSTATE_STENCILPASS**—The stencil pass state, which determines the operation to perform if both the stencil and depth tests pass. This state can be set to one of the following enumeration values:
	• **D3DSTENCILOP_KEEP**—The entry in the stencil buffer is not updated. This is the default value for this state.
	• **D3DSTENCILOP_ZERO**—The entry in the stencil buffer is set to 0.
	• **D3DSTENCILOP_REPLACE**—The entry in the stencil buffer is replaced with the stencil reference value.
	• **D3DSTENCILOP_INCRSAT**—The entry in the stencil buffer is incremented, unless it has already reached its maximum value. The maximum value for a stencil buffer is given by the equation 2^n-1, where n is the bit depth of the stencil buffer.
	• **D3DSTENCILOP_DECRSAT**—The entry in the stencil buffer is decremented, unless it has already reached 0.
	• **D3DSTENCILOP_INVERT**—The bits of the entry in the stencil buffer are inverted.
	• **D3DSTENCILOP_INCR**—The entry in the stencil buffer is incremented. If the entry is already at maximum value, it is reset to 0. The maximum value for a stencil buffer is given by the equation 2^n-1, where n is the bit depth of the stencil buffer.
	• **D3DSTENCILOP_DECR**—The entry in the stencil buffer is decremented. If the entry is already at 0, it is set to the maximum value. The maximum value for a stencil buffer is given by the equation 2^n-1, where n is the bit depth of the stencil buffer.

(continued)

IDirect3DDevice7::GetRenderState () *(continued)*	
Parameter	Description
	• **D3DRENDERSTATE_STENCILFUNC**—The stencil function state, which determines the function to use when comparing the stencil reference value (governed by the **D3DRENDER-STATE_STENCILREF** state) to a stencil buffer entry. This state can be set to one of the following enumeration values: • **D3DCMP_NEVER**—The function always evaluates to false. The operation Direct3D takes when the function evaluates to **FALSE** depends on the **D3DRENDER STATE_STENCIL-FAIL** and **D3DRENDERSTATE_STENCILZFAIL** under states. • **D3DCMP_LESS**—The function evaluates to **TRUE** only if the new pixel has a stencil value less than the stencil reference value. Otherwise, the function evaluates to **FALSE**. The operation Direct3D takes when the function evaluates to **TRUE** or **FALSE** depends on the **D3DRENDERSTATE_STENCILFAIL**, **D3DRENDERSTATE_STENCILZFAIL** and **D3DRENDER-STATE_STENCILPASS** under states. • **D3DCMP_EQUAL**—The function evaluates to **TRUE** only if the new pixel has a stencil value equal to the stencil reference value. Otherwise, the function evaluates to **FALSE**. The operation Direct3D takes when the function evaluates to **TRUE** or **FALSE** depends on the **D3DRENDERSTATE_STENCILFAIL**, **D3DRENDERSTATE_STENCILZFAIL** and **D3DRENDER-STATE_STENCILPASS** under states. • **D3DCMP_LESSEQUAL**—The function evaluates to **TRUE** only if the new pixel has a stencil value less than or equal to the stencil reference value. Otherwise, the function evaluates to **FALSE**. The operation Direct3D takes when the function evaluates to **TRUE** or **FALSE** depends on the **D3DRENDERSTATE_STENCILFAIL**, **D3DRENDERSTATE_STENCILZFAIL** and **D3DRENDER-STATE_STENCILPASS** under states. • **D3DCMP_GREATER**—The function evaluates to **TRUE** only if the new pixel has a stencil value greater than the stencil reference value. Otherwise, the function evaluates to **FALSE**. The operation Direct3D takes when the function evaluates to **TRUE** or **FALSE** depends on the **D3DRENDERSTATE_STENCILFAIL**, **D3DRENDERSTATE_STENCILZFAIL** and **D3DRENDER-STATE_STENCILPASS** under states.

(continued)

IDirect3DDevice7::GetRenderState () *(continued)*	
Parameter	**Description**
	• **D3DCMP_NOTEQUAL**—The function evaluates to **TRUE** only if the new pixel has a stencil value not equal to the stencil reference value.
	Otherwise, the function evaluates to **FALSE**. The operation Direct3D takes when the function evaluates to **TRUE** or **FALSE** depends on the **D3DRENDERSTATE_STENCILFAIL**, **D3DRENDERSTATE_STENCILZFAIL** and **D3DRENDER-STATE_STENCILPASS** under states.
	• **D3DCMP_GREATEREQUAL**—The function evaluates to **TRUE** only if the new pixel has a stencil value greater than or equal to the stencil reference value.
	Otherwise, the function evaluates to **FALSE**. The operation Direct3D takes when the function evaluates to **TRUE** or **FALSE** depends on the **D3DRENDERSTATE_STENCILFAIL**, **D3DRENDERSTATE_STENCILZFAIL** and **D3DRENDER-STATE_STENCILPASS** under states.
	• **D3DCMP_ALWAYS**—The function always evaluates to **TRUE**. The operation Direct3D takes when the function evaluates to **TRUE** depends on the **D3DRENDERSTATE_-STENCILPASS** under state.
	• **D3DRENDERSTATE_STENCILREF**—The stencil reference value state, which determines the reference value for the stencil test, specified as an integer in the range of 0 to 2^n-1, where **n** is the bit depth of the stencil buffer. The default value for this state is 0.
	• **D3DRENDERSTATE_STENCILMASK**—The stencil mask state, which determines the mask applied to both the reference value and each stencil buffer entry to isolate the significant bits for the stencil test. The default value for this state is 0×FFFFFFFF, indicating all bits are significant.
	• **D3DRENDERSTATE_STENCILWRITEMASK**—The stencil write mask state, which determines the mask applied to values written into the stencil buffer. The default value for this state is 0×FFFFFFFF, indicating all bits are significant.
	• **D3DRENDERSTATE_TEXTUREFACTOR**—The texture factor state, which determines the color used for multiple texture blending with either the **D3DTA_TFACTOR** texture-blending argument or the **D3DTOP_BLENDFACTORALPHA** texture-blending operation. This is specified as a **D3DCOLOR** structure.

(continued)

IDirect3DDevice7::GetRenderState () *(continued)*	
Parameter	Description
	• **D3DRENDERSTATE_WRAP0** through **D3DRENDERSTATE_-WRAP7**—The texture wrapping state, which determines the behavior of texture wrapping for texture coordinates. This state can be set to zero or one of the following values:
	• **D3DWRAPCOORD_0**—Texture wrapping is enabled in the first, usually horizontal, dimension.
	• **D3DWRAPCOORD_1**—Texture wrapping is enabled in the second, usually vertical, dimension.
	• **D3DWRAPCOORD_2**—Texture wrapping is enabled in the third dimension.
	• **D3DWRAPCOORD_3**—Texture wrapping is enabled in the fourth dimension.
	These values are combined with the bitwise or operator ('|').
	• **D3DRENDERSTATE_CLIPPING**—The clipping state, which determines whether or not Direct3D performs primitive clipping. This state can be set to one of the following values:
	• **TRUE**—Primitive clipping is enabled. This is the default value for this state.
	• **FALSE**—Primitive clipping is disabled.
	• **D3DRENDERSTATE_LIGHTING**—The lighting state, which determines whether or not Direct3D performs lighting. This state can be set to one of the following values:
	• **TRUE**—Lighting is enabled. This applies only for vertices that include a vertex normal. This is the default value for this state.
	• **FALSE**—Lighting is disabled.
	• **D3DRENDERSTATE_EXTENTS**—The extents state, which determines whether or not the system updates the screen extents for each rendering call. This state can be set to one of the following values:
	• **TRUE**—Screen extents are updated for each rendering call.
	• **FALSE**—Screen extents are not updated. This is the default value for this state.
	• **D3DRENDERSTATE_AMBIENT**—The ambient state, which determines the ambient light color, specified as **D3DCOLOR** structure. The default value for this state is (0, 0, 0).

(continued)

IDirect3DDevice7::GetRenderState () *(continued)*	
Parameter	Description
	• **D3DRENDERSTATE_FOGVERTEXMODE**—The fog vertex mode state, which determines the fog formula to be used for vertex-based fog. This state can be set to one of the following enumeration values:
	• **D3DFOG_NONE**—There is no fog shading. This is the default value for this state.
	• **D3DFOG_EXP**—Fog shading intensifies exponentially, according to the following formula: $f = 1/e^{d*r}$, where f is the fog intensity at a point, d is the distance from the viewer to the point (either along all axes, or just the z-axis, depending on the **D3DRENDERSTATE_RANGEFOGENABLE** state), e is the base of natural logarithms (approximately 2.7182818285), and r is the density of the fog (a value that ranges from 0.0 to 1.0, as determined by the **D3DRENDERSTATE_FOGDENSITY** render state). This value is not currently supported.
	• **D3DFOG_EXP2**—Fog shading intensifies with the square of the distance, according to the following formula: $f = 1/e^{(d*r)(d*r)}$, where f is the fog intensity at a point, d is the distance from the viewer to the point (either along all axes, or just the z-axis, depending on the **D3DRENDERSTATE_RANGEFOGENABLE** state), e is the base of natural logarithms (approximately 2.7182818285), and r is the density of the fog (a value that ranges from 0.0 to 1.0, as determined by the **D3DRENDERSTATE_-FOGDENSITY** render state). This value is not currently supported.
	• **D3DFOG_LINEAR**—Fog shading intensifies linearly between the starting and ending points, according to the following formula: $f = (end - d)/(end - start)$, where f is the fog intensity at a point, d is the distance from the viewer to the point (either along all axes, or just the z-axis, depending on the **D3DRENDERSTATE_RANGEFOGENABLE** state), **start** is the distance at which fog shading begins, and **end** is the distance at which fog shading ends. This value is the only fog formula currently supported.
	• **D3DRENDERSTATE_COLORVERTEX**—The color vertex state, which determines whether or not to perform per-vertex color. If per-vertex coloring is enabled, Direct3D uses the color information for each vertex (if present) for lighting calculations.

(continued)

IDirect3DDevice7::GetRenderState () *(continued)*	
Parameter	**Description**

	This state can be set to one of the following values:
	
	• **TRUE**—Per-vertex color is enabled. This is the default value for this state.
	
	• **FALSE**—Per-vertex color is disabled.
	
	• **D3DRENDERSTATE_LOCALVIEWER**—The local viewer state, which determines whether or not camera-relative specular highlights are enabled. This state can be set to one of the following values:
	
	  • **TRUE**—Camera-relative specular highlights are enabled. This is the default value for this state.
	
	  • **FALSE**—Orthogonal specular highlights are enabled.
	
	• **D3DRENDERSTATE_NORMALIZENORMALS**—The normalize normals state, which determines whether or not vertex normals are automatically normalized. This state can be set to one of the following values:
	
	  • **TRUE**—Vertex normals are automatically normalized after the system transforms vertices into camera space. This is computationally intensive.
	
	  • **FALSE**—Vertex normals are not automatically normalized. This is the default value for this state.
	
	• **D3DRENDERSTATE_COLORKEYBLENDENABLE**—The color key blend enable state, which determines whether or not alpha-blended color keying is enabled. This state can be set to one of the following values:
	
	  • **TRUE**—Alpha-blended color keying is enabled.
	
	  • **FALSE**—Alpha-blended color keying is disabled.
	
	• **D3DRENDERSTATE_DIFFUSEMATERIALSOURCE**—The diffuse material source state, which determines the diffuse color source for lighting calculations. This state, which is valid only when the **D3DRENDERSTATE_COLORVERTEX** state is set to **TRUE**, can be set to one of the following enumeration values:
	
	  • **D3DMCS_MATERIAL**—The diffuse color for lighting calculations is taken from the current material.
	
	  • **D3DMCS_COLOR1**—The diffuse color for lighting calculations is taken from the diffuse color contained in each vertex. This is the default value for this state.
	
	  • **D3DMCS_COLOR2**—The diffuse color for lighting calculations is taken from the specular color contained in each vertex.

(continued)

IDirect3DDevice7::GetRenderState () *(continued)*	
Parameter	**Description**
	• **D3DRENDERSTATE_SPECULARMATERIALSOURCE**—The specular material source state, which determines the specular color source for lighting calculations. This state can be set to one of the following enumeration values: • **D3DMCS_MATERIAL**—The specular color for lighting calculations is taken from the current material. • **D3DMCS_COLOR1**—The specular color for lighting calculations is taken from the diffuse color contained in each vertex. • **D3DMCS_COLOR2**—The specular color for lighting calculations is taken from the specular color contained in each vertex. This is the default value for this state. • **D3DRENDERSTATE_AMBIENTMATERIALSOURCE**—The ambient material source state, which determines the ambient color source for lighting calculations. This state can be set to one of the following enumeration values: • **D3DMCS_MATERIAL**—The ambient color for lighting calculations is taken from the current material. • **D3DMCS_COLOR1**—The ambient color for lighting calculations is taken from the diffuse color contained in each vertex. • **D3DMCS_COLOR2**—The ambient color for lighting calculations is taken from the specular color contained in each vertex. This is the default value for this state. • **D3DRENDERSTATE_EMISSIVEMATERIALSOURCE**—The emissive material source state, which determines the emissive color source for lighting calculations. This state can be set to one of the following enumeration values: • **D3DMCS_MATERIAL**—The emissive color for lighting calculations is taken from the current material. This is the default value for this state. • **D3DMCS_COLOR1**—The emissive color for lighting calculations is taken from the diffuse color contained in each vertex. • **D3DMCS_COLOR2**—The emissive color for lighting calculations is taken from the specular color contained in each vertex.

(continued)

IDirect3DDevice7::GetRenderState () *(continued)*	
Parameter	**Description**
	• **D3DRENDERSTATE_ALPHASOURCE**—The alpha source state, which determines the location from which Direct3D should obtain the alpha component of output diffuse color. This state can be set to one of the following enumeration values:
	• **D3DMCS_MATERIAL**—The alpha component is taken from the current material.
	• **D3DMCS_COLOR1**—The alpha component is taken from the diffuse color contained in each vertex. This is the default value for this state.
	• **D3DMCS_COLOR2**—The alpha component is taken from the specular color contained in each vertex.
	• **D3DRENDERSTATE_FOGFACTORSOURCE**—The fog factor source state, which determines the location from which Direct3D should obtain the alpha component of output specular color. This alpha component is used for fog calculations. This state can be set to one of the following enumeration values:
	• **D3DMCS_MATERIAL**—The alpha component is taken from the current material.
	• **D3DMCS_COLOR1**—The alpha component is taken from the diffuse color contained in each vertex.
	• **D3DMCS_COLOR2**—The alpha component is taken from the specular color contained in each vertex. This is the default value for this state.
	• **D3DRENDERSTATE_VERTEXBLEND**—The verted blend state, which determines the number of matrices used in vertex blending. This state can be set to one of the following enumeration values:
	• **D3DVBLEND_DISABLE**—Vertex blending is disabled. The only matrix applied to vertices is the one specified by the **D3DTRANSFORMSTATE_WORLD** transformation matrix. Untransformed vertices are sent through this matrix and then outputted.
	This is the default value for this state.

(continued)

IDirect3DDevice7::GetRenderState () *(continued)*	
Parameter	**Description**
	• **D3DVBLEND_1WEIGHT**—Vertex blending is enabled for two matrices. The two matrices applied to vertices are the ones specified by the **D3DTRANSFORMSTATE_WORLD** and **D3DTRANSFORMSTATE_WORLD1** transformation matrices. Untransformed vertices are sent through each of these matrices. The resulting vertices are then blending according to the weighting values specified in their vertex structures. The resulting blended vertices are then outputted.
	• **D3DVBLEND_2WEIGHTS**—Vertex blending is enabled for three matrices. The three matrices applied to vertices are the ones specified by the **D3DTRANSFORMSTATE_WORLD, D3DTRANSFORMSTATE_WORLD1,** and **D3DTRANSFORM-STATE_WORLD2** transformation matrices. Untransformed vertices are sent through each of these matrices. The resulting vertices are then blending according to the weighting values specified in their vertex structures. The resulting blended vertices are then outputted**.**
	• **D3DVBLEND_3WEIGHTS**—Vertex blending is enabled for four matrices. The four matrices applied to vertices are the ones specified by the **D3DTRANSFORMSTATE_WORLD, D3DTRANSFORMSTATE_WORLD1, D3DTRANSFORM-STATE_WORLD2,** and **D3DTRANSFORMSTATE_WORLD3** transformation matrices. Untransformed vertices are sent through each of these matrices. The resulting vertices are then blending according to the weighting values specified in their vertex structures. The resulting blended vertices are then outputted.
	• **D3DRENDERSTATE_CLIPPLANEENABLE**—The clip plane enable state, which determines which user-defined clipping planes (if any) are enabled. This state is specified as a **DWORD** value, where each bit corresponds to the status of a plane (1 indicates the plane is enabled, 0 indicates it is disabled). The least significant bit identifies the first plane; the next significant bit, the second plane; and so on.
	The **D3DCLIPPLANEn** constants (defined in d3dtypes.h) can be used conveniently to enable clipping planes.
	The default value for this state is 0, which indicates no user-defined clipping planes are enabled.
lpdwRenderState	The address of a variable or structure, depending on the render state being retrieved. If this function succeeds, the variable or structure will be filled with the specified render state.
Return Value	**Description**
D3D_OK	Direct3D successfully retrieved the specified render state.
DDERR_INVALIDPARAMS	Direct3D could not retrieve the specified render state, because one or more parameters are invalid.

IDirect3DDevice7::GetRenderTarget ()

Function Description

This function retrieves a pointer to the DirectDraw surface that is currently being used as the render target. The render target surface is where 3D rendering is directed to.

Function Declaration

```
HRESULT GetRenderTarget(
  LPDIRECTDRAWSURFACE7 *lplpRenderTarget
);
```

Parameter	Description
lplpRenderTarget	The address of a pointer to a DirectDrawSurface7 object. If this function succeeds, the pointer will be set to the DirectDraw surface currently designated as the render target surface.

Return Value	Description
D3D_OK	Direct3D successfully retrieved the render target surface.
DDERR_INVALIDPARAMS	Direct3D could not retrieve the render target surface, because one or more parameters are invalid.

IDirect3DDevice7::GetTexture ()

Function Description

This function retrieves a pointer to a DirectDrawSurface7 object that identifies the texture currently assigned to a specified texture stage.

Function Declaration

```
HRESULT GetTexture(
  DWORD dwStage,
  LPDIRECTDRAWSURFACE7 * lplpTexture
);
```

Parameter	Description
dwStage	The texture stage of the texture to be retrieved, in the range of 0 to 7.
lplpTexture	The address of a pointer to a DirectDrawSurface7 object. If this function succeeds, the pointer will be set to the texture surface currently assigned to the texture stage specified by the dwStage parameter.

Return Value	Description
D3D_OK	Direct3D successfully retrieved the texture assigned to the specified texture stage.
DDERR_INVALIDOBJECT	Direct3D could not retrieve the texture assigned to the specified texture stage, because this Direct3DDevice7 object is invalid.
DDERR_INVALIDPARAMS	Direct3D could not retrieve the texture assigned to the specified texture stage, because one or more parameters are invalid.

IDirect3DDevice7::GetTextureStageState ()	

Function Description

This function retrieves a state of a specified texture stage. This function retrieves a state as a 32-bit unsigned integer. Most states are specified in this format, but some are specified as floating-point numbers and others as structures. If an application is retrieving a floating-point state, it should cast the integer to a 32-bit floating-point number. If an application is retrieving a structure-based state, it should use the value of the integer as the address of the structure.

Function Declaration

```
HRESULT GetTextureStageState(
  DWORD   dwStage,
  D3DTEXTURESTAGESTATETYPE dwState,
  LPDWORD lpdwValue
);
```

Parameter	Description
dwStage	The texture stage whose state is being retrieved, in the range of 0 to 7.
dwState	Identifies the texture stage state to be retrieved. This parameter can be set to one of the following enumeration values:

- **D3DTSS_COLOROP**—The color blending operation, which determines the operation performed when two color channels are blended. This operation determines the color output for this texture stage.

  This state can be set to one of the following enumeration values:

  - **D3DTOP_ADD**—The color output is the sum of the texture stage's two color arguments. In equation form, $S_{rgb} = Arg1 + Arg2$.
  - **D3DTOP_ADDSIGNED**—The color output is the sum of the texture stage's two color arguments, minus 0.5. The range of output values is -0.5 to 0.5. In the equation form, $S_{rgb} = Arg1 + Arg2 - 0.5$.
  - **D3DTOP_ADDSIGNED2X**—The color output is the sum of the texture stage's two color arguments, minus 0.5, all multiplied by 2. The range of output values is -1.0 to 1.0. In equation form, $S_{rgb} = (Arg1 + Arg2 - 0.5) * 2.0$.
  - **D3DTOP_ADDSMOOTH**—The color output is the sum of the texture stage's two color arguments, minus their product. In equation form, $S_{rgb} = (Arg1 + Arg2) - (Arg1 * Arg2)$.
  - **D3DTOP_BLENDDIFFUSEALPHA**—The color output is a linear blend of the first argument with the second argument, using the interpolated alpha from each vertex. In equation form, $S_{rgb} = Arg1 * Alpha + Arg2 * (1.0 - Alpha)$, where **Alpha** ranges from 0.0 to 1.0.

(continued)

IDirect3DDevice7::GetTextureStageState () *(continued)*	
Parameter	**Description**
	• **D3DTOP_BLENDTEXTUREALPHA**—The color output is a linear blend of the first color argument with the second color argument, using the alpha from this stage's texture. In equation form, $S_{rgb} = Arg1 * Alpha + Arg2 * (1.0 - Alpha)$, where **Alpha** ranges from 0.0 to 1.0.
	• **D3DTOP_BLENDFACTORALPHA**—The color output is a linear blend of the first color argument with the second color argument, using a scalar alpha set with the **D3DRENDERSTATE_TEXTUREFACTOR** render state. In equation form, $S_{rgb} = Arg1 * Alpha + Arg2 * (1.0 - Alpha)$, where **Alpha** ranges from 0.0 to 1.0.
	• **D3DTOP_BLENDCURRENTALPHA**—The color output is a linear blend of the first color argument with the second color argument, using the alpha from the previous texture stage. In equation form, $S_{rgb} = Arg1 * Alpha + Arg2 * (1.0 - Alpha)$, where **Alpha** ranges from 0.0 to 1.0.
	• **D3DTOP_BLENDTEXTUREALPHAPM**—The color output is a linear blend of the first color argument with the second color argument, using premultiplied alpha. In equation form, $S_{rgb} = Arg1 + Arg2 * (1.0 - Alpha)$, where **Alpha** ranges from 0.0 to 1.0.
	• **D3DTOP_BUMPENVMAP**—The color output is a per-pixel bump-mapping using the bump map associated with this texture stage to perturb the texture coordinates of the environment map of the next texture stage, without luminance.
	• **D3DTOP_BUMPENVMAPLUMINANCE**—The color output is a per-pixel bump-mapping using the bump map associated with this texture stage to perturb the texture coordinates of the environment map of the next texture stage, with luminance.
	• **D3DTOP_DISABLE**—Color output from this texture stage and all texture stages with a higher index is disabled. Disabling the first texture stage (with index 0) disables texture mapping. This value is the default for the second and higher texture stages.
	• **D3DTOP_DOTPRODUCT3**—The color output is the dot product of the first and second arguments, replicated to all components, including alpha. In equation form, $S = Arg1_r * Arg2_r + Arg1_g * Arg2_g + Arg1_b * Arg2_b$, where $Arg1_r$, $Arg1_g$, and $Arg1_b$ are the red, green, and blue components of the first argument, respectively, and $Arg2_r$, $Arg2_g$, and $Arg2_b$ are the red, green, and blue components of the second argument, respectively.

(continued)

IDirect3DDevice7::GetTextureStageState () *(continued)*	
Parameter	**Description**
	• **D3DTOP_MODULATE**—The color output is the product of the texture stage's two color arguments. In equation form, S_{rgb} = **Arg1 * Arg2**. This value is the default for the first texture stage (texture stage index 0).
	• **D3DTOP_MODULATE2X**—The color output is the product of the texture stage's two color arguments, multiplied by 2. In equation form, S_{rgb} = **2.0 * Arg1 * Arg2**.
	• **D3DTOP_MODULATE4X**—The color output is the product of the texture stage's two color arguments, multiplied by 4. In equation form, S_{rgb} = **4.0 * Arg1 * Arg2**.
	• **D3DTOP_MODULATEALPHA_ADDCOLOR**—The color output is the sum of the first color argument and the product of the first color's alpha component and the second color argument. In equation form, S_{rgb} = **Arg1 + Arg1$_a$ * Arg2**, where **Arg1$_a$** is the alpha component of the first color argument.
	• **D3DTOP_MODULATECOLOR_ADDALPHA**—The color output is the sum of the first argument's alpha component and the product of the first color argument and the second color argument. In equation form, S_{rgb} = **Arg1 * Arg2 + Arg1$_a$**, where **Arg1$_a$** is the alpha component of the first color argument.
	• **D3DTOP_MODULATEINVALPHA_ADDCOLOR**—The color output is the sum of the first color argument and the product of the inverse of the first color's alpha component and the second color argument. In equation form, S_{rgb} = **Arg1 + (1.0 - Arg1$_a$) * Arg2**, where **Arg1$_a$** is the alpha component of the first color argument.
	• **D3DTOP_MODULATEINVCOLOR_ADDALPHA**—The color output is the sum of the first argument's alpha component and the product of the inverse of the first color argument and the second color argument. In equation form, S_{rgb} = **(1.0 - Arg1) * Arg2 + Arg1$_a$**, where **Arg1$_a$** is the alpha component of the first color argument.
	• **D3DTOP_PREMODULATE**—The color output is the product of this texture stage with the next texture stage.
	• **D3DTOP_SELECTARG1**—The color output is the color of the texture stage's first argument, unmodified.
	• **D3DTOP_SELECTARG2**—The color output is the color of the texture stage's second argument, unmodified.

(continued)

IDirect3DDevice7::GetTextureStageState () *(continued)*	
Parameter	**Description**
	• **D3DTOP_SUBTRACT**—The color output is the difference of the texture stage's two color arguments. In equation form, S_{rgb} = **Arg1 - Arg2**.
	• **D3DTSS_COLORARG1**—The first color argument, which determines the source of the color components for the texture stage's first argument. This state can be one of the following enumeration values:
	• **D3DTA_ALPHAREPLICATE**—Alpha information should be replicated to all color components before the operation completes. This value modifies another enumeration value that itself specifies the source for the argument's information.
	• **D3DTA_COMPLEMENT**—The first color argument should be inverted; that is, a color S_{rgba} should be translated to **1.0** - S_{rgba} before being used. This value modifies another enumeration value that itself specifies the source for the argument's information.
	• **D3DTA_CURRENT**—The first color argument is the output from the previous texture stage. For the first texture stage (stage index 0), this argument defaults to **D3DTA_DIFFUSE**.
	• **D3DTA_DIFFUSE**—The first color argument is the diffuse color interpolated from vertex components during Gouraud shading. If the primitive's vertices do not include a diffuse color, the default color is white.
	• **D3DTA_SELECTMASK**—The mask value for all arguments.
	• **D3DTA_SPECULAR**—The first color argument is the specular color interpolated from vertex components during Gouraud shading. If the vertices of the primitive do not include a specular color, the default is white.
	• **D3DTA_TEXTURE**—The first color argument is the color of the texture associated with this texture stage. This is the default value for this state.
	• **D3DTA_TFACTOR**—The first color argument is the texture factor as specified by the **D3DRENDERSTATE_TEXTURE** render state.
	• **D3DTSS_COLORARG2**—The second color argument, which determines the source of the color components for the texture stage's second argument. This state can be one of the following enumeration values:

(continued)

IDirect3DDevice7::GetTextureStageState () *(continued)*	
Parameter	**Description**
	• **D3DTA_ALPHAREPLICATE**—Alpha information should be replicated to all color components before the operation completes. This value modifies another enumeration value that itself specifies the source for the argument's information.
	• **D3DTA_COMPLEMENT**—The second color argument should be inverted; that is, a color S_{rgba} should be translated to **1.0 - S_{rgba}** before being used. This value modifies another enumeration value that itself specifies the source for the argument's information.
	• **D3DTA_CURRENT**—The second color argument is the output from the previous texture stage. For the first texture stage (stage index 0), this argument defaults to **D3DTA_DIFFUSE**.
	This is the default value for this state.
	• **D3DTA_DIFFUSE**—The second color argument is the diffuse color interpolated from vertex components during Gouraud shading. If the primitive's vertices do not include a diffuse color, the default color is white.
	• **D3DTA_SELECTMASK**—The mask value for all arguments.
	• **D3DTA_SPECULAR**—The second color argument is the specular color interpolated from vertex components during Gouraud shading. If the vertices of the primitive do not include a specular color, the default is white.
	• **D3DTA_TFACTOR**—The second color argument is the texture factor as specified by the **D3DRENDERSTATE_TEXTURE** render state.
	• **D3DTSS_ALPHAOP**— The alpha blending operation, which determines the operation performed when two alpha channels are blended. This operation determines the alpha output for this texture stage.
	This state can be set to one of the following enumeration values:
	• **D3DTOP_ADD**—The alpha output is the sum of the texture stage's two alpha arguments. In equation form, S_a = **Arg1 + Arg2**.
	• **D3DTOP_ADDSIGNED**—The alpha output is the sum of the texture stage's two alpha arguments, minus 0.5. The range of output values is -0.5 to 0.5. In the equation form, S_a = **Arg1 + Arg2 - 0.5**.

(continued)

IDirect3DDevice7::GetTextureStageState () *(continued)*	
Parameter	**Description**
	• **D3DTOP_ADDSIGNED2X**—The alpha output is the sum of the texture stage's two alpha arguments, minus 0.5, all multiplied by 2. The range of output values is -1.0 to 1.0. In equation form, $S_a = (Arg1 + Arg2 - 0.5) * 2.0$.
	• **D3DTOP_ADDSMOOTH**—The alpha output is the sum of the texture stage's two alpha arguments, minus their product. In equation form, $S_a = (Arg1 + Arg2) - (Arg1 * Arg2)$.
	• **D3DTOP_BLENDDIFFUSEALPHA**—The alpha output is a linear blend of the first argument with the second argument, using the interpolated alpha from each vertex. In equation form, $S_a = Arg1 * Alpha + Arg2 * (1.0 - Alpha)$, where **Alpha** ranges from 0.0 to 1.0.
	• **D3DTOP_BLENDTEXTUREALPHA**—The alpha output is a linear blend of the first alpha argument with the second alpha argument, using the alpha from this stage's texture. In equation form, $S_a = Arg1 * Alpha + Arg2 * (1.0 - Alpha)$, where **Alpha** ranges from 0.0 to 1.0.
	• **D3DTOP_BLENDFACTORALPHA**—The alpha output is a linear blend of the first alpha argument with the second alpha argument, using a scalar alpha set with the **D3DRENDERSTATE_TEXTUREFACTOR** render state. In equation form, $S_a = Arg1 * Alpha + Arg2 * (1.0 - Alpha)$, where **Alpha** ranges from 0.0 to 1.0.
	• **D3DTOP_BLENDCURRENTALPHA**—The alpha output is a linear blend of the first alpha argument with the second alpha argument, using the alpha from the previous texture stage. In equation form, $S_a = Arg1 * Alpha + Arg2 * (1.0 - Alpha)$, where **Alpha** ranges from 0.0 to 1.0.
	• **D3DTOP_BLENDTEXTUREALPHAPM**—The alpha output is a linear blend of the first alpha argument with the second alpha argument, using premultiplied alpha. In equation form, $S_a = Arg1 + Arg2 * (1.0 - Alpha)$, where **Alpha** ranges from 0.0 to 1.0.
	• **D3DTOP_DISABLE**—Alpha output from this texture stage and all texture stages with a higher index is disabled. Disabling the first texture stage (with index 0) disables alpha blending. This value is the default for the second and higher texture stages.

(continued)

IDirect3DDevice7::GetTextureStageState () *(continued)*	
Parameter	**Description**
	• **D3DTOP_DOTPRODUCT3**—The alpha output is the dot product of the first and second arguments. In equation form, $S_a = Arg1_r * Arg2_r + Arg1_g * Arg2_g + Arg1_b * Arg2_b$, where $Arg1_r$, $Arg1_g$, and $Arg1_b$ are the red, green, and blue components of the first argument, respectively; and $Arg2_r$, $Arg2_g$, and $Arg2_b$ are the red, green, and blue components of the second argument, respectively.
	• **D3DTOP_MODULATE**—The alpha output is the product of the texture stage's two alpha arguments. In equation form, $S_a = Arg1 * Arg2$.
	• **D3DTOP_MODULATE2X**—The alpha output is the product of the texture stage's two alpha arguments, multiplied by 2. In equation form, $S_a = 2.0 * Arg1 * Arg2$.
	• **D3DTOP_MODULATE4X**—The alpha output is the product of the texture stage's two alpha arguments, multiplied by 4. In equation form, $S_a = 4.0 * Arg1 * Arg2$.
	• **D3DTOP_PREMODULATE**—The alpha output is the product of this texture stage with the next texture stage.
	• **D3DTOP_SELECTARG1**—The alpha output is the alpha of the texture stage's first argument, unmodified. This value is the default for the first texture stage (texture stage index 0).
	• **D3DTOP_SELECTARG2**—The alpha output is the alpha of the texture stage's second argument, unmodified.
	• **D3DTOP_SUBTRACT**—The alpha output is the difference of the texture stage's two alpha arguments. In equation form, $S_a = Arg1 - Arg2$.
	• **D3DTSS_ALPHAARG1**—The first alpha argument, which determines the source of the alpha component for the texture stage's first argument. This state can be one of the following enumeration values:
	• **D3DTA_ALPHAREPLICATE**—Alpha information should be replicated to all components before the operation completes. This value modified another enumeration value that itself specifies the source for the argument's information.
	• **D3DTA_COMPLEMENT**—The first alpha argument should be inverted; that is, an alpha S_a should be translated to $1.0 - S_a$ before being used. This value modified another enumeration value that itself specifies the source for the argument's information.
	• **D3DTA_CURRENT**—The first alpha argument is the output from the previous texture stage. For the first texture stage (stage index 0), this argument defaults to **D3DTA_DIFFUSE**.

(continued)

IDirect3DDevice7::GetTextureStageState () *(continued)*	
Parameter	**Description**
	• **D3DTA_DIFFUSE**—The first alpha argument is the diffuse alpha interpolated from vertex components during Gouraud shading. If the primitive's vertices do not include diffuse alpha information, the default alpha is 0×FFFFFFFF. This is the default value if no texture is associated with this texture stage; otherwise, the default is **D3DTA_TEXTURE**. • **D3DTA_SELECTMASK**—The mask value for all arguments. • **D3DTA_SPECULAR**—The first alpha argument is the specular alpha interpolated from vertex components during Gouraud shading. If the vertices of the primitive do not include specular alpha information, the default is 0×FFFFFFFF. • **D3DTA_TEXTURE**—The first alpha argument is the alpha of the texture associated with this texture stage. This is the default value unless no texture is associated with this texture stage, in which case the default value is **D3DTA_DIFFUSE**. • **D3DTA_TFACTOR**—The first alpha argument is the texture factor as specified by the **D3DRENDERSTATE_TEXTURE** render state. • **D3DTSS_ALPHAARG2**—The second alpha argument, which determines the source of the alpha component for the texture stage's second argument. This state can be one of the following enumeration values: • **D3DTA_ALPHAREPLICATE**—Alpha information should be replicated to all alpha components before the operation completes. This value modified another enumeration value that itself specifies the source for the argument's information. • **D3DTA_COMPLEMENT**—The second alpha argument should be inverted; that is, an alpha **S** should be translated to **1.0 - S** before being used. This value modified another enumeration value that itself specifies the source for the argument's information. • **D3DTA_CURRENT**—The second alpha argument is the output from the previous texture stage. For the first texture stage (stage index 0), this argument defaults to **D3DTA_-DIFFUSE**. This is the default value for this state. • **D3DTA_DIFFUSE**—The second alpha argument is the diffuse alpha interpolated from vertex components during Gouraud shading. If the primitive's vertices do not include diffuse alpha information, the default alpha is 0×FFFFFFFF.

(continued)

IDirect3DDevice7::GetTextureStageState () *(continued)*	
Parameter	**Description**
	• **D3DTA_SELECTMASK**—The mask value for all arguments.
	• **D3DTA_SPECULAR**—The second alpha argument is the specular alpha interpolated from vertex components during Gouraud shading. If the vertices of the primitive do not include specular alpha information, the default is 0×FFFFFFFF.
	• **D3DTA_TFACTOR**—The second alpha argument is the texture factor as specified by the **D3DRENDERSTATE_-TEXTURE** render state.
	• **D3DTSS_BUMPENVMAT00**—The [0][0] coefficient in the bump-mapping matrix, specified as a **D3DVALUE**. This 2×2 matrix is applied to bump-map values and can be used by an application to scale, offset, or otherwise transform bump-map values.
	The default value for this state is 0.0.
	• **D3DTSS_BUMPENVMAT01**—The [0][1] coefficient in the bump-mapping matrix, specified as a **D3DVALUE**. This 2×2 matrix is applied to bump-map values and can be used by an application to scale, offset, or otherwise transform bump-map values.
	The default value for this state is 0.0.
	• **D3DTSS_BUMPENVMAT10**—The [1][0] coefficient in the bump-mapping matrix, specified as a **D3DVALUE**. This 2×2 matrix is applied to bump-map values and can be used by an application to scale, offset, or otherwise transform bump-map values.
	The default value for this state is 0.0.
	• **D3DTSS_BUMPENVMAT11**—The [1][1] coefficient in the bump-mapping matrix, specified as a **D3DVALUE**. This 2×2 matrix is applied to bump-map values and can be used by an application to scale, offset, or otherwise transform bump-map values.
	The default value for this state is 0.0.
	• **D3DTSS_TEXCOORDINDEX**—The index of the texture coordinate set to be used with this texture stage. The default value for this state is 0, indicating the first texture coordinate set will be used.
	If a texture is associated with this texture stage, then the texture coordinate set specified by this state will be used to determine the texture coordinates for a primitive's vertices. If a vertex does not specify texture coordinate information for a given set, the default *u-*, *v*-coordinates are (0, 0).

(continued)

IDirect3DDevice7::GetTextureStageState () *(continued)*	
Parameter	**Description**
	The current maximum for this state is seven, allowing a total of eight texture coordinate sets.
	This state can also include with the texture coordinate set index one of a series of predefined flags. If an application includes one of these flags, then the texture coordinate set specified will be used only to determine the texture wrapping mode for the specified texture stage. It will not be used to extract texture coordinate information.
	The predefined constants are listed below:
	• **D3DTSS_TCI_CAMERASPACENORMAL**—Direct3D uses the transformed, camera-space vertex normal of a vertex to determine the texture coordinates for that vertex.
	This flag is primarily useful for environment mapping.
	• **D3DTSS_TCI_CAMERASPACEPOSITION**— Direct3D uses the transformed, camera-space vertex position of a vertex to determine the texture coordinates for that vertex.
	This flag is primarily useful for environment mapping.
	• **D3DTSS_TCI_CAMERASPACEREFLECTIONVECTOR**—Direct3D calculates a reflection vector to determine the texture coordinates for a vertex. The reflection vector is calculated in the following manner: A vector (representing a ray of light) is sent out from the camera to the vertex, and then reflected off the plane determined by the vertex normal at that vertex. The reflected vector then intersects the environment map, and the resulting intersection is used to determine the texture coordinates for the vertex.
	This flag is primarily useful for cubic environment mapping. Applications should use this flag rather than calculate their own texture coordinates because on some hardware devices this operation is accelerated.
	To specify the second texture coordinate set and the **D3DTSS_TCI_CAMERASPACENORMAL** flag, an application would use the render state generated by the following code: (**1** | **D3DTSS_TCI_CAMERASPACENORMAL**).
	• **D3DTSS_ADDRESS**—The texture addressing method for both *u*- and *v*-texture coordinates. This determines how the system treats *u*- and *v*-values outside the [0.0, 1.0] range.
	This state can be set to one of the following enumeration values:
	• **D3DTADDRESS_WRAP**—Textures are tiled at every integer junction. This is the default value for this state.

(continued)

IDirect3DDevice7::GetTextureStageState () *(continued)*	
Parameter	**Description**

Description column:

- **D3DTADDRESS_MIRROR**—Textures are tiled at every integer junction, but are mirrored (flipped) at every other junction to facilitate seamless texture wrapping.
- **D3DTADDRESS_CLAMP**—Texture coordinates outside the [0.0, 1.0] range are clamped to 0.0 and 1.0, respectively.
- **D3DTADDRESS_BORDER**—Texture coordinates outside the [0.0, 1.0] range are set to the border color, which is determined by the **D3DTSS_BORDERCOLOR** texture stage state.

- **D3DTSS_ADDRESSU**—The texture addressing method for *u*-texture coordinates. This determines how the system treats *u*-values outside the [0.0, 1.0] range.

This state can be set to one of the following enumeration values:

- **D3DTADDRESS_WRAP**—Textures are tiled at every integer junction. This is the default value for this state.
- **D3DTADDRESS_MIRROR**—Textures are tiled at every integer junction, but are mirrored (flipped) at every other junction to facilitate seamless texture wrapping.
- **D3DTADDRESS_CLAMP**—Texture coordinates outside the [0.0, 1.0] range are clamped to 0.0 and 1.0, respectively.
- **D3DTADDRESS_BORDER**—Texture coordinates outside the [0.0, 1.0] range are set to the border color, which is determined by the **D3DTSS_BORDERCOLOR** texture stage state.

- **D3DTSS_ADDRESSV**—The texture addressing method for *v*-texture coordinates. This determines how the system treats *v*-values outside the [0.0, 1.0] range.

This state can be set to one of the following enumeration values:

- **D3DTADDRESS_WRAP**—Textures are tiled at every integer junction. This is the default value for this state.
- **D3DTADDRESS_MIRROR**—Textures are tiled at every integer junction, but are mirrored (flipped) at every other junction to facilitate seamless texture wrapping.
- **D3DTADDRESS_CLAMP**—Texture coordinates outside the [0.0, 1.0] range are clamped to 0.0 and 1.0, respectively.
- **D3DTADDRESS_BORDER**—Texture coordinates outside the [0.0, 1.0] range are set to the border color, which is determined by the **D3DTSS_BORDERCOLOR** texture stage state.

(continued)

IDirect3DDevice7::GetTextureStageState () *(continued)*

Parameter	Description
	• **D3DTSS_BORDERCOLOR**—The border color, which determines the color to be used for rasterizing texture coordinates in the [0.0,1.0] range, when the texture addressing mode is set to **D3DTADDRESS_BORDER**. The default color is 0×00000000, or black.
	• **D3DTSS_MAGFILTER**—The filter the system uses when a texel (a pixel in a texture map) is mapped to more than one screen coordinate. This occurs when a primitive occupies more screen space than the primitive's texture. The filter determines how the system handles this case.
	This state can be set to one or, on occasion, more of the following enumeration values:
	• **D3DTFG_POINT**—Nearest point filtering. The system selects the texel with coordinates nearest to the calculated texel. This is the default value for this state.
	• **D3DTFG_LINEAR**—Bilinear interpolation filtering. The system generates a weighted average of a 2×2 area of texels surrounding the calculated texel.
	• **D3DTFG_ANISOTROPIC**—Anisotropic texture filtering, which compensates for the difference in angle between the polygon and the camera. This value may be used in combination with **D3DTFN_POINT** or **D3DTFN_LINEAR**.
	• **D3DTSS_MINFILTER**—The filter the system uses when a pixel in the render-target surface is mapped to more than one texel (a pixel in a texture map). This occurs when a primitive occupies less screen space than the primitive's texture. The filter determines how the system handles this case.
	This state can be set to one or, on occasion, more of the following enumeration values:
	• **D3DTFN_POINT**—Nearest point filtering. The system selects the texel with coordinates nearest to the calculated texel. This is the default value for this state.
	• **D3DTFN_LINEAR**—Bilinear interpolation filtering. The system generates a weighted average of a 2×2 area of texels surrounding the calculated texel.
	• **D3DTFN_ANISOTROPIC**—Anisotropic texture filtering, which compensates for the difference in angle between the polygon and the camera. This value may be used in combination with **D3DTFN_POINT** or **D3DTFN_LINEAR**.
	• **D3DTSS_MIPFILTER**—The filter the system uses when performing mipmapping. The filter determines how the system selects the appropriate texel (a pixel in a texture map) when performing mipmapping.

(continued)

IDirect3DDevice7::GetTextureStageState () (continued)	
Parameter	**Description**
	This state can be set to one of the following enumeration values:
	• **D3DTFP_NONE**—Mipmapping is disabled. This is the default value for this state.
	• **D3DTFP_POINT**—Nearest point filtering. The system selects the texel of the nearest mipmap texture.
	• **D3DTFP_LINEAR**—Trilinear mipmap filtering. The system linearly interpolates pixel color using the calculated texels of the two nearest mipmap textures.
	• **D3DTSS_MIPMAPLODBIAS**—The level-of-detail bias for mipmapping, which can be used to make textures appear more or less pixelated. The default value for this state is 0.
	• **D3DTSS_MAXMIPLEVEL**—The maximum mipmap level of detail that the system should use, specified as a zero-based index, where 0 corresponds to the highest level of detail in the mipmap chain. The default value for this state is 0, indicating all mipmap levels can be used.
	• **D3DTSS_MAXANISOTROPY**—The maximum level of anisotropy. The default value for this state is 1.
	• **D3DTSS_BUMPENVLSCALE**—The bump-map luminance scale, which is used to scale bump-map values. This is specified as a **D3DVALUE**, whose default is 0.0.
	• **D3DTSS_BUMPENVLOFFSET**—The offset for bump-map luminance, added to bump-map luminance values. This is specified as a **D3DVALUE**, whose default is 0.0.
	• **D3DTSS_TEXTURETRANSFORMFLAGS**—The texture transformation flags, which determine if and how texture coordinates are transformed.
	This state can be set to one or, on occasion, more of the following values:
	• **D3DTTFF_DISABLE**—Texture transformation is disabled. This is the default value for this state.
	• **D3DTTFF_COUNT1**—The rasterizer should expect 1D texture coordinates.
	• **D3DTTFF_COUNT2**—The rasterizer should expect 2D texture coordinates.
	• **D3DTTFF_COUNT3**—The rasterizer should expect 3D texture coordinates.
	• **D3DTTFF_COUNT4**—The rasterizer should expect 4D texture coordinates.

(continued)

IDirect3DDevice7::GetTextureStageState () *(continued)*

Parameter	Description
	• **D3DTTFF_PROJECTED**—Texture coordinates should all be divided by their last component before being sent to the rasterizer.
lpdwValue	The address of a variable or structure, depending on the texture stage state being retrieved. If this function succeeds, the variable or structure will be filled with the state of the texture stage specified by **dwStage**.

Return Value	Description
D3D_OK	Direct3D successfully retrieved the state of the specified texture stage.
DDERR_INVALIDOBJECT	Direct3D could not retrieve the state of the specified render stage, because this Direct3DDevice7 object is invalid.
DDERR_INVALIDPARAMS	Direct3D could not retrieve the state of the specified render stage, because one or more parameters are invalid.

IDirect3DDevice7::GetTransform ()

Function Description

This function retrieves the matrix associated with a specified transformation stage.

Function Declaration

```
HRESULT GetTransform(
  D3DTRANSFORMSTATETYPE dtstTransformStateType,
  LPD3DMATRIX lpD3DMatrix
);
```

Parameter	Description
dtstTransformStateType	The transformation matrix being retrieved. This parameter can be one of the following enumeration values:
	• **D3DTRANSFORMSTATE_WORLD**—The world transformation matrix is being retrieved. The default value for this matrix is the identity matrix.
	• **D3DTRANSFORMSTATE_WORLD1** through **D3DTRANSFORMSTATE_WORLD3**—World transformation matrices 1 through 3, which are used when blending vertices.
	• **D3DTRANSFORMSTATE_VIEW**—The view transformation matrix is being retrieved. The default value for this matrix is the identity matrix.
	• **D3DTRANSFORMSTATE_PROJECTION**—The projection transformation matrix is being retrieved. The default value for this matrix is the identity matrix.

(continued)

IDirect3DDevice7::GetTransform () *(continued)*

Parameter	Description
	• **D3DTRANSFORMSTATE_TEXTURE0** through **D3DTRANS-FORMSTATE_TEXTURE7**—The transformation matrix associated with the 0 through 7th texture coordinate transformation stage is being retrieved.
lpD3DMatrix	A pointer to a **D3DMATRIX** structure. If this function succeeds, the structure will be filled with the coefficients of the matrix for the specified transformation stage.
Return Value	**Description**
D3D_OK	Direct3D successfully retrieved the specified transformation matrix.
DDERR_INVALIDPARAMS	Direct3D could not retrieve the specified transformation matrix, because one or more parameters are invalid.

IDirect3DDevice7::GetViewport ()

Function Description

This function retrieves the current viewport parameters for the device represented by this **Direct3DDevice7** object. The viewport defines the range of x-, y-, and z-values that primitives will be rendered into.

After undergoing the projection transformation stage, the horizontal, vertical, and depth components of a primitive's vertices will be scaled into the horizontal, vertical, and depth ranges specified by the viewport. Unless an application wishes to render to only a portion of the render-target surface, the horizontal and vertical viewport ranges will correspond to the width and height of the render-target surface, respectively, while the depth range will typically be set to [0.0, 1.0].

Function Declaration

```
HRESULT GetViewport(
  LPD3DVIEWPORT7 lpViewport
);
```

Parameter	Description
lpViewport	A pointer to a **D3DVIEWPORT7** structure. If this function succeeds, the structure will be filled with the current viewport parameters.
Return Value	**Description**
D3D_OK	Direct3D successfully retrieved the current viewport parameters.
DDERR_INVALIDPARAMS	Direct3D could not retrieve the current viewport parameters, because one or more parameters are invalid.

IDirect3DDevice7::LightEnable ()

Function Description

This function enables or disables a light source.

Function Declaration

```
HRESULT LightEnable(
  DWORD dwLightIndex,
  BOOL bEnable
);
```

Parameter	Description
dwLightIndex	The zero-based index of the light source being enabled or disabled. If this index is greater than the index of the last light source created, this function will create a new directional light source, colored white, that points along the positive z-axis.
bEnable	A Win32 **BOOL** value that indicates whether Direct3D should enable or disable the specified light source. If this parameter is **TRUE**, Direct3D enables the light source. If it is set to **FALSE**, Direct3D disables it.

Return Value	Description
D3D_OK	Direct3D successfully enabled or disabled the specified light source.
DDERR_INVALIDPARAMS	Direct3D could not enable or disable the specified light source, because one or more parameters are invalid.

IDirect3DDevice7::Load ()

Function Description

This function loads a rectangular area of a source texture to a specified point on a destination texture or to faces of a cubic environment map. The destination texture and source texture need not have been created by the same device.

This function can be hardware accelerated and is recommended over blit operations for loading textures into video memory.

Function Declaration

```
HRESULT Load(
  LPDIRECTDRAWSURACE7 lpDestTex,
  LPPOINT lpDestPoint,
  LPDIRECTDRAWSURACE7 lpSrcTex,
  LPRECT lprcSrcRect,
  DWORD dwFlags
);
```

Parameter	Description
lpDestTex	A pointer to a DirectDrawSurface7 object that identifies the destination texture. This texture may be a cubic environment map.

(continued)

IDirect3DDevice7::Load () *(continued)*	
Parameter	**Description**
lpDestPoint	A pointer to a Win32 **POINT** structure that identifies the point on the destination texture at which Direct3D should load the source texture. This parameter may be **NULL**, in which case the destination point is assumed to be the origin of the destination texture.
lpSrcTex	A pointer to a DirectDrawSurface7 object that identifies the source texture.
lprcSrcRect	A pointer to a Win32 **RECT** structure that identifies the area within the source texture that should be loaded onto the destination texture. This parameter may be **NULL**, in which case the source rectangle is assumed to cover the entire source texture.
dwFlags	Describes which face of the destination texture should receive the image data. This parameter, which must be 0 unless the source texture is being loaded onto a cubic environment map, can be one of the following flags:
	• **DDSCAPS2_CUBEMAP_ALLFACES**—All faces should receive the image data of the source texture.
	• **DDSCAPS2_CUBEMAP_NEGATIVEX**—The face oriented toward the negative x-axis should receive the image data of the source texture.
	• **DDSCAPS2_CUBEMAP_NEGATIVEY**—The face oriented toward the negative y-axis should receive the image data of the source texture.
	• **DDSCAPS2_CUBEMAP_NEGATIVEZ**—The face oriented toward the negative z-axis should receive the image data of the source texture.
	• **DDSCAPS2_CUBEMAP_POSITIVEX**—The face oriented toward the positive x-axis should receive the image data of the source texture.
	• **DDSCAPS2_CUBEMAP_POSITIVEY**—The face oriented toward the positive y-axis should receive the image data of the source texture.
	• **DDSCAPS2_CUBEMAP_POSITIVEZ**—The face oriented toward the positive z-axis should receive the image data of the source texture.
Return Value	**Description**
D3D_OK	Direct3D successfully loaded the specified texture.
DDERR_INVALIDOBJECT	Direct3D could not load the specified texture, because this Direct3DDevice7 object is invalid.
DDERR_INVALIDPARAMS	Direct3D could not load the specified texture, because one or more parameters are invalid.

IDirect3DDevice7::MultiplyTransform ()

Function Description

This function concatenates the device's world, view, or projection matrix with a specified matrix. This is useful for hierarchical transformations.

The order of multiplication is **lpbD3DMatrix** times **dtstTransformStateType**.

Function Declaration

```
HRESULT MultiplyTransform(
  D3DTRANSFORMSTATETYPE dtstTransformStateType,
  LPD3DMATRIX lpD3DMatrix
);
```

Parameter	Description
dtstTransformStateType	The matrix that should be used in the concatenation. This parameter can be one of the following enumeration values: • **D3DTRANSFORMSTATE_WORLD**—The world transformation matrix is being used. • **D3DTRANSFORMSTATE_VIEW**—The view transformation matrix is being used. • **D3DTRANSFORMSTATE_PROJECTION**—The projection transformation matrix is being used.
lpD3DMatrix	A pointer to a **D3DMATRIX** structure that identifies the matrix to be used in the concatenation.

Return Value	Description
D3D_OK	Direct3D successfully performed the matrix multiplication.
DDERR_INVALIDPARAMS	Direct3D could not perform the matrix multiplication, because one or more parameters are invalid.

IDirect3DDevice7::PreLoad ()

Function Description

This function forces Direct3D to load a managed texture into video memory, causing other textures to be evicted if sufficient free memory is not available. This function is valid only for managed textures.

Function Declaration

```
HRESULT PreLoad(
  LPDIRECTDRAWSURFACE7 lpddsTexture
);
```

Parameter	Description
lpddsTexture	A pointer to a DirectDrawSurface7 object that identifies the texture to be loaded into video memory. This texture must be managed by Direct3D, or else this function will fail.

(continued)

IDirect3DDevice7::PreLoad () *(continued)*	
Return Value	**Description**
D3D_OK	Direct3D successfully preloaded the specified texture.
DDERR_INVALIDOBJECT	Direct3D could not preload the specified texture, because this Direct3DDevice7 object is invalid.
DDERR_INVALIDPARAMS	Direct3D could not preload the specified texture, because one or more parameters are invalid.

IDirect3DDevice7::SetClipPlane ()

Function Description

This function sets the coefficients of the plane equation for an application-defined clipping plane. Application-defined clipping planes are nonstandard clipping planes used to delineate the boundaries of the geometry that should be visible.

The coefficients retrieved by this equation are the A, B, C, and D coefficients of the plane equation. All points that, when plugged into the plane equation, result in a negative value ($Ax + By + Cz + Dw < 0$) and, hence, lie on the side of the plane opposite the direction of its normal, are considered to lie outside the plane and are therefore clipped from the scene.

An application can retrieve arbitrary clipping planes by calling the **IDirect3DDevice7::GetClipPlane ()** function.

Function Declaration

```
HRESULT SetClipPlane(
  DWORD dwIndex,
  D3DVALUE* pPlaneEquation
);
```

Parameter	Description
dwIndex	The index designating the clipping plane whose plane equation coefficients are being set.
pPlaneEquation	An array of four floating-point integers that specify the clipping plane's coefficients.
Return Value	**Description**
D3D_OK	Direct3D successfully set the plane equation coefficients for the specified user-defined clipping plane.
DDERR_INVALIDPARAMS	Direct3D could not set the plane equation coefficients for the specified user-defined clipping plane, because one or more parameters are invalid.

IDirect3DDevice7::SetClipStatus ()

Function Description

This function sets the clip status for the device.

Function Declaration

```
HRESULT SetClipStatus(
  LPD3DCLIPSTATUS lpD3DClipStatus
);
```

Parameter	Description
lpD3DClipStatus	A pointer to a **D3DCLIPSTATUS** structure that describes the new settings for the clip status.

Return Value	Description
D3D_OK	Direct3D successfully set the clip status for the device.
DDERR_INVALIDPARAMS	Direct3D could not set the clip status, because one or more parameters are invalid.

IDirect3DDevice7::SetLight ()

Function Description

This function sets the parameters of an existing light source or creates a new one for the device.

Function Declaration

```
HRESULT SetLight(
  DWORD dwLightIndex,
  LPD3DLIGHT7 lpLight
);
```

Parameter	Description
dwLightIndex	The zero-based index that identifies the light source whose parameters are being set. If this index is greater than the index of the last light source set, this function will create a new light source with the specified settings.
lpLight	A pointer to a **D3DLIGHT7** structure that describes the parameters of the light to be set or created.

Return Value	Description
D3D_OK	Direct3D successfully set the parameters of the light source.
DDERR_INVALIDOBJECT	Direct3D could not set the parameters of the light source, because this Direct3DDevice object is invalid.
DDERR_INVALIDPARAMS	Direct3D could not set the parameters of the light source, because one or more parameters are invalid.
DDERR_OUTOFMEMORY	Direct3D could not set the parameters of the light source, because sufficient memory is not available.

IDirect3DDevice7::SetMaterial ()

Function Description

This function sets the material properties for all rendered primitives.

Function Declaration

```
HRESULT SetMaterial(
  LPD3DMATERIAL7 lpMaterial
);
```

Parameter	Description
lpMaterial	A pointer to a **D3DMATERIAL7** structure that describes the material properties to be set.

Return Value	Description
D3D_OK	Direct3D successfully set the material properties for the device.
DDERR_INVALIDOBJECT	Direct3D could not set the material properties for the device, because this Direct3DDevice7 object is invalid.
DDERR_INVALIDPARAMS	Direct3D could not set the material properties for the device, because one or more parameters are invalid.

IDirect3DDevice7::SetRenderState ()

Function Description

This function retrieves a single rendering state parameter for the device represented by this **Direct3DDevice7** object.

Function Declaration

```
HRESULT SetRenderState(
  D3DRENDERSTATETYPE dwRenderStateType,
  DWORD dwRenderState
);
```

Parameter	Description
dwRenderStateType	Describes the state to be set. This parameter can be one of the following enumeration values:
	• **D3DRENDERSTATE_ANTIALIAS**—The full-scene antialias state, which determines the desired type of full-scene antialiasing. Full-scene antialiasing is when polygons are rendered with antialiased edges in one pass, as they are rendered into the target surface. This type of antialiasing does not work for lines, and is valid only for devices that support the **D3DPRASTERCAPS_ANTIALIASSORTINDEPENDENT** or **D3DPRASTERCAPS_ANTIALIASSORTDEPENDENT** capabilities.
	This state can be set to one of the following enumeration values:

(continued)

IDirect3DDevice7::SetRenderState () *(continued)*

Parameter	Description
	• **D3DANTIALIAS_NONE**—No full-scene antialiasing is performed. This is the default value for this state.
	• **D3DANTIALIAS_SORTDEPENDENT**—Sort dependent full-scene antialiasing is performed. In sort dependent antialiasing, the order in which the polygons are displayed matters—the application must display them in the proper order, whether front to back, or back to front, as determined by the capabilities of the hardware device.
	• **D3DANTIALIAS_SORTINDEPENDENT**—Sort independent full-scene antialiasing is performed. In sort independent antialiasing, the order in which the polygons are displayed does not matter. Sort independent full-scene antialiasing is slower them sort dependent antialiasing on some hardware devices.
	• **D3DRENDERSTATE_TEXTUREPERSPECTIVE**—The texture perspective state, which determines whether or not perspective-corrected texture mapping is enabled. Perspective-correct texture mapping is more accurate than linear texture mapping, the alternative.
	This state can be set to one of the following values:
	• **TRUE**—Perspective-corrected texture mapping is enabled. This is the default value for this state.
	• **FALSE**—Perspective-corrected texture mapping is disabled.
	• **D3DRENDERSTATE_ZENABLE**—The depth enable state, which determines whether or not depth buffering is enabled, and if so, what type of depth buffering is enabled. This state can be set to one of the following enumeration values:
	• **D3DZB_TRUE**—z-based depth buffering is enabled. This is the default value for this state if a depth buffer is attached to the render-target surface.
	• **D3DZB_USEW**—w-based depth buffering is enabled.
	• **D3DZB_FALSE**—Depth buffering is not enabled.
	• **D3DRENDERSTATE_FILLMODE**—The fill mode state, which describes how primitives are rendered. This state can be set to one of the following enumeration values:
	• **D3DFILL_POINT**—The vertices of primitives are rendered as points.
	• **D3DFILL_WIREFRAME**—Primitives are rendered in wireframe (that is, the edges of polygons are displayed as lines). This state does not work for clipped primitives.

(continued)

IDirect3DDevice7::SetRenderState () *(continued)*	
Parameter	**Description**
	• **D3DFILL_SOLID**—The primitives are rendered solid. This is the default value for this state.
	• **D3DRENDERSTATE_SHADEMODE**—The shade mode state, which describes how triangles are shaded. This state can be set to one of the following enumeration values:
	• **D3DSHADE_FLAT**—Triangles are rendered in flat shade mode. In this mode, the entire face of a triangle is shaded the same color, determined by the color and specular component of the first vertex in the triangle.
	• **D3DSHADE_GOURAUD**—Triangles are rendered in Gouraud shade mode. In this mode, the color and specular components of a pixel in the triangle are determined by a linear interpolation between the color and specular components of all three of the triangle's vertices. This is the default value for this state.
	• **D3DSHADE_PHONG**—Triangles are rendered in Phong shade mode. This mode is not currently supported.
	• **D3DRENDERSTATE_LINEPATTERN**—The line pattern state, which describes the pattern used when Direct3D draws lines. This is specified by a **D3DLINEPATTERN** structure.
	The default value for this state is a **D3DLINEPATTERN** structure whose **wRepeatPattern** and **wLinePattern** members are 0.
	• **D3DRENDERSTATE_ZWRITEENABLE**—The depth buffer write enable state, which describes whether or not writing to the depth buffer is enabled. This state can be set to one of the following values:
	• **TRUE**—Writing to the depth buffer is enabled. This is the default value for this state.
	• **FALSE**—Writing to the depth buffer is disabled. Depth comparisons will still take place if enabled, but depth values will not be written to the depth buffer.
	• **D3DRENDERSTATE_ALPHATESTENABLE**—The alpha test enable state, which determines whether or not alpha comparisons are enabled. Alpha comparisons, if enabled, prevent alpha blending from occurring unless the alpha comparison function succeeds.
	This state can be set to one of the following values:
	• **TRUE**—Alpha comparisons are enabled.
	• **FALSE**—Alpha comparisons are disabled. This is the default value for this state.

(continued)

IDirect3DDevice7::SetRenderState () *(continued)*	
Parameter	**Description**
	• **D3DRENDERSTATE_LASTPIXEL**—The draw last pixel state, which determines whether or not Direct3D fills the last pixel in a line or row of a triangle. This state can be set to one of the following values:
	• **TRUE**—Last-pixel filling is enabled. This is the default value for this state.
	• **FALSE**—Last-pixel filling is disabled.
	• **D3DRENDERSTATE_SRCBLEND**—The source blend state, which determines the blend factor for source blend operations. The blend factor is a series of four floating-point values that range from 0.0 (completely transparent) to 1.0 (completely opaque). These values describe the proportions of red, green, blue, and alpha in the source that will be used when blending the source pixels with those in the destination.
	This state can be set to one of the following enumeration values:
	• **D3DBLEND_ZERO**—The blend factor is (0, 0, 0, 0).
	• **D3DBLEND_ONE**—The blend factor is (1, 1, 1, 1). This is the default value for this state.
	• **D3DBLEND_SRCCOLOR**—The blend factor is (R_s, G_s, B_s, A_s), where R_s, G_s, B_s, and A_s are the red, green, blue, and alpha components of the source, respectively.
	• **D3DBLEND_INVSRCCOLOR**—The blend factor is ($1-R_s$, $1-G_s$, $1-B_s$, $1-A_s$), where R_s, G_s, B_s, and A_s are the red, green, blue, and alpha components of the source, respectively.
	• **D3DBLEND_SRCALPHA**—The blend factor is (A_s, A_s, A_s, A_s), where A_s is the alpha component of the source.
	• **D3DBLEND_INVSRCALPHA**—The blend factor is ($1-A_s$, $1-A_s$, $1-A_s$, $1-A_s$), where A_s is the alpha component of the source.
	• **D3DBLEND_DESTALPHA**—The blend factor is (A_d, A_d, A_d, A_d), where A_d is the alpha component of the destination.
	• **D3DBLEND_INVDESTALPHA**—The blend factor is ($1-A_d$, $1-A_d$, $1-A_d$, $1-A_d$), where A_d is the alpha component of the destination.
	• **D3DBLEND_DESTCOLOR**—The blend factor is (R_d, G_d, B_d, A_d), where R_d, G_d, B_d, and A_d are the red, green, blue, and alpha components of the destination, respectively.

(continued)

IDirect3DDevice7::SetRenderState () *(continued)*	
Parameter	**Description**
	• **D3DBLEND_INVDESTCOLOR**—The blend factor is $(1-R_d, 1-G_d, 1-B_d, 1-A_d)$, where R_d, G_d, B_d, and A_d are the red, green, blue, and alpha components of the destination, respectively.
	• **D3DBLEND_SRCALPHASAT**—The blend factor is (f, f, f, f), where $f = A_s$ (the alpha component of the source) or $1-A_d$ (the inverse of the alpha component of the destination), whichever is lower.
	• **D3DBLEND_BOTHINVSRCALPHA**—This value controls both source and destination blend values. The destination blend value is overridden.
	The source blend factor is $(1-A_s, 1-A_s, 1-A_s, 1-A_s)$, where A_s is the alpha component of the source. The destination blend factor is (A_s, A_s, A_s, A_s).
	• **D3DRENDERSTATE_DESTBLEND**—The destination blend state, which determines the blend factor for destination blend operations. The blend factor is a series of four floating-point values that range from 0.0 (completely transparent) to 1.0 (completely opaque). These values describe the proportions of red, green, blue, and alpha in the destination surface that will be used when blending the source pixels with those in the source.
	This state can be set to one of the following enumeration values:
	• **D3DBLEND_ZERO**—The blend factor is (0, 0, 0, 0). This is the default value for this state.
	• **D3DBLEND_ONE**—The blend factor is (1, 1, 1, 1).
	• **D3DBLEND_DESTALPHA**—The blend factor is (A_d, A_d, A_d, A_d), where A_d is the alpha component of the destination.
	• **D3DBLEND_INVDESTALPHA**—The blend factor is $(1-A_d, 1-A_d, 1-A_d, 1-A_d)$, where A_d is the alpha component of the destination.
	• **D3DBLEND_DESTCOLOR**—The blend factor is (R_d, G_d, B_d, A_d), where R_d, G_d, B_d, and A_d are the red, green, blue, and alpha components of the destination, respectively.
	• **D3DBLEND_INVDESTCOLOR**—The blend factor is $(1-R_d, 1-G_d, 1-B_d, 1-A_d)$, where R_d, G_d, B_d, and A_d are the red, green, blue, and alpha components of the destination, respectively.

(continued)

IDirect3DDevice7::SetRenderState () *(continued)*	
Parameter	**Description**
	• **D3DRENDERSTATE_CULLMODE**—The cull mode state, which determines whether and in what manner back-face culling is performed. This state can be set to one of the following enumeration values:
	• **D3DCULL_NONE**—Back-face culling is not performed.
	• **D3DCULL_CW**—Back-face culling is performed on all polygons whose vertices are defined in a clockwise fashion when viewed from the direction pointed to by their surface normals.
	• **D3DCULL_CCW**—Back-face culling is performed on all polygons whose vertices are defined in a counterclockwise fashion when viewed from the direction pointed to by their surface normals. This is the default value for this state.
	• **D3DRENDERSTATE_ZFUNC**—The depth compare function state, which determines the function used when comparing depth values. This function is used only when depth buffering is enabled.
	This state can be one of the following enumeration values:
	• **D3DCMP_NEVER**—The function always evaluates to false. No new pixels are displayed.
	• **D3DCMP_LESS**—The function evaluates to **TRUE** only if the new pixel has a depth less than that of the current pixel.
	Otherwise, the function evaluates to **FALSE**, and the new pixel is not displayed.
	• **D3DCMP_EQUAL**—The function evaluates to **TRUE** only if the new pixel has a depth value equal to that of the current pixel.
	Otherwise, the function evaluates to **FALSE**, and the new pixel is not displayed.
	• **D3DCMP_LESSEQUAL**—The function evaluates to **TRUE** only if the new pixel has a depth value less than or equal to that of the current pixel.
	Otherwise, the function evaluates to **FALSE**, and the new pixel is not displayed.
	This is the default value for this state.

(continued)

IDirect3DDevice7::SetRenderState () *(continued)*	
Parameter	**Description**
	• **D3DCMP_GREATER**—The function evaluates to **TRUE** only if the new pixel has a depth greater than that of the current pixel.
	Otherwise, the function evaluates to **FALSE**, and the new pixel is not displayed.
	• **D3DCMP_NOTEQUAL**—The function evaluates to **TRUE** only if the new pixel has a depth value not equal to that of the current pixel.
	Otherwise, the function evaluates to **FALSE**, and the new pixel is not displayed.
	• **D3DCMP_GREATEREQUAL**—The function evaluates to **TRUE** only if the new pixel has a depth value greater than or equal to that of the current pixel.
	Otherwise, the function evaluates to **FALSE**, and the new pixel is not displayed.
	• **D3DCMP_ALWAYS**—The function always evaluates to **TRUE**. All new pixels are displayed.
	• **D3DRENDERSTATE_ALPHAREF**—The alpha reference value state, which determines the reference value against which pixels are tested when alpha-testing is enabled. This state is described by an eight-bit value in the low eight bits of the **DWORD** render state. Valid values range from 0×00000000 to 0×000000FF.
	• **D3DRENDERSTATE_ALPHAFUNC**—The alpha compare function state, which determines the function used when comparing alpha values. This state can be set to one of the following enumeration values:
	• **D3DCMP_NEVER**—The function always evaluates to false. No new pixels are displayed.
	• **D3DCMP_LESS**—The function evaluates to **TRUE** only if the new pixel has an alpha less than that of the current pixel.
	Otherwise, the function evaluates to **FALSE**, and the new pixel is not displayed.
	• **D3DCMP_EQUAL**—The function evaluates to **TRUE** only if the new pixel has an alpha value equal to that of the current pixel.

(continued)

IDirect3DDevice7::SetRenderState () *(continued)*	
Parameter	**Description**
	Otherwise, the function evaluates to **FALSE**, and the new pixel is not displayed.
	• **D3DCMP_LESSEQUAL**—The function evaluates to **TRUE** only if the new pixel has an alpha value less than or equal to that of the current pixel.
	Otherwise, the function evaluates to **FALSE**, and the new pixel is not displayed.
	• **D3DCMP_GREATER**—The function evaluates to **TRUE** only if the new pixel has an alpha greater than that of the current pixel.
	Otherwise, the function evaluates to **FALSE**, and the new pixel is not displayed.
	• **D3DCMP_NOTEQUAL**—The function evaluates to **TRUE** only if the new pixel has an alpha value not equal to that of the current pixel.
	Otherwise, the function evaluates to **FALSE**, and the new pixel is not displayed.
	• **D3DCMP_GREATEREQUAL**—The function evaluates to **TRUE** only if the new pixel has an alpha value greater than or equal to that of the current pixel.
	Otherwise, the function evaluates to **FALSE**, and the new pixel is not displayed.
	• **D3DCMP_ALWAYS**—The function always evaluates to **TRUE**. All new pixels are displayed. This is the default value for this state.
	• **D3DRENDERSTATE_DITHERENABLE**—The dither enable state, which determines whether or not dithering is enabled. This state can be set to one of the following values:
	• **TRUE**—Dithering is enabled.
	• **FALSE**—Dithering is disabled. This is the default value for this state.
	• **D3DRENDERSTATE_ALPHABLENDENABLE**—The alpha blend enable state, which determines whether or not alpha-blended transparency is enabled. This state can be set to one of the following values:
	• **TRUE**—Alpha-blended transparency is enabled.
	• **FALSE**—Alpha-blended transparency is disabled. This is the default value for this state.

(continued)

IDirect3DDevice7::SetRenderState () *(continued)*	
Parameter	**Description**
	• **D3DRENDERSTATE_FOGENABLE**—The fog enable state, which determines whether or not fog shading is enabled. This state can be set to one of the following values:
	• **TRUE**—Fog shading is enabled.
	• **FALSE**—Fog shading is disabled. This is the default value for this state.
	• **D3DRENDERSTATE_SPECULARENABLE**—The specular enable state, which determines whether or not specular highlights are enabled. The specular highlights as generated by Direct3D tend to work best when the object is centered on the origin in model space and is far away from the light source.
	This state can be one of the following values:
	• **TRUE**—Specular highlights are enabled.
	• **FALSE**—Specular highlights are disabled. This is the default value for this state.
	• **D3DRENDERSTATE_STIPPLEDALPHA**—The stippled alpha state, which determines whether or not stippled alpha blending is enabled. This state can be set to one of the following values:
	• **TRUE**—Stippled alpha blending is enabled.
	• **FALSE**—Stippled alpha blending is disabled.
	• **D3DRENDERSTATE_FOGCOLOR**—The fog color state, which determines the color used for fog shading. This state is described by a **D3DCOLOR** structure. The default setting for this state is the color (0, 0, 0).
	• **D3DRENDERSTATE_FOGTABLEMODE**—The fog table mode state, which determines the equation used for pixel-based fog shading, if any. This state can be set to one of the following enumeration values:
	• **D3DFOG_NONE**—There is no fog shading. This is the default value for this state.
	• **D3DFOG_EXP**—Fog shading intensifies exponentially, according to the following formula: $\mathbf{f} = 1/e^{d*r}$, where **f** is the fog intensity at a point, **d** is the distance from the viewer to the point (either along all axes, or just the z-axis, depending on the **D3DRENDERSTATE_RANGE FOGENABLE** state), **e** is the base of natural logarithms (approximately 2.7182818285), and **r** is the density of the fog (a value that ranges from 0.0 to 1.0, as determined by the **D3DRENDERSTATE_FOGDENSITY** render state).

(continued)

IDirect3DDevice7::SetRenderState () *(continued)*

Parameter	Description
	• **D3DFOG_EXP2**—Fog shading intensifies with the square of the distance, according to the following formula: $f = 1/e^{(d*r)(d*r)}$, where **f** is the fog intensity at a point, **d** is the distance from the viewer to the point (either along all axes, or just the z-axis, depending on the **D3DRENDERSTATE_-RANGEFOGENABLE** state), **e** is the base of natural logarithms (approximately 2.7182818285), and **r** is the density of the fog (a value that ranges from 0.0 to 1.0, as determined by the **D3DRENDERSTATE_FOGDENSITY** render state).
	This value is not currently supported.
	• **D3DFOG_LINEAR**—Fog shading intensifies linearly between the starting and ending points, according to the following formula: $f = (end - d)/(end - start)$, where **f** is the fog intensity at a point, **d** is the distance from the viewer to the point (either along all axes, or just the z-axis, depending on the **D3DRENDERSTATE_RANGEFOGENABLE** state), **start** is the distance at which fog shading begins, and **end** is the distance at which fog shading ends.
	This value is the only fog formula currently supported.
	• **D3DRENDERSTATE_FOGSTART**—The fog begin depth state, which determines the depth at which fog shading begins for linear fog mode. This depth is specified in world space for hardware devices or in device space (0.0 to 1.0) for software devices.
	• **D3DRENDERSTATE_FOGEND**—The fog end depth state, which determines the depth at which fog shading ends for linear fog mode. This depth is specified in world space for hardware devices or in device space (0.0 to 1.0) for software devices.
	• **D3DRENDERSTATE_FOGDENSITY**—The fog density state, which determines the density of the fog, used in exponential fog modes (**D3DFOG_EXP** and **D3DFOG_EXP2**). Valid values for this state range from 0.0 to 1.0, inclusive, the default being 1.0.
	• **D3DRENDERSTATE_COLORKEYENABLE**—The color key enable state, which determines whether or not color-keyed transparency is enabled. This state can be set to one of the following values:
	• **TRUE**—Color-keyed transparency is enabled. This affects only texture surfaces created with the **DDSD_CKSRCBLT** flag. Surfaces created without this flag will exhibit color-keyed transparency.

IDirect3DDevice7::SetRenderState () *(continued)*	
Parameter	**Description**
	• **FALSE**—Color-keyed transparency is disabled. This is the default value for this state.
	• **D3DRENDERSTATE_ZBIAS**—The z-bias state for rendered polygons, specified as an integer in the range of 0 to 16, the default being 0. The z-bias is used to put into order of priority polygons that are coplanar (lying on the same three-dimensional plane). Polygons with higher z-biases are rendered in front of coplanar polygons with lower z-biases. The rendering order for coplanar polygons with identical z-biases is undefined.
	• **D3DRENDERSTATE_RANGEFOGENABLE**—The range fog enable state, which determines whether or not range-based fog is enabled. This state, which is valid for unlit untransformed vertices only, can be set to one of the following values:
	• **TRUE**—Range-based fog is enabled. In this mode, points are shaded according to their actual distance from the viewer. This is the most realistic method of fog shading, but is more computationally expensive than depth-based fog.
	• **FALSE**—Depth-based fog is enabled. In this mode, points are shaded according to their depths (z-coordinates). This is the default value for this state.
	• **D3DRENDERSTATE_TRANSLUCENTSORTINDEPENDENT**—The translucent sort independent state, which determines whether or not sort-independent transparency is enabled. This state can be set to one of the following values:
	• **TRUE**—Sort-independent transparency is enabled.
	• **FALSE**—Sort-independent transparency is disabled.
	• **D3DRENDERSTATE_STENCILENABLE**—The stencil enable state, which determines if stenciling is enabled. This state can be one of the following values:
	• **TRUE**—Stenciling is enabled.
	• **FALSE**—Stenciling is disabled. This is the default value for this state.
	• **D3DRENDERSTATE_STENCILFAIL**—The stencil fail operation state, which determines the operation to perform if the stencil test fails. This state can be one of the following enumeration values:
	• **D3DSTENCILOP_KEEP**—The entry in the stencil buffer is not updated. This is the default value for this state.
	• **D3DSTENCILOP_ZERO**—The entry in the stencil buffer is set to 0.

(continued)

IDirect3DDevice7::SetRenderState () *(continued)*	
Parameter	**Description**
	• **D3DSTENCILOP_REPLACE**—The entry in the stencil buffer is replaced with the stencil reference value.
	• **D3DSTENCILOP_INCRSAT**—The entry in the stencil buffer is incremented, unless it has already reached its maximum value. The maximum value for a stencil buffer is given by the equation $2^n\text{-}1$, where n is the bit depth of the stencil buffer.
	• **D3DSTENCILOP_DECRSAT**—The entry in the stencil buffer is decremented, unless it has already reached 0.
	• **D3DSTENCILOP_INVERT**—The bits of the entry in the stencil buffer are inverted.
	• **D3DSTENCILOP_INCR**—The entry in the stencil buffer is incremented. If the entry is already at maximum value, it is reset to 0. The maximum value for a stencil buffer is given by the equation $2^n\text{-}1$, where n is the bit depth of the stencil buffer.
	• **D3DSTENCILOP_DECR**—The entry in the stencil buffer is decremented. If the entry is already at 0, it is set to the maximum value. The maximum value for a stencil buffer is given by the equation $2^n\text{-}1$, where n is the bit depth of the stencil buffer.
	• **D3DRENDERSTATE_STENCILZFAIL**—The stencil *z* fail operation state, which determines the operation to perform if the stencil test passes but the depth test fails. This state can be set to one of the following enumeration values:
	• **D3DSTENCILOP_KEEP**—The entry in the stencil buffer is not updated. This is the default value for this state.
	• **D3DSTENCILOP_ZERO**—The entry in the stencil buffer is set to 0.
	• **D3DSTENCILOP_REPLACE**—The entry in the stencil buffer is replaced with the stencil reference value.
	• **D3DSTENCILOP_INCRSAT**—The entry in the stencil buffer is incremented, unless it has already reached its maximum value. The maximum value for a stencil buffer is given by the equation $2^n\text{-}1$, where n is the bit depth of the stencil buffer.
	• **D3DSTENCILOP_DECRSAT**—The entry in the stencil buffer is decremented, unless it has already reached 0.
	• **D3DSTENCILOP_INVERT**—The bits of the entry in the stencil buffer are inverted.

(continued)

IDirect3DDevice7::SetRenderState () *(continued)*	
Parameter	**Description**
	• **D3DSTENCILOP_INCR**—The entry in the stencil buffer is incremented. If the entry is already at maximum value, it is reset to 0. The maximum value for a stencil buffer is given by the equation 2^n-1, where n is the bit depth of the stencil buffer.
	• **D3DSTENCILOP_DECR**—The entry in the stencil buffer is decremented. If the entry is already at 0, it is set to the maximum value. The maximum value for a stencil buffer is given by the equation 2^n-1, where n is the bit depth of the stencil buffer.
	• **D3DRENDERSTATE_STENCILPASS**—The stencil pass state, which determines the operation to perform if both the stencil and depth tests pass. This state can be set to one of the following enumeration values:
	• **D3DSTENCILOP_KEEP**—The entry in the stencil buffer is not updated. This is the default value for this state.
	• **D3DSTENCILOP_ZERO**—The entry in the stencil buffer is set to 0.
	• **D3DSTENCILOP_REPLACE**—The entry in the stencil buffer is replaced with the stencil reference value.
	• **D3DSTENCILOP_INCRSAT**—The entry in the stencil buffer is incremented, unless it has already reached its maximum value. The maximum value for a stencil buffer is given by the equation 2^n-1, where n is the bit depth of the stencil buffer.
	• **D3DSTENCILOP_DECRSAT**—The entry in the stencil buffer is decremented, unless it has already reached 0.
	• **D3DSTENCILOP_INVERT**—The bits of the entry in the stencil buffer are inverted.
	• **D3DSTENCILOP_INCR**—The entry in the stencil buffer is incremented. If the entry is already at maximum value, it is reset to 0. The maximum value for a stencil buffer is given by the equation 2^n-1, where n is the bit depth of the stencil buffer.
	• **D3DSTENCILOP_DECR**—The entry in the stencil buffer is decremented. If the entry is already at 0, it is set to the maximum value. The maximum value for a stencil buffer is given by the equation 2^n-1, where n is the bit depth of the stencil buffer.

(continued)

IDirect3DDevice7::SetRenderState () *(continued)*

Parameter	Description
	• **D3DRENDERSTATE_STENCILFUNC**—The stencil function state, which determines the function to use when comparing the stencil reference value (governed by the **D3DRENDERSTATE_STENCILREF** state) with a stencil buffer entry. This state can be set to one of the following enumeration values:
	• **D3DCMP_NEVER**—The function always evaluates to false. No new pixels are displayed.
	• **D3DCMP_LESS**—The function evaluates to **TRUE** only if the new pixel has a stencil value less than the stencil reference value.
	Otherwise, the function evaluates to **FALSE**, and the new pixel is not displayed.
	• **D3DCMP_EQUAL**—The function evaluates to **TRUE** only if the new pixel has a stencil value equal to the stencil reference value.
	Otherwise, the function evaluates to **FALSE**, and the new pixel is not displayed.
	• **D3DCMP_LESSEQUAL**—The function evaluates to **TRUE** only if the new pixel has a stencil value less than or equal to the stencil reference value.
	Otherwise, the function evaluates to **FALSE**, and the new pixel is not displayed.
	• **D3DCMP_GREATER**—The function evaluates to **TRUE** only if the new pixel has a stencil value strictly greater than the stencil reference value.
	Otherwise, the function evaluates to **FALSE**, and the new pixel is not displayed.
	• **D3DCMP_NOTEQUAL**—The function evaluates to **TRUE** only if the new pixel has a stencil value not equal to the stencil reference value.
	Otherwise, the function evaluates to **FALSE**, and the new pixel is not displayed.
	• **D3DCMP_GREATEREQUAL**—The function evaluates to **TRUE** only if the new pixel has a stencil value greater than or equal to the stencil reference value.
	Otherwise, the function evaluates to **FALSE**, and the new pixel is not displayed.

(continued)

IDirect3DDevice7::SetRenderState () *(continued)*	
Parameter	**Description**
	• **D3DCMP_ALWAYS**—The function always evaluates to **TRUE**. All new pixels are displayed. This is the default value for this state.
	• **D3DRENDERSTATE_STENCILREF**—The stencil reference value state, which determines the reference value for the stencil test, specified as an integer in the range of 0 to $2n-1$, where **n** is the bit depth of the stencil buffer. The default value for this state is 0.
	• **D3DRENDERSTATE_STENCILMASK**—The stencil mask state, which determines the mask applied to both the reference value and each stencil buffer entry to isolate the significant bits for the stencil test. The default value for this state is 0×FFFFFFFF, indicating all bits are significant.
	• **D3DRENDERSTATE_STENCILWRITEMASK**—The stencil write mask state, which determines the mask applied to values written into the stencil buffer. The default value for this state is 0×FFFFFFFF, indicating all bits are significant.
	• **D3DRENDERSTATE_TEXTUREFACTOR**—The texture factor state, which determines the color used for multiple texture blending with either the **D3DTA_TFACTOR** texture-blending argument or the **D3DTOP_BLENDFACTORALPHA** texture-blending operation. This is specified as a **D3DCOLOR** structure.
	• **D3DRENDERSTATE_WRAP0** through **D3DRENDERSTATE_-WRAP7**—The texture wrapping state, which determines the behavior of texture wrapping for texture coordinates. This state can be set to zero or more of the following values:
	• **D3DWRAPCOORD_0**—Texture wrapping is enabled in the first, usually horizontal, dimension.
	• **D3DWRAPCOORD_1**—Texture wrapping is enabled in the second, usually vertical, dimension.
	• **D3DWRAPCOORD_2**—Texture wrapping is enabled in the third dimension.
	• **D3DWRAPCOORD_3**—Texture wrapping is enabled in the fourth dimension.
	These values are combined with the bitwise or operator ('|').

(continued)

IDirect3DDevice7::SetRenderState () *(continued)*	
Parameter	**Description**
	• **D3DRENDERSTATE_CLIPPING**—The clipping state, which determines whether or not Direct3D performs primitive clipping. This state can be set to one of the following values:
	• **TRUE**—Primitive clipping is enabled. This is the default value for this state.
	• **FALSE**—Primitive clipping is disabled.
	• **D3DRENDERSTATE_LIGHTING**—The lighting state, which determines whether or not Direct3D performs lighting. This state can be set to one of the following values:
	• **TRUE**—Lighting is enabled. This applies only for vertices that include a vertex normal.
	This is the default value for this state.
	• **FALSE**—Lighting is disabled.
	• **D3DRENDERSTATE_EXTENTS**—The extents state, which determines whether or not the system updates the screen extents for each rendering call. This state can be set to one of the following values:
	• **TRUE**—Screen extents are updated for each rendering call.
	• **FALSE**—Screen extents are not updated. This is the default value for this state.
	• **D3DRENDERSTATE_AMBIENT**—The ambient state, which determines the ambient light color, specified as a **D3DCOLOR** structure. The default value for this state is (0, 0, 0).
	• **D3DRENDERSTATE_FOGVERTEXMODE**—The fog vertex mode state, which determines the fog formula to be used for vertex-based fog. This state can be set to one of the following enumeration values:
	• **D3DFOG_NONE**—There is no fog shading. This is the default value for this state.
	• **D3DFOG_EXP**—Fog shading intensifies exponentially, according to the following formula: $f = 1/e^{d*r}$, where **f** is the fog intensity at a point, **d** is the distance from the viewer to the point (either along all axes, or just the *z*-axis, depending on the **D3DRENDERSTATE_RANGEFOGENABLE** state), **e** is the base of natural logarithms (approximately 2.7182818285), and **r** is the density of the fog (a value that ranges from 0.0 to 1.0, as determined by the **D3DRENDERSTATE_FOGDENSITY** render state).
	This value is not currently supported.

(continued)

IDirect3DDevice7::SetRenderState () (continued)	
Parameter	**Description**
	• **D3DFOG_EXP2**—Fog shading intensifies with the square of the distance, according to the following formula: $f = 1/e^{(d*r)(d*r)}$, where f is the fog intensity at a point, d is the distance from the viewer to the point (either along all axes, or just the z-axis, depending on the **D3DRENDERSTATE_-RANGEFOGENABLE** state) , e is the base of natural logarithms (approximately 2.7182818285), and r is the density of the fog (a value that ranges from 0.0 to 1.0, as determined by the **D3DRENDERSTATE_FOGDENSITY** render state).
	This value is not currently supported.
	• **D3DFOG_LINEAR**—Fog shading intensifies linearly between the starting and ending points, according to the following formula: **f = (end - d)/(end - start)**, where **f** is the fog intensity at a point, **d** is the distance from the viewer to the point (either along all axes, or just the z-axis, depending on the **D3DRENDERSTATE_RANGEFOGENABLE** state), **start** is the distance at which fog shading begins, and **end** is the distance at which fog shading ends.
	This value is the only fog formula currently supported.
	• **D3DRENDERSTATE_COLORVERTEX**—The color vertex state, which determines whether or not to perform per-vertex color. If per-vertex coloring is enabled, Direct3D uses the color information for each vertex (if present) for lighting calculations.
	This state can be set to one of the following values:
	• **TRUE**—Per-vertex color is enabled. This is the default value for this state.
	• **FALSE**—Per-vertex color is disabled.
	• **D3DRENDERSTATE_LOCALVIEWER**—The local viewer state, which determines whether or not camera-relative specular highlights are enabled. This state can be set to one of the following values:
	• **TRUE**—Camera-relative specular highlights are enabled. This is the default value for this state.
	• **FALSE**—Orthogonal specular highlights are enabled.

(continued)

IDirect3DDevice7::SetRenderState () *(continued)*	
Parameter	**Description**
	• **D3DRENDERSTATE_NORMALIZENORMALS**—The normalize normals state, which determines whether or not vertex normals are automatically normalized. This state can be set to one of the following values:
	• **TRUE**—Vertex normals are automatically normalized after the system transforms vertices into camera space. This is computationally intensive.
	• **FALSE**—Vertex normals are not automatically normalized. This is the default value for this state.
	• **D3DRENDERSTATE_COLORKEYBLENDENABLE**—The color key blend enable state, which determines whether or not alpha-blended color keying is enabled. This state can be set to one of the following values:
	• **TRUE**—Alpha-blended color keying is enabled.
	• **FALSE**—Alpha-blended color keying is disabled.
	• **D3DRENDERSTATE_DIFFUSEMATERIALSOURCE**—The diffuse material source state, which determines the diffuse color source for lighting calculations. This state, which is valid only when the **D3DRENDERSTATE_COLORVERTEX** state is set to **TRUE**, can be set to one of the following enumeration values:
	• **D3DMCS_MATERIAL**—The diffuse color for lighting calculations is taken from the current material.
	• **D3DMCS_COLOR1**—The diffuse color for lighting calculations is taken from the diffuse color contained in each vertex. This is the default value for this state.
	• **D3DMCS_COLOR2**—The diffuse color for lighting calculations is taken from the specular color contained in each vertex.
	• **D3DRENDERSTATE_SPECULARMATERIALSOURCE**—The specular material source state, which determines the specular color source for lighting calculations. This state can be set to one of the following enumeration values:
	• **D3DMCS_MATERIAL**—The specular color for lighting calculations is taken from the current material.
	• **D3DMCS_COLOR1**—The specular color for lighting calculations is taken from the diffuse color contained in each vertex.

(continued)

IDirect3DDevice7::SetRenderState () (continued)

Parameter	Description
	• **D3DMCS_COLOR2**—The specular color for lighting calculations is taken from the specular color contained in each vertex. This is the default value for this state.
	• **D3DRENDERSTATE_AMBIENTMATERIALSOURCE**—The ambient material source state, which determines the ambient color source for lighting calculations. This state can be set to one of the following enumeration values:
	• **D3DMCS_MATERIAL**—The ambient color for lighting calculations is taken from the current material.
	• **D3DMCS_COLOR1**—The ambient color for lighting calculations is taken from the diffuse color contained in each vertex.
	• **D3DMCS_COLOR2**—The ambient color for lighting calculations is taken from the specular color contained in each vertex. This is the default value for this state.
	• **D3DRENDERSTATE_EMISSIVEMATERIALSOURCE**—The emissive material source state, which determines the emissive color source for lighting calculations. This state can be set to one of the following enumeration values:
	• **D3DMCS_MATERIAL**—The emissive color for lighting calculations is taken from the current material. This is the default value for this state.
	• **D3DMCS_COLOR1**—The emissive color for lighting calculations is taken from the diffuse color contained in each vertex.
	• **D3DMCS_COLOR2**—The emissive color for lighting calculations is taken from the specular color contained in each vertex.
	• **D3DRENDERSTATE_ALPHASOURCE**—The alpha source state, which determines the location from which Direct3D should obtain the alpha component of output diffuse color. This state can be set to one of the following enumeration values:
	• **D3DMCS_MATERIAL**—The alpha component is taken from the current material.
	• **D3DMCS_COLOR1**—The alpha component is taken from the diffuse color contained in each vertex. This is the default value for this state.
	• **D3DMCS_COLOR2**—The alpha component is taken from the specular color contained in each vertex.

(continued)

IDirect3DDevice7::SetRenderState () *(continued)*	
Parameter	**Description**
	• **D3DRENDERSTATE_FOGFACTORSOURCE**—The fog factor source state, which determines the location from which Direct3D should obtain the alpha component of output specular color. This alpha component is used for fog calculations. This state can be set to one of the following enumeration values:
	• **D3DMCS_MATERIAL**—The alpha component is taken from the current material.
	• **D3DMCS_COLOR1**—The alpha component is taken from the diffuse color contained in each vertex.
	• **D3DMCS_COLOR2**—The alpha component is taken from the specular color contained in each vertex. This is the default value for this state.
	• **D3DRENDERSTATE_VERTEXBLEND**—The verted blend state, which determines the number of matrices used in vertex blending. This state can be set to one of the following enumeration values:
	• **D3DVBLEND_DISABLE**—Vertex blending is disabled. The only matrix applied to vertices is the one specified by the **D3DTRANSFORMSTATE_WORLD** transformation matrix. Untransformed vertices are sent through this matrix and then outputted.
	This is the default value for this state.
	• **D3DVBLEND_1WEIGHT**—Vertex blending is enabled for two matrices. The two matrices applied to vertices are the ones specified by the **D3DTRANSFORMSTATE_WORLD** and **D3DTRANSFORMSTATE_WORLD1** transformation matrices. Untransformed vertices are sent through each of these matrices. The resulting vertices are then blending according to the weighting values specified in their vertex structures. The resulting blended vertices are then outputted.
	• **D3DVBLEND_2WEIGHTS**—Vertex blending is enabled for three matrices. The three matrices applied to vertices are the ones specified by the **D3DTRANSFORMSTATE_WORLD, D3DTRANSFORMSTATE_WORLD1,** and **D3DTRANSFORMSTATE_WORLD2** transformation matrices. Untransformed vertices are sent through each of these matrices. The resulting vertices are then blending according to the weighting values specified in their vertex structures. The resulting blended vertices are then outputted.

(continued)

IDirect3DDevice7::SetRenderState () *(continued)*	
Parameter	**Description**
	• **D3DVBLEND_3WEIGHTS**—Vertex blending is enabled for four matrices. The four matrices applied to vertices are the ones specified by the **D3DTRANSFORMSTATE_WORLD**, **D3DTRANSFORMSTATE_WORLD1**, **D3DTRANSFORM-STATE_WORLD2**, and **D3DTRANSFORMSTATE_WORLD3** transformation matrices. Untransformed vertices are sent through each of these matrices. The resulting vertices are then blending according to the weighting values specified in their vertex structures. The resulting blended vertices are then outputted.
	• **D3DRENDERSTATE_CLIPPLANEENABLE**—The clip plane enable state, which determines which user-defined clipping planes (if any) are enabled. This state is specified as a **DWORD** value, where each bit corresponds to the status of a plane (1 indicates the plane is enabled, 0 indicates it is disabled). The least significant bit identifies the first plane; the next significant bit, the second plane; and so on.
	The **D3DCLIPPLANEn** constants (defined in d3dtypes.h) can be used to conveniently enable clipping planes.
	The default value for this state is 0, which indicates no user-defined clipping planes are enabled.
dwRenderState	The new value for the specified render state, specified as either a **DWORD** value or the address of data that contains the state's new value, depending on the specific state being set.
Return Value	**Description**
D3D_OK	Direct3D successfully set the specified render state for the device.
DDERR_INVALIDPARAMS	Direct3D could not set the specified render state, because one or more parameters are invalid.

IDirect3DDevice7::SetRenderTarget ()

Function Description

This function sets the new render target surface for the device. The render target surface is where 3D rendering is directed to.

Function Declaration

```
HRESULT SetRenderTarget(
  LPDIRECTDRAWSURFACE7 lpNewRenderTarget,
  DWORD dwFlags
);
```

Parameter	Description
lpNewRenderTarget	A pointer to a DirectDrawSurface7 object that identifies the new render target surface. This surface must have been created with 3D rendering capabilities (specified by the **DDSCAPS_3D-DEVICE** flag).
	This surface must match the existing render target surface in depth buffer presence. If the existing render target surface has an attached depth buffer, then the new one must also have a depth buffer; and if the existing render target surface does not have an attached depth buffer, then neither can the new one.
	No more than one depth buffer can be attached to the new surface.
dwFlags	This parameter, which is not currently used, must be set to 0.

Return Value	Description
D3D_OK	Direct3D successfully set the new render target surface.
DDERR_INVALIDPARAMS	Direct3D could not set the new render target surface, because one or more parameters are invalid.
DDERR_INVALIDSURFACETYPE	Direct3D could not set the new render target surface, because the type of the specified surface is invalid.

IDirect3DDevice7::SetTexture ()

Function Description

This function associates a texture surface with a specified texture stage. Software devices do not support associating a texture surface to more than one texture stage at a time.

Function Declaration

```
HRESULT SetTexture(
  DWORD dwStage,
  LPDIRECTDRAWSURFACE7 lpTexture
);
```

(continued)

	IDirect3DDevice7::SetTexture () *(continued)*
Parameter	**Description**
dwStage	The texture stage with which the texture specified by **lpTexture** will be associated, in the range of 0 to 7.
lpTexture	A pointer to a DirectDrawSurface7 object that identifies the texture to be associated with the specified texture stage.
Return Value	**Description**
D3D_OK	Direct3D successfully associated the specified texture with the specified texture stage.
DDERR_INVALIDOBJECT	Direct3D could not associate the specified texture with the specified stage, because this Direct3DDevice7 object is invalid.
DDERR_INVALIDPARAMS	Direct3D could not associate the specified texture with the specified stage, because one or more parameters are invalid.

IDirect3DDevice7::SetTextureStageState ()

Function Description

This function sets a state of a specified texture stage. This function sets a state as a 32-bit unsigned integer. Most states are specified in this format, but some are specified as floating-point numbers and others as structures. If an application is setting a floating-point state, it should cast the 32-bit floating-point number to an integer (it should *not* convert the number into an integer). If an application is setting a structure-based state, it should pass the address of the structure as an integer.

Function Declaration

```
HRESULT SetTextureStageState(
    DWORD dwStage,
    D3DTEXTURESTAGESTATETYPE dwState,
    DWORD dwValue
);
```

Parameter	**Description**
dwStage	The texture stage whose state is being set, in the range of 0 to 7.
dwState	Identifies the texture stage state to be set. This parameter can be set to one of the following enumeration values: • **D3DTSS_COLOROP**—The color blending operation, which determines the operation performed when two color channels are blended. This operation determines the color output for this texture stage. This state can be set to one of the following enumeration values: • **D3DTOP_ADD**—The color output is the sum of the texture stage's two color arguments. In equation form, $\mathbf{S_{rgb}} = \mathbf{Arg1} + \mathbf{Arg2}$.

(continued)

IDirect3DDevice7::SetTextureStageState () *(continued)*	
Parameter	Description
	• **D3DTOP_ADDSIGNED**—The color output is the sum of the texture stage's two color arguments, minus 0.5. The range of output values is -0.5 to 0.5. In the equation form, $S_{rgb} = \textbf{Arg1} + \textbf{Arg2} - \textbf{0.5}$.
	• **D3DTOP_ADDSIGNED2X**—The color output is the sum of the texture stage's two color arguments, minus 0.5, all multiplied by 2. The range of output values is -1.0 to 1.0. In equation form, $S_{rgb} = (\textbf{Arg1} + \textbf{Arg2} - \textbf{0.5}) * \textbf{2.0}$.
	• **D3DTOP_ADDSMOOTH**—The color output is the sum of the texture stage's two color arguments, minus their product. In equation form, $S_{rgb} = (\textbf{Arg1} + \textbf{Arg2}) - (\textbf{Arg1} * \textbf{Arg2})$.
	• **D3DTOP_BLENDDIFFUSEALPHA**—The color output is a linear blend of the first argument with the second argument, using the interpolated alpha from each vertex. In equation form, $S_{rgb} = \textbf{Arg1} * \textbf{Alpha} + \textbf{Arg2} * (\textbf{1.0} - \textbf{Alpha})$, where **Alpha** ranges from 0.0 to 1.0.
	• **D3DTOP_BLENDTEXTUREALPHA**—The color output is a linear blend of the first color argument with the second color argument, using the alpha from this stage's texture. In equation form, $S_{rgb} = \textbf{Arg1} * \textbf{Alpha} + \textbf{Arg2} * (\textbf{1.0} - \textbf{Alpha})$, where **Alpha** ranges from 0.0 to 1.0.
	• **D3DTOP_BLENDFACTORALPHA**—The color output is a linear blend of the first color argument with the second color argument, using a scalar alpha set with the **D3DRENDERSTATE_TEXTUREFACTOR** render state. In equation form, $S_{rgb} = \textbf{Arg1} * \textbf{Alpha} + \textbf{Arg2} * (\textbf{1.0} - \textbf{Alpha})$, where **Alpha** ranges from 0.0 to 1.0.
	• **D3DTOP_BLENDCURRENTALPHA**—The color output is a linear blend of the first color argument with the second color argument, using the alpha from the previous texture stage. In equation form, $S_{rgb} = \textbf{Arg1} * \textbf{Alpha} + \textbf{Arg2} * (\textbf{1.0} - \textbf{Alpha})$, where **Alpha** ranges from 0.0 to 1.0.
	• **D3DTOP_BLENDTEXTUREALPHAPM**—The color output is a linear blend of the first color argument with the second color argument, using premultiplied alpha. In equation form, $S_{rgb} = \textbf{Arg1} + \textbf{Arg2} * (\textbf{1.0} - \textbf{Alpha})$, where **Alpha** ranges from 0.0 to 1.0.
	• **D3DTOP_BUMPENVMAP**—The color output is a per-pixel bump-mapping using the bump map associated with this texture stage to perturb the texture coordinates of the environment map of the next texture stage, without luminance.

(continued)

IDirect3DDevice7::SetTextureStageState () *(continued)*	
Parameter	**Description**
	• **D3DTOP_BUMPENVMAPLUMINANCE**—The color output is a per-pixel bump-mapping using the bump map associated with this texture stage to perturb the texture coordinates of the environment map of the next texture stage, with luminance.
	• **D3DTOP_DISABLE**—Color output from this texture stage and all texture stages with a higher index is disabled. Disabling the first texture stage (with index 0) disables texture mapping. This value is the default for the second and higher texture stages.
	• **D3DTOP_DOTPRODUCT3**—The color output is the dot product of the first and second arguments, replicated to all components, including alpha. In equation form, $S = Arg1_r * Arg2_r + Arg1_g * Arg2_g + Arg1_b * Arg2_b$, where $Arg1_r$, $Arg1_g$, and $Arg1_b$ are the red, green, and blue components of the first argument, respectively, and $Arg2_r$, $Arg2_g$, and $Arg2_b$ are the red, green, and blue components of the second argument, respectively.
	• **D3DTOP_MODULATE**—The color output is the product of the texture stage's two color arguments. In equation form, $S_{rgb} = Arg1 * Arg2$. This value is the default for the first texture stage (texture stage index 0).
	• **D3DTOP_MODULATE2X**—The color output is the product of the texture stage's two color arguments, multiplied by 2. In equation form, $S_{rgb} = 2.0 * Arg1 * Arg2$.
	• **D3DTOP_MODULATE4X**—The color output is the product of the texture stage's two color arguments, multiplied by 4. In equation form, $S_{rgb} = 4.0 * Arg1 * Arg2$.
	• **D3DTOP_MODULATEALPHA_ADDCOLOR**—The color output is the sum of the first color argument and the product of the first color's alpha component and the second color argument. In equation form, $S_{rgb} = Arg1 + Arg1_a * Arg2$, where $Arg1_a$ is the alpha component of the first color argument.
	• **D3DTOP_MODULATECOLOR_ADDALPHA**—The color output is the sum of the first argument's alpha component and the product of the first color argument and the second color argument. In equation form, $S_{rgb} = Arg1 * Arg2 + Arg1_a$, where $Arg1_a$ is the alpha component of the first color argument.

(continued)

IDirect3DDevice7::SetTextureStageState () *(continued)*

Parameter	Description
	• **D3DTOP_MODULATEINVALPHA_ADDCOLOR**—The color output is the sum of the first color argument and the product of the inverse of the first color's alpha component and the second color argument. In equation form, $S_{rgb} = Arg1 + (1.0 - Arg1_a) * Arg2$, where $Arg1_a$ is the alpha component of the first color argument.
	• **D3DTOP_MODULATEINVCOLOR_ADDALPHA**—The color output is the sum of the first argument's alpha component and the product of the inverse of the first color argument and the second color argument. In equation form, $S_{rgb} = (1.0 - Arg1) * Arg2 + Arg1_a$, where $Arg1_a$ is the alpha component of the first color argument.
	• **D3DTOP_PREMODULATE**—The color output is the product of this texture stage with the next texture stage.
	• **D3DTOP_SELECTARG1**—The color output is the color of the texture stage's first argument, unmodified.
	• **D3DTOP_SELECTARG2**—The color output is the color of the texture stage's second argument, unmodified.
	• **D3DTOP_SUBTRACT**—The color output is the difference of the texture stage's two color arguments. In equation form, $S_{rgb} = Arg1 - Arg2$.
	• **D3DTSS_COLORARG1**—The first color argument, which determines the source of the color components for the texture stage's first argument. This state can be one of the following enumeration values:
	• **D3DTA_ALPHAREPLICATE**—Alpha information should be replicated to all color components before the operation completes. This value modifies another enumeration value that itself specifies the source for the argument's information.
	• **D3DTA_COMPLEMENT**—The first color argument should be inverted; that is, a color S_{rgba} should be translated to $1.0 - S_{rgba}$ before being used. This value modifies another enumeration value that itself specifies the source for the argument's information.
	• **D3DTA_CURRENT**—The first color argument is the output from the previous texture stage. For the first texture stage (stage index 0), this argument defaults to **D3DTA_DIFFUSE**.
	• **D3DTA_DIFFUSE**—The first color argument is the diffuse color interpolated from vertex components during Gouraud shading. If the primitive's vertices do not include a diffuse color, the default color is white.
	• **D3DTA_SELECTMASK**—The mask value for all arguments.

(continued)

IDirect3DDevice7::SetTextureStageState () *(continued)*	
Parameter	**Description**
	• **D3DTA_SPECULAR**—The first color argument is the specular color interpolated from vertex components during Gouraud shading. If the vertices of the primitive do not include a specular color, the default is white.
	• **D3DTA_TEXTURE**—The first color argument is the color of the texture associated with this texture stage. This is the default value for this state.
	• **D3DTA_TFACTOR**—The first color argument is the texture factor as specified by the **D3DRENDERSTATE_TEXTURE** render state.
	• **D3DTSS_COLORARG2**—The second color argument, which determines the source of the color components for the texture stage's second argument. This state can be one of the following enumeration values:
	• **D3DTA_ALPHAREPLICATE**—Alpha information should be replicated to all color components before the operation completes. This value modifies another enumeration value that itself specifies the source for the argument's information.
	• **D3DTA_COMPLEMENT**—The second color argument should be inverted; that is, a color S_{rgba} should be translated to $1.0 - S_{rgba}$ before being used. This value modifies another enumeration value that itself specifies the source for the argument's information.
	• **D3DTA_CURRENT**—The second color argument is the output from the previous texture stage. For the first texture stage (stage index 0), this argument defaults to **D3DTA_DIFFUSE**. This is the default value for this state.
	• **D3DTA_DIFFUSE**—The second color argument is the diffuse color interpolated from vertex components during Gouraud shading. If the primitive's vertices do not include a diffuse color, the default color is white.
	• **D3DTA_SELECTMASK**—The mask value for all arguments.
	• **D3DTA_SPECULAR**—The second color argument is the specular color interpolated from vertex components during Gouraud shading. If the vertices of the primitive do not include a specular color, the default is white.
	• **D3DTA_TFACTOR**—The second color argument is the texture factor as specified by the **D3DRENDERSTATE_-TEXTURE** render state.

(continued)

IDirect3DDevice7::SetTextureStageState () *(continued)*	
Parameter	**Description**

	• **D3DTSS_ALPHAOP**—The alpha blending operation, which determines the operation performed when two alpha channels are blended. This operation determines the alpha output for this texture stage.
	
	This state can be set to one of the following enumeration values:
	
	  • **D3DTOP_ADD**—The alpha output is the sum of the texture stage's two alpha arguments. In equation form, $S_a = Arg1 + Arg2$.
	
	  • **D3DTOP_ADDSIGNED**—The alpha output is the sum of the texture stage's two alpha arguments, minus 0.5. The range of output values is -0.5 to 0.5. In the equation form, $S_a = Arg1 + Arg2 - 0.5$.
	
	  • **D3DTOP_ADDSIGNED2X**—The alpha output is the sum of the texture stage's two alpha arguments, minus 0.5, all multiplied by 2. The range of output values is -1.0 to 1.0. In equation form, $S_a = (Arg1 + Arg2 - 0.5) * 2.0$.
	
	  • **D3DTOP_ADDSMOOTH**—The alpha output is the sum of the texture stage's two alpha arguments, minus their product. In equation form, $S_a = (Arg1 + Arg2) - (Arg1 * Arg2)$.
	
	  • **D3DTOP_BLENDDIFFUSEALPHA**—The alpha output is a linear blend of the first argument with the second argument, using the interpolated alpha from each vertex. In equation form, $S_a = Arg1 * Alpha + Arg2 * (1.0 - Alpha)$, where **Alpha** ranges from 0.0 to 1.0.
	
	  • **D3DTOP_BLENDTEXTUREALPHA**—The alpha output is a linear blend of the first alpha argument with the second alpha argument, using the alpha from this stage's texture. In equation form, $S_a = Arg1 * Alpha + Arg2 * (1.0 - Alpha)$, where **Alpha** ranges from 0.0 to 1.0.
	
	  • **D3DTOP_BLENDFACTORALPHA**—The alpha output is a linear blend of the first alpha argument with the second alpha argument, using a scalar alpha set with the **D3DRENDERSTATE_TEXTUREFACTOR** render state. In equation form, $S_a = Arg1 * Alpha + Arg2 * (1.0 - Alpha)$, where **Alpha** ranges from 0.0 to 1.0.
	
	  • **D3DTOP_BLENDCURRENTALPHA**—The alpha output is a linear blend of the first alpha argument with the second alpha argument, using the alpha from the previous texture stage. In equation form, $S_a = Arg1 * Alpha + Arg2 * (1.0 - Alpha)$, where **Alpha** ranges from 0.0 to 1.0.

(continued)

IDirect3DDevice7::SetTextureStageState () *(continued)*	
Parameter	**Description**
	• **D3DTOP_BLENDTEXTUREALPHAPM**—The alpha output is a linear blend of the first alpha argument with the second alpha argument, using premultiplied alpha. In equation form, S_a = **Arg1** + **Arg2** * (**1.0** - **Alpha**), where **Alpha** ranges from 0.0 to 1.0.
	• **D3DTOP_DISABLE**—Alpha output from this texture stage and all texture stages with a higher index is disabled. Disabling the first texture stage (with index 0) disables alpha blending.
	This value is the default for the second and higher texture stages.
	• **D3DTOP_DOTPRODUCT3**—The alpha output is the dot product of the first and second arguments. In equation form, S_a = **Arg1**$_r$ * **Arg2**$_r$ + **Arg1**$_g$ * **Arg2**$_g$ + **Arg1**$_b$ * **Arg2**$_b$, where **Arg1**$_r$, **Arg1**$_g$, and **Arg1**$_b$ are the red, green, and blue components of the first argument, respectively, and **Arg2**$_r$, **Arg2**$_g$, and **Arg2**$_b$ are the red, green, and blue components of the second argument, respectively.
	• **D3DTOP_MODULATE**—The alpha output is the product of the texture stage's two alpha arguments. In equation form, S_a = **Arg1** * **Arg2**.
	• **D3DTOP_MODULATE2X**—The alpha output is the product of the texture stage's two alpha arguments, multiplied by 2. In equation form, S_a = **2.0** * **Arg1** * **Arg2**.
	• **D3DTOP_MODULATE4X**—The alpha output is the product of the texture stage's two alpha arguments, multiplied by 4. In equation form, S_a = **4.0** * **Arg1** * **Arg2**.
	• **D3DTOP_PREMODULATE**—The alpha output is the product of this texture stage with the next texture stage.
	• **D3DTOP_SELECTARG1**—The alpha output is the alpha of the texture stage's first argument, unmodified. This value is the default for the first texture stage (texture stage index 0).
	• **D3DTOP_SELECTARG2**—The alpha output is the alpha of the texture stage's second argument, unmodified.
	• **D3DTOP_SUBTRACT**—The alpha output is the difference of the texture stage's two alpha arguments. In equation form, S_a = **Arg1** - **Arg2**.
	• **D3DTSS_ALPHAARG1**—The first alpha argument, which determines the source of the alpha component for the texture stage's first argument. This state can be one of the following enumeration values:

(continued)

IDirect3DDevice7::SetTextureStageState () *(continued)*

Parameter	Description
	• **D3DTA_ALPHAREPLICATE**—Alpha information should be replicated to all components before the operation completes. This value modifies another enumeration value that itself specifies the source for the argument's information.
	• **D3DTA_COMPLEMENT**—The first alpha argument should be inverted; that is, an alpha S_a should be translated to **1.0 - S_a** before being used. This value modifies another enumeration value that itself specifies the source for the argument's information.
	• **D3DTA_CURRENT**—The first alpha argument is the output from the previous texture stage. For the first texture stage (stage index 0), this argument defaults to **D3DTA_DIFFUSE**.
	• **D3DTA_DIFFUSE**—The first alpha argument is the diffuse alpha interpolated from vertex components during Gouraud shading. If the primitive's vertices do not include diffuse alpha information, the default alpha is 0×FFFFFFFF.
	This is the default value if no texture is associated with this texture stage; otherwise, the default is **D3DTA_TEXTURE**.
	• **D3DTA_SELECTMASK**—The mask value for all arguments.
	• **D3DTA_SPECULAR**—The first alpha argument is the specular alpha interpolated from vertex components during Gouraud shading. If the vertices of the primitive do not include specular alpha information, the default is 0×FFFFFFFF.
	• **D3DTA_TEXTURE**—The first alpha argument is the alpha of the texture associated with this texture stage. This is the default value unless no texture is associated with this texture stage, in which case the default value is **D3DTA_DIFFUSE**.
	• **D3DTA_TFACTOR**—The first alpha argument is the texture factor as specified by the **D3DRENDERSTATE_TEXTURE** render state.
	• **D3DTSS_ALPHAARG2**—The second alpha argument, which determines the source of the alpha component for the texture stage's second argument. This state can be one of the following enumeration values:
	• **D3DTA_ALPHAREPLICATE**—Alpha information should be replicated to all alpha components before the operation completes. This value modifies another enumeration value that itself specifies the source for the argument's information.

(continued)

IDirect3DDevice7::SetTextureStageState () (continued)

Parameter	Description
	• **D3DTA_COMPLEMENT**—The second alpha argument should be inverted; that is, an alpha **S** should be translated to **1.0 - S** before being used. This value modifies another enumeration value that itself specifies the source for the argument's information.
	• **D3DTA_CURRENT**—The second alpha argument is the output from the previous texture stage. For the first texture stage (stage index 0), this argument defaults to **D3DTA_DIFFUSE**.
	This is the default value for this state.
	• **D3DTA_DIFFUSE**—The second alpha argument is the diffuse alpha interpolated from vertex components during Gouraud shading. If the primitive's vertices do not include diffuse alpha information, the default alpha is 0×FFFFFFFF.
	• **D3DTA_SELECTMASK**—The mask value for all arguments.
	• **D3DTA_SPECULAR**—The second alpha argument is the specular alpha interpolated from vertex components during Gouraud shading. If the vertices of the primitive do not include specular alpha information, the default is 0×FFFFFFFF.
	• **D3DTA_TFACTOR**—The second alpha argument is the texture factor as specified by the **D3DRENDERSTATE_-TEXTURE** render state.
	• **D3DTSS_BUMPENVMAT00**—The [0][0] coefficient in the bump-mapping matrix, specified as a **D3DVALUE**. This 2×2 matrix is applied to bump-map values and can be used by an application to scale, offset, or otherwise transform bump-map values.
	The default value for this state is 0.0.
	• **D3DTSS_BUMPENVMAT01**—The [0][1] coefficient in the bump-mapping matrix, specified as a **D3DVALUE**. This 2×2 matrix is applied to bump-map values and can be used by an application to scale, offset, or otherwise transform bump-map values.
	The default value for this state is 0.0.
	• **D3DTSS_BUMPENVMAT10**—The [1][0] coefficient in the bump-mapping matrix, specified as a **D3DVALUE**. This 2×2 matrix is applied to bump-map values and can be used by an application to scale, offset, or otherwise transform bump-map values.
	The default value for this state is 0.0.

(continued)

IDirect3DDevice7::SetTextureStageState () *(continued)*	
Parameter	**Description**
	• **D3DTSS_BUMPENVMAT11**—The [1][1] coefficient in the bump-mapping matrix, specified as a **D3DVALUE**. This 2×2 matrix is applied to bump-map values and can be used by an application to scale, offset, or otherwise transform bump-map values.
	The default value for this state is 0.0.
	• **D3DTSS_TEXCOORDINDEX**—The index of the texture coordinate set to be used with this texture stage. The default value for this state is 0, indicating the first texture coordinate set will be used.
	If a texture is associated with this texture stage, then the texture coordinate set specified by this state will be used to determine the texture coordinates for a primitive's vertices. If a vertex does not specify texture coordinate information for a given set, the default *u*-, *v*-coordinates are (0, 0).
	The current maximum for this state is seven, allowing a total of eight texture coordinate sets.
	This state can also include with the texture coordinate set index one of a series of predefined flags. If an application includes one of these flags, then the texture coordinate set specified will be used only to determine the texture wrapping mode for the specified texture stage. It will not be used to extract texture coordinate information.
	The predefined constants are listed below:
	• **D3DTSS_TCI_CAMERASPACENORMAL**—Direct3D uses the transformed, camera-space vertex normal of a vertex to determine the texture coordinates for that vertex.
	This flag is primarily useful for environment mapping.
	• **D3DTSS_TCI_CAMERASPACEPOSITION**—Direct3D uses the transformed, camera-space vertex position of a vertex to determine the texture coordinates for that vertex.
	This flag is primarily useful for environment mapping.
	• **D3DTSS_TCI_CAMERASPACEREFLECTIONVECTOR**—Direct3D calculates a reflection vector to determine the texture coordinates for a vertex. The reflection vector is calculated in the following manner: A vector (representing a ray of light) is sent out from the camera to the vertex, and then reflected off the plane determined by the vertex normal at that vertex. The reflected vector then intersects the environment map, and the resulting intersection is used to determine the texture coordinates for the vertex.

(continued)

IDirect3DDevice7::SetTextureStageState () *(continued)*	
Parameter	**Description**
	This flag is primarily useful for cubic environment mapping. Applications should use this flag rather than calculate their own texture coordinates because on some hardware devices this operation is accelerated.
	To specify the second texture coordinate set and the **D3DTSS_TCI_CAMERASPACENORMAL** flag, an application would use the render state generated by the following code: (**1 | D3DTSS_TCI_CAMERASPACENORMAL**).
	• **D3DTSS_ADDRESS**—The texture addressing method for both *u*- and *v*-texture coordinates. This determines how the system treats *u*- and *v*-values outside the [0.0, 1.0] range.
	This state can be set to one of the following enumeration values:
	• **D3DTADDRESS_WRAP**—Textures are tiled at every integer junction. This is the default value for this state.
	• **D3DTADDRESS_MIRROR**—Textures are tiled at every integer junction, but are mirrored (flipped) at every other junction to facilitate seamless texture wrapping.
	• **D3DTADDRESS_CLAMP**—Texture coordinates outside the [0.0, 1.0] range are clamped to 0.0 and 1.0, respectively.
	• **D3DTADDRESS_BORDER**—Texture coordinates outside the [0.0, 1.0] range are set to the border color, which is determined by the **D3DTSS_BORDERCOLOR** texture stage state.
	• **D3DTSS_ADDRESSU**—The texture addressing method for *u*-texture coordinates. This determines how the system treats *u*-values outside the [0.0, 1.0] range.
	This state can be set to one of the following enumeration values:
	• **D3DTADDRESS_WRAP**—Textures are tiled at every integer junction. This is the default value for this state.
	• **D3DTADDRESS_MIRROR**—Textures are tiled at every integer junction, but are mirrored (flipped) at every other junction to facilitate seamless texture wrapping.
	• **D3DTADDRESS_CLAMP**—Texture coordinates outside the [0.0, 1.0] range are clamped to 0.0 and 1.0, respectively.
	• **D3DTADDRESS_BORDER**—Texture coordinates outside the [0.0, 1.0] range are set to the border color, which is determined by the **D3DTSS_BORDERCOLOR** texture stage state.

(continued)

IDirect3DDevice7::SetTextureStageState () *(continued)*	
Parameter	**Description**
	• **D3DTSS_ADDRESSV**—The texture addressing method for *v* texture coordinates. This determines how the system treats *v* values outside the [0.0, 1.0] range.
	This state can be set to one of the following enumeration values:
	• **D3DTADDRESS_WRAP**—Textures are tiled at every integer junction. This is the default value for this state.
	• **D3DTADDRESS_MIRROR**—Textures are tiled at every integer junction, but are mirrored (flipped) at every other junction to facilitate seamless texture wrapping.
	• **D3DTADDRESS_CLAMP**—Texture coordinates outside the [0.0, 1.0] range are clamped to 0.0 and 1.0, respectively.
	• **D3DTADDRESS_BORDER**—Texture coordinates outside the [0.0, 1.0] range are set to the border color, which is determined by the **D3DTSS_BORDERCOLOR** texture stage state.
	• **D3DTSS_BORDERCOLOR**—The border color, which determines the color to be used for rasterizing texture coordinates in the [0.0,1.0] range, when the texture addressing mode is set to **D3DTADDRESS_BORDER**. The default color is 0×00000000, or black.
	• **D3DTSS_MAGFILTER**—The filter the system uses when a texel (a pixel in a texture map) is mapped to more than one screen coordinate. This occurs when a primitive occupies more screen space than the primitive's texture. The filter determines how the system handles this case.
	This state can be set to one or, on occasion, more of the following enumeration values:
	• **D3DTFG_POINT**—Nearest point filtering. The system selects the texel with coordinates nearest to the calculated texel. This is the default value for this state.
	• **D3DTFG_LINEAR**—Bilinear interpolation filtering. The system generates a weighted average of a 2×2 area of texels surrounding the calculated texel.
	• **D3DTFG_ANISOTROPIC**—Anisotropic texture filtering, which compensates for the difference in angle between the polygon and the camera. This value may be used in combination with **D3DTFN_POINT** or **D3DTFN_LINEAR**.

(continued)

IDirect3DDevice7::SetTextureStageState () *(continued)*

Parameter	Description
	• **D3DTSS_MINFILTER**—The filter the system uses when a pixel in the render-target surface is mapped to more than one texel (a pixel in a texture map). This occurs when a primitive occupies less screen space than the primitive's texture. The filter determines how the system handles this case.
	This state can be set to one or, on occasion, more of the following enumeration values:
	• **D3DTFN_POINT**—Nearest point filtering. The system selects the texel with coordinates nearest to the calculated texel. This is the default value for this state.
	• **D3DTFN_LINEAR**—Bilinear interpolation filtering. The system generates a weighted average of a 2×2 area of texels surrounding the calculated texel.
	• **D3DTFN_ANISOTROPIC**—Anisotropic texture filtering, which compensates for the difference in angle between the polygon and the camera. This value may be used in combination with **D3DTFN_POINT** or **D3DTFN_LINEAR**.
	• **D3DTSS_MIPFILTER**—The filter the system uses when performing mipmapping. The filter determines how the system selects the appropriate texel (a pixel in a texture map) when performing mipmapping.
	This state can be set to one of the following enumeration values:
	• **D3DTFP_NONE**—Mipmapping is disabled. This is the default value for this state.
	• **D3DTFP_POINT**—Nearest point filtering. The system selects the texel of the nearest mipmap texture.
	• **D3DTFP_LINEAR**—Trilinear mipmap filtering. The system linearly interpolates pixel color using the calculated texels of the two nearest mipmap textures.
	• **D3DTSS_MIPMAPLODBIAS**—The level-of-detail bias for mipmapping, which can be used to make textures appear more or less pixelated. The default value for this state is 0.
	• **D3DTSS_MAXMIPLEVEL**—The maximum mipmap level-of-detail that the system should use, specified as a zero-based index, where 0 corresponds to the highest level of detail in the mipmap chain. The default value for this state is 0, indicating all mipmap levels can be used.
	• **D3DTSS_MAXANISOTROPY**—The maximum level of anisotropy. The default value for this state is 1.

(continued)

IDirect3DDevice7::SetTextureStageState () *(continued)*	
Parameter	**Description**
	• **D3DTSS_BUMPENVLSCALE**—The bump-map luminance scale, which is used to scale bump-map values. This is specified as a **D3DVALUE**, whose default is 0.0.
	• **D3DTSS_BUMPENVLOFFSET**—The offset for bump-map luminance, added to bump-map luminance values. This is specified as a **D3DVALUE**, whose default is 0.0.
	• **D3DTSS_TEXTURETRANSFORMFLAGS**—The texture transformation flags, which determine if and how texture coordinates are transformed.
	This state can be set to one or, on occasion, more of the following values:
	• **D3DTTFF_DISABLE**—Texture transformation is disabled. This is the default value for this state.
	• **D3DTTFF_COUNT1**—The rasterizer should expect 1D texture coordinates.
	• **D3DTTFF_COUNT2**—The rasterizer should expect 2D texture coordinates.
	• **D3DTTFF_COUNT3**—The rasterizer should expect 3D texture coordinates.
	• **D3DTTFF_COUNT4**—The rasterizer should expect 4D texture coordinates.
	• **D3DTTFF_PROJECTED**—Texture coordinates should all be divided by their last component before being sent to the rasterizer.
dwValue	The new value for the specified texture stage state, specified as either a **DWORD** value or as the address of data that contains the state's new value, depending on the specific state being set.
Return Value	**Description**
D3D_OK	Direct3D successfully set the specified texture stage state.
DDERR_INVALIDOBJECT	Direct3D could not set the specified texture stage state, because this Direct3DDevice7 object is invalid.
DDERR_INVALIDPARAMS	Direct3D could not set the specified texture stage state, because one or more parameters are invalid.

IDirect3DDevice7::SetTransform ()	

Function Description

This function sets the matrix associated with a specified transformation stage.

Function Declaration

```
HRESULT SetTransform(
  D3DTRANSFORMSTATETYPE dtstTransformStateType,
  LPD3DMATRIX lpD3DMatrix
);
```

Parameter	Description
dtstTransformStateType	The transformation matrix being set. This parameter can be one of the following enumeration values:
	• **D3DTRANSFORMSTATE_WORLD**—The world transformation matrix is being set. The default value for this matrix is the identity matrix.
	• **D3DTRANSFORMSTATE_WORLD1** through **D3DTRANSFORMSTATE_WORLD3**—World transformation matrices 1 through 3, which are used when blending vertices.
	• **D3DTRANSFORMSTATE_VIEW**—The view transformation matrix is being set. The default value for this matrix is the identity matrix.
	• **D3DTRANSFORMSTATE_PROJECTION**—The projection transformation matrix is being set. The default value for this matrix is the identity matrix.
	• **D3DTRANSFORMSTATE_TEXTURE0** through **D3DTRANSFORMSTATE_TEXTURE7**—The transformation matrix associated with the zero through seventh texture coordinate transformation stage is being set.
lpD3DMatrix	A pointer to a **D3DMATRIX** structure that specifies the new matrix for the specified matrix transformation stage.

Return Value	Description
D3D_OK	Direct3D successfully set the specified matrix transformation stage.
DDERR_INVALIDPARAMS	Direct3D could not set the specified matrix transformation stage, because one or more parameters are invalid.

IDirect3DDevice7::SetViewport ()

Function Description

This function sets the current viewport parameters for the device represented by this **Direct3DDevice7** object. The viewport defines the range of *x*-, *y*-, and *z*-values that primitives will be rendered into.

After undergoing the projection transformation stage, the horizontal, vertical, and depth components of a primitive's vertices will be scaled into the horizontal, vertical, and depth ranges specified by the viewport. Unless an application wishes to render to only a portion of the render-target surface, the horizontal and vertical viewport ranges will correspond to the width and height of the render-target surface, respectively, while the depth range will typically be set to [0.0, 1.0].

Function Declaration

```
HRESULT SetViewport(
  LPD3DVIEWPORT7 lpViewport
);
```

Parameter	Description
lpViewport	A pointer to a **D3DVIEWPORT7** structure that describes the new viewport parameters. If the window dimensions in this structure exceed the boundaries of the render target surface, this function will fail.

Return Value	Description
D3D_OK	Direct3D successfully set the viewport parameters.
DDERR_INVALIDPARAMS	Direct3D could not set the viewport parameters, because one or more parameters are invalid.

IDirect3DDevice7::ValidateDevice ()

Function Description

This function tests the device's ability to render the currently set texture blending operations and arguments in a single pass.

Function Declaration

```
HRESULT ValidateDevice(
  LPDWORD lpdwPasses
);
```

Parameter	Description
lpdwPasses	The address of a **DWORD** variable. If this function succeeds, the variable will be set to the number of passes required to render a primitive with the currently set texture blending operations and arguments.

Return Value	Description
D3D_OK	Direct3D successfully tested the device.
DDERR_INVALIDOBJECT	Direct3D could not test the device, because this Direct3DDevice7 object is invalid.

(continued)

IDirect3DDevice7::ValidateDevice () *(continued)*	
Return Value	**Description**
DDERR_INVALIDPARAMS	Direct3D could not test the device, because one or more parameters are invalid.
D3DERR_CONFLICTINGTEXTUREFILTER	Direct3D could not test the device, because the current texture filters conflict.
D3DERR_CONFLICTINGTEXTUREPALETTE	Direct3D could not test the device, because the current textures cannot be used together.
D3DERR_TOOMANYOPERATIONS	Direct3D could not test the device, because the device does not support the required number of filtering operations.
D3DERR_UNSUPPORTEDALPHAARG	Direct3D could not test the device, because one or more alpha arguments are unsupported.
D3DERR_UNSUPPORTEDALPHAOPERATION	Direct3D could not test the device, because one or more alpha operations are unsupported.
D3DERR_UNSUPPORTEDCOLORARG	Direct3D could not test the device, because one or more color arguments are unsupported.
D3DERR_UNSUPPORTEDCOLOROPERATION	Direct3D could not test the device, because one or more color operations are unsupported.
D3DERR_UNSUPPORTEDFACTORVALUE	Direct3D could not test the device, because the required texture factor is unsupported.
D3DERR_UNSUPPORTEDTEXTUREFILTER	Direct3D could not test the device, because the required texture filter is unsupported.
D3DERR_WRONGTEXTUREFORMAT	Direct3D could not test the device, because the required texture format is invalid.

IDirect3DVertexBuffer7 Reference

This section documents the IDirect3DVertexBuffer7 interface, which applications may obtain by calling the **IDirect3D7::CreateVertexBuffer ()** function.

The GUID for this interface is **IID_IDirect3DVertexBuffer7**.

IDirect3DVertexBuffer7::GetVertexBufferDesc ()
Function Description
This function retrieves a description of the vertex buffer.
Function Declaration

```
HRESULT GetVertexBufferDesc(
  LPD3DVERTEXBUFFERDESC lpVBDesc
);
```

(continued)

IDirect3DVertexBuffer7::GetVertexBufferDesc () *(continued)*

Parameter	Description
lpVBDesc	A pointer to a **D3DVERTEXBUFFERDESC** structure. If this function succeeds, the structure will be filled with a description of the vertex buffer.

Return Value	Description
D3D_OK	Direct3D successfully retrieved a description of the vertex buffer.
DDERR_INVALIDPARAMS	Direct3D could not retrieve a description of the vertex buffer, because one or more parameters are invalid.

IDirect3DVertexBuffer7::Lock ()

Function Description

This function locks the vertex buffer and retrieves a pointer to the vertex buffer memory, which allows applications to manipulate vertex data. After an application is done with the vertex buffer memory, it must unlock the vertex buffer by calling the **IDirect3DVertexBuffer7::Unlock** () function. Vertex buffers must be unlocked before their vertex data can be used with the **DrawPrimitive** functions.

This function often halts multithreading by holding the Win16Mutex. Graphical debuggers cannot operate while the Win16Mutex is held.

Function Declaration

```
HRESULT Lock(
  DWORD   dwFlags,
  LPVOID* lplpData,
  LPDWORD lpdwSize
);
```

Parameter	Description
dwFlags	Describes how the vertex buffer memory should be locked. This parameter can be one or more of the following flags: • **DDLOCK_DISCARDCONTENTS**—The application makes no assumptions about the contents of the vertex buffer during the period of the lock. If this flag is specified, Direct3D is free to use an alternate memory area for the vertex buffer. • **DDLOCK_NOOVERWRITE**—The application will not overwrite any existing vertices during the period of the lock. If the application modifies the contents of the vertex buffer, it will only be appending new vertices to the end of the vertex buffer. • **DDLOCK_NOSYSLOCK**—Direct3D should attempt to lock the vertex buffer memory without holding the Win16Mutex. If Direct3D succeeds, multithreading will not halt, as it otherwise would. • **DDLOCK_READONLY**—The vertex buffer memory will be strictly read from, not written to.

(continued)

IDirect3DVertexBuffer7::Lock () *(continued)*	
Parameter	**Description**
	• **DDLOCK_SURFACEMEMORYPTR**—Direct3D should retrieve a valid pointer to the vertex buffer memory. This is the default behavior.
	• **DDLOCK_WAIT**—Direct3D should wait until either it can lock the vertex buffer or an error occurs before returning. If this flag is not specified, and Direct3D cannot immediately lock the vertex buffer, then it returns immediately with the **DDERR_SURFACEBUSY** error code.
	• **DDLOCK_WRITEONLY**—The vertex memory will be strictly written to, not read from.
lplpData	The address of a pointer. If this function succeeds, the pointer will be set to the vertex buffer memory.
lpdwSize	A pointer to a 32-bit unsigned integer. If this function succeeds, the integer will be set to the size of the vertex buffer pointed to by **lplpData**. This parameter may be **NULL**, in which case the buffer size is not retrieved.
Return Value	**Description**
D3D_OK	Direct3D successfully locked the vertex buffer.
D3DERR_VERTEXBUFFER OPTIMIZED	Direct3D could not lock the vertex buffer, because the vertex buffer is optimized. Optimized vertex buffers cannot be modified.
DDERR_INVALIDPARAMS	Direct3D could not lock the vertex buffer, because one or more parameters are invalid.
DDERR_OUTOFMEMORY	Direct3D could not lock the vertex buffer, because sufficient memory is not available.
DDERR_SURFACEBUSY	Direct3D could not lock the vertex buffer, because it is currently being accessed.
DDERR_SURFACELOST	Direct3D could not lock the vertex buffer, because the memory associated with it has been lost. It must be re-created.

IDirect3DVertexBuffer7::Optimize ()	
Function Description	
This function optimizes the contents of a vertex buffer. Optimized vertex buffers, though more efficient than unoptimized buffers, cannot be modified, because the way that a vertex buffer is optimized is device-specific.	
Function Declaration	

```
HRESULT Optimize(
  LPDIRECT3DDEVICE7 lpD3DDevice,
  DWORD dwFlags
);
```

(continued)

IDirect3DVertexBuffer7::Optimize () *(continued)*

Parameter	Description
lpD3DDevice	A pointer to the Direct3DDevice7 object that identifies the device for which this vertex buffer should be optimized.
dwFlags	This parameter, which is not currently used, must be set to 0.

Return Value	Description
D3D_OK	Direct3D successfully optimized the vertex buffer.
D3DERR_VERTEXBUFFER OPTIMIZED	Direct3D could not optimize the vertex buffer, because it is already optimized.
D3DERR_VERTEXBUFFERLOCKED	Direct3D could not optimize the vertex buffer, because it is locked. It must be unlocked with the **IDirect3DVertexBuffer7::- Unlock** () function.
DDERR_INVALIDPARAMS	Direct3D could not optimize the vertex buffer, because one or more parameters are invalid.
DDERR_OUTOFMEMORY	Direct3D could not optimize the vertex buffer, because sufficient memory is not available.

IDirect3DVertexBuffer7::ProcessVertices ()

Function Description

This function processes an untransformed vertex buffer and stores the resulting transformed vertex data in this vertex buffer, optionally lighting and clipping the vertices as requested. The untransformed vertex buffer is referred to as the source vertex buffer, and this vertex buffer as the destination vertex buffer, which must have a transformed vertex format.

Function Declaration

```
HRESULT ProcessVertices(
  DWORD dwVertexOp,
  DWORD dwDestIndex,
  DWORD dwCount,
  LPDIRECT3DVERTEXBUFFER7 lpSrcBuffer,
  DWORD dwSrcIndex,
  LPDIRECT3DDEVICE7       lpD3DDevice,
  DWORD dwFlags
);
```

Parameter	Description
dwVertexOp	Describes how the source vertex buffer should be processed. This parameter can be one or more of the following flags:
	• **D3DVOP_CLIP**—Direct3D should clip the vertices from the source vertex buffer to the viewing frustum. If this flag is specified, the destination vertex buffer must support clipping information, and therefore cannot have been created with the **D3DVBCAPS_DONOTCLIP** flag.

(continued)

IDirect3DVertexBuffer7::ProcessVertices () *(continued)*	
Parameter	**Description**
	• **D3DVOP_EXTENTS**—Direct3D should update the extents of the screen rectangle when the vertices of the destination vertex buffer are rendered.
	• **D3DVOP_LIGHT**—Direct3D should light the vertices and include that lighting information in the destination vertex buffer. If this flag is specified, the destination vertex buffer format must support lighting information.
	• **D3DVOP_TRANSFORM**—Direct3D should transform the vertices of the source vertex buffer using the world, view, and projection matrices. This flag must always be set. Otherwise, the function will fail.
dwDestIndex	An index into this vertex buffer that identifies the position where the vertices of the source vertex buffer will be stored after processing.
dwCount	The number of vertices in the source vertex buffer to process.
lpSrcBuffer	A pointer to a Direct3DVertexBufffer7 object that identifies the source vertex buffer.
dwSrcIndex	An index into the source vertex buffer that identifies the position of the first vertex to be processed.
lpD3DDevice	A pointer to a Direct3DDevice7 object that identifies the device to be used to process the vertices.
dwFlags	Describes the processing options. This parameter may be set to 0, which indicates default processing, or the following flag:
	• **D3DPV_DONOTCOPYDATA**—Direct3D should not copy into the destination vertex buffer data that is not affected by the current vertex operation. If this flag is not specified, then components that the application does not request to be processed (such as lighting components) will be copied from the source vertex buffer to the destination vertex buffer (assuming the format of the destination vertex buffer supports this). If this information is not required, an application should specify this flag to avoid needless copying of data.
Return Value	**Description**
D3D_OK	Direct3D successfully processed the source vertex buffer, storing the result in the destination vertex buffer.
D3DERR_INVALIDVERTEX FORMAT	Direct3D could not process the source vertex buffer, because the format of one or more vertex buffers are invalid.
DDERR_INVALIDOBJECT	Direct3D could not process the source vertex buffer, because this Direct3DVertexBuffer object is invalid.
DDERR_INVALIDPARAMS	Direct3D could not process the source vertex buffer, because one or more parameters are invalid.

(continued)

IDirect3DVertexBuffer7::ProcessVertices () *(continued)*

Return Value	Description
DDERR_OUTOFMEMORY	Direct3D could not process the source vertex buffer, because sufficient memory is not available.
DDERR_SURFACEBUSY	Direct3D could not process the source vertex buffer, because one or more vertex buffers are being accessed.
DDERR_SURFACELOST	Direct3D could not process the source vertex buffer, because the memory associated with one or more buffers has been lost.

IDirect3DVertexBuffer7::ProcessVerticesStrided ()

Function Description

This function processes untransformed, strided vertices and stores the resulting transformed vertex data in this vertex buffer, optionally lighting and clipping the vertices as requested. The strided vertices are referred to as the source vertex data, while this vertex buffer is referred to as the destination vertex buffer. The destination vertex buffer must have a transformed vertex format.

Function Declaration

```
HRESULT ProcessVerticesStrided(
  DWORD dwVertexOp,
  DWORD dwDestIndex,
  DWORD dwCount,
  LPD3DDRAWPRIMITIVESTRIDEDDATA lpVertexArray,
  DWORD dwSrcIndex,
  LPDIRECT3DDEVICE7 lpD3DDevice,
  DWORD dwFlags
);
```

Parameter	Description
dwVertexOp	Describes how the source vertex data should be processed. This parameter can be one or more of the following flags:
	• **D3DVOP_CLIP**—Direct3D should clip the vertices from the source vertex data to the viewing frustum. If this flag is specified, the destination vertex buffer must support clipping information and, therefore, cannot have been created with the **D3DVBCAPS_DONOTCLIP** flag.
	• **D3DVOP_EXTENTS**—Direct3D should update the extents of the screen rectangle when the vertices of the destination vertex buffer are rendered.
	• **D3DVOP_LIGHT**—Direct3D should light the vertices and include that lighting information in the destination vertex buffer. If this flag is specified, the destination vertex buffer format must support lighting information.

(continued)

IDirect3DVertexBuffer7::ProcessVerticesStrided () *(continued)*

Parameter	Description
	• **D3DVOP_TRANSFORM**—Direct3D should transform the vertices of the source vertex data using the world, view, and projection matrices. This flag must always be set. Otherwise, the function will fail.
dwDestIndex	An index into this vertex buffer that identifies the position where the vertices of the source vertex data will be stored after processing.
dwCount	The number of vertices in the source vertex data to process.
lpVertexArray	A pointer to a **D3DDRAWPRIMITIVESTRIDEDDATA** structure that contains the untransformed, strided vertex data to be used as the source for the vertex processing operation.
dwSrcIndex	An index into the source vertex data that identifies the position of the first vertex to be processed.
lpD3DDevice	A pointer to a Direct3DDevice7 object that identifies the device to be used to process the vertices.
dwFlags	Describes the processing options. This parameter may be set to 0, which indicates default processing, or the following flag:
	• **D3DPV_DONOTCOPYDATA**—Direct3D should not copy into the destination vertex buffer data that is not affected by the current vertex operation. If this flag is not specified, then components that the application does not request to be processed (such as lighting components) will be copied from the source vertex data to the destination vertex buffer (assuming the format of the destination vertex buffer supports this). If this information is not required, an application should specify this flag to avoid needless copying of data.

Return Value	Description
D3D_OK	Direct3D successfully processed the source vertex data, storing the result in the destination vertex buffer.
D3DERR_INVALIDVERTEX FORMAT	Direct3D could not process the source vertex data, because this vertex buffer is invalid.
DDERR_INVALIDOBJECT	Direct3D could not process the source vertex data, because this Direct3DVertexBuffer object is invalid.
DDERR_INVALIDPARAMS	Direct3D could not process the source vertex data, because one or more parameters are invalid.
DDERR_OUTOFMEMORY	Direct3D could not process the source vertex data, because sufficient memory is not available.
DDERR_SURFACEBUSY	Direct3D could not process the source vertex data, because this vertex buffer is being accessed.
DDERR_SURFACELOST	Direct3D could not process the source vertex data, because the memory associated with this vertex buffer has been lost.

IDirect3DVertexBuffer7::Unlock ()

Function Description

This function unlocks a vertex buffer previously locked with the **IDirect3DVertexBuffer7::Lock ()** function.

Function Declaration

```
HRESULT Unlock();
```

Parameter	Description
None	

Return Value	Description
D3D_OK	Direct3D successfully unlocked the vertex buffer.
D3DERR_VERTEXBUFFERUNLOCKFAILED	Direct3D could not unlock the vertex buffer.
DDERR_GENERIC	Direct3D could not unlock the vertex buffer, because of a generic error.
DDERR_INVALIDOBJECT	Direct3D could not unlock the vertex buffer, because this Direct3DVertexBuffer7 object is invalid.
DDERR_INVALIDPARAMS	Direct3D could not unlock the vertex buffer, because one or more parameters are invalid.
DDERR_SURFACEBUSY	Direct3D could not unlock the vertex buffer because it is being accessed.
DDERR_SURFACELOST	Direct3D could not unlock the vertex buffer, because the memory associated with it has been lost.

Callbacks Reference

This section documents application-defined functions that Direct3D uses to pass information to applications.

D3DEnumDevicesCallback7 ()

Function Description

This function is an application-defined function that Direct3D calls for every device it enumerates. The enumeration is initiated by the **IDirect3D7::EnumDevices ()** function.

Function Declaration

```
HRESULT CALLBACK D3DEnumDevicesCallback7(
  LPSTR lpDeviceDescription,
  LPSTR lpDeviceName,
  LPD3DDEVICEDESC7 lpD3DDeviceDesc,
  LPVOID lpContext
);
```

(continued)

D3DEnumDevicesCallback7 () *(continued)*	
Parameter	**Description**
lpDeviceDescription	A pointer to a string containing a textual description of the device.
lpDeviceName	A pointer to a string containing the device name.
lpD3DDeviceDesc	A pointer to a **D3DDEVICEDESC7** structure that describes the hardware capabilities of the device.
lpContext	A pointer to application-defined data sent to this function through the **IDirect3D7::EnumDevices** () function.
Return Value	**Description**
D3DENUMRET_OK	Direct3D should continue the enumeration process.
D3DENUMRET_CANCEL	Direct3D should stop the enumeration process.

D3DEnumPixelFormatsCallback ()

This function is an application-defined function that Direct3D calls for every pixel format it enumerates. The enumeration is initiated by the **IDirect3D7::EnumZBufferFormat** () or **IDirect3DDevice7::EnumTextureFormats** () functions.

Function Declaration

```
HRESULT CALLBACK D3DEnumPixelFormatsCallback(
  LPDDPIXELFORMAT lpDDPixFmt,
  LPVOID          lpContext
);
```

Parameter	**Description**
lpDDPixFmt	A pointer to a **DDPIXELFORMAT** structure that describes the enumerated pixel format.
lpContext	A pointer to application-defined data sent to this function through the **IDirect3D7::EnumZBufferFormat** () or **IDirect3D7::EnumTextureFormats** () function.
Return Value	**Description**
D3DENUMRET_OK	Direct3D should continue the enumeration process.
D3DENUMRET_CANCEL	Direct3D should stop the enumeration process.

D3D_OVERLOADS Reference

This section documents the overloaded functions and other miscellaneous routines that are available to all C++ programmers who define **D3D_OVERLOADS** before including the Direct3D header file (for example, **#define D3D_OVERLOADS**).

Table B.1 lists helper functions for the **D3DVECTOR** type, which enable applications to calculate the dot product, cross product, and magnitude of vectors, among other functions. Table B.2 documents the overloaded operators for the **D3DVECTOR** type that enable applications to use **D3DVECTOR** types as they would built-in types. Table B.3 provides references for a few useful constructors for the **D3DVECTOR** type. Table B.4 documents the overloaded operator for the **D3DMATRIX** type.

Table B.1 Helper functions for the D3DVECTOR type.

Function Name	Description
CrossProduct ()	Returns the cross product of two vector types.
DotProduct ()	Returns the dot product of two vectors.
Magnitude ()	Returns the magnitude of a vector.
Max ()	Returns the maximum component of a vector.
Maximize ()	Returns a vector made up of the largest components of two vectors.
Min ()	Returns the minimum component of a vector.
Minimize ()	Returns a vector made up of the smallest components of two vectors.
Normalize ()	Normalizes a vector (makes its magnitude 1).
SquareMagnitude ()	Returns the square of the magnitude of a vector.

Table B.2 Overloaded operator for the D3DVECTOR type.

Operator Name	Description
[n]	Returns the **n**th vector component; 0 indicates the x- component, 1, the y- component, and 2, the z-component.
+	Returns the addition of two vectors.
+=	Adds one vector to another.
-=	Subtracts one vector from another.
*=	Multiplies one vector by another.
/=	Divides one vector by another.
*=	Multiplies a vector by a scalar.
/=	Divides a vector by a scalar.
==	Determines if two vectors are identical, component for component.
/	Returns the division of one vector by another.
/	Returns the division of a vector by a scalar.
*	Returns the multiplication of one vector by another.
*	Returns the multiplication of a vector by a scalar.
-	Returns the subtraction of one vector from another.
+	Returns a vector.
-	Returns the negation of a vector.
<	Returns true if all components of the first vector are less than the corresponding components of the second vector.
<= to	Returns true if all components of the first vector are less than or equal the corresponding components of the second vector.

Table B.3 Constructors for the D3DVECTOR type.

Constructor	Description
(f)	Initializes all components of the vector to **f**.
(i, j, k)	Initializes the vector's x-, y-, and z-components to **i**, **j**, and **k**, respectively.
(f[3])	Initializes the vector's x-, y-, and z-components to **f[0]**, **f[1]**, and **f[2]**, respectively, where **f** is an array of three floating-point values.

Table B.4 Overloaded operator for the D3DMATRIX type.

Operator Name	Description
(i, j)	Returns a reference to the element at the **i**th row and **j**th column of the matrix. This allows assignments, such as **X = Matrix(i,j)** and **Matrix(i,j)=1.0**.

Structure Reference

This section documents the structures used by Direct3D functions.

D3DCLIPSTATUS	
Structure Description	
This function describes the current clip status.	
Structure Declaration	

```
typedef struct _D3DCLIPSTATUS {
    DWORD dwFlags;
    DWORD dwStatus;
    float minx, maxx;
    float miny, maxy;
    float minz, maxz;
} D3DCLIPSTATUS, *LPD3DCLIPSTATUS;
```

Member	Description
dwFlags	Describes the information content of this structure. This member can be one or more of the following flags: • **D3DCLIPSTATUS_STATUS**—The structure contains the current clip status. • **D3DCLIPSTATUS_EXTENTS2**—The structure contains the current 2D extents. This flag cannot be used with the **D3DCLIPSTATUS_EXTENTS3** flag. • **D3DCLIPSTATUS_EXTENTS3**—The structure contains the current 3D extents. This flag cannot be used with the **D3DCLIPSTATUS_EXTENTS2** flag. This flag is not currently implemented.

(continued)

D3DCLIPSTATUS *(continued)*	
Member	**Description**
dwStatus	Describes the current clip status. This member can be one or more of the following flags:
	• **D3DSTATUS_CLIPINTERSECTIONALL**—This flag is a combination of all **D3DSTATUS_CLIPINTERSECTION*** flags.
	• **D3DSTATUS_CLIPUNIONALL**—This flag is a combination of all **D3DSTATUS_CLIPUNION*** flags.
	• **D3DSTATUS_DEFAULT**—This flag is a combination of the **D3DSTATUS_CLIPINTERSECTIONALL** and **D3DSTATUS_-ZNOTVISIBLE** flags. This flag is the default clip status.
	• **D3DSTATUS_ZNOTVISIBLE**—The rendered primitive is not visible.
	• **D3DCLIP_BACK**—Vertices are clipped by the viewing frustum's back clipping plane.
	• **D3DCLIP_BOTTOM**—Vertices are clipped by the viewing frustum's bottom clipping plane.
	• **D3DCLIP_FRONT**—Vertices are clipped by the viewing frustum's front clipping plane.
	• **D3DCLIP_LEFT**—Vertices are clipped by the viewing frustum's left clipping plane.
	• **D3DCLIP_RIGHT**—Vertices are clipped by the viewing frustum's right clipping plane.
	• **D3DCLIP_TOP**—Vertices are clipped by the viewing frustum's top clipping plane.
	• **D3DSTATUS_CLIPUNIONBACK**—This flag is identical to **D3DCLIP_BACK**.
	• **D3DSTATUS_CLIPUNIONBOTTOM**—This flag is identical to **D3DCLIP_BOTTOM**.
	• **D3DSTATUS_CLIPUNIONFRONT**—This flag is identical to **D3DCLIP_FRONT**.
	• **D3DSTATUS_CLIPUNIONGEN0** through **D3DSTATUS_-CLIPUNIONGEN5**—These flags are identical to **D3DCLIP_-GEN0** through **D3DCLIP_GEN5**.
	• **D3DSTATUS_CLIPUNIONLEFT**—This flag is equal to **D3DCLIP_LEFT**.

(continued)

D3DCLIPSTATUS *(continued)*	
Member	**Description**
	• **D3DSTATUS_CLIPUNIONRIGHT**—This flag is equal to **D3DCLIP_RIGHT**.
	• **D3DSTATUS_CLIPUNIONTOP**—This flag is equal to **D3DCLIP_TOP**.
	• **D3DCLIP_GEN0** through **D3DCLIP_GEN5**—Vertices are clipped by the application-defined clipping planes 0 through 5, respectively.
	• **D3DSTATUS_CLIPINTERSECTIONBACK**—The logical AND of the clip flags for the vertices when compared with the viewing frustum's back clipping plane.
	• **D3DSTATUS_CLIPINTERSECTIONBOTTOM**—The logical AND of the clip flags for the vertices when compared with the viewing frustum's bottom clipping plane.
	• **D3DSTATUS_CLIPINTERSECTIONFRONT**—The logical AND of the clip flags for the vertices when compared with the viewing frustum's front clipping plane.
	• **D3DSTATUS_CLIPINTERSECTIONGEN0** through **D3DSTATUS_CLIPINTERSECTIONGEN5**—The logical AND of the clip flags for the vertices when compared with the application-defined clipping planes 0 through 5, respectively.
	• **D3DSTATUS_CLIPINTERSECTIONLEFT**—The logical AND of the clip flags for the vertices when compared with the viewing frustum's left clipping plane.
	• **D3DSTATUS_CLIPINTERSECTIONRIGHT**—The logical AND of the clip flags for the vertices when compared with the viewing frustum's right clipping plane.
	• **D3DSTATUS_CLIPINTERSECTIONTOP**—The logical AND of the clip flags for the vertices when compared with the viewing frustum's top clipping plane.
minx	The minimum x-coordinate of the current clipping region.
maxx	The maximum x-coordinate of the current clipping region.
miny	The minimum y-coordinate of the current clipping region.
maxy	The maximum y-coordinate of the current clipping region.
minz	The minimum z-coordinate of the current clipping region.
maxz	The maximum z-coordinate of the current clipping region.

D3DCOLORVALUE

Structure Description

This function describes a color value. Though the range of each component is typically [0.0, 1.0], applications may select values outside this range to achieve special effects (negative values for a light's color, for example, produce lights that darken a scene).

Structure Declaration

```
typedef struct _D3DCOLORVALUE {
    union {
        D3DVALUE r;
        D3DVALUE dvR;
    };
    union {
        D3DVALUE g;
        D3DVALUE dvG;
    };
    union {
        D3DVALUE b;
        D3DVALUE dvB;
    };
    union {
        D3DVALUE a;
        D3DVALUE dvA;
    };
} D3DCOLORVALUE;
```

Member	Description
r, dvR	The red component of the color, typically in the [0.0, 1.0] range, where 0.0 corresponds to no intensity, and 1.0 corresponds to full intensity.
g, dvG	The green component of the color, typically in the [0.0, 1.0] range, where 0.0 corresponds to no intensity, and 1.0 corresponds to full intensity.
b, dvB	The blue component of the color, typically in the [0.0, 1.0] range, where 0.0 corresponds to no intensity, and 1.0 corresponds to full intensity.
a, dvA	The alpha component of the color, typically in the [0.0, 1.0] range, where 0.0 corresponds to completely transparent, and 1.0 corresponds to fully opaque.

D3DDEVICEDESC7

Structure Description

This structure describes the current device.

Structure Declaration

```
typedef struct _D3DDeviceDesc7 {
    DWORD           dwDevCaps;
    D3DPRIMCAPS     dpcLineCaps;
    D3DPRIMCAPS     dpcTriCaps;
    DWORD           dwDeviceRenderBitDepth;
    DWORD           dwDeviceZBufferBitDepth;
    DWORD           dwMinTextureWidth, dwMinTextureHeight;
    DWORD           dwMaxTextureWidth, dwMaxTextureHeight;
    DWORD           dwMaxTextureRepeat;
    DWORD           dwMaxTextureAspectRatio;
    DWORD           dwMaxAnisotropy;
    D3DVALUE        dvGuardBandLeft;
    D3DVALUE        dvGuardBandTop;
    D3DVALUE        dvGuardBandRight;
    D3DVALUE        dvGuardBandBottom;
    D3DVALUE        dvExtentsAdjust;
    DWORD           dwStencilCaps;
    DWORD           dwFVFCaps;
    DWORD           dwTextureOpCaps;
    WORD            wMaxTextureBlendStages;
    WORD            wMaxSimultaneousTextures;
    DWORD           dwMaxActiveLights;
    D3DVALUE        dvMaxVertexW;
    GUID            deviceGUID;
    WORD            wMaxUserClipPlanes;
    WORD            wMaxVertexBlendMatrices;
    DWORD           dwVertexProcessingCaps;
    DWORD           dwReserved1;
    DWORD           dwReserved2;
    DWORD           dwReserved3;
    DWORD           dwReserved4;
} D3DDEVICEDESC7, *LPD3DDEVICEDESC7;
```

Member	Description
dwDevCaps	Describes the capabilities of the device. This member can be one or more of the following flags: • **D3DDEVCAPS_CANBLTSYSTONONLOCAL**—The device supports blits from system-memory textures to nonlocal video-memory textures.

(continued)

D3DDEVICEDESC7 *(continued)*	
Member	**Description**
	• **D3DDEVCAPS_CANRENDERAFTERFLIP**—The device can schedule rendering commands after a page flip, indicating the device is relatively fast. Applications should not change this capability.
	• **D3DDEVCAPS_DRAWPRIMTLVERTEX**—The device exports a **DrawPrimitive**-aware Hardware Abstraction Layer (HAL).
	• **D3DDEVCAPS_EXECUTESYSTEMMEMORY**—The device can execute buffers from system memory. This capability cannot be used with the IDirect3DDevice7 interface, because this interface does not support execute buffers.
	• **D3DDEVCAPS_EXECUTEVIDEOMEMORY**—The device can execute buffers from video memory. This capability cannot be used with the IDirect3DDevice7 interface, because this interface does not support execute buffers.
	• **D3DDEVCAPS_FLOATTLVERTEX**—The device accepts floating-point for post-transformation vertex data.
	• **D3DDEVCAPS_HWRASTERIZATION**—The device supports hardware acceleration for scene rasterization.
	• **D3DDEVCAPS_HWTRANSFORMANDLIGHT**—The device supports transformation and lighting in hardware.
	• **D3DDEVCAPS_SEPARATETEXTUREMEMORIES**—The device uses separate memory pools for each texture stage. Textures must be explicitly assigned a texture stage when they are created. Applications may do this by setting the **dwTextureStage** member of the **DDSURFACEDESC2** structure used for texture creation to the appropriate texture stage number.
	• **D3DDEVCAPS_SORTDECREASINGZ**—The device requires data sorted by decreasing depth.
	• **D3DDEVCAPS_SORTEXACT**—The device requires data sorted exactly.
	• **D3DDEVCAPS_SORTINCREASINGZ**—The device requires data sorted by increasing depth.
	• **D3DDEVCAPS_STRIDEDVERTICES**—The device supports strided vertex data for transformation and lighting in hardware.
	• **D3DDEVCAPS_TEXREPEATNOTSCALEDBYSIZE**—The device waits to scale texture coordinates by the texture size until after the texture address mode is applied.
	• **D3DDEVCAPS_TEXTURENONLOCALVIDMEM**—The device can retrieve textures from nonlocal video memory.

(continued)

D3DDEVICEDESC7 *(continued)*

Member	Description
	• **D3DDEVCAPS_TEXTURESYSTEMMEMORY**—The device can retrieve textures from system memory.
	• **D3DDEVCAPS_TEXTUREVIDEOMEMORY**—The device can retrieve textures from local video memory.
	• **D3DDEVCAPS_TLVERTEXSYSTEMMEMORY**—The device can use buffers existing in system memory for transformed and lit vertices.
	• **D3DDEVCAPS_TLVERTEXVIDEOMEMORY**—The device can use buffers existing in video memory for transformed and lit vertices.
dpcLineCaps	A **D3DPRIMCAPS** structure that describes the extent of the device's support for line-drawing primitives.
dpcTriCaps	A **D3DPRIMCAPS** structure that describes the extent of the device's support for triangle primitives.
dwDeviceRenderBitDepth	The rendering bit depths supported by the device, which can be one or more of the following predefined bit depth constants: **DDBD_8**, **DDBD_16**, **DDBD_24**, or **DDBD_32**.
dwDeviceZBufferBitDepth	The depth-buffer bit depths supported by the device, which can be one or more of the following predefined bit depth constants: **DDBD_8**, **DDBD_16**, **DDBD_24**, or **DDBD_32**.
dwMinTextureWidth	The minimum texture width supported by the device, in pixels.
dwMinTextureHeight	The minimum texture height supported by the device, in pixels.
dwMaxTextureWidth	The maximum texture width supported by the device, in pixels.
dwMaxTextureHeight	The maximum texture height supported by the device, in pixels.
dwMaxTextureRepeat	The maximum texture repeat for post-normalized texture coordinates, rounded down to the nearest integer. Post-normalized texture coordinates are those that have been multiplied by size of the texture.
	If the **D3DDEVCAPS_TEXREPEATNOTSCALEDBYSIZE** capability is present, the device waits to scale texture coordinates by the texture size until after the texture address mode is applied. Otherwise, the device scales texture coordinates immediately prior to interpolation.
dwMaxTextureAspectRatio	The maximum texture aspect ratio supported by the device, typically a power of 2.
dwMaxAnisotropy	The maximum value for the **D3DRENDERSTATE_ANISOTROPY** render state.
dvGuardBandLeft	The leftmost pixel of the guard-band clipping region. Coordinates inside the guard-band region but outside the viewport rectangle will be automatically clipped.

(continued)

D3DDEVICEDESC7 *(continued)*

Member	Description
dvGuardBandTop	The topmost pixel of the guard-band clipping region. Coordinates inside the guard-band region but outside the viewport rectangle will be automatically clipped.
dvGuardBandRight	The rightmost pixel of the guard-band clipping region. Coordinates inside the guard-band region but outside the viewport rectangle will be automatically clipped.
dvGuardBandBottom	The bottom-most pixel of the guard-band clipping region. Coordinates inside the guard-band region but outside the viewport rectangle will be automatically clipped.
dvExtentsAdjust	The number of pixels to adjust the extents of the rectangle outward for accommodating anti-aliasing kernels.
dwStencilCaps	The stencil-buffer operations supported for the **D3DRENDERSTATE_STENCILFAIL**, **D3DRENDERSTATE_-STENCILPASS**, and **D3DRENDERSTATE_STENCILFAILZFAIL** render states. This member can be set to zero or one of the following flags: • **D3DSTENCILCAPS_DECR**—The device supports the **D3DSTENCILOP_DECR** operation. • **D3DSTENCILCAPS_DECRSAT**—The device supports the **D3DSTENCILOP_DECRSAT** operation. • **D3DSTENCILCAPS_INCR**—The device supports the **D3DSTENCILOP_INCR** operation. • **D3DSTENCILCAPS_INCRSAT**—The device supports the **D3DSTENCILOP_INCRSAT** operation. • **D3DSTENCILCAPS_INVERT**—The device supports the **D3DSTENCILOP_INVERT** operation. • **D3DSTENCILCAPS_KEEP**—The device supports the **D3DSTENCILOP_KEEP** operation. • **D3DSTENCILCAPS_REPLACE**—The device supports the **D3DSTENCILOP_REPLACE** operation. • **D3DSTENCILCAPS_ZERO**—The device supports the **D3DSTENCILOP_ZERO** operation.
dwFVFCaps	Describes the flexible vertex format capabilities supported by the device. This member can be zero or one of the following flags: • **D3DFVFCAPS_DONOTSTRIPELEMENTS**—The device prefers that unused vertex components not be stripped from the vertex data. If this flag is not present, the device will perform rendering faster if extraneous components are stripped from the vertex data.

(continued)

D3DDEVICEDESC7 *(continued)*	
Member	**Description**
	• **D3DFVFCAPS_TEXCOORDCOUNTMASK**—This is not a flag, but, rather, a mask that, when applied to **dwFVFCaps**, produces an integer that describes the total number of texture coordinate sets that the device can simultaneously use for texture blending operations.
dwTextureOpCaps	Describes the texture operations supported by the device. This member can be one or more of the following flags:
	• **D3DTEXOPCAPS_ADD**—The device supports the **D3DTOP_ADD** texture blending operation.
	• **D3DTEXOPCAPS_ADDSIGNED**—The device supports the **D3DTOP_ADDSIGNED** texture blending operation.
	• **D3DTEXOPCAPS_ADDSIGNED2X**—The device supports the **D3DTOP_ADDSIGNED2X** texture blending operation.
	• **D3DTEXOPCAPS_ADDSMOOTH**—The device supports the **D3DTOP_ADDSMOOTH** texture blending operation.
	• **D3DTEXOPCAPS_BLENDCURRENTALPHA**—The device supports the **D3DTOP_BLENDCURRENTALPHA** texture blending operation.
	• **D3DTEXOPCAPS_BLENDDIFFUSEALPHA**—The device supports the **D3DTOP_BLENDDIFFUSEALPHA** texture blending operation.
	• **D3DTEXOPCAPS_BLENDFACTORALPHA**—The device supports the **D3DTOP_BLENDFACTORALPHA** texture blending operation.
	• **D3DTEXOPCAPS_BLENDTEXTUREALPHA**—The device supports the **D3DTOP_BLENDTEXTUREALPHA** texture blending operation.
	• **D3DTEXOPCAPS_BLENDTEXTUREALPHAPM**—The device supports the **3DTOP_BLENDTEXTUREALPHAPM** texture blending operation.
	• **D3DTEXOPCAPS_BUMPENVMAP**—The device supports the **D3DTOP_BUMPENVMAP** texture blending operation.
	• **D3DTEXOPCAPS_BUMPENVMAPLUMINANCE**—The device supports the **D3DTOP_BUMPENVMAPLUMINANCE** texture blending operation.
	• **D3DTEXOPCAPS_DISABLE**—The device supports the **D3DTOP_DISABLE** texture blending operation.
	• **D3DTEXOPCAPS_DOTPRODUCT3**—The device supports the **D3DTOP_DOTPRODUCT3** texture blending operation.

(continued)

D3DDEVICEDESC7 *(continued)*	
Member	**Description**
	• **D3DTEXOPCAPS_MODULATE**—The device supports the **D3DTOP_MODULATE** texture blending operation.
	• **D3DTEXOPCAPS_MODULATE2X**—The device supports the **D3DTOP_MODULATE2X** texture blending operation.
	• **D3DTEXOPCAPS_MODULATE4X**—The device supports the **D3DTOP_MODULATE4X** texture blending operation.
	• **D3DTEXOPCAPS_MODULATEALPHA_ADDCOLOR**— The device supports the **D3DTOP_MODULATEALPHA_-ADDCOLOR** texture blending operation.
	• **D3DTEXOPCAPS_MODULATECOLOR_ADDALPHA**—The device supports the **D3DTOP_MODULATECOLOR_-ADDALPHA** texture blending operation.
	• **D3DTEXOPCAPS_MODULATEINVALPHA_ADDCOLOR**— The device supports the **D3DTOP_MODULATEINVALPHA_-ADDCOLOR** texture blending operation.
	• **D3DTEXOPCAPS_MODULATEINVCOLOR_ADDALPHA**— The device supports the **D3DTOP_MODULATEINVCOLOR_-ADDALPHA** texture blending operation.
	• **D3DTEXOPCAPS_PREMODULATE**—The device supports the **D3DTOP_PREMODULATE** texture blending operation.
	• **D3DTEXOPCAPS_SELECTARG1**—The device supports the **D3DTOP_SELECTARG1** texture blending operation.
	• **D3DTEXOPCAPS_SELECTARG2**—The device supports the **D3DTOP_SELECTARG2** texture blending operation.
	• **D3DTEXOPCAPS_SUBTRACT**—The device supports the **D3DTOP_SUBTRACT** texture blending operation.
wMaxTextureBlendStages	The maximum number of texture stages supported by the device.
wMaxSimultaneousTextures	The number of texture stages that can simultaneously have textures assigned to them by the **IDirect3DDevice7::SetTexture** () function.
dwMaxActiveLights	The maximum number of light sources that can be active simultaneously.
dvMaxVertexW	The maximum *w*-based depth value supported by the device.
deviceGUID	A GUID that uniquely identifies the device.

(continued)

D3DDEVICEDESC7 *(continued)*

Member	Description
wMaxUserClipPlanes	The maximum number of user-defined clipping planes, which can range from 0 to **D3DMAXUSERCLIPPLANES**.
wMaxVertexBlendMatrices	The maximum number of matrices that can be used for multi-matrix vertex blending.
dwVertexProcessingCaps	Describes the vertex processing capabilities of the device. This member can be zero or more of the following flags: • **D3DVTXPCAPS_TEXGEN**—The device can generate texture coordinates. • **D3DVTXPCAPS_MATERIALSOURCE7**—The device supports selectable vertex color sources. Applications can choose the source for the ambient, diffuse, and specular lighting information. • **D3DVTXPCAPS_VERTEXFOG**—The device supports vertex-based fog. • **D3DVTXPCAPS_DIRECTIONALLIGHTS**—The device supports directional light sources. • **D3DVTXPCAPS_POSITIONALLIGHTS**—The device supports positional light sources, including both point lights and spotlights. • **D3DVTXPCAPS_NONLOCALVIEWER**—The device supports orthogonal specular highlights, governed by the **D3DRENDERSTATE_LOCALVIEWER** render state.
dwReserved1-dwReserved4	These members are reserved for future use and must be 0.

D3DDEVINFO_TEXTUREMANAGER

Structure Description

This structure describes the current state of the texture manager.

Structure Declaration

```
typedef struct _D3DDEVINFO_TEXTUREMANAGER {
    BOOL    bThrashing;
    DWORD   dwNumEvicts;
    DWORD   dwNumVidCreates;
    DWORD   dwNumTexturesUsed;
    DWORD   dwNumUsedTexInVid;
    DWORD   dwWorkingSet;
    DWORD   dwWorkingSetBytes;
    DWORD   dwTotalManaged;
```

(continued)

D3DDEVINFO_TEXTUREMANAGER *(continued)*

Structure Declaration

```
    DWORD    dwTotalBytes;
    DWORD    dwLastPri;
} D3DDEVINFO_TEXTUREMANAGER, *LPD3DDEVINFO_TEXTUREMANAGER;
```

Member	Description
bThrashing	The thrashing status, which can be **TRUE** if texture thrashing (swapping) occurred during the last frame, or **FALSE** otherwise.
dwNumEvicts	The number of textures that were evicted from video memory during the last frame.
dwNumVidCreates	The number of textures that were created in video memory during the last frame.
dwNumTexturesUsed	The number of textures that were used during the last frame.
dwNumUsedTexInVid	The number of video memory textures that were used during the last frame.
dwWorkingSet	The number of textures that currently reside in video memory.
dwWorkingSetBytes	The number of bytes used for textures currently residing in video memory.
dwTotalManaged	The total number of managed textures.
dwTotalBytes	The total number of bytes allocated for managed textures.
dwLastPri	The priority number of the last texture that was evicted.

D3DDEVINFO_TEXTURING

Structure Description

This structure describes the texturing activity of the application.

Structure Declaration

```
typedef struct _D3DDEVINFO_TEXTURING {
    DWORD    dwNumLoads;
    DWORD    dwApproxBytesLoaded;
    DWORD    dwNumPreLoads;
    DWORD    dwNumSet;
    DWORD    dwNumCreates;
    DWORD    dwNumDestroys;
    DWORD    dwNumSetPriorities;
    DWORD    dwNumSetLODs;
    DWORD    dwNumLocks;
    DWORD    dwNumGetDCs;
} D3DDEVINFO_TEXTURING, *LPD3DDEVINFO_TEXTURING;
```

(continued)

D3DDEVINFO_TEXTURING (continued)

Member	Description
dwNumLoads	The number of times textures have been loaded by the **IDirect3DDevice7::Load** () function.
DwApproxBytesLoaded	The approximate number of bytes loaded by the **IDirect3DDevice7::Load** () function.
DwNumPreLoads	The number of times automatically managed textures have been explicitly loaded by the **IDirect3DDevice7::PreLoad** () function.
DwNumSet	The number of times textures have been associated with texture-blending stages by the **IDirect3DDevice7::SetTexture** () function.
DwNumCreates	The number of texture surfaces created by the application.
DwNumDestroys	The number of texture surfaces destroyed by the application.
DwNumSetPriorities	The number of times the texture-management priority level has been set by the **IDirectDrawSurface7::SetPriority** () function.
DwNumSetLODs	The number of times the maximum mipmap level of detail has been set by the **IDirectDrawSurface7::SetLOD** () function for mipmapped texture surfaces.
DwNumLocks	The number of times texture surfaces have been locked by the **IDirectDrawSurface7::Lock** () function.
DwNumGetDCs	The number of times a device context has been created for a texture surface by the **IDirectDrawSurface7::GetDC** () function.

D3DDP_PTRSTRIDE

Structure Description

This structure describes the stride between two elements of a component in a strided vertex format. Strided vertices are those whose individual components (such as x or the vertical texture coordinate v, for example) are defined by both a memory location and a stride, the latter indicating the distance (in bytes) from one component to the next. Strided vertices allow an application to store its vertex components in any arrangement possible, even storing individual components in their own separate arrays.

This structure is used by the **D3DDRAWPRIMITIVESTRIDEDDATA** structure.

Structure Declaration

```
typedef struct _D3DDP_PTRSTRIDE {
    LPVOID lpvData;
    DWORD  dwStride;
} D3DDP_PTRSTRIDE;
```

Member	Description
lpvData	A pointer to the first component.
dwStride	The number of bytes between components in the array specified by **lpvData**.

D3DDRAWPRIMITIVESTRIDEDDATA

Structure Description

This structure describes strided vertices. Strided vertices are those whose individual components (such as *x* or the vertical texture coordinate *v*, for example) are defined by both a memory location and a stride, the latter indicating the distance (in bytes) from one component to the next. Strided vertices allow an application to store its vertex components in any arrangement possible, even storing individual components in their own separate arrays.

Structure Declaration

```
typedef struct D3DDRAWPRIMITIVESTRIDEDDATA  {
    D3DDP_PTRSTRIDE position;
    D3DDP_PTRSTRIDE normal;
    D3DDP_PTRSTRIDE diffuse;
    D3DDP_PTRSTRIDE specular;
    D3DDP_PTRSTRIDE textureCoords[D3DDP_MAXTEXCOORD];
} D3DDRAWPRIMITIVESTRIDEDDATA , *LPD3DDRAWPRIMITIVESTRIDEDDATA;
```

Member	Description
position	A pointer to a **D3DDP_PTRSTRIDE** structure that specifies the memory location for the first vertex position component and the distance (in bytes) between consecutive vertex position components.
	Each vertex position component is a 64-64-64 floating-point triplet.
normal	A pointer to a **D3DDP_PTRSTRIDE** structure that specifies the memory location for the first vertex normal component and the distance (in bytes) between consecutive vertex normal components.
	Each vertex normal component is a 64-64-64 floating-point triplet.
diffuse	A pointer to a **D3DDP_PTRSTRIDE** structure that specifies the memory location for the first vertex diffuse component and the distance (in bytes) between consecutive vertex diffuse components.
	Each diffuse component is an 8-8-8-8 RGBA value.
specular	A pointer to a **D3DDP_PTRSTRIDE** structure that specifies the memory location for the first vertex specular component and the distance (in bytes) between consecutive vertex specular components.
	Each specular component is an 8-8-8-8 RGBA value.
textureCoords	A pointer to an eight-element array of **D3DDP_PTRSTRIDE** structures, one for each texture coordinate set. Each structure specifies the memory location for the first texture coordinate in that set, and the distance (in bytes) between consecutive texture coordinates.
	The **D3DTSS_TEXCOORDINDEX** texture stage state determines how many of the **D3DDP_PTRSTRIDE** structures must contain valid data.
	The format of a texture coordinate depends on how many dimensions it has, which is specified by the flexible vertex format.

D3DLIGHT7

Structure Description

This structure describes a light source.

Structure Declaration

```
typedef struct _D3DLIGHT7 {
    D3DLIGHTTYPE    dltType;
    D3DCOLORVALUE   dcvDiffuse;
    D3DCOLORVALUE   dcvSpecular;
    D3DCOLORVALUE   dcvAmbient;
    D3DVECTOR       dvPosition;
    D3DVECTOR       dvDirection;
    D3DVALUE        dvRange;
    D3DVALUE        dvFalloff;
    D3DVALUE        dvAttenuation0;
    D3DVALUE        dvAttenuation1;
    D3DVALUE        dvAttenuation2;
    D3DVALUE        dvTheta;
    D3DVALUE        dvPhi;
} D3DLIGHT7, *LPD3DLIGHT7;
```

Member	Description
dltType	The type of light source. This member can be one of the following enumeration values: • **D3DLIGHT_POINT**—The light is a point light source, which has a position but no orientation and, therefore, emits light equally in all directions. • **D3DLIGHT_SPOT**—The light is a spotlight source, which has a position, orientation, and light cone, which determines where the light falls. • **D3DLIGHT_DIRECTIONAL**—The light is a directional light source, which has a direction but no position. • **D3DLIGHT_PARALLELPOINT**—The light is a parallel light source, which has a position. The direction of a parallel light is the vector from the position of the light to the origin of the object being illuminated.
dcvDiffuse	A **D3DCOLORVALUE** structure that specifies the diffuse color emitted by the light source.
dcvSpecular	A **D3DCOLORVALUE** structure that specifies the specular color emitted by the light source.
dcvAmbient	A **D3DCOLORVALUE** structure that specifies the ambient color emitted by the light source.

(continued)

D3DLIGHT7 *(continued)*	
Member	Description
dvPosition	A **D3DVECTOR** structure that specifies position of the light source in world space. This member is not valid for directional light sources.
dvDirection	A **D3DVECTOR** structure that specifies the direction of the light source in world space. This member is valid only for directional and spotlights, in which cases it must be non-**NULL**.
dvRange	The maximum range of the light, which ranges from 0 to **D3DLIGHT_RANGE_MAX**. This member is not valid for directional light sources.
dvFalloff	The decrease in intensity between the spotlight's inner and outer cones (specified by **dvTheta** and **dvPhi**, respectively). This member, which is valid only for spotlights, may slightly degrade performance unless it is set to 1.0.
dvAttenuation0	A coefficient in the equation Direct3D uses to attenuate light. This equation is **A=1/(dvAttenuation0 + D*dvAttenuation1 + D²*Attenuation2)**, where **A** is the attenuation, **D** is the distance from the viewer to the point, and the rest of terms are the attenuation coefficients. Valid values for this member are 0 to infinity.
dvAttenuation1	A coefficient in the equation Direct3D uses to attenuate light. This equation is **A=1/(dvAttenuation0 + D*dvAttenuation1 + D²*Attenuation2)**, where **A** is the attenuation, **D** is the distance from the viewer to the point, and the rest of terms are the attenuation coefficients. Valid values for this member are 0 to infinity.
dvAttenuation2	A coefficient in the equation Direct3D uses to attenuate light. This equation is **A=1/(dvAttenuation0 + D*dvAttenuation1 + D²*Attenuation2)**, where **A** is the attenuation, **D** is the distance from the viewer to the point, and the rest of terms are the attenuation coefficients. Valid values for this member are 0 to infinity.
dvTheta	The angle, specified in radians, of the spotlight's inner cone. All points falling in this cone will be fully illuminated. The range of this value is [0, **dvPhi**], where **dvPhi** is the angle of the spotlight's outer cone. This member is valid only for spotlights.
dvPhi	The angle, specified in radians, of the spotlight's outer cone. All points falling outside this cone will not be lit by the spotlight. The range of this value is [**dvTheta**, p], where **dvTheta** is the angle of the spotlight's inner cone.

D3DLIGHTINGCAPS

Structure Description

This structure describes the lighting capabilities of a device.

Structure Declaration

```
typedef struct _D3DLIGHTINGCAPS {
    DWORD dwSize;
    DWORD dwCaps;
    DWORD dwLightingModel;
    DWORD dwNumLights;
} D3DLIGHTINGCAPS, *LPD3DLIGHTINGCAPS;
```

Member	Description
dwSize	The size of this structure, in bytes. This member must be initialized before this structure can be used.
dwCaps	Describes the capabilities of the lighting module. This member can be zero or one of the following flags: • **D3DLIGHTCAPS_DIRECTIONAL**—The device supports directional light sources. • **D3DLIGHTCAPS_POINT**—The device supports point light sources. • **D3DLIGHTCAPS_SPOT**—The device supports spotlights.
dwLightingModel	Describes the lighting models supported by the device. This member can be one or more of the following flags: • **D3DLIGHTINGMODEL_MONO**—The device supports the monochromatic lighting model, where the color of the light is assumed to be white, and only the intensity of the light may be specified. • **D3DLIGHTINGMODEL_RGB**—The device supports the RGB lighting model, where both color and intensity of the light may be specified.
dwNumLights	The number of light sources the device supports.

D3DLINEPATTERN

Structure Description

This structure describes a line pattern. A line pattern describes how a line is drawn by specifying the state (whether on or off) of 16 consecutive pixels.

Structure Declaration

```
typedef struct _D3DLINEPATTERN {
    WORD wRepeatFactor;
    WORD wLinePattern;
} D3DLINEPATTERN;
```

(continued)

D3DLINEPATTERN *(continued)*

Member	Description
wRepeatFactor	The number of times each series of 1s and 0s specified by **wLinePattern** should be replicated. This member allows line patterns to be stretched.
wLinePattern	The line pattern, specified as a 16-bit integer value, where each bit corresponds to the state of a pixel. A value of 1 for a bit indicates the pixel should be drawn, whereas a value of 0 indicates it should not be drawn. A pattern for a dotted line of four drawn pixels followed by four pixels not drawn, for example, can be encoded by the following binary number: 1111000011110000.

D3DLVERTEX

Structure Description

This structure describes an untransformed, lit vertex.

Structure Declaration

```
typedef struct _D3DLVERTEX {
    union {
        D3DVALUE x;
        D3DVALUE dvX;
    };
    union {
        D3DVALUE y;
        D3DVALUE dvY;
    };
    union {
        D3DVALUE z;
        D3DVALUE dvZ;
    };
    DWORD       dwReserved;
    union {
        D3DCOLOR color;
        D3DCOLOR dcColor;
    };
    union {
        D3DCOLOR specular;
        D3DCOLOR dcSpecular;
    };
    union {
        D3DVALUE tu;
        D3DVALUE dvTU;
```

(continued)

D3DLVERTEX *(continued)*

Structure Declaration

```
    };
    union {
        D3DVALUE tv;
        D3DVALUE dvTV;
    };
} D3DLVERTEX, *LPD3DLVERTEX;
```

Member	Description
x, dvX	The *x*-component of the vertex, typically specified in model space.
y, dvY	The *y*-component of the vertex, typically specified in model space.
z, dvZ	The *z*-component of the vertex, typically specified in model space.
dwReserved	This member is reserved for future use and must be set to 0.
color, dcColor	A **D3DCOLOR** structure that describes the color of the vertex.
specular, dcSpecular	A **D3DCOLOR** structure that describes the specular color of the vertex.
tu, dvTU	A floating-point value that specifies the horizontal texture coordinate of the vertex, typically in the [0.0, 1.0] range.
tv, dvTV	A floating-point value that specifies the vertical texture coordinate of the vertex, typically in the [0.0, 1.0] range.

D3DMATERIAL7

Structure Description

This structure describes the material used to render primitives.

Structure Declaration

```
typedef struct _D3DMATERIAL7 {
    union {
        D3DCOLORVALUE   diffuse;
        D3DCOLORVALUE   dcvDiffuse;
    };
    union {
        D3DCOLORVALUE   ambient;
        D3DCOLORVALUE   dcvAmbient;
    };
    union {
        D3DCOLORVALUE   specular;
        D3DCOLORVALUE   dcvSpecular;
    };
```

(continued)

D3DMATERIAL7 *(continued)*

Structure Declaration

```
    union {
        D3DCOLORVALUE    emissive;
        D3DCOLORVALUE    dcvEmissive;
    };
    union {
        D3DVALUE         power;
        D3DVALUE         dvPower;
    };
} D3DMATERIAL7, *LPD3DMATERIAL7;
```

Member	Description
diffuse, dcvDiffuse	A **D3DCOLOR** structure that describes the diffuse color of the material. This is the color best reflected by the material when illuminated by diffuse light sources.
ambient, dcvAmbient	A **D3DCOLOR** structure that describes the ambient color of the material. This is the color best reflected by the material when illuminated by ambient light sources.
specular, dcvSpecular	A **D3DCOLOR** structure that describes the specular color of the material. This color is used for specular highlights.
emissive, dcvEmissive	A **D3DCOLOR** structure that describes the emissive color of the material. The material appears to emit this color.
power, dvPower	The sharpness of the specular highlights, which typically ranges from 0 (indicating no highlight) to 10 (indicating a sharp highlight) or more.

D3DMATRIX

Structure Description

This structure describes a 4×4 transformation matrix.

Structure Declaration

```
typedef struct _D3DMATRIX {
    D3DVALUE _11, _12, _13, _14;
    D3DVALUE _21, _22, _23, _24;
    D3DVALUE _31, _32, _33, _34;
    D3DVALUE _41, _42, _43, _44;
} D3DMATRIX, *LPD3DMATRIX;
```

Member	Description
_11	The 1st-row, 1st-column entry of the matrix.
_12	The 1st-row, 2nd-column entry of the matrix.
_13	The 1st-row, 3rd-column entry of the matrix.

(continued)

D3DMATRIX *(continued)*

Member	Description
_14	The 1st-row, 4th-column entry of the matrix.
_21	The 2nd-row, 1st-column entry of the matrix.
_22	The 2nd-row, 2nd-column entry of the matrix.
_23	The 2nd-row, 3rd-column entry of the matrix.
_24	The 2nd-row, 4th-column entry of the matrix.
_31	The 3rd-row, 1st-column entry of the matrix.
_32	The 3rd-row, 2nd-column entry of the matrix.
_33	The 3rd-row, 3rd-column entry of the matrix.
_34	The 3rd-row, 4th-column entry of the matrix. This entry cannot be a negative value. Applications that wish to use a negative value in this entry should instead negate the whole matrix by multiplying it by -1.
_41	The 4th-row, 1st-column entry of the matrix.
_42	The 4th-row, 2nd-column entry of the matrix.
_43	The 4th-row, 3rd-column entry of the matrix.
_44	The 4th-row, 4th-column entry of the matrix.

D3DPRIMCAPS

Structure Description

This structure describes the capabilities for each primitive type. This structure appears in the **D3DDEVICEDESC7** structure.

Structure Declaration

```
typedef struct _D3DPrimCaps {
    DWORD dwSize;              // size of structure
    DWORD dwMiscCaps;         // miscellaneous caps
    DWORD dwRasterCaps;       // raster caps
    DWORD dwZCmpCaps;         // z-comparison caps
    DWORD dwSrcBlendCaps;     // source blending caps
    DWORD dwDestBlendCaps;    // destination blending caps
    DWORD dwAlphaCmpCaps;     // alpha-test comparison caps
    DWORD dwShadeCaps;        // shading caps
    DWORD dwTextureCaps;      // texture caps
    DWORD dwTextureFilterCaps; // texture filtering caps
    DWORD dwTextureBlendCaps; // texture blending caps
    DWORD dwTextureAddressCaps; // texture addressing caps
    DWORD dwStippleWidth;     // stipple width
    DWORD dwStippleHeight;    // stipple height
} D3DPRIMCAPS, *LPD3DPRIMCAPS;
```

(continued)

D3DPRIMCAPS *(continued)*	
Member	**Description**
dwSize	The size of this structure, in bytes. This member must be initialized before this structure can be used.
dwMiscCaps	Describes general capabilities for the primitive. This member can be zero or one of the following flags:
	• **D3DPMISCCAPS_CONFORMANT**—The device conforms to the OpenGL standard.
	• **D3DPMISCCAPS_CULLCCW**—The device can cull triangles whose vertices are defined in a counterclockwise order when viewed from the direction of their surface normals.
	• **D3DPMISCCAPS_CULLCW**—The device can cull triangles whose vertices are defined in a clockwise order when viewed from the direction of their surface normals.
	• **D3DPMISCCAPS_CULLNONE**—The device cannot perform triangle culling.
	• **D3DPMISCCAPS_LINEPATTERNREP**—The driver supports values other than 1 for the **wRepeatFactor** member of the **D3DLINEPATTERN** structure. This value is valid only for the line primitive.
	• **D3DPMISCCAPS_MASKPLANES**—The device can mask color planes.
	• **D3DPMISCCAPS_MASKZ**—The device can enable and disable modification of the depth-buffer for pixel operations.
dwRasterCaps	Describes the raster-drawing capabilities for the primitive. This member can be zero or one of the following flags:
	• **D3DPRASTERCAPS_ANISOTROPY**—The device supports anisotropic filtering for the primitive.
	• **D3DPRASTERCAPS_ANTIALIASEDGES**—The device can anti-alias the edges of the primitive.
	• **D3DPRASTERCAPS_ANTIALIASSORTDEPENDENT**—The device can anti-alias primitives if they are depth-sorted in the right order (front-to-back or back-to-front).
	• **D3DPRASTERCAPS_ANTIALIASSORTINDEPENDENT**—The device can anti-alias primitives regardless of their depth-based order.
	• **D3DPRASTERCAPS_COLORKEYBLEND**—The device supports alpha-blended color keying, as governed by the **D3DRENDERSTATE_COLORKEYBLENDENABLE** render state.

(continued)

D3DPRIMCAPS *(continued)*	
Member	Description
	• **D3DPRASTERCAPS_DITHER**—The device can perform color dithering to improve the appearance of rendered primitives.
	• **D3DPRASTERCAPS_FOGRANGE**—The device supports range-based fog for primitives, where the distance from the viewer to a point is used to compute the fog density at that point, rather than the depth of the point.
	• **D3DPRASTERCAPS_FOGTABLE**—The device calculates fog density using a look-up table filled with fog values, each indexed to a specific depth value.
	• **D3DPRASTERCAPS_FOGVERTEX**—The device calculates fog on a per-vertex basis, storing the fog value in the alpha component of each vertex's specular color member. The fog values are then interpolated during rendering.
	• **D3DPRASTERCAPS_MIPMAPLODBIAS**—The device supports level-of-detail (LOD) bias adjustments, enabling applications to make a mipmapped texture appear sharper or blurrier than it normally would.
	The LOD bias is governed by the **D3DRENDERSTATE_-MIPMAPLODBIAS** render state.
	• **D3DPRASTERCAPS_PAT**—The driver can perform patterned drawing for the primitive.
	• **D3DPRASTERCAPS_ROP2**—The device supports raster operations other than **R2_COPYPEN** for the primitive. If this flag is present, the device supports XOR operations.
	• **D3DPRASTERCAPS_STIPPLE**—The device can perform polygon stippling to simulate transparency.
	• **D3DPRASTERCAPS_SUBPIXEL**—The device performs subpixel calculations for depth, color, and texture data. This capability indicates superior quality.
	• **D3DPRASTERCAPS_SUBPIXELX**—The device performs subpixel calculations for depth, color, and texture data, but only along the *x*-axis.
	• **D3DPRASTERCAPS_TRANSLUCENTSORTINDEPENDENT**—The device supports translucency that is independent of the depth-order of the polygons.
	• **D3DPRASTERCAPS_WBUFFER**—The device supports *w*-based depth buffering.

(continued)

D3DPRIMCAPS *(continued)*	
Member	**Description**
	• **D3DPRASTERCAPS_WFOG**—The device supports *w*-based fog when a perspective projection matrix is specified. Projection matrices that contain a nonzero entry for the [3][4] element are considered to be perspective projection matrices.
	• **D3DPRASTERCAPS_XOR**—The device supports XOR operations.
	• **D3DPRASTERCAPS_ZBIAS**—The device supports *z*-biases, which are used to identify the rendering order for coplanar polygons (polygons that lie on the same plane).
	• **D3DPRASTERCAPS_ZBUFFERLESSHSR**—The device can perform hidden-surface removal (HSR) without forcing the application to sort polygons and without the use of a depth buffer. This device-specific method of HSR will be employed if no depth-buffer surface is attached to the render-target surface and the depth-buffer comparison test is enabled.
	• **D3DPRASTERCAPS_ZFOG**—The device supports depth-based fog.
	• **D3DPRASTERCAPS_ZTEST**—The device can perform *z*-test operations.
dwZCmpCaps	Describes the *z*-buffer comparison functions that the device supports. This member can be zero or one of the following flags:
	• **D3DPCMPCAPS_ALWAYS**—The device supports the **D3DCMP_ALWAYS** comparison function for *z*-comparisons.
	• **D3DPCMPCAPS_EQUAL**—The device supports the **D3DCMP_EQUAL** comparison function for *z*-comparisons.
	• **D3DPCMPCAPS_GREATER**—The device supports the **D3DCMP_GREATER** comparison function for *z*-comparisons.
	• **D3DPCMPCAPS_GREATEREQUAL**—The device supports the **D3DCMP_GREATEREQUAL** comparison function for *z*-comparisons.
	• **D3DPCMPCAPS_LESS**—The device supports the **D3DCMP_LESS** comparison function for *z*-comparisons.
	• **D3DPCMPCAPS_LESSEQUAL**—The device supports the **D3DCMP_LESSEQUAL** comparison function for *z*-comparisons.
	• **D3DPCMPCAPS_NEVER**—The device supports the **D3DCMP_NEVER** comparison function for *z*-comparisons.
	• **D3DPCMPCAPS_NOTEQUAL**—The device supports the **D3DCMP_NOTEQUAL** comparison function for *z*-comparisons.

(continued)

D3DPRIMCAPS *(continued)*	
Member	**Description**
dwSrcBlendCaps	Describes the source-blending capabilities. This member can be one or more of the following flags: • **D3DPBLENDCAPS_BOTHINVSRCALPHA**—The device supports the **D3DBLEND_BOTHINVSRCALPHA** blending operation for source blending. • **D3DPBLENDCAPS_DESTALPHA**—The device supports the **D3DBLEND_DESTALPHA** blending operation for source blending. • **D3DPBLENDCAPS_DESTCOLOR**—The device supports the **D3DBLEND_DESTCOLOR** blending operation for source blending. • **D3DPBLENDCAPS_INVDESTALPHA**—The device supports the **D3DBLEND_INVDESTALPHA** blending operation for source blending. • **D3DPBLENDCAPS_INVDESTCOLOR**—The device supports the **D3DBLEND_INVDESTCOLOR** blending operation for source blending. • **D3DPBLENDCAPS_INVSRCALPHA**—The device supports the **D3DBLEND_INVSRCALPHA** blending operation for source blending. • **D3DPBLENDCAPS_INVSRCCOLOR**—The device supports the **D3DBLEND_INVSRCCOLOR** blending operation for source blending. • **D3DPBLENDCAPS_ONE**—The device supports the **D3DBLEND_ONE** blending operation for source blending. • **D3DPBLENDCAPS_SRCALPHA**—The device supports the **D3DBLEND_SRCALPHA** blending operation for source blending. • **D3DPBLENDCAPS_SRCALPHASAT**—The device supports the **D3DBLEND_SRCALPHASAT** blending operation for source blending. • **D3DPBLENDCAPS_SRCCOLOR**—The device supports the **D3DBLEND_SRCCOLOR** blending operation for source blending. • **D3DPBLENDCAPS_ZERO**—The device supports the **D3DBLEND_ZERO** blending operation for source blending.
dwDestBlendCaps	Describes the destination-blending capabilities. This member can be one or more of the following flags: • **D3DPBLENDCAPS_BOTHINVSRCALPHA**—The device supports the **D3DBLEND_BOTHINVSRCALPHA** blending operation for destination blending.

(continued)

D3DPRIMCAPS *(continued)*	
Member	Description
	• **D3DPBLENDCAPS_DESTALPHA**—The device supports the **D3DBLEND_DESTALPHA** blending operation for destination blending.
	• **D3DPBLENDCAPS_DESTCOLOR**—The device supports the **D3DBLEND_DESTCOLOR** blending operation for destination blending.
	• **D3DPBLENDCAPS_INVDESTALPHA**—The device supports the **D3DBLEND_INVDESTALPHA** blending operation for destination blending.
	• **D3DPBLENDCAPS_INVDESTCOLOR**—The device supports the **D3DBLEND_INVDESTCOLOR** blending operation for destination blending.
	• **D3DPBLENDCAPS_INVSRCALPHA**—The device supports the **D3DBLEND_INVSRCALPHA** blending operation for destination blending.
	• **D3DPBLENDCAPS_INVSRCCOLOR**—The device supports the **D3DBLEND_INVSRCCOLOR** blending operation for destination blending.
	• **D3DPBLENDCAPS_ONE**—The device supports the **D3DBLEND_ONE** blending operation for destination blending.
	• **D3DPBLENDCAPS_SRCALPHA**—The device supports the **D3DBLEND_SRCALPHA** blending operation for destination blending.
	• **D3DPBLENDCAPS_SRCALPHASAT**—The device supports the **D3DBLEND_SRCALPHASAT** blending operation for destination blending.
	• **D3DPBLENDCAPS_SRCCOLOR**—The device supports the **D3DBLEND_SRCCOLOR** blending operation for destination blending.
	• **D3DPBLENDCAPS_ZERO**—The device supports the **D3DBLEND_ZERO** blending operation for destination blending.
dwAlphaCmpCaps	Describes the alpha comparison functions that the device supports. This member can be zero or one of the following flags:
	• **D3DPCMPCAPS_ALWAYS**—The device supports the **D3DCMP_ALWAYS** comparison function for alpha comparisons. If only this and the **D3DPCMPCAPS_NEVER** flags are present, the driver does not support alpha tests.

(continued)

D3DPRIMCAPS *(continued)*	
Member	**Description**
	• **D3DPCMPCAPS_EQUAL**—The device supports the **D3DCMP_EQUAL** comparison function for alpha comparisons.
	• **D3DPCMPCAPS_GREATER**—The device supports the **D3DCMP_GREATER** comparison function for alpha comparisons.
	• **D3DPCMPCAPS_GREATEREQUAL**—The device supports the **D3DCMP_GREATEREQUAL** comparison function for alpha comparisons.
	• **D3DPCMPCAPS_LESS**—The device supports the **D3DCMP_LESS** comparison function for alpha comparisons.
	• **D3DPCMPCAPS_LESSEQUAL**—The device supports the **D3DCMP_LESSEQUAL** comparison function for alpha comparisons.
	• **D3DPCMPCAPS_NEVER**—The device supports the **D3DCMP_NEVER** comparison function for alpha comparisons. If only this and the **D3DPCMPCAPS_ALWAYS** flags are present, the driver does not support alpha tests.
	• **D3DPCMPCAPS_NOTEQUAL**—The device supports the **D3DCMP_NOTEQUAL** comparison function for alpha comparisons.
dwShadeCaps	Describes the shading operations the device supports. This member can be zero or one of the following flags:
	• **D3DPSHADECAPS_ALPHAFLATBLEND**—The device supports flat-blended transparency. The alpha component for a primitive is taken from the alpha value assigned to the primitive's first vertex.
	• **D3DPSHADECAPS_ALPHAFLATSTIPPLED**—The device supports stippled transparency. The alpha component for a primitive is taken from the alpha value assigned to the primitive's first vertex.
	• **D3DPSHADECAPS_ALPHAGOURAUDBLEND**—The device supports Gouraud alpha blending. The alpha component for a pixel is calculated by linearly interpolating the alpha values specified by the primitive's vertices.
	• **D3DPSHADECAPS_ALPHAGOURAUDSTIPPLED**—The device supports Gouraud stippled alpha blending. The alpha component for a pixel is calculated by linearly interpolating the alpha values specified by the primitive's vertices.

(continued)

D3DPRIMCAPS *(continued)*	
Member	Description
	• **D3DPSHADECAPS_COLORFLATMONO**—The device supports colored flat shading in the monochromatic lighting model. The lighting color for a primitive is taken from the blue component of the color value of the primitive's first vertex, which is used to determine the intensity of the lighting across the face of the polygon.
	• **D3DPSHADECAPS_COLORFLATRGB**—The device supports colored flat shading in the RGB lighting model. The lighting color for a primitive is taken from the color value of the primitive's first vertex, which is used to determine both the intensity and color of the lighting across the face of the polygon.
	• **D3DPSHADECAPS_COLORGOURAUDMONO**—The device supports colored Gouraud shading in the monochromatic lighting model. The intensity of light at a pixel is calculated by linearly interpolating the blue component of the color values of the primitive's vertices.
	• **D3DPSHADECAPS_COLORGOURAUDRGB**—The device supports colored Gouraud shading in the RGB lighting model. The intensity and color of light at a pixel are calculated by linearly interpolating the color values of the primitive's vertices.
	• **D3DPSHADECAPS_COLORPHONGMONO**—The device supports colored Phong shading in the monochromatic lighting model. The intensity of light at a pixel is calculated by interpolating the blue component of the color values of the primitive's vertices. This capability is not currently supported.
	• **D3DPSHADECAPS_COLORPHONGRGB**—The device supports colored Phong shading in the RGB lighting model. The intensity and color of light at a pixel are calculated by interpolating the color values of the primitive's vertices. This capability is not currently supported.
	• **D3DPSHADECAPS_FOGFLAT**—The device supports fog shading for the flat shading model.
	• **D3DPSHADECAPS_FOGGOURAUD**—The device supports fog shading for the Gouraud shading model.
	• **D3DPSHADECAPS_FOGPHONG**—The device supports fog shading for the Phong shading model. This capability is not currently supported.

(continued)

D3DPRIMCAPS *(continued)*	
Member	**Description**
	• **D3DPSHADECAPS_SPECULARFLATMONO**—The device supports specular highlights for the flat, monochromatic shading model.
	• **D3DPSHADECAPS_SPECULARFLATRGB**—The device supports specular highlights for the flat, RGB shading model.
	• **D3DPSHADECAPS_SPECULARGOURAUDMONO**—The device supports specular highlights for the Gouraud, monochromatic shading model.
	• **D3DPSHADECAPS_SPECULARGOURAUDRGB**—The device supports specular highlights for the Gouraud, RGB shading model.
	• **D3DPSHADECAPS_SPECULARPHONGMONO**—The device supports specular highlights for the Phong, monochromatic shading model. This capability is not currently supported.
	• **D3DPSHADECAPS_SPECULARPHONGRGB**—The device supports specular highlights for the Phong, RGB shading model. This capability is not currently supported.
dwTextureCaps	Describes miscellaneous texture-mapping capabilities. This member can be zero or one of the following flags:
	• **D3DPTEXTURECAPS_ALPHA**—The device supports textures with an alpha pixel component in the **D3DTBLEND_DECAL** and **D3DTBLEND_MODULATE** texture filtering modes.
	• **D3DPTEXTURECAPS_ALPHAPALETTE**—The device supports textures whose palettes contain alpha information.
	• **D3DPTEXTURECAPS_CUBEMAP**—The device supports cubic environment mapping.
	• **D3DPTEXTURECAPS_NONPOW2CONDITIONAL**—The device supports texture dimensions that are not powers of 2, but only if all of the following conditions are met: The texture-addressing mode for the texture stage is set to **D3DTADDRESS_CLAMP**; texture wrapping for the stage is disabled; mipmapping is disabled; and anisotropic texture filtering is disabled.
	• **D3DPTEXTURECAPS_PERSPECTIVE**—The device supports perspective-corrected texture mapping.
	• **D3DPTEXTURECAPS_POW2**—The device requires all textures that are not mipmaps to have dimensions that are powers of 2. Mipmapped textures must always have dimensions that are powers of 2.

(continued)

D3DPRIMCAPS *(continued)*	
Member	**Description**
	• **D3DPTEXTURECAPS_PROJECTED**—The device supports the **D3DTTFF_PROJECTED** texture transformation flag, which directs the device to divide each texture component by the last texture component. Applications may set this flag with the **D3DTSS_TEXTURETRANSFORMFLAGS** render state.
	• **D3DPTEXTURECAPS_SQUAREONLY**—The device requires that all textures be square.
	• **D3DPTEXTURECAPS_TEXREPEATNOTSCALEDBYSIZE**—The device does not scale texture coordinates by texture size prior to interpolation.
	• **D3DPTEXTURECAPS_TEXTURETRANSFORM**—The device supports texture coordinate transformations.
	• **D3DPTEXTURECAPS_TRANSPARENCY**—The device supports texture transparency. Texels that match the current transparent color are not displayed.
dwTextureFilterCaps	Describes texture map-filtering capabilities for the **D3DTSS_MAGFILTER**, **D3DTSS_MINFILTER** and **D3DTSS_-MIPFILTER** texture stage states. This member can be zero or one of the following flags:
	• **D3DPTFILTERCAPS_LINEAR**—The device supports bilinear interpolation filtering. The system generates a weighted average of a 2×2 area of texels surrounding the calculated texel.
	• **D3DPTFILTERCAPS_LINEARMIPLINEAR**—The device supports trilinear interpolation filtering. The system performs bilinear filtering on the two nearest mipmaps and then linearly interpolates these two colors to calculate the final color.
	• **D3DPTFILTERCAPS_LINEARMIPNEAREST**—The device supports linear interpolation between the two nearest point-filtered texels. The system performs point filtering on the two nearest mipmaps and then linearly interpolates these two colors to calculate the final color.
	• **D3DPTFILTERCAPS_MIPLINEAR**—The device supports nearest mipmapping with bilinear filtering. The system chooses the nearest texel from the closest mipmap and then performs bilinear filtering on the result.
	• **D3DPTFILTERCAPS_MIPNEAREST**—The device supports nearest mipmapping filtering. The system chooses the nearest texel from the closest mipmap.

(continued)

D3DPRIMCAPS *(continued)*	
Member	**Description**
	• **D3DPTFILTERCAPS_NEAREST**—The device supports point filtering. The system chooses the texel with the coordinates nearest the desired texel.
	• **D3DPTFILTERCAPS_MAGFAFLATCUBIC**—The device supports per-stage, flat cubic filtering when magnifying textures.
	• **D3DPTFILTERCAPS_MAGFANISOTROPIC**—The device supports per-stage, anisotropic filtering when magnifying textures.
	• **D3DPTFILTERCAPS_MAGFGAUSSIANCUBIC**—The device supports per-stage, Gaussian-cubic filtering when magnifying textures.
	• **D3DPTFILTERCAPS_MAGFLINEAR**—The device supports per-stage, bilinear interpolation filtering when magnifying textures.
	• **D3DPTFILTERCAPS_MAGFPOINT**—The device supports per-stage, point filtering when magnifying textures.
	• **D3DPTFILTERCAPS_MINFANISOTROPIC**—The device supports per-stage, anisotropic filtering when reducing textures.
	• **D3DPTFILTERCAPS_MINFLINEAR**—The device supports per-stage, bilinear interpolation filtering when reducing textures.
	• **D3DPTFILTERCAPS_MINFPOINT**—The device supports per-stage, point filtering for reducing textures.
	• **D3DPTFILTERCAPS_MIPFLINEAR**—The device supports per-stage, trilinear interpolation filtering for mipmaps.
	• **D3DPTFILTERCAPS_MIPFPOINT**—The device supports per-stage, point filtering for mipmaps.
dwTextureBlendCaps	Describes obsolete capabilities.
dwTextureAddressCaps	Describes the texture addressing capabilities of the device. This member can be zero or one of the following flags:
	• **D3DPTADDRESSCAPS_BORDER**—The device supports the **D3DTADDRESS_BORDER** texture addressing mode. The texture addressing mode is governed by the **D3DTSS_-ADDRESS**, **D3DTSS_ADDRESSU**, and **D3DTSS_ADDRESSV** render states.
	• **D3DPTADDRESSCAPS_CLAMP**—The device supports the **D3DTADDRESS_CLAMP** texture addressing mode. The texture addressing mode is governed by the **D3DTSS_-ADDRESS**, **D3DTSS_ADDRESSU**, and **D3DTSS_ADDRESSV** render states.

(continued)

D3DPRIMCAPS *(continued)*

Member	Description
	• **D3DPTADDRESSCAPS_INDEPENDENTUV**—The device supports the **D3DTADDRESS_INDEPENDENTUV** texture addressing mode. The texture addressing mode is governed by the **D3DTSS_ADDRESS**, **D3DTSS_ADDRESSU**, and **D3DTSS_ADDRESSV** render states.
	• **D3DPTADDRESSCAPS_MIRROR**—The device supports the **D3DTADDRESS_MIRROR** texture addressing mode. The texture addressing mode is governed by the **D3DTSS_-ADDRESS**, **D3DTSS_ADDRESSU**, and **D3DTSS_ADDRESSV** render states.
	• **D3DPTADDRESSCAPS_WRAP**—The device supports the **D3DTADDRESS_WRAP** texture addressing mode. The texture addressing mode is governed by the **D3DTSS_ADDRESS**, **D3DTSS_ADDRESSU**, and **D3DTSS_ADDRESSV** render states.
dwStippleWidth	The maximum width of the supported stipple, up to 32.
dwStippleHeight	The maximum height of the supported stipple, up to 32.

D3DRECT

Structure Description

This structure describes a 2D rectangle.

Structure Declaration

```
typedef struct _D3DRECT {
    union {
        LONG x1;
        LONG lX1;
    };
    union {
        LONG y1;
        LONG lY1;
    };
    union {
        LONG x2;
        LONG lX2;
    };
    union {
        LONG y2;
        LONG lY2;
    };
} D3DRECT, *LPD3DRECT;
```

(continued)

D3DRECT *(continued)*	
Member	**Description**
x1, lX1	The left of the rectangle.
y1, lY1	The top of the rectangle.
x2, lX2	The right of the rectangle.
y2, lY2	The bottom of the rectangle.

D3DTLVERTEX

Structure Description

This structure describes a transformed, lit vertex.

Structure Declaration

```
typedef struct _D3DTLVERTEX {
    union {
        D3DVALUE sx;
        D3DVALUE dvSX;
    };
    union {
        D3DVALUE sy;
        D3DVALUE dvSY;
    };
    union {
        D3DVALUE sz;
        D3DVALUE dvSZ;
    };
    union {
        D3DVALUE rhw;
        D3DVALUE dvRHW;
    };
    union {
        D3DCOLOR color;
        D3DCOLOR dcColor;
    };
    union {
        D3DCOLOR specular;
        D3DCOLOR dcSpecular;
    };
    union {
        D3DVALUE tu;
        D3DVALUE dvTU;
```

(continued)

D3DTLVERTEX *(continued)*

Structure Declaration

```
    };
    union {
        D3DVALUE tv;
        D3DVALUE dvTV;
    };
} D3DTLVERTEX, *LPD3DTLVERTEX;
```

Member	Description
sx, dvSX	The horizontal screen coordinate of the vertex, in pixels.
sy, dvSY	The vertical screen coordinate of the vertex, in pixels.
sz, dvSZ	The z-coordinate for the vertex. For visible vertices, the maximum value this member can be is 0.99999.
rhw, dvRHW	The reciprocal of the homogenous w from the vertex's homogenous coordinate. This value is typically 1 divided by the depth of the vertex.
color, dcColor	The color component of the vertex.
specular, dcSpecular	The specular component of the vertex. The alpha value of this member may be used for fog shading.
tu, dvTU	The horizontal component of the texture coordinate for the vertex, typically in the range [0.0, 1.0].
tv, dvTV	The vertical component of the texture coordinate for the vertex, typically in the range [0.0, 1.0].

D3DTRANSFORMCAPS

Structure Description

This structure describes the transformation capabilities of a device.

Structure Declaration

```
typedef struct _D3DTransformCaps {
    DWORD dwSize;
    DWORD dwCaps;
} D3DTRANSFORMCAPS, *LPD3DTRANSFORMCAPS;
```

Member	Description
dwSize	The size of this structure, in bytes. This member must be initialized before this structure can be used.
dwCaps	The transformation capabilities of the device. This member may or may not be the following flag: • **D3DTRANSFORMCAPS_CLIP**—The system clips primitives during transformation.

D3DVECTOR

Structure Description

This structure describes a vector.

Structure Declaration

```
typedef struct _D3DVECTOR {
    union {
        D3DVALUE x;
        D3DVALUE dvX;
    };
    union {
        D3DVALUE y;
        D3DVALUE dvY;
    };
    union {
        D3DVALUE z;
        D3DVALUE dvZ;
    };
} D3DVECTOR, *LPD3DVECTOR;
```

Member	Description
dvX	The horizontal component of the vector.
dvY	The vertical component of the vector.
dvZ	The depth component of the vector.

D3DVERTEX

Structure Description

This structure describes an untransformed, unlit vertex.

Structure Declaration

```
typedef struct _D3DVERTEX {
    union {
        D3DVALUE x;
        D3DVALUE dvX;
    };
    union {
        D3DVALUE y;
        D3DVALUE dvY;
    };
    union {
        D3DVALUE z;
        D3DVALUE dvZ;
    };
```

(continued)

D3DVERTEX *(continued)*

Structure Declaration

```
    union {
        D3DVALUE nx;
        D3DVALUE dvNX;
    };
    union {
        D3DVALUE ny;
        D3DVALUE dvNY;
    };
    union {
        D3DVALUE nz;
        D3DVALUE dvNZ;
    };
    union {
        D3DVALUE tu;
        D3DVALUE dvTU;
    };
    union {
        D3DVALUE tv;
        D3DVALUE dvTV;
    };
} D3DVERTEX, *LPD3DVERTEX;
```

Member	Description
dvX	The horizontal component of the position of the vertex, in model space.
dvY	The vertical component of the position of the vertex, in model space.
dvZ	The depth component of the position of the vertex, in model space.
dvNX	The horizontal component of the normal of a plane orthogonal to the object at the location of the vertex. This is used for lighting calculations.
dvNY	The vertical component of the normal of a plane orthogonal to the object at the location of the vertex. This is used for lighting calculations.
dvNZ	The depth component of the normal of a plane orthogonal to the object at the location of the vertex. This is used for lighting calculations.
dvTU	The horizontal component of the texture coordinate for the vertex, typically in the range [0.0, 1.0].
dvTV	The vertical component of the texture coordinate for the vertex, typically in the range [0.0, 1.0].

D3DVERTEXBUFFERDESC

Structure Description

This structure describes a vertex buffer.

Structure Declaration

```
typedef struct _D3DVERTEXBUFFERDESC {
    DWORD dwSize;
    DWORD dwCaps;
    DWORD dwFVF;
    DWORD dwNumVertices;
} D3DVERTEXBUFFERDESC, *LPD3DVERTEXBUFFERDESC;
```

Member	Description
dwSize	The size of this structure, in bytes. This member must be initialized before this structure can be used.
dwCaps	Describes the capabilities of the vertex buffer. This member can be one of the following values:
	• **0**—If the flag is 0, the vertex buffer should be created in whatever kind of memory allows efficient read operations, as determined by the system. This value is valid only when creating vertex buffers.
	• **D3DVBCAPS_DONOTCLIP**—The vertex buffer cannot contain clipping information.
	• **D3DVBCAPS_OPTIMIZED**—The vertex buffer can contain optimized vertex data. This flag is not valid when creating vertex buffers.
	• **D3DVBCAPS_SYSTEMMEMORY**—The vertex buffer should be created in system memory. This flag should be used for software devices.
	• **D3DVBCAPS_WRITEONLY**—The application intends strictly to write to the vertex buffer. This allows the system to choose the best memory location for efficient write operations and rendering.
	Performance will be degraded if an application attempts to read from a vertex buffer that was created with this flag.
dwFVF	Describes the flexible vertex format the vertex buffer should use.
	A flexible vertex format structure may include a number of components; however, if these components are present, they must appear in a certain order. This order is reflected in the following list (that is, the following list specifies the order in which the components must appear in the structure).

(continued)

D3DVERTEXBUFFERDESC *(continued)*	
Member	Description
	These are the relevant flags, constants, and macros that can be used to create a flexible vertex format: • **D3DFVF_XYZ**—The vertex format includes the position of an untransformed vertex, specified as three floating-point values (*x*, *y*, and *z*). This format is for 3D applications that use Direct3D to transform and light their vertices. This flag, which cannot be used with the **D3DFVF_XYZRHW** flag, requires the application to specify a vertex normal (**D3DFVF_NORMAL**), a vertex color component (**D3DFVF_DIFFUSE** or **D3DFVF_SPECULAR**), or at least one set of texture coordinates (**D3DFVF_TEX1** through **D3DFVF_TEX8**). • **D3DFVF_XYZRHW**—The vertex format includes the position of a transformed vertex, specified as four floating-point values (*x*, *y*, *z*, and *1/w*). This format is for 3D applications that transform and light their own vertices. This flag, which cannot be used with the **D3DFVF_XYZ** or **D3DFVF_NORMAL** flags, requires the application to specify a vertex color component (**D3DFVF_DIFFUSE** or **D3DFVF_SPECULAR**) or at least one set of texture coordinates (**D3DFVF_TEX1** through **D3DFVF_TEX8**). • **D3DFVF_XYZB1** through **D3DFVF_XYZB5**—These flags specify the number of floating-point weighting ("beta") values included in the vertex format to be used for multi-matrix vertex blending operations. By changing these weighting values, and modifying as necessary the matrices to be used in blending operations, applications can animate vertices. Direct3D currently supports a maximum of three weighting values. • **D3DFVF_NORMAL**—The vertex format includes a normal vector. This normal vector describes the orientation of a plane tangent to the object at the location of the vertex. This flag, which cannot be used with the **D3DFVF_XYZRHW** flag, is used by Direct3D for lighting vertices. If this flag is not specified, Direct3D does not light vertices. • **D3DFVF_DIFFUSE**—The vertex format includes a diffuse color component, specified as a **DWORD** value containing red, green, blue, and alpha components. The diffuse component specifies the light color and intensity falling on the vertex.

D3DVERTEXBUFFERDESC *(continued)*	
Member	**Description**
	Neither transformed nor untransformed vertices need to include the diffuse component. Transformed vertices, however, are not lit by Direct3D, so applications using them typically specify their own lighting information to Direct3D by using the diffuse and specular components of their vertex formats. Untransformed vertices do not need to specify this information to be lit, because Direct3D will by default use the material of the object for diffuse lighting information. They may wish to do so anyway, however, for enhanced realism.

• **D3DFVF_SPECULAR**—The vertex format includes a specular color component, specified as a **DWORD** value containing red, green, blue, and alpha components. The specular component describes how shiny the object is at a vertex and what the color of the shine is. The alpha component of the specular value is used for fog effects.

Neither transformed nor untransformed vertices need to include the specular component. Transformed vertices, however, are not lit by Direct3D, so applications using them typically specify their own lighting information to Direct3D by using the diffuse and specular components of their vertex formats. Untransformed vertices do not need to specify this information to be lit, because Direct3D will by default use the material of the object for specular lighting information. They may wish to do so anyway, however, for enhanced realism.

• **D3DFVF_TEX0** through **D3DFVF_TEX8**—These flags specify the number of texture coordinates for the vertex. Texture coordinates may be specified using one, two, or three floating-point values, as indicated by the flags generated by the **D3DFVF_TEXCOORDSIZE*** macros listed in this section.

• **D3DFVF_TEXCOUNT_SHIFT**—This value is not used directly as a flag, but it can be used to generate a flag that specifies the number of texture coordinates for the vertex. This flag can be used in place of the **D3DFVF_TEX0** through **D3DFVF_TEX8** flags.

If a vertex uses **N** sets of texture coordinates, the flag describing this information can be calculated by the code **(N<<D3DFVF_TEXCOUNT_SHIFT)**.

• **D3DFVF_TEXTUREFORMAT1** through **D3DFVF_TEXTUREFORMAT4**—These constants indicate the number of floating-point values used to describe a texture coordinate set of a vertex. The constant **D3DFVF_TEXTUREFORMAT1** indicates one floating-point value is used, and so on. |

D3DVERTEXBUFFERDESC *(continued)*	
Member	**Description**
	These constants are rarely used directly, but instead are used implicitly by these **D3DFVF_TEXCOORDSIZE*** macros:
	• **D3DFVF_TEXCOORDSIZE1(N)**—This macro is used to generate a flag that tells Direct3D that one floating-point value is used for the texture coordinate information in the **N**th texture coordinate set of a vertex. For example, if the first texture coordinate set of a vertex uses one floating-point value, then the flexible vertex format for the vertex would include the flag produced by the code **D3DFVF_-TEXCOORDSIZE1(0)**.
	• **D3DFVF_TEXCOORDSIZE2(N)**—This macro is used to generate a flag that tells Direct3D that two floating-point values are used for the texture coordinate information in the **N**th texture coordinate set of a vertex. For example, if the first texture coordinate set of a vertex uses two floating-point values, then the flexible vertex format for the vertex would include the flag produced by the code **D3DFVF_-TEXCOORDSIZE2(0)**.
	• **D3DFVF_TEXCOORDSIZE3(N)**—This macro is used to generate a flag that tells Direct3D that three floating-point values are used for the texture coordinate information in the **N**th texture coordinate set of a vertex. For example, if the first texture coordinate set of a vertex uses three floating-point values, then the flexible vertex format for the vertex would include the flag produced by the code **D3DFVF_TEXCOORDSIZE3(0)**.
	• **D3DFVF_TEXCOORDSIZE4(N)**—This macro is used to generate a flag that tells Direct3D that four floating-point values are used for the texture coordinate information in the **N**th texture coordinate set of a vertex. For example, if the first texture coordinate set of a vertex uses four floating-point values, then the flexible vertex format for the vertex would include the flag produced by the code **D3DFVF_-TEXCOORDSIZE4(0)**.
dwNumVertices	The maximum number of vertices the vertex buffer can contain. The maximum value for this member is **D3DMAXNUM-VERTICES**, currently defined as 0×FFFF.

D3DVIEWPORT7

Structure Description

This structure describes the current viewport. The viewport defines the range of x-, y-, and z-values that primitives will be rendered into.

After undergoing the projection transformation stage, the horizontal, vertical, and depth components of a primitive's vertices will be scaled into the horizontal, vertical, and depth ranges specified by the viewport. Unless an application wishes to render to only a portion of the render-target surface, the horizontal and vertical viewport ranges will correspond to the width and height of the render-target surface, respectively, while the depth range will typically be set to [0.0, 1.0].

Structure Declaration

```
typedef struct _D3DVIEWPORT7{
    DWORD       dwX;
    DWORD       dwY;
    DWORD       dwWidth;
    DWORD       dwHeight;
    D3DVALUE    dvMinZ;
    D3DVALUE    dvMaxZ;
} D3DVIEWPORT7, *LPD3DVIEWPORT7
```

Member	Description
dwX	The left of the viewport on the render-target surface, in pixels.
dwY	The top of the viewport on the render-target surface, in pixels.
dwWidth	The width of the viewport on the render-target surface, in pixels.
dwHeight	The height of the viewport on the render-target surface, in pixels.
dvMinZ	The minimum depth value to be generated. This member is typically set to 0.0.
	Together, the **dvMinZ** and **dvMaxZ** members define the range of depth values into which a scene will be rendered.
dvMaxZ	The maximum depth value to be generated. This member is typically set to 1.0.
	Together, the **dvMinZ** and **dvMaxZ** members define the range of depth values into which a scene will be rendered.

Appendix C

DirectSound Reference

This appendix is divided into four main reference sections: interface, function, callback, and structure.

The interface reference documents in detail all of the methods of the DirectSound interfaces, except those derived from the IUnknown interface, which is documented in Chapter 3. The function reference does the same for all functions in DirectSound that do not belong to an interface (such as **DirectSoundCreate ()**). The callback reference describes the format of application-defined functions that DirectSound calls. Finally, the structure reference documents all of the structures included in the DirectSound API.

For a conceptual overview of DirectSound, see Chapter 10. For sample code, see Chapter 11 or the DirectX SDK.

Interface Reference

The interfaces documented in this section include IDirectSound, IDirectSoundBuffer, IDirectSound3DBuffer, IDirectSound3D Listener, IDirectSoundCapture, IDirectSoundCaptureBuffer, IDirectSoundNotify, and IKsPropertySet.

IDirectSound

Applications can obtain the IDirectSound interface by calling **DirectSoundCreate ()** or **CoCreateInstance ()**.

The Globally Unique Identifier (GUID) for the IDirectSound interface is IID_IDirectSound.

IDirectSound: Compact ()

Function Description

This function moves all unused memory on a sound card into one location to free the largest continuous amount of memory possible. It can be called only by applications with priority-level access to the sound hardware and will fail if the sound card's memory is being accessed (for example, sounds are playing).

Function Declaration

```
HRESULT Compact ();
```

Parameter	Description
None	

Return Value	Description
DS_OK	DirectSound successfully compacted the memory.
DSERR_INVALIDPARAM	DirectSound could not compact the memory, because one or more parameters are invalid.
DSERR_PRIOLEVELNEEDED	DirectSound could not compact the memory, because the application does not have priority-level access to the sound hardware.
DSERR_UNINITIALIZED	DirectSound could not compact the memory, because this DirectSound object is uninitialized. It must be initialized with **DirectSound: Initialize** () before this function can be called.

IDirectSound::CreateSoundBuffer ()

Function Description

This function creates a DirectSoundBuffer object given a structure describing its attributes. Before calling this function, you must set the cooperative level of the application.

Function Declaration

```
HRESULT CreateSoundBuffer (
  LPCDSBUFFERDESC lpcDSBufferDesc,
  LPLPDIRECTSOUNDBUFFER lplpDirectSoundBuffer,
  IUnknown FAR * pUnkOuter
);
```

Parameter	Description
lpcDSBufferDesc	A pointer to a **DSBUFFERDESC** structure describing the attributes of the sound buffer to be created.
lplpDirectSoundBuffer	The address of a pointer to a DirectSoundBuffer object. If this function succeeds, the pointer will be set to the newly created DirectSound object.
pUnkOuter	Exists for compatibility with COM. This parameter must be set to **NULL**.

(continued)

IDirectSound::CreateSoundBuffer () *(continued)*

Return Value	Description
DS_OK	DirectSound successfully created the DirectSoundBuffer object.
DSERR_ALLOCATED	DirectSound could not create the sound buffer, because of insufficient resources.
DSERR_CONTROLUNAVAIL	DirectSound could not create the sound buffer, because the hardware does not support one or more control flags specified by **lpcDSBufferDesc**.
DSERR_BADFORMAT	DirectSound could not create the sound buffer, because the hardware does not support the wave format specified by **lpcDSBufferDesc**.
DSERR_INVALIDPARAM	DirectSound could not create the sound buffer, because one or more parameters are invalid.
DSERR_NOAGGREGATION	DirectSound could not create the sound buffer, because the **pUnkOuter** parameter is not **NULL**.
DSERR_OUTOFMEMORY	DirectSound could not create the sound buffer, because sufficient memory is not available.
DSERR_UNINITIALIZED	DirectSound could not create the sound buffer, because this DirectSound object is uninitialized. It must be initialized with **DirectSound::Initialize** () before this function can be called.
DSERR_UNSUPPORTED	DirectSound could not create the sound buffer, because the action is not supported.

IDirectSound::DuplicateSoundBuffer ()

Function Description

This function duplicates an existing sound buffer. The attributes of the original sound buffer are duplicated in the new sound buffer and can later be modified independently, but the memory used for storing the sound data of the original sound buffer is shared with the memory of the duplicate sound buffer. Any changes to the sound data of one are immediately reflected in the sound data of the other.

Because the memory of the original and the duplicate are shared, this function will fail if it cannot create the duplicate in the same memory type as the original.

Function Declaration

```
HRESULT DuplicateSoundBuffer (
  LPDIRECTSOUNDBUFFER lpDsbOriginal,
  LPLPDIRECTSOUNDBUFFER lplpDsbDuplicate
);
```

Parameter	Description
lpDsbOriginal	A pointer to the DirectSoundBuffer object to be duplicated.
lplpDsbDuplicate	The address of a pointer to a DirectSoundBuffer object. If this function succeeds, the pointer will be set to the duplicated DirectSound object.

(continued)

IDirectSound::DuplicateSoundBuffer () *(continued)*

Return Value	Description
DS_OK	DirectSound successfully duplicated the sound buffer.
DSERR_ALLOCATED	DirectSound could not duplicate the sound buffer, because of insufficient resources.
DSERR_INVALIDCALL	DirectSound could not duplicate the sound buffer, because the current state of this DirectSound object does not permit the operation.
DSERR_INVALIDPARAM	DirectSound could not duplicate the sound buffer, because one or more parameters are invalid.
DSERR_OUTOFMEMORY	DirectSound could not duplicate the sound buffer, because sufficient memory is not available.
DSERR_UNINITIALIZED	DirectSound could not duplicate the sound buffer, because this DirectSound object is uninitialized. It must be initialized with **DirectSound::Initialize** () before this function can be called.

IDirectSound::GetCaps ()

Function Description

This function retrieves the capabilities of the sound hardware represented by this DirectSound object.

Function Declaration

```
HRESULT GetCaps (
  LPDSCAPS lpDSCaps
);
```

Parameter	Description
lpDSCaps	A pointer to a **DSCAPS** structure. If this function succeeds, the structure will be filled with the capabilities of the sound hardware represented by this DirectSound object.

Return Value	Description
DS_OK	DirectSound successfully retrieved the capabilities of the sound hardware.
DSERR_GENERIC	DirectSound could not retrieve the capabilities of the sound hardware, because of a generic error.
DSERR_INVALIDPARAM	DirectSound could not retrieve the capabilities of the sound hardware, because one or more parameters are invalid.
DSERR_UNINITIALIZED	DirectSound could not retrieve the capabilities of the sound hardware, because this DirectSound object is uninitialized. It must be initialized with **DirectSound::Initialize** () before this function can be called.

IDirectSound::GetSpeakerConfig ()

Function Description

This function retrieves the configuration of the speakers. DirectSound uses this setting, which can be configured through the Windows Control Panel or overridden by the **IDirectSound::SetSpeaker-Config** () function, to determine how to represent 3D sound to the user.

Function Declaration

```
HRESULT GetSpeakerConfig (
  LPDWORD lpdwSpeakerConfig
);
```

Parameter	Description

lpdwSpeakerConfig	A pointer to 32-bit integer. If the function succeeds, the least significant 16 bits of this integer will be set to one of the following values:
	
	• **DSSPEAKER_5POINT1**—Sound is played through five surround sound speakers and one subwoofer.
	
	• **DSSPEAKER_HEADPHONE**—Sound is played through a headphone.
	
	• **DSSPEAKER_MONO**—Sound is played through one speaker.
	
	• **DSSPEAKER_QUAD**—Sound is played through four speakers.
	
	• **DSSPEAKER_STEREO**—Sound is played through two speakers. If this value is specified, the high 16 bits of the integer may be one of the following values:
	
	  • **DSSPEAKER_GEOMETRY_WIDE**—The speakers span an arc of 20 degrees.
	
	  • **DSSPEAKER_GEOMETRY_NARROW**—The speakers span an arc of 10 degrees.
	
	  • **DSSPEAKER_GEOMETRY_MIN**—The speakers span an arc of 5 degrees.
	
	  • **DSSPEAKER_GEOMETRY_MAX**—The speakers span an arc of 180 degrees.
	
	• **DSSPEAKER_SURROUND**—Sound is played through surround speakers (usually five).

Return Value	Description
DSERR_INVALIDPARAM	DirectSound could not retrieve the speaker configuration, because one or more parameters are invalid.
DSERR_UNINITIALIZED	DirectSound could not retrieve the speaker configuration, because this DirectSound object is uninitialized. It must be initialized with **DirectSound: Initialize** () before this function can be called.

IDirectSound::Initialize ()

Function Description

This function initializes an object created with **CoCreateInstance** (). Applications that use
DirectSoundCreate () to obtain a pointer to a DirectSound object do not need to call this function.

Function Declaration

```
HRESULT Initialize (
  LPGUID lpGuid
);
```

Parameter	Description
lpGuid	A pointer to a GUID that identifies the sound device to be represented by this DirectSound object. This can be set to **NULL** to select the primary sound device.

Return Value	Description
DS_OK	DirectSound successfully initialized the DirectSound object.
DSERR_ALREADYINITIALIZED	DirectSound could not initialize the DirectSound object, because it is already initialized, either by this function or implicitly by the **DirectSoundCreate** () function.
DSERR_GENERIC	DirectSound could not initialize the DirectSound object, because of a generic error.
DSERR_INVALIDPARAM	DirectSound could not initialize the DirectSound object, because one or more parameters are invalid.
DSERR_NODRIVER	DirectSound could not initialize the DirectSound object, because there is no sound driver.

IDirectSound::SetCooperativeLevel ()

Function Description

This function sets the cooperative level for the DirectSound object. Applications should set the
cooperative level immediately after creating a DirectSound object.

Function Declaration

```
HRESULT SetCooperativeLevel (
  HWND hwnd,
  DWORD dwLevel
);
```

Parameter	Description
hwnd	A handle to the application's foreground window. If the application is using DirectDraw, then this must be the same handle as passed to **IDirectDraw4::SetCooperativeLevel** ().

(continued)

IDirectSound::SetCooperativeLevel () *(continued)*

Parameter	Description
dwLevel	The cooperative level to be set. This parameter can be one of the following values:
	• **DSSCL_EXCLUSIVE**—Sets the application's cooperative level to exclusive. Exclusive cooperative level mutes all other sounds when the application has input focus. In addition, this level has all privileges of **DSSCL_PRIORITY**.
	• **DSSCL_NORMAL**—Sets the application's cooperative level to normal. Normal cooperative level allows other applications equal access to the sound device's resources, but does not allow the application to change the output format from the default (an 8-bit format) or perform memory management.
	• **DSSCL_PRIORITY**—Sets the application's cooperative level to priority. Priority cooperative level allows other background applications to be audible, but allows the application to change the output format and perform memory management.
	• **DSSCL_WRITEPRIMARY**—Sets the application's cooperative level to write primary. Write primary cooperative level does not allow secondary buffers, but does allow the application to write data directly to the primary sound buffer. It is not recommended for most applications, because none of DirectSound's advanced features are available.

Return Value	Description
DS_OK	DirectSound successfully set the cooperative level.
DSERR_ALLOCATED	DirectSound could not set the cooperative level, because of insufficient resources.
DSERR_INVALIDPARAM	DirectSound could not set the cooperative level, because one or more parameters are invalid.
DSERR_UNINITIALIZED	DirectSound could not set the cooperative level, because this DirectSound object is uninitialized. It must be initialized with **DirectSound: Initialize** () before this function can be called.
DSERR_UNSUPPORTED	DirectSound could not set the cooperative level, because the action is not supported.

IDirectSound: SetSpeakerConfig ()	
Function Description	
This function overrides the current configuration of the speakers. DirectSound uses the speaker configuration setting to determine how to represent 3D sound to the user.	
Function Declaration	

```
HRESULT SetSpeakerConfig (
  DWORD dwSpeakerConfig
);
```

Parameter	Description

dwSpeakerConfig	The speaker configuration to be set. The least significant 16 bits of this integer can be one of the following values:
	
	• **DSSPEAKER_5POINT1**—Sound is played through five surround sound speakers and one subwoofer.
	
	• **DSSPEAKER_HEADPHONE**—Sound is played through a headphone.
	
	• **DSSPEAKER_MONO**—Sound is played through one speaker.
	
	• **DSSPEAKER_QUAD**—Sound is played through four speakers.
	
	• **DSSPEAKER_STEREO**—Sound is played through two speakers. If this value is specified, the high 16 bits of the integer may be one of the following values:
	
	  • **DSSPEAKER_GEOMETRY_WIDE**—The speakers span an arc of 20 degrees (that is, the sound played through the speakers is directed over an arc of 20 degrees).
	
	  • **DSSPEAKER_GEOMETRY_NARROW**—The speakers span an arc of 10 degrees.
	
	  • **DSSPEAKER_GEOMETRY_MIN**—The speakers span an arc of 5 degrees.
	
	  • **DSSPEAKER_GEOMETRY_MAX**—The speakers span an arc of 180 degrees.
	
	• **DSSPEAKER_SURROUND**—Sound is played through surround speakers (usually five).

Return Value	**Description**
DS_OK	DirectSound successfully set the speaker configuration.
DSERR_INVALIDPARAM	DirectSound could not set the speaker configuration, because one or more parameters are invalid.
DSERR_UNINITIALIZED	DirectSound could not set the speaker configuration, because this DirectSound object is uninitialized. It must be initialized with **DirectSound::Initialize** () before this function can be called.

IDirectSound3DBuffer

You can obtain the IDirectSound3DBuffer interface by querying an IDirectSoundBuffer interface whose sound buffer was created with 3D capabilities.

The GUID for the IDirectSound3DBuffer interface is **IID_IDirectSound3DBuffer**.

IDirectSound3DBuffer::GetAllParameters ()

Function Description

This retrieves all parameters of the 3D sound buffer.

Function Declaration

```
HRESULT GetAllParameters (
 LPDS3DBUFFER lpDs3dBuffer
);
```

Parameter	Description
lpDs3dBuffer	A pointer to a **DS3DBUFFER** structure. If the function succeeds, the structure will be filled with all parameters of the 3D sound buffer.

Return Value	Description
DS_OK	DirectSound successfully retrieved all parameters of the 3D sound buffer.
DSERR_INVALIDPARAM	DirectSound could not retrieve all parameters of the 3D sound buffer, because one or more of the parameters are invalid.

IDirectSound3DBuffer::GetConeAngles ()

Function Description

This function retrieves the 3D sound buffer's two sound-cone angles for the inner and outer sound cones. Sounds inside the inner sound cone are heard at the loudest intensity, while sounds outside the outer sound cone are heard at the lowest intensity; in-between sounds have in-between intensities.

Function Declaration

```
HRESULT GetConeAngles (
  LPDWORD lpdwInsideConeAngle,
  LPDWORD lpdwOutsideConeAngle
);
```

Parameter	Description
lpdwInsideConeAngle	A pointer to an integer. If this function succeeds, this integer will be set to the inside cone angle, measured in degrees. The minimum, maximum, and default angles for this value are **DS3D_MINCONEANGLE**, **DS3D_MAXCONEANGLE**, and **DS3D_DEFAULTCONEANGLE**, respectively. The default cone angle is currently defined as 360 degrees, indicating the sound has no particular direction.

(continued)

IDirectSound3DBuffer::GetConeAngles () *(continued)*	
Parameter	**Description**
lpdwOutsideConeAngle	A pointer to an integer. If this function succeeds, this integer will be set to the outside cone angle, measured in degrees. The minimum, maximum, and default angles for this value are **DS3D_MINCONEANGLE**, **DS3D_MAXCONEANGLE**, and **DS3D_DEFAULTCONEANGLE**, respectively. The default cone angle is currently defined as 360 degrees, indicating the sound has no particular direction.
Return Value	**Description**
DS_OK	DirectSound successfully retrieved the cone angles.
DSERR_INVALIDPARAM	DirectSound could not retrieve the cone angles, because one or more parameters are invalid.

IDirectSound3DBuffer::GetConeOrientation ()

Function Description

This function retrieves the orientation of the 3D sound buffer's two sound cones, inner and outer. Sounds inside the inner sound cone are heard at the loudest intensity, while sounds outside the outer sound cone are heard at the lowest intensity; in-between sounds have in-between intensities.

Function Declaration

```
HRESULT GetConeOrientation (
  LPD3DVECTOR lpvOrientation
);
```

Parameter	**Description**
lpvOrientation	A pointer to a **D3DVECTOR** structure. If this function is successful, the structure will be filled with the orientation of the cones.
Return Value	**Description**
DS_OK	DirectSound successfully retrieved the cone orientation.
DSERR_INVALIDPARAM	DirectSound could not retrieve the cone orientation, because one or more parameters are invalid.

IDirectSound3DBuffer::GetConeOutsideVolume ()

Function Description

This function retrieves the volume level used for sounds outside the 3D sound buffer's sound cones.

Function Declaration

```
HRESULT GetConeOutsideVolume (
  LPLONG lplConeOutsideVolume
);
```

(continued)

IDirectSound3DBuffer::GetConeOutsideVolume () *(continued)*	
Parameter	**Description**
lplConeOutsideVolume	A pointer to an integer. If this function succeeds, the integer will be set to the volume level used for sounds outside the 3D sound buffer's sound cones. This can range from **DSBVOLUME_MIN**, which silences the sound, to **DSBVOLUME_MAX**, which indicates the volume level is normal.
Return Value	**Description**
DS_OK	DirectSound successfully retrieved the outside cone volume.
DSERR_INVALIDPARAM	DirectSound could not retrieve the outside cone volume, because one or more parameters are invalid.

IDirectSound3DBuffer::GetMaxDistance ()

Function Description

This function retrieves the 3D sound buffer's maximum distance (the distance from the listener beyond which the sound is not heard).

Function Declaration

```
HRESULT GetMaxDistance (
  LPD3DVALUE lpflMaxDistance
);
```

Parameter	**Description**
lpflMaxDistance	A pointer to a floating-point value. If this function succeeds, the value will be set to the 3D sound buffer's maximum distance. The default maximum distance is **DS3D_DEFAULTMAXDISTANCE**, which is effectively infinite.
Return Value	**Description**
DS_OK	DirectSound successfully retrieved the 3D sound buffer's maximum distance.
DSERR_INVALIDPARAM	DirectSound could not retrieve the 3D sound buffer's maximum distance, because one or more parameters are invalid.

IDirectSound3DBuffer::GetMinDistance ()

Function Description

This function retrieves the 3D sound buffer's minimum distance (the distance from the listener closer than which the sound volume level is not increased).

(continued)

IDirectSound3DBuffer::GetMinDistance () *(continued)*	
Function Declaration	

`HRESULT GetMinDistance (`
`  LPD3DVALUE lpflMinDistance`
`);`	

Parameter	**Description**
lpflMinDistance	A pointer to a floating-point value. If this function succeeds, the value will be set to the 3D sound buffer's minimum distance. The default minimum distance is **DS3D_DEFAULTMINDISTANCE**, which is currently defined as 1.0 (one meter under the default DirectSound measurement system).
Return Value	**Description**
DS_OK	DirectSound successfully retrieved the 3D sound buffer's minimum distance.
DSERR_INVALIDPARAM	DirectSound could not retrieve the 3D sound buffer's minimum distance, because one or more parameters are invalid.

IDirectSound3DBuffer::GetMode ()	
Function Description	
This function retrieves the operation mode of the 3D sound buffer.	
Function Declaration	

`HRESULT GetMode (`
`  LPDWORD lpdwMode`
`);`	

Parameter	**Description**
lpdwMode	A pointer to an integer. If this function is successful, the integer will be set to one of the following flags, which indicate the operation mode of the 3D sound buffer: • **DS3DMODE_DISABLE**—3D sound processing is disabled. • **DS3DMODE_HEADRELATIVE**—The position, velocity, and orientation of the 3D sound buffer are relative to the head of the listener. • **DS3DMODE_NORMAL**—The position, velocity, and orientation of the 3D sound buffer are absolute.
Return Value	**Description**
DS_OK	DirectSound successfully retrieved the operation mode of the 3D sound buffer.
DSERR_INVALIDPARAM	DirectSound could not retrieve the operation mode of the 3D sound buffer, because one or more parameters are invalid.

IDirectSound3DBuffer::GetPosition ()

Function Description

This function retrieves the 3D position of the 3D sound buffer in terms of an *x*-, *y*-, and *z*-component. DirectSound uses this position to play the 3D sound effect realistically.

Function Declaration

```
HRESULT GetPosition (
  LPD3DVECTOR lpvPosition
);
```

Parameter	Description
lpvPosition	A pointer to a **D3DVECTOR** structure. If this function succeeds, the structure will be filled with the position of the 3D sound buffer.

Return Value	Description
DS_OK	DirectSound successfully retrieved the position of the 3D sound buffer.
DSERR_INVALIDPARAM	DirectSound could not retrieve the position of the 3D sound buffer, because one or more parameters are invalid.

IDirectSound3DBuffer: GetVelocity ()

Function Description

This function retrieves the velocity of the 3D sound buffer. The velocity is used by DirectSound to calculate the Doppler effect; it does not actually move the position of the 3D sound buffer.

Function Declaration

```
HRESULT GetVelocity (
  LPD3DVECTOR lpvVelocity
);
```

Parameter	Description
lpvVelocity	A pointer to a **D3DVECTOR** structure. If this function is successful, this structure will be filled with the velocity of the 3D sound buffer.

Return Value	Description
DS_OK	DirectSound successfully retrieved the velocity of the 3D sound buffer.
DSERR_INVALIDPARAM	DirectSound could not retrieve the velocity of the 3D sound buffer, because one or more parameters are invalid.

IDirectSound3DBuffer::SetAllParameters ()

Function Description

This function sets all parameters of the 3D sound buffer.

Function Declaration

```
HRESULT SetAllParameters (
  LPCDS3DBUFFER lpcDs3dBuffer,
  DWORD dwApply
);
```

Parameter	Description
lpcDs3dBuffer	A pointer to a **DS3DBUFFER** structure that describes all of the parameters of the 3D sound buffer.
dwApply	Describes how the setting is to be applied. This parameter can be one of the following flags: • **DS3D_DEFERRED**—The setting will not be applied until the **IDirectSound3DListener::CommitDeferredSettings** () function is called. • **DS3D_IMMEDIATE**—The setting will be applied immediately. This flag forces Direct3D to recalculate 3D sound information for all 3D sounds. Unless an application must change only a single parameter, it should instead use the **DS3D_DEFERRED** flag and call the **IDirectSound3D-Listener::CommitDeferredSettings** () function when all changes are complete, thus avoiding unnecessary calculations.
Return Value	**Description**
DS_OK	DirectSound successfully set all parameters of the 3D sound buffer.
DSERR_INVALIDPARAM	DirectSound could not set all parameters of the 3D sound buffer, because one or more parameters are invalid.

IDirectSound3DBuffer::SetConeAngles ()

Function Description

This function sets the 3D sound buffer's two sound-cone angles for the inner and outer sound cones. Sounds inside the inner sound cone are heard at the loudest intensity, while sounds outside the outer sound cone are heard at the lowest intensity; in-between sounds have in-between intensities.

Function Declaration

```
HRESULT SetConeAngles (
  DWORD dwInsideConeAngle,
  DWORD dwOutsideConeAngle,
  DWORD dwApply
);
```

(continued)

IDirectSound3DBuffer::SetConeAngles () *(continued)*

Parameter	Description
dwInsideConeAngle	The inside cone angle, measured in degrees. The minimum, maximum, and default angles for this value are **DS3D_-MINCONEANGLE**, **DS3D_MAXCONEANGLE**, and **DS3D_-DEFAULTCONEANGLE**, respectively. The default cone angle is currently defined as 360 degrees, indicating the sound has no particular direction.
dwOutsideConeAngle	The outside cone angle, measured in degrees. The minimum, maximum, and default angles for this value are **DS3D_-MINCONEANGLE**, **DS3D_MAXCONEANGLE**, and **DS3D_-DEFAULTCONEANGLE**, respectively. The default cone angle is currently defined as 360 degrees, indicating the sound has no particular direction.
dwApply	Describes how the setting is to be applied. This parameter can be one of the following flags: • **DS3D_DEFERRED**—The setting will not be applied until the **IDirectSound3DListener::CommitDeferredSettings ()** function is called. • **DS3D_IMMEDIATE**—The setting will be applied immediately. This flag forces Direct3D to recalculate 3D sound information for all 3D sounds. Unless an application must change only a single parameter, it should instead use the **DS3D_DEFERRED** flag and call the **IDirectSound3DListener::CommitDeferredSettings ()** function when all changes are complete, thus avoiding unnecessary calculations.

Return Value	Description
DS_OK	DirectSound successfully set the cone angles.
DSERR_INVALIDPARAM	DirectSound could not set the cone angles, because one or more parameters are invalid.

IDirectSound3DBuffer::SetConeOrientation ()

Function Description

This function sets the orientation of the 3D sound buffer's two sound cones. Sounds inside the inner sound cone are heard at the loudest intensity, while sounds outside the outer sound cone are heard at the lowest intensity; in-between sounds have in-between intensities.

Function Declaration

```
HRESULT SetConeOrientation (
  D3DVALUE x,
  D3DVALUE y,
  D3DVALUE z,
  DWORD dwApply
);
```

IDirectSound3DBuffer::SetConeOrientation () *(continued)*

Parameter	Description
x	The x-axis component of the vector representing the orientation of the sound cones.
y	The y-axis component of the vector describing the orientation of the sound cones.
z	The z-axis component of the vector describing the orientation of the sound cones.
dwApply	Describes how the setting is to be applied. This parameter can be one of the following flags: • **DS3D_DEFERRED**—The setting will not be applied until the **IDirectSound3DListener::CommitDeferredSettings** () function is called. • **DS3D_IMMEDIATE**—The setting will be applied immediately. This flag forces Direct3D to recalculate 3D sound information for all 3D sounds. Unless an application must change only a single parameter, it should instead use the **DS3D_DEFERRED** flag and call the **IDirectSound3DListener::CommitDeferredSettings** () function when all changes are complete, thus avoiding unnecessary calculations.

Return Value	Description
DS_OK	DirectSound successfully set the orientation of the sound cones.
DSERR_INVALIDPARAM	DirectSound could not set the orientation of the sound cones, because one or more parameters are invalid.

IDirectSound3DBuffer::SetConeOutsideVolume ()

Function Description

This function sets the volume level used for sounds outside the 3D sound buffer's sound cones.

Function Declaration

```
HRESULT SetConeOutsideVolume (
  LONG lConeOutsideVolume,
  DWORD dwApply
);
```

Parameter	Description
lConeOutsideVolume	A 32-bit signed integer describing the volume level used for sounds outside the 3D sound buffer's sound cones. This can range from **DSBVOLUME_MIN**, which silences the sound, to **DSBVOLUME_MAX**, which indicates the volume level is normal.

(continued)

IDirectSound3DBuffer::SetConeOutsideVolume () *(continued)*

Parameter	Description
dwApply	Describes how the setting is to be applied. This parameter can be one of the following flags:
	• **DS3D_DEFERRED**—The setting will not be applied until the **IDirectSound3DListener::CommitDeferredSettings ()** function is called.
	• **DS3D_IMMEDIATE**—The setting will be applied immediately. This flag forces Direct3D to recalculate 3D sound information for all 3D sounds. Unless an application must change only a single parameter, it should instead use the **DS3D_DEFERRED** flag and call the **IDirectSound3DListener::CommitDeferredSettings ()** function when all changes are complete, thus avoiding unnecessary calculations.

Return Value	Description
DS_OK	DirectSound successfully set the outside cone volume.
DSERR_INVALIDPARAM	DirectSound could not set the outside cone volume, because one or more parameters are invalid.

IDirectSound3DBuffer::SetMaxDistance ()

Function Description

This function sets the 3D sound buffer's maximum distance (the distance from the listener beyond which the sound is not heard).

Function Declaration

```
HRESULT SetMaxDistance (
 D3DVALUE flMaxDistance,
 DWORD dwApply
);
```

Parameter	Description
flMaxDistance	A floating-point value describing the 3D sound buffer's maximum distance. The default maximum distance is **DS3D_-DEFAULTMAXDISTANCE**, which is effectively infinite.
dwApply	Describes how the setting is to be applied. This parameter can be one of the following flags:
	• **DS3D_DEFERRED**—The setting will not be applied until the **IDirectSound3DListener::CommitDeferredSettings ()** function is called.

(continued)

IDirectSound3DBuffer::SetMaxDistance () *(continued)*

Parameter	Description
	• **DS3D_IMMEDIATE**—The setting will be applied immediately. This flag forces Direct3D to recalculate 3D sound information for all 3D sounds. Unless an application must change only a single parameter, it should instead use the **DS3D_DEFERRED** flag and call the **IDirectSound3DListener::CommitDeferredSettings** () function when all changes are complete, thus avoiding unnecessary calculations.

Return Value	Description
DS_OK	DirectSound successfully set the 3D sound buffer's maximum distance.
DSERR_INVALIDPARAM	DirectSound could not set the 3D sound buffer's maximum distance, because one or more parameters are invalid.

IDirectSound3DBuffer::SetMinDistance ()

Function Description

This function sets the 3D sound buffer's minimum distance (the distance from the listener closer than which the sound volume level is not increased).

Function Declaration

```
HRESULT SetMinDistance (
  D3DVALUE flMinDistance,
  DWORD dwApply
);
```

Parameter	Description
flMinDistance	The 3D sound buffer's minimum distance. The default minimum distance is **DS3D_DEFAULTMINDISTANCE**, which is currently defined as 1.0 (one meter under the default DirectSound measurement system).
dwApply	Describes how the setting is to be applied. This parameter can be one of the following flags:
	• **DS3D_DEFERRED**—The setting will not be applied until the **IDirectSound3DListener::CommitDeferredSettings** () function is called.
	• **DS3D_IMMEDIATE**—The setting will be applied immediately. This flag forces Direct3D to recalculate 3D sound information for all 3D sounds. Unless an application must change only a single parameter, it should instead use the **DS3D_DEFERRED** flag and call the **IDirectSound3DListener::CommitDeferredSettings** () function when all changes are complete, thus avoiding unnecessary calculations.

(continued)

IDirectSound3DBuffer::SetMinDistance () *(continued)*

Return Value	Description
DS_OK	DirectSound successfully set the 3D sound buffer's minimum distance.
DSERR_INVALIDPARAM	DirectSound could not set the 3D sound buffer's minimum distance, because one or more parameters are invalid.

IDirectSound3DBuffer::SetMode ()

Function Description

This function sets the operation mode of the 3D sound buffer.

Function Declaration

```
HRESULT SetMode (
  DWORD dwMode,
  DWORD dwApply
);
```

Parameter	Description
dwMode	The operation mode of the 3D sound buffer. This parameter can be one of the following flags: • **DS3DMODE_DISABLE**—DirectSound should disable 3D sound processing. • **DS3DMODE_HEADRELATIVE**—DirectSound should interpret the position and velocity of the 3D sound buffer as relative to the head of the listener. • **DS3DMODE_NORMAL**—DirectSound should interpret the position and velocity of the 3D sound buffer as absolute.
dwApply	Describes how the setting is to be applied. This parameter can be one of the following flags: • **DS3D_DEFERRED**—The setting will not be applied until the **IDirectSound3DListener::CommitDeferredSettings ()** function is called. • **DS3D_IMMEDIATE**—The setting will be applied immediately. This flag forces Direct3D to recalculate 3D sound information for all 3D sounds. Unless an application must change only a single parameter, it should instead use the **DS3D_DEFERRED** flag and call the **IDirectSound3DListener::CommitDeferredSettings ()** function when all changes are complete, thus avoiding unnecessary calculations.

(continued)

IDirectSound3DBuffer::SetMode () *(continued)*	
Return Value	**Description**
DS_OK	DirectSound successfully set the operation mode of the 3D sound buffer.
DSERR_INVALIDPARAM	DirectSound could not set the operation mode of the 3D sound buffer, because one or more parameters are invalid.

IDirectSound3DBuffer::SetPosition ()

Function Description

This function sets the position of the 3D sound buffer in terms of an *x*-, *y*-, and *z*-component. DirectSound uses this position to play the 3D sound effect realistically.

Function Declaration

```
HRESULT SetPosition (
  D3DVALUE x,
  D3DVALUE y,
  D3DVALUE z,
  DWORD dwApply
);
```

Parameter	Description
x	The position of the 3D sound buffer along the *x*-axis.
y	The position of the 3D sound buffer along the *y*-axis.
z	The position of the 3D sound buffer along the *z*-axis.
dwApply	Describes how the setting is to be applied. This parameter can be one of the following flags:
	• **DS3D_DEFERRED**—The setting will not be applied until the **IDirectSound3DListener::CommitDeferredSettings ()** function is called.
	• **DS3D_IMMEDIATE**—The setting will be applied immediately. This flag forces Direct3D to recalculate 3D sound information for all 3D sounds. Unless an application must change only a single parameter, it should instead use the **DS3D_DEFERRED** flag and call the **IDirectSound3DListener::-CommitDeferredSettings ()** function when all changes are complete, thus avoiding unnecessary calculations.
Return Value	**Description**
DS_OK	DirectSound successfully set the position of the 3D sound buffer.
DSERR_INVALIDPARAM	DirectSound could not set the position of the 3D sound buffer, because one or more parameters are invalid.

IDirectSound3DBuffer::SetVelocity ()

Function Description

This function sets the velocity of the 3D sound buffer. DirectSound uses the velocity to calculate the Doppler effect; it does not actually move the position of the 3D sound buffer.

Function Declaration

```
HRESULT SetVelocity (
  D3DVALUE x,
  D3DVALUE y,
  D3DVALUE z,
  DWORD dwApply
);
```

Parameter	Description
x	The component of the velocity vector along the x-axis.
y	The component of the velocity vector along the y-axis.
z	The component of the velocity vector along the z-axis.
dwApply	Describes how the setting is to be applied. This parameter can be one of the following flags:
	• **DS3D_DEFERRED**—The setting will not be applied until the **IDirectSound3DListener::CommitDeferredSettings** () function is called.
	• **DS3D_IMMEDIATE**—The setting will be applied immediately. This flag forces Direct3D to recalculate 3D sound information for all 3D sounds. Unless an application must change only a single parameter, it should instead use the **DS3D_DEFERRED** flag and call the **IDirectSound3DListener::-CommitDeferredSettings** () function when all changes are complete, thus avoiding unnecessary calculations.

Return Value	Description
DS_OK	DirectSound successfully set the velocity of the 3D sound buffer.
DSERR_INVALIDPARAM	DirectSound could not set the velocity of the 3D sound buffer, because one or more parameters are invalid.

IDirectSound3DListener

You can obtain the IDirectSound3DListener interface by querying an IDirectSoundBuffer interface whose sound buffer is a primary sound buffer with 3D capabilities.

The GUID for the IDirectSound3DListener interface is **IID_IDirectSound3DListener**.

IDirectSound3DListener::CommitDeferredSettings ()

Function Description

This function commits settings that have been deferred.

Function Declaration

```
HRESULT CommitDeferredSettings ();
```

Parameter	Description
None	

Return Value	Description
DS_OK	DirectSound successfully committed the deferred settings.
DSERR_INVALIDPARAM	DirectSound could not commit the deferred settings, because one or more parameters are invalid.

IDirectSound3DListener::GetAllParameters ()

Function Description

This function retrieves all parameters of the 3D listener.

Function Declaration

```
HRESULT GetAllParameters (
  LPDS3DLISTENER lpListener
);
```

Parameter	Description
lpListener	A pointer to a **DS3DLISTENER** structure. If this function succeeds, the structure will be filled with all parameters of the 3D listener.

Return Value	Description
DS_OK	DirectSound successfully retrieved all parameters of the 3D listener.
DSERR_INVALIDPARAM	DirectSound could not retrieve all parameters of the 3D listener, because one or more parameters are invalid.

IDirectSound3DListener::GetDistanceFactor ()

Function Description

This function retrieves the 3D listener's distance factor. By default, DirectSound measures position and velocity in meters. But if an application is using some other unit of measurement, it can inform Direct3D to use this unit by calling the **IDirectSound3DListener::GetDistanceFactor ()** function.

Function Declaration

```
HRESULT GetDistanceFactor (
  LPD3DVALUE lpflDistanceFactor
);
```

(continued)

IDirectSound3DListener::GetDistanceFactor () *(continued)*

Parameter	Description
lpflDistanceFactor	A pointer to a floating-point value. If this function succeeds, this value will be set to the distance factor, specified in meters/unit, where unit represents the unit of measurement currently being used. For feet, this value would be 0.3048, because 0.3048 meters go in to one foot (0.3048/1).

Return Value	Description
DS_OK	DirectSound successfully retrieved the distance factor.
DSERR_INVALIDPARAM	DirectSound could not retrieve the distance factor, because one or more parameters are invalid.

IDirectSound3DListener::GetDopplerFactor ()

Function Description

This function retrieves the Doppler factor. The Doppler factor describes how pronounced the Doppler effect is.

Function Declaration

```
HRESULT GetDopplerFactor (
  LPD3DVALUE lpflDopplerFactor
);
```

Parameter	Description
lpflDopplerFactor	A pointer to a floating-point value. If this function succeeds, this value will be set to the Doppler factor. This can range from **DS3D_MINDOPPLERFACTOR** (0.0), which specifies no Doppler effects, to **DS3D_MAXDOPPLERFACTOR** (10.0), which specifies Doppler effects 10 times as pronounced as they are in the real world. The default value is **DS3D_DEFAULTDOPPLERFACTOR** (1.0), which specifies real-world Doppler effects.

Return Value	Description
DS_OK	DirectSound successfully retrieved the Doppler factor.
DSERR_INVALIDPARAM	DirectSound could not retrieve the Doppler factor, because one or more parameters are invalid.

IDirectSound3DListener::GetOrientation ()

Function Description

This function retrieves the orientation of the 3D listener. Two vectors describe the orientation: a front vector, which specifies the direction the listener's face is pointing; and a top vector, which specifies the direction the top of the listener's head is pointing. The top and front vectors are perpendicular to one another.

(continued)

IDirectSound3DListener::GetOrientation () *(continued)*

Function Declaration

```
HRESULT GetOrientation (
  LPD3DVECTOR lpvOrientFront,
  LPD3DVECTOR lpvOrientTop
);
```

Parameter	Description
lpvOrientFront	A pointer to a **D3DVECTOR** structure. If this function succeeds, this structure will be filled with the front vector, describing the direction of the listener's face.
lpvOrientTop	A pointer to a **D3DVECTOR** structure. If this function succeeds, this structure will be filled with the top vector, describing the direction of the top of the listener's head.
Return Value	**Description**
DS_OK	DirectSound successfully retrieved the orientation of the 3D listener.
DSERR_INVALIDPARAM	DirectSound could not successfully retrieve the orientation of the 3D listener, because one or more parameters are invalid.

IDirectSound3DListener::GetPosition ()

Function Description

This function retrieves the position of the 3D listener.

Function Declaration

```
HRESULT GetPosition (
  LPD3DVECTOR lpvPosition
);
```

Parameter	Description
lpvPosition	A pointer to a **D3DVECTOR** structure. If this function succeeds, this structure will be filled with the position of the 3D listener.
Return Value	**Description**
DS_OK	DirectSound successfully retrieved the position of the 3D listener.
DSERR_INVALIDPARAM	DirectSound could not successfully retrieve the position of the 3D listener, because one or more parameters are invalid.

IDirectSound3DListener::GetRolloffFactor ()

Function Description

This function retrieves the rolloff factor. The rolloff factor determines the rate at which a sound's intensity falls off as that sound becomes farther away from the listener.

Function Declaration

```
HRESULT GetRolloffFactor (
  LPD3DVALUE lpflRolloffFactor
);
```

Parameter	Description
lpflRolloffFactor	A pointer to a floating-point value. If this function succeeds, this value will be set to the rolloff factor, which can range from **DS3D_MINROLLOFFFACTOR** (0.0), indicating no rolloff, to **DS3D_MAXROLLOFFFACTOR**, indicating rolloff 10 times more pronounced than in the real world. The default value is **DS3D_-DEFAULTROLLOFFFACTOR** (1.0), indicating real-world rolloff.

Return Value	Description
DS_OK	DirectSound successfully retrieved the rolloff factor.
DSERR_INVALIDPARAM	DirectSound could not retrieve the rolloff factor, because one or more parameters are invalid.

IDirectSound3DListener::GetVelocity ()

Function Description

This function retrieves the velocity of the 3D listener. DirectSound uses the velocity to calculate the Doppler effect; it does not actually move the position of the 3D listener.

Function Declaration

```
HRESULT GetVelocity (
  LPD3DVECTOR lpvVelocity
);
```

Parameter	Description
lpvVelocity	A pointer to a **D3DVECTOR** structure. If this function succeeds, this structure will be filled with the velocity of the 3D listener.

Return Value	Description
DS_OK	DirectSound successfully retrieved the velocity of the 3D listener.
DSERR_INVALIDPARAM	DirectSound could not retrieve the velocity of the 3D listener, because one or more parameters are invalid.

IDirectSound3DListener::SetAllParameters ()

Function Description

This function sets all parameters of the 3D listener.

Function Declaration

```
HRESULT SetAllParameters (
  LPCDS3DLISTENER lpcListener,
  DWORD dwApply
);
```

Parameter	Description
lpcListener	A pointer to a **DS3DLISTENER** structure that describes the parameters of the 3D sound buffer.
dwApply	Describes how the setting is to be applied. This parameter can be one of the following flags:
	• **DS3D_DEFERRED**—The setting will not be applied until the **IDirectSound3DListener::CommitDeferredSettings ()** function is called.
	• **DS3D_IMMEDIATE**—The setting will be applied immediately. This flag forces Direct3D to recalculate 3D sound information for all 3D sounds. Unless an application must change only a single parameter, it should instead use the **DS3D_DEFERRED** flag and call the **IDirectSound3DListener::-CommitDeferredSettings ()** function when all changes are complete, thus avoiding unnecessary calculations.

Return Value	Description
DS_OK	DirectSound successfully set all parameters of the 3D listener.
DSERR_INVALIDPARAM	DirectSound could not set all parameters of the 3D listener, because one or more parameters are invalid.

IDirectSound3DListener::SetDistanceFactor ()

Function Description

This function sets the 3D listener's distance factor. By default, DirectSound measures position and velocity in meters. This function retrieves the 3D listener's distance factor. By default, DirectSound measures position and velocity in meters. But if an application is using some other unit of measurement, it can inform Direct3D to use this unit by calling this function.

Function Declaration

```
HRESULT SetDistanceFactor (
  D3DVALUE flDistanceFactor,
  DWORD dwApply
);
```

(continued)

IDirectSound3DListener::SetDistanceFactor () *(continued)*

Parameter	Description
flDistanceFactor	The distance factor, specified in meters/unit, where unit represents the new unit of measurement. For feet, this value would be 0.3048, because 0.3048 meters go in to one foot (0.3048/1).
dwApply	Describes how the setting is to be applied. This parameter can be one of the following flags: • **DS3D_DEFERRED**—The setting will not be applied until the **IDirectSound3DListener::CommitDeferredSettings** () function is called. • **DS3D_IMMEDIATE**—The setting will be applied immediately. This flag forces Direct3D to recalculate 3D sound information for all 3D sounds. Unless an application must change only a single parameter, it should instead use the **DS3D_DEFERRED** flag and call the **IDirectSound3DListener::CommitDeferredSettings** () function when all changes are complete, thus avoiding unnecessary calculations.
Return Value	**Description**
DS_OK	DirectSound successfully set the distance factor.
DSERR_INVALIDPARAM	DirectSound could not set the distance factor, because one or more parameters are invalid.

IDirectSound3DListener::SetDopplerFactor ()

Function Description

This function sets the Doppler factor. The Doppler factor describes how pronounced the Doppler effect is.

Function Declaration

```
HRESULT SetDopplerFactor (
  D3DVALUE flDopplerFactor,
  DWORD dwApply
);
```

Parameter	Description
flDopplerFactor	The Doppler factor. This can range from **DS3D_MINDOPPLERFACTOR** (0.0), which specifies no Doppler effects, to **DS3D_MAXDOPPLERFACTOR** (10.0), which specifies Doppler effects 10 times as pronounced as they are in the real world. The default value is **DS3D_DEFAULTDOPPLERFACTOR** (1.0), which specifies real-world Doppler effects.
dwApply	Describes how the setting is to be applied. This parameter can be one of the following flags: • **DS3D_DEFERRED**—The setting will not be applied until the **IDirectSound3DListener::CommitDeferredSettings** () function is called.

(continued)

IDirectSound3DListener::SetDopplerFactor () *(continued)*

Parameter	Description
	• **DS3D_IMMEDIATE**—The setting will be applied immediately. This flag forces Direct3D to recalculate 3D sound information for all 3D sounds. Unless an application must change only a single parameter, it should instead use the **DS3D_DEFERRED** flag and call the **IDirectSound3DListener::CommitDeferredSettings** () function when all changes are complete, thus avoiding unnecessary calculations.

Return Value	Description
DS_OK	DirectSound successfully set the Doppler factor.
DSERR_INVALIDPARAM	DirectSound could not set the Doppler factor, because one or more parameters are invalid.

IDirectSound3DListener::SetOrientation ()

Function Description

This function sets the orientation of the 3D listener. Two vectors describe the orientation: a front vector, which specifies the direction the listener's face is pointing; and a top vector, which specifies the direction the top of the listener's head is pointing. The top and front vectors must be perpendicular to one another.

Function Declaration

```
HRESULT SetOrientation (
  D3DVALUE xFront,
  D3DVALUE yFront,
  D3DVALUE zFront,
  D3DVALUE xTop,
  D3DVALUE yTop,
  D3DVALUE zTop,
  DWORD dwApply
);
```

Parameter	Description
xFront	The x-component of the front vector.
yFront	The y-component of the front vector.
zFront	The z-component of the front vector.
xTop	The x-component of the top vector.
yTop	The y-component of the top vector.
zTop	The z-component of the top vector.
dwApply	Describes how the setting is to be applied. This parameter can be one of the following flags:
	• **DS3D_DEFERRED**—The setting will not be applied until the **IDirectSound3DListener::CommitDeferredSettings** () function is called.

(continued)

IDirectSound3DListener::SetOrientation () *(continued)*

Parameter	Description
	• **DS3D_IMMEDIATE**—The setting will be applied immediately. This flag forces Direct3D to recalculate 3D sound information for all 3D sounds. Unless an application must change only a single parameter, it should instead use the **DS3D_DEFERRED** flag and call the **IDirectSound3DListener::CommitDeferredSettings** () function when all changes are complete, thus avoiding unnecessary calculations.

Return Value	Description
DS_OK	DirectSound successfully set the orientation of the 3D listener.
DSERR_INVALIDPARAM	DirectSound could not set the orientation of the 3D listener, because one or more parameters are invalid.

IDirectSound3DListener::SetPosition ()

Function Description

This function sets the position of the 3D listener.

Function Declaration

```
HRESULT SetPosition (
  D3DVALUE x,
  D3DVALUE y,
  D3DVALUE z,
  DWORD dwApply
);
```

Parameter	Description
x	The position of the 3D listener along the x-axis.
y	The position of the 3D listener along the y-axis.
z	The position of the 3D listener along the z-axis.
dwApply	Describes how the setting is to be applied. This parameter can be one of the following flags:
	• **DS3D_DEFERRED**—The setting will not be applied until the **IDirectSound3DListener::CommitDeferredSettings** () function is called.
	• **DS3D_IMMEDIATE**—The setting will be applied immediately. This flag forces Direct3D to recalculate 3D sound information for all 3D sounds. Unless an application must change only a single parameter, it should instead use the **DS3D_DEFERRED** flag and call the **IDirectSound3DListener::CommitDeferredSettings** () function when all changes are complete, thus avoiding unnecessary calculations.

Return Value	Description
DS_OK	DirectSound successfully set the position of the 3D listener.
DSERR_INVALIDPARAM	DirectSound could not set the position of the 3D listener, because one or more parameters are invalid.

IDirectSound3DListener::SetRolloffFactor ()

Function Description

This function sets the rolloff factor. The rolloff factor determines the rate at which a sound's intensity falls off as that sound becomes farther away from the listener.

Function Declaration

```
HRESULT SetRolloffFactor (
  D3DVALUE flRolloffFactor,
  DWORD dwApply
);
```

Parameter	Description
flRolloffFactor	The rolloff factor. This parameter can range from **DS3D_-MINROLLOFFFACTOR** (0.0), indicating no rolloff, to **DS3D_-MAXROLLOFFFACTOR**, indicating rolloff 10 times more pronounced than in the real world. The default value is **DS3D_-DEFAULTROLLOFFFACTOR** (1.0), indicating real-world rolloff.
dwApply	Describes how the setting is to be applied. This parameter can be one of the following flags:
	• **DS3D_DEFERRED**—The setting will not be applied until the **IDirectSound3DListener::CommitDeferredSettings ()** function is called.
	• **DS3D_IMMEDIATE**—The setting will be applied immediately. This flag forces Direct3D to recalculate 3D sound information for all 3D sounds. Unless an application must change only a single parameter, it should instead use the **DS3D_DEFERRED** flag and call the **IDirectSound3DListener::-CommitDeferredSettings ()** function when all changes are complete, thus avoiding unnecessary calculations.

Return Value	Description
DS_OK	DirectSound successfully set the rolloff factor.
DSERR_INVALIDPARAM	DirectSound could not set the rolloff factor, because one or more parameters are invalid.

IDirectSound3DListener::SetVelocity ()

Function Description

This function sets the velocity of the 3D listener. DirectSound uses the velocity to calculate the Doppler effect; it does not actually move the position of the 3D listener.

Function Declaration

```
HRESULT SetVelocity (
  D3DVALUE x,
  D3DVALUE y,
  D3DVALUE z,
  DWORD dwApply
);
```

(continued)

IDirectSound3DListener::SetVelocity () *(continued)*	
Parameter	**Description**
x	The component of the velocity vector along the *x*-axis.
y	The component of the velocity vector along the *y*-axis.
z	The component of the velocity vector along the *z*-axis.
dwApply	Describes how the setting is to be applied. This parameter can be one of the following flags:
	• **DS3D_DEFERRED**—The setting will not be applied until the **IDirectSound3DListener::CommitDeferredSettings ()** function is called.
	• **DS3D_IMMEDIATE**—The setting will be applied immediately. This flag forces Direct3D to recalculate 3D sound information for all 3D sounds. Unless an application must change only a single parameter, it should instead use the **DS3D_DEFERRED** flag and call the **IDirectSound3DListener::CommitDeferredSettings ()** function when all changes are complete, thus avoiding unnecessary calculations.
Return Value	**Description**
DS_OK	DirectSound successfully set the velocity of the 3D listener.
DSERR_INVALIDPARAM	DirectSound could not set the velocity of the 3D listener, because one or more parameters are invalid.

IDirectSoundBuffer

You can obtain the IDirectSoundBuffer interface by calling the **IDirectSound::CreateSoundBuffer ()** function.

The GUID for the IDirectSoundBuffer interface is **IID_IDirectSoundBuffer**.

IDirectSoundBuffer::GetCaps ()	
Function Description	
This function retrieves the capabilities of the sound buffer.	
Function Declaration	
``` HRESULT GetCaps (LPDSBCAPS lpDSBufferCaps); ```	
Parameter	**Description**
lpDSBufferCaps	A pointer to a **DSBCAPS structure.** If this function succeeds, this structure will be filled with the capabilities of the sound buffer.

(continued)

IDirectSoundBuffer::GetCaps () *(continued)*	
Return Value	**Description**
DS_OK	DirectSound successfully retrieved the capabilities of the sound buffer.
DSERR_INVALIDPARAM	DirectSound could not retrieve the capabilities of the sound buffer, because one or more parameters are invalid.

IDirectSoundBuffer::GetCurrentPosition ()

Function Description

This function retrieves the current play and write positions. The play position indicates the position in the sound buffer where DirectSound is currently playing. The write position indicates a position in the sound buffer after the play position where it is safe to write sound data to (typically this is about 15ms worth of sound data ahead of the play position). An application can always write data to the sound buffer behind the current play position.

Function Declaration

```
HRESULT GetCurrentPosition (
  LPDWORD lpdwCurrentPlayCursor,
  LPDWORD lpdwCurrentWriteCursor
);
```

Parameter	Description
lpdwCurrentPlayCursor	A pointer to an integer. If the function succeeds, this integer will be set to the current play position. This parameter can also be **NULL**, indicating that DirectSound should not retrieve the current play position.
lpdwCurrentWriteCursor	A pointer to an integer. If this function succeeds, this integer will be set to the current write position.
	This parameter can also be **NULL**, indicating that DirectSound should not retrieve the current write position.
Return Value	**Description**
DS_OK	DirectSound successfully retrieved the current position.
DSERR_INVALIDPARAM	DirectSound could not retrieve the current position, because one or more parameters are invalid.
DSERR_PRIOLEVELNEEDED	DirectSound could not retrieve the current position, because priority-level access is required for the operation (see **IDirectSound::SetCooperativeLevel** ()).

IDirectSoundBuffer::GetFormat ()	

Function Description

This function retrieves the format of the sound buffer.

Function Declaration

```
HRESULT GetFormat (
  LPWAVEFORMATEX lpwfxFormat,
  DWORD dwSizeAllocated,
  LPDWORD lpdwSizeWritten
);
```

Parameter	Description
lpwfxFormat	A pointer to a Win32 **WAVEFORMATEX** structure. If this function succeeds, the structure will be filled with the format of the sound buffer. Note that for some WAV formats, extra data is appended to the end of the standard **WAVEFORMATEX** structure (**dwSizeAllocated** should reflect these extra bytes). This parameter may be **NULL**, in which case DirectSound merely stores the number of bytes necessary to contain the structure in **lpdwSizeWritten**.
dwSizeAllocated	The size of the structure pointed to by **lpwfxFormat**.
lpdwSizeWritten	A pointer to an integer. If this function succeeds, this integer will be set to the number of bytes actually written to **lpwfxFormat**.
Return Value	Description
DS_OK	DirectSound successfully retrieved the format of the sound buffer.
DSERR_INVALIDPARAM	DirectSound could not retrieve the format of the sound buffer, because one or more parameters are invalid.

IDirectSoundBuffer::GetFrequency ()	

Function Description

This function retrieves the playback frequency of the sound buffer.

Function Declaration

```
HRESULT GetFrequency (
  LPDWORD lpdwFrequency
);
```

Parameter	Description
lpdwFrequency	A pointer to an integer. If this function succeeds, this integer will be set to the playback frequency of the sound buffer. The frequency is measured in Hertz (Hz), or samples per second. The range for the frequency is **DSBFREQUENCY_MIN** (currently defined as 100) to **DSBFREQUENCY_MAX** (currently defined as 100,000).

(continued)

IDirectSoundBuffer::GetFrequency () *(continued)*	
Return Value	**Description**
DS_OK	DirectSound successfully retrieved the frequency of the sound buffer.
DSERR_CONTROLUNAVAIL	DirectSound could not retrieve the frequency of the sound buffer, because the operation is not supported.
DSERR_INVALIDPARAM	DirectSound could not retrieve the frequency of the sound buffer, because one or more parameters are invalid.
DSERR_PRIOLEVELNEEDED	DirectSound could not retrieve the frequency of the sound buffer, because priority-level access is required for the operation.

IDirectSoundBuffer::GetPan ()	
Function Description	
This function retrieves the pan of the sound buffer.	

Function Declaration

```
HRESULT GetPan (
  LPLONG lplPan
);
```

Parameter	Description
lplPan	A pointer to a signed 32-bit integer. If this function succeeds, the integer will be set to the pan of the sound buffer. The range of the pan is **DSBPAN_LEFT** (-10,000) to **DSBPAN_CENTER** (0) to **DSBPAN_RIGHT** (10,000), measured in hundredths of a decibel. Negative values reduce the volume of the right speaker. If the pan is -5,000, for example, the right speaker's volume is reduced by 50 decibels. Conversely, positive values reduce the volume of the left speaker. If the pan is 2,000, the left speaker's volume is reduced by 20 decibels.
Return Value	**Description**
DS_OK	DirectSound successfully retrieved the pan of the sound buffer.
DSERR_CONTROLUNAVAIL	DirectSound could not retrieve the pan of the sound buffer, because the operation is not supported.
DSERR_INVALIDPARAM	DirectSound could not retrieve the pan of the sound buffer, because one or more parameters are invalid.
DSERR_PRIOLEVELNEEDED	DirectSound could not retrieve the pan of the sound buffer, because the operation requires priority-level access.

IDirectSoundBuffer::GetStatus ()

Function Description

This function retrieves the status of the sound buffer.

Function Declaration

```
HRESULT GetStatus (
  LPDWORD lpdwStatus
);
```

Parameter	Description
lpdwStatus	A pointer to an integer. If this function succeeds, the integer will be set to the status of the sound buffer. This can be 0, indicating the sound is not playing, or a combination of one or more of the following values: • **DSBSTATUS_BUFFERLOST**—The memory storing the sound data has been lost and must be restored with the **IDirectSoundBuffer::Restore** () function. • **DSBSTATUS_LOCSOFTWARE**—The sound is playing in local software. This flag is valid only for buffers created with the **DSBCAPS_LOCDEFER** flag. • **DSBSTATUS_LOCHARDWARE**—The sound is playing in local hardware. This flag is valid for buffers created with the **DSBCAPS_LOCDEFER** flag. • **DSBSTATUS_LOOPING**—The sound is looping. This value is always specified with **DSBSTATUS_PLAYING**. • **DSBSTATUS_PLAYING**—The sound is playing. • **DSBSTATUS_TERMINATED**—The playing of the sound was prematurely terminated due to the voice management logic. This flag is valid only for buffers created with the **DSBCAPS_-LOCDEFER** flag.

Return Value	Description
DS_OK	DirectSound successfully retrieved the status of the sound buffer.
DSERR_INVALIDPARAM	DirectSound could not retrieve the status of the sound buffer, because one or more parameters are invalid.

IDirectSoundBuffer::GetVolume ()

Function Description

This function retrieves the volume of the sound buffer.

Function Declaration

```
HRESULT GetVolume (
  LPLONG lplVolume
);
```

(continued)

IDirectSoundBuffer::GetVolume () *(continued)*

Parameter	Description
lplVolume	A pointer to a 32-bit signed integer. If this function succeeds, the integer will be set to the volume of the sound buffer. The range of the volume is **DSBVOLUME_MIN** (-10,000) to **DSBVOLUME_MAX** (0), measured in hundredths of a decibel. A value of 0 indicates the volume of the sound buffer is unchanged. A value of -10,000 indicates the volume of the sound buffer is reduced by 100 decibels (which silences all but the loudest of sounds).

Return Value	Description
DS_OK	DirectSound successfully retrieved the volume of the sound buffer.
DSERR_CONTROLUNAVAIL	DirectSound could not retrieve the frequency of the sound buffer, because the operation is not supported.
DSERR_INVALIDPARAM	DirectSound could not retrieve the volume of the sound buffer, because one or more parameters are invalid.
DSERR_PRIOLEVELNEEDED	DirectSound could not retrieve the volume of the sound buffer, because priority-level access is required for the operation (see **IDirectSound::SetCooperativeLevel** ()).

IDirectSoundBuffer::Initialize ()

Function Description

This function initializes a DirectSoundBuffer object created with **CoCreateInstance** (). Applications that use **IDirectSound::CreateSoundBuffer** () to obtain a pointer to a **DirectSoundBuffer** object do not need to call this function.

Function Declaration

```
HRESULT Initialize (
  LPDIRECTSOUND lpDirectSound,
  LPCDSBUFFERDESC lpcDSBufferDesc
);
```

Parameter	Description
lpDirectSound	A pointer to a DirectSound object that identifies the sound device associated with this DirectSoundBuffer object.
lpcDSBufferDesc	A pointer to a **DSBUFFERDESC** structure that describes the attributes of the sound buffer to be initialized.

Return Value	Description
DS_OK	DirectSound successfully initialized the sound buffer object.
DSERR_INVALIDPARAM	DirectSound could not initialize the sound buffer object, because one or more parameters are invalid.
DSERR_ALREADYINITIALIZED	DirectSound could not initialize the DirectSoundBuffer object, because it is already initialized, either by this function or implicitly by the **IDirectSound::CreateSoundBuffer** () function.

IDirectSoundBuffer::Lock ()

Function Description

This function locks a portion of the memory of the sound buffer for writing data to it. The application must unlock the memory when it is finished by calling **IDirectSoundBuffer::Unlock ()**.

Function Declaration

```
HRESULT Lock (
  DWORD dwWriteCursor,
  DWORD dwWriteBytes,
  LPVOID lplpvAudioPtr1,
  LPDWORD lpdwAudioBytes1,
  LPVOID lplpvAudioPtr2,
  LPDWORD lpdwAudioBytes2,
  DWORD dwFlags
);
```

Parameter	Description
dwWriteCursor	The position of the first byte in the sound buffer to be locked. If this function succeeds, **lplpvAudioPtr1** will point to memory representing the location of this byte.
dwWriteBytes	The number of bytes to be locked. The sound buffer is conceptually circular, so this is not always the number of bytes pointed to by **lplpvAudioPtr1**. If this parameter exceeds the number of bytes in the buffer from the **dwWriteCursor** position, then **lplpvAudioPtr2** points to the beginning of the sound buffer and **lpdwAudioBytes2** describes the remaining number of bytes.
lplpvAudioPtr1	The address of a pointer. If this function succeeds, the pointer will be set to a piece of memory representing the first byte of the locked portion of the sound buffer.
lpdwAudioBytes1	A pointer to an integer. If this function succeeds, the integer will be set to the number of bytes pointed to by **lplpvAudioPtr1**. This is not equal to **dwWriteBytes** if **dwWriteCursorBytes** specifies a segment longer than the end of the sound buffer.
lplpvAudioPtr2	The address of a pointer. If this function succeeds, the pointer will be set to a piece of memory representing the first byte in the sound buffer. This parameter may be **NULL** if **dwWriteBytes** does not specify a segment beyond the end of the sound buffer.
lpdwAudioBytes2	A pointer to an integer. If this function succeeds, the integer will be set to the number of bytes pointed to by **lplpvAudioPtr2**. This parameter may be **NULL** if **dwWriteBytes** does not specify a segment beyond the end of the sound buffer.
dwFlags	Describes how the lock operation is to be performed. This parameter can be one of the following flags: • **DSBLOCK_FROMWRITECURSOR**—The lock operation occurs from the current write position (the position ahead of the play position where it is safe to write sound data to). If this flag is specified, **dwWriteCursor** is ignored.

(continued)

IDirectSoundBuffer::Lock () *(continued)*	
Parameter	**Description**
	• **DSBLOCK_ENTIREBUFFER**—The lock operation occurs from the start of the sound buffer and extends its entire length. If this flag is specified, **dwWriteCursorBytes** is ignored.
	• **DSBPLAY_LOCHARDWARE**—The sound should be played in a hardware buffer only; the function will fail if sufficient hardware resources to play the sound are not available. This flag is valid only for sound buffers created with the **DSBPLAY_LOCSOFTWARE** flag.
	• **DSBPLAY_LOCSOFTWARE**—The sound should be played only in a software buffer. This flag is valid only for sound buffers created with the **DSBPLAY_LOCSOFTWARE** flag, and cannot be used with the **DSBPLAY_LOCHARDWARE** flag.
	• **DSBPLAY_TERMINATEBY_TIME**—This flag guarantees the sound will be played in hardware. If this flag is used, and there are no resources left for playing the sound in hardware, the sound buffer with the least remaining time left to play will be terminated to free up resources for this sound. This flag is valid only for sound buffers created with the **DSBCAPS_LOCDEFER** flag.
	• **DSBPLAY_TERMINATEBY_DISTANCE**—This flag guarantees the sound will be played in hardware. If this flag is used, and there are no resources left for playing the sound in hardware, the sound buffer the farthest away from the listener will be terminated to free up resources for this sound. This flag is valid only for sound buffers created with the **DSBCAPS_LOCDEFER** flag.
	• **DSBPLAY_TERMINATEBY_PRIORITY**—This flag guarantees the sound will be played in hardware. If this flag is used, and there are no resources left for playing the sound in hardware, the sound buffer with the lowest priority level will be terminated to free up resources for this sound. This flag is valid only for sound buffers created with the **DSBCAPS_LOCDEFER** flag.
Return Value	**Description**
DS_OK	DirectSound successfully locked the sound buffer.
DSERR_BUFFERLOST	DirectSound could not lock the sound buffer, because its memory is lost. It must first be restored with **IDirectSoundBuffer::Restore ()**.
DSERR_INVALIDCALL	DirectSound could not lock the sound buffer, because the current state of this DirectSoundBuffer object does not permit the operation.
DSERR_INVALIDPARAM	DirectSound could not lock the sound buffer, because one or more parameters are invalid.
DSERR_PRIOLEVELNEEDED	DirectSound could not lock the sound buffer, because the operation requires priority-level access.

IDirectSoundBuffer::Play ()

Function Description

This function plays the contents of the sound buffer.

Function Declaration

```
HRESULT Play (
  DWORD dwReserved1,
  DWORD dwReserved2,
  DWORD dwFlags
);
```

Parameter	Description
dwReserved1	An integer reserved for future use. Must be 0.
dwReserved2	An integer reserved for future use. Must be 0.
dwFlags	Describes how the sound is to be played. This can be 0, in which case the sound is played once, or the following parameter: • **DSBPLAY_LOOPING**—The sound should be played continually.

Return Value	Description
DS_OK	DirectSound successfully started playing the sound buffer.
DSERR_BUFFERLOST	DirectSound could not play the sound buffer, because its memory is lost. It must first be restored with **IDirectSoundBuffer::Restore** ().
DSERR_INVALIDCALL	DirectSound could not play the sound buffer, because the current state of this DirectSoundBuffer object does not permit the operation.
DSERR_INVALIDPARAM	DirectSound could not play the sound buffer, because one or more parameters are invalid.
DSERR_PRIOLEVELNEEDED	DirectSound could not play the sound buffer, because the operation requires priority-level access.
DSERR_HWUNAVAIL	DirectSound could not play the sound buffer because sufficient hardware resources are not available.

IDirectSoundBuffer::Restore ()

Function Description

This function restores sound buffer memory that has been lost.

Function Declaration

```
HRESULT Restore ();
```

Parameter	Description
None	

(continued)

IDirectSoundBuffer::Restore () *(continued)*

Return Value	Description
DS_OK	DirectSound successfully restored the memory of the sound buffer.
DSERR_BUFFERLOST	DirectSound could not restore the memory of the sound buffer.
DSERR_INVALIDCALL	DirectSound could not restore the sound buffer, because the current state of this DirectSoundBuffer object does not permit the operation.
DSERR_INVALIDPARAM	DirectSound could not restore the sound buffer, because one or more parameters are invalid.
DSERR_PRIOLEVELNEEDED	DirectSound could not restore the memory of the sound buffer, because the operation requires priority-level access.

IDirectSoundBuffer::SetCurrentPosition ()

Function Description

This function sets the current play position. The play position indicates the position in the sound buffer where DirectSound is currently playing.

Function Declaration

```
HRESULT SetCurrentPosition (
  DWORD dwNewPosition
);
```

Parameter	Description
dwNewPosition	The new play position. If the sound is playing, it will immediately skip to this new position. Otherwise, the next time the sound is played, it will start with the position.

Return Value	Description
DS_OK	DirectSound successfully set the play position of the sound buffer.
DSERR_INVALIDCALL	DirectSound could not set the play position of the sound buffer, because the current state of this DirectSoundBuffer object does not permit the operation.
DSERR_INVALIDPARAM	DirectSound could not set the play position of the sound buffer, because one or more parameters are invalid.
DSERR_PRIOLEVELNEEDED	DirectSound could not set the current play position of the sound buffer, because the operation requires priority-level access.

IDirectSoundBuffer::SetFormat ()

Function Description

This function sets the format for the primary sound buffer. It is not valid for secondary sound buffers. In write-primary cooperative level, the sound playback must be explicityly stopped before this function can be called.

Function Declaration

```
HRESULT SetFormat (
  LPCWAVEFORMATEX lpcfxFormat
);
```

(continued)

IDirectSoundBuffer::SetFormat () *(continued)*

Parameter	Description
lpcfxFormat	A pointer to a Win32 **WAVEFORMATEX** structure that describes the new format of the sound buffer.

Return Value	Description
DS_OK	DirectSound successfully set the format of the sound buffer.
DSERR_BADFORMAT	DirectSound could not set the format of the sound buffer, because the hardware does not support the WAV format specified by **lpcfxFormat**.
DSERR_INVALIDCALL	DirectSound could not set the format of the sound buffer, because the current state of this DirectSoundBuffer object does not permit the operation.
DSERR_INVALIDPARAM	DirectSound could not set the format of the sound buffer, because one or more parameters are invalid.
DSERR_OUTOFMEMORY	DirectSound could not set the format of the sound buffer, because sufficient memory for the new format is not available.
DSERR_PRIOLEVELNEEDED	DirectSound could not set the format of the sound buffer, because the operation requires priority-level access.
DSERR_UNSUPPORTED	DirectSound could not set the format of the sound buffer, because the action is not supported.

IDirectSoundBuffer::SetFrequency ()

Function Description

This function sets the playback frequency of the sound buffer.

Function Declaration

```
HRESULT SetFrequency (
  DWORD dwFrequency
);
```

Parameter	Description
dwFrequency	The new playback frequency of the sound buffer. This parameter may also be **DSBFREQUENCY_ORIGINAL**, in which case the frequency is set to default, as specified when the sound was created.

Return Value	Description
DS_OK	DirectSound successfully set the frequency of the sound buffer.
DSERR_CONTROLUNAVAIL	DirectSound could not set the frequency of the sound buffer, because the operation is not supported.
DSERR_GENERIC	DirectSound could not set the frequency of the sound buffer, because of a generic error.
DSERR_INVALIDPARAM	DirectSound could not set the frequency of the sound buffer, because one or more parameters are invalid.
DSERR_PRIOLEVELNEEDED	DirectSound could not set the frequency of the sound buffer, because the operation requires priority-level access.

IDirectSoundBuffer::SetPan ()

Function Description

This function sets the pan of the sound buffer.

Function Declaration

```
HRESULT SetPan (
  LONG lPan
);
```

Parameter	Description
lPan	A signed 32-bit integer that describes the new pan of the sound buffer. The range of the pan is **DSBPAN_LEFT** (-10,000) to **DSBPAN_CENTER** (0) to **DSBPAN_RIGHT** (10,000), measured in hundredths of a decibel. Negative values reduce the volume of the right speaker. If the pan is -5,000, for example, the right speaker's volume is reduced by 50 decibels. Conversely, positive values reduce the volume of the left speaker. If the pan is 2,000, the left speaker's volume is reduced by 20 decibels.

Return Value	Description
DS_OK	DirectSound successfully set the pan of the sound buffer.
DSERR_CONTROLUNAVAIL	DirectSound could not set the pan of the sound buffer, because the operation is not supported.
DSERR_GENERIC	DirectSound could not set the pan of the sound buffer, because of a generic error.
DSERR_INVALIDPARAM	DirectSound could not set the pan of the sound buffer, because one or more parameters are invalid.
DSERR_PRIOLEVELNEEDED	DirectSound could not set the pan of the sound buffer, because the operation requires priority-level access.

IDirectSoundBuffer::SetVolume ()

Function Description

This function sets the volume of the sound buffer.

Function Declaration

```
HRESULT SetVolume (
  LONG lVolume
);
```

Parameter	Description
lVolume	The new volume of the sound buffer. The range of the volume is **DSBVOLUME_MIN** (-10,000) to **DSBVOLUME_MAX** (0), measured in hundredths of a decibel. A value of 0 indicates the volume of the sound buffer is unchanged. A value of -10,000 indicates the volume of the sound buffer is reduced by 100 decibels (which silences all but the loudest of sounds).

(continued)

IDirectSoundBuffer::SetVolume () *(continued)*

Return Value	Description
DS_OK	DirectSound successfully set the volume of the sound buffer.
DSERR_CONTROLUNAVAIL	DirectSound could not set the volume of the sound buffer, because the operation is not supported.
DSERR_GENERIC	DirectSound could not set the volume of the sound buffer, because of a generic error.
DSERR_INVALIDPARAM	DirectSound could not set the volume of the sound buffer, because one or more parameters are invalid.
DSERR_PRIOLEVELNEEDED	DirectSound could not set the volume of the sound buffer, because the operation requires priority-level access.

IDirectSoundBuffer::Stop ()

Function Description

This function stops the sound buffer from playing.

Function Declaration

```
HRESULT Stop ();
```

Parameter	Description
None	

Return Value	Description
DS_OK	DirectSound successfully stopped playing the sound buffer.
DSERR_INVALIDPARAM	DirectSound could not stop the sound buffer, because one or more parameters are invalid.
DSERR_PRIOLEVELNEEDED	DirectSound could not stop the sound buffer, because the operation requires priority-level access.

IDirectSoundBuffer::Unlock ()

Function Description

This function unlocks memory locked with **IDirectSoundBuffer::Lock** (). It must be called when an application is done writing to the sound buffer.

Function Declaration

```
HRESULT Unlock (
  LPVOID lpvAudioPtr1,
  DWORD dwAudioBytes1,
  LPVOID lpvAudioPtr2,
  DWORD dwAudioBytes2
);
```

(continued)

IDirectSoundBuffer::Unlock () *(continued)*	
Parameter	**Description**
lpvAudioPtr1	The address of the pointer by the same name retrieved by **IDirectSoundBuffer::Lock** ().
dwAudioBytes1	An integer specifying the number of bytes actually written to **lpvAudioPtr1**.
lpvAudioPtr2	The address of the pointer by the same name retrieved by **IDirectSoundBuffer::Lock** ().
dwAudioBytes2	An integer specifying the number of bytes actually written to **lpvAudioPtr2**.
Return Value	**Description**
DS_OK	DirectSound successfully unlocked the sound buffer.
DSERR_INVALIDCALL	DirectSound could not unlock the sound buffer, because the current state of this DirectSoundBuffer object does not permit the operation.
DSERR_INVALIDPARAM	DirectSound could not unlock the sound buffer, because one or more parameters are invalid.
DSERR_PRIOLEVELNEEDED	DirectSound could not unlock the sound buffer, because the operation requires priority-level access.

IDirectSoundCapture

You can obtain the IDirectSoundCapture interface by calling the **DirectSoundCapture-Create ()** function.

The GUID for the IDirectSoundCapture interface is **IID_IDirectSoundCapture**.

IDirectSoundCapture::CreateCaptureBuffer ()	
Function Description	
This function creates a sound-capture buffer, given a structure describing its attributes.	
Function Declaration	
<pre>HRESULT CreateCaptureBuffer (
LPDSCBUFFERDESC lpDSCBufferDesc,
LPLPDIRECTSOUNDCAPTUREBUFFER lplpDirectSoundCaptureBuffer,
LPUNKNOWN pUnkOuter
);</pre>	
Parameter	**Description**
lpDSCBufferDesc	A pointer to a **DSCBUFFERDESC** structure that describes the attributes of the sound-capture buffer to be created.

(continued)

IDirectSoundCapture::CreateCaptureBuffer () *(continued)*

Parameter	Description
lplpDirectSoundCaptureBuffer	The address of a pointer to a DirectSoundCaptureBuffer object. If this function succeeds, the pointer will be set to the newly created DirectSoundCaptureBuffer object.
pUnkOuter	Exists for compatibility with COM. This parameter must be set to **NULL**.

Return Value	Description
DS_OK	DirectSound successfully created the sound-capture buffer.
DSERR_INVALIDPARAM	DirectSound could not create the sound-capture buffer, because one or more parameters are invalid.
DSERR_BADFORMAT	DirectSound could not create the sound-capture buffer, because the hardware does not support the WAV format specified by **lpDSCBufferDesc**.
DSERR_GENERIC	DirectSound could not create the sound-capture buffer, because of a generic error.
DSERR_NODRIVER	DirectSound could not create the sound-capture buffer, because there is no sound-capture driver.
DSERR_OUTOFMEMORY	DirectSound could not create the sound-capture buffer, because sufficient memory is not available.
DSERR_UNINITIALIZED	DirectSound could not create the sound-capture buffer, because this DirectSoundCapture object is uninitialized. It must be initialized with **DirectSoundCapture::Initialize ()** before this function can be called.

IDirectSoundCapture::GetCaps ()

Function Description

This function retrieves the capabilities of the sound-capture device.

Function Declaration

```
HRESULT GetCaps (
  LPDSCCAPS lpDSCCaps
);
```

Parameter	Description
lpDSCCaps	A pointer to a **DSCCAPS** structure. If this function succeeds, this structure will be filled with the capabilities of the sound-capture device.

Return Value	Description
DS_OK	DirectSound successfully retrieved the capabilities of the sound-capture hardware.
DSERR_INVALIDPARAM	DirectSound could not retrieve the capabilities of the sound-capture device, because one or more parameters are invalid.

(continued)

IDirectSoundCapture::GetCaps () *(continued)*

Parameter	Description
DSERR_UNSUPPORTED	DirectSound could not retrieve the capabilities of the sound buffer, because the action is not supported.
DSERR_NODRIVER	DirectSound could not retrieve the capabilities of the sound buffer, because there is no sound-capture driver to perform the operation.
DSERR_OUTOFMEMORY	DirectSound could not retrieve the capabilities of the sound-capture device, because sufficient memory is not available.
DSERR_UNINITIALIZED	DirectSound could not retrieve the capabilities of the sound-capture device, because this DirectSoundCapture object is uninitialized. It must be initialized with **DirectSoundCapture::Initialize** () before this function can be called.

IDirectSoundCapture::Initialize ()

Function Description

This function initializes a **DirectSoundCapture** object created with **CoCreateInstance** (). Applications that use **DirectSoundCaptureCreate** () to obtain a pointer to a **DirectSoundCapture** object do not need to call this function.

Function Declaration

```
HRESULT Initialize(
  LPGUID lpGuid
);
```

Parameter	Description
lpGuid	The address of a GUID that describes the sound-capture hardware to be represented by this DirectSoundCapture object.

Return Value	Description
DS_OK	DirectSound successfully initialized the sound-capture object.
DSERR_INVALIDPARAM	DirectSound could not initialize the sound-capture object, because one or more parameters are invalid.
DSERR_NODRIVER	DirectSound could not initialize the sound-capture object, because there is no sound-capture driver.
DSERR_OUTOFMEMORY	DirectSound could not initialize the DirectSoundCapture, object, because sufficient memory is not available.
DSERR_ALREADYINITIALIZED	DirectSound could not initialize the DirectSoundCapture object, because it is already initialized, either by this function or implicitly by the **DirectSoundCaptureCreate** () function.

IDirectSoundCaptureBuffer

You can obtain the IDirectSoundCaptureBuffer interface by calling the **IDirectSound-Capture::CreateCaptureBuffer ()** function.

The GUID for the IDirectSoundCaptureBuffer interface is **IID_IDirectSoundCapture-Buffer**.

IDirectSoundCaptureBuffer::GetCaps ()

Function Description

This function retrieves the capabilities of the sound-capture buffer.

Function Declaration

```
HRESULT GetCaps (
  LPDSCBCAPS lpDSCBCaps
);
```

Parameter	Description
lpDSCBCaps	A pointer to a **DSCBCAPS** structure. If this function succeeds, this structure will be filled with the capabilities of the sound-capture buffer.
Return Value	**Description**
DS_OK	DirectSound successfully retrieved the capabilities of the sound-capture buffer.
DSERR_INVALIDPARAM	DirectSound could not retrieve the capabilities of the sound-capture buffer, because one or more parameters are invalid.
DSERR_UNSUPPORTED	DirectSound could not retrieve the capabilities of the sound-capture buffer, because the action is not supported.
DSERR_OUTOFMEMORY	DirectSound could not retrieve the capabilities of the sound-capture buffer, because sufficient memory is not available.

IDirectSoundCaptureBuffer::GetCurrentPosition ()

Function Description

This function retrieves the current capture and read positions of the sound-capture buffer. The capture position indicates the position in the sound-capture buffer where data is being written to by the sound-capture hardware. The read position indicates the position in the sound-capture buffer that data can safely be read from.

Function Declaration

```
HRESULT GetCurrentPosition (
  LPDWORD lpdwCapturePosition,
  LPDWORD lpdwReadPosition
);
```

(continued)

IDirectSoundCaptureBuffer::GetCurrentPosition () *(continued)*

Parameter	Description
lpdwCapturePosition	A pointer to an integer. If this function succeeds, the integer will be set to the current capture position.
	This parameter can also be **NULL**, indicating that DirectSound should not retrieve the current capture position.
lpdwReadPosition	A pointer to an integer. If this function succeeds, the integer will be set to the current read position.
	This parameter can also be **NULL**, indicating that DirectSound should not retrieve the current read position.

Return Value	Description
DS_OK	DirectSound successfully retrieved the capture and read positions of the sound capture buffer.
DSERR_INVALIDPARAM	DirectSound could not retrieve the capture and read positions of the sound-capture buffer, because one or more parameters are invalid.
DSERR_NODRIVER	DirectSound could not retrieve the capture and read positions of the sound-capture buffer, because there is no sound-capture driver.
DSERR_OUTOFMEMORY	DirectSound could not retrieve the capture and read positions of the sound-capture buffer, because sufficient memory is not available.

IDirectSoundCaptureBuffer::GetFormat ()

Function Description

This function retrieves the format of the sound-capture buffer.

Function Declaration

```
HRESULT GetFormat (
  LPWAVEFORMATEX lpwfxFormat,
  DWORD dwSizeAllocated,
  LPDWORD lpdwSizeWritten
);
```

Parameter	Description
lpwfxFormat	A pointer to a Win32 **WAVEFORMATEX** structure. If this function succeeds, this structure will be filled with the format of the sound-capture buffer. Note that for some WAV formats, extra data is appended to the end of the standard **WAVEFORMATEX** structure (**dwSizeAllocated** should reflect these extra bytes).
dwSizeAllocated	The size of the structure pointed to by **lpwfxFormat**.
lpdwSizeWritten	A pointer to an integer. If this function succeeds, this integer will be set to the number of bytes actually written to **lpwfxFormat**.

(continued)

IDirectSoundCaptureBuffer::GetFormat () *(continued)*

Return Value	Description
DS_OK	DirectSound successfully retrieved the format of the sound-capture buffer.
DSERR_INVALIDPARAM	DirectSound could not retrieve the format of the sound-capture buffer, because one or more parameters are invalid.

IDirectSoundCaptureBuffer::GetStatus ()

Function Description
This function retrieves the status of the sound capture buffer.

Function Declaration
```
HRESULT GetStatus (
  DWORD *lpdwStatus
);
```

Parameter	Description
lpdwStatus	A pointer to an integer. If this function succeeds, the integer will be set to the status of the sound-capture buffer. This can be 0, indicating that sound is not being captured, or one of the following flags: • **DSCBSTATUS_CAPTURING**—Sound is being captured into the buffer. • **DSCBSTATUS_LOOPING**—Sound is being continually captured into the buffer.

Return Value	Description
DS_OK	DirectSound successfully retrieved the status of the sound-capture buffer.
DSERR_INVALIDPARAM	DirectSound could not retrieve the status of the sound-capture buffer, because one or more parameters are invalid.

IDirectSoundCaptureBuffer::Initialize ()

Function Description
This function initializes a DirectSoundCaptureBuffer object created with **CoCreateInstance** (). Applications that use **IDirectSoundCapture::CreateCaptureBuffer** () to obtain a pointer to a DirectSoundCaptureBuffer object do not need to call this function.

Function Declaration
```
HRESULT Initialize (
  LPDIRECTSOUNDCAPTURE lpDirectSoundCapture,
  LPCDSBUFFERDESC lpcDSBufferDesc
);
```

(continued)

IDirectSoundCaptureBuffer::Initialize () *(continued)*

Parameter	Description
lpDirectSoundCapture	A pointer to a DirectSoundCapture object that identifies the sound-capture device associated with this DirectSoundCapture-Buffer object.
lpcDSBufferDesc	A pointer to a **DSCBUFFERDESC** structure that describes the attributes of the sound-capture buffer to be initialized.

Return Value	Description
DS_OK	DirectSound successfully initialized the sound-capture buffer.
DSERR_INVALIDPARAM	DirectSound could not initialize the sound-capture buffer, because one or more parameters are invalid.
DSERR_ALREADYINITIALIZED	DirectSound could not initialize the DirectSoundCaptureBuffer object, because it is already initialized, either by this function or implicitly by the **IDirectSoundCapture::CreateCaptureBuffer ()** function.

IDirectSoundCaptureBuffer::Lock ()

Function Description

This function locks the sound-capture buffer to read data from it. Applications that use this function must call the **IDirectSoundCaptureBuffer::Unlock ()** function when finished reading data.

Function Declaration

```
HRESULT Lock (
  DWORD dwReadCursor,
  DWORD dwReadBytes,
  LPVOID *lplpvAudioPtr1,
  LPDWORD lpdwAudioBytes1,
  LPVOID *lplpvAudioPtr2,
  LPDWORD lpdwAudioBytes2,
  DWORD dwFlags
);
```

Parameter	Description
dwReadCursor	The position of the first byte in the sound-capture buffer to be locked. If this function succeeds, **lplpvAudioPtr1** will point to memory representing the location of this byte.
dwReadBytes	The number of bytes to be locked. The sound buffer is conceptually circular, so this is not always the number of bytes pointed to by **lplpvAudioPtr1**. If this parameter exceeds the number of bytes in the buffer from the **dwReadCursor** position, then **lplpvAudioPtr2** points to the tbeginning of the sound buffer and **lpdwAudioBytes2** describes the remaining number of bytes.

IDirectSoundCaptureBuffer::Lock () *(continued)*

Parameter	Description
lplpvAudioPtr1	The address of a pointer. If this function succeeds, the pointer will be set to a piece of memory representing the first byte of the locked portion of the sound-capture buffer.
lpdwAudioBytes1	A pointer to an integer. If this function succeeds, the integer will be set to the number of bytes pointed to by **lplpvAudioPtr1**. This is not equal to **dwReadCursorBytes** if **dwReadCursorBytes** specifies a segment longer than the end of the sound-capture buffer.
lplpvAudioPtr2	The address of a pointer. If this function succeeds, the pointer will be set to a piece of memory representing the first byte in the sound-capture buffer. This parameter may be **NULL** if **dwReadCursorBytes** does not specify a segment beyond the end of the sound-capture buffer.
lpdwAudioBytes2	A pointer to an integer. If this function succeeds, the integer will be set to the number of bytes pointed to by **lplpvAudioPtr2**. This parameter may be **NULL** if **dwReadCursorBytes** does not specify a segment beyond the end of the sound-capture buffer.
dwFlags	Describes how the lock operation is to be performed. This parameter can be 0 or the following flag: • **DSCBLOCK_ENTIREBUFFER**—The lock operation occurs from the start of the sound buffer and extends its entire length. If this flag is specified, **dwReadCursorBytes** is ignored.
Return Value	**Description**
DS_OK	DirectSound successfully locked the sound-capture buffer.
DSERR_INVALIDPARAM	DirectSound could not lock the sound-capture buffer, because one or more parameters are invalid.
DSERR_INVALIDCALL	DirectSound could not lock the sound-capture buffer, because the current state of this DirectSoundCaptureBuffer object does not permit the operation.

IDirectSoundCaptureBuffer::Start ()

Function Description

This function starts capturing sound data into the sound-capture buffer.

Function Declaration

```
HRESULT Start (
  DWORD dwFlags
);
```

(continued)

IDirectSoundCaptureBuffer::Start () *(continued)*	
Parameter	**Description**
dwFlags	A 32-bit integer that specifies how the capture operation is to proceed:
	• **DSCBSTART_LOOPING**—The capture operation should be continual. When DirectSound reaches the end of the sound-capture buffer, it starts again at the beginning.
Return Value	**Description**
DS_OK	DirectSound successfully started capturing sound data.
DSERR_INVALIDPARAM	DirectSound could not start capturing sound data, because one or more parameters are invalid.
DSERR_NODRIVER	DirectSound could not start capturing sound data, because there is no sound-capture driver.
DSERR_OUTOFMEMORY	DirectSound could not start capturing sound data, because sufficient memory is not available.

IDirectSoundCaptureBuffer::Stop ()	
Function Description	
This function stops capturing sound data.	
Function Declaration	
`HRESULT Stop ();`	
Parameter	**Description**
None	
Return Value	**Description**
DS_OK	DirectSound successfully stopped capturing sound data.
DSERR_NODRIVER	DirectSound could not stop capturing sound data, because there is no sound-capture driver.
DSERR_OUTOFMEMORY	DirectSound could not stop capturing sound data, because sufficient memory is not available.

IDirectSoundCaptureBuffer::Unlock ()

Function Description

This function unlocks memory locked with **IDirectSoundCaptureBuffer::Lock ()**. It must be called when an application is done writing to the sound buffer.

Function Declaration

```
HRESULT Unlock (
  LPVOID lpvAudioPtr1,
  DWORD dwAudioBytes1,
  LPVOID lpvAudioPtr2,
  DWORD dwAudioBytes2
);
```

Parameter	Description
lpvAudioPtr1	The address of the pointer by the same name retrieved by **IDirectSoundCaptureBuffer::Lock ()**.
dwAudioBytes1	An integer specifying the number of bytes actually read from **lpvAudioPtr1**.
lpvAudioPtr2	The address of the pointer by the same name retrieved by **IDirectSoundCaptureBuffer::Lock ()**.
dwAudioBytes2	An integer specifying the number of bytes actually read from **lpvAudioPtr2**.
Return Value	**Description**
DS_OK	DirectSound successfully unlocked the sound-capture buffer.
DSERR_INVALIDPARAM	DirectSound could not unlock the sound-capture buffer, because one or more parameters are invalid.
DSERR_INVALIDCALL	DirectSound could not unlock the sound-capture buffer, because the current state of this DirectSoundCaptureBuffer object does not permit the operation.

IDirectSoundNotify

You can obtain the IDirectSoundNotify interface by querying an existing IDirectSoundBuffer interface.

The GUID for the IDirectSoundNotify interface is **IID_IDirectSoundNotify**.

IDirectSoundNotify::SetNotificationPositions ()

Function Description

This function sets the notification positions for the sound buffer.

Function Declaration

```
HRESULT SetNotificationPositions (
  DWORD cPositionNotifies,
  LPCDSBPOSITIONNOTIFY lpcPositionNotifies
);
```

Parameter	Description
cPositionNotifies	The number of **DSBPOSITIONNOTIFY** structures pointed to by **lpcPositionNotifies**.
lpcPositionNotifies	A pointer to an array of **DSBPOSITIONNOTIFY** structures that describe the notification positions.
Return Value	**Description**
DS_OK	DirectSound successfully set the notification positions for the sound buffer.
DSERR_INVALIDPARAM	DirectSound could not set the notification positions for the sound buffer, because one or more parameters are invalid.
DSERR_OUTOFMEMORY	DirectSound could not set the notification positions for the sound buffer, because sufficient memory is not available.

IKsPropertySet

You can obtain the IKsPropertySet interface by querying an existing IDirectSoundBuffer interface.

The GUID for the IKsPropertySet interface is **IID_IKsPropertySet**.

IKsPropertySet::Get ()

Function Description

This function retrieves a property of the sound hardware device.

Function Declaration

```
HRESULT Get (
  REFGUID rguidPropSet,
  ULONG ulId,
  LPVOID pInstanceData,
  ULONG ulInstanceLength,
  LPVOID pPropertyData,
  ULONG ulDataLength,
  ULONG * pulBytesReturned
);
```

(continued)

IKsPropertySet::Get () *(continued)*

Parameter	Description
rguidPropSet	A reference to a GUID that describes the property set to which the property to be retrieved belongs.
ulId	The zero-based index of the property to be retrieved.
pInstanceData	A pointer to instance data.
ulInstanceLength	The number of bytes pointed to by **pInstanceData**.
pPropertyData	A pointer to a piece of memory. If this function succeeds, the memory will be filled with the data of the property.
ulDataLength	The number of bytes pointed to by **pPropertyData**.
pulBytesReturned	A pointer to an integer. If this function succeeds, this integer will be set to the number of bytes written into **pPropertyData**.
Return Value	**Description**
S_OK	DirectSound retrieved the property.
E_POINTER	DirectSound could not retrieve the property.

IKsPropertySet::QuerySupport ()

Function Description

This function queries the sound hardware device for support for a property.

Function Declaration

```
HRESULT QuerySupport (
  REFGUID rguidPropSet,
  ULONG ulId,
  ULONG* pulTypeSupport
);
```

Parameter	Description
rguidPropSet	A reference to a GUID that describes the property set containing the property whose support is to be queried for.
ulId	The zero-based index of the property whose support is to be queried for.
pulTypeSupport	A pointer to an integer. If the function succeeds, this integer will be set to 0, which indicates no support for the specified property, or one or more of the following values: • **KSPROPERTY_SUPPORT_GET**—The property can be retrieved. • **KSPROPERTY_SUPPORT_SET**—The property can be set.
Return Value	**Description**
S_OK	DirectSound successfully queried for support for the property.
E_NOTIMPL	The property is not implemented on the hardware device.
E_POINTER	DirectSound could not query for support for the property.

IKsPropertySet::Set ()	
Function Description	
This function sets a property of the sound hardware device.	
Function Declaration	

```
HRESULT Set (
  REFGUID rguidPropSet,
  ULONG ulId,
  LPVOID pInstanceData,
  ULONG ulInstanceLength,
  LPVOID pPropertyData,
  ULONG pulDataLength
);
```

Parameter	Description
rguidPropSet	A reference to a GUID that describes the property set to which the property to be set belongs.
ulId	The zero-based index of the property to be set.
pInstanceData	A pointer to instance data.
ulInstanceLength	The number of bytes pointed to by **pInstanceData**.
pPropertyData	A pointer to a piece of memory that describes the data to be set for the property.
pulDataLength	The number of bytes pointed to by **pPropertyData**.
Return Value	**Description**
S_OK	DirectSound set a property of the hardware device.
E_POINTER	DirectSound could not set the property.

Function Reference

This section documents the functions of DirectSound that do not belong to any interfaces.

DirectSoundCaptureCreate ()
Function Description
This function creates a sound-capture object representing a sound-capture hardware device.
Function Declaration

```
HRESULT WINAPI DirectSoundCaptureCreate (
  LPGUID lpGUID,
  LPDIRECTSOUNDCAPTURE *lplpDSC,
  LPUNKNOWN pUnkOuter
);
```

(continued)

DirectSoundCaptureCreate () *(continued)*

Parameter	Description
lpGUID	A pointer to a GUID that identifies the sound-capture device to be represented by the new DirectSoundCapture object.
lplpDSC	The address of a pointer to a DirectSoundCapture object. If this function succeeds, the pointer will be set to the newly created DirectSoundCapture object.
pUnkOuter	Exists for compatibility with COM. This parameter must be set to **NULL**.

Return Value	Description
DS_OK	DirectSound successfully created a sound-capture device.
DSERR_INVALIDPARAM	DirectSound could not create a sound-capture object, because one or more parameters are invalid.
DSERR_NOAGGREGATION	DirectSound could not create the sound-capture object, because the **pUnkOuter** parameter is not **NULL**.
DSERR_OUTOFMEMORY	DirectSound could not create a sound-capture buffer object, because sufficient memory is not available.

DirectSoundCaptureEnumerate ()

Function Description

This function enumerates the sound-capture devices on the system that can be represented by **DirectSoundCapture** objects.

Function Declaration

```
HRESULT WINAPI DirectSoundCaptureEnumerate (
  LPDSENUMCALLBACK lpDSEnumCallback,
  LPVOID lpContext
);
```

Parameter	Description
lpDSEnumCallback	The address of a **DSEnumCallback ()** function to be called for every enumerated sound-capture device.
lpContext	A pointer to application-defined data to be passed to the callback function every time it is called.

Return Value	Description
DS_OK	DirectSound successfully enumerated the sound-capture devices on the system.
DSERR_INVALIDPARAM	DirectSound could not enumerate the sound-capture device buffer, because one or more parameters are invalid.

DirectSoundCreate ()

Function Description

This function creates a DirectSound object that represents sound hardware.

Function Declaration

```
HRESULT WINAPI DirectSoundCreate (
  LPGUID lpGuid,
  LPDIRECTSOUND * ppDS,
  LPUNKNOWN pUnkOuter
);
```

Parameter	Description
lpGuid	A pointer to a GUID that identifies the sound device to be represented by the new DirectSound object.
ppDS	The address of a pointer to a DirectSound object. If this function succeeds, the pointer will be set to the newly created DirectSound object.
pUnkOuter	Exists for compatibility with COM. This parameter must be set to **NULL**.

Return Value	Description
DS_OK	DirectSound successfully created a DirectSound object.
DSERR_ALLOCATED	DirectSound could not create the DirectSound object, because the resources required to do so are allocated already.
DSERR_INVALIDPARAM	DirectSound could not create a DirectSound object, because one or more parameters are invalid.
DSERR_NOAGGREGATION	DirectSound could not create the DirectSound object, because the **pUnkOuter** parameter is not **NULL**.
DSERR_NODRIVER	DirectSound could not create a DirectSound object, because there is no sound driver.
DSERR_OUTOFMEMORY	DirectSound could not create a DirectSound object, because sufficient memory is not available.

DirectSoundEnumerate ()

Function Description

This function enumerates the sound devices on the system capable of being represented by DirectSound objects.

Function Declaration

```
HRESULT WINAPI DirectSoundEnumerate (
  LPDSENUMCALLBACK lpDSEnumCallback,
  LPVOID lpContext
);
```

(continued)

DirectSoundEnumerate () *(continued)*	
Parameter	**Description**
lpDSEnumCallback	The address of a **DSEnumCallback** () function to be called for every enumerated sound device.
lpContext	A pointer to application-defined data to be passed to the callback function every time it is called.
Return Value	**Description**
DS_OK	DirectSound successfully enumerated the sound devices on the system capable of being represented by DirectSound objects.
DSERR_INVALIDPARAM	DirectSound could not enumerate the sound devices, because one or more parameters are invalid.

Callback Function Reference

This section documents the application-defined callback function used by DirectSound during device enumeration.

DSEnumCallback ()	
Function Description	
This function is an application-defined function that DirectSound calls for every device it enumerates.	
Function Declaration	

```
BOOL CALLBACK DSEnumCallback (
  LPGUID lpGuid,
  LPCSTR lpcstrDescription,
  LPCSTR lpcstrModule,
  LPVOID lpContext
);
```

Parameter	**Description**
lpGuid	A pointer to a GUID that identifies the device being enumerated.
lpcstrDescription	A pointer to a **NULL**-terminated string that identifies the device being enumerated.
lpcstrModule	A pointer to a **NULL**-terminated string that specifies the name of the module for the driver of the device being enumerated.
lpContext	A pointer to application-defined data sent to this function through the **DirectSoundEnumerate** () or **DirectSoundCapture-Enumerate** () function.
Return Value	**Description**
TRUE	DirectSound should continue enumerating devices.
FALSE	DirectSound should stop the enumeration process.

Structure Reference

This section documents the structures used by DirectSound functions.

DS3DBUFFER

Structure Description

This structure is used to store the attributes of 3D sound buffers.

Structure Declaration

```
typedef struct {
  DWORD    dwSize;
  D3DVECTOR vPosition;
  D3DVECTOR vVelocity;
  DWORD    dwInsideConeAngle;
  DWORD    dwOutsideConeAngle;
  D3DVECTOR vConeOrientation;
  LONG     lConeOutsideVolume;
  D3DVALUE flMinDistance;
  D3DVALUE flMaxDistance;
  DWORD    dwMode;
} DS3DBUFFER, *LPDS3DBUFFER;

typedef const DS3DBUFFER *LPCDS3DBUFFER;
```

Member	Description
dwSize	The size of the structure, in bytes. This member must be initialized before the structure is used.
vPosition	A **D3DVECTOR** structure that describes the position of the 3D sound buffer.
vVelocity	A **D3DVECTOR** structure that describes the velocity of the 3D sound buffer. The velocity of the 3D sound buffer is used for calculating Doppler effects only; DirectSound does not alter the position of the sound based on its velocity.
dwInsideConeAngle	The cone angle of the inside sound cone.
dwOutsideConeAngle	The cone angle of the outside sound cone.
vConeOrientation	A **D3DVECTOR** structure that describes the orientation of the 3D sound buffer's two sound cones.
lConeOutsideVolume	The volume level used for sounds outside the 3D sound buffer's sound cones. This can range from **DSBVOLUME_MIN**, which silences the sound, to **DSBVOLUME_MAX**, which indicates the volume level is normal.
flMinDistance	The 3D sound buffer's minimum distance.
flMaxDistance	The 3D sound buffer's maximum distance.

(continued)

DS3DBUFFER *(continued)*

Member	Description
dwMode	The operation mode of the 3D sound buffer. This member can be one of the following values: • **DS3DMODE_DISABLE**—3D sound processing is disabled. • **DS3DMODE_HEADRELATIVE**—The position and velocity of the 3D sound buffer are relative to the head of the listener. • **DS3DMODE_NORMAL**—The position and velocity of the 3D sound buffer are absolute.

DS3DLISTENER

Structure Description

This structure describes the attributes of the 3D listener.

Structure Declaration

```
typedef struct {
  DWORD    dwSize;
  D3DVECTOR vPosition;
  D3DVECTOR vVelocity;
  D3DVECTOR vOrientFront;
  D3DVECTOR vOrientTop;
  D3DVALUE  flDistanceFactor;
  D3DVALUE  flRolloffFactor;
  D3DVALUE  flDopplerFactor;
} DS3DLISTENER, *LPDS3DLISTENER;

typedef const DS3DLISTENER *LPCDS3DLISTENER;
```

Member	Description
dwSize	The size of the structure, in bytes. This member must be initialized before the structure is used.
vPosition	A **D3DVECTOR** structure that describes the position of the 3D listener.
vVelocity	A **D3DVECTOR** structure that describes the velocity of the 3D listener. The velocity of the 3D listener is used for calculating Doppler effects only; DirectSound does not alter the position of the listener based on its velocity.
vOrientFront	A **D3DVECTOR** structure that describes the 3D listener's front vector. The front vector specifies which direction the front of the listener's head is facing.
vOrientTop	A **D3DVECTOR** structure that describes the 3D listener's top vector. The top vector specifies which direction the top of the listener's head is facing.

(continued)

DS3DLISTENER *(continued)*

Member	Description
flDistanceFactor	The distance factor, specified in meters/unit, where unit represents the unit of measurement currently being used. For meters, this value would be 1. For feet, this value would be 0.3048, because 0.3048 meters go in to one foot (0.3048/1).
flRolloffFactor	The rolloff factor, which can range from **DS3D_MINROLLOFF-FACTOR** (0.0), indicating no rolloff, to **DS3D_MAXROLLOFF-FACTOR**, indicating rolloff 10 times more pronounced than in the real world. The default value is **DS3D_DEFAULTROLLOFF-FACTOR** (1.0), indicating real-world rolloff.
flDopplerFactor	The Doppler factor. This can range from **DS3D_MINDOPPLER-FACTOR** (0.0), which specifies no Doppler effects, to **DS3D_-MAXDOPPLERFACTOR** (10.0), which specifies Doppler effects 10 times as pronounced as they are in the real world. The default value is **DS3D_DEFAULTDOPPLERFACTOR** (1.0), which specifies real-world Doppler effects.

DSBCAPS

Structure Description

This structure describes the capabilities of a DirectSound buffer.

Structure Declaration

```
typedef struct {
  DWORD dwSize;
  DWORD dwFlags;
  DWORD dwBufferBytes;
  DWORD dwUnlockTransferRate;
  DWORD dwPlayCpuOverhead;
} DSBCAPS, *LPDSBCAPS;

typedef const DSBCAPS *LPCDSBCAPS;
```

Member	Description
dwSize	The size of the structure, in bytes. This member must be initialized before the structure is used.
dwFlags	Describes some of the attributes of the sound buffer. This member can be zero or more of the following flags: • **DSBCAPS_CTRL3D**—The sound buffer is capable of 3D control. • **DSBCAPS_CTRLALL**—The sound buffer is capable of all **DSBCAPS_CTRL** flags.

(continued)

DSBCAPS *(continued)*	
Member	**Description**
	• **DSBCAPS_CTRLDEFAULT**—The sound buffer is capable of pan, volume, and frequency control (this flag is equivalent to the **DSBCAPS_CTRLPAN**, **DSBCAPS_CTRLVOLUME**, and **DSBCAPS_-CTRLFREQUENCY** flags).
	• **DSBCAPS_CTRLFREQUENCY**—The sound buffer is capable of frequency control.
	• **DSBCAPS_CTRLPAN**—The sound buffer is capable of pan control.
	• **DSBCAPS_CTRLPOSITIONNOTIFY**—The sound buffer is capable of position notify control.
	• **DSBCAPS_CTRLVOLUME**—The sound buffer is capable of volume control.
	• **DSBCAPS_GETCURRENTPOSITION2**—The sound buffer retrieves the currently playing position more accurately than it otherwise would for an emulated sound device.
	• **DSBCAPS_GLOBALFOCUS**—The sound buffer is a global sound, meaning it is heard even when the application loses input focus. The exception to this occurs upon the activation of another DirectSound application whose cooperative level is either exclusive or write primary. In this case, not even global sounds from another application are audible.
	• **DSBCAPS_LOCDEFER**—The buffer can be assigned to hardware or software resource when it is played through the **IDirectSoundBuffer::-Play()** function.
	• **DSBCAPS_LOCHARDWARE**—The sound buffer is located in hardware memory and uses hardware mixing.
	• **DSBCAPS_LOCSOFTWARE**—The sound buffer is located in software memory and uses software mixing.
	• **DSBCAPS_MUTE3DATMAXDISTANCE**—The 3D sound is muted at its maximum distance. This improves the performance of DirectSound 3D applications.
	• **DSBCAPS_PRIMARYBUFFER**—The sound buffer is the primary one. If this flag is not specified, the sound buffer is a secondary sound buffer.
	• **DSBCAPS_STATIC**—The sound buffer has static sound data, meaning that it rarely, if ever, changes.
	• **DSBCAPS_STICKYFOCUS**—The sound buffer has sticky focus, meaning that unless another DirectSound application is activated, the sound is always audible.
dwBufferBytes	The size of the sound buffer, in bytes.
dwUnlockTransferRate	The rate, in kilobytes per second, at which DirectSound transfers memory from the system to the sound card for unlocking operations.
dwPlayCpuOverhead	The percentage of CPU cycles used for sound processing (only present for software buffers).

DSBPOSITIONNOTIFY

Structure Description

This structure is used to set notification positions for a sound buffer.

Structure Declaration

```
typedef struct {
  DWORD  dwOffset;
  HANDLE hEventNotify;
} DSBPOSITIONNOTIFY, *LPDSBPOSITIONNOTIFY;

typedef const DSBPOSITIONNOTIFY *LPCDSBPOSITIONNOTIFY;
```

Member	Description
dwOffset	The offset into the buffer at which DirectSound is to set the Win32event designated by **hEventNotify**.
hEventNotify	The Win32 event DirectSound is to set when it reaches the position designated by **dwOffset**.

DSBUFFERDESC

Structure Description

This structure is used for creating a sound buffer.

Structure Declaration

```
typedef struct {
  DWORD        dwSize;
  DWORD        dwFlags;
  DWORD        dwBufferBytes;
  DWORD        dwReserved;
  LPWAVEFORMATEX lpwfxFormat;
  GUID         guid3DAlgorithm;
} DSBUFFERDESC, *LPDSBUFFERDESC;

typedef const DSBUFFERDESC *LPCDSBUFFERDESC;
```

Member	Description
dwSize	The size of the structure, in bytes. This member must be initialized before the structure is used.
dwFlags	Describes some of the attributes of the sound buffer. It can be one or more of the following values:
	• **DSBCAPS_CTRL3D**—The sound buffer will be capable of 3D control.
	• **DSBCAPS_CTRLALL**—The sound buffer will be capable of all **DSBCAPS_CTRL** flags.

(continued)

DSBUFFERDESC *(continued)*	
Member	**Description**
	• **DSBCAPS_CTRLDEFAULT**—The sound buffer will be capable of pan, volume, and frequency control (this flag is equivalent to the **DSBCAPS_CTRLPAN**, **DSBCAPS_CTRLVOLUME**, and **DSBCAPS_CTRLFREQUENCY** flags).
	• **DSBCAPS_CTRLFREQUENCY**—The sound buffer will be capable of frequency control.
	• **DSBCAPS_CTRLPAN**—The sound buffer will be capable of pan control.
	• **DSBCAPS_CTRLPOSITIONNOTIFY**—The sound buffer will be capable of position notify control.
	• **DSBCAPS_CTRLVOLUME**—The sound buffer will be capable of volume control.
	• **DSBCAPS_GETCURRENTPOSITION2**—The sound buffer will retrieve the currently playing position more accurately than it otherwise would for an emulated sound device.
	• **DSBCAPS_GLOBALFOCUS**—The sound buffer will be a global sound, meaning it will be heard even when the application loses input focus. The exception to this occurs upon the activation of another DirectSound application whose cooperative level is either exclusive or write primary. In this case, not even global sounds from another application are audible.
	• **DSBCAPS_LOCDEFER**—The buffer can be assigned to a hardware or software resource when it is played through the **IDirectSoundBuffer::Play()** function.
	• **DSBCAPS_LOCHARDWARE**—The sound buffer will be stored in hardware memory and will use hardware mixing.
	• **DSBCAPS_LOCSOFTWARE**—The sound buffer will use software memory and software mixing.
	• **DSBCAPS_MUTE3DATMAXDISTANCE**—The 3D sound will be muted at its maximum distance. This improves the performance of DirectSound 3D applications.
	• **DSBCAPS_PRIMARYBUFFER**—The sound buffer will be the primary one. If this flag is not specified, the sound buffer is assumed to be a secondary sound buffer.
	• **DSBCAPS_STATIC**—The sound buffer will have static sound data, meaning that it will rarely, if ever, change.
	• **DSBCAPS_STICKYFOCUS**—The sound buffer will have sticky focus, meaning that unless another DirectSound application is activated, the sound will always be audible.

(continued)

DSBUFFERDESC *(continued)*

Member	Description
dwBufferBytes	The size of the buffer, in bytes. For primary buffers, this member must be 0 (DirectSound automatically selects the size of the primary buffer). For secondary buffers, it must be between **DSBSIZE_MIN** and **DSBSIZE_MAX**.
dwReserved	Reserved for future use and must be 0.
lpwfxFormat	A pointer to a **WAVEFORMATEX** structure that specifies the format of the sound data.
guid3DAlgorithm	A Globally-Unique Identifier (GUID) that describes the algorithm used for processing 3D sounds with two-speaker or headphone configurations. This member must be **GUID_NULL** if the sound does not have 3D capabilities, but otherwise may be one of the following predefined GUIDs:
	• **DS3DALG_DEFAULT**—The default algorithm which is currently **DS3DALG_NO_VIRTUALIZATION**. This algorithm applies only to software mixing, and is available on both WDM and Vxd drivers.
	• **DS3DALG_NO_VIRTUALIZATION**—Three-dimensional sounds are mapped to normal left/right stereo panning. This algorithm, though efficient, provides no virtual 3D audio effect. This algorithm applies only to software mixing, and is available on both WDM and Vxd drivers.
	• **DS3DALG_HRTF_FULL**—The highest quality algorithm. This algorithm provides the fullest 3D audio effect possible, but is slower than **DS3DALG_NO_VIRTUALIZATION**. This algorithm applies only to software devices, and is available only on WDM drivers.
	• **DS3DALG_HRTF_LIGHT**—An algorithm in-between **DS3DALG_NO_VIRTUALIZATION** and **DS3DALG_HRTF_-FULL** in terms of both quality and speed. This algorithm applies only to software mixing, and is available only on WDM drivers.

DSCAPS

Structure Description

This structure is used for describing the capabilities of a sound device.

Structure Declaration

```
typedef {
  DWORD dwSize;
  DWORD dwFlags;
  DWORD dwMinSecondarySampleRate;
  DWORD dwMaxSecondarySampleRate;
```

(continued)

DSCAPS *(continued)*

Structure Declaration

```
DWORD dwPrimaryBuffers;
  DWORD dwMaxHwMixingAllBuffers;
  DWORD dwMaxHwMixingStaticBuffers;
  DWORD dwMaxHwMixingStreamingBuffers;
  DWORD dwFreeHwMixingAllBuffers;
  DWORD dwFreeHwMixingStaticBuffers;
  DWORD dwFreeHwMixingStreamingBuffers;
  DWORD dwMaxHw3DAllBuffers;
  DWORD dwMaxHw3DStaticBuffers;
  DWORD dwMaxHw3DStreamingBuffers;
  DWORD dwFreeHw3DAllBuffers;
  DWORD dwFreeHw3DStaticBuffers;
  DWORD dwFreeHw3DStreamingBuffers;
  DWORD dwTotalHwMemBytes;
  DWORD dwFreeHwMemBytes;
  DWORD dwMaxContigFreeHwMemBytes;
  DWORD dwUnlockTransferRateHwBuffers;
  DWORD dwPlayCpuOverheadSwBuffers;
  DWORD dwReserved1;
  DWORD dwReserved2;
} DSCAPS, *LPDSCAPS;

typedef const DSCAPS *LPCDSCAPS;
```

Member	Description
dwSize	The size of the structure, in bytes. This member must be initialized before the structure is used.
dwFlags	Describes some of the attributes of the sound device. This member can be one or more of the following flags: • **DSCAPS_CERTIFIED**—The driver has been tested and certified by Microsoft. • **DSCAPS_CONTINUOUSRATE**—The driver supports all sample rates between **dwMinSecondarySampleRate** and **dwMaxSecondarySampleRate**, usually within +/- 10 Hz. • **DSCAPS_EMULDRIVER**—The DirectSound driver is emulated. This causes sound data to be passed through Windows, resulting in suboptimal performance. • **DSCAPS_PRIMARY16BIT**—The device supports primary sound buffers with 16 bits per sample. • **DSCAPS_PRIMARY8BIT**—The device supports primary sound buffers with 8 bits per sample.

(continued)

DSCAPS *(continued)*	
Member	**Description**
	• **DSCAPS_PRIMARYMONO**—The device supports mono sound output through the primary sound buffer.
	• **DSCAPS_PRIMARYSTEREO**—The device supports stereo sound output through the primary sound buffer.
	• **DSCAPS_SECONDARY16BIT**—The device supports secondary (non-primary) sound buffers with 16 bits per sample.
	• **DSCAPS_SECONDARY8BIT**—The device supports secondary (non-primary) sound buffers with 8 bits per sample.
	• **DSCAPS_SECONDARYMONO**—The device supports mono secondary (non-primary) sound buffers.
	• **DSCAPS_SECONDARYSTEREO**— The device supports stereo secondary (non-primary) sound buffers.
dwMinSecondarySampleRate	The minimum sample rate supported by the device, in samples per second.
dwMaxSecondarySampleRate	The maximum sample rate supported by the device, in samples per second.
dwPrimaryBuffers	The maximum number of primary buffers. This value is always 1.
dwMaxHwMixingAllBuffers	The total number of sounds that can be played at once. This may be less than the sum of **dwMaxHwMixingStaticBuffers** and **dwMaxHwMixingStreamingBuffers** because of a resource tradeoff.
dwMaxHwMixingStaticBuffers	The number of static sound buffers that can be played at once.
dwMaxHwMixingStreamingBuffers	The number of dynamic sound buffers (sounds whose data continuously changes) that can be played at once.
dwFreeHwMixingAllBuffers	The total number of free buffers. This may be less than the sum of **dwFreeHwMixingStaticBuffers** and **dwFreeHwMixingStreamingBuffers** because of a resource tradeoff.
dwFreeHwMixingStaticBuffers	The number of free static sound buffers.
dwFreeHwMixingStreamingBuffers	The number of free dynamic sound buffers.
dwMaxHw3DAllBuffers	The total number of 3D hardware buffers that can exist simultaneously. This may be less than the sum of **dwMaxHw3DStaticBuffers** and **dwMaxHw3DStreamingBuffers** because of a resource tradeoff.
dwMaxHw3DStaticBuffers	The number of static 3D sound buffers that can exist simultaneously.
dwMaxHw3DStreamingBuffers	The number of dynamic 3D sound buffers (sounds whose data continuously changes) that can exist simultaneously.

(continued)

DSCAPS *(continued)*

Member	Description
dwFreeHw3DAllBuffers	The total number of free buffers. This may be less than the sum of **dwFreeHw3DStaticBuffers** and **dwFreeHw3DStreaming-Buffers** because of a resource tradeoff.
dwFreeHw3DStaticBuffers	The number of free static 3D sound buffers.
dwFreeHw3DStreamingBuffers	The number of free dynamic 3D sound buffers.
dwTotalHwMemBytes	The total number of bytes on the sound device.
dwFreeHwMemBytes	The free number of bytes on the sound device.
dwMaxContigFreeHwMemBytes	The maximum number of consecutive bytes on the sound device.
dwUnlockTransferRateHwBuffers	The rate, in kilobytes per second, at which DirectSound transfers memory from the system to the sound card for unlocking operations.
dwPlayCpuOverheadSwBuffers	The percentage of CPU cycles used for sound processing for software buffers.
dwReserved1	Reserved for future use. Must be 0.
dwReserved2	Reserved for future use. Must be 0.

DSCBCAPS

Structure Description

This structure describes the capabilities of a sound-capture buffer.

Structure Declaration

```
typedef struct {
  DWORD dwSize;
  DWORD dwFlags;
  DWORD dwBufferBytes;
  DWORD dwReserved;
} DSCBCAPS, *LPDSCBCAPS;

typedef const DSCBCAPS *LPCDSCBCAPS;
```

Member	Description
dwSize	The size of the structure, in bytes. This member must be initialized before the structure is used.
dwFlags	Describes some of the capabilities of the sound-capture device. This member can be 0 or the following flag: • **DSCBCAPS_WAVEMAPPED**—The Win32 wave mapper is used for formats not natively supported by the sound device.
dwBufferBytes	The size of the sound capture buffer, in bytes.
dwReserved	Reserved for future use. Must be 0.

DSCBUFFERDESC

Structure Description

This structure is used for creating a sound-capture buffer.

Structure Declaration

```
typedef struct {
    DWORD       dwSize;
    DWORD       dwFlags;
    DWORD       dwBufferBytes;
    DWORD       dwReserved;
    LPWAVEFORMATEX lpwfxFormat;
} DSCBUFFERDESC, *LPDSCBUFFERDESC;

typedef const DSCBUFFERDESC *LPCDSCBUFFERDESC;
```

Member	Description
dwSize	The size of the structure, in bytes. This member must be initialized before the structure is used.
dwFlags	Describes some of the capabilities of the sound-capture device. This member can be 0 or the following flag: • **DSCBCAPS_WAVEMAPPED**—The Win32 wave mapper will be used for formats not natively supported by the sound device.
dwBufferBytes	The size of the buffer, in bytes.
dwReserved	Reserved for future use. Must be 0.
lpwfxFormat	A pointer to a **WAVEFORMATEX** structure describing the format of the sound-capture buffer.

DSCCAPS

Structure Description

This structure describes the capabilities of a sound-capture device.

Structure Declaration

```
typedef struct {
    DWORD dwSize;
    DWORD dwFlags;
    DWORD dwFormats;
    DWORD dwChannels;
} DSCCAPS, *LPDSCCAPS;

typedef const DSCCAPS *LPCDSCCAPS;
```

(continued)

DSCCAPS *(continued)*	
Member	**Description**
dwSize	The size of the structure, in bytes. This member must be initialized before the structure is used.
dwFlags	Describes some of the sound-capture device's capabilities. This member can be 0 or the following flag: • **DSCCAPS_CERTIFIED**—The device's driver is a certified WDM driver. • **DSCCAPS_EMULDRIVER**—The DirectSound driver is emulated. This causes sound data to be passed through Windows, resulting in suboptimal performance.
dwFormats	The format supported by the sound-capture device. This member can be one or more of the following values: • **WAVE_FORMAT_1M08**—The sound-capture device supports 11.025-kHz, mono, 8-bit. • **WAVE_FORMAT_1M16**—The sound-capture device supports 11.025-kHz, mono, 16-bit. • **WAVE_FORMAT_1S08**—The sound-capture device supports 11.025-kHz, stereo, 8-bit. • **WAVE_FORMAT_1S16**—The sound-capture device supports 11.025-kHz, stereo, 16-bit. • **WAVE_FORMAT_2M08**—The sound-capture device supports 22.05-kHz, mono, 8-bit. • **WAVE_FORMAT_2M16**—The sound-capture device supports 22.05-kHz, mono, 16-bit. • **WAVE_FORMAT_2S08**—The sound-capture device supports 22.05-kHz, stereo, 8-bit. • **WAVE_FORMAT_2S16**—The sound-capture device supports 22.05-kHz, stereo, 16-bit. • **WAVE_FORMAT_4M08**—The sound-capture device supports 44.1-kHz, mono, 8-bit. • **WAVE_FORMAT_4M16**—The sound-capture device supports 44.1-kHz, mono, 16-bit. • **WAVE_FORMAT_4S08**—The sound-capture device supports 44.1-kHz, stereo, 8-bit. • **WAVE_FORMAT_4S16**—The sound-capture device supports 44.1-kHz, stereo, 16-bit.
dwChannels	The number of channels the sound-capture device can capture from. A value of 1 indicates mono, 2 indicates stereo, and so on.

Appendix D
DirectInput Reference

This appendix is divided into five main reference sections: interface, function, callback, macro, and structure.

The interface reference documents in detail all of the methods of the DirectInput interfaces, except those derived from the IUnknown interface, which is documented in Chapter 3. The function reference does the same for all functions in DirectInput that do not belong to an interface (such as **DirectInputCreate ()**). The callback reference describes the format of application-defined functions that DirectInput calls. The macro section describes the macros defined in the DirectInput header file that speed the development of applications. Finally, the structure reference documents all of the structures included in the DirectInput API.

For a conceptual overview of DirectInput, see Chapter 12. For sample code, see Chapter 13 or the DirectX SDK.

Interface Reference

The interfaces documented in this section are IDirectInput, IDirectInputDevice2, and IDirectInputEffect.

IDirectInput

Applications can obtain the IDirectInput interface by calling **DirectInputCreate ()** or **CoCreateInstance ()**. Objects created with **CoCreateInstance ()** must be initialized by the **IDirectInput::Initialize ()** function.

The globally unique identifier (GUID) for the IDirectInput interface is **IID_IDirectInput**.

IDirectInput::CreateDevice ()	
Function Description	
This function creates and initializes a DirectInputDevice object to represent an input device on the system.	
Function Declaration	

```
HRESULT CreateDevice(
    REFGUID rguid,
    LPDIRECTINPUTDEVICE *lplpDirectInputDevice,
    LPUNKNOWN pUnkOuter
);
```

Parameter	Description
rguid	A reference to a GUID that identifies the desired input device. This can be one of the values obtained by calling **IDirectInput::EnumDevices** () or one of the following predefined GUIDs:
	• **GUID_SysKeyboard**—Selects the default system keyboard.
	• **GUID_SysMouse**—Selects the default system mouse.
lplpDirectInputDevice	The address of a pointer to a DirectInputDevice object. If this function succeeds, the pointer will be set to the newly created DirectInputDevice object.
pUnkOuter	A pointer to the controlling object's IUnknown interface. Unless an application is using COM aggregation features, this parameter should be **NULL**.
Return Value	**Description**
DI_OK	DirectInput successfully created the device object.
DIERR_DEVICENOTREG	DirectInput could not create the device object, because the specified device is not registered with DirectInput.
DIERR_INVALIDPARAM	DirectInput could not create the device object, because one or more parameters are invalid.
DIERR_NOINTERFACE	DirectInput could not create the device object, because the specified interface is not valid for the object.
DIERR_NOTINITIALIZED	DirectInput could not create the device object, because this DirectInput object is not initialized. It must be initialized with the **IDirectInput::Initialize** () function.
DIERR_OUTOFMEMORY	DirectInput could not create the device object, because sufficient memory is not available.

IDirectInput::EnumDevices ()

Function Description

This function enumerates the input devices supported by the system. It can enumerate devices physically attached to the system, devices that are supported by the system but not physically attached, or both.

Function Declaration

```
HRESULT EnumDevices(
   DWORD dwDevType,
   LPDIENUMCALLBACK lpCallback,
   LPVOID pvRef,
   DWORD dwFlags
);
```

Parameter	Description
dwDevType	If this parameter is 0, then DirectInput enumerates all input devices. Otherwise, the least significant byte of this parameter describes which device types DirectInput should enumerate. It can be one of the following flags: • **DIDEVTYPE_MOUSE**—Mouse devices • **DIDEVTYPE_KEYBOARD**—Keyboard devices • **DIDEVTYPE_JOYSTICK**—Joystick devices • **DIDEVTYPE_DEVICE**—Other devices The next significant byte is optional and describes the device subtype. These are some of the more common values: • **DIDEVTYPEMOUSE_TRADITIONA**L—Traditional mouse devices. This subtype can be used only when the device type is set to **DIDEVTYPE_MOUSE**. • **DIDEVTYPEMOUSE_FINGERSTICK**—Fingerstick devices. This subtype can be used only when the device type is set to **DIDEVTYPE_MOUSE**. • **DIDEVTYPEMOUSE_TOUCHPAD**—Touchpad devices. This subtype can be used only when the device type is set to **DIDEVTYPE_MOUSE**. • **DIDEVTYPEMOUSE_TRACKBALL**—Trackball devices. This subtype can be used only when the device type is set to **DIDEVTYPE_MOUSE**. • **DIDEVTYPEKEYBOARD_PCENH**—Standard 101-key keyboards. This subtype can be used only when the device type is set to **DIDEVTYPE_KEYBOARD**. • **DIDEVTYPEJOYSTICK_TRADITIONAL**—Traditional joystick devices. This subtype can be used only when the device type is set to **DIDEVTYPE_JOYSTICK**.

(continued)

IDirectInput::EnumDevices () *(continued)*	
Parameter	**Description**
	• **DIDEVTYPEJOYSTICK_FLIGHTSTICK**—Flight stick devices. This subtype can be used only when the device type is set to **DIDEVTYPE_JOYSTICK**.
	• **DIDEVTYPEJOYSTICK_GAMEPAD**—Gamepad devices. This subtype can be used only when the device type is set to **DIDEVTYPE_JOYSTICK**.
	• **DIDEVTYPEJOYSTICK_RUDDER**—Rudder devices. This subtype can be used only when the device type is set to **DIDEVTYPE_JOYSTICK**.
	• **DIDEVTYPEJOYSTICK_WHEEL**—Wheel devices. This subtype can be used only when the device type is set to **DIDEVTYPE_JOYSTICK**.
	• **DIDEVTYPEJOYSTICK_HEADTRACKER**—Head-tracking devices. This subtype can be used only when the device type is set to **DIDEVTYPE_JOYSTICK**.
	The next significant byte can be 0 or **DIDEVTYPE_HID**, in which case only Human Interface Device (HID)-compliant devices are enumerated.
lpCallback	A pointer to a **DIEnumDevicesProc** function. This function will be called with each device enumerated.
pvRef	A pointer to application-defined data that will be passed to the callback function every time it is called.
dwFlags	Describes the extent of the enumeration. This parameter can be 0, or one or more of the following flags:
	• **DIEDFL_ALLDEVICES**—All supported devices will be enumerated, attached or not. This is the default behavior and need not be explicitly specified.
	• **DIEDFL_ATTACHEDONLY**—Only attached devices will be enumerated.
	• **DIEDFL_FORCEFEEDBACK**—Only devices that support force-feedback will be enumerated.
	• **DIEDFL_INCLUDEALIASES**—Devices that have more than one name will be listed uniquely for each name.
	• **DIEDFL_INCLUDEPHANTOMS**—Phantom devices, those that do not yet exist but that have placeholder names and may exist in the future, will be enumerated.

(continued)

IDirectInput::EnumDevices () *(continued)*

Return Value	Description
DI_OK	DirectInput successfully enumerated the input devices available on the system.
DIERR_INVALIDPARAM	DirectInput could not enumerate available devices, because one or more parameters are invalid.
DIERR_NOTINITIALIZED	DirectInput could not enumerate available devices, because this DirectInput object is not initialized. It must be initialized with the **IDirectInput::Initialize** () function.

IDirectInput::GetDeviceStatus ()

Function Description
This function retrieves the status of a device. The status indicates whether the device is attached or not.

Function Declaration
```
HRESULT GetDeviceStatus(
   REFGUID rguidInstance
);
```

Parameter	Description
rguidInstance	A reference to a GUID that describes the device whose status will be checked. This can be any GUID obtained by calling **IDirectInput::EnumDevices** ().

Return Value	Description
DI_OK	The device is physically attached to the system.
DI_NOTATTACHED	The device is not physically attached to the system.
DIERR_GENERIC	DirectInput could not retrieve the status of the device, because of a generic error.
DIERR_INVALIDPARAM	DirectInput could not retrieve the status of the device, because one or more parameters are invalid.
DIERR_NOTINITIALIZED	DirectInput could not retrieve the status of the device, because this DirectInput object is not initialized. It must be initialized with the **IDirectInput::Initialize** () function.

IDirectInput::Initialize ()

Function Description

This function initializes a DirectInput object created with **CoCreateInstance** (). Applications that obtain their IDirectInput interfaces by calling **DirectInputCreate** () do not need to call this function.

Function Declaration

```
HRESULT Initialize(
    HINSTANCE hinst,
    DWORD dwVersion
);
```

Parameter	Description
hinst	A handle to the instance of the application. DLLs calling this function must pass their own handles, not the handles of their container applications.
dwVersion	The version of DirectInput that the application is using. This should normally be the constant **DIRECTINPUT_-VERSION** (defined in the DirectInput header file), unless the application wants DirectInput to emulate a previous version.

Return Value	Description
DI_OK	DirectInput successfully initialized the object.
DIERR_BETADIRECTINPUTVERSION	DirectInput could not initialize the object, because the application is designed for an unsupported beta version of DirectInput.
DIERR_OLDDIRECTINPUTVERSION	DirectInput could not initialize the object, because the application is designed for a newer version of DirectInput than is installed.

IDirectInput::RunControlPanel ()

Function Description

This function runs the Windows Control Panel. This allows users to install new input devices or modify the settings of those already installed.

Function Declaration

```
HRESULT RunControlPanel(
    HWND hwndOwner,
    DWORD dwFlags
);
```

Parameter	Description
hwndOwner	A handle to the window to be used as the parent window for the control panel. This parameter may be **NULL**.
dwFlags	This parameter is reserved for future use and must be set to 0.

(continued)

IDirectInput::RunControlPanel () *(continued)*	
Return Value	**Description**
DI_OK	DirectInput successfully launched the control panel.
DIERR_INVALIDPARAM	DirectInput could not run the control panel, because one or more parameters are invalid.
DIERR_NOTINITIALIZED	DirectInput could not run the control panel, because this DirectInput object is not initialized. It must be initialized with the **IDirectInput::Initialize** () function.

IDirectInputDevice2

Applications can obtain the IDirectInputDevice interface by calling the **IDirectInput::-CreateDevice** () function and subsequently query this interface for the IDirectInputDevice2 interface.

The GUID for the IDirectInputDevice interface is **IID_IDirectInputDevice**, while the GUID for the IDirectInputDevice2 interface is **IID_IDirectInputDevice2**.

IDirectInputDevice2::Acquire ()	
Function Description	
This function acquires access to an input device. An application must call this function before it can retrieve data from a device with the **IDirectInputDevice2::GetDeviceState** () or **IDirectInputDevice2::GetDeviceData** () functions.	
Function Declaration	
`HRESULT Acquire ();`	
Parameter	**Description**
None	
Return Value	**Description**
DI_OK	DirectInput successfully acquired access to the input device.
DIERR_INVALIDPARAM	DirectInput could not acquire access to the input device, because one or more parameters are invalid.
DIERR_NOTINITIALIZED	DirectInput could not acquire access to the input device, because this DirectInputDevice object is not initialized. It must be initialized with the **IDirectInputDevice2::Initialize** () function.
DIERR_OTHERAPPHASPRIO	DirectInput could not acquire access to the input device, because another application has priority-level access to the input device.
S_FALSE	DirectInput could not acquire access to the input device, because access to the device has already been acquired.

IDirectInputDevice2::CreateEffect ()

Function Description
This function creates a force-feedback effect object.

Function Declaration

```
HRESULT CreateEffect(
    REFGUID rguid,
    LPCDIEFFECT lpeff,
    LPDIRECTINPUTEFFECT * ppdeff,
    LPUNKNOWN punkOuter
);
```

Parameter	Description
rguid	A reference to a GUID that identifies the effect to be created. This can be any GUID obtained by **IDirectInputDevice2::-EnumEffects ()** or one of the following predefined effect GUIDs:
	• **GUID_ConstantForce**—A constant force
	• **GUID_RampForce**—A ramp force, having initial and final force values
	• **GUID_Square**—A force whose amplitude varies as a square wave
	• **GUID_Sine**—A force whose amplitude varies as a sine wave
	• **GUID_Triangle**—A force whose amplitude varies as a triangular wave
	• **GUID_SawtoothUp**—A force whose amplitude varies as a sawtooth wave, where the spike of the wave corresponds to an increase in force
	• **GUID_SawtoothDown**—A force whose amplitude varies as a sawtooth wave, where the spike of the wave corresponds to a decrease in force
	• **GUID_Spring**—A force whose amplitude increases as the distance from an axis to a defined neutral point increases
	• **GUID_Damper**—A force whose amplitude increases as the velocity with which the user moves an axis increases
	• **GUID_Inertia**—A force whose amplitude increases as the acceleration with which the user moves an axis increases
	• **GUID_Friction**—A force applied to an axis with its movement
	• **GUID_CustomForce**—A force whose properties are explicitly defined by the application and applied to an axis

(continued)

IDirectInputDevice2::CreateEffect () *(continued)*

Parameter	Description
lpeff	A pointer to a **DIEFFECT** structure that describes the specific parameters of the effect to be created. This may be **NULL**, in which case the parameters of the effect must be set later by the **IDirectInputEffect::SetParameters** () function.
ppdeff	The address of a pointer to a **DirectInputEffect** object. If this function succeeds, the pointer will be set to the newly created DirectInputEffect object.
punkOuter	A pointer to the controlling object's IUnknown interface. Unless an application is using COM aggregation features, this parameter should be **NULL**.
Return Value	Description
DI_OK	DirectInput successfully created the force-feedback effect object.
S_FALSE	DirectInput successfully created the force-feedback effect and set its parameters as requested, but could not download the effect, because the application does not have exclusive-level access to the device.
DIERR_DEVICENOTREG	DirectInput could not create the force-feedback effect, because the specified device is not registered.
DIERR_DEVICEFULL	DirectInput could not create the force-feedback effect, because the device has no additional room for effects.
DIERR_INVALIDPARAM	DirectInput could not create the force-feedback effect, because one or more parameters are invalid.
DIERR_NOTINITIALIZED	DirectInput could not create the force-feedback effect, because this DirectInputDevice2 object is not initialized. It must be initialized with the **IDirectInputDevice2::Initialize** () function.

IDirectInputDevice2::EnumCreatedEffectObjects ()

Function Description

This function enumerates all effects that have been created by the **IDirectInput::CreateEffect** () function.

Function Declaration

```
HRESULT EnumCreatedEffectObjects(
    LPDIENUMCREATEDEFFECTOBJECTSCALLBACK lpCallback,
    LPVOID pvRef,
    DWORD fl
);
```

(continued)

IDirectInputDevice2::EnumCreatedEffectObjects () *(continued)*

Parameter	Description
lpCallback	The address of a **DIEnumCreatedEffectObjectsProc** () callback function. This function will be called for every effect enumerated.
pvRef	A pointer to application-defined data passed to the callback function every time it is called.
fl	This parameter is not currently used and must be 0.

Return Value	Description
DI_OK	DirectInput successfully enumerated the effects.
DIERR_INVALIDPARAM	DirectInput could not enumerate the effects, because one or more parameters are invalid.
DIERR_NOTINITIALIZED	DirectInput could not enumerate the effects, because this DirectInputDevice2 object is not initialized. It must be initialized with the **IDirectInputDevice2::Initialize** () function.

IDirectInputDevice2::EnumEffects ()

Function Description

This function enumerates all of the effect types that the input device supports.

Function Declaration

```
HRESULT EnumEffects(
    LPDIENUMEFFECTSCALLBACK lpCallback,
    LPVOID pvRef,
    DWORD dwEffType
);
```

Parameter	Description
lpCallback	The address of a **DIEnumEffectsProc** () callback function. This function will be called for every effect type enumerated.
pvRef	A pointer to application-defined data passed to the callback function every time it is called.
dwEffType	Describes the effect type. This parameter can be one of the following values: • **DIEFT_ALL**—Enumerates all effects. • **DIEFT_CONDITION**—Enumerates condition effects. Condition effects are defined by the **DICONDITION** structure. • **DIEFT_CONSTANTFORCE**—Enumerates constant force effects. Constant force effects are defined by the **DICONSTANTFORCE** structure.

(continued)

IDirectInputDevice2::EnumEffects () *(continued)*

Parameter	Description
	• **DIEFT_CUSTOMFORCE**—Enumerates custom force effects. Custom force effects are defined by the **DICUSTOMFORCE** structure.
	• **DIEFT_HARDWARE**—Enumerates hardware-specific effects.
	• **DIEFT_PERIODIC**—Enumerates periodic force effects. Periodic force effects are defined by the **DIPERIODIC** structure.
	• **DIEFT_RAMPFORCE**—Enumerates ramp force effects. Ramp force effects are defined by the **DIRAMPFORCE** structure.

Return Value	Description
DI_OK	DirectInput successfully enumerated the effects.
DIERR_INVALIDPARAM	DirectInput could not enumerate the effects, because one or more parameters are invalid.
DIERR_NOTINITIALIZED	DirectInput could not enumerate the effects, because this DirectInputDevice2 object is not initialized. It must be initialized with the **IDirectInputDevice2::Initialize** () function.

IDirectInputDevice2::EnumObjects ()

Function Description

This function enumerates the objects on the input device, whether input objects (such as buttons or axes) or output objects (such as force-feedback actuators).

Function Declaration

```
HRESULT EnumObjects(
    LPDIENUMDEVICEOBJECTSCALLBACK lpCallback,
    LPVOID pvRef,
    DWORD dwFlags
);
```

Parameter	Description
lpCallback	The address of a **DIEnumDeviceObjectsProc** () callback function. This function will be called for every object enumerated.
pvRef	A pointer to application-defined data passed to the callback function every time it is called.
dwFlags	Describes the types of objects to be enumerated. This parameter can be one or more of the following flags:
	• **DIDFT_ABSAXIS**—Absolute axes.
	• **DIDFT_ALL**—All objects.

(continued)

IDirectInputDevice2::EnumObjects () *(continued)*	
Parameter	**Description**
	• **DIDFT_AXIS**—All axes, whether relative or absolute.
	• **DIDFT_BUTTON**—Push or toggle buttons.
	• **DIDFT_COLLECTION**—Objects that belong to an HID collection.
	• **DIDFT_FFACTUATOR**—Objects that have force-feedback actuators. Forces can be applied to such objects.
	• **DIDFT_FFEFFECTTRIGGER**—Objects that can be used to trigger force-feedback effects. Buttons, for example, can often trigger the playback of a force-feedback effect.
	• **DIDFT_NOCOLLECTION**—Objects that do not belong to any HID link collection.
	• **DIDFT_NODATA**—Objects that do not produce data.
	• **DIDFT_OUTPUT**—Output objects, to which data can be sent.
	• **DIDFT_POV**—Point-of-View (POV) controllers.
	• **DIDFT_PSHBUTTON**—Pushbuttons.
	• **DIDFT_RELAXIS**—Relative axes.
	• **DIDFT_TGLBUTTON**—Toggle buttons.
Return Value	**Description**
DI_OK	DirectInput successfully enumerated the input device's objects.
DIERR_INVALIDPARAM	DirectInput could not enumerate the input device's objects, because one or more parameters are invalid.
DIERR_NOTINITIALIZED	DirectInput could not enumerate the input device's objects, because this DirectInputDevice object is not initialized. It must be initialized with the **IDirectInputDevice2::Initialize ()** function.

IDirectInputDevice2::Escape ()	
Function Description	
This function sends a hardware-specific command to an input device.	
Function Declaration	

```
HRESULT Escape(
   LPDIEFFESCAPE pesc
);
```

(continued)

IDirectInputDevice2::Escape () *(continued)*

Parameter	Description
pesc	A pointer to a **DIEFFESCAPE** structure that describes the command to be sent to the input device.

Return Value	Description
DI_OK	DirectInput successfully sent the hardware-specific command to the input device.
DIERR_DEVICEFULL	DirectInput could not send the command, because the device is full.
DIERR_NOTINITIALIZED	DirectInput could not send the command, because this DirectInputDevice2 object is not initialized. It must be initialized with the **IDirectInputDevice2::Initialize** () function.

IDirectInputDevice2::GetCapabilities ()

Function Description

This function retrieves the capabilities of the input device.

Function Declaration

```
HRESULT GetCapabilities(
    LPDIDEVCAPS lpDIDevCaps
);
```

Parameter	Description
lpDIDevCaps	A pointer to a **DIDEVCAPS** structure. If this function succeeds, the structure will be filled with the capabilities of the input device.

Return Value	Description
DI_OK	DirectInput successfully retrieved the device's capabilities.
DIERR_INVALIDPARAM	DirectInput could not retrieve the device's capabilities, because one or more parameters are invalid.
DIERR_NOTINITIALIZED	DirectInput could not retrieve the device's capabilities, because this DirectInputDevice object is not initialized. It must be initialized with the **IDirectInputDevice2::Initialize** () function.

IDirectInputDevice2::GetDeviceData ()	

Function Description

This function retrieves buffered data from the input device. Before using this function, an application must set the cooperative level, set the size and format of the buffer, and acquire access to the input device.

Function Declaration

```
HRESULT GetDeviceData(
    DWORD cbObjectData,
    LPDIDEVICEOBJECTDATA rgdod,
    LPDWORD pdwInOut,
    DWORD dwFlags
);
```

Parameter	Description
cbObjectData	The size of the **DIDEVICEOBJECTDATA** structure, in bytes.
rgdod	An array of **DIDEVICEOBJECTDATA** structures. If this function succeeds, the structures will be filled with buffered data. This parameter may be **NULL**, in which case data is removed from the buffer, but is not stored.
pdwInOut	A pointer to an integer that describes either the number of **DIDEVICEOBJECTDATA** structures pointed to by the **rgdod** parameter or, if **rgdod** is **NULL**, the number of structures that should be removed from the buffer. The integer may be set to the constant **INFINITE**.
	When this function returns, the integer will be set to the number of data items actually retrieved. Note that if **dwFlags** is set to **DIGDD_PEEK**, no items are actually removed from the buffer; the integer is merely set to the number of items it contains.
dwFlags	Describes how the data is retrieved. This parameter can be zero or the following flag:
	• **DIGDD_PEEK**—The data items read should not be removed from the buffer.

Return Value	Description
DI_OK	DirectInput successfully retrieved buffered data.
DI_BUFFEROVERFLOW	DirectInput successfully retrieved buffered data, but because the size of the device's buffer was insufficient, some input data was lost. Applications receiving this error message should either increase the size of the buffer by calling **IDirectInputDevice2::SetProperty** () or call this function more frequently.
DIERR_INPUTLOST	DirectInput could not retrieve buffered data, because input to the device has been lost. It must be reacquired with the **IDirectInputDevice2::Acquire** () function.

(continued)

IDirectInputDevice2::GetDeviceData () *(continued)*

Return Value	Description
DIERR_INVALIDPARAM	DirectInput could not retrieve buffered data, because one or more parameters are invalid.
DIERR_NOTACQUIRED	DirectInput could not retrieve buffered data, because access to the device has not been acquired. It must be acquired with the **IDirectInputDevice2::Acquire** () function.
DIERR_NOTBUFFERED	DirectInput could not retrieve buffered data, because the size of the buffer has not been set. It must be set with the **IDirectInputDevice2::SetProperty** () function.
DIERR_NOTINITIALIZED	DirectInput could not retrieve buffered data, because this **DirectInputDevice** object is not initialized. It must be initialized with the **IDirectInputDevice2::Initialize** () function.

IDirectInputDevice2::GetDeviceInfo ()

Function Description

This function retrieves information describing the input device's identity.

Function Declaration

```
HRESULT GetDeviceInfo(
    LPDIDEVICEINSTANCE pdidi
);
```

Parameter	Description
pdidi	A pointer to a **DIDEVICEINSTANCE** structure. If this function succeeds, the structure will be filled with information describing the identity of the device.

Return Value	Description
DI_OK	DirectInput successfully retrieved the device information.
DIERR_INVALIDPARAM	DirectInput could not retrieve the device information, because one or more parameters are invalid.
DIERR_NOTINITIALIZED	DirectInput could not retrieve the device information, because this DirectInputDevice object is not initialized. It must be initialized with the **IDirectInputDevice2::Initialize** () function.

IDirectInputDevice2::GetDeviceState ()

Function Description

This function retrieves immediate data from the input device. Before an application can call this function, it must set the cooperative level and acquire access to the input device.

Function Declaration

```
HRESULT GetDeviceState(
    DWORD cbData,
    LPVOID lpvData
);
```

Parameter	Description
cbData	The size of the buffer pointed to by **lpvData**, in bytes.
lpvData	A pointer to a structure. If this function succeeds, the structure will be filled with the instantaneous state of the device. An application establishes the format of the structure by calling **IDirectInputDevice2::SetDataFormat** ().
	The pointer should point to a **DIMOUSESTATE** structure for the **c_dfDIMouse** format, a **DIMOUSESTATE2** structure for the **c_dfDIMouse2** format, an array of 256 bytes for the **c_dfDIKeyboard** format, a **DIJOYSTICK** structure for the **c_dfDIJoystick** format, and a **DIJOYSTATE2** structure for the **c_dfDIJoystick2** format.

Return Value	Description
DI_OK	DirectInput successfully retrieved immediate data from the input device.
DIERR_INPUTLOST	DirectInput could not retrieve immediate data, because input to the device has been lost. It must be reacquired with the **IDirectInputDevice2::Acquire** () function.
DIERR_INVALIDPARAM	DirectInput could not retrieve immediate data, because one or more parameters are invalid.
DIERR_NOTACQUIRED	DirectInput could not retrieve immediate data, because access to the device has not been acquired. It must be acquired with the **IDirectInputDevice2::Acquire** () function.
DIERR_NOTINITIALIZED	DirectInput could not retrieve immediate data, because this DirectInputDevice object is not initialized. It must be initialized with the **IDirectInputDevice2::Initialize** () function.
E_PENDING	DirectInput could not retrieve immediate data, because data is not yet available from the device.

IDirectInputDevice2::GetEffectInfo ()

Function Description

This function retrieves information describing a force-feedback effect.

Function Declaration

```
HRESULT GetEffectInfo(
    LPDIEFFECTINFO pdei,
    REFGUID rguid
);
```

Parameter	Description
pdei	A pointer to a **DIEFFECTINFO** structure. If this function succeeds, the structure will be filled with information describing the force-feedback effect specified by **rguid**.
rguid	A reference to a GUID that identifies the force-feedback effect whose information is being retrieved. This can be any value obtained by calling **IDirectInputDevice2::EnumEffects** ().

Return Value	Description
DI_OK	DirectInput successfully retrieved information describing the effect.
DIERR_DEVICENOTREG	DirectInput could not retrieve the effect information, because the specified device is not registered.
DIERR_INVALIDPARAM	DirectInput could not retrieve the effect information, because one or more parameters are invalid.
DIERR_NOTINITIALIZED	DirectInput could not retrieve the effect information, because this DirectInputDevice2 object is not initialized. It must be initialized with the **IDirectInputDevice2::Initialize** () function.

IDirectInputDevice2::GetForceFeedbackState ()

Function Description

This function retrieves the state of the input device's force-feedback system.

Function Declaration

```
HRESULT GetForceFeedbackState(
    LPDWORD pdwOut
);
```

Parameter	Description
pdwOut	A pointer to an integer. If this function succeeds, the integer will be set to the state of the force-feedback system, designated by one or more of the following constants: • **DIGFFS_ACTUATORSOFF**—The input device's force-feedback actuators are disabled.

(continued)

IDirectInputDevice2::GetForceFeedbackState () *(continued)*	
Parameter	**Description**
	• **DIGFFS_ACTUATORSON**—The input device's force-feedback actuators are enabled.
	• **DIGFFS_DEVICELOST**—The device is in an indeterminate state because of an unexpected failure. To reset the device, either access must be unacquired and reacquired or a **DISFFC_RESET** command must be sent to the device by calling the **IDirectInputDevice2::SendForceFeedback-Command** () function.
	• **DIGFFS_EMPTY**—No effects have been downloaded to the input device.
	• **DIGFFS_PAUSED**—The playback of all force-feedback effects has been paused.
	• **DIGFFS_POWEROFF**—The force-feedback system is unavailable, possibly because the user has shut off power to the system.
	• **DIGFFS_POWERON**—The force-feedback system is receiving power (note that this flag may be returned even if the system is not receiving power, if the input device is incapable of reporting power information).
	• **DIGFFS_SAFETYSWITCHOFF**—The force-feedback system's safety switch is off, preventing the system from operating.
	• **DIGFFS_SAFETYSWITCHON**—The force-feedback system's safety switch is on, allowing the system to operate.
	• **DIGFFS_STOPPED**—No effects are playing, and the device is not paused.
	• **DIGFFS_USERFFSWITCHOFF**—The switch controlling the force-feedback system is off, preventing the system from operating.
	• **DIGFFS_USERFFSWITCHON**—The switch controlling the force-feedback system is on, allowing the system to operate.
Return Value	**Description**
DI_OK	DirectInput successfully retrieved the state of the force-feedback system.
DIERR_INPUTLOST	DirectInput could not retrieve the force-feedback system's state, because input to the device has been lost. It must be reacquired with the **IDirectInputDevice2::Acquire** () function.
DIERR_INVALIDPARAM	DirectInput could not retrieve the force-feedback system's state, because one or more parameters are invalid.

(continued)

IDirectInputDevice2::GetForceFeedbackState () *(continued)*

Return Value	Description
DIERR_NOTEXCLUSIVEACQUIRED	DirectInput could not retrieve the force-feedback system's state, because exclusive-level access is required for all force-feedback devices.
DIERR_NOTINITIALIZED	DirectInput could not retrieve the force-feedback system's state, because this DirectInputDevice2 object is not initialized. It must be initialized with the **IDirectInputDevice2::Initialize** () function.
DIERR_UNSUPPORTED	DirectInput could not retrieve the force-feedback system's state, because the operation is not supported.

IDirectInputDevice2::GetObjectInfo ()

Function Description

This function retrieves information describing an object on the input device.

Function Declaration

```
HRESULT GetObjectInfo(
    LPDIDEVICEOBJECTINSTANCE pdidoi,
    DWORD dwObj,
    DWORD dwHow
);
```

Parameter	Description
pdidoi	A pointer to a **DIDEVICEOBJECTINSTANCE** structure. If this function succeeds, the structure will be filled with information describing the specified object.
dwObj	The object whose information is to be retrieved. The object can be identified either by its offset into the device's data format (see **IDirectInputDevice2::SetDataFormat** ()) or by its type identifier, depending on the value of **dwHow**.
dwHow	Describes how the object is identified. This parameter can be one of the following values: • **DIPH_BYOFFSET**—The object specified by **dwObj** is identified by its offset into the device's data format, measured in bytes. • **DIPH_BYID**—The object specified by **dwObj** is identified by its type identifier, as retrieved by **IDirectInputDevice2::EnumObjects** () in the **dwType** member of the **DIDEVICEOBJECTINSTANCE** structure.

(continued)

IDirectInputDevice2::GetObjectInfo () *(continued)*	
Return Value	**Description**
DI_OK	DirectInput successfully retrieved the object's information.
DIERR_INVALIDPARAM	DirectInput could not retrieve the object's information, because one or more parameters are invalid.
DIERR_NOTINITIALIZED	DirectInput could not retrieve the object's information, because this DirectInputDevice object is not initialized. It must be initialized with the **IDirectInputDevice2::Initialize** () function.
DIERR_OBJECTNOTFOUND	DirectInput could not retrieve the object's information, because the specified object was not found on the input device.

IDirectInputDevice2::GetProperty ()

Function Description

This function retrieves a property of either the device itself or one of its objects.

Function Declaration

```
HRESULT GetProperty(
    REFGUID rguidProp,
    LPDIPROPHEADER pdiph
);
```

Parameter	Description
rguidProp	Identifies the property to be retrieved. This can be a reference to a GUID that identifies the property or one of the following predefined property constants: • **DIPROP_AUTOCENTER**—The device's auto-center property is being retrieved. If this property is specified, the **pdiph** parameter must point to a **DIPROPDWORD** structure, whose **dwHow** member is set to **DIPH_DEVICE**. If this function succeeds, the **dwData** member of this structure will be set to **DIPROPAUTOCENTER_OFF** or **DIPROPAUTOCENTER_ON**. • **DIPROP_AXISMODE**—The device's axis mode property is being retrieved. If this property is specified, the **pdiph** parameter must point to a **DIPROPDWORD** structure whose **dwHow** member is set to **DIPH_DEVICE**. If this function succeeds, the **dwData** member of this structure will be set to **DIPROPAXISMODE_ABS** or **DIPROPAXISMODE_REL**. • **DIPROP_BUFFERSIZE**—The device's buffer size is being retrieved. If this property is specified, the **pdiph** parameter must point to a **DIPROPDWORD** structure whose **dwHow** member is set to **DIPH_DEVICE**. If this function succeeds, the **dwData** member of this structure will specify the size of the buffer, in items (**DIDEVICEOBJECTDATA** structures).

(continued)

IDirectInputDevice2::GetProperty () *(continued)*	
Parameter	**Description**
	• **DIPROP_DEADZONE**—The dead zone of the device or one of its objects is being retrieved. If this property is specified, the **pdiph** parameter must point to a **DIPROPDWORD** structure that either describes the object whose property is being retrieved or whose **dwHow** member is set to **DIPH_DEVICE**, indicating the property of the entire device is being retrieved. If this function succeeds, the **dwData** member of this structure will specify the dead zone, in the range of 0 (no dead zone) to 10,000 (100-percent dead zone). The dead zone indicates the neutral center region for a joystick. Any axis in this region is reported as being in the exact center.
	• **DIPROP_FFGAIN**—The device's force-feedback gain is being retrieved. If this property is specified, the **pdiph** parameter must point to a **DIPROPDWORD** structure whose **dwHow** member is set to **DIPH_DEVICE**. If this function succeeds, the **dwData** member of this structure will specify the force-feedback gain. A value of 0 indicates force-feedback effects are reduced by 100 percent and a value of 10,000 indicates no reduction. A value of 7,000 would indicate a 30-percent reduction.
	• **DIPROP_FFLOAD**—The device's memory load is being retrieved. If this property is specified, the **pdiph** parameter must point to a **DIPROPDWORD** structure whose **dwHow** member is set to **DIPH_DEVICE**. If this function succeeds, the **dwData** member of this structure will indicate the percentage (0 to 100) of memory in use on the device.
	• **DIPROP_GRANULARITY**—An object's granularity is being retrieved. If this property is specified, the **pdiph** parameter must point to a **DIPROPDWORD** structure that identifies the object. If this function succeeds, the **dwData** member of this structure will describe the granularity of the device. A granularity of 120 means the smallest change reported by the object is 120.
	• **DIPROP_GUIDANDPATH**—The class GUID and device interface (path), which may be used with the Win32 function **CreateFile ()** to access the device directly. If this property is specified, the **pdiph** parameter must point to a **DIPROPGUIDANPATH** structure, which contains the GUID and path. The **dwHow** member of this structure's **diph** member must be set to **DIPH_DEVICE**.
	• **DIPROP_INSTANCENAME**—The instance name of the device. If this property is specified, the **pdiph** paramater must point to a **DIPROPSTRING** structure, which contains a pointer to a string. The **dwHow** member of this structure's **diph** member must be set to **DIPH_DEVICE**.

(continued)

IDirectInputDevice2::GetProperty () *(continued)*	
Parameter	**Description**
	• **DIPROP_PRODUCTNAME**—The product name of the device. If this property is specified, the **pdiph** parameter must point to a **DIPROPSTRING** structure, which contains a pointer to a string. The **dwHow** member of this structure's **diph** member must be set to **DIPH_DEVICE**.
	• **DIPROP_RANGE**—An object's range is being retrieved. If this property is specified, the **pdiph** parameter must point to a **DIPROPRANGE** structure that identifies the object. If this function succeeds, the **lMin** and **lMax** members of this structure will describe the minimum and maximum values possible for the object.
	• **DIPROP_SATURATION**—The saturation of the device or one of its objects is being retrieved. If this property is specified, the **pdiph** parameter must point to a **DIPROPDWORD** structure that either describes the object whose property is being retrieved or whose **dwHow** member is set to **DIPH_DEVICE**, indicating the property of the entire device is being retrieved. If this function succeeds, the **dwData** member of this structure will be set to the device's saturation, in the range of 0 (no saturation) to 10,000 (100-percent saturation). The saturation indicates how far an axis must be from its center position before it is reported to be at its most extreme position.
pdiph	A pointer to a structure, such as **DIPROPRANGE** or **DIPROPDWORD**, as determined by the property being retrieved. The first portion of this structure will always include a **DIPROPHEADER** structure.
Return Value	**Description**
DI_OK	DirectInput successfully retrieved the property.
DIERR_INVALIDPARAM	DirectInput could not retrieve the property, because one or more parameters are invalid.
DIERR_NOTINITIALIZED	DirectInput could not retrieve the property, because this DirectInputDevice object is not initialized. It must be initialized with the **IDirectInputDevice2::Initialize** () function.
DIERR_OBJECTNOTFOUND	DirectInput could not retrieve the property, because the specified object was not found on the input device.
DIERR_UNSUPPORTED	DirectInput could not retrieve the property, because the operation is not supported.

IDirectInputDevice2::Initialize ()

Function Description

This function initializes a DirectInputDevice object created with **CoCreateInstance** (). Applications that obtain their IDirectInputDevice interfaces by calling **IDirectInput::CreateDevice** () do not need to call this function.

Function Declaration

```
HRESULT Initialize(
    HINSTANCE hinst,
    DWORD dwVersion,
    REFGUID rguid
);
```

Parameter	Description
hinst	A handle to the instance of the application. DLLs calling this function must pass their own handles, not the handles of their container applications.
dwVersion	The version of DirectInput the application is using. This should normally be the constant **DIRECTINPUT_VERSION** (defined in the DirectInput header file), unless the application wants DirectInput to emulate an earlier version.
rguid	A reference to a GUID that identifies the device to be associated with this DirectInputDevice object.

Return Value	Description
DI_OK	DirectInput successfully initialized the object.
DIERR_ACQUIRED	DirectInput could not initialize the object, because access to the device is acquired.
DIERR_DEVICENOTREG	DirectInput could not initialize the object, because the specified device is not registered.
S_FALSE	DirectInput could not initialize the object, because it has already been initialized.

IDirectInputDevice2::Poll ()

Function Description

This function polls the input device. Some joysticks and other input devices are not event-driven, meaning they do not inform DirectInput when their states change. These devices must be polled at regular intervals, or else buffered data will not be available and event notification will be disabled.

Function Declaration

```
HRESULT Poll();
```

Parameter	Description
None	

(continued)

IDirectInputDevice2::Poll () *(continued)*

Return Value	Description
DI_OK	DirectInput successfully polled the input device.
DIERR_INPUTLOST	DirectInput could not poll the input device, because input to the device has been lost. It must be reacquired with the **IDirectInputDevice2::Acquire** () function.
DIERR_NOTACQUIRED	DirectInput could not poll the input device, because access to the device has not been acquired. It must be acquired with the **IDirectInputDevice2::Acquire** () function.
DIERR_NOTINITIALIZED	DirectInput could not poll the input device, because this DirectInputDevice2 object is not initialized. It must be initialized with the **IDirectInputDevice2::Initialize** () function.

IDirectInputDevice2::RunControlPanel ()

Function Description

This function runs the DirectInput control panel associated with the input device, or the default device control panel if one is not associated.

Function Declaration

```
HRESULT RunControlPanel(
    HWND hwndOwner,
    DWORD dwFlags
);
```

Parameter	Description
hwndOwner	A handle to the window that will own the launched control panel. This parameter may be **NULL**.
dwFlags	This parameter is not used and must be 0.

Return Value	Description
DI_OK	DirectInput successfully launched the control panel associated with the input device.
DIERR_INVALIDPARAM	DirectInput could not run the control panel, because one or more parameters are invalid.
DIERR_NOTINITIALIZED	DirectInput could not run the control panel, because this DirectInputDevice object is not initialized. It must be initialized with the **IDirectInputDevice2::Initialize** () function.

IDirectInputDevice2::SendDeviceData ()

Function Description

This function sends data to one or more output objects on the device.

Function Declaration

```
HRESULT SendDeviceData(
    DWORD cbObjectData,
    LPCDIDEVICEOBJECTDATA rgdod,
    LPDWORD pdwInOut,
    DWORD fl
);
```

Parameter	Description
cbObjectData	The size of the **DIDEVICEOBJECTDATA** structure in bytes.
rgdod	An array of **DIDEVICEOBJECTDATA** structures. Each structure specifies both an object to which data will be sent and the output data for that object. To avoid ambiguity, no two structures should reference the same object.
pdwInOut	A pointer to an integer that describes the number of **DIDEVICEOBJECTDATA** structures pointed to by **rgdod**. When this function returns, the integer will be set to the number of data items actually sent to the device.
fl	Describes how the data is sent. This parameter may be 0 or the following flag: • **DISDD_CONTINUE**—The data to be sent, if it does not contain information for all outputs, will affect only the outputs that are specified by **rgdod**. If this flag is not specified, outputs for which data is not specified will be reset to default values.

Return Value	Description
DI_OK	DirectInput successfully sent the data.
DIERR_INPUTLOST	DirectInput could not send the data, because input to the device has been lost. It must be reacquired with the **IDirectInput-Device2::Acquire** () function.
DIERR_NOTACQUIRED	DirectInput could not send the data, because access to the device has not been acquired. It must be acquired with the **IDirectInputDevice2::Acquire** () function.
DIERR_REPORTFULL	DirectInput could not send the data, because more information was requested to be sent to the input device than supported.
DIERR_UNPLUGGED	DirectInput could not send the data, because the input device is not physically plugged in.

IDirectInputDevice2::SendForceFeedbackCommand ()

Function Description

This function sends a command to the input device's force-feedback system.

Function Declaration

```
HRESULT SendForceFeedbackCommand(
    DWORD dwFlags
);
```

Parameter	Description
dwFlags	Describes the command to be sent to the input device. This parameter can be one of the following flags: • **DISFFC_CONTINUE**—Resumes paused playback. • **DISFFC_PAUSE**—Pauses playback of force-feedback effects. • **DISFFC_RESET**—Resets the input device, removing all force-feedback effects from memory, disabling force-feedback actuators, and restoring defaults. • **DISFFC_SETACTUATORSOFF**—Turns the input device's force-feedback actuators off. • **DISFFC_SETACTUATORSON**—Turns the input device's force-feedback actuators on. • **DISFFC_STOPALL**—Stops all playback of force-feedback effects.

Return Value	Description
DI_OK	DirectInput successfully sent the command.
DIERR_INPUTLOST	DirectInput could not send the command, because input to the device has been lost. It must be reacquired with the **IDirectInputDevice2::Acquire** () function.
DIERR_INVALIDPARAM	DirectInput could not send the command, because one or more parameters are invalid.
DIERR_NOTEXCLUSIVEACQUIRED	DirectInput could not send the command, because exclusive-level access is required for all force-feedback devices.
DIERR_NOTINITIALIZED	DirectInput could not send the command, because this DirectInputDevice2 object is not initialized. It must be initialized with the **IDirectInputDevice2::Initialize** () function.
DIERR_UNSUPPORTED	DirectInput could not send the command, because the operation is not supported.

IDirectInputDevice2::SetCooperativeLevel ()

Function Description

This function sets the cooperative level for the input device. This must be done separately for each DirectInputDevice object before access to the device can be acquired and input retrieved.

Function Declaration

```
HRESULT SetCooperativeLevel(
    HWND hwnd,
    DWORD dwFlags
);
```

Parameter	Description
hwnd	A handle to the application's main window.
dwFlags	Describes the cooperative level. This parameter must be a combination of one of the first two and one of the second two flags listed here: • **DISCL_BACKGROUND**—The application will receive input even when it does not have the input focus. This flag cannot be used with **DISCL_FOREGROUND**. • **DISCL_FOREGROUND**—The application will receive input only when it has input focus. This flag cannot be used with **DISCL_BACKGROUND**. • **DISCL_EXCLUSIVE**—The application will receive exclusive-level access. Exclusive-level access can be acquired by only one application, but does not prevent other applications from acquiring nonexclusive access to the device. This flag cannot be used with **DISCL_NONEXCLUSIVE**. • **DISCL_NONEXCLUSIVE**—The application will receive nonexclusive access to the device. This flag cannot be used with **DISCL_EXCLUSIVE**.

Return Value	Description
DI_OK	DirectInput successfully set the cooperative level for the input device.
DIERR_INVALIDPARAM	DirectInput could not set the cooperative level, because one or more parameters are invalid.
DIERR_NOTINITIALIZED	DirectInput could not set the cooperative level, because this DirectInputDevice object is not initialized. It must be initialized with the **IDirectInputDevice2::Initialize** () function.

IDirectInputDevice2::SetDataFormat ()

Function Description

This function sets the data format for the input device. The data format describes where each input device object appears in a buffer. Objects may be identified by their offsets into the buffer.

Function Declaration

```
HRESULT SetDataFormat(
    LPCDIDATAFORMAT lpdf
);
```

(continued)

IDirectInputDevice2::SetDataFormat () *(continued)*

Parameter	Description
lpdf	A pointer to a **DIDATAFORMAT** structure that describes the data format to be set. Applications can create their own data formats or, more typically, use one of the following predefined formats: • **c_dfDIKeyboard**—The default keyboard data format • **c_dfDIMouse**—The default mouse data format • **c_dfDIMouse2**—The enhanced default mouse data format • **c_dfDIJoystick**—The default joystick data format • **c_dfDIJoystick2**—An enhanced default joystick data format with support for more objects

Return Value	Description
DI_OK	DirectInput successfully set the data format of the input device.
DIERR_ACQUIRED	DirectInput could not set the data format, because access to the device is acquired. It must be unacquired with **IDirectInput-Device2::Unacquire** () before this function can succeed.
DIERR_INVALIDPARAM	DirectInput could not set the data format, because one or more parameters are invalid.
DIERR_NOTINITIALIZED	DirectInput could not set the data format, because this DirectInputDevice object is not initialized. It must be initialized with the **IDirectInputDevice2::Initialize** () function.

IDirectInputDevice2::SetEventNotification ()

Function Description

This function sets the event notification. This is a standard Win32 event (created with **CreateEvent** ()) that is set by DirectInput whenever the state of the input device changes.

Function Declaration

```
HRESULT SetEventNotification(
    HANDLE hEvent
);
```

Parameter	Description
hEvent	A handle to the event. This event, created with the Win32 **CreateEvent** () function, is set by DirectInput whenever the state of the input device changes. The status of the event (whether set or not set) can be checked by the Win32 function **WaitForSingleObject** (). If the event was created with automatic reset property, then after its status has been checked, it will automatically be reset; otherwise, an application must reset the event explicitly by calling the Win32 function **ResetEvent** ().

(continued)

IDirectInputDevice2::SetEventNotification () *(continued)*

Return Value	Description
DI_OK	DirectInput successfully set the event notification.
DI_POLLEDDEVICE	DirectInput successfully set the event notification. Because the device is polled, however, the event will not be set and no data will be generated for the device unless the **IDirectInput Device2::Poll** () function is called continuously throughout the life of the application.
DIERR_ACQUIRED	DirectInput could not set the event notification, because access to the device is acquired. It must be unacquired with **IDirectInputDevice2::Unacquire** () before this function can succeed.
DIERR_HANDLEEXISTS	DirectInput could not set the event notification, because an event is already associated with device state changes.
DIERR_INVALIDPARAM	DirectInput could not set the event notification, because one or more parameters are invalid.
DIERR_NOTINITIALIZED	DirectInput could not set the event notification, because this DirectInputDevice object is not initialized. It must be initialized with the **IDirectInputDevice2::Initialize** () function.

IDirectInputDevice2::SetProperty ()

Function Description

This function sets a property of either the input device itself or one of its objects.

Function Declaration

```
HRESULT SetProperty(
    REFGUID rguidProp,
    LPCDIPROPHEADER pdiph
);
```

Parameter	Description
rguidProp	Identifies the property to be set. This can be a reference to a GUID that identifies the property or one of the following predefined property constants: • **DIPROP_AUTOCENTER**—The device's auto-center property is being set. If this property is specified, the **pdiph** parameter must point to a **DIPROPDWORD** structure, whose **dwHow** member is set to **DIPH_DEVICE** and whose **dwData** member is set to **DIPROPAUTOCENTER_OFF** or **DIPROPAUTOCENTER_ON**.

(continued)

IDirectInputDevice2::SetProperty () *(continued)*	
Parameter	**Description**
	• **DIPROP_AXISMODE**—The device's axis mode property is being set. If this property is specified, the **pdiph** parameter must point to a **DIPROPDWORD** structure, whose **dwHow** member is set to **DIPH_DEVICE** and whose **dwData** member is set to **DIPROPAXISMODE_ABS** or **DIPROPAXISMODE_REL**.
	• **DIPROP_BUFFERSIZE**—The device's buffer size is being set. If this property is specified, the **pdiph** parameter must point to a **DIPROPDWORD** structure, whose **dwHow** member is set to **DIPH_DEVICE** and whose **dwData** member specifies the size of the buffer, in items (**DIDEVICEOBJECTDATA** structures).
	• **DIPROP_CALIBRATIONMODE**—The calibration mode of either the device or one of its objects is being set. If this property is specified, the **pdiph** parameter must point to a **DIPROPDWORD** structure that specifies the object whose property is being set or whose **dwHow** member is set to **DIPH_DEVICE**, indicating the property will be set for the entire device. The **dwData** member of this structure must be set to either **DIPROPCALIBRATIONMODE_COOKED** (indicating DirectInput should calibrate input data according to the device's control panel before reporting it) or **DIPROPCALIBRATIONMODE_RAW** (indicating DirectInput should not calibrate the data before reporting it). Setting the calibration mode to **DIPROPCALIBRATIONMODE_RAW** causes all dead-zone, saturation, and range settings to be ignored.
	• **DIPROP_DEADZONE**—The device's dead zone is being set. If this property is specified, the **pdiph** parameter must point to a **DIPROPDWORD** structure that describes the object whose property is being retrieved or whose **dwHow** member is set to **DIPH_DEVICE**, indicating the property will be set for the entire device. The **dwData** member of this structure must specify the dead zone, in the range of 0 (no dead zone) to 10,000 (100-percent dead zone). The dead zone indicates the neutral center region for a joystick. Any axis in this region is reported as being in the exact center.
	• **DIPROP_FFGAIN**—The device's force-feedback gain is being set. If this property is specified, the **pdiph** parameter must point to a **DIPROPDWORD** structure, whose **dwHow** member is set to **DIPH_DEVICE** and whose **dwData** member specifies the force-feedback gain. A value of 0 indicates force-feedback effects are reduced by 100 percent and a value of 10,000 indicates no reduction. A value of 7,000 would indicate 30-percent reduction.

(continued)

IDirectInputDevice2::SetProperty () *(continued)*	
Parameter	**Description**
	• **DIPROP_INSTANCE**—The instance name of the device. If this property is specified, the **pdiph** parameter must point to a **DIPROPSTRING** structure, which contains a pointer to a string. The **dwHow** member of this structure's **diph** member must be set to **DIPH_DEVICE**.
	• **DIPROP_PRODUCTNAME**—The porduct name of the device. If this is specified, the **pdiph** parameter must point to a **DIPROPSTRING** structure, which contains a pointer to a string. The **dwHow** member of this structure's **diph** member must be set to **DIPH_DEVICE**.
	• **DIPROP_RANGE**—An object's range is being set. If this property is specified, the **pdiph** parameter must point to a **DIPROPRANGE** structure that both identifies the object and whose **lMin** and **lMax** members describe the minimum and maximum values possible for the object.
	• **DIPROP_SATURATION**—The saturation for the device or one of its objects is being set. If this property is specified, the **pdiph** parameter must point to a **DIPROPDWORD** structure that describes the object whose property is being set or whose **dwHow** member is set to **DIPH_DEVICE**, indicating the saturation will be set for the entire device. The **dwData** member of this structure must be set to the device's saturation, in the range of 0 (no saturation) to 10,000 (100-percent saturation). The saturation indicates how far an axis must be from its center position before it is reported to be at its most extreme position.
pdiph	A pointer to a structure such as **DIPROPRANGE** or **DIPROPDWORD**, as determined by the property being set. The first portion of this structure will always be a **DIPROPHEADER** structure.
Return Value	**Description**
DI_OK	DirectInput successfully set the property of the input device.
DI_PROPNOEFFECT	DirectInput successfully set the property of the input device, but it had no effect.
DIERR_INVALIDPARAM	DirectInput could not set the property, because one or more parameters are invalid.
DIERR_NOTINITIALIZED	DirectInput could not set the property, because this **DirectInputDevice** object is not initialized. It must be initialized with the **IDirectInputDevice2::Initialize ()** function.
DIERR_OBJECTNOTFOUND	DirectInput could not set the property, because the specified object was not found on the input device.
DIERR_UNSUPPORTED	DirectInput could not set the property, because the operation is not supported.

IDirectInputDevice2::Unacquire ()	
Function Description	
This function unacquires access to the input device.	
Function Declaration	
);	
Parameter	**Description**
None	
Return Value	**Description**
DI_OK	DirectInput successfully unacquired access to the input device.

IDirectInputEffect

Applications can obtain the IDirectInputEffect interface by calling the **IDirectInputDevice2::CreateEffect ()** function.

The GUID for the IDirectInputEffect interface is **IID_IDirectInputEffect**.

IDirectInputEffect::Download ()	
Function Description	
This function downloads the force-feedback effect onto the input device.	
Function Declaration	
Download();	
Parameter	**Description**
None	
Return Value	**Description**
DI_OK	DirectInput successfully downloaded the force-feedback effect.
DIERR_NOTINITIALIZED	DirectInput could not download the force-feedback effect, because this DirectInputEffect object is not initialized. It must be initialized with the **IDirectInputEffect::Initialize ()** function.
DIERR_DEVICEFULL	DirectInput could not download the force-feedback effect, because the device is full.

IDirectInputEffect::Escape ()

Function Description

This function sends a hardware-specific command to an input device.

Function Declaration

```
HRESULT Escape(
    LPDIEFFESCAPE pesc
);
```

Parameter	Description
pesc	A pointer to a **DIEFFESCAPE** structure that describes the command to be sent.

Return Value	Description
DI_OK	DirectInput successfully sent the command to the driver.
DIERR_NOTINITIALIZED	DirectInput could not send the command, because this DirectInputEffect object is not initialized. It must be initialized with the **IDirectInputEffect::Initialize** () function.
DIERR_DEVICEFULL	DirectInput could send the command, because the device is full.

IDirectInputEffect::GetEffectGuid ()

Function Description

This function retrieves the force-feedback effect's GUID.

Function Declaration

```
HRESULT GetEffectGuid(
    LPGUID pguid
);
```

Parameter	Description
pguid	A pointer to a GUID structure. If this function is successful, the structure will be filled with the GUID of the DirectInputEffect object.

Return Value	Description
DI_OK	DirectInput successfully retrieved the effect GUID.
DIERR_INVALIDPARAM	DirectInput could not retrieve the effect GUID, because one or more parameters are invalid.
DIERR_NOTINITIALIZED	DirectInput could not retrieve the effect GUID, because this DirectInputEffect object is not initialized. It must be initialized with the **IDirectInputEffect::Initialize** () function.

IDirectInputEffect::GetEffectStatus ()

Function Description

This function retrieves the status of the force-feedback effect.

Function Declaration

```
HRESULT GetEffectStatus(
    LPDWORD pdwFlags
);
```

Parameter	Description
pdwFlags	A pointer to an integer. If this function succeeds, the integer will be set to 0, or one or more of the following flags: • **DIEGES_PLAYING**—The force-feedback effect is playing. • **DIEGES_EMULATED**—The force-feedback effect is emulated.

Return Value	Description
DI_OK	DirectInput successfully retrieved the effect's status.
DIERR_INVALIDPARAM	DirectInput could not retrieve the effect's status, because one or more parameters are invalid.
DIERR_NOTINITIALIZED	DirectInput could not retrieve the effect's status, because this DirectInputEffect object is not initialized. It must be initialized with the **IDirectInputEffect::Initialize** () function.

IDirectInputEffect::GetParameters ()

Function Description

This function retrieves the parameters of the force-feedback effect.

Function Declaration

```
HRESULT GetParameters(
    LPDIEFFECT peff,
    DWORD dwFlags
);
```

Parameter	Description
peff	The address of a **DIEFFECT** structure. If this function succeeds, the structure will be filled with the parameters of the force-feedback effect.
dwFlags	Describes which parameters of the force-feedback effect are to be retrieved. This parameter can be 0, or one or more of the following flags: • **DIEP_ALLPARAMS**—All parameters are to be retrieved. • **DIEP_ALLPARAMS_DX5**—All parameters as of DirectX 5 are to be retrieved.

IDirectInputEffect::GetParameters () *(continued)*	
Parameter	**Description**
	• **DIEP_AXES**—The **cAxes** and **rgdwAxes** members of the **DIEFFECT** structure pointed to by **peff** are to be retrieved.
	• **DIEP_DIRECTION**—The **cAxes** and **rglDirection** members of the **DIEFFECT** structure pointed to by **peff** are to be retrieved.
	• **DIEP_DURATION**—The **dwDuration** member of the **DIEFFECT** structure pointed to by **peff** is to be retrieved.
	• **DIEP_ENVELOPE**—The **lpEnvelope** member of the **DIEFFECT** structure pointed to by **peff** is to be retrieved.
	• **DIEP_GAIN**—The **dwGain** member of the **DIEFFECT** structure pointed to by **peff** is to be retrieved.
	• **DIEP_SAMPLEPERIOD**—The **dwSamplePeriod** member of the **DIEFFECT** structure pointed to by **peff** is to be retrieved.
	• **DIEP_STARTDELAY**—The **dwStartDelay** member of the **DIEFFECT** structure pointed to be **peff** is to be retrieved.
	• **DIEP_TRIGGERBUTTON**—The **dwTriggerButton** member of the **DIEFFECT** structure pointed to by **peff** is to be retrieved.
	• **DIEP_TRIGGERREPEATINTERVAL**—The **dwTriggerRepeatInterval** member of the **DIEFFECT** structure pointed to by **peff** is to be retrieved.
	• **DIEP_TYPESPECIFICPARAMS**—The **lpvTypeSpecificParams** member of the **DIEFFECT** structure pointed to by **peff** points to a buffer whose size is specified by the structure's **cbTypeSpecificParams** member. The buffer will be filled with type-specific data.
Return Value	**Description**
DI_OK	DirectInput successfully retrieved the effect's parameters.
DIERR_INVALIDPARAM	DirectInput could not retrieve the effect's parameters, because one or more parameters are invalid.
DIERR_MOREDATA	DirectInput could not retrieve the effect's parameters because the buffer is too small.
DIERR_NOTINITIALIZED	DirectInput could not retrieve the effect's parameters, because this DirectInputEffect object is not initialized. It must be initialized with the **IDirectInputEffect::Initialize** () function.

IDirectInputEffect::Initialize ()

Function Description

This function initializes a DirectInputEffect object created with **CoCreateInstance** (). Applications that obtain their IDirectInputEffect interfaces by calling **IDirectInputDevice2::CreateEffect** () do not need to call this function.

Function Declaration

```
HRESULT Initialize(
    HINSTANCE hinst,
    DWORD dwVersion,
    REFGUID rguid
);
```

Parameter	Description
hinst	A handle to the instance of the application. DLLs calling this function must pass their own handles, not the handles of their container applications.
dwVersion	The version of DirectInput the application is using. This should normally be the constant **DIRECTINPUT_VERSION** (defined in the DirectInput header file), unless the application wants DirectInput to emulate an earlier version.
rguid	A reference to a GUID that identifies the effect to be associated with this DirectInputEffect object. This can be any GUID obtained by calling **IDirectInputDevice2::EnumEffects** ().

Return Value	Description
DI_OK	DirectInput successfully initialized the object.
DIERR_DEVICENOTREG	DirectInput could not initialize the object, because the specified device is not registered.

IDirectInputEffect::SetParameters ()

Function Description

This function sets the parameters of the force-feedback effect.

Function Declaration

```
HRESULT SetParameters(
    LPCDIEFFECT peff,
    DWORD dwFlags
);
```

(continued)

IDirectInputEffect::SetParameters () *(continued)*	
Parameter	**Description**
peff	The address of a **DIEFFECT** structure that holds the parameters to be set.
dwFlags	Describes which parameters are to be set. This parameter can be 0, or one or more of the following flags:
	• **DIEP_AXES**—The **cAxes** and **rgdwAxes** members of the **DIEFFECT** structure pointed to by **peff** are valid.
	• **DIEP_DIRECTION**—The **cAxes** and **rglDirection** members of the **DIEFFECT** structure pointed to by **peff** are valid. If this flag is specified, the direction type (Cartesian, polar, or spherical) must be specified in **peff**.
	• **DIEP_DURATION**—The **dwDuration** member of the **DIEFFECT** structure pointed to by **peff** is valid.
	• **DIEP_ENVELOPE**—The **lpEnvelope** member of the **DIEFFECT** structure pointed to by **peff** is valid.
	• **DIEP_GAIN**—The **dwGain** member of the **DIEFFECT** structure pointed to by **peff** is valid.
	• **DIEP_NODOWNLOAD**—DirectInput should not automatically download the effect to the device after updating its parameters. If this flag is not specified, then DirectInput attempts to download the effect to the device after updating its parameters.
	• **DIEP_NORESTART**—DirectInput should not change the parameters of the device if the hardware cannot do so without restarting the effect. If this flag is specified and the hardware is so limited, this function returns **DIERR_EFFECTPLAYING**.
	• **DIEP_SAMPLEPERIOD**—The **dwSamplePeriod** member of the **DIEFFECT** structure pointed to by **peff** is valid.
	• **DIEP_START**—DirectInput should start or restart the effect after changing its parameters.
	• **DIEP_STARTDELAY**—The **dwStartDelay** member of the **DIEFFECT** structure pointed to by **peff** is valid.
	• **DIEP_TRIGGERBUTTON**—The **dwTriggerButton** member of the **DIEFFECT** structure pointed to by **peff** is valid.

(continued)

IDirectInputEffect::SetParameters () *(continued)*	
Return Value	**Description**
	• **DIEP_TRIGGERREPEATINTERVAL**—The **dwTriggerRepeatInterval** member of the **DIEFFECT** structure pointed to by **peff** is valid.
	• **DIEP_TYPESPECIFICPARAMS**—The **lpvTypeSpecificParams** member of the **DIEFFECT** structure pointed to by **peff** points to a buffer whose size is specified by the structure's **cbTypeSpecificParams** member. The buffer is filled with type-specific data.
DI_OK	DirectInput successfully set the effect's parameters.
DI_EFFECTRESTARTED	DirectInput successfully restarted the effect after stopping and updating its parameters.
DI_DOWNLOADSKIPPED	DirectInput successfully set the parameters of the effect, but could not download the effect to the input device, because it was not acquired with exclusive cooperative level.
DI_TRUNCATED	DirectInput successfully set some parameters of the effect, but others were not supported by the device and were therefore truncated to the nearest supported value.
DI_TRUNCATEDANDRESTARTED	This return value is equivalent to **DI_RESTARTED** and **DI_TRUNCATED**.
DIERR_NOTINITIALIZED	DirectInput could not set the effect's parameters, because this **DirectInputEffect** object is not initialized. It must be initialized with the **IDirectInputEffect::Initialize ()** function.
DIERR_INCOMPLETEEFFECT	DirectInput could not set the effect's parameters, because essential information is missing.
DIERR_INPUTLOST	DirectInput could not set the effect's parameters, because input to the device has been lost. It must be reacquired with the **IDirectInputEffect::Acquire ()** function.
DIERR_INVALIDPARAM	DirectInput could not set the effect's parameters, because one or more parameters are invalid.
DIERR_EFFECTPLAYING	DirectInput could not set the effect's parameters, because the effect is playing.

DIPROPGUIDANPATH

Function Description

This function describes a GUID and a path. It is used when retrieving the **DIPROP_GUIDANPATH** property.

Function Declaration

```
typedef struct DIPROPGUIDANPATH{
  DIPROPHEADER diph;
  GUID    guidClass;
  WCHAR   wszPath[MAX_PATH];
  }DIPROPGUIDANPATH, *LPDIPROPGUIDANPATH;
```

Parameter	Description
diph	A pointer to a **DIPROPHEADER** structure whose **dwHow** member is set to **DIPH_DEVICE**.
guidClass	The class **GUID** for the device.
wszPath	A Unicode string that specified the path for the device. This may be used with the Win32 function **CreateFile()** to access the device directly.

IDirectInputEffect::Start ()

Function Description

This function starts playback of the force-feedback effect or restarts one that is already playing. Note that DirectInput automatically downloads the effect to the device if it has not already been downloaded.

Function Declaration

```
HRESULT Start(
   DWORD dwIterations,
   DWORD dwFlags
);
```

Parameter	Description
dwIterations	Specifies the number of times to play the effect or **INFINITE** to play it continually.
dwFlags	Describes how the effect should be played. This parameter can be one or more of the following flags:
	• **DIES_SOLO**—The effect should be played solo. This flag causes all other currently playing effects to stop. If this flag is not specified, the effect is combined with those already playing on the device.
	• **DIES_NODOWNLOAD**—The effect should not automatically be downloaded to the device.

(continued)

IDirectInputEffect::Start () *(continued)*	
Return Value	**Description**
DI_OK	DirectInput successfully started playback of the force-feedback effect.
DIERR_INVALIDPARAM	DirectInput could not start the effect, because one or more parameters are invalid.
DIERR_INCOMPLETEEFFECT	DirectInput could not start the effect, because essential information is missing.
DIERR_NOTEXCLUSIVEACQUIRED	DirectInput could not start the effect, because exclusive-level access is required for all force-feedback devices.
DIERR_NOTINITIALIZED	DirectInput could not start the effect, because this DirectInputEffect object is not initialized. It must be initialized with the **IDirectInputEffect::Initialize** () function.
DIERR_UNSUPPORTED	DirectInput could not start the effect, because the operation is not supported.

IDirectInputEffect::Stop ()	
Function Description	
This function stops playback of the force-feedback effect.	
Function Declaration	
`HRESULT Stop(void);`	
Parameter	**Description**
None	
Return Value	**Description**
DI_OK	DirectInput successfully stopped playback of the force-feedback effect.
DIERR_NOTEXCLUSIVEACQUIRED	DirectInput could not stop the effect, because exclusive-level access is required for all force-feedback devices.
DIERR_NOTINITIALIZED	DirectInput could not stop the effect, because this DirectInputEffect object is not initialized. It must be initialized with the **IDirectInputEffect::Initialize** () function.

IDirectInputEffect::Unload ()

Function Description

This function unloads the force-feedback effect from memory, stopping it if necessary.

Function Declaration

```
HRESULT Unload(void);
```

Parameter	Description
None	

Return Value	Description
DI_OK	DirectInput successfully unloaded the force-feedback effect from memory.
DIERR_INPUTLOST	DirectInput could not unload the effect, because input to the device has been lost. It must be reacquired with the **IDirectInputEffect::Acquire** () function.
DIERR_INVALIDPARAM	DirectInput could not unload the effect, because one or more parameters are invalid.
DIERR_NOTEXCLUSIVEACQUIRED	DirectInput could not unload the effect, because exclusive-level access is required for all force-feedback devices.
DIERR_NOTINITIALIZED	DirectInput could not unload the effect, because this DirectInputEffect object is not initialized. It must be initialized with the **IDirectInputEffect::Initialize** () function.

Function Reference

This section documents the functions of DirectInput that do not belong to any interfaces.

DirectInputCreate ()

Function Description

This function creates and initializes a **DirectInput** object.

Function Declaration

```
HRESULT WINAPI DirectInputCreate(
    HINSTANCE hinst,
    DWORD dwVersion,
    LPDIRECTINPUT *lplpDirectInput,
    LPUNKNOWN punkOuter
);
```

Parameter	Description
hinst	A handle to the instance of the application. DLLs calling this function must pass their own handles, not the handles of their container applications.

(continued)

DirectInputCreate () *(continued)*	
Parameter	**Description**
dwVersion	The version of DirectInput that the application is using. This should normally be the constant **DIRECTINPUT_VERSION** (defined in the DirectInput header file), unless the application wants DirectInput to emulate a previous version.
lplpDirectInputDevice	The address of a pointer to a DirectInput object. If this function succeeds, the pointer will be set to the newly created DirectInput object.
pUnkOuter	A pointer to the controlling object's IUnknown interface. Unless an application is using COM aggregation features, this parameter should be **NULL**.
Return Value	**Description**
DI_OK	DirectInput successfully created and initialized the DirectInput object.
DIERR_BETADIRECTINPUTVERSION	DirectInput could not create the object, because the application is designed for an unsupported beta version of DirectInput.
DIERR_INVALIDPARAM	DirectInput could not create the object, because one or more parameters is invalid.
DIERR_OLDDIRECTINPUTVERSION	DirectInput could not create the object, because the application is designed for a newer version of DirectInput than is installed.
DIERR_OUTOFMEMORY	DirectInput could not create the object, because sufficient memory is not available.

Callback Function Reference

This section documents the application-defined callback functions used by DirectInput during enumeration processes.

DIEnumCreatedEffectObjectsProc ()
Function Description
This is an application-defined function that DirectInput calls for every created effect it enumerates.
Function Declaration

```
BOOL CALLBACK DIEnumCreatedEffectObjectsProc(
   LPDIRECTINPUTEFFECT peff,
   LPVOID pvRef
);
```

(continued)

DIEnumCreatedEffectObjectsProc () *(continued)*

Parameter	Description
peff	A pointer to a DirectInputEffect object previously created by the **IDirectInputDevice2::CreateEffect** () function. Applications must release the interface when they are done using it.
pvRef	A pointer to application-defined data sent to this function through the **IDirectInputDevice2::EnumCreatedEffectObjects** () function.

Return Value	Description
DIENUM_CONTINUE	DirectInput should continue the enumeration process.
DIENUM_STOP	DirectInput should stop the enumeration process.

DIEnumDeviceObjectsProc ()

Function Description

This function is an application-defined function that DirectInput calls for every object it enumerates.

Function Declaration

```
BOOL CALLBACK DIEnumDeviceObjectsProc(
    LPCDIDEVICEOBJECTINSTANCE lpddoi,
    LPVOID pvRef
);
```

Parameter	Description
lpddoi	A pointer to a **DIDEVICEOBJECTINSTANCE** structure in this that describes the object being enumerated.
pvRef	A pointer to application-defined data sent to this function through the **IDirectInputDevice2::EnumObjects** () function.

Return Value	Description
DIENUM_CONTINUE	DirectInput should continue the enumeration process.
DIENUM_STOP	DirectInput should stop the enumeration process.

DIEnumDevicesProc ()

Function Description

This is an application-defined function that DirectInput calls for every input device it enumerates.

Function Declaration

```
BOOL CALLBACK DIEnumDevicesProc(
    LPCDIDEVICEINSTANCE lpddi,
    LPVOID pvRef
);
```

Parameter	Description
lpddi	A pointer to a **DIDEVICEINSTANCE** structure that describes the device being enumerated.
pvRef	A pointer to application-defined data sent to this function through the **IDirectInput::EnumDevices** () function.

Return Value	Description
DIENUM_CONTINUE	DirectInput should continue the enumeration process.
DIENUM_STOP	DirectInput should stop the enumeration process.

DIEnumEffectsProc ()

Function Description

This function is an application-defined function that DirectInput calls for every supported effect it enumerates.

Function Declaration

```
BOOL CALLBACK DIEnumEffectsProc(
    LPCDIEFFECTINFO pdei,
    LPVOID pvRef
);
```

Parameter	Description
pdei	A pointer to a **DIEFFECTINFO** structure that describes the effect being enumerated. The input device can create this effect.
pvRef	A pointer to application-defined data sent to this function through the **IDirectInputDevice2::EnumEffects** () function.

Return Value	Description
DIENUM_CONTINUE	DirectInput should continue the enumeration process.
DIENUM_STOP	DirectInput should stop the enumeration process.

Macro Reference

This section documents the macros defined in the DirectInput header file. These provide shortcuts to some of the mundane tasks of writing DirectInput applications.

DIDFT_GETINSTANCE ()

Macro Description

This macro takes the **dwType** member of the **DIOBJECTDATAFORMAT** structure and extracts from it the object instance number, which is located in the member's middle 16 bits.

Macro Declaration

```
DIDFT_GETINSTANCE(n) LOWORD((n) >> 8)
```

Parameter	Description
n	The **dwType** member of a **DIOBJECTDATAFORMAT** structure.
Return Value	Description
WORD	The object instance number.

DIDFT_GETTYPE ()

Macro Description

This macro takes the **dwType** member of the **DIOBJECTDATAFORMAT** structure and extracts from it the object type code, which is located in the member's low 8 bits.

Macro Declaration

```
DIDFT_GETTYPE(n)   LOBYTE(n)
```

Parameter	Description
n	The **dwType** member of a **DIOBJECTDATAFORMAT** structure.
Return Value	Description
BYTE	The object type code.

DIDFT_MAKEINSTANCE ()

Macro Description

This macro takes an object instance number and packs it into the middle 16 bits of a **DWORD**. This is the format used by the **dwType** member of the **DIOBJECTDATAFORMAT** structure for storing object instance numbers.

Macro Declaration

```
DIDFT_MAKEINSTANCE(n) ((WORD)(n) << 8)
```

Parameter	Description
n	The object instance number.
Return Value	Description
DWORD	The packed object instance number.

DIEFT_GETTYPE ()

Macro Description

This macro takes the **dwEffType** member of the **DIEFFECTINFO** structure and extracts from it the effect type code, which is located in the member's low 8 bits.

Macro Declaration

```
DIEFT_GETTYPE(n)   LOBYTE(n)
```

Parameter	Description
n	The **dwEffType** member of a **DIEFFECTINFO** structure.
Return Value	**Description**
BYTE	The effect type code.

DISEQUENCE_COMPARE ()

Macro Description

This macro compares two sequence numbers generated by DirectInput for a buffered data item, taking into account wraparound.

Macro Declaration

```
DISEQUENCE_COMPARE(dwSequence1, cmp, dwSequence2) \
   ((int)((dwSequence1) - (dwSequence2)) cmp 0)
```

Parameter	Description
dwSequence1	The first sequence.
cmp	The comparison operator, such as '<', '>', or '=='.
dwSequence2	The second sequence.
Return Value	**Description**
int	This will be nonzero if the comparison evaluates to true or 0 if it evaluates to false.

GET_DIDEVICE_SUBTYPE ()

Macro Description

This macro takes the **dwDevType** member of the **DIDEVICEINSTANCE** structure and extracts from it the device subtype code, which is located in the member's next-to-least significant byte.

Macro Declaration

```
GET_DIDEVICE_SUBTYPE(dwDevType)   HIBYTE(dwDevType)
```

Parameter	Description
dwDevType	The **dwDevType** member of a **DIDEVICEINSTANCE** structure.
Return Value	**Description**
BYTE	The device subtype code.

GET_DIDEVICE_TYPE ()

Macro Description

This macro takes the **dwDevType** member of the **DIDEVICEINSTANCE** structure and extracts from it the device type code, which is located in the member's least significant byte.

Macro Declaration

```
GET_DIDEVICE_TYPE(dwDevType)  LOBYTE(dwDevType)
```

Parameter	Description
dwDevType	The **dwDevType** member of a **DIDEVICEINSTANCE** structure.

Return Value	Description
BYTE	The device type code.

Structure Reference

This section documents the structures used by DirectInput functions.

DICONDITION

Structure Description

This structure describes a condition force-feedback effect. A condition effect is dependent on the position, velocity, or acceleration of an axis. Effects that depend on position are called *spring conditions*, those that depend on velocity, *damper conditions*, and those that depend on acceleration, *inertia conditions*.

A condition effect varies in proportion to the difference between an axis value (position, velocity, or acceleration, depending on the condition type) and a neutral value. You can use different scaling values for positive and negative differences, and a deadband (where no force is present) is supported.

Structure Declaration

```
typedef struct DICONDITION {
    LONG lOffset;
    LONG lPositiveCoefficient;
    LONG lNegativeCoefficient;
    DWORD dwPositiveSaturation;
    DWORD dwNegativeSaturation;
    LONG lDeadBand;
} DICONDITION, *LPDICONDITION;

typedef const DICONDITION *LPCDICONDITION;
```

Member	Description
lOffset	The neutral axis value, in the range of -10,000 to 10,000.
lPositiveCoefficient	The scaling factor applied to positive differences, in the range of -10,000 to 10,000. Devices that do not support different scaling factors for positive and negative differences use the positive scaling factor for both.

(continued)

DICONDITION *(continued)*

Member	Description
lNegativeCoefficient	The scaling factor applied to negative differences, in the range of -10,000 to 10,000. Devices that do not support negative scaling factors will use the positive scaling factor instead.
dwPositiveSaturation	The maximum saturation for positive differences, in the range of 0 to 10,000. Forces equal to or above this value are adjusted to 10,000.
dwNegativeSaturation	The maximum saturation for negative differences, in the range of 0 to 10,000. Forces equal to or above this value are adjusted to 10,000.
lDeadBand	The deadband region, from 0 to 10,000, centered on **lOffset**.

DICONSTANTFORCE

Structure Description

This structure describes a constant force.

Structure Declaration

```
typedef struct DICONSTANTFORCE {
    LONG lMagnitude;
} DICONSTANTFORCE, *LPDICONSTANTFORCE;

typedef const DICONSTANTFORCE *LPCDICONSTANTFORCE;
```

Member	Description
lMagnitude	The magnitude of the force, in the range of -10,000 to 10,000.

DICUSTOMFORCE

Structure Description

The structure describes a custom force, defined by an array of force magnitudes.

Structure Declaration

```
typedef struct DICUSTOMFORCE {
    DWORD cChannels;
    DWORD dwSamplePeriod;
    DWORD cSamples;
    LPLONG rglForceData;
} DICUSTOMFORCE, *LPDICUSTOMFORCE;

typedef const DICUSTOMFORCE *LPCDICUSTOMFORCE;
```

(continued)

DICUSTOMFORCE *(continued)*

Member	Description
cChannels	The number of axes to which this effect applies. This member should be set to 1 if the effect is being rotated.
dwSamplePeriod	The sample period, specified in microseconds (1/1,000,000 of a second).
cSamples	The number of samples in the **rglForceData** array.
rglForceData	An array of samples that designate the force magnitudes to be applied to the axes. Each sample, which ranges from -10,000 to 10,000, is applied to the axes for an amount of time given by **dwSamplePeriod**
	If more than one axis is specified by **cChannels**, then the samples are interleaved. For example, in the case of two axes, the order of the data would be as follows: Sample 1 for the first axis, Sample 1 for the second axis, Sample 2 for the first axis, Sample 2 for the second axis, and so on.

DIDATAFORMAT

Structure Description

This structure describes a device's data format.

Structure Declaration

```
typedef struct DIDATAFORMAT {
    DWORD dwSize;
    DWORD dwObjSize;
    DWORD dwFlags;
    DWORD dwDataSize;
    DWORD dwNumObjs;
    LPDIOBJECTDATAFORMAT rgodf;
} DIDATAFORMAT, *LPDIDATAFORMAT;

typedef const DIDATAFORMAT *LPCDIDATAFORMAT;
```

Member	Description
dwSize	The size of the structure, in bytes. This member must be initialized before the structure is used.
dwObjSize	The size of the **DIOBJECTDATAFORMAT** structure, in bytes.
dwFlags	Describes additional attributes of the device's data format. This member can be 0, or one of the following flags:
	• **DIDF_ABSAXIS**—Axes described by the data format are in absolute mode.
	• **DIDF_RELAXIS**—Axes described by the data format are in relative mode.

(continued)

DIDATAFORMAT (continued)

Member	Description
dwDataSize	The size of the device's data packet, in bytes. This member must be a multiple of 4 bytes and large enough to describe the offset of the last object in the data packet.
dwNumObjs	The number of **DIOBJECTDATAFORMAT** structures pointed to by the **rgdodf** array.
rgdodf	A pointer to an array of **DIOBJECTDATAFORMAT** structures. Each structure in this array specifies an object's type and location in the device's data packet.

DIDEVCAPS

Structure Description

This structure describes the capabilities of an input device.

Structure Declaration

```
typedef struct DIDEVCAPS {
    DWORD dwSize;
    DWORD dwFlags;
    DWORD dwDevType;
    DWORD dwAxes;
    DWORD dwButtons;
    DWORD dwPOVs;
    DWORD dwFFSamplePeriod;
    DWORD dwFFMinTimeResolution;
    DWORD dwFirmwareRevision;
    DWORD dwHardwareRevision;
    DWORD dwFFDriverVersion;
} DIDEVCAPS, *LPDIDEVCAPS;
```

Member	Description
dwSize	The size of the structure, in bytes. This member must be initialized before the structure can be used.
dwFlags	Describes attributes of the device. This flag can be 0, or one or more of the following flags: • **DIDC_ALIAS**—The device is another name for some other device on the system. • **DIDC_ATTACHED**—The device is physically attached to the system. • **DIDC_DEADBAND**—The device supports a dead zone for, at minimum, one force-feedback condition effect. • **DIDC_EMULATED**—The device's functionality is emulated.

DIDEVCAPS *(continued)*	
Member	**Description**
	• **DIDC_FORCEFEEDBACK**—The device is a force-feedback device.
	• **DIDC_FFFADE**—The device supports the fade parameter of an envelope.
	• **DIDC_FFATTACK**—The device supports the attack parameter of an envelope.
	• **DIDC_POLLEDDATAFORMAT**—At least one object specified in the data format must be polled.
	• **DIDC_POLLEDDEVICE**—The device has objects that must be polled.
	• **DIDC_POSNEGCOEFFICIENTS**—The device supports both positive and negative scaling factors for at least one condition effect.
	• **DIDC_POSNEGSATURATION**—The device supports both positive and negative saturation values for at least one condition effect.
	• **DIDC_PHANTOM**— The device is a phantom device—one that does not yet exist, but that has a placeholder name and may exist in the future.
	• **DIDC_SATURATION**—The device supports saturation values for at least one condition effect.
	• **DIDC_STARTDELAY**—The device supports the start delay for, at minimum, one force-feedback effect.
dwDevType	The device type and subtype information. The least significant byte of this member describes the device type. It can be one of the following flags:
	• **DIDEVTYPE_MOUSE**—Mouse device
	• **DIDEVTYPE_KEYBOARD**—Keyboard device
	• **DIDEVTYPE_JOYSTICK**—Joystick device
	• **DIDEVTYPE_DEVICE**—Other device
	The next significant byte is optional and describes the device subtype. These are some of the more common values:
	• **DIDEVTYPEMOUSE_TRADITIONAL**—Traditional mouse device. This subtype can be present only when the device type is set to **DIDEVTYPE_MOUSE**.
	• **DIDEVTYPEMOUSE_FINGERSTICK**—Fingerstick device. This subtype can be present only when the device type is set to **DIDEVTYPE_MOUSE**.

(continued)

DIDEVCAPS *(continued)*	
Member	**Description**
	• **DIDEVTYPEMOUSE_TOUCHPAD**—Touchpad device. This subtype can be present only when the device type is set to **DIDEVTYPE_MOUSE**.
	• **DIDEVTYPEMOUSE_TRACKBALL**—Trackball device. This subtype can be present only when the device type is set to **DIDEVTYPE_MOUSE**.
	• **DIDEVTYPEKEYBOARD_PCENH**—Standard 101-key keyboard. This subtype can be present only when the device type is set to **DIDEVTYPE_KEYBOARD**.
	• **DIDEVTYPEJOYSTICK_TRADITIONAL**—Traditional joystick device. This subtype can be present only when the device type is set to **DIDEVTYPE_JOYSTICK**.
	• **DIDEVTYPEJOYSTICK_FLIGHTSTICK**—Traditional joystick device. This subtype can be present only when the device type is set to **DIDEVTYPE_JOYSTICK**.
	• **DIDEVTYPEJOYSTICK_GAMEPAD**—Gamepad device. This subtype can be present only when the device type is set to **DIDEVTYPE_JOYSTICK**.
	• **DIDEVTYPEJOYSTICK_RUDDER**—Rudder device. This subtype can be present only when the device type is set to **DIDEVTYPE_JOYSTICK**.
	• **DIDEVTYPEJOYSTICK_WHEEL**—Wheel device. This subtype can be present only when the device type is set to **DIDEVTYPE_JOYSTICK**.
	• **DIDEVTYPEJOYSTICK_HEADTRACKER**—Head-tracking device. This subtype can be present only when the device type is set to **DIDEVTYPE_JOYSTICK**.
	The next significant byte can be 0 or **DIDEVTYPE_HID**, in which case the device is HID-compliant.
dwAxes	The number of axes on the device.
dwButtons	The number of buttons on the device.
dwPOVs	The number of POV controllers on the device.
dwFFSamplePeriod	The minimum sample period for playback of force-feedback effects, specified in microseconds (1/1,000,000 of a second).
dwFFMinTimeResolution	The smallest amount of time the device can resolve, specified in microseconds (1/1,000,000 of a second). All times specified at a higher resolution than this are rounded.
dwFirmwareRevision	The firmware revision of the device.
dwFFDriverVersion	The version number of the device.

DIDEVICEINSTANCE

Structure Description

This structure is used to store information about a device's identity.

Structure Declaration

```
typedef struct DIDEVICEINSTANCE {
    DWORD dwSize;
    GUID  guidInstance;
    GUID  guidProduct;
    DWORD dwDevType;
    TCHAR tszInstanceName[MAX_PATH];
    TCHAR tszProductName[MAX_PATH];
    GUID guidFFDriver;
    WORD wUsagePage;
    WORD wUsage;
} DIDEVICEINSTANCE, *LPDIDEVICEINSTANCE;

typedef const DIDEVICEINSTANCE  *LPCDIDEVICEINSTANCE;
```

Member	Description
dwSize	The size of the structure, in bytes. This member must be initialized before the structure can be used.
guidInstance	The instance GUID of the device. Instance GUIDs uniquely identify devices on a system; they are not, however, constant across different computer systems (two identical devices on two different systems will probably have different instance GUIDs).
guidProduct	The product GUID of the device. The manufacturer of the device chooses this GUID, which is constant across different computer systems.
dwDevType	The device type and subtype information. The least significant byte of this member describes the device type. It can be one of the following flags: • **DIDEVTYPE_MOUSE**—Mouse device • **DIDEVTYPE_KEYBOARD**—Keyboard device • **DIDEVTYPE_JOYSTICK**—Joystick device • **DIDEVTYPE_DEVICE**—Other device The next significant byte is optional and describes the device subtype. These are some of the more common values: • **DIDEVTYPEMOUSE_TRADITIONAL**—Traditional mouse device. This subtype can be present only when the device type is set to **DIDEVTYPE_MOUSE**. • **DIDEVTYPEMOUSE_FINGERSTICK**—Fingerstick device. This subtype can be present only when the device type is set to **DIDEVTYPE_MOUSE**.

(continued)

DIDEVICEINSTANCE *(continued)*	
Member	**Description**
	• **DIDEVTYPEMOUSE_TOUCHPAD**—Touchpad device. This subtype can be present only when the device type is set to **DIDEVTYPE_MOUSE**.
	• **DIDEVTYPEMOUSE_TRACKBALL**—Trackball device. This subtype can be present only when the device type is set to **DIDEVTYPE_MOUSE**.
	• **DIDEVTYPEKEYBOARD_PCENH**—Standard 101-key keyboard. This subtype can be present only when the device type is set to **DIDEVTYPE_KEYBOARD**.
	• **DIDEVTYPEJOYSTICK_TRADITIONAL**—Traditional joystick device. This subtype can be present only when the device type is set to **DIDEVTYPE_JOYSTICK**.
	• **DIDEVTYPEJOYSTICK_FLIGHTSTICK**—Traditional joystick device. This subtype can be present only when the device type is set to **DIDEVTYPE_JOYSTICK**.
	• **DIDEVTYPEJOYSTICK_GAMEPAD**—Gamepad device. This subtype can be present only when the device type is set to **DIDEVTYPE_JOYSTICK**.
	• **DIDEVTYPEJOYSTICK_RUDDER**—Rudder device. This subtype can be present only when the device type is set to **DIDEVTYPE_JOYSTICK**.
	• **DIDEVTYPEJOYSTICK_WHEEL**—Wheel device. This subtype can be present only when the device type is set to **DIDEVTYPE_JOYSTICK**.
	• **DIDEVTYPEJOYSTICK_HEADTRACKER**—Head-tracking device. This subtype can be present only when the device type is set to **DIDEVTYPE_JOYSTICK**. The next significant byte can be 0 or **DIDEVTYPE_HID**, in which case the device is HID-compliant.
tszInstanceName	A string designating the name of the device.
tszProductName	A string designating the product name of the device as established by the manufacturer.
guidFFDriver	The force-feedback driver GUID of the device. The manufacturer of the force-feedback device chooses this GUID, which is constant across different computer systems.
wUsagePage	The HID usage page code for HID devices. A HID device is a type of USB input device.
wUsage	The HID usage code for HID devices. A HID device is a type of USB input device.

DIDEVICEOBJECTDATA

Structure Description

This structure describes an object and its state. It can be used when receiving input from a device or when sending a command to an object.

Structure Declaration

```
typedef struct DIDEVICEOBJECTDATA {
    DWORD dwOfs;
    DWORD dwData;
    DWORD dwTimeStamp;
    DWORD dwSequence;
} DIDEVICEOBJECTDATA, *LPDIDEVICEOBJECTDATA;

typedef const DIDEVICEOBJECTDATA *LPCDIDEVICEOBJECTDATA;
```

Member	Description
dwOfs	The offset into the device's data format where the object is located. This offset is used to identify the object. See Tables 13.1 - 13.3 in Chapter 13 for the offset values for the data formats **c_dfDIKeyboard**, **c_dfDIMouse**, and **c_dfDIJoystick**.
dwData	The state of the object referred to by **dwOfs**.
dwTimeStamp	The time at which the event was generated, as measured in milliseconds from when Windows was last restarted. This value wraps around every 50 days.
	If the structure is being sent to the **IDirectInputDevice2::SendDeviceData** () function, this member should be set to 0.
dwSequence	A sequence number generated by DirectInput that can be used for chronological comparisons between two different input events. Because this value wraps around, the macro **DISEQUENCE_COMPARE** should be used to compare the two sequences.
	If the structure is being sent to the **IDirectInputDevice2::SendDeviceData** () function, this member should be set to 0.

DIDEVICEOBJECTINSTANCE

Structure Description

This structure is used to describe an instance of an object on an input device.

Structure Declaration

```
typedef struct DIDEVICEOBJECTINSTANCE {
    DWORD dwSize;
    GUID  guidType;
    DWORD dwOfs;
    DWORD dwType;
    DWORD dwFlags;
    TCHAR tszName[MAX_PATH];
    DWORD dwFFMaxForce;
    DWORD dwFFForceResolution;
    WORD wCollectionNumber;
    WORD wDesignatorIndex;
    WORD wUsagePage;
    WORD wUsage;
    DWORD dwDimension;
    WORD wExponent;
    WORD wReserved;
} DIDEVICEOBJECTINSTANCE, *LPDIDEVICEOBJECTINSTANCE;

typedef const DIDEVICEOBJECTINSTANCE *LPCDIDEVICEOBJECTINSTANCE;
```

Member	Description
dwSize	The size of the structure, in bytes. This member must be initialized before the structure can be used.
guidType	A GUID that identifies the class to which the object belongs. This can be one of the following values: • **GUID_XAxis**—The *x*-axis • **GUID_YAxis**—The *y*-axis • **GUID_ZAxis**—The *z*-axis • **GUID_RxAxis**—The rotational *x*-axis • **GUID_RyAxis**—The rotational *y*-axis • **GUID_RzAxis**—The rotational *z*-axis • **GUID_Slider**—A slider • **GUID_Button**—A button • **GUID_Key**—A key • **GUID_POV**—A POV controller • **GUID_Unknown**—An unknown object type
dwOfs	The offset into the device's data format where the object resides. This is used to identify the object.

(continued)

DIDEVICEOBJECTINSTANCE (continued)

Member	Description
dwType	Describes the object type. This member can be one or more of the following flags:
	• **DIDFT_ABSAXIS**—An absolute axis.
	• **DIDFT_AXIS**—An axis, whether relative or absolute.
	• **DIDFT_BUTTON**—A push- or toggle button.
	• **DIDFT_COLLECTION**—An object that belongs to an HID collection.
	• **DIDFT_FFACTUATOR**—An object that has a force-feedback actuator. Forces can be applied to this object.
	• **DIDFT_FFEFFECTTRIGGER**—An object that can be used to trigger force-feedback effects. Buttons, for example, can often trigger the playback of a force-feedback effect.
	• **DIDFT_NOCOLLECTION**—An object that does not belong to any HID link collection.
	• **DIDFT_NODATA**—An object that does not produce data.
	• **DIDFT_OUTPUT**—An output object, to which data can be sent.
	• **DIDFT_PSHBUTTON**—A pushbutton.
	• **DIDFT_RELAXIS**—A relative axis.
	• **DIDFT_TGLBUTTON**—A toggle button.
dwFlags	Describes additional attributes of the object. This member can be one or more of the following flags:
	• **DIDOI_ASPECTACCEL**—The object reports acceleration information.
	• **DIDOI_ASPECTFORCE**—The object reports force information.
	• **DIDOI_ASPECTPOSITION**—The object reports position information.
	• **DIDOI_ASPECTVELOCITY**—The object reports velocity information.
	• **DIDOI_FFACTUATOR**—The object contains a force-feedback actuator and can have effects applied to it.
	• **DIDOI_FEFFECTTRIGGER**—The object can trigger the playback of force-feedback effects.
	• **DIDOI_POLLED**—The object is polled, not event-driven.
tszName	A string designating the name of the object.

(continued)

DIDEVICEOBJECTINSTANCE *(continued)*

Member	Description
dwFFMaxForce	The maximum force the object's force-feedback actuator can apply, in newtons.
dwFFForceResolution	The resolution of the object's force-feedback actuator. If the actuator can apply all forces, from 0 to the maximum force (typically 10,000), then this member will be 0.
wCollectionNumber	The HID link collection the object belongs to.
wDesignatorIndex	The object's designator in the HID physical descriptor.
wUsagePage	The object's HID usage page.
wUsage	The object's HID usage.
dwDimension	The dimensional units the object's value is reported in, or 0 if this information is not known.
wExponent	The exponent to associate with the dimension, or 0 if this information is not unknown.
wReserved	This member is reserved for future use.

DIEFFECT

Structure Description

This structure describes a force-feedback effect.

Structure Declaration

```
typedef struct DIEFFECT {
    DWORD dwSize;
    DWORD dwFlags;
    DWORD dwDuration;
    DWORD dwSamplePeriod;
    DWORD dwGain;
    DWORD dwTriggerButton;
    DWORD dwTriggerRepeatInterval;
    DWORD cAxes;
    LPDWORD rgdwAxes;
    LPLONG rglDirection;
    LPDIENVELOPE lpEnvelope;
    DWORD cbTypeSpecificParams;
    LPVOID lpvTypeSpecificParams;
} DIEFFECT, *LPDIEFFECT;

typedef const DIEFFECT *LPCDIEFFECT;
```

(continued)

DIEFFECT *(continued)*

Member	Description
dwSize	The size of this structure, in bytes. This member must be initialized before the structure can be used.
dwFlags	Describes some attributes of the effect. This member can be one or more of the following flags:
	• **DIEFF_CARTESIAN**—The **rglDirection** member contains Cartesian coordinate information. When this flag is specified, the effect can be applied to any number of axes.
	• **DIEFF_OBJECTIDS**—The **dwTriggerButton** and **rgdwAxes** members are identified by their type identifiers, as retrieved by **IDirectInputDevice2::EnumObjects** () in the **dwType** member of the **DIDEVICEOBJECTINSTANCE** structure.
	• **DIEFF_OBJECTOFFSETS**—The **dwTriggerButton** and **rgdwAxes** members are identified by their offsets into the device's data format.
	• **DIEFF_POLAR**—The **rglDirection** member contains polar coordinates. When this flag is specified, the effect should be applied to exactly two axes.
	• **DIEFF_SPHERICAL**—The **rglDirection** member contains spherical coordinates. When this flag is specified, the effect should be applied to three or more axes.
dwDuration	The duration of the effect, specified in microseconds (1/1,000,000 of a second), or **INFINITE**, in which case the effect plays until stopped. If this member is **INFINITE**, then the fade parameter of any envelope applied to the effect is ignored.
dwSamplePeriod	The sample period, specified in microseconds (1/1,000,000 of a second).
dwGain	The effect's gain. A value of 0 indicates force-feedback effects are reduced by 100 percent, and a value of 10,000 indicates no reduction. A value of 7,000 would indicate a 30-percent reduction.
dwTriggerButton	The button object that should trigger playback of the force-feedback effect. The object is identified by its type identifier (if **dwFlags** includes **DIEFF_OBJECTIDS**) or its position in the device's data format (if **dwFlags** includes **DIEFF_OBJECTOFFSETS**). This member may be 0 if this feature is not desired.
dwTriggerRepeatInterval	The minimum duration between each playback of the effect triggered by the **dwTriggerButton** member, or **INFINITE** if the effect should be played only once, the first time the button is pressed.
cAxes	The number of axes the effect applies to. The maximum value for this member is 32.

(continued)

DIEFFECT *(continued)*	
Member	**Description**
rgdwAxes	A pointer to an array of 32-bit unsigned integers. Each integer identifies an axis to which the affect applies, either by the axis' type identifier or by its offset into the device's data format, depending on the value of **dwFlags**.
rglDirection	An array of 32-bit signed integers, with exactly one element for each axis specified by **rgdwAxes**. The array describes the direction from which the effect comes. The precise content of the array depends on which of the following three flags are included in **dwFlags**:
	• **DIEFF_CARTESIAN**—The array is a Cartesian coordinate that describes the direction of the force. Each element in the array corresponds to one coordinate. For example, if **cAxes** is 2, then the content of the array for a north force would be { 0, -1 }, the first element typically representing the component of the force on the x axis, and the second element typically representing the component of the force on the y axis.
	• **DIEFF_POLAR**—The first element in the array indicates the direction of the force in polar coordinates, measured clockwise in hundredths of a degree from north. The last element in the array is set to 0. For example, the content of the array for a south force would be { 180 • 1000, 0 }.
	• **DIEFF_SPHERICAL**—The first element in the array indicates the direction of the force in the x-y plane, measured in hundredths of a degree from the (1, 0) direction toward the (0, 1) direction. The second element in the array indicates the direction of the force in the x-z plane, measured in hundredths of a degree from the (1, 0, 0) direction toward the (0, 0, 1) direction. The last element in the array is set to 0.
lpEnvelope	A pointer to a **DIENVELOPE** structure that identifies the envelope to be applied to the effect. This may be **NULL** if no envelope is desired.
cbTypeSpecificParams	The number of bytes pointed to by the **lpvTypeSpecificParams** member.
lpvTypeSpecificParams	A pointer to data that describes parameters of the effect that depend on the effect's type.
	For condition effects (identified with the **DIEFT_CONDITION** flag), the pointer should be set to an array of **DICONDITION** structures, one for each axis the effect is being applied to. A single **DICONDITION** structure can be used for all axes if the effect is not being rotated.
	For custom effects (identified with the **DIEFT_CUSTOMFORCE** flag), the pointer should be set to a **DICUSTOMFORCE** structure.

(continued)

DIEFFECT *(continued)*	
Member	**Description**
	For periodic effects (identified with the **DIEFT_PERIODIC** flag), the pointer should be set to a **DIPERIODIC** structure.
	For ramp effects (identified with the **DIEFT_RAMPFORCE** flag), the pointer should be set to a **DIRAMPFORCE** structure.
	For constant effects (identified by the **DIEFT_CONSTANT** flag), the pointer should be set to a **DICONSTANTFORCE** structure).
dwStartDelay	The time, in microseconds, that the device should wait for after the IDirectInputEffect::Start<mk:@MSITStore:C\mssdk\doc\DirectX7\directx.chm::/devdoc/live/directx/diref_4b04.htm>() function has been called before playing a force-feedback effect. This may be 0, in chich case playback begins immediately after the function is called.

DIEFFECTINFO

Structure Description

This structure is used to describe a force-feedback effect.

Structure Declaration

```
typedef struct DIEFFECTINFO {
    DWORD dwSize;
    GUID guid;
    DWORD dwEffType;
    DWORD dwStaticParams;
    DWORD dwDynamicParams;
    TCHAR tszName[MAX_PATH];
} DIEFFECTINFO, *LPDIEFFECTINFO;


typedef const DIEFFECTINFO  *LPCDIEFFECTINFO;
```

Member	**Description**
dwSize	The size of this structure, in bytes. This member must be initialized before the structure can be used.
guid	The GUID for the effect.
dwEffType	Describes the effect type. The least significant byte of this member may be 0, or one or more of the following flags:
	• **DIEFT_ALL**—All effects. This flag may be used only when the structure is being sent to **IDirectInputDevice2::EnumEffects** ().
	• **DIEFT_CONDITION**—The effect is a condition effect.
	• **DIEFT_CONSTANTFORCE**—The effect is a constant force effect.

(continued)

DIEFFECTINFO (continued)	
Member	**Description**
	• **DIEFT_CUSTOMFORCE**—The effect is a custom force effect.
	• **DIEFT_DEADBAND**—The deadband for the condition effect, supported by the effect generator.
	• **DIEFT_FFATTACK**—The attack parameters of an envelope can be applied to the effect.
	• **DIEFT_FFFADE**—The fade parameters of an envelope can be applied to the effect.
	• **DIEFT_HARDWARE**—The effect is hardware-specific.
	• **DIEFT_PERIODIC**—The effect is periodic.
	• **DIEFT_POSNEGCOEFFICIENTS**—The positive and negative scaling-factor parameters for the condition are supported by the effect generator.
	• **DIEFT_POSNEGSATURATION**—The positive and negative saturation parameters for the condition are supported by the effect generator.
	• **DIEFT_RAMPFORCE**—The effect is a ramp effect.
	• **DIEFT_SATURATION**—Saturation for the condition is supported by the effect generator.
dwStaticParams	Describes the parameters supported by the effect. This member can be 0, or one or more of the following flags:
	• **DIEP_ALLPARAMS**—All parameters are supported by the effect.
	• **DIEP_ALLPARAMS_DX5**—All parameters as of DirectX 5 are supported by the effect.
	• **DIEP_AXES**—The **cAxes** and **rgdwAxes** members of the **DIEFFECT** structure are supported by the effect.
	• **DIEP_DIRECTION**—The **cAxes** and **rglDirection** members of the **DIEFFECT** structure are supported by the effect.
	• **DIEP_DURATION**—The **dwDuration** member of the **DIEFFECT** structure is supported by the effect.
	• **DIEP_ENVELOPE**—The **lpEnvelope** member of the **DIEFFECT** structure is supported by the effect.
	• **DIEP_GAIN**—The **dwGain** member of the **DIEFFECT** structure is supported by the effect.
	• **DIEP_SAMPLEPERIOD**—The **dwSamplePeriod** member of the **DIEFFECT** structure is supported by the effect.

(continued)

DIEFFECTINFO *(continued)*

Member	Description
	• **DIEP_TRIGGERBUTTON**—The **dwTriggerButton** member of the **DIEFFECT** structure is supported by the effect.
	• **DIEP_TRIGGERREPEATINTERVAL**—The **dwTriggerRepeatInterval** member of the **DIEFFECT** structure is supported by the effect.
	• **DIEP_TYPESPECIFICPARAMS**—The **lpvTypeSpecificParams** member of the **DIEFFECT** structure is supported by the effect.
dwDynamicParams	Describes the parameters supported by the effect that can be changed while the effect is playing. This member can be 0, or one or more of the following flags:
	• **DIEP_ALLPARAMS**—All parameters can be modified while the effect is playing.
	• **DIEP_ALLPARAMS_DX5**—All parameters as of DirectX 5 can be modified while the effect is playing.
	• **DIEP_AXES**—The **cAxes** and **rgdwAxes** members of the **DIEFFECT** structure can be modified while the effect is playing.
	• **DIEP_DIRECTION**—The **cAxes** and **rglDirection** members of the **DIEFFECT** structure can be modified while the effect is playing.
	• **DIEP_DURATION**—The **dwDuration** member of the **DIEFFECT** structure can be modified while the effect is playing.
	• **DIEP_ENVELOPE**—The **lpEnvelope** member of the **DIEFFECT** structure can be modified while the effect is playing.
	• **DIEP_GAIN**—The **dwGain** member of the **DIEFFECT** structure can be modified while the effect is playing.
	• **DIEP_SAMPLEPERIOD**—The **dwSamplePeriod** member of the **DIEFFECT** structure can be modified while the effect is playing.
	• **DIEP_TRIGGERBUTTON**—The **dwTriggerButton** member of the **DIEFFECT** structure can be modified while the effect is playing.
	• **DIEP_TRIGGERREPEATINTERVAL**—The **dwTriggerRepeatInterval** member of the **DIEFFECT** structure can be modified while the effect is playing.
	• **DIEP_TYPESPECIFICPARAMS**—The **lpvTypeSpecificParams** member of the **DIEFFECT** structure can be modified while the effect is playing.
tszName	A string designating the name of the effect, such as "Constant force" or "Custom force".

DIEFFESCAPE

Structure Description

This structure is used to send a command directly to an input device.

Structure Declaration

```
typedef struct DIEFFESCAPE {
    DWORD dwSize;
    DWORD dwCommand;
    LPVOID lpvInBuffer;
    DWORD cbInBuffer;
    LPVOID lpvOutBuffer;
    DWORD cbOutBuffer;
} DIEFFESCAPE, *LPDIEFFESCAPE;
```

Member	Description
dwSize	The size of this structure, in bytes. This member must be initialized before the structure can be used.
dwCommand	The command to be sent to the input device.
lpvInBuffer	The address of a buffer to be sent to the device.
cbInBuffer	The size of the buffer pointed to by **lpvInBuffer**, in bytes.
lpvOutBuffer	The address of a buffer to receive information from the device.
cbOutBuffer	The size of the buffer pointed to by **lpvOutBuffer**, in bytes. When the function returns, this member will be set to the number of bytes actually written to the buffer.

DIENVELOPE

Structure Description

This structure describes an envelope. Envelopes can be applied to force-feedback effects to change the way they start and end. Envelopes consist of an *attack*, where the amplitude starts at a value specified by the envelope and ends at the effect's true amplitude; a *sustain*, where the true amplitude of the effect is played; and a *fade*, where the amplitude starts at the effect's true amplitude and ends at a value specified by the envelope.

Structure Declaration

```
typedef struct DIENVELOPE {
    DWORD dwSize;
    DWORD dwAttackLevel;
    DWORD dwAttackTime;
    DWORD dwFadeLevel;
    DWORD dwFadeTime;
} DIENVELOPE, *LPDIENVELOPE;

typedef const DIENVELOPE *LPCDIENVELOPE;
```

(continued)

DIENVELOPE (continued)

Member	Description
dwSize	The size of this structure, in bytes. This member must be initialized before the structure can be used.
dwAttackLevel	The amplitude of the attack value, in the range of 0 to 10,000. This is measured relative to the effect's baseline, or 0 if the effect does not have a baseline.
dwAttackTime	The duration of the attack, specified in microseconds (1/1,000,000 of a second).
dwFadeLevel	The amplitude of the fade value, in the range of 0 to 10,000. This is measured relative to the effect's baseline, or 0 if the effect does not have a baseline.
dwFadeTime	The duration of the fade, specified in microseconds (1/1,000,000 of a second).

DIJOYSTATE

Structure Description

This structure is used to retrieve the state of a joystick whose data format is set to **c_dfDIJoystick**.

Structure Declaration

```
typedef struct DIJOYSTATE {
    LONG    lX;
    LONG    lY;
    LONG    lZ;
    LONG    lRx;
    LONG    lRy;
    LONG    lRz;
    LONG    rglSlider[2];
    DWORD   rgdwPOV[4];
    BYTE    rgbButtons[32];
} DIJOYSTATE, *LPDIJOYSTATE;
```

Member	Description
lX	The horizontal movement of the joystick. This can be relative to the last horizontal position or absolute, depending on the axis mode. You can determine the range of this axis by calling the **IDirectInputDevice2::GetProperty** () function.
lY	The vertical movement of the joystick. This can be relative to the last vertical position or absolute, depending on the axis mode. You can determine the range of this axis by calling the **IDirectInputDevice2::GetProperty** () function.
lZ	The movement of the joystick's z-axis, usually a throttle control. This can be relative to the last position or absolute, depending on the axis mode. You can determine the range of this axis by calling the **IDirectInputDevice2::GetProperty** () function.

(continued)

DIJOYSTATE *(continued)*

Member	Description
lRx	The rotation of the joystick's x-axis. This can be relative to the last x-rotation or absolute, depending on the axis mode. You can determine the range of this axis calling the **IDirectInput-Device2::GetProperty** () function.
lRy	The rotation of the joystick's y axis. This can be relative to the last y rotation or absolute, depending on the axis mode. You can determine the range of this axis by calling the **IDirectInput-Device2::GetProperty** () function.
lRz	The rotation of the joystick's z-axis, usually a rudder control. This can be relative to the last z-rotation or absolute, depending on the axis mode. You can determine the range of this axis by calling the **IDirectInputDevice2::GetProperty** () function.
rglSlider	The state of up to two joystick sliders, each represented by a 32-bit signed integer. You can determine the range of the sliders by calling the **IDirectInputDevice2::GetProperty** () function.
rgdwPOV	The state of up to four POV controls, each represented by a 32-bit unsigned integer. In a neutral position, the least significant 16 bits of this integer will be set to 0xFFFF. Otherwise, the integer will contain the direction of the POV control in hundredths of a degree clockwise from north.
rgbButtons	The state of up to 32 joystick buttons, represented by one byte per button. The high bit of the byte is 1 if the button is down, or 0 otherwise.

DIJOYSTATE2

Structure Description

This structure is used to retrieve the state of a joystick whose data format is set to **c_dfDIJoystick2**.

Structure Declaration

```
typedef struct DIJOYSTATE2 {
    LONG    lX;
    LONG    lY;
    LONG    lZ;
    LONG    lRx;
    LONG    lRy;
    LONG    lRz;
    LONG    rglSlider[2];
    DWORD   rgdwPOV[4];
    BYTE    rgbButtons[128];
    LONG    lVX;
    LONG    lVY;
```

(continued)

DIJOYSTATE2 *(continued)*

Structure Declaration

```
LONG    lVZ;
    LONG    lVRx;
    LONG    lVRy;
    LONG    lVRz;
    LONG    rglVSlider[2];
    LONG    lAX;
    LONG    lAY;
    LONG    lAZ;
    LONG    lARx;
    LONG    lARy;
    LONG    lARz;
    LONG    rglASlider[2];
    LONG    lFX;
    LONG    lFY;
    LONG    lFZ;
    LONG    lFRx;
    LONG    lFRy;
    LONG    lFRz;
    LONG    rglFSlider[2];
} DIJOYSTATE2, *LPDIJOYSTATE2;
```

Member	Description
lX	The horizontal movement of the joystick. This can be relative to the last horizontal position or absolute, depending on the axis mode. You can determine the range of this axis by calling the **IDirectInputDevice2::GetProperty** () function.
lY	The vertical movement of the joystick. This can be relative to the last vertical position or absolute, depending on the axis mode. You can determine the range of this axis by calling the **IDirectInputDevice2::GetProperty** () function.
lZ	The movement of the joystick's *z*-axis, usually a throttle control. This can be relative to the last position or absolute, depending on the axis mode. You can determine the range of this axis by calling the **IDirectInputDevice2::GetProperty** () function.
lRx	The rotation of the joystick's *x*-axis. This can be relative to the last *x*-rotation or absolute, depending on the axis mode. You can determine the range of this axis by calling the **IDirectInputDevice2::GetProperty** () function.
lRy	The rotation of the joystick's *y*-axis. This can be relative to the last *y*-rotation or absolute, depending on the axis mode. You can determine the range of this axis by calling the **IDirectInput-Device2::GetProperty** () function.

(continued)

Member	Description
lRz	The rotation of the joystick's z-axis, usually a rudder control. This can be relative to the last z-rotation or absolute, depending on the axis mode. You can determine the range of this axis by calling the **IDirectInputDevice2::GetProperty** () function.
rglSlider	The state of up to two joystick sliders, each represented by a 32-bit signed integer. You can determine the range of the sliders by calling the **IDirectInputDevice2::GetProperty** () function.
rgdwPOV	The state of up to four POV controls, each represented by a 32-bit unsigned integer. In a neutral position, the least significant 16 bits of this integer will be set to 0xFFFF. Otherwise, the integer will contain the direction of the POV control in hundredths of a degree clockwise from north.
rgbButtons	The state of up to 128 joystick buttons, represented by one byte per button. The high bit of the byte is 1 if the button is down, or 0 otherwise.
lVX	The joystick's velocity for the x-axis. You can determine the range of this axis by calling the **IDirectInputDevice2::GetProperty** () function.
lVY	The joystick's velocity for the y-axis. You can determine the range of this axis by calling the **IDirectInputDevice2::-GetProperty** () function.
lVZ	The joystick's velocity for the z-axis. You can determine the range of this axis by calling the **IDirectInputDevice2::-GetProperty** () function.
lVRx	The joystick's angular velocity for the x-axis. You can determine the range of this axis by calling the**IDirectInputDevice2::-GetProperty** () function.
lVRy	The joystick's angular velocity for the y-axis. You can determine the range of this axis by calling the **IDirectInputDevice2::-GetProperty** () function.
lVRz	The joystick's angular velocity for the z-axis. You can determine the range of this axis by calling the **IDirectInputDevice2::-GetProperty** () function.
rglVSlider	The state of up to two joystick sliders that contain additional velocity information, each represented by a 32-bit signed integer. You can determine the range of the sliders by calling the **IDirectInputDevice2::GetProperty** () function.
lAX	The joystick's acceleration for the x-axis. You can determine the range of this axis by calling the **IDirectInputDevice2::-GetProperty** () function.
lAY	The joystick's acceleration for the y-axis. You can determine the range of this axis by calling the **IDirectInputDevice2::-GetProperty** () function.

(continued)

DIJOYSTATE2 *(continued)*	
Member	**Description**
lAZ	The joystick's acceleration for the *z*-axis. You can determine the range of this axis by calling the **IDirectInputDevice2::-GetProperty** () function.
lARx	The joystick's angular acceleration for the *x*-axis. You can determine the range of this axis by calling the **IDirectInputDevice2::GetProperty** () function.
lARy	The joystick's angular acceleration for the *y*-axis. You can determine the range of this axis by calling the **IDirectInputDevice2::GetProperty** () function.
lARz	The joystick's angular acceleration for the *z*-axis. You can determine the range of this axis by calling the **IDirectInputDevice2::GetProperty** () function.
rglASlider	The state of up to two joystick sliders that contain additional acceleration information, each represented by a 32-bit signed integer. You can determine the range of the sliders by calling the **IDirectInputDevice2::GetProperty** () function.
lFX	The joystick's force for the *x*-axis. You can determine the range of this axis by calling the **IDirectInputDevice2::GetProperty** () function.
lFY	The joystick's force for the *y*-axis. You can determine the range of this axis by calling the **IDirectInputDevice2::GetProperty** () function.
lFZ	The joystick's force for the *z*-axis. You can determine the range of this axis by calling the **IDirectInputDevice2::GetProperty** () function.
lFRx	The joystick's angular force (torque) for the *x*-axis. You can determine the range of this axis by calling the **IDirectInput-Device2::GetProperty** () function.
lFRy	The joystick's angular force (torque) for the *y*-axis. You can determine the range of this axis by calling the **IDirectInput-Device2::GetProperty** () function.
lFRz	The joystick's angular force (torque) for the *z*-axis. You can determine the range of this axis by calling the **IDirectInput-Device2::GetProperty** () function.
rglFSlider	The state of up to two joystick sliders that contain additional force information, each represented by a 32-bit signed integer. You can determine the range of the sliders by calling the **IDirectInputDevice2::GetProperty** () function.

DIMOUSESTATE

Structure Description

This structure is used to retrieve the state of a mouse, whose data format is set to **c_dfDIMouse**.

Structure Declaration

```
typedef struct DIMOUSESTATE {
    LONG lX;
    LONG lY;
    LONG lZ;
    BYTE rgbButtons[4];
} DIMOUSESTATE, *LPDIMOUSESTATE;
```

Member	Description
lX	The horizontal movement of the mouse, in mickeys (*mickeys* are the unit of movement reported by the mouse driver and are not equivalent to pixels). This can be relative to the last horizontal position or absolute, depending on the axis mode.
lY	The vertical movement of the mouse, in mickeys. This can be relative to the last vertical position or absolute, depending on the axis mode.
lZ	The movement of the mouse wheel. This can be relative to the last wheel position or absolute, depending on the axis mode.
rgbButtons	The state of each of the mouse's buttons, represented by one byte per button. The high bit of the byte is 1 if the button is down, or 0 otherwise.

DIMOUSESTATE2

Structure Description

This structure is used to retrieve the state of a mouse, whose data format is set to **c_dfDIMouse2**.

Structure Declaration

```
typedef struct DIMOUSESTATE2 {
    LONG lX;
    LONG lY;
    LONG lZ;
    BYTE rgbButtons[8];
} DIMOUSESTATE2, *LPDIMOUSESTATE2;
```

Member	Description
lX	The horizontal movement of the mouse, in mickeys (*mickeys* are the unit of movement reported by the mouse driver and are not equivalent to pixels). This can be relative to the last horizontal position or absolute, depending on the axis mode.
lY	The vertical movement of the mouse, in mickeys. This can be relative to the last vertical position or absolute, depending on the axis mode.

(continued)

DIMOUSESTATE2 *(continued)*

Member	Description
lZ	The movement of the mouse wheel. This can be relative to the last wheel position or absolute, depending on the axis mode.
rgbButtons	The state of each of the mouse's buttons, represented by one byte per button. The high bit of the byte is 1 if the button is down, or 0 otherwise.

DIOBJECTDATAFORMAT

Structure Description
This structure describes the data format of an object on an input device.

Structure Declaration

```
typedef struct DIOBJECTDATAFORMAT {
    const GUID * pguid;
    DWORD       dwOfs;
    DWORD       dwType;
    DWORD       dwFlags;
} DIOBJECTDATAFORMAT, *LPDIOBJECTDATAFORMAT;


typedef const DIOBJECTDATAFORMAT *LPCDIOBJECTDATAFORMAT;
```

Member	Description
pguid	A pointer to a GUID that identifies the object. This member may be **NULL**, in which case any object is allowed.
dwOfs	The offset into the device's data packet, where the object is stored.
dwType	This member is a combination of the object instance and the object type. The middle 16 bits of this member indicate the object instance (from 0 to the number of objects of this type on the device). The object type can be one or more of the following flags: • **DIDFT_ABSAXIS**—An absolute axis. • **DIDFT_AXIS**—Any axis, whether relative or absolute. • **DIDFT_BUTTON**—A push- or toggle button. • **DIDFT_FFACTUATOR**—An object that has force-feedback actuators. Forces can be applied to this object. • **DIDFT_FFEFFECTTRIGGER**—An object that can be used to trigger force-feedback effects. Buttons, for example, can often trigger the playback of a force-feedback effect. • **DIDFT_POV**—A POV controller. • **DIDFT_PSHBUTTON**—A pushbutton.

(continued)

DIOBJECTDATAFORMAT *(continued)*	
Member	**Description**
dwFlags	• **DIDFT_RELAXIS**—A relative axis.
	• **DIDFT_TGLBUTTON**—A toggle button.
	Describes additional information about the object. This member can be 0, or one or more of the following flags:
	DIDOI_ASPECTACCEL—The object must report acceleration information.
	DIDOI_ASPECTFORCE—The object must report force information.
	DIDOI_ASPECTPOSITION—The object must report position information.
	DIDOI_ASPECTVELOCITY—The object must report velocity information.

DIPERIODIC

Structure Description

This structure describes a periodic force-feedback effect.

Structure Declaration

```
typedef struct DIPERIODIC {
    DWORD dwMagnitude;
    LONG lOffset;
    DWORD dwPhase;
    DWORD dwPeriod;
} DIPERIODIC, *LPDIPERIODIC;

typedef const DIPERIODIC *LPCDIPERIODIC;
```

Member	**Description**
dwMagnitude	The magnitude of the effect, in the range of 0 to 10,000. If an envelope is being applied to the effect, then this member describes the magnitude of the envelope's sustain parameter. Otherwise, the member describes the magnitude of the entire effect.
lOffset	The offset of the effect. All force-feedback magnitudes will be offset by this amount, and any envelope uses this as its baseline.
dwPhase	The position in the cycle of the period effect where playback should begin. Unsupported positions are rounded to the nearest supported values.
dwPeriod	The period of the effect, specified in microseconds (1/1,000,000 of a second).

DIPROPDWORD

Structure Description

This structure describes a 32-bit integer property of either an input device or one of its objects.

Structure Declaration

```
typedef struct DIPROPDWORD {
    DIPROPHEADER    diph;
    DWORD           dwData;
} DIPROPDWORD, *LPDIPROPDWORD;

typedef const DIPROPDWORD *LPCDIPROPDWORD;
```

Member	Description
diph	A **DIPROPHEADER** structure that specifies an object or the input device itself.
dwData	The data of the property. The value of this member depends on the property being set or retrieved.

DIPROPHEADER

Structure Description

This structure identifies an object or the input device itself. It is the first member in all property structures, such as **DIPROPRANGE** and **DIPROPDWORD**.

Structure Declaration

```
typedef struct DIPROPHEADER {
    DWORD    dwSize;
    DWORD    dwHeaderSize;
    DWORD    dwObj;
    DWORD    dwHow;
} DIPROPHEADER, *LPDIPROPHEADER;

typedef const DIPROPHEADER *LPCDIPROPHEADER;
```

Member	Description
dwSize	The size of the enclosing structure (the structure in which this structure is located), in bytes. This member must be initialized before the structure can be used.
dwHeaderSize	The size of this structure, in bytes. This member must be initialized before the structure can be used.
dwObj	The object being identified, or 0 if **dwHow** is set to **DIPH_DEVICE**. The object can be identified either by its offset into the device's data format or by its type identifier, depending on the value of **dwHow**.

(continued)

DIPROPHEADER *(continued)*	
Member	**Description**
dwHow	Describes how the object is identified. This member can be one of the following values:
	• **DIPH_BYID**—The object specified by **dwObj** is identified by its type identifier, as retrieved by **IDirectInputDevice2::-EnumObjects** () in the **dwType** member of the **DIDEVICE-OBJECTINSTANCE** structure.
	• **DIPH_BYOFFSET**—The object specified by **dwObj** is identified by its offset into the device's data format, measured in bytes.
	• **DIPH_DEVICE**—The enclosing structure describes a property of the input device itself, not one of its objects.

DIPROPRANGE

Structure Description

This structure describes the range of an object.

Structure Declaration

```
typedef struct DIPROPRANGE {
    DIPROPHEADER diph;
    LONG         lMin;
    LONG         lMax;
} DIPROPRANGE, *LPDIPROPRANGE;

typedef const DIPROPRANGE *LPCDIPROPRANGE;
```

Member	**Description**
diph	Identifies the object.
lMin	The minimum value for the object, or **DIPROPRANGE_NOMIN** if the object has no minimum value.
lMax	The maximum value for the object, or **DIPROPRANGE_NOMAX** if the object has no maximum value.

DIPROPSTRING

Structure Description

This structure is used to describe string properties.

Structure Declaration

```
typedef struct{
DIPROPHEADER diph;
WCHAR wsz;

}DIPROPSTRING;
```

Member	Description
diph	A pointer to a **DIPROPHEADER** structure that identifies the object or device itself.
wsz	The string property in Unicode format.

DIRAMPFORCE

Structure Description

This structure describes a ramp force-feedback effect.

Structure Declaration

```
typedef struct DIPROPRANGE {
    LONG lStart;
    LONG lEnd;
} DIRAMPFORCE, *LPDIRAMPFORCE;

typedef const DIRAMPFORCE *LPCDIRAMPFORCE;
```

Member	Description
lStart	The magnitude of the force when it starts, in the range of -10,000 to 10,000.
lEnd	The magnitude of the force when it ends, in the range of -10,000 to 10,000.

PART IV

TRIG, POINTS, AND VECTORS

Appendix E
Points And Vectors

Geometry, mathematics, and physics—the principles, theorems, and equations in these fields provide the sturdy foundation on which all three-dimensional games are built. Geometry gives objects their virtual existence, and mathematics makes those objects visible and, through physics, gives them motion and lets them interact realistically. This appendix covers two concepts extremely important for all three fields: points and vectors.

Points

The two most common methods of defining points rely on the *polar coordinate system* and the *Cartesian coordinate system*. These systems use *axes*. An axis is an infinite, imaginary straight line. In the third dimension, we define three axes that travel in each of the six directions—left and right, up and down, and forward and backward, as shown in Figure E.1. In the computer world, the axis traveling left and right is usually called x, the one traveling up and down y, and the one traveling forward and backward z. The place where these three axes intersect is called the *origin*, because all points are measured from this spot.

The Polar Coordinate System

The polar coordinate system measures a three-dimensional point with two angles and one number. Each of the angles is given in terms of rotation around one of the axes; any two axes will work. The one number indicates how far the point is from the origin, in the direction specified by the two angles, as shown in Figure E.2.

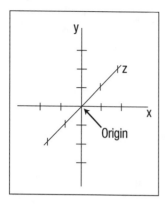

Figure E.1
The three axes of coordinate systems.

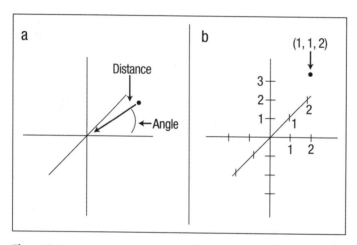

Figure E.2
A two-dimensional point measured in polar coordinates.

The Cartesian Coordinate System

The Cartesian coordinate system measures a three-dimensional point with three values—the first called x, the second y, and the third z, specified in that order. These three values indicate how far the point is along each of the three axes.

In the Cartesian coordinate system, the x-axis is positive to the right of the origin; and the y-axis is positive above the origin. If the z-axis is positive on the far side of the origin, the coordinate system is called left-handed. If z is negative on the far side of the origin, the system is called right-handed. Direct3D supports both the left-handed and the right-handed coordinate system. The left-handed coordinate system, shown in Figure E.3, is the default; it is the one programmers use most commonly.

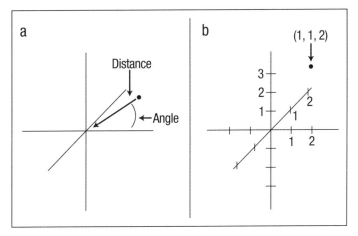

Figure E.3
A point measured in left-handed Cartesian coordinates.

Most games, and Direct3D, use the Cartesian coordinate system, because it is more straightforward than the polar coordinate system, and it lends itself to advanced 3D work. Even in Direct3D games, however, Cartesian points are sometimes converted to polar points for certain operations that are easier using polar coordinates.

Manipulating Points

Common methods of manipulating a point are:

- *Translating*—Moving it in a certain direction.
- *Rotating*—Rotating it around a certain axis (often *x*, *y*, or *z*, but not necessarily).
- *Scaling*—Uniformly enlarging or reducing the point's *x*-, *y*-, and *z*-values (thus moving it closer or farther from the origin).
- *Skewing*—Scaling it *nonuniformly* (that is, enlarging or reducing the point's *x*-, *y*-, and *z*-values by different proportions).

The Mathematics Behind Manipulations

This section covers the mathematics behind point manipulations. Direct3D will often handle the math for you, but extending the features that Direct3D provides requires you to be familiar with exactly how points are transformed.

Translating

In the Cartesian coordinate system, translating is easy. Moving a point in a direction merely requires adding three offsets (representing the direction) to that point—one offset each for *x*, *y*, and *z*. Translating the point (5, 5, 0) to (10, 10, 0) requires adding 5 to each component except *z*, as shown in Figure E.4.

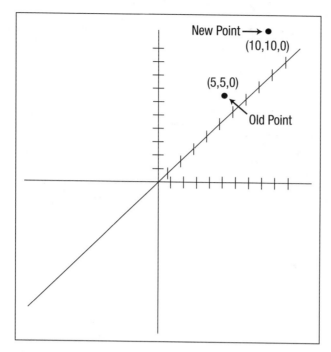

Figure E.4
Translating a point.

Rotating

Rotating, the most difficult operation for Cartesian points, requires trigonometry (see Appendix F for a trigonometry refresher). For three-dimensional space, you can rotate a point around any one of the three axes—x, y, or z.

The equations for rotating a point around the z-axis by θ degrees are as follows:

```
x' = x * cos ( θ ) - y * sin ( θ )
y' = y * cos ( θ ) + x * sin ( θ )
z' = z
```

Here x, y, and z were the original point, and x', y', and z' are the new point. Notice that rotating on the z-axis does not move the z-component of the point, as expected, just as rotating on the x- and y-axes does not move the x- and y-components of the point, respectively. The equations for rotating on the other axes are the same as the previous example, except the variable names are changed.

Scaling

Scaling a point involves multiplying each of its x-, y-, and z-components by a single number. Scaling the point (5, 10, 10) by 2, for example, produces (10, 20, 20). You can scale a point by any number (positive, negative, or fractional), except 0. If you scale a point by 0,

you lose all of its information (no amount of positive or negative scaling afterward can move the point from the origin).

Skewing

Skewing a point, also called *shearing*, is like scaling it, except that you can multiply each x-, y-, and z-component by a different number. The point $(2, 4, 2)$ skewed by the numbers $(2, 3, 1)$ results in the location $(4, 12, 2)$. Skewing an object distorts it and is useful for simulating underwater environments, for example.

Vectors

Vectors, one of the most important concepts in 3D games, are mathematical entities that describe a direction and a magnitude (which can stand for anything, such as speed). These contrast with *scalars*—numbers that describe a magnitude alone. You could use a vector to describe which direction an airplane is flying *and* how fast it is going; you could use a scalar to describe the temperature inside the airplane.

A general-purpose vector consists of two coordinates. You can see the direction of these vectors by drawing a line between the two coordinates; the magnitude is the distance between the points. The first coordinate is called the *initial point*, and the second is the *final point*. Figure E.5 illustrates a general-purpose vector.

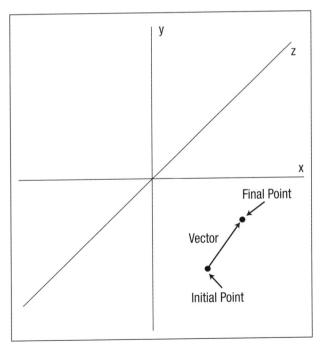

Figure E.5
A general-purpose vector with an initial point and a final point.

General-purpose vectors sometimes contain too much information; thus, three-dimensional games often use a more specific kind of vector—the *free vector*. Its initial point is assumed to be the origin, and only the final point is specified (so only three numbers are required to describe a free vector). In this book, I primarily use free vectors; hence, all manipulations assume these vectors.

Representation Of Vectors

In mathematics, vectors are usually designated by capital, bold letters, such as **A** or **V**. Their components are often written as enclosed by angle brackets—for example, <3, 2, 1>. A few vectors have special names because of their usefulness. The *null vector* is one whose components are zero—<0, 0, 0>. The **i** vector is <1, 0, 0>, the 1 pointing along the axis of x in the positive direction. Similarly, the **j** vector is <0, 1, 0>, and the **k** vector is <0, 0, 1>. The **i**, **j**, and **k** vectors are useful for algebraically manipulating vectors. A number of mathematical operations are defined for vectors.

Magnitude Of Vectors

You calculate the magnitude of vectors using the Pythagorean theorem, which for three dimensions, looks like the following:

```
x² + y² + z² = m²
```

where M is the magnitude. Thus, the distance is simply the square root of this quantity:

```
x² + y² + z²
```

The magnitude of a vector has a special symbol in mathematics: two vertical bars that surround the vector. The magnitude of vector **A**, for example, is designated as |**A**|.

Addition Of Vectors

Adding two vectors involves adding their components. Thus:

```
<10, 2, 5> + <2, 0, 2> = <12, 2, 7>
```

Visually, you can think of adding two vectors as moving the first so that its initial point touches the second one's final point. The ending point of the second vector is the final point of the new vector (which is called the *resultant*), as seen in Figure E.6. If the two vectors being added have the same magnitudes, the vector that results from their addition equally divides the two vectors.

Because the addition of vectors is nothing more than the addition of numbers, the addition of vectors is *commutative*, meaning the order of addition does not affect the result. Thus,

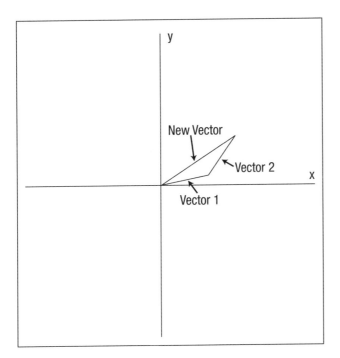

Figure E.6
The addition of two vectors, visually.

A + B

is the same as:

B + A

Further, the addition of vectors is *associative*:

A + (B + C) = A + B + C

Subtraction Of Vectors

Subtracting two vectors is performed by subtracting one vector's components from the other's (<2, 2, 2> − <4, 4, 4> = <-2, -2, -2>). The subtraction of vectors is, like addition, both commutative and associative. You can think of the result of vector subtraction as the line connecting the end points of two vectors, thus forming a triangle. Of course, the resulting vector does not actually connect the end points of the vectors (because the initial point of a free vector is always at the origin), but it has the same direction and magnitude as a line drawn between the end points of the two vectors.

Vector subtraction undoes vector addition, as can be shown from their similar definitions: One adds the components; the other subtracts them. Figure E.7 illustrates this concept. The vectors are called **A** and **B**, and the resultant is **C**. The mathematical relationship is as follows:

```
A + B = C
```

By adding **-A** to both sides of the equation, the equation becomes the following:

```
B = C - A
```

From this equation (depicted in Figure E.7), you can see that addition and subtraction, because one undoes the other, can be used with the normal rules of algebra.

Multiplication And Division Of Vectors By A Scalar

The multiplication of a vector by a scalar changes the vector's magnitude—the distance from the vector's initial point to its final point. You perform this operation, which does not affect the vector's direction, by multiplying each of the vector's components by the scalar, as demonstrated here:

```
<100, 50, 20> * 2 = <200, 100, 40>
```

You perform division of a vector in the same way.

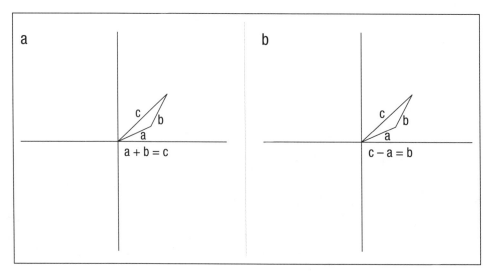

Figure E.7
The addition of two vectors (a) and the subtraction of two vectors (b).

One special vector division uses the magnitude as the scalar. This produces a *normalized* vector—a vector that has a length of 1. The vector <2, 2, 2>, for example, has a magnitude of roughly 3.5. Dividing each of the vector's components by 3.5 results in the new vector, <0.57..., 0.57..., 0.57...>. The magnitude of this new vector is, as expected, 1. Normalized vectors are useful in computer graphics because they often simplify equations, such as the dot product (covered below).

Scalar multiplication allows a useful representation of vectors. Any vector can be represented as the sum of three scalar multiplications with the vectors **i**, **j**, and **k** mentioned earlier, as shown here,

```
A = ai + bj + ck
```

where *a*, *b*, and *c* are the scalars. The advantage to this way of describing vectors is that it lets you manipulate vectors as a single mathematical entity (when you add two vectors, for example, you can add separately the **i** components, the **j** components, and the **k** components). This frees you from keeping track of vector components when you perform many manipulations in a row.

The Dot Product Of Two Vectors

The *dot product* of two vectors is designated by the dot symbol (•), as in **A** • **B** (pronounced "**A** dot **B**"). This is defined as:

```
A · B = |A||B| cos (A, B)
```

The calculation of the dot product is performed as follows:

```
A · B = X₁X₂ + Y₁Y₂ + Z₁Z₂
```

The proof of this equation is straightforward. Figure E.8 shows vectors **A** and **B**, the angle between them being **q**. The vector **C** connects the final points of the two vectors and, by the properties of the subtraction of vectors, is equal to **B** – **A**. Notice the triangle formed by these three vectors: The length of each side is the magnitude of its vector.

The law of cosines states that for a triangle, such as the one formed by the vectors **A**, **B**, and **C** (where **a**, **b**, and **c** are the lengths of the sides of the triangle), the following holds true:

```
c² = a² + b² - 2ab cos θ
```

The lengths of the sides are the magnitudes of their vectors, so:

```
|C|² = |A|² + |B|² - 2|A|B| cos θ
```

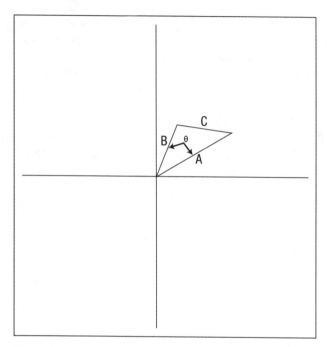

Figure E.8
Three vectors. **C** connects **A** and **B**.

Notice the product $|A||B|\cos\theta$ on the right side of the equation, which is the dot product. By adding $-|C|^2$ and $2|A||B|\cos\theta$ to both sides of the equation, the equation becomes:

```
2|A||B| cos θ = |A|² + |B|² - |C|²
```

Finally, by multiplying both sides by 1/2, you isolate the dot product:

```
|A||B| cos θ = (|A|² + |B|² - |C|²)/2
```

Assuming X_1, Y_1, and Z_1 designate the vector **A**; X_2, Y_2, and Z_2 designate **B**; and X_3, Y_3, and Z_3 designate **C**, expanding the right side gives the following:

```
( (X₁² + Y₁² + Z₁²) + (X₂² + Y₂² + Z₂²) - (X₃² + Y₃² + Z₃²) ) / 2
```

(The square root used to calculate the magnitude of a vector dropped out, because the result is immediately squared: $|A|^2$, $|B|^2$, and $|C|^2$.)

The vector **C**, as observed earlier, is merely **B** – **A**. Thus, X^3 is $X^2 - X^1$ (that is, X^3, the x component of **C**, is equal to the subtraction of the x components of **B** and **A**), Y^3 is $Y^2 - Y^1$, and Z^3 is $Z^2 - Z^1$, producing:

((X$_1^2$ + Y$_1^2$ + Z$_1^2$) + (X$_2^2$ + Y$_2^2$ + Z$_2^2$) - ((X$_2$ - X$_1$)^2 +
(Y$_2$ - Y$_1$)^2 + (Z$_2$ - Z$_1$)^2)) / 2

Simplifying the results gives:

((X$_1^2$ + Y$_1^2$ + Z$_1^2$) + (X$_2^2$ + Y$_2^2$ + Z$_2^2$) -
(X$_2^2$ - 2X$_2$X$_1$ + X$_1^2$ + Y$_2^2$ - 2Y$_2$Y$_1$ + Y$_1^2$ + Z$_2^2$ - 2Z$_2$Z$_1$ + Z$_1^2$))
 / 2

Carrying the negative sign through and canceling produces:

(2X$_2$X$_1$ + 2Y$_2$Y$_1$ + 2Z$_2$Z$_1$) / 2

After dividing by 2, the equation yields the expected form:

X$_2$X$_1$ + Y$_2$Y$_1$ + Z$_2$Z$_1$

From this equation, you will immediately see that the dot product is commutative, associative, and *distributive* (that is, **A** • (**B** + **C**) = **A** • **B** + **A** • **C**). Thus, you can manipulate dot products as normal integers in algebra.

One helpful application of the dot product is obtaining the angle between two vectors. The definition of the dot product is, again, as follows:

A • B = |A||B| cos θ

Dividing both sides by |**A**| |**B**| produces the following equation:

cos θ = (A • B)/|A||B|

By using the inverse cosine function on the right quantity, you can find the angle between the two vectors. This equation is used for shading polygons and producing many other effects.

The Cross Product Of Two Vectors

The cross product of two vectors is called a *normal vector*, which points in the direction of the plane formed by those two vectors (that is, it is perpendicular to the plane formed by the two vectors). This is not the same as a normalized vector, although normal vectors are often normalized. Figure E.9 shows this graphically.

Any two vectors with unique directions and nonzero magnitudes can describe a plane in three-dimensional space. The plane rests on the two vectors and is thus oriented by them. The cross product lets you determine, from these two vectors, which direction the plane faces.

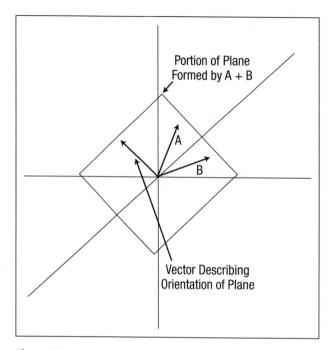

Figure E.9
The vector describing the orientation of the plane formed by the two vectors **A** and **B**.

The cross product of two vectors is designated by **A x B** (read "**A** cross **B**") and can be determined as follows:

$$A \times B = \langle Y_1 Z_2 - Z_1 Y_2, \ Z_1 X_2 - X_1 Z_2, \ X_1 Y_2 - Y_1 X_2 \rangle$$

The proof for this equation is too complex to list here. *Calculus* (1996, Addison-Wesley) is an excellent reference if you are interested in why this equation is true. Note that the cross product is not commutative: **A x B** is not the same as **B x A**. The results of both are indeed vectors describing the orientation of the plane formed by them, but they point in opposite directions.

Appendix F
Trigonometry Refresher

Trigonometry is the study of the relationship between the sides and angles of triangles. Trigonometry has its formal roots in the work of the Greek astronomers Hipparchus and Ptolemy, but took its present form only much later. It has proven an invaluable discipline in all areas of applied mathematics, and even more so in computer science, where physics, graphics, and geometry manipulations all draw from its principles.

A right triangle is shown in Figure F.1. The length of its sides are designated by **o**, **h**, and **a**, and its angle is represented by the Greek letter θ (pronounced "thay-tuh"). The names of the sides are not arbitrary: **o** stands for opposite, because that side is opposite to the two sides that form the angle; **h** stands for hypotenuse (the standard name given to this side, the only side that is neither horizontal or vertical); and **a** stands for adjacent, because that side is adjacent to the angle (that is, it is one of the sides that form the angle).

Note

*The angles used in trigonometry are not specified in degrees (**360** of which define a complete rotation), but rather, in radians. Under this system, a complete revolution is defined as **2p** radians; **90** degrees is **p/2**; 45 degrees is **p/4**, and so on. A general equation that expresses this relationship is as follows: **radians = degrees × 2p/360**.*

Trigonometry exists because for a given angle, the proportions of a right triangle do not change, even if the lengths of the sides do (see Figure F.2). Mathematicians define certain functions (mathematical equations that accept one or more inputs and give an

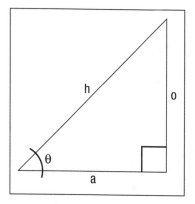

Figure F.1
A right triangle.

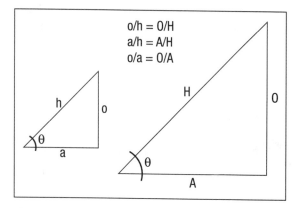

Figure F.2
Right triangles that share the same angle are proportionate to one another.

output, much like a C++ function) to express these ratios. The most common are listed in Table F.1.

You will notice that some trigonometric functions are redundant. Because the **sine** function is defined as **o/h** and **cosine** as **a/h**, **sine** divided by **cosine** is **(o/h)/(a/h)**, which is just **o/a**, or the **tangent** function. The redundancy is more than made up for by the added convenience, however.

The arc functions (**arc sine**, for example) are *inverse functions*—that is, they take the output of a normal function and return the input that would have been required to produce that output value. Another way of looking at an inverse function is by this mathematical relationship: $f^{-1}(f(x))=x$. In words, the inverse function outputs **x** when its input is the result of the function **f** evaluated at **x**. The inverse functions allow you to

Table F.1   Commonly used trigonometric functions.

Name Of Function	Abbreviated Name	Input	Output
sine	sin	θ	o/h
cosine	cos	θ	a/h
tangent	tan	θ	o/a
arc sine	sin⁻¹	o/h	θ
arc cosine	cos⁻¹	a/h	θ
arc tangent	tan⁻¹	o/a	θ

calculate the angle knowing only a ratio. If you knew the ratio **o/a**, then inputting this value for the **arc sine** function would give you θ, the angle required to produce such an angle.

Other Relationships

Many relationships between the trigonometric functions and the geometry of triangles have proven valuable, including the Law of Sines, the Law of Cosines, and the Fundamental Identities, among others. In this book, all laws and equations are introduced as they are needed, but readers interested in pursuing a greater knowledge of trigonometry should purchase a precalculus book.

Using Trigonometry

The trigonometry functions allow you to solve problems that are otherwise impossible. This section presents and solves a few of these problems.

Problem: Given the right triangle in Figure F.3, find (a) the length of the hypotenuse and (b) the length of the adjacent side.

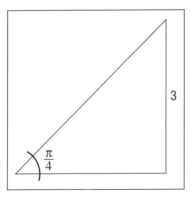

Figure F.3
In this triangle, the angle and the adjacent side are known, but the length of the hypotenuse is not.

Solution:

(a) You know the length of the opposite side is **3** and the angle is π/4. The tangent of π/4 is o/a, expressed mathematically as follows:

```
tan (π/4) = o/a
```

Dividing both sides by **o** produces:

```
tan (π/4)/o = 1/a
```

Finally, inverting both sides solves for **a**:

```
o/tan(π/4) = a
```

As your calculator will show, **tan(π/4)** is **3**. Hence the length of the adjacent side is **3**.

(b) You could use the straightforward Pythagorean theorem (**h² = o² + a²**), but this is not strictly necessary. The **cosine** or **sine** functions can also be used. Because the length of the adjacent side is **3**, and the angle is π/4, the following relationships hold true:

```
cos (π/4) = 3/h
```

Solving for **h** gives:

```
h = 3/cos (π/4)
```

Your calculator will show this to be approximately **4.243**, the exact value produced by the Pythagorean theorem. This calculation could just as easily have been done with the **sine** function.

Problem: Find the angle θ in the right triangle shown in Figure F.4.

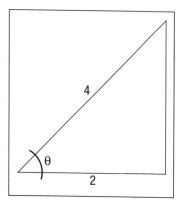

Figure F.4
In this triangle, the hypotenuse and adjacent side are known, but the angle θ is not.

Solution: The length of the hypotenuse is **4**, while the length of the adjacent side is **2**. Using the **arc cosine** function (which accepts **a/h**) gives an angle of $\pi/3$.

The applications in this appendix included only right triangles, but by dividing other kinds of triangles into right triangles, it is possible to use trigonometry on any triangle where enough information is known.

Index

What's On The CD-ROM

The *3D Game Programming with* C++'s companion CD-ROM contains elements specifically selected to enhance the usefulness of this book, including the following:

♦ *DirectX 7 SDK*—The DirectX 7 SDK from Microsoft Corporation. The latest version of DirectX is faster than ever and supports advanced features like bump mapping, cubic environment mapping, multitexturing, and more. Comes with help files, source code examples, and all the libraries and headers you need to write your own DirectX 7 games.

♦ *trueSpace 4.2*—An evaluation version of the application from Caligari Corporation. trueSpace 4.2 is the hottest 3D tool on the market for creating realtime 3D game worlds. It supports Microsoft's X file format and automatic detail reduction, critical features for all game-oriented development systems.

♦ *Adobe PhotoShop 5*—A 30-day-trial edition of Photoshop 5 from Adobe. Create, paint, correct, and retouch textures for your Direct3D games.

♦ *Cool Edit 96*—Digital audio software from Syntrillium Software Corporation that can manipulate, modify, convert, and mix all the sounds effects your 3D games will need.

♦ *Source code for the book's projects*—High-quality, feature-rich encapsulations for DirectDraw, DirectSound, and DirectInput, as well as software for physics simulation, artificial intelligence, and advanced 3D optimizations.

System Requirements

Software:

♦ Your operating system must be Windows 95, 98 or higher to install and use DirectX 7 or the included trial applications.

♦ You must have a Win32 compiler compatible with DirectX 7 to compile the included source code.

Hardware:

♦ A 100% DirectX 7 compatible sound card, input device, and graphics card are required for using DirectX 7 and the included source code examples.

W